Contributions to Management Science

More information about this series at http://www.springer.com/series/1505

Volker Nissen
Editor

Advances in Consulting Research

Recent Findings and Practical Cases

Springer

Editor
Volker Nissen
Economic Sciences and Media
Ilmenau University of Technology
Ilmenau, Germany

ISSN 1431-1941 ISSN 2197-716X (electronic)
Contributions to Management Science
ISBN 978-3-030-07125-7 ISBN 978-3-319-95999-3 (eBook)
https://doi.org/10.1007/978-3-319-95999-3

Softcover reprint of the hardcover 1st edition 2019

This Springer imprint is published by the registered company Springer Nature Switzerland AG
The registered company address is: Gewerbestrasse 11, 6330 Cham, Switzerland

I dedicate this book to my mother Heidrun Nissen.
Volker Nissen

Preface

Over the last few decades, business consulting has recorded continuous and significant dynamic growth. Despite its great economic relevance and the fact that many young professionals are attracted to consulting as a career opportunity, the scientific community that looks at consulting from an academic perspective is still comparatively small. Moreover, there are only few dedicated outlets to publish research on consulting.

Even though consulting seems to be driven by practice, there are many useful points of contact between practical consulting and a scientific research discipline dealing with consultancy (consulting research). This closeness calls for a fruitful, mutual relationship where both sides benefit from that cooperation. Recently, the classical delivery model of consulting is challenged by new technology-driven approaches. A digital transformation process of the consulting industry is in progress. In this situation, many interesting research questions arise that are of immediate practical relevance.

This book brings together recent research contributions on consulting by a range of experts in one volume. It aims to be a building block toward making the current state of the art in the field of consulting research more accessible while looking at consulting from different angles and with a variety of methods. The wide range of topics includes consulting research as a discipline, general issues in consulting, developments in different consulting fields, consulting processes and approaches, the consulting market and clients, as well as the future of consulting and current trends.

This volume will be beneficial reading for consultants who want to critically reflect on their own methods and approaches in light of scientific results. Furthermore, it will be a helpful orientation for students of management and IT-related courses, who either think about a professional career in consulting or want to be reflective clients of consultants. Finally, this collection of scientific results should foster future contributions in this important research field.

I would like to thank all the people who contributed to this book! This not only includes the various authors but also my doctoral students and staff at the Ilmenau

University of Technology, in particular Mr. Julian Schulte and Mrs. Anne Füßl, as well as the editorial office at Springer, in particular Mr. Christian Rauscher as the executive editor. I truly enjoyed working with you on this project! Moreover, I sincerely appreciate the financial support from the former Gesellschaft für Consulting Research (GCR) e.V.

Hopefully, this volume provides not only some scientific contribution in the field of consulting research but also concrete practical hints to consulting companies in their struggle for competitive advantage and long-term success. If you have comments on the book, or want to get in touch, please contact me at volker.nissen@tu-ilmenau.de.

Enjoy the book!

Ilmenau, Germany
March 2018

Volker Nissen

Contents

Part III Consulting Fields and Approaches

Part IV Consulting Clients and Market

Part V Future of Consulting

Editor and Contributors

About the Editor

Volker Nissen holds the Chair of Information Systems Engineering in Services at Technische Universität Ilmenau, Germany, since 2005. Prior to this, he pursued a consulting career, including positions as manager at IDS Scheer AG, director at DHC GmbH, and CEO of NISSCON Ltd, Germany. In 1994, he received a PhD degree in economic sciences with distinction from the University of Goettingen, Germany. His current research interests include the digital transformation of the consulting industry, the management of IT agility, metaheuristic optimization, and process acceptance research. He is author and editor of 20 books and some 200 other publications, including papers in *Business & Information Systems Engineering*, *Information Systems Frontiers*, *IEEE Transactions on EC*, *IEEE Transactions on NN*, *OR Spectrum*, and *Annals of OR*.

Contributors

Rainer Alt Leipzig University, Leipzig, Germany

Gunnar Auth Hochschule für Telekommunikation Leipzig, Leipzig, Germany

Frank Bensberg Osnabrück University of Applied Sciences, Osnabrück, Germany

Arne Buchwald EBS Business School, Wiesbaden, Germany

Gandalf Buscher HfT Leipzig University of Applied Sciences, Leipzig, Germany

Christian Czarnecki HfT Leipzig University of Applied Sciences, Leipzig, Germany

Thomas Deelmann University of Applied Sciences for Public Administration and Management of North Rhine-Westphalia—Fachhochschule für öffentliche Verwaltung (FHöV), Cologne, Germany

Johannes Dittler INVERTO GmbH, Munich, Germany

Anne Füßl Technische Universität Ilmenau, Ilmenau, Germany

Florian Glaser Karlsruhe Institute of Technology (KIT), Karlsruhe, Germany

Kristina Gugler AWS Institut, Saarbrücken, Germany

Lisa Hannemann University of Oldenburg, Oldenburg, Germany

Julia Hautz IMP Network of Excellence, University of Innsbruck, Innsbruck, Austria

Martin Hillebrand CO(13), Berlin, Germany

Dominik Jung Karlsruhe Institute of Technology (KIT), Karlsruhe, Germany

Christoph Kögler T-Systems Multimedia Solutions GmbH, Dresden, Germany

Willi Köpplin Karlsruhe Institute of Technology (KIT), Karlsruhe, Germany

Thomas Müllerleile Technische Universität Ilmenau, Ilmenau, Germany

Tino Machts Rudolf-Breitscheid-Str. 2 b, Jena, Germany

Kurt Matzler Free University of Bolzano, Bolzano, Italy

Christian Mauerer Technische Universität Ilmenau, Ilmenau, Germany

Stefan Mette BNP Paribas Personal Finance, Bremen, Germany

Christian Neu AWS Institut, Saarbrücken, Germany

Volker Nissen Economic Sciences and Media, Ilmenau University of Technology, Ilmenau, Germany

Severin Oesterle University of Bayreuth, Bayreuth, Germany

Ferdinando Piumelli mindsquare GmbH, Bielefeld, Germany

Christian Stummeyer Technical University of Ingolstadt, Ingolstadt, Germany

Frank Termer Bitkom, Berlin, Germany

Christoph Treichler Cardea AG, Zurich, Switzerland

Nils Urbach University of Bayreuth, Bayreuth, Germany

Stephan Friedrich von den Eichen University of Bremen, Bremen, Germany

Dirk Werth AWS Institut, Saarbrücken, Germany

Consulting Research: A Scientific Perspective on Consulting

Volker Nissen

Abstract Consulting clearly is one of the major service industries with an ever growing turnover and considerable influence on the development of virtually all other branches of industry. Consultancies are also one of the most attractive employers to highly qualified young people. Despite this significant practical impact, the amount of research on consulting is only moderate, and scientific outlets exclusively dedicated to consulting issues are scarce. In this introductory paper, the necessity, requirements and benefits of a scientific perspective on consulting are highlighted. This 'Consulting Research', while sustaining academic rigor, must closely cooperate with consulting practice to simultaneously achieve relevance. As an academic stream it must be supported by an active and well organized research community, cooperatively acting at national as well as international level.

1 Context and Fundamentals of Business Consulting[1]

1.1 The Term and Forms of Business Consulting

The term 'business consulting' is inconsistently defined in the scientific literature. Ernst even refers to the search of an established and consistent definition as an 'impossible undertaking' (Ernst 2002). The reason for this is, on the one side the fragmented condition of the research community with various research objectives and demarcation purposes (Ernst 2002; Mohe 2003). On the other side the widespread, colloquial understanding of consulting contributes to the conceptual confusion. Furthermore, 'business consultant' is not a protected job description. Everyone can basically be a business consultant, without having any certified proof of a

[1]This revised text builds on Nissen (2007).

V. Nissen (✉)
Economic Sciences and Media, Ilmenau University of Technology, Ilmenau, Germany
e-mail: volker.nissen@tu-ilmenau.de

V. Nissen (ed.), *Advances in Consulting Research*, Contributions to Management Science, https://doi.org/10.1007/978-3-319-95999-3_1

specific qualification. This contributes to a confusing consulting market and a heterogeneous understanding of business consulting.

Business consulting (brief: consulting) is defined here as a professional service, which is done by one or more persons, generally professionally qualified, and hierarchically independent from the advised client. This service is time-limited and usually paid for. The objectives are to define, structure and analyze business issues of the commissioning company interactively with the client to develop solutions for problems and, if wanted, to plan their implementation together with representatives of the client and to realize them in the company.

Consulting is hence a matter of providing support in the processing of business-related issues.[2] For this purpose, various aspects of the client can be investigated, for example strategy topics, organization and business processes, information technology or staff related aspects. Accordingly, there are various consulting focus areas, in particular (according to the classification of the BDU e.V.—the Association of German Business Consultants):

- strategy consulting,
- organization consulting (including process improvement),
- IT-oriented consulting
- HR consulting.

A distinction is sometimes made between strategic and functional consulting in the literature.[3] Thus, strategic consulting is particularly characterized by badly structured problems, which present extra high challenges for innovative solution concepts. Purchaser of strategic consulting services is normally the client's executive board. In comparison, functional consulting is rather assigned to the level of specialist departments or business units. The tasks, which need to be processed, often are better structured.

This characterization of relevant problems can only be a rough approximation, which may not apply to an individual case. Generally, it is assumed that consulting, in whatever form, is characterized by client-individual, usually complex tasks and framework conditions, which require corresponding solutions, even when the individuality can vary depending on the type of project, respectively consulting focus. Thus, consciously a unifying perspective on business consulting is taken in this contribution.

On an abstract level, four types (modes) of business consulting can be differentiated: advisory consulting, expert consulting, organizational development/coaching and systemic consulting (Walger 1995; Nissen 2007; Deelmann 2012). They differ mainly in the way the client organization is viewed and, consequently, the role of the consultant in the transformation process.

---

[2]There are also other forms of consulting e.g. in the technical area, which is here only of marginal importance.

[3]For an example see Peterson (2001, pp. 40–41).

Very briefly, in advisory consulting, the consultant, based on specific knowledge, suggests a solution to a client problem in the form of a report (Bamberger and Wrona 2012). He is usually not involved during the (optional) implementation of these proposals. Expert consulting is the dominant type of consulting today. It assumes a doctor-patient relationship between consultant and client. Here the expert solves complex problems due to superior knowledge, and together with the client's executives, he actively realizes a change in the client company. In organizational development client employees essentially solve the business problems by themselves, but consultants help them through external reflection and active guidance. The consultant is seen as a coordinator in this development, and an initiator of the clients' learning processes. In the view of systemic consulting, which is based on systems theory, organizations are regarded as social autopoietic systems. Such systems are recursively closed and self-regulative. They cannot be specifically changed from the outside. Consultants in this approach take on the role of an observer who tries to find out the client organizations' characteristic behavior and communication patterns that reproduce the problem. He then attempts to 'irritate' constitutive perceptual and explanatory models of the client's system, also pointing to complex interrelationships in the effect of potential actions. As a result processes are disturbed that generate the problem. Of central importance in systemic consulting is also the self-reflection of clients on their modes of observation, communicative and behavioral patterns.

1.2 Embedding in the Context of Professional Service Firms

Consulting is a professional service often characterized by the following features:

- immateriality and intangibility (performance result related delimitation),
- marketing of service promises (potential oriented delimitation),
- integration of internal and external production factors in the process of service performance (process-related delimitation).

On this basis, the distinction between services and material goods is not without problems. Therefore, some authors suggested to forego the separation entirely and to speak of output bundles as sales objects instead.[4] These output bundles consist of component services, which are performed on the basis of a predisposed performance potential. They integrate external factors to various extents into a service construction process and their results are marked by varying shares of material and immaterial components. The emphasized differentiation of service as a result or service as a process is important. In this logic consulting services are marked by both a large share of immaterial components in the service result and by an intensive integration of external factors in the shape of the client's employees (see Fig. 1).

[4]See, for instance, Kleinaltenkamp (2001).

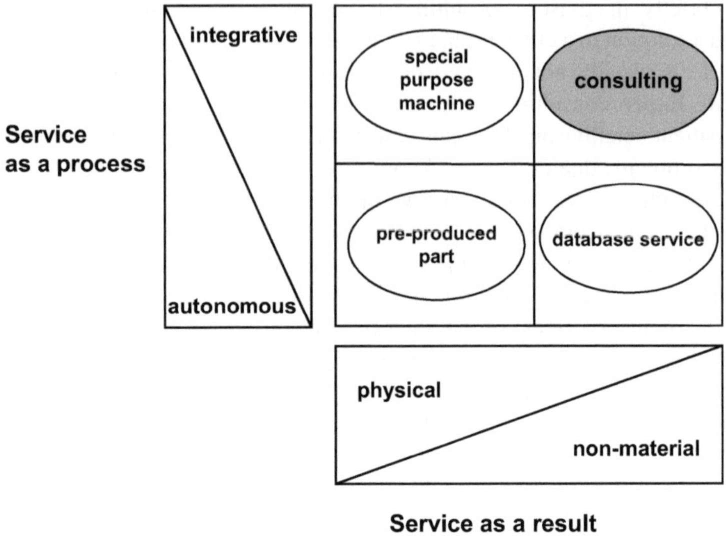

Fig. 1 Position of consulting in a service typology [based on Engelhardt et al. (1994)]

Here the definition of Müller-Stewens et al. (1999) will be used. Thus, professional services are *services which are custom-designed for individual requirements and usually are performed in close collaboration with the client. This is done by bringing in a high level of expertise and experience of highly qualified employees.*

Professional service firms are increasingly seen as an independent group within service companies. They can be characterized by means of the following three features (Müller-Stewens et al. 1999). They provide professional services. These are knowledge-intensive companies in which the creation of value depends primarily on highly qualified, performance-oriented employees. Professional service firms provide services exclusively in the B2B business, i. e. they only work for other private or public companies and organisations.

In the age of knowledge-based competition professional service firms are more and more turning into a model for other companies, even beyond the service sector:

> Professional service firms may represent the pinnacle of the information age. (...) As competence is becoming an increasingly important resource even in traditional manufacturing firms, Many of the challenges that are typical to professional service firms are becoming increasingly prevalent in other types of organizations as well (Løwendahl 1997).

Not only in the case of professional service firms, the management interest does increasingly shift from a material economy to an economy of the non-material (Schüppel 1996). This is an additional motivation to scientifically be more intensively occupied with the specific challenges of consulting and other professional service firms.

2 Changing Conditions in Consulting Practice[5]

The global consulting sector is one of the largest and most mature markets within the professional services industry, according to Consultancy.uk (2017). Figure 2 shows exemplary the rise in total turnover in the German consulting market between 2010 and 2016 (BDU 2017). And the positive development continues. For 2017, the Association of German Business Consultants expects another increase of 8.3%, reaching a total German consulting market volume of an estimated 31.4 billion € (personal communication). On an international level the turnover increased from $205 billion (including financial advisory) in 2011 to around $250 billion in 2016.

The figures seem to suggest that all is well in the consulting sector and steady growth for most companies can be anticipated for the next years, too. However, continued success can make you lazy and inattentive for potentially disruptive competitors. Or, as Christensen et al. (2013) put it, "there may be nothing as vulnerable as entrenched success". Much of the growth we see in consulting today may be attributed to some form of co-management or 'body leasing', where clients essentially remove management layers and replace permanent staff by support services from consultancies.

Some of the most important current megatrends that also have an effect on consulting providers refer to complementary technological developments. Technologies like mobile devices and virtual personal assistants (VPAs) add to the channels to reach customers, while also changing the habits how people want to consume services. Moreover, these technologies enable instant responses and access to vast amounts of information that could be used on the client as well as on the consultant side.

The consulting and IT services industries meanwhile face a truly global competition while traditional boundaries between market segments are disappearing. As a result, vendor's offerings are converging and clients find it increasingly difficult to perceive differences between service providers in each segment (Parakala 2015). This reduces the pricing power of consulting firms as they become more exchangeable. Furthermore, concerning standard services ('commodity consulting'), the

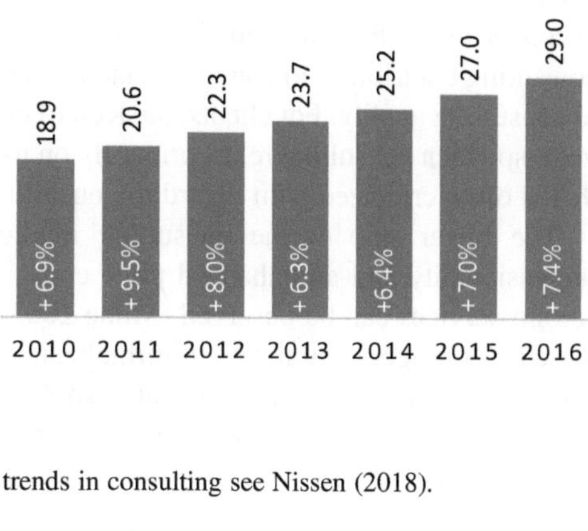

Fig. 2 Total turnover in the German consulting market 2010–2016 (BDU 2017)

[5]For a more detailed elaboration on current trends in consulting see Nissen (2018).

market is characterized by massive pressure on margins from freelancers and providers from low-wage countries (Nissen 2013). Aggressive competition in the area of commoditized services is seriously impacting the profitability of many consulting companies (Parakala 2015).

The situation is further aggravated by the clients growing tendency to unbundle consulting engagements and buy modular pieces from different providers, aiming for best-of-breed solutions in all aspects. A particular reaction to this best-of-breed attitude of clients is the business model of consulting providers like Eden McCallum (EMC). They analyze every project and compile a team of experienced freelance consultants to tackle it. For clients, that means tailored expertise at highly competitive rates, while consultants remain free from internal demands of traditional consulting companies and can opt to work on those projects they are really interested in.

This setting also helps new competitors with innovative business models and technology-driven consulting concepts to enter the market, challenging incumbent firms in the long run (Christensen et al. 2013). Many of them do not aim to be providers of overarching 'one-stop-shopping' consulting services, but rather supply innovative solutions for a particular step in the consulting process, such as automated data analysis and interpretation (e.g. Narrative Science, BeyondCore or Experient), process mining and modeling (e.g. Celonis), or creating innovative solutions with the help of an international community of experts (e.g. 10EQS, Wikistrat, Kaggle). The functional spectrum of services reaches from quickly connecting a client to an expert to provide on demand business advice (e.g. Clarity) to processing an entire consulting project in a fully digital manner. Many of these new consulting providers rely on web-based IT-platforms as a medium of communication and data exchange.

A group of new competitors in the consulting market provides asset-based consulting solutions. This consulting approach heavily relies on software solutions, tools, models, algorithms and data-based assets. Consequently, the amount of human intervention is generally less than what traditional consulting requires. As a result, these services can be multiplied and scale much better than traditional consulting. Asset-based consulting is generally provided at a lower price than traditional people-based consulting, because of a substantial increase in efficiency, speed and productivity.

Asset and platform-based consulting concepts render geographic borders and distances irrelevant, thus extending the reach of providers. Expert knowledge becomes instantly and globally available. Additionally, in particular asset-based consulting contributes to consistent and repeatable project output, potentially adding to consulting quality. For clients, the ROI of consulting engagements becomes easier to grasp when consulting relies primarily on tools and software, reducing the opacity that is often criticized with regard to consulting.

The buyer side of the consulting market has also changed. An increasing professionality and an enhanced price consciousness of the clients regarding consulting services can be observed (Mohe 2003). In the realm of consulting purchase there is a stronger centralization, formalization and standardization of the processes. The client organizations' increasing sophistication about consulting services is often attributed to the vast number of former consultants now working inside client organizations.

The megatrend digitalization further changed the buying behavior of consulting customers significantly. Following a general trend in B2C trade, clients increasingly use digital channels to search information on eligible consulting providers for their projects. Here, digital marketplaces and online communities already exceed the importance of the known search engines and portals (e.g., LinkedIn, XING) according to a survey by Cardea and Newcoventure (2016). Consequently, there is a stronger need for active (digital) marketing in consulting to increase the marketplace visibility and improve brand recognition and reputation.

Where large service providers are unable to meet expectations, clients are willing to explore partnerships with smaller, more agile and innovative consulting companies. Clients demand leveraging digital technologies to streamline operational processes and bring about fundamental changes in the business model. This requires consulting and IT service providers to increasingly co-create solutions in close cooperation with clients that face a globalized and volatile business environment.

In this situation, the clients have become more demanding and professional, and they are more closely examining whether they really need consulting services and which consulting company they want to use (Cardea 2016). Moreover, new and potentially disruptive consulting delivery models become more acceptable with clients, when they better account for their needs and provide a clearer ROI.

The recent study conducted by Cardea (2016) revealed that almost two third of the surveyed clients stated that it is difficult or very difficult for them to find the right consultants for their businesses. At the same time, the majority of clients in this study said that digital media and channels are gaining importance for seeking the right consulting service providers. As a consequence, a further increase in market share for digital matching platforms (such as consultingsearcher, COMATCH, and KLAITON) can be expected that aim to provide transparency over the consulting market and intermediate between companies searching for consultants, and consultants (including independent freelancers) seeking project engagements.

3 Consulting Research

3.1 A Quick Assessment of Consulting Publications and Lecturing

With Armbrüster and Kieser (2001) the literature on consulting can be differentiated into:

1. Research oriented literature,
2. Practice oriented literature (for consultant or client), Wolf speaks here of guideline literature (Wolf 2000),
3. 'Tell-it-all' literature, often with biased, not really differentiated presentations about the consulting sector.

Examples of practice oriented guidelines for consultants in the German-speaking region are Niedereichholz (2010, 2012), and Lippold (2015). Examples of tell-it-all literature include Staute (1996), Zimmermann (1997), and in English Craig (2005).

Despite the large practical significance of professional service firms, only moderate attention is given to this sector in research and teaching, though in the past years, the scientific involvement with this topic experienced a certain recovery. For the German-speaking area Mohe (2004) stated that there is an extensive isolation of individual research groups, and ascribes this to the fact that these research fields are not anchored in institutions. This leads to relatively disconnected ‘research islands’. The situation prevails until today, although there have been (partly unsuccessful) attempts to create such organizational anchors (see the contribution of Deelmann and Nissen 2018).

The majority of scientific publication on consulting addresses aspects of strategy- or organization consulting. There is hardly any scientific involvement in the topic of IT-oriented consulting as well as HR consulting. This contrasts with the practical importance of these consulting fields. For instance, the share of the 2016 consulting turnover in Germany was 21.6% for IT consulting and 10.0% for HR consulting, respectively. In an analogous way the research concentrates on large consulting firms, while the specific problems of small and medium consulting providers are rather neglected. Simultaneously, according to the BDU, small and medium consultancies (below an annual turnover of 45 Mio €) currently account for nearly 58% of the consulting turnover in Germany (BDU 2017).

Consulting practice has a greater influence on teaching than on research (Shugan 2004). However, there are occasional relevant research publications from larger consulting firms as for example ‘The McKinsey Quarterly’. An intensive mutual exchange between consulting practice and Consulting Research does currently, at least in the German-speaking area, not really exist. Whether this will happen in future is open. For this purpose, a transition of consultant’s self-conception is necessary, which currently prevents the demand of scientific support on the part of consulting practice. Consultants often see scientific research on consulting as ‘bloodless’ and redundant.[6] Here more dialogue and good argumentation is needed. Finally, it would be helpful if it could be proven that science can add value to consulting practice. Equally, it is sometimes still necessary to work on reservations and prejudices against consulting practice amongst academics.

In the following, a stepwise approach to scientific research in consulting, in the following termed as ‘Consulting Research’, will be discussed. For this purpose the objectives and self-conception is explained in more detail and the question on the relevance to consulting practice will be critically examined.

[6]Personal communication with various consultants.

3.2 Concept and Goals of Consulting Research (CR)[7]

In short, the term Consulting Research is understood to refer to the scientific treatment of the service of business consulting, the consultancy firms as organisations as well as the consultancy market and its various participants on the supply and demand sides. Consulting Research forms a sub-field of general research on advisory within the social sciences (see Fig. 3).

Shugan does use the term Consulting Research but without a concrete definition, simply writing: "Sometimes, it is possible to bridge scholarly research with consulting to create Consulting Research." (Shugan 2004) He further names some tasks and points of emphasis of Consulting Research: "Consulting Research can often bridge well-known academic research with the immediate problems faced by practitioners. That contribution is both an immediate gain for the client as well as new knowledge for the academic literature. However, that new knowledge might be more related to implementation issues, ideas for future research, information about priorities faced by practitioners, and the adequacy of current theories than to the development of new abstract theories in the so-called state of the art. (...) In my opinion, the most important part of the bridging function is the identification of irrelevant variables." (Shugan 2004).

These points are hardly sufficient for forming a definitional basis for CR. They are not specific to the field of business consulting; rather, they are usable for every form of close cooperation between science and practice, as they are expressed in the

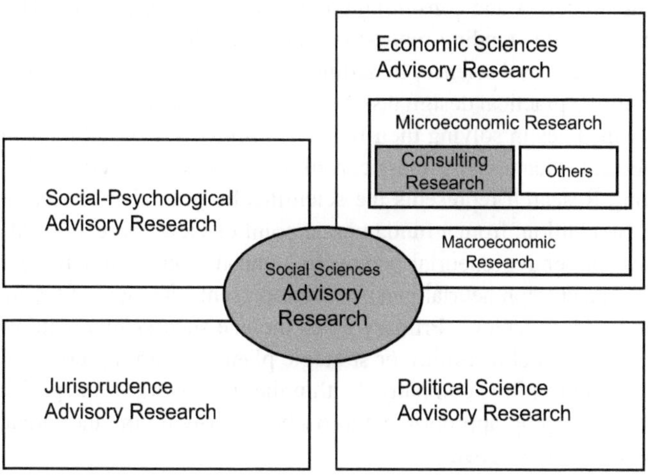

Fig. 3 Consulting Research as a branch of general research on advisory within the social sciences [inspired by Jeschke (2002)]

[7]It is unknown who first coined the phrase 'Consulting Research'.

approaches of action research or design science research, which are also relevant outside of business consulting.

Shugan continues his reflections on Consulting Research by introducing the additional term 'scholarly Consulting Research', which differs from 'simple' Consulting Research in that the results are more theoretically beneficial because existing theories are further developed while solving practical problems: "Beyond Consulting Research, there is research that excels on relevance as well as rigor and innovativeness." (Shugan 2004) However, this differentiation does not actually significantly improve the definition.

Niehaves and Becker close in on the term Consulting Research on the basis of the works of Kieser (1999) and Mohe (2005b) by separating off from the practice of consultancy: "Consulting Research is supposed to be aiming at producing true knowledge whereas consulting practice is supposed to bring this knowledge to application." (Niehaves and Becker 2006) Consulting Research would therefore be above all a service provider of consulting practice, which at the same time has to maintain a critical distance to practice ['*practically uninvolved research*' (Niehaves and Becker 2006)]. This understanding seems to be unnaturally shortened, but it refers to the appropriateness of making the desired relationship between science and practical business consulting explicit as part of one's own research.

Consulting Research as understood in the present contribution has two central issues. The first is the scientific penetration of the subject of business consulting, in which the focus is on gaining abstract scientific knowledge from individual consultancy projects. Second, scientific theories, results and methods need to be transferred to the practice of consulting, with the aim of solving tasks and problems in the realm of consulting processes and consulting companies better than before. The latter goal comes from the understanding represented here that the study of business management is an applied social science. In addition to a theoretical explanatory function, it also has to fulfil a practical design task by providing concrete assistance to decision-makers in companies in solving their business problems. Consulting Research aims at a management science of business consulting, as was demanded in the literature.[8]

Consulting Research represents the scientifically grounded concept of business consulting. In addition, from a fundamental point of view, there are further consulting concepts: the entrepreneurial perspective and the problem solving perspective (see Fig. 4). The entrepreneurial perspective represents the view of the management of consultancy organisations. Primary goals include successfully handling business tasks such as personnel recruiting or strategic planning, earning profit and securing the long-term future of the company. Within the framework of the problem solving perspective, developing appropriate approaches to solving the individual problems of clients is the primary goal.

Consulting Research recognises the great importance of business consulting for the development of companies on the one hand and as a high-turnover business sector on the other. From the point of view of gaining knowledge, it is not a matter of

[8]Compare Kaas and Schade (1995), Mohe and Pfriem (2002) and Fritz and Effenberger (2002).

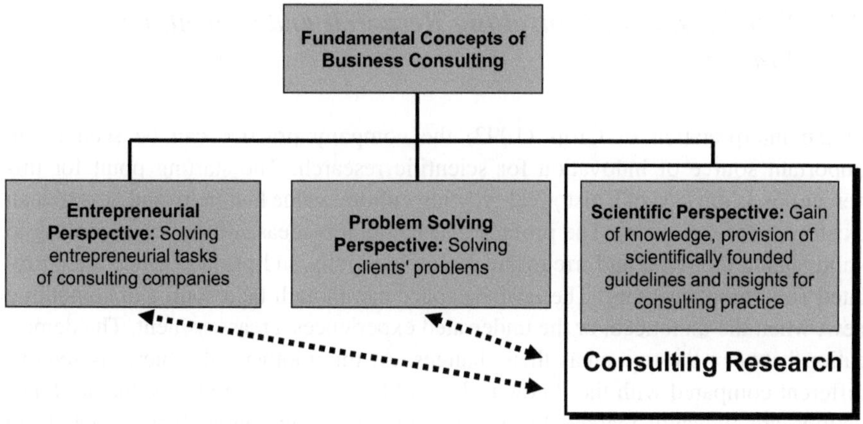

Fig. 4 Fundamental concepts of business consulting

collecting arguments for or against the use of consulting services. Rather, the goal is a better understanding of the phenomenon of business consulting in all its facets. A management science that largely excludes consulting firms from its considerations should be considered incomplete.

In addition to economic sciences, related disciplines such as sociology, psychology and (in particular in IT-oriented consulting) business informatics can also contribute to Consulting Research. Equally, various categories of research efforts within CR are conceivable and desirable:

- theory-oriented or conceptual contributions: development of concepts, models and theories covering the functioning of consulting and the consultancy market; application or adaptation of existing socio-scientific theories to peculiarities within consulting; derivation of normative design considerations,
- empirical contributions: survey of current states; quantitative analysis of empirical data; qualitative empirical Consulting Research; evaluation of model projects,
- methodological and instrumental contributions: development of methods and instruments for supporting consulting practice.[9]

With regard to the last point, CR should strive to offer effective methods and instruments for solving entrepreneurial questions within consultancy firms as well as for working on concrete consulting tasks. At the same time CR should receive suggestions for research activities, both from the entrepreneurial perspective and from the perspective of problem solving. This makes it clear that there are important points of contact and potential synergies between CR and the two other fundamental concepts of business consulting (indicated by arrows in Fig. 4).

[9]See Nissen (2003) for an example of a methodological contribution to CR.

3.3 Relationship of Consulting Research and Consulting Practice

In the interpretation of Grojs (1992) the company practice can be seen as an important source of innovation for scientific research. The starting point for this perception is the idea of a historical growing cultural value hierarchy and next to it an existing 'profane space'. The profane space contains ideas, which are according to valid standards trivial and irrelevant. Value hierarchy and profane space are correlated and complementary. The profane space can though be a source of something new, when the unnoticed, or the underrated experiences a reassessment. The demarcation between the two areas then changes. At this moment, the 'new' is seen as different compared with the 'known', but is likewise considered as valuable. Innovations are typically marked by actions among various hierarchies, which form profane spaces for each other (Grojs 1992).

Scheytt (1998) transfers this consideration to the question about innovation in business administration, and comes to the conclusion that company practice for the value hierarchy of business research can be seen as the location of the profane (and *vice versa*). Changed demarcations between business research and company practice, as well as the exchange of values between these spheres allow the 'trivial' practice to be significant for science. Innovation emerges from the reassessment of the known. Practice, as an independent domain, is therefore significant for innovation in science—for that matter it is also *vice versa*.

This conception suggests an intensive mutual involvement between Consulting Research and consulting practice. In the course of this, it is considered that the practice does not need a preliminary scientific theory to be capable of acting. Likewise, Consulting Research does not develop separately from the practice, but independent and self-reflective. It has its own picture of company practice. Scheytt (1998) demands, therefore, to acknowledge in the practical action, a concrete expressed intent to consider the seemingly trivial, worthless and profane, which determines the situation in the practice as a sphere of the trivial. This needs substantial efforts because of reservations and various conception worlds. Developing irritations, differences and paradoxes in dealing with practice would be *an incitement (driving force) for the process of self-reflexive renewal in science* (Scheytt 1998). One should though not go that far, that practice is the only source for the new in science.

Schrädler (1996) discusses the question on using scientific perceptions in consulting practice. Besides scientific aspiration and interdisciplinarity he demands research to be able to connect to consulting practice. Similar to Scheytt, Schrädler also sees the necessity to avoid inadmissible simplifications in Consulting Research and to illustrate the object of investigation in its entire complexity. This may give rise to the problem that research results are more difficult to understand and to be taken up by consulting practice (Schrädler 1996). Consulting Research shares this problem with other areas in science. The self-reflexive development of scientific systems is automatically accompanied by a certain distance from practice (Knyphausen 1988;

Schrädler 1996). To find a solution for this situation, science is encouraged to participate in consulting practice (internal perspective) and to recondition gained knowledge scientifically, in order to critically reflect the theory-driven results on consulting (external perspective) repeatedly.

In the context of the rigor versus relevance debate in management sciences, Nicolai (2004) estimates that an application concept is that much removed from the practitioner's conception, as itself is scientifically reflected. Consulting Research is in Nicolai's understanding of science a self-referential, closed sense-system. Above all, it would have to aim at developing alternative argumentation and action patterns to current consulting practice as well as at providing unrecognized correlations and deviating interpretations of practical facts. Similar to Scheytt and Schrädler, Nicolai also demands that communication between consulting science and practice is necessary. Thus differences among the perspectives should not be disclaimed but should be used productively and by doing this, new opportunities for action are made available for the consulting practice.

The totally different target systems of both spheres should though be noticed, as emphasized by Kieser (2002a). Consulting providers do not search for some scientific truth, but they do want to achieve economic targets. According to Kieser, scientists particularly aim at raising their scientific reputation. Therefore, they publish preferably in renowned professional journals with high requirements concerning the way an article is presented. This, by tendency, leads to an increasing complexity of science, which again builds a communication barrier to consulting practice. Even when the motivation of scientists can be more broadly established than in the interpretation of Kieser, it needs to be recorded that science and practice follow different objectives and values. This must be considered in their interaction and communication. It can, by tendency, lead to problems and misconceptions.

Wolf (2000) vehemently argues for a stronger theoretical foundation for consulting. Through continuous scientific support, he sees the opportunity to correct fundamental misconceptions (e.g. the independence of consultants) and gaps in practical business consulting and to avoid a crisis in the industry with lasting economic and business damage. Basically, this crisis has occurred in the meantime, in particular under the aspects of public view and the reputation of this industry. In the long term, a stronger theoretical foundation of consulting intervention in companies could have a very positive impact on the consulting industry's image, project quality and thus indirectly also on the economic situation of the consulting industry.

Mohe (2005a) also feels that a strong theoretical foundation is useful for consulting practice. On the other side, he refers to a certain 'consulting resistance' of business consultants themselves. Here it would be necessary that the consultants attitude changes. Consultants have to be prepared to complement their present approaches and instruments, which are lacking in theoretical foundations. They will only do this if the resulting economic benefits for practical business consulting can be credible. However, this should be possible in view of the professionalization of clients and increasingly critical consideration of current consulting methods. Exner et al. (1987) justify the need for theory of business consulting with the practical expediency to not allow oneself to be drawn into the consulted system and to be instrumentalized on the one hand, and on the other hand to make the consulting success more objectifiable.[10]

In addition to its significance for consulting practice, Consulting Research can also make important contributions to a more professional client approach to business consultants and the 'demystification' (Mohe and Pfriem 2002) of consultancy as a service. Mohe (2003) suggests the concept of 'meta consulting' as an example of a concrete application of Consulting Research. Meta consulting addresses itself as 'consulting on consulting processes' especially to consulting clients, who should be enabled to deal with consultants in a more professional way.

Mohe also demands a strong inclusion of the clients in Consulting Research (Mohe 2003). An integration of the consultants in research projects of Consulting Research is equally meaningful. Various forms of practical academic research are conceivable. Here a view on similar aspirations of the academic discipline 'business informatics' (Wirtschaftsinformatik) in the German-speaking area can be helpful.

The close connection between science and practice of consulting should simultaneously be supported by the integration of research results in the (university) education of future consultants (and their clients).

3.4 Requirements for Consulting Research

Some requirements for contributions to Consulting Research can be derived from the current discussion. First and foremost is the demand for *academic soundness* in the sense of being oriented toward established scientific conventions. This especially includes:

- defining the terms used,
- clear objective of the investigation, but impartiality regarding the result,
- consideration of the *status quo* of research,
- methodologically sound, systematic and critically reflecting approach,
- willingness to disclose all results and details of the research procedure for the purpose of a possible review by others.

According to Schrädler (1996), consideration of the research *status quo* means to strive to prevent different research methods from being simply set up next to each other. Instead, there should be active engagement with the ideas of others. The additional 'critical distance from the object under consideration' required by Wolf (2000) needs to be generally recognized as a property of academic rigor but different levels should be allowed depending on the research approach. For example, action research requires the combination of practical action and critical reflection with the cooperative inclusion of practitioners. The researcher can therefore be both observer

[10]Wolf (2000) also argues for a better, i.e. theoretically profound training for future business consultants.

and agent at the same time (Wolf and Priebe 2001). Even if the explanatory power of action research is debatable, it is encouraged here not to dismiss the soundness of it from the outset as it seems to be a promising approach for Consulting Research.

The criteria listed here for academic soundness do not automatically exclude research funded by third parties, including from the private sector, but it does point to potential problems, especially in the aspects of impartiality and disclosure.

A further 'ought-to' requirement in the context of scholarly work and academic soundness is the generation of completely new knowledge, i.e. *innovation*. Connected to that is the demand to not only publish existing concepts under new names but to actually ask new questions and find answers to them. The requirement sounds more trivial than it is, as expressly shown in the past discussion regarding 'fashion' and sustainability in business informatics and information systems research.[11] Consulting Research is particularly at risk because its subject matter, business consulting, is characterized by numerous management fashions and pseudo-innovations as well as a scientifically undisciplined, artificial language.

Another research demand is a *strong application reference*. The term is purposely not listed as 'practical relevance'. As the discussion has previously made clear, the scientific results are often not immediately practically relevant due to differing value systems and terminologies. They should however contain relevant results regarding the practice or at least be able to be transferred to relevant patterns of practical action, methods or concepts. The combination of *relevance* and *rigor* is considered here to be possible and worthwhile depending on the chosen topic and research approach.[12]

Cooperation and integration of science and practical work in consulting (consultants and clients) is also a part of the aim rooted in this requirement. It should have become clear that all sides can profit from this cooperation. According to Schrädler (1996) it can even be considered indispensable for assuring further developments on the theoretical side of consultancy and simultaneously for preventing research from becoming meaningless for practice.

A necessary condition and therefore a requirement for researchers in Consulting Research is, in addition to familiarity with science, *exact knowledge of the specifics in the application field of business consulting*. This especially concerns the values system, goals, terminology and methods of consultancy as well as comparable knowledge of the client side. This can be achieved for example through one's own experiences in consulting which should be gained through activity outside of the higher education system as much as possible in order to achieve the necessary authenticity. This increases the likelihood that, in Grojs's sense, it will be possible to successfully mediate and act between different value hierarchies, thus generating scientific innovation.

Also, the research results must *flow back into education*. In addition to scientifically rooted reflective knowledge (Moldaschl 2001), practical instrumental knowledge belongs in the educational repertoire of future consultants at institutes of higher

[11]See the essay by Mertens (2006) for a discussion within business informatics.

[12]This estimation is also shared by Shugan for example Shugan (2004).

education. There is no reason that this knowledge should remain exclusively in the domain of consulting firms.

4 Scientific Approaches to Consulting

4.1 Selected Theoretical Approaches to Consulting Research at a Glance

It is impossible to go into all theoretical approaches to the topic consulting. The following examples highlight some important theoretical perspectives on the subject.

4.1.1 Perspective of (New) Systems Theory

From a system theoretical perspective, a central topic of consulting is the possibility of intervention by consultants in companies. Closely related to that is the question how the interaction between consultants and clients should be organized. Essential is the perception of organizations as social autopoietic systems. According to that, organizations are operatively closed and self-regulating. They orientate their actions towards themselves, select and process environmental influences from their own perspective. A direct external influence on the organization is impossible. The foundation of these scientific investigations stems from Maturana and Varela (2006), as well as the systems theory of Luhmann (2006).

At the same time recent systems theory forms the foundation of systemic consulting. Wimmer (1992) defines interrelated objectives of this form of consulting:

- assisting a client system to attain an appropriate perspective on an actual problem, so that the survival chances of the company are maintained,
- to encourage the development of variants to deal with the problem on the basis of a changed problem view,
- to promote an organizational process, which mobilizes the system internal potential to process problems; in this way, the problem processing capacity of the client system is enlarged.

The claim to direct influence or change on the part of the consultants is abandoned. Instead, the self-reflection of the client system is the objective, from which changes may result that remove existing problems.

4.1.2 Perspective of New Institutional Economics

From the view of New Institutional Economics, consulting is a contract asset. Such assets are marked, in that they demand an investment in a specific, complex and high-value asset from a party involved, whose profitability depends on the future behavior of the other party (Kaas and Schade 1995). Consulting and other professional services are typical immaterial contract assets, which are initially marketed as service promises and are afterwards created by a close cooperation between the provider and the client.

Institutional economics deals with the imperfectness of actual markets - and institutions, which are suitable to overcome such imperfectness (Kaas 1992). Sub-disciplines of institutional economics are, in particular, the transaction cost theory, the property-rights theory and the principal-agent theory.[13]

The market of consulting services is characterized by information asymmetry of the providers and the clients. Therefore experience and trust features are very significant. Possible institutions, which can moderate the problems on the market for consulting or can even overcome them are lasting business relations, and the reputation of a consulting provider, but also contractual regulations and ‘signals’ (plausible information) (Kaas and Schade 1995).

Armbrüster and Kieser (2001) believe that institutional economics’ organizational theoretical instruments are a good way of not only describing the mechanisms of the consulting market but also explaining them, as in the case of the consultant-client relationship.[14] The perspective of institutional economics can moreover provide a practical contribution to improve the professionality of the clients and the efficiency of the consulting marketing and projects.

4.1.3 Perspective of Service Theory

The terms, essence and significance of professional services were already discussed in Sect. 1.2 of this contribution. For this consulting is a typical example. The features of professional services result in meaningful research questions for example in the areas of:

- the design process of consulting products,
- options of standardizing consulting services (Dichtl 1998),
- professional consulting marketing (Jeschke 2002),
- optimal integration of the client into the consulting process,
- capacity management in consulting companies,
- quality management in the case of consulting services.

[13]For a detailed overview on institutional economics and criticism on this theoretical perspective, see e.g. Schade (1997) and Barchewitz and Armbrüster (2004).

[14]Examples of contributions based on institutional economics are e.g. given by Kaas and Schade (1995), Schade (1997) and Stegemeyer (2002).

4.1.4 Perspective of the Resource-Based Management Approach

The resource-based view of strategic management (RBV) goes back to the papers by Penrose (1959), Wernerfelt (1984), Barney (1991) and others. From a theoretical point of view, it can be assigned to the area of competition theory. The RBV places the heterogeneous equipment of companies with internal resources as a source of competitive advantage in the center. It is argued that not the sole possession of these resources is the cause of the success of a company, but additionally appropriate employee skills and management skills are needed who know to take advantage of the potential of resources, which can be understood as a refinement process.

Following Schneider (1997) strategic resources within the meaning of RBV can be defined as: production factors purchased in markets, altered or enhanced by able management, employees or external specialists to create company-specific characteristics of competitiveness. While production factors can be bought by all competitors in markets, resources embody specific tangible and especially intangible assets of a firm. Their main characteristic is a more difficult acquisition by competitors.

For characterization of (strategically relevant) resources, various properties were defined in the course of academic discourse. According to the VRIS-framework of Barney (1991), a resource is valuable, rare (or even unique), inimitable and non-substitutable, i.e. cannot be replaced by other equivalents. Other authors have varied these properties and added in particular the usability and immobility aspects (see for instance Wade and Hulland 2004).

In terms of the RBV, strategic resources can be of both the material and the immaterial kind (tangible and intangible assets). Knowledge, capabilities and skills are immaterial resources and are exemplary for the fact that soft factors can also present a source of possible competitive advantages. The importance of intangible resources in the competitive environment is constantly increasing. In many industries, the knowledge and skills of employees have become the basis for company-related core competencies (Prahalad and Hamel 1990) and thus a source of long-term competitive advantages.

The original, rather production oriented concept of core competences, can also be transmitted to consulting, whereas the 'production capabilities' are here determined by human capital. One of the main tasks of the consulting management is to create conditions under which competitive relevant consulting competences can be established and expanded. The resource, respectively competence-oriented management approach can specifically provide important research contributions in the following areas of consulting:

- the establishment of unique differentiating factors in competition (a) in consulting as well as (b) via business consultants at their clients,
- strategic planning for consulting (Binnewies 2002),
- knowledge management, in particular the design of favorable conditions for individual and organizational learning in consulting.

4.1.5 Perspective of Procurement Theory

From the perspective of procurement theory consulting presents a valuable investment asset. Contrary to other investment assets the provision process of consulting reaches much further than the selection of suitable transaction partners, because the service generation is a longer interactive process, which happens among various persons from the provider and the client side. Additionally, the provision situation (e.g. the perceived risk) and company related context factors (e.g. size of the client firm) have an influence on the transaction behavior during the different process phases.

Kißling (1999) develops in his paper, which is exemplary for this perspective, a transaction model for purchasing professional services from a merging of knowledge of service marketing with concepts and results on organizational procurement behavior. The fundamental characteristic of his transaction model is the connection between a structural and a process-related viewpoint.

The procurement theoretical perspective provides implications for topics such as customer relationship management of business consultancies, project management in the consulting process and client professionalization in consulting procurement.

4.1.6 Perspective of Sociological Theory

Different theories from the sociological context have been applied to business consulting. The sociological point of view is characterised by the emphasis on values, norms and social relations within the framework of individual decisions. Such decisions are accordingly not made in a strict, rational way, but are based on experiences and internalized behavior patterns. Armbrüster and co-workers describe consulting performances from the sociological perspective of embeddedness (Glückler and Armbrüster 2003; Barchewitz and Armbrüster 2004). The embeddedness-approach (Granovetter 1985) understands both the actions of individuals as well as those of larger economic entities as influenced by networks of social relationships.

In this perspective, consulting is characterized above all by the uncertainty associated with it. Both the confidence in the market system and the institutions of the consulting market is low among market participants. For this reason, informal social institutions play an important role in reducing uncertainty. Such institutions are in particular the trust built up by positive personal experience with a transaction partner, the general reputation of a consulting firm in the market and, as a third form, information (e.g. recommendations) of trustworthy persons within the own social network (Barchewitz and Armbrüster 2004). The embeddedness approach has explanatory and design potential, especially in the context of consulting marketing, client relationship management and the selection of consultants.

In contrast, Kieser (2002b) uses sociological fashion theories to show how consulting firms generate demand for their services by creating and promoting management fashions. He creates a link with the individual career of managers who pick up on emerging fashions and implement them in their companies in order to ultimately make progress in their own professions.

Another example of the relevance of sociological theories in the consulting environment is Gidden's structuration theory (Giddens 1984). Giddens basically argues that actors (described as human agents) and social structure (rules and resources) are interrelated. Structure is thereby reproduced by repeated actions of individual agents taking place within a structured framework. A basic assumption formulated there is the duality of structure and action. All actions of the actors in a social system therefore relate to structures of this system. At the same time, the structures are reproduced by reference in actions. The social system therefore behaves recursively. A distinction is made between the three structural dimensions of legitimacy (authorization), domination (rule) and signification (meaning). These correspond to normative, power-related and communicative aspects of actions.

Iding (2000) uses this theoretical approach to analyze the influence of power in the consulting process in the context of hospital consulting. Mauerer and Nissen (2014) argue in their paper that the consultant-client relationship is of central importance for consulting engagements. The paper therefore outlines the social dimensions that are inherent in the consulting system due to its characteristics that create social complexity. They propose to utilize structuration theory for the compilation of the social context of a consulting system, as this provides a framework for incorporating the social determinants, focuses on actions of human-beings, and additionally allows the identification of interrelated dependencies of structure and actions.

Since the structuration theory principally addresses the question of understanding and controlling social systems, other possible applications are seen, for example, in the areas of personnel and project management of consulting firms as well as in the development of best practices.

4.2 Selected Practice-Oriented Research Conceptions

4.2.1 Action Research

Action research is a concept of applied management research and can be understood as an alternative to classical, quantitative empirical research (Wolf and Priebe 2001). It is characterized by its focus on practice-oriented benefit criteria that guide the scientific research process. Action research combines practical action and critical reflection. Through the direct participation of practitioners in research, the prospect of realizable solutions to problems and practical research results is enhanced. In this context, Probst and Raub (1995) speak of the equal pursuit of the two objectives problem solution and knowledge gained.

Typical research methods are self-evaluation and other qualitative survey methods (qualitative interviews, participatory observation, single-case study, and group discussion). Investigated persons have, as part of a 'discourse', the opportunity to comment on the research results and research interpretation. The results, which were verified in the discourse, are preliminary and can be questioned by new discourses. The results of such research should therefore not be misunderstood as irrevocable truths. Rather, a good part of their validity results from the feasibility and confirmation in entrepreneurial practice. In this sense, research is a continuous learning process that must remain critical and reflect on itself.

4.2.2 Design Science Research

Design science research is an approach with emphasis on practical research, in the tradition of engineering sciences. It is understood as being complementary to the development of suitable theories, which explain or predict human or organizational behavior. The design science paradigm seeks to extend the boundaries of human and organizational capabilities by creating new and innovative artifacts. In the design science paradigm, knowledge and understanding of a problem domain and its solution are achieved in the building and application of the designed artifact (Hevner et al. 2004). Various forms of artifacts are conceivable (March and Smith 1995), in particular:

- Construct: constitutes a (formal or informal) conceptualization used to describe and communicate on problems within a given domain and to specify their solutions.
- Model: a set of propositions or statements expressing relationships among constructs.
- Method: a set of steps used to perform a task or solve a problem.
- Instantiation: the realization of an artifact in its environment. It proves the practical realizability of constructs, models and methods.

Peffers et al. (2007, p. 47) define design as "the act of creating an explicitly applicable solution to a problem" while Hevner et al. (2004) describe design as a process as well as a product (artifact). In the concrete course of the research process one can, for instance, orientate on the widespread Design Science Research Process Model (see Fig. 5) according to Peffers et al. (2007). Initially, the problem must be identified and research activities motivated. This first step defines the research question and explains why a solution is worthwhile. An important issue here is to demonstrate the practical relevance of the problem. Then, in step 2, the objectives of a solution to be developed should be made clear. By designing an artifact to address the relevant practical problem, an improvement over the current situation must be attainable. In addition scientific goals should be pursued and clarified at this step. The third step is the actual design and development of the artifact. The functionality and structure of the artifact is first of all designed and then the artifact itself. During the design step, different methods may be applied depending on the concrete problem and issue. These may include, for instance, literature reviews, quantitative and qualitative research approaches, or any other scientifically sound method to

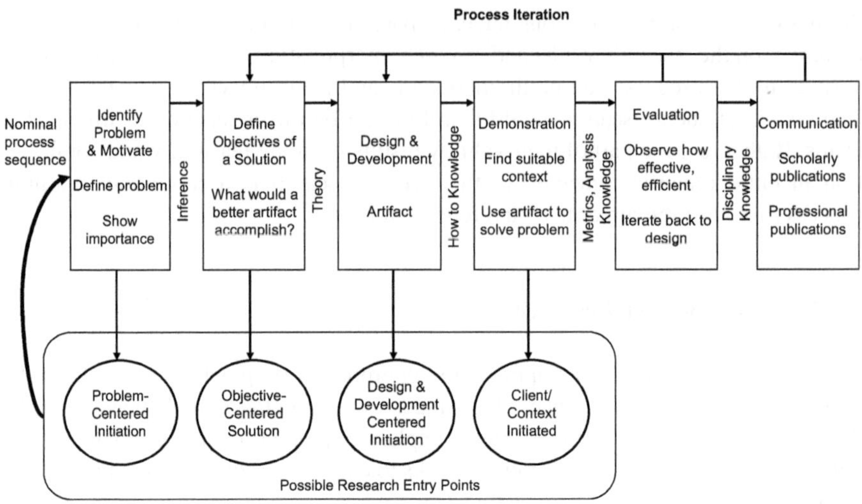

Fig. 5 Design science research process model after Peffers et al. (2007)

design the artifact. Then, the usefulness of the artifact in solving the practical problem addressed must be demonstrated. Again, various methods can be applied during this demonstration step. These may include experiments, simulations, case studies or formal evidence. After the construction and demonstration of an artifact the next step in the design process is the evaluation (March and Storey 2008). The evaluation should prove the quality and effectiveness of the artifact (Hevner et al. 2004). Applicable methods include e.g. performance measurements, user surveys, expert interviews or simulations. In a final step, it is intended to communicate the problem and its meaning as well as the developed artifact and its benefits. Target groups are researchers and practitioners alike.

The Design Science Research Process Model after Peffers et al. has different possible entry points, as can be seen in Fig. 5. Moreover, it is of an iterative nature so that a design result can incrementally be optimized while integrating results in particular from the evaluation phase in the next design cycle.

Design science is of interest for Consulting Research as it bridges the gap between science and practice. Moreover, it can effectively supplement the more theoretical or empirical contributions in Consulting Research (Niehaves and Becker 2006). These research paradigms benefit from each other and should be seen as complementary.

4.3 Empirical Research

Of course, classical empirical research is also of great importance for the field of Consulting Research. These studies, which are based on quantitative and qualitative survey methods (e.g. questionnaires, interviews or document analysis) use statistical data analyses to determine structural correlations between influencing and result variables, for example, or to test previously formulated hypotheses. A typical example is the research of success factors, which can also be found in the context of business consulting (Effenberger 1998; Fritz and Effenberger 1998).

5 Conclusions

Consulting is an important branch of industry, not so much in terms of total turnover, but more in the sense that it influences virtually all other industries. Moreover, consulting is very attractive as an employer to highly qualified young people. By contrast, the amount of scientific research interest in consulting is only moderate, and dedicated scientific outlets for results of Consulting Research are scarce. The proportionally small amount of scientific publications on the topic of consultancy fades into the mass of other contributions in the business-oriented journals.

The scientific community of Consulting Research is divided. They are referred to as ‘islands of research’ (Mohe 2004) and ‘lone wolfs’, not only in the German-speaking areas. It would therefore be desirable to more strongly bundle the research efforts in Consulting Research and to make it more visible to the outside. This applies both to the relationship with other sub-fields of management research and with regard to consulting practice and its clients. As an academic stream it must be supported by an active and well organized research community, cooperatively acting at national as well as international level. In addition, subjects and results of Consulting Research should find a stronger place in academic education to grow an audience of reflective practitioners.

The research field neither carries the weight appropriate to its true importance nor does the consulting profession enjoy an especially positive reputation. Guideline- and disclosure-oriented literature, which has a much higher volume, dominates the perception of the public. In this contribution we argue for a change towards a better theoretical understanding of consulting and a closer cooperation between science and practice in this field. Design Science appears to be a particularly attractive research paradigm to reach the latter goal.

However, at this stage, there is no closed universal theory of business consulting nor can any superiority of a specific theoretical foundation be proven. The search for a universal, timelessly valid theory can be judged critically in the sense of Feyerabend (2001). With a multitude of alternative theoretical approaches, however, the pressure of arbitrariness can quickly arise. Similarly, the isolated and sometimes contradictory results of different approaches make it more difficult to achieve connectivity in consulting practice.

The diversity of theories on the subject of consulting not only presents the risk of research being fragmented, but also offers an opportunity for progress in knowledge. Scientific innovations are often generated at the interface of neighboring disciplines. By looking at the same facts simultaneously from different perspectives, synergies and new insights can arise. However, competing approaches must be known and critically integrated into one's own considerations.

According to Schrädler (1996), the ideal form of theory development in Consulting Research is a reflexive circle of cooperative and competing theoretical approaches, whereby the contents of other disciplines and impulses from practice are also integrated into the research process. Such a state of evolutionary theory development has not yet been reached. As the above explanations have made clear, there are indeed different proposals for a theoretical approach to the topic. However, these are largely unconnected to each other, so that it is left to everyone to decide for themselves which approach promises the greatest potential under which conditions. It is also unclear which theories are compatible with each other and where they can complement each other.

The phenomenon of business consulting is complex and has many facets that may require different theoretical foundations and research methods. Therefore, from a research-theoretical perspective, research approaches should not be excluded from the outsets which remove the strict separation of science and practice. Action Research and Design Science Research can provide valuable insights. Consulting practice is an indispensable source of stimulation and critical reflection for science.

The continual dialog and close integration of consulting practice and its clients must be a continuous foundation within Consulting Research. All sides can profit from that cooperation. More readiness would be necessary on the part of the consultants to critically reflect on their own methods and approaches in light of scientific results and to adapt them where appropriate. A stronger theoretical foundation of consulting can in the long run also contribute to improving the image of consultants in the public eye.

References

Armbrüster T, Kieser A (2001) Unternehmensberatung—Analysen einer Wachstumsbranche. DBW 61(6):688–709

Bamberger I, Wrona T (2012) Konzeptionen der strategischen Unternehmensberatung. In: Wrona T (ed) Strategische Unternehmensberatung, 6th edn. Gabler, Wiesbaden, pp 1–44

Barchewitz C, Armbrüster T (2004) Unternehmensberatung. Marktmechanismen, Marketing, Auftragsakquisition. DUV, Wiesbaden

Barney J (1991) Firm resources and sustained competitive advantage. J Manag 17(1):99–120

BDU (2017) Facts and figures zum deutschen Beratungsmarkt 2016/17. BDU e.V, Bonn

Binnewies S (2002) Strategisches Management professioneller Dienstleistungen am Beispiel der Unternehmensberatung. Duehrkohp and Radicke, Göttingen

Cardea (2016) Trends in the consulting market 2016. Cardea AG. https://www.consultingsearcher.com/eng/Cardea-competence-centre/The-consulting-market/Executive-Survey-Consulting-Market-Trends. Accessed 12 Aug 2017

Cardea & Newcoventure (2016) Consulting 4.0—die marktorientierte Digitalisierung. Research report. Cardea AG & Newcoventure GmbH, Zurich and Neckarhausen

Christensen CM, Wang D, van Bever D (2013) Consulting on the cusp of disruption. Harv Bus Rev 91(10):106–114

Consultancy.uk (2017) Global consulting market development. And other publically available information on the website http://www.consultancy.uk/consulting-industry/global. Accessed 18 Jul 2017
Craig D (2005) Rip-off! The scandalous inside story of the management consulting money machine. Original Book Company, London
Deelmann T (2012) Organisations- und Prozessberatung. In: Nissen V, Klauk B (eds) Studienführer Consulting. Gabler, Wiesbaden
Deelmann T, Nissen V (2018) Institutionalization of consulting research—review and comparison of two approaches in Germany over the period 2007–2017. In: Nissen V (ed) Advances in consulting research. Springer, Heidelberg
Dichtl M (1998) Standardisierung von Beratungsleistungen. DUV, Wiesbaden
Effenberger J (1998) Erfolgsfaktoren der Strategieberatung. Die Analyse einer Leistung von Unternehmensberatern aus Klientensicht. Poeschel, Stuttgart
Engelhardt WH, Kleinaltenkamp M, Reckenfelderbäumer M (1994) Leistungsbündel als Absatzobjekte. Ein Ansatz zur Überwindung der Dichotomie von Sach- und Dienstleistungen. In: Corsten H (ed) Integratives Dienstleistungsmanagement. Gabler, Wiesbaden, pp 31–69
Ernst B (2002) Die evaluation von Beratungsleistungen—Prozesse der Wahrnehmung und Bewertung. DUV, Wiesbaden
Exner A, Königswieser R, Titscher S (1987) Unternehmensberatung—systemisch. DBW 47 (3):265–284
Feyerabend PK (2001) Wider den Methodenzwang, 8th edn. Suhrkamp, Frankfurt am Main
Fritz W, Effenberger J (1998) Strategische Unternehmensberatung. Verlauf und Erfolg von Projekten der Strategieberatung. Die Betriebswirtschaft 58(1):103–118
Fritz W, Effenberger J (2002) Strategische Unternehmensberatung. Verlauf und Erfolg von Projekten der Strategieberatung. In: Bamberger I (ed) Strategische Unternehmensberatung. Konzeptionen – Prozesse – Methoden, 3rd edn. Gabler, Wiesbaden, pp 273–298
Giddens A (1984) The constitution of society. Outline of the theory of structuration. Polity Press, Cambridge
Glückler J, Armbrüster T (2003) Bridging uncertainty in management consulting. The mechanisms of trust and networked reputation. Organ Stud 24(2):269–297
Granovetter M (1985) Economic action and social structure. The problem of Ebeddedness. Am J Sociol 91(3):481–510
Grojs B (1992) Über das Neue. Versuch einer Kulturökonomie
Hevner A, March ST, Park J, Ram S (2004) Design science research in information systems. MIS Q 28(1):75–105
Iding H (2000) Hinter den Kulissen der Organisationsberatung. Qualitative Fallstudien von Beratungsprozessen im Krankenhaus. Leske und Budrich, Opladen
Jeschke K (2002) Theorie und Praxis der Unternehmensberatung. Teil 2: Theoretische Grundlagen der Unternehmensberatung. Vorlesungsfolien der ebs European Business School, Reichartshausen
Kaas KP (1992) Marketing und Neue Institutionenlehre. Working paper, Frankfurt am Main University, Chair of Marketing
Kaas KP, Schade C (1995) Unternehmensberater im Wettbewerb. Eine empirische Untersuchung aus der Perspektive der Neuen Institutionslehre. ZfB 65(10):1067–1089
Kieser A (1999) Kommunikationsprobleme zwischen Wissenschaft, Unternehmensberatung und Praxis bei der Konzeptionierung praktikabler Organisationsmodelle. In: Egger A, Grün O, Moser R (eds) Managementinstrumente und -konzepte. Entstehung, Verbreitung und Bedeutung für die Betriebswirtschaftslehre. Schäffer-Poeschel, Stuttgart, pp 63–88
Kieser A (2002a) Wissenschaft und Beratung. C. Winter, Heidelberg
Kieser A (2002b) Managers as marionettes? Using fashion theories to explain the success of consultancies. In: Kipping M, Engwall L (eds) Management consulting. Emergence and dynamics of a knowledge industry. Oxford University Press, Oxford, pp 167–183
Kißling V (1999) Beschaffung professioneller Dienstleistungen. Eine empirische Untersuchung zum Transaktionsverhalten. Duncker und Humblot, Berlin

Kleinaltenkamp M (2001) Begriffsabgrenzungen und Erscheinungsformen von Dienstleistungen. In: Bruhn M, Meffert H (eds) Handbuch Dienstleistungsmanagement. Von der strategischen Konzeption zur praktischen Umsetzung, 2nd edn. Gabler, Wiesbaden, pp 27–50

Knyphausen D (1988) Unternehmungen als evolutionsfähige Systeme. Überlegungen zu einem evolutionären Konzept für die Organisationstheorie. Kirsch, München

Lippold D (2015) Die Unternehmensberatung: Von der strategischen Konzeption zur praktischen Umsetzung, 2nd edn. Springer Gabler, Wiesbaden

Løwendahl BR (1997) Strategic management of professional service firms. Handelshøjskolens Forlag, Kopenhagen

Luhmann N (2006) Soziale Systeme. Grundriß einer allgemeinen Theorie, 12th edn. Suhrkamp, Frankfurt am Main

March ST, Smith G (1995) Design and natural science research on information technology. Decis Support Syst 15(4):251–266

March ST, Storey VC (2008) Design science in the information systems discipline: an introduction to the special issue on design science research. MIS Q 32(4):725–730

Maturana H, Varela FJ (2006) Der Baum der Erkenntnis, 12th edn. Goldmann, München

Mauerer C, Nissen V (2014) Portraying the social dimensions of consulting with structuration theory. J Serv Sci Manag 2(7):110–130

Mertens P (2006) Moden und Nachhaltigkeit in der Wirtschaftsinformatik. HMD Praxis der Wirtschaftsinformatik 250:109–118

Mohe M (2003) Klientenprofessionalisierung. Strategien und Perspektiven eines professionellen Umgangs mit Unternehmensberatung. Metropolis, Marburg

Mohe M (2004) Stand und Entwicklungstendenzen der empirischen Beratungsforschung. Eine qualitative Meta-Analyse für den deutschsprachigen Raum. DBW 64(6):693–713

Mohe M (2005a) Meta-Beratung. In: Mohe M (ed) Innovative Beratungskonzepte. Ansätze, Fallbeispiele, Reflexionen. Rosenberger, Leonberg, pp 285–311

Mohe M (2005b) Der systemische Klient. Was passiert, wenn Klienten ihre Berater beobachten? Organ 24(2):44–51

Mohe M, Pfriem R (2002) Where are the Professional Clients? Möglichkeiten zur konzeptionellen Weiterentwicklung von Meta-Beratung. In: Mohe M, Heinecke HJ, Pfriem R (eds) Consulting—Problemlösung als Geschäftsmodell. Klett-Cotta, Stuttgart, pp 25–40

Moldaschl M (2001) Reflexive Beratung. Einer Alternative zu strategischen und systemischen Ansätzen. In: Degele N, Münch T, Pongratz HJ, Saam NJ (eds) Soziologische Beratungsforschung. Perspektiven für Theorie und Praxis der Organisationsforschung. Leske und Budrich, Opladen, pp 133–157

Müller-Stewens G, Drolshammer J, Kriegmeier J (1999) Professional Service Firms—Branchenmerkmale und Gestaltungsfelder des Managements. In: Müller-Stewens G, Drolshammer J, Kriegmeier J (eds) Professional service firms. FAZ, Frankfurt am Main, pp 11–153

Nicolai AT (2004) Der „trade-off" zwischen „rigour" und „relevance" und seine Konsequenzen für die Managementwissenschaften. Z Betriebswirt 74(2):99–118

Niedereichholz C (2010) Unternehmensberatung. Vol. 1: Beratungsmarketing und Auftragsakquisition, 5th edn. R. Oldenbourg, München und Wien

Niedereichholz C (2012) Unternehmensberatung. Vol. 2: Auftragsdurchführung und Qualitätssicherung, 6th edn. R. Oldenbourg, München und Wien

Niehaves B, Becker J (2006) Design science perspectives on IT-consulting. In: Lehner F, Nösekabel H, Kleinschmidt P (eds) Proceedings of MKWI 2006. GITO, Berlin, pp 7–17

Nissen V (2003) Wissenskonservierung mittels eines fuzzy-regelbasierten Systems für die Aufwandsplanung von Beratungsprojekten. Zeitschrift für Planung & Unternehmenssteuerung 14(3):243–258

Nissen V (2007) Consulting Research—eine Einführung. In: Nissen V (ed) Consulting Research. Unternehmensberatung aus wissenschaftlicher Perspektive. DUV, Wiesbaden, pp 3–38

Nissen V (2013) Stand und Perspektiven der informationsverarbeitungsbezogenen Beratung. HMD Praxis der Wirtschaftsinformatik 50(4):23–32

Nissen V (2018) Digital transformation of the consulting industry—introduction and overview. In: Nissen V (ed) Digital transformation of the consulting industry. Extending the traditional delivery model. Springer, Berlin, pp 1–58
Parakala K (2015) Global consulting and IT service providers trends, an industry perspective. Technova, Australia
Peffers K, Tuunanen T, Rothenberger MA, Und Chatterjee S (2007) A design science research methodology for information systems research. J Manag Inf Syst 24(3):45–77
Penrose ET (1959) The theory of the growth of the firm. Wiley, New York
Peterson M (2001) Wissensmanagement in der strategischen Unternehmensberatung: Erfolgsfaktoren, Methoden und Konzepte. DUV, Wiesbaden
Prahalad CK, Hamel G (1990) The core competence of the corporation. Harv Bus Rev 68(3):79–91
Probst G, Raub S (1995) Action research: Ein Konzept angewandter Managementforschung. Die Unternehmung 49(1):3–19
Schade C (1997) Marketing für Unternehmensberatung. Ein institutionenökonomischer Ansatz, 2nd edn. DUV, Wiesbaden
Scheytt T (1998) Innovation in der Betriebswirtschaftslehre. In: Gerum E (ed) Innovation in der Betriebswirtschaftslehre. Gabler, Wiesbaden, pp 23–49
Schneider D (1997) Betriebswirtschaftslehre. Vol. 3: Theorie der Unternehmung. Oldenbourg, München
Schrädler J (1996) Unternehmensberatung aus organisationstheoretischer Sicht. DUV, Wiesbaden
Schüppel J (1996) Wissensmanagement. Organisatorisches Lernen im Spannungsfeld von Wissens– und Lernbarrieren. Gabler, Wiesbaden
Shugan SM (2004) Consulting, research, and consulting research (editorial). Mark Sci 23 (2):173–179
Staute J (1996) Der Consulting-Report. Vom Versagen der Manager zum Reibach der Berater, 2nd edn. Campus, Frankfurt am Main
Stegemeyer W (2002) Der Vergleich von Abschlussprüfung und Unternehmensberatung aus der Perspektive der Agency- und der Signalling-Theorie. Tectum, Marburg
Wade M, Hulland J (2004) The resource-based view and information systems research: review, extension, and suggestions for future research. MIS Q 28(1):107–142
Walger G (1995) Idealtypen der Unternehmensberatung. In: Walger G (ed) Formen der Unternehmensberatung: Systemische Unternehmensberatung, Organisationsabwicklung, Expertenberatung und gutachterliche Beratungstätigkeit in Theorie und Praxis. Otto Schmidt, Cologne, pp 1–18
Wernerfelt B (1984) A resource-based view of the firm. Strateg Manag J 5:171–180
Wimmer R (1992) Was kann Beratung leisten? Zum Interventionsrepertoire und Interventionsverständnis der systemischen Organisationsberatung. In: Wimmer R (ed) Organisationsberatung. Neue Wege und Konzepte. Gabler, Wiesbaden, pp 59–111
Wolf G (2000) Die Krisis der Unternehmensberatung. DUV, Wiesbaden
Wolf B, Priebe M (2001) Wissenschaftstheoretische Richtungen, 2nd edn. Empirische Pädagogik, Landau
Zimmermann KA (1997) Kasse ohne Klasse. MVG-Verlag, Landsberg am Lech

Volker Nissen holds the Chair of Information Systems Engineering in Services at Technische Universität Ilmenau, Germany, since 2005. Prior to this, he pursued a consulting career, including positions as manager at IDS Scheer AG, director at DHC GmbH, and CEO of NISSCON Ltd., Germany. In 1994 he received a PhD degree in Economic Sciences with distinction from the University of Goettingen, Germany. His current research interests include the digital transformation of the consulting industry, the management of IT-agility, metaheuristic optimization, and process acceptance research. He is author and editor of 20 books and some 200 other publications, including papers in Business and Information Systems Engineering, Information Systems Frontiers, IEEE Transactions on EC, IEEE Transactions on NN, OR Spectrum, and Annals of OR.

Part I
Consulting Research as a Discipline

Consulting: Characterization of Concepts and Connections

Thomas Deelmann

Abstract Consulting is highly popular but a semantic consensus does not seem to exist—neither in theory nor in praxis. Even at a high level, the differences between the terms of e.g. consulting, business consulting, management consulting, and top management consulting are not always clear. This paper aims to characterize and connect various existing concepts in the consulting business. It can be interpreted as a discussion proposal and as a basis for a clearer understanding. For this purpose, the consultancy system is separated from the client system. Subsequently, the consultancy system with its roles, forms, structure and skills is presented. The last part describes the client system with its roles, types of requirements and characteristics. Links between the individual concepts are drawn.

1 Introduction[1]

Consulting has been enjoying an increasing popularity for several decades. For example, the market volume for organizational consulting services in Germany rose by an annual average of 9% from 1963 to 2015 (CAGR; data taken from Deelmann 2018). In parallel, one can articulate that the theoretical foundation of this business practice is inadequate and needs further detailing (e.g. Nissen 2007; Armbrüster 2006; Zirkler 2005; Heuermann and Herrmann 2003; Mohe et al. 2002). One example for this missing foundation might be the lack of a semantic consensus: Leading German market researchers distinguish between Management Consulting and IT Consulting & Systems Integration,[2] resp. between Strategy, Organization &

---

[1]This paper is an updated, translated, and shortened version of Deelmann (2015).

[2]This enumeration refers to the so called 'Lünendonk-Listen', online at: www.luenendonk.de

T. Deelmann (✉)
University of Applied Sciences for Public Administration and Management of North Rhine-Westphalia—Fachhochschule für öffentliche Verwaltung (FHöV), Cologne, Germany
e-mail: thomas.deelmann@fhoev.nrw.de

V. Nissen (ed.), *Advances in Consulting Research*, Contributions to Management Science, https://doi.org/10.1007/978-3-319-95999-3_2

Processes, HR, and IT consulting.[3] Similarities or differences between the approaches are hard to define. Additionally, authors often use the terms of Management Consulting, Top-Management Consulting, and Strategy Consulting while referring to consultancies like McKinsey, Boston Consulting Group and Bain—only to name a few prominent representatives. One can only speculate about the reasons of this semantic confusion: It might either be a matter of pure carelessness or the hope of getting more attention for a publication due to the usage of verbal add-ons like Strategy or Top-Management.

Wolf (2013) offers emerging scientific domains a way out of this situation. He sees the compilation of a conceptual apparatus as constitutional work for a given domain. Currently consulting research lacks such a conceptual model. However, some authors have already compiled extensive collections of single definitions, e.g. for consulting (cf. Kohr 2000; Sangüesa Sanchez 2003; Heuermann and Herrmann 2003).

This paper wants to elaborate various concepts in the context of organizational consulting rather than to discuss single terms intensively. As a result, it will propose a conceptual apparatus or model that can serve as a basis for a better understanding of the term consulting with its related concepts and connections. Therefore, a larger total scope of terms is preferred over an in-depth comparison of existing definitions. The individual concepts will be connected in text form and with the help of visual representations.

After this introductory section, a working definition for organizational consulting is presented and the basic relationship between the so-called consultancy system and the client system is introduced (Sect. 2). Section 3 then describes the consultancy system in detail. After an overview, details on the forms of intervention (or forms of consulting), the structure of a consultancy, and its skills are discussed. Section 4 focuses on the client system. It starts with an overview and goes on with the client's internal roles, types of demand, and characteristics. A short summary (Sect. 5) completes this paper.

2 Point of Departure

2.1 *Working Definition of "Consulting"*

The following working definition of consulting will be used as a starting point for subsequent explanations and discussions.[4]

[3]This enumeration refers to the 'Facts & Figures' studies of the BDU, online at: www.bdu.de

[4]This section is taken with minor adoptions from Deelmann et al. (2006a, pp. 199–200).

Consulting is a professional, contractually appointed service and transformation process of an intervening attendance by a consultancy system for the description, analysis, and solution of a problem of the client system with the goal of transformation.

The individual aspects of the definition are briefly sketched out first and referred to within the conceptual model later on. Beneath the point that consulting refers not only to businesses of all sizes but also to e.g. governments, municipalities, and churches, there are several relevant elements in this definition:

Professionalism This attribute distinguishes consulting as a (mostly) for-profit and regular activity from various other support activities.

Contractual Appointment Is a relevant criterion due to formalistic reasons. The relationship between client and consultant is initialized and stands out against other working relationships, e. g. employer-employee-relationship.

Process Organizational consulting is being understood as a process and distinguishes from singular events such as lectures, training sessions etc.

Intervening Attendance This is an open genus with respect to the several types of consulting, containing different kinds of intervention: expertise-oriented consulting, expert-oriented consulting, process-oriented consulting, and systemic consulting. The term 'attendance' distinguishes from other forms of cooperation (e.g. co-management) or replacing work (e.g. interim management).

Consultancy System This depicts a marked system—consisting of one or more persons and their emergent interaction relationships—which is not identical with the client system.

Description, Analysis, and Solution These terms describe the main tasks of a consultancy. One has to indicate that there—in principle—is an information asymmetry towards the client. Therefore, consulting has to support the client's awareness for change and the self-description of problem situations, and should not give recommendations only based on external and environmental knowledge.

Problem of the Client System This is to stress that not projected problems of the consultancy (perhaps with a root in available solutions) have to be solved. Rather virulent problems of the client have to be solved in co-operation. It is important to note that the client is the only one who can decide for the client organization within a consultant-client-relationship. The act of consulting only supports the realization, evaluation, and (if necessary) change of existing decisions. This situation points out the relevant difference between consultancies and the client: The decision is exclusively made by the client. This is also true if the consultant influences the client in a more or less strong way.

Transformation The primary goal of consulting is to support a self-driven change of the client system.

2.2 Relation Between Consultant and Client

Section 2.1 pointed out that consulting is an *intervention*, i.e. an interaction between a *consultancy system* (consultant) and a *client system* (client). Together they are the *participants of the intervention*. The rather technical terms of a consultancy system and a client system are used in order to signal that the systems could consist of only one member each but are not limited to this size.

The participants can be grouped into a consulting system in a narrower and a broader sense. The *consulting system in a narrower sense* is a sub-system and only contains the members of the consultancy system and the client system which are active participants of the above mentioned intervention, often called project members. The *consulting system in a broader sense* is a super-system and contains all members of the consultancy systems and the client system—it has therefore not only active but also passive elements for a given intervention (Mohe 2003).

Organizational consulting is often conducted in the form of a project. The Project Management Institute defines a *project* as "a temporary endeavor undertaken to create a unique product, service or result. A project is temporary in that it has a defined beginning and end in time, and therefore defined scope and resources. And a project is unique in that it is not a routine operation, but a specific set of operations designed to accomplish a singular goal." (Project Management Institute 2017, emphasis removed by the author) Sect. 4.3 demonstrates that not all kinds of consulting interventions have a specific target. Organizational consulting could be a project but it does not have to. A project on the other hand is always an intervention.

Organizational consulting has the *contractual appointment* as a relevant criterion because at this point the relationship between the consultancy system and the client system is initialized (cf. above). Any given intervention can rely on a contract; the consulting intervention needs a contract. In praxis a differentiation between an initial contract and a follow-up contract (or: follow-up order) is often considered being relevant.

Figure 1 summarizes the discussed concepts and their connections. The format of the visualization is explained in Sect. 2.3.

2.3 Remarks on the Graphical Notation

The individual concepts and their connections in this paper will be emphasized in italics within the text as well in a visual form. Within the figures, each concept is represented by a single square (e.g. *organizational consulting* at the top of Fig. 1).

The connections between the concepts are represented by lines. These lines can be semantic links in the form of an arrow. They have little notes describing the connection (e.g. can be at the arrow from *organizational consulting* towards *project* in the upper left corner of Fig. 1).

A second kind of connection is the generalization resp. specialization which is represented by a triangle pointing towards the more general concept (e.g. the triangle in the upper right hand corner of Fig. 1 points towards *contractual appointment* in

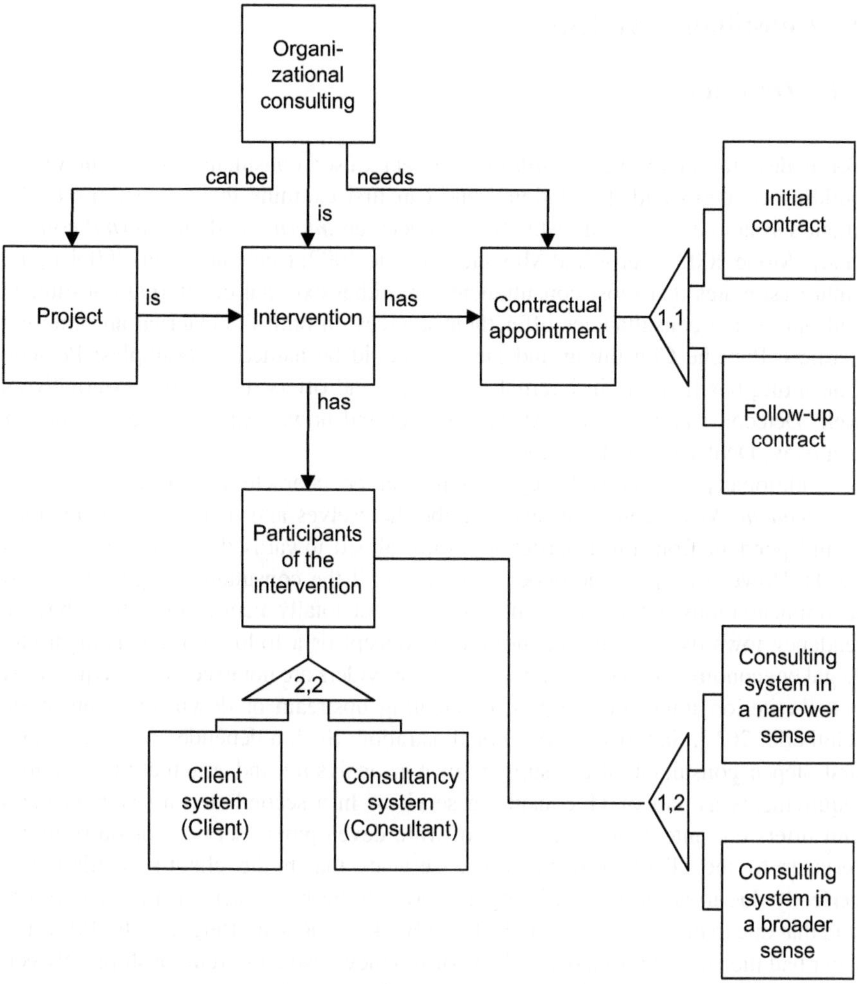

Fig. 1 Connections towards client system and consultancy system

order to symbolize that this concept is more abstract than the two concepts of *initial contract* and *follow-up contract* which are connected to the flat side of the triangle).

Each triangle contains two numbers which state the minimum and the maximum of specializations a concept can adopt (e.g. the 1,1 in the triangle mentioned above: A *contractual appointment* is at least one and also at most one of the two more specialized concepts—it is either an *initial contract* or a *follow-up contract* but it cannot be both at the same time. The 1,2 in the triangle in the bottom right corner says that a *participant of an intervention* has to be part of a *consulting system in a narrower sense* or it has to be part of a *consulting system in a broader sense* or it can be part of both).

The figures will be combined in one summarizing figure at the end of this paper.

3 Consultancy System

3.1 Overview

For a description of the *consultancy system* (also: consultant, consultancy), its building concepts and its relations, one can first examine the connections to the client's system and make a distinction between an *internal* and an *external* consultancy (Mohe 2002; Wurps and Musone Crispino 2002; Deelmann et al. 2006b). The author estimates that most consultancies are either external or internal consultants and only some consultancies offer their services on both the external and internal markets. Porsche Consulting and Detecon could be named as examples: Porsche Consulting has its roots in internal consulting and offers its services externally as well; Detecon started on the external market and nowadays works for its mother company, Deutsche Telekom, too.

Additionally, the consultancy system can be characterized as *dependent* or *independent*. Many consultancies describe themselves and their recommendations as independent from third parties and only aimed towards the individual client's needs. However, a possible dependency exists if the consultant's suggestions and recommendations for a client's problem are not totally neutral or if they have a tendency towards a certain technological concept or a follow-up engagement etc. Legal or economic ties between two service providers are not necessarily required. A better criterion might be the goal of creating upstream or downstream business. (Gutberlet 2012; Sandberg 2003) For illustration: Such a dependency exists if in a first step a consultant offers support in e.g. analysing and articulating customer requirements as part of IT consulting services. In a second step a sister business unit offers e.g. integration services, software development services or outsourcing services to the client systems. These services match the client's requirements perfectly due to an optimized interplay between the two sister business units. It is said that due to the investment of Deutsche Bank into Roland Berger in the 1990s the latter had the character of a dependent consultancy; also close relationships between e.g. tax and audit firms and consultancies tend to bind the consultants.

While intervening in the client system, the consultancy system takes over a *role*. This is an externalized mode of behaviour during the intervention. Examples for a role are: Scapegoat, guru, legitimization authority, doctor, pilot, and architect. The describing labels can be used for conclusions by analogy between the role model and the performed role. These labels help all involved parties to get a better understanding about the actions of the consultancy system. (Friedrich von den Eichen 2005; Neuberger 2002) An agreement about the role can be made on an explicit or an implicit level. A contract or a simple understanding between the consultant and the client would be explicit; actions implied by conduct would be implicit. Disagreements about the offered and performed role by the consultancy system and the requested and perceived role by the client are likely to lead to misunderstandings of all kinds and to different opinions about the success of the consulting engagement (Friedrich von den Eichen 2005). Of course, the roles can overlap in various ways.

In addition to these rather descriptive attributes, there are several connections highly relevant for the inner workings of the consultancy systems. Firstly, there is the *form of intervention* a consultant uses. The form determines the way in which the consultant interacts with the client (cf. Sect. 3.2). Secondly, the consultancy system offers *skills* towards client systems. Thirdly, it has an individual *structure*. The *organizational dimensions* build on skills and structures.

Regularly, one, two or more skills are combined in a divisional, matrix or intermeshed organization. Together with hierarchical and geographical structures, an internal structure for the leadership team and the employees can be designed. One member of the leadership team takes over the responsibility for a single segment of the created organization. The number of segments is not determined but regularly reflects the type, the breadth and the depth of the service offerings and the size of the leadership team.

The form of intervention, the structure, and the skills of the consultancy systems will be discussed in more detail below; Fig. 2 gives a visual summary.

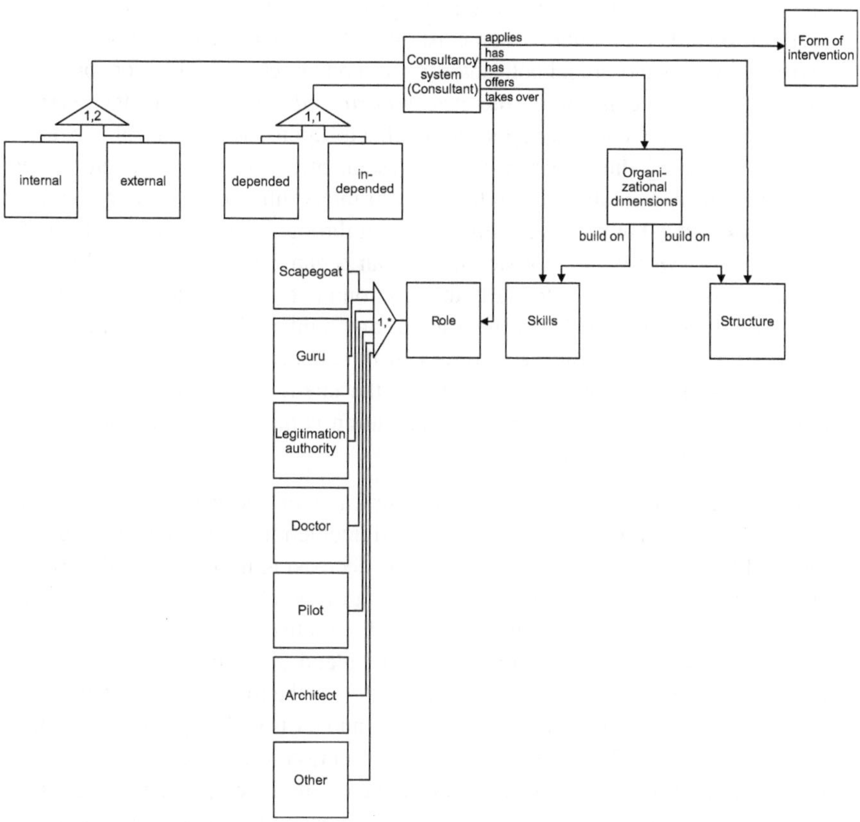

Fig. 2 Overview of concepts and their connections in the consultancy system

3.2 Form of Intervention

The *form of intervention* or *form of consulting* focuses on the interaction between the consultancy system and the client system. The selected form determines significantly the approach and the mode of cooperation between the two parties. There are four basic kinds of intervention: Expertise-oriented consulting, expert-oriented consulting, process-oriented consulting, and systemic consulting [for the following description see esp. (Walger 1995) but also (Heinecke 2002; Hübscher and Schneidewind 2002; Canbäck 1998)]:

- The form of *expertise-oriented consulting* interprets an organization purely as an instrument for reaching a target. Consulting in this context is more or less the collection of information, the analysis of data, and the evaluation of alternatives. Furthermore, it answers questions which support the decision making process in the client system. Members of the client system ask a question and members of the consultancy system reply with an answer.
- The form of *expert-oriented consulting* sees an organization as a socio-technical and open system. Members of the consultancy system and the client system are working together towards the solution of an existing problem. The interaction between the two systems gets closer and both share a common target of the intervention.
- The overarching concept of the *process-oriented consulting* is the learning organization. The consultancy system reflects upon the actions of the client system. By doing this, the consultancy system offers help to the client system to help itself. A consultant using this kind of intervention offers no or very little content expertise but wants to guide the client through a process of self-learning.
- The *systemic consulting* approach defines an organization with the help of the organization's boundaries towards the environment. Additionally the approach builds on interdependencies of the organization's internal functions. The consultant does not reflect upon the activities of the client systems (like the process-oriented consulting), but wants to enable the client system to perform a self-reflection. Relevant for this kind of intervention is the so-called irritation of the client system by the consultancy system.

This sequence of the description of the four kinds of intervention is determined (1) due to the increasing degree of intimacy and interaction between the consultancy system and the client system. It (2) reflects the decreasing necessity for the consultancy system to know details of the environment of the client system, e.g. industry knowledge or details of the organization itself. In practice, one can identify the four kinds of intervention in a pure form as well as a blend of them.

Based on this relatively abstract characterization of the four kinds of intervention, the concepts of consulting approaches, methods, and tools will be presented in a next step (Werr et al. 1997). Every form of intervention uses a certain *consulting approach* in order to gain an overall perspective on the given problem situation. A consultancy system using the expert-oriented consulting style could consider e.g. portfolio management as a consulting approach. An example for process-oriented interventions could be the necessary simultaneous change of social and technical systems during the change management.

The consulting approach accesses several methods and uses them. A *method* gives operational guidance to the members of the consultancy system, often in form of step-by-step instructions and clear roles and responsibilities.[5] The above mentioned portfolio management example could be updated for the expert-oriented consulting interventions e.g. with the method of the growth-share-matrix (known as BCG matrix). The process-oriented example could be updated with the methods of the change curve, business mediation, or the neuro-linguistic programming for the steering of change management processes.

A method finally refers to *tools* in order to fulfil specific tasks. Tools are often focussed on very explicit aspects. However, it can be used by various methods. If we continue the examples from above, the tools of data analysis or conducting interviews could be used for mapping a portfolio. And formats like group discussions, interviews, or questionnaires could be used for supporting the work with the change curve.

Figure 3 shows the discussed concepts and their connections.

3.3 Structure

The *structure* of a consultancy system can be described with the help of three aspects: Membership structure (or hierarchy), leadership structure, and geographical structure.

The *membership structure* towards the client covers the vertical or hierarchical set-up of the consultancy system (Ringlstetter et al. 2004). At consultancies with a

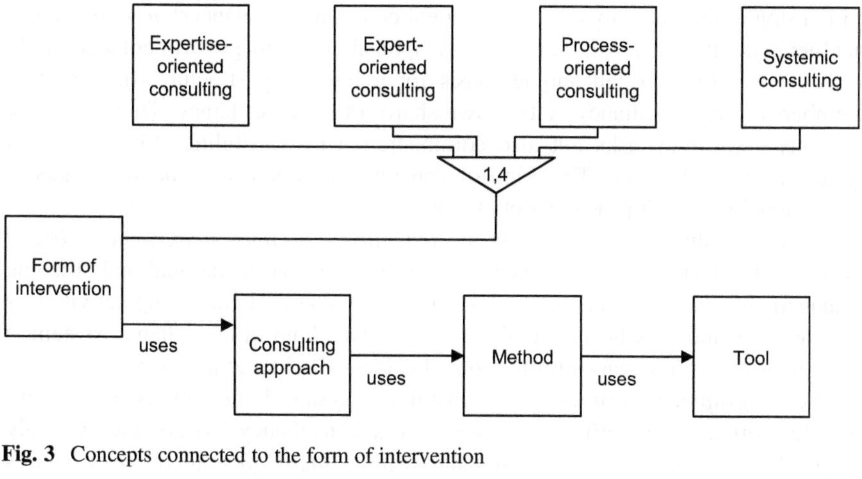

Fig. 3 Concepts connected to the form of intervention

[5]A method is often a skill of a consultancy system; cf. Sect. 3.4.

single-tier hierarchy, all members of the consultancy system are on the same level. Typically, they have identical rights and duties; a division of labour can be performed.

A separation of the members of a consultancy system is made by a *two-tier hierarchy*. The responsibilities of the management (executives, managing directors) are clearly allocated to a certain group. In some consultancies, members of this group are called partners. Separated from the management is the group of the consultants.

In a *three-tier hierarchy* it is usual to split up the group of non-partners again. It is common to place a group of (project) managers between the partners at the top and the consultants at the bottom of the hierarchy. They take over the responsibility for a certain intervention at a client system—in a consultancy with this kind of structure and the respective size, one can assume that these interventions have the form of a project—and consultants are responsible for the operational work while partners oversee the whole work.

Consultancy systems with a *five-tier hierarchy* split their members into five separate groups: *senior partner*, *junior partner*, *project manager*, *senior consultant*, and *junior consultant*. Especially the large expert-oriented consultancy systems—which comprise a large share of all individual consultants in a market like Germany—are organized this way. Therefore, a typical characterization of each seniority level (or hierarchy, consultant level) is given in Table 1.

The author estimates that the four mentioned membership structures are widely spread in practice. However, other structures and *other levels* can be established; other names are widely common. An increase in members of a consultancy system typically requires an increase in hierarchy levels. Different skills (cf. Sect. 3.4) lead to different spans of control which are determined by the leverage ratio, i.e. the ratio between partners and other members.

The *leadership structure* reflects the composition and role allocation within the consultancy system's executive team. A *one-person leadership structure* concentrates the management functions to only one member of the system. This could be the case with a single-tier hierarchy (e.g. independent consultant, freelancer) or with a multi-tier hierarchy (if the necessity for a shared responsibility is not given or not identified).

A *partnership* is often another basis for a leadership structure. In this case, members of the consultancy system own shares of the consultancy. They take over not only consulting tasks but also administrative responsibilities for the overall system at the same time. This kind of consultancy system is sometimes called a professional partnership (Richter et al. 2005).

At a consultancy system with a *dedicated, full-time management board* (or executive board) the board members focus solely on operational and strategic management activities. They are unburdened from classical consulting activities as long as their duties as board members persist. This kind of consultancy system is sometimes called a managed professional business (Richter et al. 2005).

The *geographical structure* of a consultancy system is determined by its subsidiaries, often called offices. Members of a consultancy system are typically assigned to one office. Beneath companies with a *single office*, there are structures with several *national offices* or even several *international offices*. Using the potential of the information and communication technology, members are also able to form a *virtual office*. Reasonable combinations out of these variations as well as additions

Table 1 Seniority levels and corresponding job characteristics (Kraus 2005)

Seniority level	Job description, characteristics
Senior partner	Is decision maker and member of the leadership team of the consultancy system
	Only takes over selective engagements during individual projects
	Has experience in managing large consulting projects with high complexity and strategic relevance
	Has overarching functional knowledge as well as deep industry know-how
	Has special knowledge about the organizational and strategic environment of the client systems to be consulted
	Possesses of at least 10 years of professional experience (post graduate)
	Is the contact person for significant issues arising in the overall cooperation between client system and consultancy system
Junior partner	Has experience in managing large consulting projects with high complexity
	Has experience in managing resp. steering of project teams
	Has overarching functional knowledge as well as deep industry know-how
	Has special, project-relevant knowledge about the environment of the client systems to be consulted
	Possesses of at least 7 years of professional experience (post graduate)
	Is the contact person for issues arising within the project team
Project manager	Has experience in managing medium-sized and small consulting projects
	Has special, project-relevant knowledge
	Has distinctive analytical capabilities
	Develops solutions and implementation concepts independently
	Has excellent social skills
	Possesses of at least 5 years of professional experience, thereof 1 year in a leadership position (post graduate)
Senior consultant	Executes project modules
	Leads working teams effectively
	Has distinctive analytical capabilities
	Has excellent IT knowledge
	Uses consulting tools and methods proficiently
	Creates presentation material and presents convincingly
	Moderates workshops in a professional manner
	Has excellent social skills
	Possesses of at least 3 years of professional experience (post graduate)
Junior consultant	Executes project work packages, especially documentation work
	Has distinctive analytical capabilities
	Has excellent IT knowledge
	Uses consulting tools and methods on a trained basis
	Has gained a full academic qualification (or comparable experience)
	Possesses of excellent social skills (communication, team work, flexibility)

are possible. In practice one can observe that the number of offices increases with the number of the consultancy system's members.

Figure 4 shows the discussed concepts and their connections.

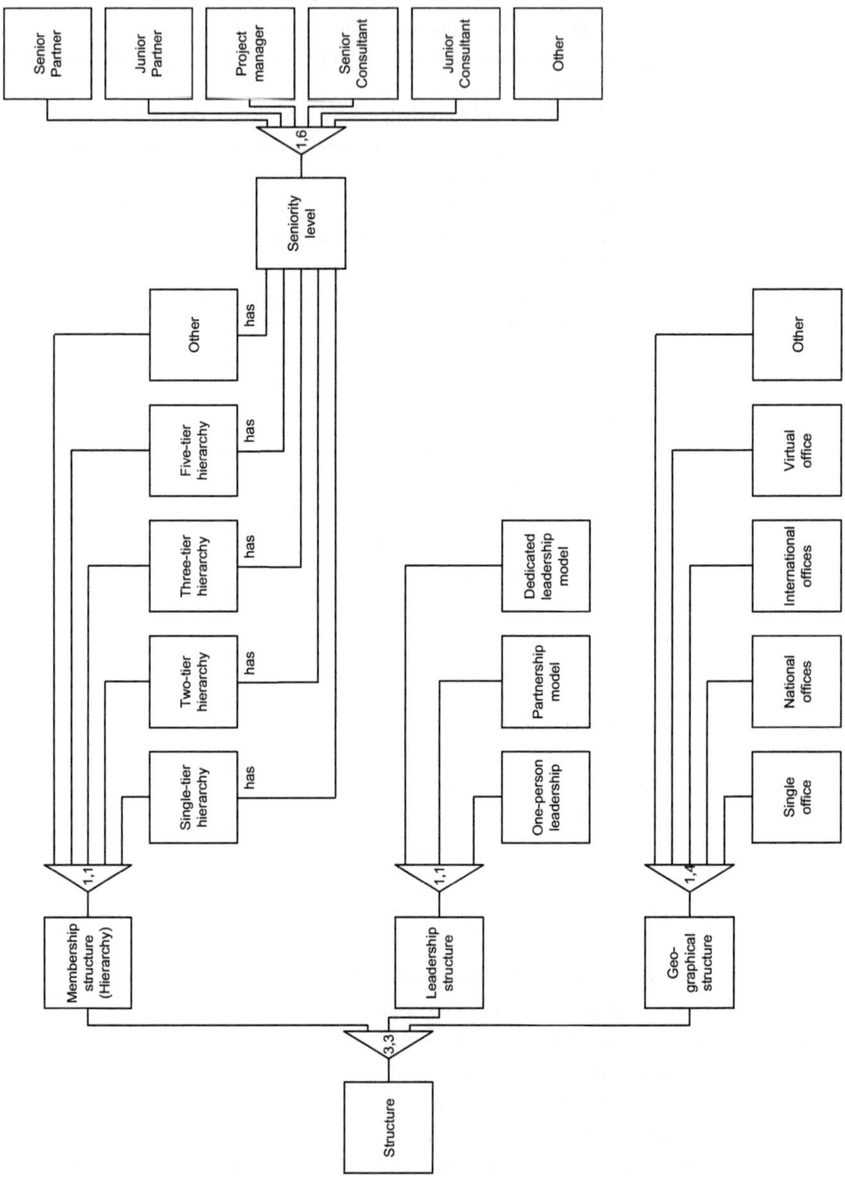

Fig. 4 Concepts connected to the structure of the consultancy system

3.4 Skills

Consultancy systems have *skills* which are finally used to offer services and to work on problems and their solutions. Skills might exist for different industries, client sizes, hierarchy levels, methods, service lines, and others.

A consultancy system has an *industry skill* if there is an asymmetry of information towards one or more industries. This asymmetry could exist within the consultancy if there is e.g. more knowledge about one industry than there is about other industries. Additionally, the asymmetry could exist externally as well, if there is more knowledge about an industry within the consultancy system than in the client system.

Beneath an industry skill consultancy systems can possess *client size skills*. This is a strength which exists in the consultancy system for one or more categories of size of their clients. The definition of client sizes can be made based on headcount, annual turnover, balance sheet volume etc. Following the EU, it can be differentiated between *large organizations*, *medium-sized organizations*, *small organizations* and *micro organizations* (European Commission 2015).

The focus on certain members of the client systems can be a skill of the consultancy system as well. This could be called the *hierarchy of target group skill*. In this case there is strength in the consultancy system for working with one or more hierarchy-defined target groups in the client systems, i.e. the consultancy systems works better or easier with one hierarchy level than with another. Target groups could be the *top-management*, the *middle management*, the *lower management*, and the non-management employees or *staff* (Chandler 1994).

A *methodical skill* exists if there is an asymmetry in the consultancy system towards one or more consulting methods. This asymmetry can be internal if the skill within the consultancy for one method is stronger than for other methods. The asymmetry can also be external if the skill is stronger at the consultancy system than at the client system. As discussed above, methods support consulting approaches, which in turn are used as part of a certain kind of intervention (cf. Sect. 3.2). Therefore one can specify *methods of expertise-oriented consulting*, *methods of expert-oriented consulting*, *methods of process-oriented consulting*, and *methods of systemic consulting*.

Common areas of skills are the *service lines* (or: fields of consulting). Again, asymmetries are the driving force behind the service line skill. Asymmetries can exist within a consultancy system if there are greater skills for one or more service lines than for others. Asymmetries can exist between a consultancy system and a client system as well if the skills are greater at the consultancy than at the client. The Association of German Business Consultants (BDU e.V.) works with the following service lines: Strategy consulting, organizational & process consulting (or: operations), information technology consulting, and human resources consulting (BDU 2017). This is a starting point but misses the recurrence of the large tax and audit firms with their advisory businesses (NN 2012). In accordance with the European Federation of Management Consultancies Associations (FEACO), the service line finance should be added (FEACO 2016).[6] It is important to state that the single service lines are interfering with each other and are often shaped by the most prominent representatives.

---

[6]Please note: FEACO calls the service line 'organizational & process' 'operations' and works with a rather small service line 'sales & marketing' which the BDU encloses into the service line 'strategy'.

In detail, *strategy consulting* has the goal to drive long-term and strategic improvements of client systems. Examples are strategic planning or restructuring. *Operations consulting* wants to improve organizational aspects and processes of client systems, e.g. business process reengineering, re-organizations etc. *HR consulting* targets the human factor and helps e.g. with HR development measures and salary structures. *Financial consulting* consists of e.g. the help with risk advisory, mergers & acquisitions, and financial advisory. *IT consulting* wants to improve the usage of data and information with the help of technology. Examples are projects in the field of IT architecture management and business-IT-alignment (Petmecky and Deelmann 2004).

Figure 5 summarizes the concepts and connections of this section. Please note: The transformation is the link to the client system and is therefore depicted as a dotted box.

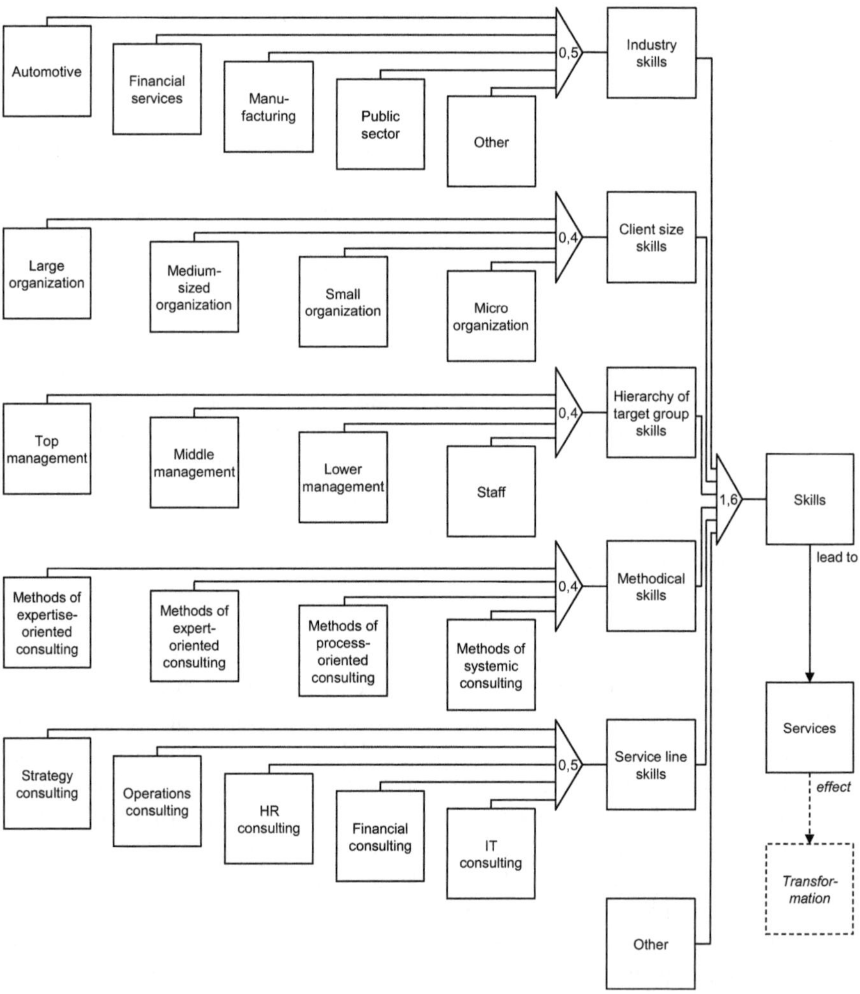

Fig. 5 Concepts connected to the skills of the consultancy system

4 Client System

4.1 Overview

The *client system* literally serves as the counterpart to the consultancy system discussed above. Therefore some of the concepts and connections discussed in this section have a similarity to those discussed in the last section. This becomes obvious with the *internal roles* which are staffed at client systems and the *characteristics* of the client systems as they are mirrored by the seniority levels resp. the skills of the consultancy systems.

The client system articulates its *problem* via a *demand* at the market. The demand can be a blend or a mixture of several demand types. The demand is met by a transformation which additionally solves the problem, too. As stated in Sect. 2.1 the *transformation* has the goal "to support a self-driven change of the client system" (Deelmann et al. 2006a, p. 200). Taking this into account, the transformation has to be part of the client system. Additionally, it is a direct link to the consultancy system which in turn causes and drive the transformation.

Figure 6 illustrates this overview. Please note: The *services* are the link to the consultancy system and are therefore depicted as a dotted box.

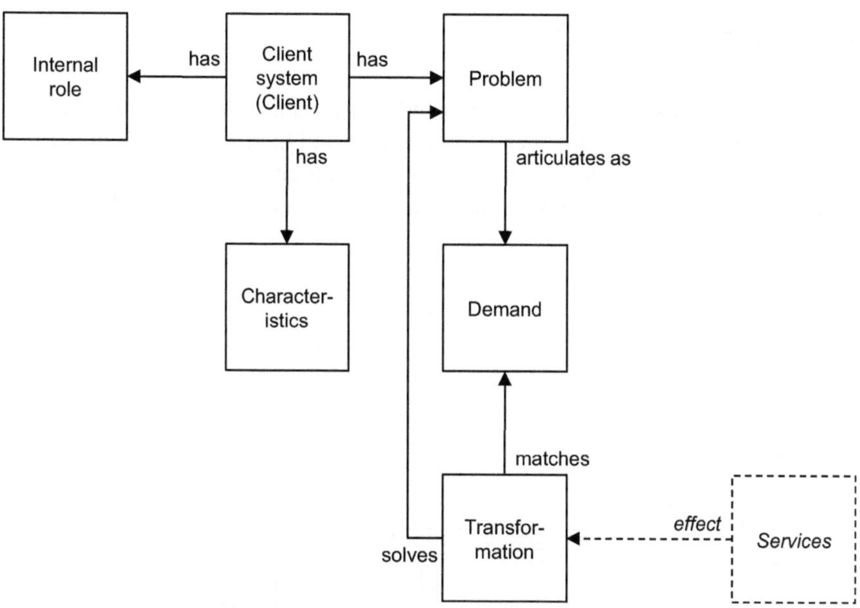

Fig. 6 Overview of concepts and their connections in the client system

4.2 Internal Roles

During an intervention a client system can fill several *internal roles*. The following roles can be found in consulting projects and help to understand and design the internal organisation of a client system (Wegmann and Winklbauer 2006). The *sponsor* typically initiates the intervention resp. the consulting project and gives overall support. The sponsor has seldom a long-term active role but is regularly part of a so-called steering committee and monitors the progress. The *customer* is the person who is responsible for the contractual assignment of the consultancy system. This role owns the budget and instructs e.g. the purchasing department to place a formal purchase order. The role of the customer can coincide with the role of the sponsor or the role of the project leader. The *project leader* is the person who is responsible for the management of the intervention. The *project members* resume—together with the project leader—the active work as part of the intervention. While each of the first three roles is typically staffed with one single member of the client system, the project member role can be assigned to a plurality of persons. This holds true for the members of the client system who are *affected by the intervention*, too. They are substantially affected by the result of the intervention. *Other roles* can be created as the client system demands this.

Figure 7 gives an overview of the roles.

4.3 Types of Demands

The problem of the client system is expressed via a *demand*. This paper differentiates between two basic types of demand. On the one hand there is the *explicitly articulated demand* (Type A). A demand of this type can focus on (1) a lack of *expertise* (Type A1), e.g. in case of novel questions or (2) a lack of *resources* (Type A2),

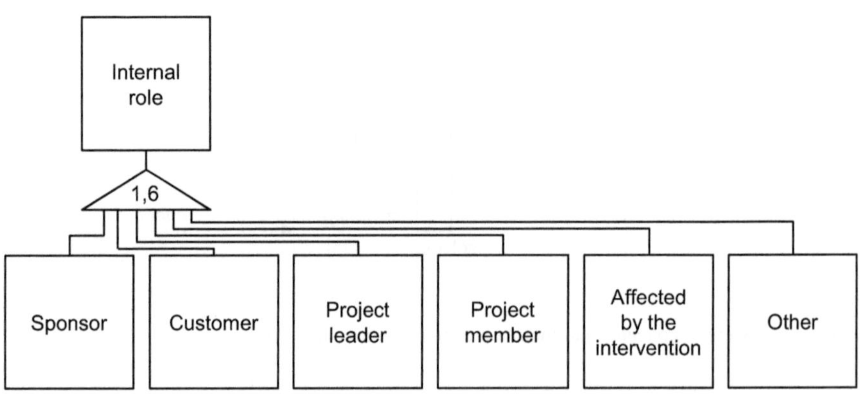

Fig. 7 Concepts connected to the internal roles of the client systems

e.g. in case more headcount will solve a problem faster. While these two sub-types focus on a kind of shortage, Type A3 focuses on a kind of redundant work if there are *tasks executed* by the consultancy system *without an existing shortage* at the client system. This can happen if e.g. the client asks the consultant to perform a research on a topic which is in parallel conducted by the client organization itself or if the client just won't use existing internal resources and prefers to work with the consultant.

Beneath the explicitly articulated demand there is often a *non-explicitly articulated demand* (Type B). Examples are the scapegoat, a guru or a legitimation authority. The non-explicitly articulated demand can appear alone (e.g. a precise demand cannot (yet) be articulated) or together with a demand Type A (e.g. a hidden agenda requires a scapegoat).[7]

Figure 8 presents the introduced types of demand.

4.4 Characteristics

Client systems have *characteristics*. Consultancy systems use them and design their skills accordingly in order to better match the above mentioned demands and to better sell their services. There are several classes of characteristics, e.g. industry, size of the organization, sector types, and purpose of the client system.

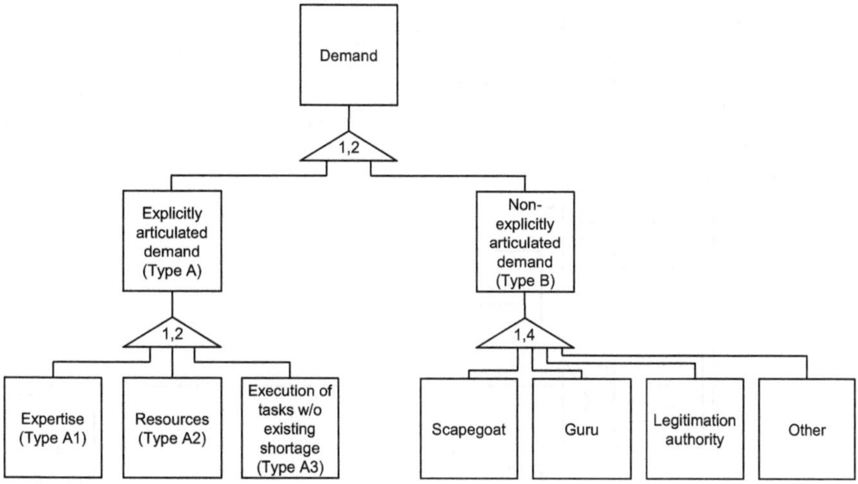

Fig. 8 Concepts connected to the demand

[7]Conrad and Trummer speak of official and latent functions resp. of direct and indirect objectives (Conrad and Trummer 2007).

The *industry* is the environment which the client system typically operates in. Industries could be *automotive*, *financial services*, *manufacturing*, *public sector* etc. Other splits are feasible.

Client systems can be differentiated by their size, too. This can be done based on headcount, annual turnover, balance sheet volume etc. According to the EU, one can differentiate into *large organizations*, *medium-sized organizations*, *small organizations*, and *micro organizations* (European Commission 2015).

The *hierarchy* of an organization determines a third characteristic. It typically consists of the *top-management*, the *middle management*, the *lower management*, and the non-management employees or *staff* (Chandler 1994).

Client systems are part of either the public sector or the private sector.

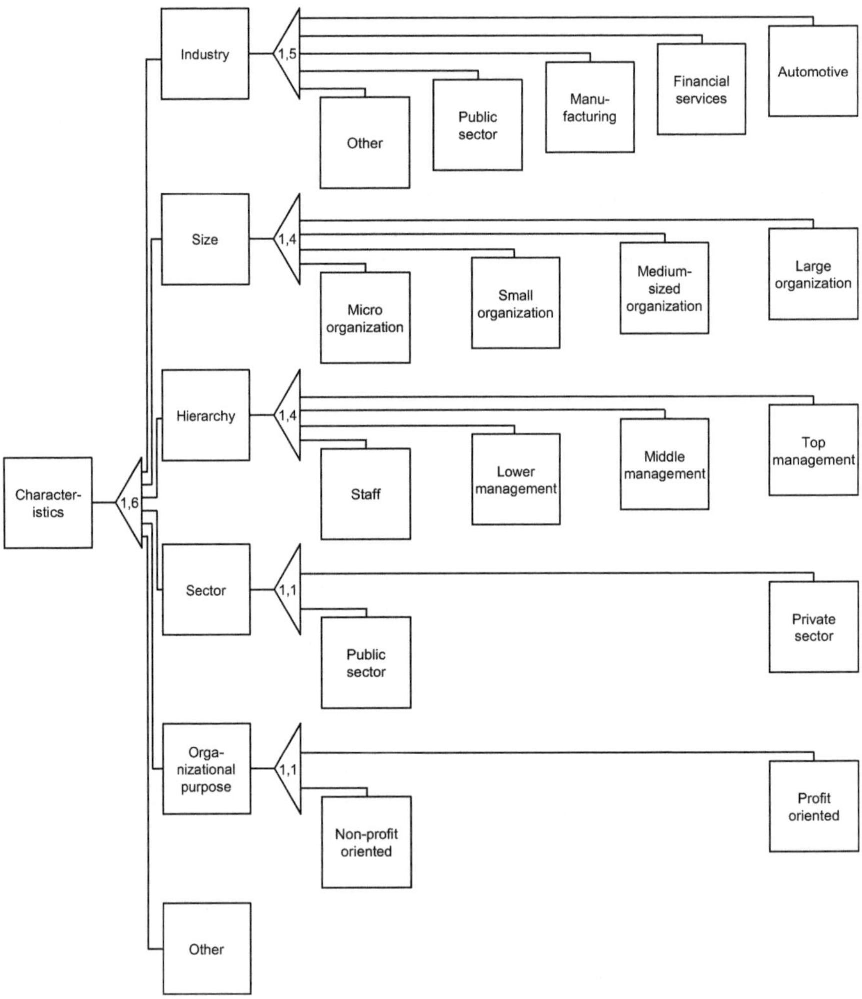

Fig. 9 Concepts connected to the characteristics of a client system

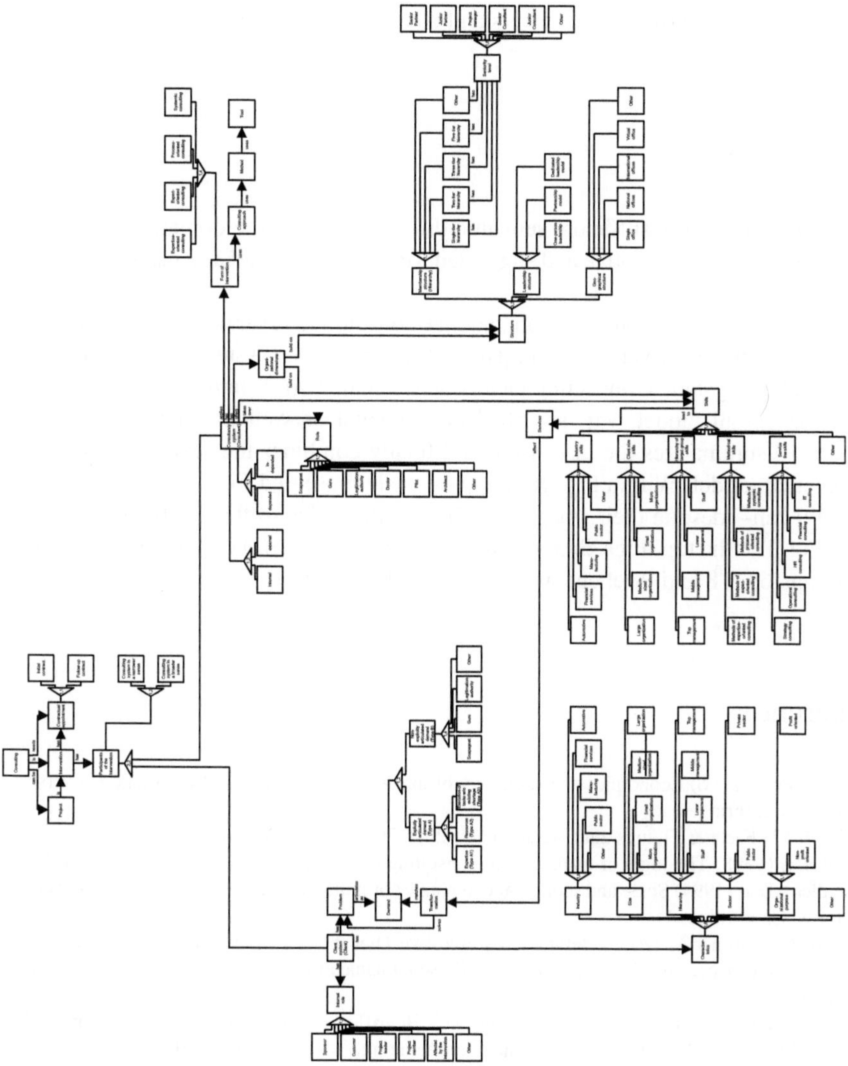

Fig. 10 Overview of the conceptual model for concepts and connections of organizational consulting

The *purpose of an organization* has a close connection to the sector characteristic. The purpose can be *profit* oriented or *non-profit* orientated. It can be assumed that most interventions will take place either in for-profit oriented client systems in the private sector or in not-for-profit oriented client systems in the public sector. However, the characteristics might be twisted (e.g. a profit-oriented company in the public sector) and therefore this separation is needed.

Figure 9 summarizes the concepts and connections of this section.

5 Summary

This paper took an insufficient semantic differentiation in the domain of organizational consulting as a motive and suggested a conceptual model as a basis for a better understanding.

Based on a definition of organizational consulting, several concepts and their connections were derived; firstly regarding the consultancy system, secondly regarding the client system. Connecting factors between the two systems were pointed out. The conceptual model was described on a textual as well as on a visual basis. Figure 10 summarizes the discussion and finally combines the several parts of the conceptual model. Within Fig. 10, the previously presented Figs. 1, 2, 3, 4, 5, 6, 7, 8 and 9 can—despite their small size—be identified due to their individual shapes with Fig. 1 at the top, Figs. 2, 3, 4 and 5 (consultancy system) on the right hand side and Figs. 6, 7, 8 and 9 (client side) on the left hand side.

References

Armbrüster T (2006) Economics and sociology of management consulting. Cambridge University Press, Cambridge

BDU (2017) Facts & Figures zum Beratermarkt 2016/2017. BDU e.V., Bonn

Canbäck S (1998) The logic of management consulting (part one). J Manag Consult 10(2):3–11

Chandler AD Jr (1994) Scale and scope—the dynamics of industrial capitalism. Harvard University Press, Cambridge

Conrad P, Trummer M (2007) Beratung als investive Dienstleistung—eine kritische Einführung. Discussion papers no 3/2007, Institut für Personalmanagement, Helmut-Schmidt-Universität, Hamburg

Deelmann T (2015) Beratung—Beschreibung von Begriffen und Beziehungen. In: Deelmann T, Ockel DM (eds) Handbuch der Unternehmensberatung. Erich Schmidt, Berlin, p 1101

Deelmann T (2018) Does digitization matter? Reflections on a possible transformation of the consulting business. In: Nissen V (ed) The digital transformation of the consulting industry. Springer, Berlin, pp 75–99

Deelmann T, Huchler A, Jansen SA, Petmecky A (2006a) An empirical analysis of internal corporate consultancies. In: Deelmann T, Mohe M (eds) Selection and evaluation of consultants. Rainer Hampp, Munich & Mering, pp 197–210

Deelmann T, Huchler A, Jansen SA, Petmecky A (2006b) Internal corporate consulting—Thesen, empirische Analysen und theoriegeleitete Prognosen zum Markt für Interne Beratungen. Discussion papers no 5. Zeppelin University, Friedrichshafen

European Commission (2015) User guide to the SME definition. https://ec.europa.eu/docsroom/documents/15582/attachments/1/translations/en/renditions/pdf. Accessed 8 Jul 2017

FEACO (2016) Survey of the European management consultancy 2015/2016, Brussels

Friedrich von den Eichen S (2005) Der Berater und seine Rollen—Höhere Klientenzufriedenheit durch erwartungszentrierte Beratung. In: Seidl D, Kirsch W, Linder M (eds) Grenzen der Strategieberatung—Eine Gegenüberstellung der Perspektiven von Wissenschaft, Beratung und Klienten. Haupt, Bern, pp 369–389

Gutberlet M (2012) IT & Technologie Beratung. Unpublished paper, Iserlohn. Presented 25 Oct 2012

Heinecke HJ (2002) Methodische Differenzierung der Geschäftsstrategie—Prozeßberatung in der Praxis. In: Mohe M, Heinecke HJ, Pfriem R (eds) Consulting—Problemlösung als Geschäftsmodell. Klett-Cotta, Stuttgart, pp 225–242

Heuermann R, Herrmann F (2003) Unternehmensberatung—Anatomie und Perspektiven einer Dienstleistungselite. Vahlen, Munich

Hübscher M, Schneidewind U (2002) Unternehmensethikberatung—Betriebswirtschaftliche Notwendigkeit in Fusionsprozessen oder akademische Fiktion? In: Mohe M, Heinecke HJ, Pfriem R (eds) Consulting—Problemlösung als Geschäftsmodell. Klett-Cotta, Stuttgart, pp 262–280

Kohr J (2000) Die Auswahl von Unternehmensberatungen. Rainer Hampp, Munich & Mering

Kraus A (2005) Der Einkauf als Intermediär zwischen Berater und Beratenem. In: Petmecky A, Deelmann T (eds) Arbeiten mit Managementberatern—Bausteine für eine erfolgreiche Zusammenarbeit. Springer, Heidelberg, pp 65–75

Mohe M (2002) Inhouse consulting: Gestern, heute—und morgen? In: Mohe M, Heinecke HJ, Pfriem R (eds) Consulting—Problemlösung als Geschäftsmodell. Klett-Cotta, Stuttgart, pp 320–343

Mohe M (2003) Klientenprofessionalisierung—Strategien und Perspektiven eines professionellen Umgangs mit Unternehmensberatung. Metropolis, Marburg

Mohe M, Heinecke HJ, Pfriem R (2002) Zukunft des Consulting—Consulting für die Zukunft. In: Mohe M, Heinecke HJ, Pfriem R (eds) Consulting—Problemlösung als Geschäftsmodell. Klett-Cotta, Stuttgart, pp 377–386

Neuberger O (2002) Rate mal! Phantome, Philosophien und Phasen der Beratung. In: Mohe M, Heinecke HJ, Pfriem R (eds) Consulting—Problemlösung als Geschäftsmodell. Klett-Cotta, Stuttgart, pp 135–161

Nissen V (2007) Consulting Research—Eine Einführung. In: Nissen V (ed) Consulting research—Unternehmensberatung aus wissenschaftlicher Perspektive. Gabler, Wiesbaden, pp 3–38

NN (2012) The big four accounting firms—shape shifters—with the audit market maturing, accounting firms become consultancies. De Economist, 29 Sept 2012

Petmecky A, Deelmann T (2004) Zur Entwicklung des Unternehmensberatungsmarktes. OrganisationsEntwicklung 13(2):38–43

Project Management Institute (2017) What is project management. https://www.pmi.org/about/learn-about-pmi/what-is-project-management. Accessed 7 Jun 2017

Richter A, Schmidt SL, Treichler C (2005) Organisation und Mitarbeiterentwicklung als Differenzierungsfaktoren. In: Deelmann T, Ockel DM (eds) Handbuch der Unternehmensberatung. Erich Schmidt, Berlin, p 7220

Ringlstetter M, Kaiser S, Bürger B (2004) Eine Einführung in die Welt der Professional Service Firms. In: Ringlstetter M, Bürger B, Kaiser S (eds) Strategien und management für professional service firms. Wiley-VCH, Weinheim, pp 11–35

Sandberg R (2003) Corporate consulting for customer solutions—bridging diverging business logics, Doctoral thesis. Handelshögskolan, Stockholm

Sangüesa Sanchez M (2003) Modell zur Evaluierung von Beratungsprojekten, Doctoral thesis. TU, Berlin
Walger G (1995) Idealtypen der Unternehmensberatung. In: Walger G (ed) Formen der Unternehmensberatung—Systemische Unternehmensberatung, Organisationsentwicklung. Expertenberatung und gutachterliche Beratungstätigkeit in Theorie und Praxis. Dr. Otto Schmidt, Cologne, pp 1–18
Wegmann C, Winklbauer H (2006) Projektmanagement für Unternehmensberatungen. Gabler, Wiesbaden
Werr A, Stjernberg T, Docherty P (1997) The functions of methods of change in management consulting. J Organ Chang Manag 10(4):288–307
Wolf J (2013) Organisation, Management, Unternehmensführung—Theorien. In: Praxisbeispiele und Kritik, 5th edn. Springer Gabler, Wiesbaden
Wurps J, Musone Crispino B (2002) Inhouse Consulting in der Praxis—Ein Erfahrungsbericht der Volkswagen Consulting. In: Mohe M, Heinecke HJ, Pfriem R (eds) Consulting—Problemlösung als Geschäftsmodell. Klett-Cotta, Stuttgart, pp 344–356
Zirkler M (2005) State-of-the-art der Forschung zur Organisationsberatung: Zusammenfassung und Analyse der Forschungsergebnisse der letzten Jahre. WWZ research paper 10/05, Basel

Thomas Deelmann is Professor for Public Management at the University of Applied Sciences for Public Administration and Management of North Rhine-Westphalia (FHöV) in Cologne, Germany. Until 2016, he was Professor for Corporate Consulting and Management at BiTS Iserlohn as well as the head of the strategy development department for a leading global ICT service provider. His professional experiences as a consultant at one of the largest international consultancies, as an in house consultant, as a strategic source for consulting services and as a client of consulting services form the basis for his teaching and research. Currently, he serves as the editor for a consulting handbook and as a jury member of the WirtschaftsWoche's "Best of Consulting" award.

Institutionalization of Consulting Research: Review and Comparison of Two Approaches in Germany Over the Period 2007–2017

Thomas Deelmann and Volker Nissen

Abstract In an assessment of the German research community some 10 years ago, we realized that there was virtually no institutionalization in research on consulting. As an immediate consequence of this unsatisfactory situation we decided, together with others, to lay the foundations of two institutions on Consulting Research with slightly different focus and degree of formalism. One of them is still operational, the other one not. In our contribution, we highlight these developments and discuss why it was a rocky road to reach the goal of a better institutionalization of Consulting Research in Germany, and what appears necessary to improve further on the current situation.

1 Introduction and Motivation

Consulting Research (CR) refers to the scientific treatment of the service of consultancy and the consulting market with its various participants on both the supplier and customer sides (Nissen 2007a). Consulting Research in Germany occupies a relatively small but important niche. The smallness can be observed for example with respect to the absence of a dedicated academic journal or an annual conference on issues of CR. The importance can be observed due to its capability to insert neutrality and objectivity in an otherwise controversial topic of great practical relevance. On the one hand, many people interpret consulting critical and negative. They often reduce its results to 'headcount reduction' and describe consultants and their attitude as arrogant. On the other hand, there is a great attractiveness of the field, as

T. Deelmann (✉)
University of Applied Sciences for Public Administration and management of North Rhine-Westphalia—Fachhochschule für öffentliche Verwaltung (FHöV), Cologne, Germany
e-mail: thomas.deelmann@fhoev.nrw.de

V. Nissen
Economic Sciences and Media, Ilmenau University of Technology, Ilmenau, Germany
e-mail: volker.nissen@tu-ilmenau.de

V. Nissen (ed.), *Advances in Consulting Research*, Contributions to Management Science, https://doi.org/10.1007/978-3-319-95999-3_3

e.g. shown in the increase in market volume over the past years and the appreciation as employer for highly qualified young professionals.

Over the last decades, there were several contributions from researchers, who tried to describe and explain consulting in total or in selected fields, e.g. (Engel 1969; Witthauer 1973; Luhmann 1989; Kaas and Schade 1995; Kieser 2002; Dornheim 2015); only to name a few. However, these research activities were either often short termed (they lasted e.g. for the time of a dissertation project) or stood unfortunately relatively unrelated side by side (Nissen et al. 2009). As was already mentioned in the introductory article of this book, the scientific community of Consulting Research appears fragmented. It would therefore be desirable to more strongly bundle the research efforts in CR and to make it more visible to the outside. The assessment that the field of Consulting Research is especially relevant for the question of disciplined institutionalization is further supported by several reasons (Nissen et al. 2009):

First, there are obviously many points of contact between practical consulting and the science of management. For example Niehaves and Becker (2006) take the view that Consulting Research brings about new knowledge, which is then carried into the practice of consulting. Even if this understanding seems abbreviated (Kieser and Nicolai 2005), many managerial concepts found their beginnings in consulting practice and were only then taken up by science (Payne and Lumsdum 1987; Deelmann 2007). Some of these management concepts were themselves described as science and the science of management defines itself as an applied science offering solutions to practical problems (Nicolai 2004). This closeness urges us to critically asses a fruitful, mutual relationship between practical consulting and a scientific research discipline dealing with consultancy. It must be noted that the practical side does not depend on previously generated scientific theories in order to be operational. Similarly while Consulting Research does not develop unrelated practical activities, it is indeed separate, independent and self-reflecting (Nissen 2007a).

Second, unlike most other sectors consultancy has recorded significant dynamic growth over the last few decades. There can hardly be doubts that business consulting is flourishing, and has been so for quite a while. On an international level the turnover increased from $205 billion (including financial advisory) in 2011 to around $250 billion in 2016. Thus, the global consulting sector is one of the largest and most mature markets within the professional services industry, according to Consultancy.uk (2017).

Third, due to the enormous growth in the last few years and the influence of consulting on virtually all other branches of industry, the consulting sector not only influences the economic system but is also having an increasing effect on social and societal areas as well (Faust 2006). Terms have been coined such as the 'consulting society' (Fuchs and Pankoke 1994), the 'consultant republic' (Bittner and Niejahr 2004) or the 'McKinsey society' (Kurbjuweit 2003).

Fourth, through economic growth and its increasing area for action, consultancy has awakened the interest of science (Clark et al. 2007). This can be inferred from conferences (e.g. meetings of the Management Consulting Division of the Academy of Management) as well as from book and article publications on issues of Consulting Research.

Together, the above points offer sufficient reasons to consider the institutionalization of this research field. We first drew this conclusion in 2007, when we empirically assessed the state of play in German Consulting Research (Mohe et al. 2008; Nissen et al. 2009). One way to find a remedy for the situation of rather uncoordinated research is to institutionalize the research activities. In 2007 two approaches for such an institutionalization process were started. This paper describes and evaluates both approaches. The authors of this paper were leading figures in both approaches.

Following this introduction, the next two sections describe in detail the two approaches of founding a registered association (Sect. 2) and of creating a Special Interest Group within a larger network of professionals (Sect. 3).

The registered association ceased to exist. Therefore its life cycle serves as a structure for the documentation: Preparation activities (Sect. 2.1), founding process (Sect. 2.2), functional phase (Sect. 2.3), and termination (Sect. 2.4). A short assessment (Sect. 2.5) summarizes lessons learned.

The Special Interest Group (SIG) is still active. Sect. 3.1 therefore first describes the foundation and gives an overview of the organization. The two types of major activities of the SIG determine the section's structure: Stand-alone meetings (Sect. 3.2) and embedded workshops resp. conferences (Sect. 3.3). An intermediate evaluation (Sect. 3.4) concludes this description.

The paper concludes with summarizing the observations on institutionalizing Consulting Research in Germany and suggests future activities to further improve the situation.

2 Association: "Gesellschaft für Consulting Research (GCR) e.V."

2.1 Preparation

The *Gesellschaft für Consulting Research* (GCR; Eng.: Association for Consulting Research) was founded in 2007. Upfront this official start several activities took place. After bilateral and private discussions about the situation of the domain Consulting Research in Germany, an *initial meeting* of four researchers took place on July 20th, 2007 in Göttingen.[1] Three major topics were discussed: The foundation of a registered association, the establishment of a journal focussing on Consulting Research, and the set-up of a corresponding website.

[1]The following section is based on the meeting protocol by Nissen (2007b).

- Association: The main focus of the association was to concentrate the efforts in the area of Consulting Research. It was aimed to increase the visibility of the research domain via e.g. the organization of special conferences on a regularly basis, workshops, lecture series, offering a special reward for excellent thesis, and the publication of a journal (see below). In addition to the increase in visibility, the association should integrate different existing groups of researchers (e.g. IT consulting-oriented, management consulting-oriented, systemic consulting-oriented) under one roof in order to support networking and co-operations. A third aim was to serve as spokesperson in the dialogue with other interest groups, e.g. from consulting practice or foreign scientific organizations.
- Journal: A 'Journal of Consulting Research' was to support the aims of the association. In two to four issues per year scientific results could get published. The intention was not to give practitioners a platform for success stories or (covered) advertisements. In a first step, the journal should focus on the German-speaking countries but accept papers in German and English language. A large editorial board should be established in order to create a significant attention in the scientific community and to ensure a large number of submissions.
- Website: The third element was a website which would support the association and the journal. An open section and a closed user group were planned. Contents should be e.g. contact details of the members for fostering collaboration, calls for papers, tutorials, presentations etc.

It was agreed upon to expand the initial group of people towards a larger and stronger *core team*. However, one of the participants of this initial meeting did not want to be part of the core team while still supporting the discussed topics.

In order to get a deeper understanding of the existing needs and moods within the Consulting Research community in Germany, the remaining three participants conducted a *survey* in the second half of 2007.[2] 65 persons with an assumed affinity towards Consulting Research (i.e. a first target group of association members) were contacted and asked for the degree to which they would agree with the following statements (scale: 1 = agree completely, 5 = disagree completely):

- I would very much welcome a society for consulting research.
- I would personally involve myself strongly in the foundational phase of such a society.
- I would very much welcome the publication of a journal specifically dealing with the topic of consulting research.
- The journal should be geared toward the English language.
- I am already a member of an organisation which sufficiently covers the field of consulting research.

[2]The following section is based on Mohe et al. (2008).

47 questionnaires were returned (response rate of 72%). The responses were analysed and the results can be summarized as follows:

- The founding of an association of Consulting Research was generally appreciated.
- The willingness for a personal involvement in a founding phase of this association was strong at some individual participants. However, there was an overall reluctance at most of the respondents.
- In principle, the publication of a special interest journal was seen positive.
- In case of such a publication, the journal should focus on English-language papers.
- Most of the respondents had no membership in an association which covered the topic Consulting Research sufficiently.

There was neither noteworthy difference between the answers from participants which were of more practical or more theoretical background nor from participants with a focus on management consulting or on IT consulting.

2.2 *Foundation Process*

The official foundation of the association took place on December 19th, 2007 in Göttingen.[3] As discussed in the July meeting, the core team was able to increase the number of participants to eight. This number was important due to the fact that in Germany at least seven participants are needed in order to found a registered association (German: eingetragener Verein, e.V.).

After a welcoming address and the self-introduction of all participants, the draft of the association's charter was discussed. Key results were:

- Name: Wissenschaftliche Gesellschaft für Unternehmensberatung (WGUB; Eng.: Scientific Society for Business Consulting).[4]
- Location: Bonn.
- Character of the association: Not-for-profit; charitable.
- Purpose of the association: Promotion of science, research and teaching in the domain of business consulting.
- Levers for reaching the purpose: Support of researchers in consulting; information of the public with respect to issues of consulting and Consulting Research; on-going development of Consulting Research; support for young academics; contribution to professional education and training; organization of relevant workshops and conferences; publishing of specialized literature; and co-operation with other national and international institutions.

[3]The following section is based on Schäfer (2007).

[4]The name had later to be changed into 'Gesellschaft für Consulting Research'; cf. below.

- Dissolution: In case of the dissolution of the association, existing assets must be transferred to another charitable organization and should only be used for the means of Consulting Research.

The ballot over the charter got a unanimous positive vote.

The next agenda item was the election of the association board. The authors of this paper were elected as part of the board which consisted of three positions: A first chairman, a second chairman, and a treasurer.

Afterwards the yearly membership fee was determined. Students and doctoral students were required to pay 24 Euros; all other members had to pay 48 Euros. It was the aspiration to serve the members with a journal subscription, the access to a website, reduced entrance fees for conferences etc. Only natural persons could get a membership.

The last agenda items contained possible co-operations with other organizations, the initial plans for a special interest journal, and the first ideas for the set-up of a website. The ideas of the initial meeting in July were shared with the other participants and agreed upon.

Shortly after this inaugural meeting, the 'Wissenschaftliche Gesellschaft für Unternehmensberatung' had to change its name. The association's board came to this conclusion, after the 'Wissenschaftliche Gesellschaft für Management und Beratung mbh', a for-profit enterprise, made a request claiming a danger of confusion. After a survey among the members, the new name 'Gesellschaft für Consulting Research' was chosen and the charter was changed accordingly in July 2008 (Nissen 2009).

After the inaugural meeting the association had to be recorded at the 'register of associations' (Ger.: Vereinsregister). This was done on October 16th, 2008. The registration number was 8935 at the local court (Ger.: Amtsgericht) Bonn (Amtsgericht Bonn 2008).

In addition, the GCR applied for being recognized as a charitable association (Ger.: gemeinnütziger Verein). This goal was pursued in order to be able to give donation receipts. Membership fees and donations were expected to be the main funding source for the association. On December 2nd, 2008 the local tax authority confirmed that the GCR serves exclusively and immediate charitable and not for-profit purposes (Finanzamt Siegburg 2008).

With these three events and results (inaugural assembly, entrance in the register of associations, acceptance as charitable association) the founding process was completed.

2.3 *Functional Phase*

2.3.1 Overview

The time span in which the GCR was effectively able to work on its self-given action points can be named as the functional phase. The phase started after completion of the founding process and ended with the decision to terminate the GCR. Based on these thoughts, the functional phase included the years 2009 to 2015.

The description of this life cycle phase consists primarily of the core activities, which drove the purpose of the association (Sect. 2.3.2). Secondly, the support activities (administration, marketing) seem worth mentioning (Sect. 2.3.3). Thirdly, key data about the financial situation (Sect. 2.3.4) and the membership development (Sect. 2.3.5) are presented.

2.3.2 Core Activities

With respect to the given purpose of the association and the supporting levers for the implementation, the following core activities and results can be listed (Nissen 2009, 2010, 2011, 2012; Deelmann 2013):

- A close cooperation with a special interest group of researchers and practitioners interested in IT consulting (cf. Sect. 3) was established since 2009.
- As a result of this cooperation, a series of workshops were conducted (cf. Sects. 3.2 and 3.3 for more details). The workshops were mainly aimed on IT consulting but also open for other fields of consulting. The following scientific meetings and workshops took place:
  - In 2009 at the annual conference of the German Informatics Society (Ger.: Gesellschaft für Informatik e.V., GI) in Lübeck and at a dedicated workshop in Aschaffenburg,
  - In 2010 at the Multi-Konferenz Wirtschaftsinformatik in Göttingen and at a dedicated workshop in Hannover,
  - In 2011 as dedicated workshops in Nuremberg and Berlin,
  - In 2012 at the Multi-Konferenz Wirtschaftsinformatik in Braunschweig,
  - In 2013 as a dedicated meeting in Hamburg; and
  - In 2014 at the Multi-Konferenz Wirtschaftsinformatik in Paderborn.
- The GCR presented its founding idea and the results of the above mentioned survey at a symposium in Kassel in 2009. The presentation was corresponded by a paper (Nissen et al. 2009).
- The survey data for a campus guide consulting (Ger.: Studienführer Consulting) were presented on the GCR website (2009) and with additional information as a book in 2012 (Nissen and Klauk 2012).
- In 2011 the GCR and the market researcher Source for Consulting, represented by its co-founder and director Fiona Czerniawska, held a virtual meeting and

discussed the management consulting markets in Europe, Middle East, India and Africa with a strong focus on the German market.

2.3.3 Support Activities

In addition to the activities which generated operational outcomes and supported the purpose of the association directly, *administrative activities* required significant resources. These activities were basically centred on the annual general meeting (preparation, documentation), the collection of membership fees and the corresponding preparation of the charitable donation certificates, and the treasury and related cash auditing processes.

The *marketing related activities* of the GCR took mainly place in the first years of its existence:

- A logo was created in 2008 and used e.g. in the association's letterhead and in presentations.
- An updated logo was used for the association's internet presence (Fig. 1).

An internet presence was created in order to gain visibility and to inform members and interested third parties about the activities and goals of the GCR (Fig. 2). The presented information was grouped into several sections: News, About us, Business Consulting, Consulting Research, Studying Consulting, and a closed user group. The content was hosted at the University of Technology Ilmenau.

- In order to support the recruiting of new members, a leaflet was designed in 2009. The flyer gave a short overview of the research domain, the association and its goals. Moreover, it presented the benefits of a membership, and had an integrated postcard for a membership application. Figures 3 and 4 show the double-sided leaflet.

2.3.4 Financial Developments

The financial situation of the GCR was (with a short exception of the founding situation) always positive and overall very stable. Revenues were generated via the membership fees. The fees were initially set by the founding assembly at 48 Euros per year. Students could get a reduction to 24 Euros per year. In 2009 the general meeting agreed upon a reduction to 30 Euros per year and a reduced amount of 12 Euros for students. (Nissen 2009) Expenditures were made mainly for banking and notary fees, and a one-off financial support of the 'Studienführer Consulting'

Fig. 1 Logo of the GCR

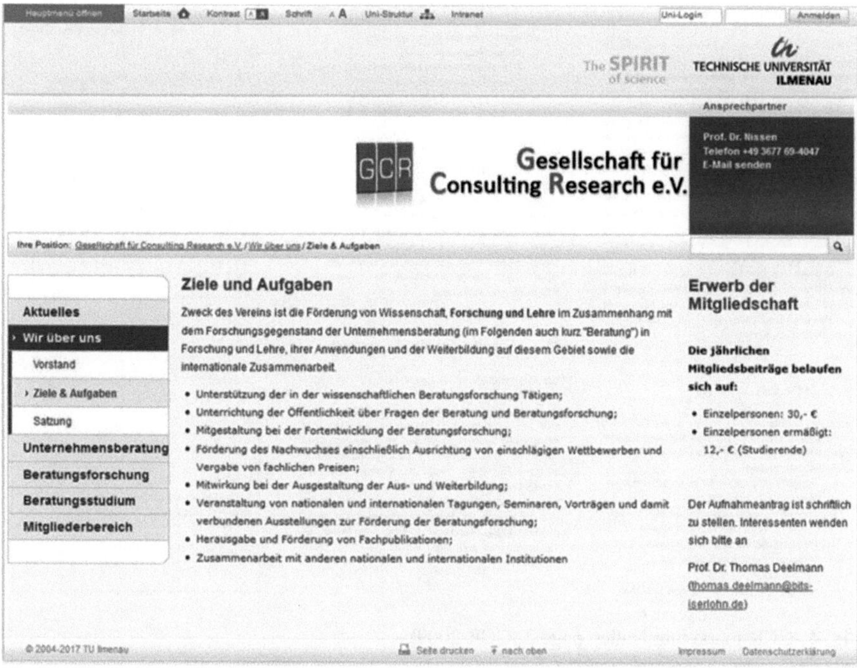

Fig. 2 Internet presence of the GCR; Screenshot (GCR 2017)

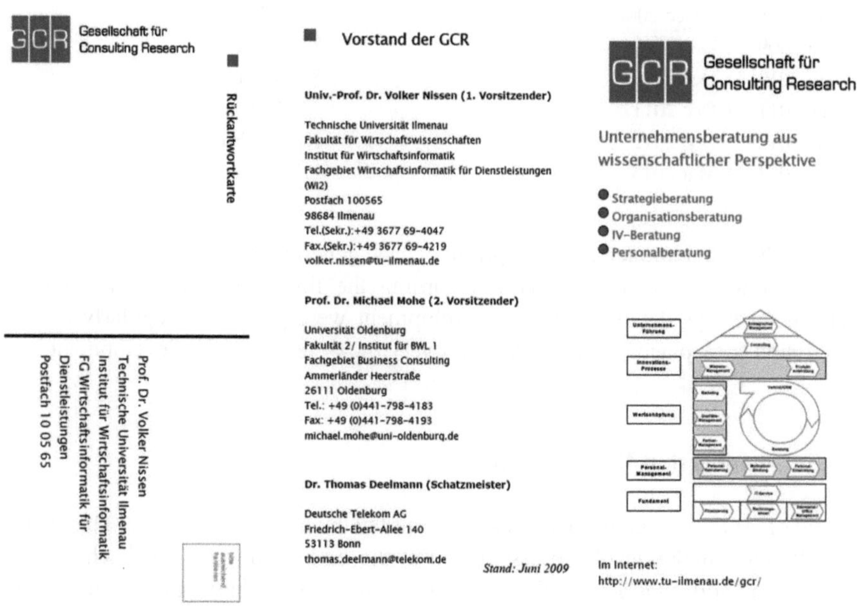

Fig. 3 GCR marketing leaflet, page 1 (GCR 2009)

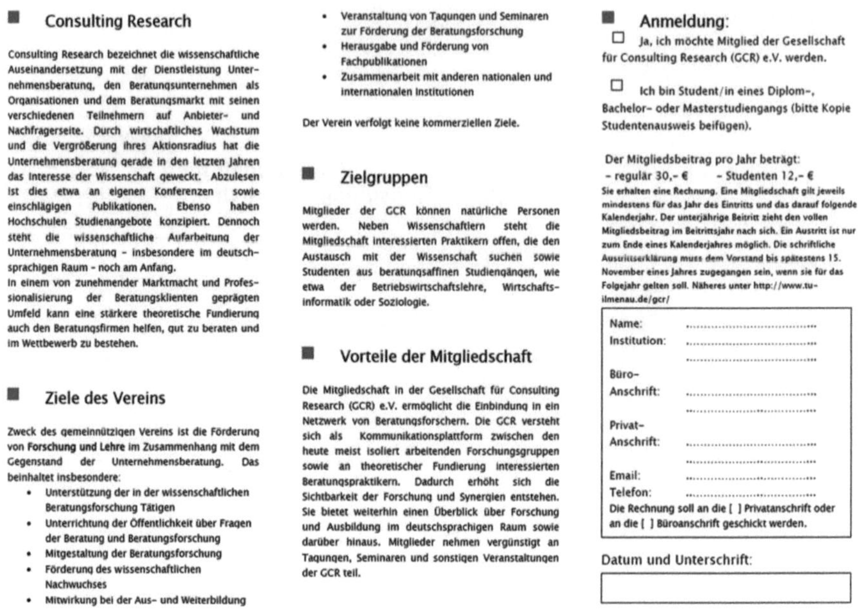

■ Consulting Research

Consulting Research bezeichnet die wissenschaftliche Auseinandersetzung mit der Dienstleistung Unternehmensberatung, den Beratungsunternehmen als Organisationen und dem Beratungsmarkt mit seinen verschiedenen Teilnehmern auf Anbieter- und Nachfragerseite. Durch wirtschaftliches Wachstum und die Vergrößerung ihres Aktionsradius hat die Unternehmensberatung gerade in den letzten Jahren das Interesse der Wissenschaft geweckt. Abzulesen ist dies etwa an eigenen Konferenzen sowie einschlägigen Publikationen. Ebenso haben Hochschulen Studienangebote konzipiert. Dennoch steht die wissenschaftliche Aufarbeitung der Unternehmensberatung - insbesondere im deutschsprachigen Raum - noch am Anfang.
In einem von zunehmender Marktmacht und Professionalisierung der Beratungsklienten geprägten Umfeld kann eine stärkere theoretische Fundierung auch den Beratungsfirmen helfen, gut zu beraten und im Wettbewerb zu bestehen.

■ Ziele des Vereins

Zweck des gemeinnützigen Vereins ist die Förderung von **Forschung und Lehre** im Zusammenhang mit dem Gegenstand der Unternehmensberatung. Das beinhaltet insbesondere:

- Unterstützung der in der wissenschaftlichen Beratungsforschung Tätigen
- Unterrichtung der Öffentlichkeit über Fragen der Beratung und Beratungsforschung
- Mitgestaltung der Beratungsforschung
- Förderung des wissenschaftlichen Nachwuchses
- Mitwirkung bei der Aus- und Weiterbildung
- Veranstaltung von Tagungen und Seminaren zur Förderung der Beratungsforschung
- Herausgabe und Förderung von Fachpublikationen
- Zusammenarbeit mit anderen nationalen und internationalen Institutionen

Der Verein verfolgt keine kommerziellen Ziele.

■ Zielgruppen

Mitglieder der GCR können natürliche Personen werden. Neben Wissenschaftlern steht die Mitgliedschaft interessierten Praktikern offen, die den Austausch mit der Wissenschaft suchen sowie Studenten aus beratungsaffinen Studiengängen, wie etwa der Betriebswirtschaftslehre, Wirtschaftsinformatik oder Soziologie.

■ Vorteile der Mitgliedschaft

Die Mitgliedschaft in der Gesellschaft für Consulting Research (GCR) e.V. ermöglicht die Einbindung in ein Netzwerk von Beratungsforschern. Die GCR versteht sich als Kommunikationsplattform zwischen den heute meist isoliert arbeitenden Forschungsgruppen sowie an theoretischer Fundierung interessierten Beratungspraktikern. Dadurch erhöht sich die Sichtbarkeit der Forschung und Synergien entstehen. Sie bietet weiterhin einen Überblick über Forschung und Ausbildung im deutschsprachigen Raum sowie darüber hinaus. Mitglieder nehmen vergünstigt an Tagungen, Seminaren und sonstigen Veranstaltungen der GCR teil.

■ Anmeldung:

☐ Ja, ich möchte Mitglied der Gesellschaft für Consulting Research (GCR) e.V. werden.

☐ Ich bin Student/in eines Diplom-, Bachelor- oder Masterstudiengangs (bitte Kopie Studentenausweis beifügen).

Der Mitgliedsbeitrag pro Jahr beträgt:
- regulär 30,- € - Studenten 12,- €
Sie erhalten eine Rechnung. Eine Mitgliedschaft gilt jeweils mindestens für das Jahr des Eintritts und das darauf folgende Kalenderjahr. Der unterjährige Beitritt zieht den vollen Mitgliedsbeitrag im Beitrittsjahr nach sich. Ein Austritt ist nur zum Ende eines Kalenderjahres möglich. Die schriftliche Austrittserklärung muss dem Vorstand bis spätestens 15. November eines Jahres zugegangen sein, wenn sie für das Folgejahr gelten soll. Näheres unter http://www.tu-ilmenau.de/gcr/

Name: ………………………
Institution: ………………………
………………………
Büro-Anschrift: ………………………
………………………
Privat-Anschrift: ………………………
………………………
Email: ………………………
Telefon: ………………………
Die Rechnung soll an die [ ] Privatanschrift oder an die [ ] Büroanschrift geschickt werden.

Datum und Unterschrift:

Fig. 4 GCR marketing leaflet, page 2 (GCR 2009)

Table 1 Development of the financial situation of the GCR

Period of time	Financial assets at year (period) end
19 Dec 2007–31 Dec 2008	−27.37 Euro
1 Jan 2009–31 Dec 2009	225.84 Euro
1 Jan 2010–31 Dec 2010	541.43 Euro
1 Jan 2011–31 Dec 2011	728.51 Euro
1 Jan 2012–31 Dec 2012	1043.66 Euro
1 Jan 2013–16 Mar 2015	1171.55 Euro

(Nissen 2012) mentioned above. Upfront of each general meeting, the members were presented with a written overview regarding the financial situation. During the general meetings details about the development were given and regularly a short discussion took place. Table 1 gives an overview of the financial development.

2.3.5 Membership Development

In mid of 2007, a group of four researchers started the preliminarily talks. They led to the official foundation of the association at the end of the year. At each general meeting, a short overview of the membership situation (joining and leaving members) was given. Table 2 presents an overview of the membership development. In 2010 two persons joined the GCR with a 'student member' status. Only for the last

Table 2 Development of the membership situation of the GCR

Point of time/time period	Members
20 Jul 2007	4 (participants)
19 Dec 2007	8
19 Dec 2007–31 Dec 2008	8
1 Jan 2009–31 Dec 2009	11
1 Jan 2010–31 Dec 2010	15
1 Jan 2011–31 Dec 2011	16
1 Jan 2012–31 Dec 2012	16
1 Jan 2013–16 Mar 2015	12

reported time period, the GCR had to record leaving members and subsequently a shrinking membership base.

At the preparation meeting, the foundation meeting and the annual general meetings a minimum of four people and a maximum of eight members participated. For the five general meetings this corresponds to a participation rate between 38 and 58%.

The association's board was stable from the foundation until 2012. The three initial board members remained on their individual positions. In 2012 the second chairman and in 2013 the treasurer stepped down but remained ordinary members of the GCR. They were replaced by two other GCR members who fulfilled their role until the dissolution in 2015 (Amtsgericht Bonn 2013).

2.4 Termination

After several bilateral discussions between the association's board members and with several other members in the years of 2013 and 2014, it became clear that the need for a special legal entity, which covers Consulting Research on a wide-ranging level, was not large enough to continue the GCR.

At the annual meeting 2015, the first chairman pushed forward the proposal to terminate the GCR. Two main reasons were mentioned. Firstly, the passivity and inactivity of the majority of the members questions the associations overarching purpose (cf. Sect. 2.2). Secondly, some of the members used the Special Interest Group IT consulting (cf. Sect. 3), which was able to create more activity, as a vehicle for their research and collaboration ambitions.

The proposal was intensively discussed, but in the end all participants agreed on the proposal. The decision to terminate the Gesellschaft für Consulting Research (GCR) e.V. as soon as possible was taken unanimously.

The association's board members subsequently informed the local court and the local tax authority over the termination. With the removal of the GCR from the register of associations it ceased to exist (officially published in Amtsblatt Regierungsbezirk Köln 41, 2015). The existing financial assets were statutory used for the means of Consulting Research; i.e. they were transferred to TU Ilmenau proWiWi e.V. which in turn forwarded the financial assets in 2017 to sponsor the present publication.

2.5 Assessment

Looking back, the situation in 2007 (at the time when the GCR founding took place) did not differ much from 2018's situation. One can still identify research islands in Germany which co-operate on a more or less opportunistic basis. There is yet no established journal for Consulting Research, and the research community is relatively scattered. Thus, despite an overall improved visibility of CR in Germany and more regular interaction amongst researchers, the targets of the GCR were not all met.

The authors identify several aspects, why the GCR was not able to satisfy the articulated demand:

- Firstly, the founding process: The timespan between the inaugural meeting (December 2007) and the first general meeting (March 2009) was probably too long. During this time, administrative and not research-driven work was prevalent—and perhaps some action spirit with some members deserted.
- Secondly, the misallocation of resources: Large amounts of manpower went into administrative task, which were required e.g. by the German legislation ('Vereinsrecht') or the tax authorities. Within a relatively small research community, this misallocation of resources towards regulatory-driven, but not content-based activities can slow down the overall research activities.
- Thirdly, the critical mass: The GCR was never able to reach a critical mass, which (in addition to administrative tasks) placed too much emphasis on activities of board members to keep the society going. Basically, too few GCR members were willing to invest a significant amount of time in the scientific development of the GCR and the institutionalization of Consulting Research. However, over the years all members were highly positive minded about the GCR—but the association was not able to translate this mind-set into enough action.

3 Special Interest Group "Arbeitskreis IV-Beratung"

3.1 Foundation and Organization

The founding process of the 'Arbeitskreis Informationsverarbeitungsbezogene Unternehmensberatung in der Gesellschaft für Informatik e.V.' (short: GI-AK IV-Beratung; Eng.: Special Interest Group (SIG) IT Consulting) was more or less in parallel to the preparation and foundation phase of the association 'Gesellschaft for Consulting Research' (cf. Sects. 2.1 and 2.2).

There were two major reasons for the foundation of the SIG:

- Building a sub-structure for IT related Consulting Research within the overarching Consulting Research community. IT consulting and other fields of consulting, e.g. HR or strategy consulting differ in several ways. A dedicated formation therefore seemed to be reasonable.
- Creating a forum within the German informatics and business informatics community, in which consulting-affine practitioners and researchers can exchange ideas, concepts, experiences and research results.

These reasons were specified and documented in a call for participation for the SIG IT Consulting, which was distributed within the German informatics and business informatics communities:

> "IT consulting is an important part of the overall consulting domain. In comparison to strategy consulting IT consulting is more operational oriented and emphasizes issues of information processing at the client side. Despite the significant practical relevance of the consulting industry, there are only little connections to research and university teaching in Germany. Additionally, the majority of Consulting Research publications focus on the areas of strategy and operations. There is a deficit in research within the area of IT consulting—despite the large share of IT consulting considering the total consulting market volume." (Nissen and Deelmann 2008; in German, translated by the authors).

The SIG IT Consulting is part of the technical committee Business informatics (Ger.: Fachbereich Wirtschaftsinformatik) of the German Informatics Society (Ger.: Gesellschaft für Informatik e.V.; short: GI). The GI is a non-profit organization with approximately 20,000 members (GI 2017a, b). In accordance with the requirements of the GI, the SIG IT Consulting is represented by a speaker and a deputy speaker. Since 2008, these two positions are held by the authors of this paper.

There is no formal membership register within the SIG. However, the call for participation was followed by six IT professionals at the first SIG meeting on 20 Feb 2009 in Ilmenau (Schäfer 2009a). Until March 2010 there were 40 people who actively signed up the mailing list (Nissen 2010). This figure remained stable thereafter.

The SIG IT consulting has an internet presence which is hosted at the University of Technology Ilmenau (Fig. 5). It does not have financial assets.

3.2 Dedicated Meetings of the Special Interest Group

The SIG IT Consulting itself organized several meetings (AK IV-Beratung 2017b). The local organization and sponsorship was typically assumed by a member of the SIG. The speakers of the SIG took care of the official announcements and invitations. The meetings itself were aimed to have a rather practice-oriented character, with e.g. best practice exchange. There was no gate keeping procedure for presentations. At the end of each meeting a focus topic for the next meeting was agreed upon. Until 2017 there were six dedicated meetings of the SIG. In the following,

Fig. 5 Internet presence of the SIG IT consulting (AK IV-Beratung 2017a)

these meetings will be shortly described. The *first dedicated meeting* of the SIG IT Consulting took place on 20 Feb 2009 at the University of Technology Ilmenau. The meeting had six participants. Three participants were also members of the association GCR (cf. Sect. 2). Two participants were practitioners and four had a research background.

Agenda items were (Schäfer 2009a):

- Presentation of the SIG IT Consulting and its background,
- Overview of an university lecture 'business administration for consultancies',
- Potentials for business informatics in the domain of tax and auditing, and
- Future topics and meetings of the SIG IT Consulting.

The *second meeting* was held on 18 Sep 2009 at T-Systems, Frankfurt/Main with seven participants. Among them were four members of the GCR; four participants came from academia, three were practitioners.

The following topics were discussed (Schäfer 2009b):

- Required competencies of consultants,
- Contents of bachelor and master studies in consulting,
- Survey on electronic recruiting in professional services firms, and
- Discussions on a Consulting Research journal and website.

The *third meeting* saw a significant increase in participants. 23 people met on 26 Feb 2010 at the Leibnitz University Hannover. 13 were affiliated with a university, nine with consultancies, and for one participant the background is not clear. Two participants were also member of the GCR.

The meeting focused on the education of consultants and had the following presentation topics (Schäfer 2010a):

- Consulting-related education at universities: overview and examples,
- Requirements of consultancies for graduates, and
- Size and building blocks of a consulting education at universities.

It was suggested to design a curriculum for the teaching of consulting core competencies, which could be used on master-level.

The *fourth meeting* had a focus on customer loyalty and customer integration. Ten participants met on 17 Sep 2010 at the University of Applied Sciences Aschaffenburg. Six of them had a university affiliation, three were practitioners and for one participant the background is unclear.

Three presentations focused on the core topic of the workshop (Schäfer 2010b):

- Value-based marketing and customer value management at consultancies,
- Requirements for a comprehensive client view as a challenge for consulting master data management, especially in the financial services sector, and
- Relevance of the personal consultant-client relationships for consulting success.

One additional presentation showed a preliminary result of the suggested consulting curriculum (cf. above). An intensive discussion followed the presentation.

A *fifth meeting* was held on 4 Mar 2011 in Nuremberg and was hosted by MID GmbH. Six out of the 14 participants were from a university, the remaining eight were practitioners. Four participants hat a GCR membership, too.

Three presentations supported the meeting's focus topic conflict and crisis management at consultancies (Schäfer 2011):

- Conflict management in consulting and IT projects—case studies and role-playing games,
- Methods and techniques for conflict detection and conflict solution in consulting processes, and
- Customer loyalty and complaint management in professional services firms.

A *sixth meeting* was organized by the University of Hamburg on 13 Sep. 2013. The overarching topics of this meeting were methods and the development of methods in IT consulting. The presentations had the following focus content (Schäfer 2013):

- Methods in IT consulting and their development—an example of a mid-sized consultancy,
- Consulting method 'WARP',
- Business transformation with agile methods,
- Research on trust within the client-consultant relationship,
- Development of methods and tools for Enterprise Architecture Modelling,
- Usage of methods, processes and standards within the application lifecycle management, and
- Recruiting criteria of IT consultancies and their relevance for the university education.

3.3 Embedded Workshops and Conferences

Upfront the official foundation of the SIG IT Consulting in 2008 there were three workshops and conferences, which one of the authors of this paper co-organized and served as co-chair. These workshops can be called embedded because they used the framing conditions (e.g. venue, catering, IT, local organization, and publication of proceedings) of a larger umbrella-conference.

Compared to the dedicated meetings, the embedded workshops/conferences were more *research-oriented*. For each presentation, a paper had to be submitted in advance of the conference date. The papers were subject to a double-blind peer review process. The *first workshop* IT consulting focused on foundations, concepts and trends and was part of the INFORMATIK 2005, the annual meeting of the German Informatics Society. Since 2000, every 2 years a team of business informatics researchers in the German-speaking countries organizes the so called Multi-Konferenz Wirtschaftsinformatik (MKWI; Eng.: multi-conference business informatics). The *second workshop* had a focus on responsibilities and challenges and was embedded in the MKWI 2006. The aim of the *third workshop* was to discuss the role of consulting as an intermediary between research and practice. It was embedded in the MKWI 2008.

The positive feedback on these workshops and the number of participants were a supporting signal for the foundation of the SIG IT Consulting. Until 2017, six embedded workshops and conferences followed the first three. For these workshops, both authors of this paper served as chairs, occasionally supported by additional co-chairs.

- The *fourth workshop* was dealing with IT consulting from a scientific perspective. It aimed at research on IT consulting from various perspectives (Nissen and Deelmann 2009). It was part of the INFORMATIK 2009, which was held from 28 Sep to 2 Oct 2009 in Lübeck. Four papers were presented (Fischer et al. 2009):
- IT consulting between transdisciplinary research and praxis,
- Development and positioning of new consulting services—challenges and approaches,
- Automation of consulting services, and
- Automation of auditing services.

The *fifth workshop* was part of the MKWI 2010 in Göttingen (23 Feb to 25 Feb 2010). The theme of the workshop focused on IT-related Consulting (Breitner et al. 2010). Six papers were presented (Schumann et al. 2010):

- VAT compliance at ERP systems,
- Formalization gaps in IT consulting,
- Procedure models in IT consulting for the selection and implementation of software,
- CRM evaluation,
- Process evaluation in consulting, and
- Business model diversification in consultancies.

Fashions and trends in IT consulting was the heading for the *sixth workshop*. It was again part of the INFORMATIK in 2011, which took place from 4 Oct to 7 Oct 2011 in Berlin (Pepper 2011).

The papers presented covered the following topics:

- Work-life-balance for women in IT consulting,
- Trends in IT consulting for notary offices,
- Professional developments between consulting and science,
- Proposal for the reflection of fashions and trends within the academic education of IT consultants, and
- Proposal of and discussion about an IT consulting curriculum for universities.

In 2012 the SIG IT Consulting used again the umbrella format of the MKWI. The MKWI 2012 was organized in Braunschweig and held from 29 Feb to 2 Mar 2012. The track heading focused on HR-related issues in IT consulting.

Three papers were presented at the *seventh workshop* (Mattfeld and Robra-Bissantz 2012):

- Job profiles in IT consulting,
- Work-life-balance—A strategic weapon for HR management in IT consultancies?, and
- Strategic workforce management as consulting competence.

The *eighth workshop* was held in Paderborn under the theme of relevance of IT innovations for IT consultancies and their clients. Consultancies have to use innovative IT in their projects and have to advise their clients in this area as well (Deelmann et al. 2014). The workshop was part of the MKWI 2014, which started on 26 Feb 2014 and lasted until 28 Feb 2014 (Kundisch et al. 2014).

The workshop topic was reflected by three presentations:

- IT consultancies' recruiting criterions and their relevance for university education,
- Types of innovations provided by management consultancies and IT consultancies, and
- Development and management of consulting methods in practice.

For the time being, the last workshop was held as part of the MKWI 2016 (9 Mar to 11 Mar 2016, Ilmenau). The *ninth workshop* focused on IT consulting in the context of digital transformation. Traditional lines and boundaries between consulting fields become blurred. This leads to new competitors in existing markets as well as the creation of completely new markets (Deelmann et al. 2016). Three papers were presented (Nissen et al. 2016):

- Digital transformation and IT trend topics reflected in job advertisements of IT consultancies,
- IT consultants as change agents in digital transformation, and
- Virtualization of the consulting industry.

At the writing of this paper, the next workshop is scheduled to be held at MKWI 2018 in Lüneburg, Germany, in March 2018. It is planned to continue the workshop series in order to create a platform for consulting-related research and information exchange. Researchers and research-affine practitioners will find an environment for exchanging ideas and discussing new developments.

3.4 Intermediate Evaluation

The Special Interest Group IT Consulting was founded for two major reasons: (1) to build a sub-structure for IT related Consulting Research within the overarching consulting community and (2) to create a Consulting Research-oriented forum within the German informatics and business informatics communities.

An intermediate assessment comes to the conclusion that (1) the creation of a (sub-) structure for IT related Consulting Research was successful. However, the once existing super-structure ceased to exist (cf. Sect. 2.4). Additionally, through the regular presence and workshops at the annual or bi-annual meetings of the German informatics and business informatics community, the SIG was (2) able to establish a forum for Consulting Research-oriented aspects.

Several aspects can be mentioned which characterize the workings of the Special Interest Group:

- Firstly, the organizational structure was lean. This starts with the founding process, goes on with the non-existent need for a large administrative overhead, and ends with the opportunity to use existing conference frameworks of e.g. the MKWI-series.
- Secondly, the Special Interest Group was founded in order to focus on the consulting field information technology. However, in the meetings and workshops contributions related to other fields of consulting were appreciated, too.
- Thirdly, a key topic is the transmission from a passive to an active engagement. For example, the willingness to organize a dedicated meeting seems to be limited. Many people rather want to attend a meeting or a workshop, but only a few can be motivated to contribute more actively. However, probably this point is true for a lot of organizations, so that the so far six meetings plus six workshops can be interpreted as a (moderate) success.

4 Conclusion

Research activities in the consulting domain exist for several decades. However, they were often not or only loosely coupled, at least in the German-speaking area. To improve this situation, an institutionalization of the research activities is helpful. This paper presented two approaches which aimed at fostering such an institutionalization process.

The first approach took place in form of a registered association (GCR). The second approach was in form of a Special Interest Group within a larger professional organization (AK IV-Beratung). A retrospective view over the last decade by the authors, who were actively involved in both approaches, leads to several conclusions:

- While the registered association had a very strong organizational stability, the Special Interest Group was more flexible due to a low administrative overhead and permeable organizational boundaries.
- The Special Interest Group had initially only limited ambitions—and was successful in reaching them.
- The association had initially greater ambitions. It was in the beginning burdened with administrative work and did little Consulting Research. This could have had a reducing effect on the overall acceptance within the relevant community.

- It was helpful to lead both institutions in personal union. The increase in (personal) work was more than compensated by the benefits of synergies.
- Despite the formal focus on IT consulting, the Special Interest Group covered partially also more general consulting topics or topics which were only loosely related to IT consulting. This can be interpreted as helpful in order to gain a critical mass.
- A national coverage with e.g. meetings, conferences and workshops is challenging due to the resulting travel costs and time of the individual participants—but supports the acceptance of these institutions.
- A critical success factor for any research institution is the personal engagement of its members. If only a small leadership team drives all the activities, the fragility is big.

Of course, these conclusions are driven by personal experience and are focused on Germany. However, the paper covers a time span of 10 years and two quite different approaches for institutionalizing Consulting Research.

Our observations and documentation could in the future be compared with institutionalization processes for Consulting Research in other countries or with processes for the institutionalization of other scientific domains in Germany. Finally, we hope that the basic results can leverage learning effects with a further institutionalization of Consulting Research in Germany and abroad.

References

AK IV-Beratung (2017a) GI-Arbeitskreis "Informationsverarbeitungsbezogene Unternehmensberatung". https://www.tu-ilmenau.de/wid/forschung/consulting-research/gi-arbeitskreis/. Accessed 9 Jun 2017

AK IV-Beratung (2017b) Aktuelles. https://www.tu-ilmenau.de/wid/forschung/consulting-research/gi-arbeitskreis/aktuelles/. Accessed 9 Jun 2017

Amtsgericht Bonn (2008) Eintragung im Vereinsregister betreffend Gesellschaft für Consulting Research (GCR) e.V. Unpublished letter form the local court Bonn to Thomas Deelmann, 16 Oct 2008

Amtsgericht Bonn (2013) Eintragung im Vereinsregister betreffend Gesellschaft für Consulting Research (GCR) e.V. Unpublished letter form the local court Bonn to the notary's office of Dr. Lohmeyer et al., 31 Jul 2013

Bittner J, Niejahr E (2004) Die Berater-Republik. Die Zeit (7):9–12

Breitner MH, Deelmann T, Loos P, Nissen V (2010) Unternehmensberatung im IT-Umfeld. In: Schumann M, Kolbe LM, Breitner MH, Frerichs A (eds) Multikonferenz Wirtschaftsinformatik 2010. Universitätsverlag Göttingen, Göttingen, pp 117–118

Clark T, Fincha R, Mohe M, Sturdy A (2007) Perspectives on management consulting research. Arbeit—Zeitschrift für Arbeitsforschung. Arbeitsgestaltung und Arbeitspolitik 16(3):255–264

Consultancy.uk (2017.) Global consulting market development and other publically available information on the website http://www.consultancy.uk/consulting-industry/global. Accessed 18 Jul 2017

Deelmann T (2007) Beratung, Wissenschaft und Gesellschaft—Interdependenzen und Gegenläufigkeiten. In: Nissen V (ed) Consulting research. DUV, Wiesbaden, pp 39–54

Deelmann T (2013) Vorabinformationen zur Mitgliederversammlung 2013. Unpublished agenda and accompanying information material for the general meeting of the GCR, 12 Feb 2013
Deelmann T, Drews P, Nissen V (2014) Bedeutung von IT-Innovationen für die IV-Unternehmensberatung und ihre Kunden. In: Kundisch D, Suhl L, Beckmann L (eds) Tagungsband Multikonferenz Wirtschaftsinformatik 2014 (MKWI 2014). Universität Paderborn, Paderborn, p 88
Deelmann T, Drews P, Nissen V (2016) IT-Beratung im Kontext digitaler transformation. In: Nissen V, Stelzer D, Straßburger S, Fischer D (eds) Multikonferenz Wirtschaftsinformatik (MKWI) 2016, Band II. Universitätsverlag Ilmenau, Ilmenau, p 1005
Dornheim LS (2015) Frauen in der Unternehmensberatung. Springer Gabler, Wiesbaden
Engel KH (1969) Mit Beratern arbeiten, Ja,—aber wie? Verlag für Unternehmensführung. Bad Homburg v.d.H, Baden-Baden
Faust M (2006) Soziologie und Beratung—Analysen und Angebote. Soziologische Revue (29):277–290
Finanzamt Siegburg (2008) Vorläufige Bescheinigung. Unpublished letter from the local tax authority Siegburg to Thomas Deelmann, 2 Dec 2008
Fischer S, Maehle E, Reischuk R (eds) (2009) Informatik 2009—Im focus das Leben. Lecture notes in informatics, P-154, Bonn
Fuchs P, Pankoke E (1994) Auf dem Weg zur Beratungsgesellschaft? Zur Theorie einer diffusen Praxis. Katholische Akademie, Schwerte
GCR (2009) Unternehmensberatung aus wissenschaftlicher Perspektive. Leaflet, Bonn
GCR (2017) Ziele & Aufgaben. https://www.tu-ilmenau.de/gcr/wir-ueber-uns/ziele-aufgaben. Accessed 9 Jun 2017
GI (2017a) At a glance—GI—Gesellschaft für Informatik e.V. https://en.gi.de/startpage/at-a-glance.html. Accessed 21 Jun 2017
GI (2017b) Technical Committees—GI—Gesellschaft für Informatik e.V. https://en.gi.de/startpage/technical-committees.html. Accessed 21 Jun 2017
Kaas KP, Schade C (1995) Unternehmensberater im Wettbewerb—Eine empirische Untersuchung aus der Perspektive der Neuen Institutionslehre. ZfB 65(10):1067–1089
Kieser A (2002) Wissenschaft und Beratung. C. Winter, Heidelberg
Kieser A, Nicolai A (2005) Success factor research: overcoming the trade-off between rigor and relevance? J Manag Inq 14(3):275–279
Kundisch D, Suhl L, Beckmann L (eds) (2014) Tagungsband Multikonferenz Wirtschaftsinformatik 2014 (MKWI 2014). Universität Paderborn, Paderborn
Kurbjuweit D (2003) Unser effizientes Leben. Die Diktatur der Ökonomie und ihre Folgen. Reinbek bei Hamburg
Luhmann N (1989) Kommunikationssperren in der Unternehmensberatung. In: Luhmann N, Fuchs P (eds) Reden und Schweigen. Suhrkamp, Frankfurt am Main, pp 209–227
Mattfeld DC, Robra-Bissantz S (eds) (2012) Multikonferenz Wirtschaftsinformatik—Proceedings. GITO, Göttingen
Mohe M, Nissen V, Deelmann T (2008) Einige Überlegungen und Daten zur Institutionalisierung des Forschungsfeldes Consulting Research. In: Loos P, Breitner M, Deelmann T (eds) IT-Beratung—Consulting zwischen Wissenschaft und Praxis. Logos, Berlin, pp 75–88
Nicolai AT (2004) The bridge to the 'real world': applied science or a 'schizophrenic tour de force'? Journal of Management Studies 41(6):951–976
Niehaves B, Becker J (2006) Design science perspectives on IT-consulting. In: Lehner F, Nösekabel H, Kleinschmidt P (eds) Tagungsband 1 der Multikonferenz Wirtschaftsinformatik in Passau 2006. GITO, Berlin, pp 7–17
Nissen V (2007a) Consulting Research—eine Einführung. In: Nissen V (ed) Consulting Research. Unternehmensberatung aus wissenschaftlicher Perspektive. Gabler Edition Wissenschaft, Wiesbaden, pp 3–38
Nissen V (2007b) Ergebnisprotokoll zum CR-Meeting vom 20.07.2007 in Göttingen. Unpublished meeting result protocol, 20 Jul 2007

Nissen V (2009) Protokoll der Hauptversammlung 2009. Unpublished result protocol of the general meeting of the GCR, 27 Mar 2009
Nissen V (2010) Protokoll der Hauptversammlung 2010. Unpublished result protocol of the general meeting of the GCR, 12 Feb 2010
Nissen V (2011) Protokoll der Mitgliederversammlung 2011. Unpublished result protocol of the general meeting of the GCR, 15 Mar 2011
Nissen V (2012) Protokoll der Mitgliederversammlung 2012. Unpublished result protocol of the general meeting of the GCR, 21 Mar 2012
Nissen V, Deelmann T (2008) Gründung des GI-Arbeitskreises, Informationsverarbeitungs-bezogene Unternehmensberatung' (IV-Beratung). Call for participation, Ilmenau & Bonn
Nissen V, Deelmann T (2009) IV-Beratung aus wissenschaftlicher Perspektive. In: Fischer S, Maehle E, Reischuk R (eds) Informatik 2009—Im Focus das Leben. Lecture notes in informatics, P-154. Bonn, pp 482–485
Nissen V, Klauk B (eds) (2012) Studienführer Consulting—Studienangebote in Deutschland, Österreich und der Schweiz. Springer Gabler, Wiesbaden
Nissen V, Mohe M, Deelmann T (2009) Ziele, Anforderungen und Institutionalisierung des Forschungsfeldes Consulting Research. In: Möller H, Hausinger B (eds) Quo vadis Beratungswissenschaft? VS Verlag für Sozialwissenschaften, Wiesbaden, pp 141–167
Nissen V, Stelzer D, Straßburger S, Fischer D (eds) (2016) Multikonferenz Wirtschaftsinformatik (MKWI) 2016, Band II. Universitätsverlag Ilmenau, Ilmenau
Payne AFT, Lumsdum C (1987) Strategy consulting—a shooting star? Long Range Plan 20 (3):53–64
Pepper P (ed) (2011) INFORMATIK 2011—Informatik schafft communities. In: Proceedings of the annual meeting of the German Informatics Society, CD-ROM
Schäfer U (2007) Gründungsversammlung des Vereins ‚Wissenschaftliche Gesellschaft für Unternehmensberatung (WGUB)'—Protokoll. Unpublished result protocol of the general meeting of the WGUB, 19 Dec 2007
Schäfer U (2009a) Workshop des Arbeitskreises IV-Beratung der Gesellschaft für Informatik e.V. am 20.2.2009. Unpublished result protocol of the meeting of the SIG IT Consulting, 20 Feb 2009
Schäfer U (2009b) 2. Workshop des Arbeitskreises IV-Beratung der Gesellschaft für Informatik e.V. am 18.9.2009. Unpublished result protocol of the meeting of the SIG IT Consulting, 18 Sep 2009
Schäfer U (2010a) 3. Workshop des Arbeitskreises IV-Beratung der Gesellschaft für Informatik e.V. am 26.2.2010. Unpublished result protocol of the meeting of the SIG IT Consulting, 26 Feb 2010
Schäfer U (2010b) 4. Workshop des Arbeitskreises IV-Beratung der Gesellschaft für Informatik e.V. am 17.9.2010. Unpublished result protocol of the meeting of the SIG IT Consulting, 17 Sep 2010
Schäfer U (2011) 5. Workshop des Arbeitskreises IV-Beratung der Gesellschaft für Informatik e.V. und der Gesellschaft für Consulting Research (GCR) e.V. am 4.3.2011. Unpublished result protocol of the joint meeting of the SIG IT Consulting and the GCR, 4 Mar 2011
Schäfer U (2013) 6. Workshop des Arbeitskreises IV-Beratung der Gesellschaft für Informatik e.V. Und der Gesellschaft für consulting research (GCR) e.V. Am 13.09.2013. Unpublished result protocol of the joint meeting of the SIG IT consulting and the GCR, 13 Sep 2013
Schumann M, Kolbe LM, Breitner MH, Frerichs A (eds) (2010) Multikonferenz Wirtschaftsinformatik 2010. Universitätsverlag Göttingen, Göttingen
Witthauer KF (1973) Betriebswirtschaftslehre der Consulting-Unternehmung. Grafenau-Döffingen, Lexika

Thomas Deelmann is Professor for Public Management at the University of Applied Sciences for Public Administration and Management of North Rhine-Westphalia (FHöV) in Cologne, Germany. Until 2016, he was Professor for Corporate Consulting and Management at BiTS Iserlohn as well as the head of the strategy development department for a leading global ICT service provider. His professional experiences as a consultant at one of the largest international consultancies, as an in house consultant, as a strategic source for consulting services and as a client of consulting services form the basis for his teaching and research. Currently, he serves as the editor for a consulting handbook and as a jury member of the WirtschaftsWoche's "Best of Consulting" award.

Volker Nissen holds the Chair of Information Systems Engineering in Services at Technische Universität Ilmenau, Germany, since 2005. Prior to this, he pursued a consulting career, including positions as manager at IDS Scheer AG, director at DHC GmbH, and CEO of NISSCON Ltd., Germany. In 1994 he received a PhD degree in Economic Sciences with distinction from the University of Goettingen, Germany. His current research interests include the digital transformation of the consulting industry, the management of IT-agility, metaheuristic optimization, and process acceptance research. He is author and editor of 20 books and some 200 other publications, including papers in Business and Information Systems Engineering, Information Systems Frontiers, IEEE Transactions on EC, IEEE Transactions on NN, OR Spectrum, and Annals of OR.

Part II
General Issues in Consulting

To Measure Is to Know: Development of an Instrument for Measuring Consulting Service Value

Severin Oesterle, Arne Buchwald, and Nils Urbach

Abstract While their fundamental business model has not changed for many decades, consulting firms are currently faced with serious challenges putting the complete market at the risk of disruption. Given that situation, it is essential for consultancies to understand how value emerges in consulting projects in the eyes of their clients. Turning to the customer perspective, it is also important to understand how value emerges from the relationship with consultancies. While previous literature provides valuable but fragmented starting points to explain the joint value creation in IT consulting projects, we suggested a synthesized conceptual model drawing on the service-dominant logic in a previous article that integrates both the service provider and client perspectives. In this article, we now put forth a measurement instrument that we subjected to a preliminary empirical validation with which the important determinants in both spheres can be assessed to ultimately explain the value of the IT consulting service in a follow-up, large-scale quantitative-empirical validation.

1 Introduction and Motivation

While their fundamental business model has not changed for many decades, consulting firms are currently faced with serious challenges putting the complete market at the risk of disruption (Christensen et al. 2013). Major triggers of this development are a general market saturation (Richter and Schmidt 2006), the trend towards digital business models (Veit et al. 2014), and the customer companies' increasing sophistication about consulting services. Looking at the domain of information technology (IT), service providers are further pressured by both a persisting competition from

S. Oesterle · N. Urbach (✉)
University of Bayreuth, Bayreuth, Germany
e-mail: severin.oesterle@uni-bayreuth.de; nils.urbach@uni-bayreuth.de

A. Buchwald
EBS Business School, Wiesbaden, Germany
e-mail: arne.buchwald@ebs.edu

V. Nissen (ed.), *Advances in Consulting Research*, Contributions to Management Science, https://doi.org/10.1007/978-3-319-95999-3_4

low-wage countries and the rise of innovative services, such as cloud computing, providing alternatives to the established business models (McCarthy and Matzke 2010). Given that situation, for consultancies, it is essential to understand the needs of their customers as good as possible. Only with a deeper comprehension of how their service provision leads to value for the customer will those companies be able to optimize their customer relationships and, finally, increase or at least keep their sales and profits as well as raise their market shares. Next to profit and sales, it becomes more and more important for consultancies to be recognized as thought leader by the customer. Turning to the customer perspective, it is also important to understand how co-created value emerges from the relationship with consultancies. In this case, client companies can arrange and staff their project teams in a way to gain the highest possible value of the delivered consulting service. Next to the understanding of how the value emerges from consulting services, it is also vital for consultancies as well as for client companies to measure which determinants relatively contribute to the emergence of consulting service value.

Our research is theoretically rooted in the insight that the value of collaboration between consulting service providers and their customers does not emerge in either the service provider (i.e. the consultancy) or the customer organization, but emerges through co-creation (Vargo and Lusch 2004), which is also long established in practice by consultancies and their interaction with clients in consulting projects. While knowledge on the underlying mechanisms between a consultancy's service provision and a customer's value receipt is surprisingly scarce, some related aspects have already been subject to academic research. Customer satisfaction with IT consultants (Das et al. 1999) is investigated but does not consider other determinants important to this setting (e.g. collaboration quality and value co-creation); IT Consulting SERVQUAL as a measurement instrument for service quality of and customer satisfaction with IT consultants (Yoon and Suh 2004) is based on a firm-centric view that is no longer state-of-the-art considering the service-dominant logic (S-D logic) (Vargo and Lusch 2004, 2008, 2016). Barrutia and Gilsanz (2013) investigate electronic service quality to explain consumer value perceptions in B2C e-commerce contexts from both, the customer and the service provider; Breidbach et al. (2013b) focuses on innovation in professional service firms drawing on the S-D logic; Chan et al. (2010) investigate customer participation in professional financial services across cultures.

While the closely related work served as valuable starting points, we advanced the scientific discourse by suggesting a structural model for explaining consulting service value (Oesterle et al. 2016) that we refine slightly and extend in this article. As we explain in more detail in the subsequent section, service providers, such as consultancies, can only provide value propositions to their clients, which can only judge ex-post the value of the provided service during its later use. Therefore, we develop an instrument to measure consulting service value and its determinants in consulting domains characterized by strong interaction between the consultancy and the client organization (such as management and IT consultancies). The remainder of this article is structured as follows: Section 2 entails the theoretical background of this research project. Subsequently, we describe the underlying research process in

Section 3. In Section 4 we briefly sketch the hypotheses synthesized in the conceptual model. Section 5 contains the detailed measurement model and results of our pre-test. In Section 6, we discuss our results and outline the next steps in the overall research project.

2 Theoretical Background

We ground our research in the service-dominant logic (S-D logic). In 2004, Vargo and Lusch (2004) published their seminal work with which the dichotomy of goods and services is overcome. They define service "as the application of specialized competences (knowledge and skills) through deeds, processes, and performances for the benefit of another entity or the entity itself" (Vargo and Lusch 2004, p. 2). In their view, goods are a distributing mechanism for services because a service represents the fundamental unit of exchange (Breidbach and Maglio 2015; Vargo and Lusch 2004, 2016). Moreover, the S-D logic and related perspectives, e.g. service logic and service science, focus on transactions in which specialized competences, such as knowledge and skills, are exchanged (Bruns and Jacob 2014) and describe the mutual interaction between the provider of a service with its customers. Therefore, it is vital to understand the S-D logic's assumptions "all economies are service economies" (Vargo and Lusch 2004, p. 10) and "enterprises cannot deliver value, but only offer value propositions" (Vargo and Lusch 2008, p. 7). Hence, the role of the customer and its resources has become more and more important. However, Heinonen et al. (2010) put forth that the S-D logic is still service provider-orientated. That is why they focus to apply a deeper customer lens. Moreover, they state that "[...] the center of interest are not exchange and service as such, but how a company's service is and becomes embedded in the customer's contexts, activities, practices, and experiences, and what implications this has for service companies" (Heinonen et al. 2010, p. 533). Hence, their customer-dominant logic places the customer in the center and not the service. In our research endeavor, we focus on the service and its mutual interactions with the client within a specific service delivery process. Consequently, we consider clients as partners in the value co-creation process and follow the view of Vargo and Lusch (2008, p. 6) that "service is the fundamental basis of exchange".

2.1 Value Propositions, Value Co-creation, and Value

Within the initial work and later revised works of S-D logic, the term value proposition has not been defined clearly (Vargo and Lusch 2004, 2008, 2016). However, looking in related works, value propositions are considered as commitments the service provider makes that value-in-exchange is connected with value-in-use (Ballantyne et al. 2011; Frow and Payne 2011; Kowalkowski 2011; Lusch et al.

2007). Similarly, Grönroos and Voima (2013) consider value propositions as "promises that customers can extract some value from an offering" (Grönroos and Voima 2013, p. 146). However, the actual evaluation whether the service contributes to the client's value in future use has to be made only by the client. Thus, the service provider cannot assure an initial value contribution (Skålén et al. 2014). Furthermore, the offered value proposition has to put the individual client in a better position. The service provider can only make suggestions how the value proposition should be used. The emergence of value, however, differs in literature. Grönroos (2006) proposes that only clients are value creators and service providers are considered value co-creators only in the case interactions exist between both parties. In other terms, a service provider is co-creator when the client invites the service provider to interact, otherwise the service provider is merely a facilitator. In contrast, Vargo and Lusch (2016, p. 9) put forth that "value is always cocreated" between a service provider and the client. Furthermore, Barrutia and Gilsanz (2013, p. 232) state that "service science suggest that company and consumer service systems simultaneously access, adapt, and integrate resources to create value for themselves and others." Summarizing, service provider cannot deliver value directly. It rather emerges in the client sphere (Ballantyne and Varey 2006; Grönroos and Ravald 2011; Gummesson 2007; Vargo and Lusch 2016) which should be seen as value-in-use (Bruns and Jacob 2014; Lusch and Nambisan 2015; Lusch et al. 2007; Vargo and Lusch 2004) because the value for clients is generated by them while using and/or consuming the provided service (Grönroos and Ravald 2011; Sandström et al. 2008).

2.2 Service Provider and Client Capabilities

In the light of the S-D logic and the closely related research fields, it is necessary to consider service provider resources as well as the resources of the client in the value co-creation process which we discuss in this article as service provider capabilities and client capabilities (Barrutia and Gilsanz 2013). Drawing on the distinction of Arnould et al. (2014), operand resources are in general e.g. physical and tangible resources, economic resources as well as goods and raw materials in their possession and which are under sole control (Chandler and Vargo 2011). In turn, there are operant resources, e.g. knowledge and skills, and openness in relation to certain activities (Alborz et al. 2003; Barrutia and Gilsanz 2013). Hence, operant resources can be defined as "[...] those that act on other [operand] resources [...]" (Vargo et al. 2008, p. 148). Vargo and Lusch (2004, 2008, 2016) state that in the S-D logic the fundamental unit of exchange is service (knowledge and skills), which is why we concentrate on these abilities and focus our approach on operant resources.

Next to certain types of expertise, such as social expertise, technological expertise, and functional expertise, that are needed by both client company and service provider, each party needs to also provide particular skills to a consulting project to maximize its value. Considering the service provider capabilities, industry expertise and methodological expertise are required to ensure a high level of consulting quality. According to the S-D logic, however, firms cannot provide value directly to their customers, but they can only offer value propositions. In the hierarchy model of Madhavaram and Hunt (2008), the service quality of an consulting firm can be established as a higher-order interconnected operant resource. They define "an interconnected operant resource as a combination of two or more distinct, basic [operand] resources in which the lower order resources significantly interact, thereby reinforcing each other in enabling the firm to produce efficiently and/or effectively valued market offerings" (Madhavaram and Hunt 2008, p. 70). Though, service quality is the major resource of professional service firms (Kaiser and Ringlstetter 2011) and should be also considered as a operant resource which is why we integrated consulting service quality into the service provider capabilities. Summarizing, the different types of expertise of the service provider outlined above contribute altogether to the consulting service quality (Alborz et al. 2003; Breidbach et al. 2013a; Goles 2003).

Similarly, a client company needs to provide a few unique capabilities. First, a client company needs to understand how the regular business with consultancies takes place. Hence an operant resource for a client is the experience made in the past with consultancies. Furthermore, clients need to be willing to change their organizational structure as well as their work and administrative processes. Otherwise, the solution suggested by a consultancy will most likely miss the planned objectives. A consulting service will only contribute to a client's value if the client has the ability to recognize the provided value and external information, transform and assimilate it, and apply it (Cohen and Levinthal 1990) which is why we also integrate the absorptive capacity of a client as an operant resource into the client capabilities.

After having introduced the two complementary capability sets, we also hypothesize that the collaboration of both parties is an additional important determinant that contributes to the consulting service value. A prerequisite for consulting services is the exchange of knowledge and information between the service provider and the client company as well as a trustworthy and courteous way of interacting with each other. This social resources comprise for instance, interpersonal trust, know-how exchange, perceived pressure, relationship proneness and social skills (Paredes et al. 2014). We suggest that the collaboration quality is determined by the social expertise of each of the parties and subsequently directly influences the consulting service value.

3 Research Process

Our research aims at explaining and measuring consulting service value on the basis of both client and service provider capabilities drawing on S-D logic as theoretical foundation. We build on Oesterle et al. (2016) in which we deductively derived a preliminary structural model. Whereas our previous article serves as a valuable starting point, we modify the previous model by including the concept of absorptive capacity (Cohen and Levinthal 1990) and by extending it with additional antecedents. To measure the proposed model, we mostly rely on existing measurement scales where possible and develop new ones where necessary. The existing measurement items were adjusted in language and phrasing to achieve consistency among the instrument. Furthermore, we conduct one round of card-sorting to test our measurement scales for clarity and a construct validity. We adopted the card-sorting procedure of Moore and Benbasat (1991) which attempts to identify any particular items which might be still ambiguous. Therefore, a small number of judges are asked to sort the items to given construct categories with the corresponding construct definitions (Davis 1989). The card-sorting procedure is conducted with a long-list of both, existing ones and new developed items. Next to the card-sorting approach, we also carry out an item prioritization which is why we can condense the long-list of items to the final measurement model.

4 Structural Model Development

After having introduced the theoretical foundations and previous works related to the investigation of value, we now derive our hypotheses to explain the value co-creation between a consultancy and its client. To examine the value co-creation in the consulting industry, we focus on the project-level, and investigate the consulting service value that emerges from the joint work of a consultancy and its client on a project level. The projects or sub-projects investigated should thus be completed, i.e. the assessment is an ex-post consideration.

As introduced in our theoretical foundation, we integrate both client and service provider capabilities to capture the co-creation process within the consulting industry. Especially, in collaboration-intensive industries like the consulting industry, it is important to consider both perspectives simultaneously. To derive our conceptual model, we were inspired by previous works of Chan et al. (2010), Breidbach et al. (2013b), and Barrutia and Gilsanz (2013). In our concept, we follow the view of Barrutia and Gilsanz (2013) of the value co-creation core model which consists of the client capabilities, service provider capabilities, and the value perception. In addition to Barrutia and Gilsanz (2013), we also integrate the collaboration quality. Our dependent variable *consulting service value* is defined as the client's evaluation of adequacy of price and value (Varki and Colgate 2001), which emerges in the S-D logic during the use of the provided service (Grönroos and Voima 2013; Vargo and Akaka 2009; Vargo and Lusch 2004).

Collaboration quality refers to the extent to which at least two entities of the service provider and the client work jointly and coordinated together (Pereira and Soares 2007). Thus, collaboration consists of personal interactions and relations between service provider and clients as well as interactional aspects like courtesy, respect, and friendliness (Kelley et al. 1990). Furthermore, collaboration depends on the mutual trustworthiness of the participants. The better these qualities, the stronger are the ties between a service provider and its client (Yi and Gong 2013), and thus, a higher value emerges. Hence, a strong relationship between client and service provider as well as a thoroughly executed relationship management are needed for a high collaboration quality (Goles 2003; Han et al. 2008). These multiple interactions are a prerequisite for successful value creation (Ennew and Binks 1999). Hence, we hypothesize:

H1: Collaboration quality has a positive impact on consulting service value.

4.1 Service Provider Capabilities

Within the service provider capabilities, the *consulting service quality* ultimately determines the consulting service value (Cronin et al. 2000; Gallarza et al. 2013). *Consulting service quality* "is best described as the result of an assessment process, in that course the client compares the expected service with the one delivered" (Kaiser and Ringlstetter 2011, p. 40). Consulting service quality is the evaluation if the expectations are met or not and differs from consulting service value. In turn, the consulting service quality depends on the operant resources of the service provider: industry expertise, methodological expertise, technological expertise, functional expertise, innovativeness, and social expertise. The assessment of the outcome, i.e. consulting service quality, is a judgment of an individual, and thus subjective impression of the regarded project (Kang 2006). Thus, we conclude:

H2: Consulting service quality has a positive impact on consulting service value.

Furthermore, the success of a consulting project depends on the consulting project team's industry knowledge. Consultants with a high industry expertise better understand the client's needs and have a thorough understanding of how business is conducted in the specific client industry (Goles 2003). We define *industry expertise* as the extent to which a consulting project team possesses expert knowledge in the domain of the client. We hypothesize:

H3: Industry expertise has a positive impact on consulting service quality.

Next to a high industry expertise, the consulting project team should provide a high *methodological expertise* to address the tasks in a structured and comprehensible way as well as usable research techniques applicable to the specific project. We define the service provider's methodological expertise as the extent to which a consulting project team possesses expert knowledge in required project skills such as systematic approach, statistical analysis, project and change management, development of surveys and measurements, or software engineering (Boh et al. 2002). The requirements of the methodological expertise can vary in each project, and it is the task of the consultancy to assess which methodological skill set is best for the project to achieve a high consulting service quality. Hence, we state:

H4: Methodological expertise has a positive impact on consulting service quality.

Furthermore, a service provider needs also *technological expertise*. Especially in the light of the ongoing digitalization, there are only few consulting projects which do not include technology issues which also stresses the importance of consultants possessing those skills. The contracting of a consultancy seems to be an easy way to get to know new technologies. Technological expertise is defined as the extent to which a consulting project team possesses expert knowledge in technology and related areas (Kirby and Dylan 1997) which facilitates the consulting service quality. We hypothesize:

H5: Technological expertise has a positive impact on consulting service quality.

Next to a technological expertise, also a functional expertise is needed to successfully complete consulting projects. Consulting projects do not only require one specific set of expert knowledge, but a heterogeneous set of expert knowledge is required. Hoffman (1998, p. 85) defines a functional expert as "one who has special skills or knowledge derived from extensive experience with subdomains" which is why we define *functional expertise* of the consultant project team as the extent to which it has expert knowledge in a specific domain. We conclude:

H6: Functional expertise of the service provider has a positive impact on consulting service quality.

Subsequent to functional expertise, *innovativeness* of the service provider contributes to the consulting service quality. We define innovativeness as the degree to which an innovative and hence novel service is able to positively influence and improve the client organization (Garcia and Calantone 2002). Furthermore, when dealing with innovativeness, it is important to notice that innovativeness depends always on whose perspective is taken, e.g. "[...] new to the world, new to the adopting unit, new to the industry, new to the market, or new to the customer" (Garcia and Calantone 2002, p. 112). Within the consultancy industry, clients rely on their service provider to figure out new ways of dealing with a specific task, process, or issue. Especially in light of the digitization of services, a certain level of innovativeness is necessary to keep track with their competitors. If the consulting project team is innovative the perception of the consulting service quality will increase. Hence, we hypothesize:

H7: Innovativeness of the service provider has a positive impact on consulting service quality.

Finally, *social expertise of the provider* is defined as the "degree to which consumers receive intelligent social support [...]" (Barrutia and Gilsanz 2013, p. 235). This conclusion remains also valid in a business-to-business context and hence, also for the consulting industry. Within the consulting project team, every team member also receives intelligent social support from his or her colleagues. This intelligent social support can be seen as knowledge transfer (Gruen et al. 2007). Consulting project teams can deploy this knowledge to complete the required service. However, the knowledge transfer will only take place if there is an interpersonal trustworthy relationship between the actors (Breidbach et al. 2013a) and if the person receiving such support has openness towards social support. Within the consulting project teams, there are various kinds of actors with different expertise and hence, the potential to receive social support from team members is high. The social expertise will facilitate the collaboration quality and furthermore enable a high level of consulting service quality. Thus, we conclude:

H8: *Social expertise of the provider has a positive impact on consulting service quality.*

H9: *Social expertise of the provider has a positive impact on collaboration quality.*

Summarizing, the service provider capabilities focus on the operant resources. We hypothesize that the determinants introduced above positively influence the client's perception of the overall consulting service quality.

4.2 Client Capabilities

In addition to the service provider capabilities, we now introduce the client company capabilities and its operant resources following the S-D logic through which the consulting service value emerges. Some determinants of the client capabilities are similar to the service provider capabilities, but are assessed from the client company's perspective. As part of the client capabilities, we include social expertise, technological expertise, and functional expertise. In addition to that, we further include the determinants willingness to change, experience with consultants, as well as the concept of absorptive capacity.

First, we suggest that absorptive capacity of the client company within a consulting project contributes to the explanation of the consulting service value. Absorptive capacity is a firm's ability to identify, assimilate, transform, and apply valuable external knowledge (Roberts et al. 2012) which is also applicable to consulting services. The consulting service is based on different kinds of expertise which needs to be absorbed by the client company. Thus, the consulting project team possesses external knowledge from the client perspective which has to be identified, assimilated, transformed, and applied to be valuable to the client firm. Therefore, we hypothesize:

H10: *Absorptive capacity has a positive impact on consulting service value.*

The *social expertise of the client*, while similar to the service provider capabilities, takes the client's perspective. According to Paredes et al. (2014, p. 128), social expertise is defined as the "knowledge available in consumer social context". In the same vein, employees of the client company receive intelligent social support from their internal workmates, i.e. colleagues from other departments or from the same department. In contrast to the service provider's social expertise, the employees of the client company receive social support from their regular team members with which they work for a longer period of time. Because of the interpersonal trust which is needed for the knowledge transfer, social expertise of the client company contributes to the collaboration quality. Furthermore, the social expertise of the client facilitates the client employees to absorb external knowledge through their interexchange. Hence, we hypothesize:

H11: *Social expertise of the client has a positive impact on collaboration quality.*

H12: *Social expertise of the client has a positive impact on absorptive capacity.*

Similar to the technological expertise of the service provider, also clients have to have *technological expertise*. Otherwise, the client does not have the abilities to absorb the new external knowledge. The client needs technological expertise to evaluate if the provided service is applicable to its firm and to judge if the transformation will be valuable. Therefore, we propose:

H13: *Technological expertise has a positive impact on absorptive capacity.*

Similar to the functional expertise of the provider, also the client needs *functional expertise*. Due to the mutual service provision, the client requires these skills to assess if the externally provided consulting service fits into the client company and if the transformation of the external knowledge is beneficial. Hence, we conclude:

H14: *Functional expertise has a positive impact on absorptive capacity.*

In addition, we also integrate the dimension experience with consultants and willingness to change. *Experience with consultants* is defined as the extent to which the client project members have developed empirical knowledge based on past interactions with consultants. This determinant is important for clients because of the learning process of how to interact, govern, judge, and transform the relationship with consultants. Hence, we hypothesize:

H15: *Experience with consultants has a positive impact on absorptive capacity.*

Finally, we integrate the *willingness to change* of the client which is defined as a positive behavioral intention of organizational change such as planned modification of an organization's structure or work and administrative processes (Metselaar 1997). Only if the client organization in total (or in parts) is willing to change and accept modifications, the external knowledge can be usefully implemented into the client's firm. Hence, we propose:

H16: *Willingness to change has a positive impact on absorptive capacity.*

Summarizing, the client capabilities focus on the client's operant resources. In our context, the client of a consulting service should also provide knowledge, skills, and social expertise as well as has to be open to change and modifications which are decisive for the value co-creation. In sum, we propose that the determinants positively influence the absorptive capacity of a client company. Figure 1 provides an overview of the derived hypotheses.

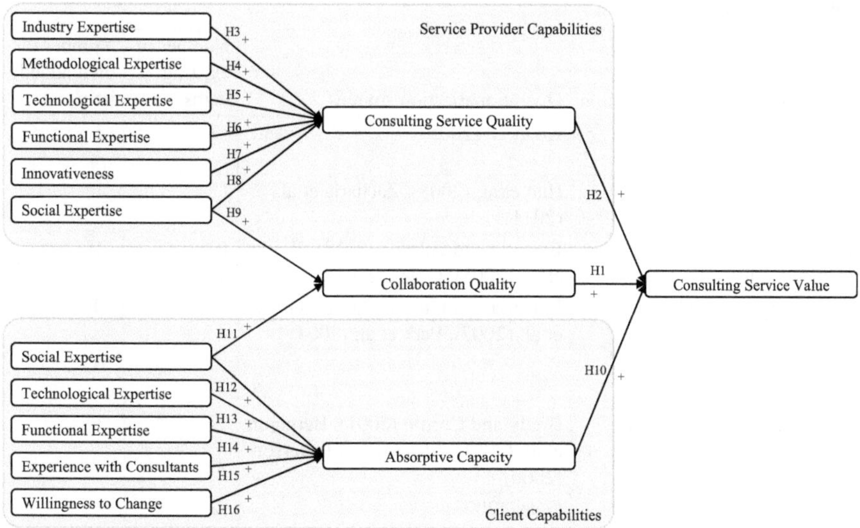

Fig. 1 Model explaining consulting service value

5 Measurement Instrument Development

5.1 Item Identification and Development

After having presented our structural model and introduced the derived hypotheses, we now enlarge on the development of the measurement instrument. For the simplification reasons, we show the item identification only once for the twofold constructs which are integrated in both, the client and the service provider capabilities (technological expertise, functional expertise, social expertise). As mentioned above, we rely on existing measurement scales where possible and develop new ones where necessary. The existing measurement scales were predominantly found in academic journals of different domains, such as outsourcing and service science literature as well as literature on behavioral science, IT and IS research, and innovation management. While the existing measurement scales serve as a good starting point, they had to be adapted to our specific context. We adjusted the existing scales in wording and language as well as in formality to have a precise measurement model. Table 1 presents the constructs for which we found existing measurement scales.

In the case that no suitable measurement scales were found, the existing measurement scales did not fit to our context, a specific aspect was not covered, or the constructs were operationalized with a single item, we developed additional items. Thus, in addition to the 77 initially found items in literature another 28 own items were added (Table 1). After a first qualitative analysis of the initially found items, we shortened our initial long-list and excluded eight items which do not fit to our context (six items of the construct *collaboration quality* and two items of the construct *consulting service quality*). Afterwards, we continued with our resulting item pool consisting of 97 items and started with the adjustment of the raw items in several rounds to fit to our context and to provide a common style.

Table 1 Initial item pool

Construct	Abbreviation	Operationalization sources	Number of existing items	Number of own added items
Absorptive capacity	AbCap	Ko et al. (2005)	7	1
Collaboration quality	CollQual	Han et al. (2008), Zacharia et al. (2011)	15	1
Consulting service quality	CoSeQual	Barrutia and Gilsanz (2013), Brady et al. (2005), Goles (2003)	10	1
Consulting service value	CoSeVal	Barrutia and Gilsanz (2013), Gruen et al. (2007), Park et al. (2004)	6	0
Experience with consultants	ExpeCon		0	6
Functional expertise	FuncExp	Brady and Cronin (2001), Bergeron et al. (2001), Sharma and Patterson (2000)	7	1
Industry expertise	IndExp	Goles (2003)	2	4
Innovativeness	Inno	Calantone et al. (2002), Wang (2008)	8	3
Methodological expertise	MethExp		0	8
Social expertise	SocExp	Barrutia and Gilsanz (2013), Gruen et al. (2007), Yi and Gong (2013)	11	1
Technological expertise	TechExp	Barrutia and Gilsanz (2013), Goles (2003)	7	1
Willingness to change	WillCha	Dayan et al. (2016), Kellermanns and Eddleston (2006)	4	1
		Items in total:	77	28

5.2 *Card-Sorting Procedure*

After having developed our initial item pool (Table 1), created new items where necessary, and adjusted them in an iteration process, we continued our instrument development with a card-sorting procedure. The aim of the card-sorting procedure is to assess the construct validity of the various scales and “to attempt to identify any particular items which still may have been ambiguous” (Moore and Benbasat 1991, p. 199). Therefore, we asked seven judges to sort the given items to constructs on basis of the construct definitions (Davis 1985, 1989). After having assigned the items to the corresponding constructs, the judges were asked to rank the items of every construct according to their representativeness. Hence, we can identify the most suitable items for each construct. We followed the card-sorting procedure proposed by Moore and Benbasat (1991) and performed the card-sorting procedure spreadsheet-based. After having received the judges’ results, we were able to evaluate the validity of our measurement model.

In Table 2, we present the results of the card-sorting procedure. The diagonal shows how many items were sorted in target, i.e. the items were correctly sorted to the corresponding construct. The last column shows the ratio of correct placed items to total, e.g. for the construct *collaboration quality* we notice a hit ratio of 95.71%. The construct collaboration quality consists of ten items, so the highest absolute matching would be 70, because of the seven judges (7 judges × 10 items). The hit ratio of 95.71% is the ratio of correct sorted items into the target construct (observations: 67) to the highest possible number.

With an overall hit ratio of 80.56% the measurement model seems to be satisfying. However, the spread of the continuum is quite wide. The lowest scores were achieved for the construct *willingness to change* with 62.86%, and the highest scores for the construct *collaboration quality* with 95.71%. However, through the integration of the elaborated long-list consisting of previously published and self-developed items, the number of items per construct is quite high. Hence, we have the possibility to only integrate those items into the final measurement instrument which were mainly sorted into the correct target construct. In a first step, we therefore analyzed the constructs with a hit ratio under 80% into detail on an item level and eliminated items which were mainly assessed into the wrong constructs. This will help us to identify the final measurement model and ensure a high validity. According to the card-sorting results presented in Table 2, the following constructs had to be considered: absorptive capacity, consulting service quality, consulting service value, functional expertise, and willingness to change. For the construct *absorptive capacity*, we identified four items which have only little target hits. Hence, we removed these items from the item pool. Furthermore, we analyzed the construct *consulting service quality*. For this construct, we identified that some of the items were ambiguous and were overlapping with consulting service value. Therefore, we removed five of the initial 9 items with the lowest target hits. Moreover, we removed two items intended to measure *consulting service value*. Both items had high overlaps with *consulting service quality*. For *functional expertise* three items had to be excluded because of their high cross loadings. Finally, the construct *willingness to change* is examined. For this construct, we examined that the judges considered three items often as innovativeness. Hence, we delete these items. In a second step, we analyzed the constructs which showed a hit ratio above 80% (collaboration quality, experience with consultants, industry expertise, innovativeness, social expertise, technological expertise, and methodological expertise) and selected those items of the long-list which were most often sorted in the target construct and ranked best according to their mean of the assessed ranks. After having identified the final items, we present an updated hit ratio in Table 3. Through the elimination of items, we gain a higher overall hit ratio, and none of the constructs have a hit ratio beneath 80%.

5.3 Final Measurement Instrument

On the basis of the presented card-sorting procedure, we identified a set of measurement items which is suitable to operationalize our structural model. The conducted procedure leads us to a measurement model consisting of 53 items (Table 4).

Table 2 Item placement ratio

Constructs		Actual													
		AbCap	CollQual	CoSeQual	CoSeVal	FuncExp	ExpeCon	IndExp	Inno	MethExp	SocExp	TechExp	WillCha	Ambig./ Unclear	Total	% Hits
Theoretical	AbCap	**36**	4	4	1	3	1	0	1	0	0	5	0	1	56	64.29%
	CollQual	0	**67**	0	0	0	0	0	0	1	0	0	1	1	70	95.71%
	CoSeQual	0	0	**43**	10	5	0	2	0	0	1	0	0	2	63	68.25%
	CoSeVal	0	0	7	**31**	0	0	1	0	1	0	0	0	2	42	73.81%
	FuncExp	0	1	9	1	**38**	1	3	0	1	0	0	0	2	56	67.86%
	ExpeCon	2	2	1	0	0	**37**	0	0	0	0	0	0	0	42	88.10%
	IndExp	0	0	1	0	2	0	**38**	0	0	0	1	0	0	42	90.48%
	Inno	0	0	0	0	4	0	0	**62**	4	1	1	5	0	77	80.52%
	MethExp	0	0	5	0	4	0	0	0	**46**	0	0	0	1	56	82.14%
	SocExp	0	3	0	1	0	0	1	0	0	**79**	0	0	0	84	94.05%
	TechExp	0	0	0	0	0	0	1	7	0	0	**48**	0	0	56	85.71%
	WillCha	0	0	1	0	0	1	0	11	0	0	0	**22**	0	35	62.86%
	Item placements:				679	Hits:	547			Overall hit ratio:			80.56%			

Table 3 Item ratio after selection

Constructs		Number items	Actual AbCap	CollQual	CoSeQual	CoSeVal	FuncExp	ExpeCon	IndExp	Inno	MethExp	SocExp	TechExp	WillCha	Ambig./ Unclear	Total	% Hits
Theoretical	AbCap	4	**25**				1						2		1	28	89.29%
	CollQual	6		**42**											1	42	100%
	CoSeQual	4			**27**	1									2	28	96.43%
	CoSeVal	4			2	**26**									2	28	92.86%
	FuncExp	5					**34**		1						2	35	97.14%
	ExpeCon	5		2				**33**							0	35	94.29%
	IndExp	3			1				**20**						0	21	95.24%
	Inno	5								**33**				2	0	35	94.29%
	MethExp	4			1						**27**				1	28	96.43%
	SocExp	5										**35**			0	35	100%
	TechExp	5							1				**34**		0	35	97.14%
	WillCha	3						1		2				**18**	0	21	85.71%
	Item placements:					371	Hits:	354	Overall hit ratio:					95.42%			

Table 4 Final measurement instrument

Absorptive capacity	
AbCap1	The client has the necessary skills to implement the delivered service
AbCap2	The client has the managerial competence to absorb the business knowledge about the delivered service
AbCap3	The client has the technical competence to absorb the technical knowledge about the delivered service
AbCap4	Overall, the client's absorptive capacity is high
Collaboration quality	
CollQual1	We and our client are interested in each other's problems
CollQual2	We and our client solve most problems together
CollQual3	We and our client are generally cooperative in conducting business
CollQual4	We and the client shared a lot of information
CollQual5	We and the client made joint decisions on most issues
CollQual6	Overall, the quality of collaboration between us and the client is high
Consulting service quality	
CoSeQual1	Our service quality is generally first class
CoSeQual2	Our performance within the project is absolutely reliable
CoSeQual3	Overall, our service quality is outstanding
CoSeQual4	Overall, the quality of the delivered service is high
Consulting service value	
CoSeVal2	The overall value you get from the provided service is worth your money and effort
CoSeVal3	Considering the price the client pays, we believe that the provided service is sufficient
CoSeVal4	The price the client pays is reasonable
CoSeVal6	Overall, the value of the provided service is high
Experience with consultants	
ExpeCon1	The client employees know how to work efficiently with consultants
ExpeCon2	The client employees often collaborate with consultants in their project domain
ExpeCon3	Working with consultants is not unusual to the client employees in their project domain
ExpeCon4	The client employees are experienced working with consultants
ExpeCon5	Overall, the client employees have much experience with consultants
Functional expertise	
FuncExp1	We understand the functional aspects of the actual problem addressed by the project
FuncExp2	We possess good functional knowledge in the project domain
FuncExp3	We are quite experienced in the functional project domain
FuncExp4	We apply our functional expertise well on the actual problem addressed by the project
FuncExp5	Overall, our functional expertise is high
Industry expertise	
IndExp1	We have a high reputation in the client's industry
IndExp2	We are well experienced in the client industry
IndExp3	Overall, our industry expertise is high

(continued)

Table 4 (continued)

Innovativeness	
Inno1	We frequently try out new ideas
Inno2	We seek out new ways doing things
Inno3	We actively seek innovative ideas
Inno4	We are willing to try new ways of doing things and seek unusual, novel solutions
Inno5	Overall, we can be considered as innovative
Methodological expertise	
MethExp1	We follow a clear project schedule
MethExp2	We follow a clear structure in our specific project methodology
MethExp3	We use methods which are appropriate for the specific project
MethExp4	Overall, our methodological expertise is high
Social expertise	
SocExp1	My colleagues and I usually speak about how to solve a specific problem
SocExp2	My colleagues and I share our knowledge with each other
SocExp3	If my colleagues and I have a useful idea on how to solve a problem, we let I let each other know
SocExp4	When my colleagues and I experience a problem, we let each other know
SocExp5	Overall, my colleagues and I have a strong social expertise
Technological expertise	
TechExp1	We give appropriate advice on relevant technologies to the client
TechExp2	We know more about relevant technologies than others
TechExp3	We have strong technological consulting capabilities
TechExp4	We have a high degree of technological competence
TechExp5	Overall, our technological expertise is high
Willingness to change	
WillCha1	The client employees are ready to take on any new challenges that they are faced with
WillCha2	The client employees find it easy to change
WillCha3	Overall, the client employees can be considered as willing to change

However, keeping in mind that we have to incorporate some of the constructs twice because of the divergent capabilities shown in Sect. 4, we will end by a total of 68 items. The resulting measurement model will help us to explain the phenomena under investigation and will be used in a matched pairs survey approach.

6 Discussion and Conclusion

With our work, we set out to develop a measurement model to explain the emergence of co-created value in consulting relationships from both the perspective of the consultancy and the client. To achieve this goal, first we deductively developed a structural model based on Oesterle et al. (2016) for which we then elaborated the presented measurement model. We were inspired by previous works and their measurement models which we adjusted to our context as well as developed new items where we did not find existing scales. In particular, the identified items were then tested in a card-sorting procedure which led us to our final measurement model. In our future research activities, our elaborated measurement model will be implemented into an online survey tool, pilot tested, and finally distributed. We attempt to follow a matched pair approach, whereby clients evaluate their service provider and vice versa on a project level. Hence, with our derived model and the corresponding measurement instrument we lay the foundation of a future empirical validation.

Before we conclude this paper by outlining our recommendations for future research and by highlighting our contributions to both theory and practice, we briefly discuss the limitations of our study. Since our study, so far, is only a conceptual piece concerning the structural model, we do not have any empirical evidence as to how far our hypotheses reflect the reality and as to how strong the proposed relationships between constructs are. Thus, while the model is deductively derived on theoretical accounts, the empirical validation remains for future research. Another aspect we want to highlight is that our study only focuses on perceived value, which can be considered as a key determinant of consulting service success. Success in that respect may also be influenced by additional factors such as price, political connections, and sales capabilities (Das et al. 1999; Oh 1999) which, however, is beyond the scope of our study. In addition to that, the conducted card-sorting procedure does not allow any further statistical analysis based on the small number of judges.

Regarding the specific next steps in this research endeavor, we deem quantitative-empirical methods as most suitable to validate our proposed model. Before we will collect survey data, we will conduct a pilot-test and analyze the first data sets and again adjust the measurement model if necessary. We will then accomplish the main study and analyze the gathered data using a structural equation modeling approach (Straub 1989; Urbach and Ahlemann 2010). For the measurement of the two spheres, we will follow a matched pairs approach (O'Farrell and Hitchins 1988; Peck 1985). Through measurement of the two spheres, we will obtain better insights and a comparison of the client's view and the provider's view is possible. To account for the particularities of the consulting domain, we aim to strengthen our statistical analysis by carrying out multi-group comparisons (Chin 2003; Henseler 2007) in a subsequent step. This will allow us to investigate not only the different value drivers' impact but also potential differences in the dynamics leading to value within consulting services considering the specific service characteristics. An additional opportunity would be the application of bottom-up segmentation procedures, such as FIMIX-PLS (Becker et al. 2013; Mohan and Urbach 2012), for further identification of heterogeneities in the dynamics leading to the emergence of value in consulting relationships.

Keeping the limitations of our work in mind, our results contribute to both theory and practice. Having finished the overall research project, our targeted contribution to research is the advancement of the theoretical discourse on the emergence of value by providing an empirically validated theory that explains consulting service value.

By proposing collaboration quality as an additional dimension in the value co-creation model next to the capabilities of service providers and client, we aim for a more differentiated view of value co-creation with which we go beyond previous approaches. Furthermore, we account for the value co-creation model in a business-to-business context that has mostly been neglected by similar studies. From a practical point of view, we expect our model after a thorough empirical evaluation to be a beneficial instrument to evaluate and predict client value with consulting services. By considering the specific service characteristics of the service provider and the client in our empirical analysis, we try to achieve a largely differentiated view of the phenomenon under investigation. Thus, our results might be useful for providing consulting firms with the necessary theoretical information and empirical findings to better understand the drivers of consulting service value, thus support their after sales process and the acquisition of follow-up projects, and finally improve or at least maintain their market position. Moreover, client companies will gain a deeper understanding which drivers of consulting service they can influence and which drivers are needed in different kinds of consulting services.

References

Alborz S, Seddon P, Scheepers R (2003) A model of studying IT outsourcing relationships. In: Proceedings of the 7th Pacific Asia conference on information systems (PACIS), Adelaide, Australia, Paper 90, 10–13 Jul

Arnould EJ, Price LL, Malshe A (2014) Toward a cultural resource-based theory of the customer. In: Lusch RF, Vargo SL (eds) The service-dominant logic of marketing: dialog, debate, and directions. Routledge, New York, pp 91–104

Ballantyne D, Varey RJ (2006) Creating value-in-use through marketing interaction: the exchange logic of relating, communicating and knowing. Mark Theory 6:335–348

Ballantyne D, Frow P, Varey RJ, Payne A (2011) Value propositions as communication practice: taking a wider view. Ind Mark Manag 40:202–210

Barrutia JM, Gilsanz A (2013) Electronic service quality and value do consumer knowledge-related resources matter. J Serv Res 16:231–246

Becker J-M, Rai A, Ringle CM, Völckner F (2013) Discovering unobserved heterogeneity in structural equation models to avert validity threats. MIS Q 37:665–694

Bergeron J, Ricard L, Perrien J (2001) Relationship marketing: the role of client knowledge, service quality and expertise. In: Proceedings of the 9th international colloquium on relationship marketing, Montréal, Canada, 24–26 Sept 2001

Boh W, Ren Y, Kiesler S (2002) Managing expertise in a distributed environment. In: Proceedings of the 23rd international conference on information systems 2002 (ICIS), Barcelona, Spain, 15–18 Dec 2002

Brady MK, Cronin JJ (2001) Some new thoughts on conceptualizing perceived service quality: a hierarchical approach. J Mark 65:34–49

Brady MK, Knight GA, Cronin JJ, Tomas G, Hult M, Keillor BD (2005) Removing the contextual Lens: a multinational, multi-setting comparison of service evaluation models. J Retail 81: 215–230

Breidbach CF, Maglio PP (2015) A service science perspective on the role of ICT in service innovation. In: Proceedings of the 23rd European conference on information systems (ECIS), Münster, Germany, 26–29 May 2015

Breidbach CF, Kolb DG, Srinivasan A (2013a) Connectivity in service systems: does technology-enablement impact the ability of a service system to co-create value? J Serv Res 16:428–441

Breidbach CF, Smith P, Callagher LJ (2013b) Advancing innovation in professional service firms: insights from the service-dominant logic. Serv Sci 5:263–275

Bruns K, Jacob F (2014) Value-in-use and mobile technologies. Bus Inf Syst Eng 6:349–359

Calantone RJ, Cavusgil ST, Zhao Y (2002) Learning orientation, firm innovation capability, and firm performance. Ind Mark Manag 31:515–524

Chan KW, Yim CK, Lam SS (2010) Is customer participation in value creation a double-edged sword? Evidence from professional financial services across cultures. J Mark 74:48–64

Chandler JD, Vargo SL (2011) Contextualization and value-in-context: how context frames exchange. Mark Theory 11:35–49

Chin WW (2003) A permutation procedure for multigroup comparison of PLS models. In: Proceedings of the PLS'03 international symposium, Lisbon, Portugal, 15–17 Sept 2003

Christensen CM, Wang D, Dv B (2013) Consulting on the cusp of disruption. Harv Bus Rev 2013:106–115

Cohen WM, Levinthal DA (1990) Absorptive capacity: a new perspective on learning and innovation. Adm Sci Q 35:128–152

Cronin JJ, Brady MK, Hult GTM (2000) Assessing the effects of quality, value, and customer satisfaction on consumer behavioral intentions in service environments. J Retail 76:193–218

Das A, Soh CWL, Lee PCB (1999) A model of customer satisfaction with information technology service providers: an empirical study. In: Proceedings of the ACM SIGCPR conference on computer personnel research, New Orleans, Louisiana, USA, 8–10 Apr 1999

Davis FD (1985) A technology acceptance model for empirically testing new end-user information systems: theory and results. Massachusetts Institute of Technology

Davis FD (1989) Perceived usefulness, perceived ease of use, and user acceptance of information technology. MIS Q 13:319–340

Dayan M, Zacca R, Husain Z, Benedetto AD, Ryan JC (2016) The effect of entrepreneurial orientation, willingness to change, and development culture on new product exploration in small enterprises. J Bus Ind Market 31:668–683

Ennew CT, Binks MR (1999) Impact of participative service relationships on quality, satisfaction and retention: an exploratory study. J Bus Res 46:121–132

Frow P, Payne A (2011) A stakeholder perspective of the value proposition concept. Eur J Mark 45:223–240

Gallarza MG, Gil Saura I, Arteaga Moreno F (2013) The quality-value-satisfaction-loyalty chain: relationships and impacts. Tour Rev 68:3–20

Garcia R, Calantone R (2002) A critical look at technological innovation typology and innovativeness terminology: a literature review. J Prod Innov Manag 19:110–132

Goles T (2003) Vendor capabilities and outsourcing success: a resource-based view. Wirtschaftsinformatik 45:199–206

Grönroos C (2006) Adopting a service logic for marketing. Mark Theory 6:317–333

Grönroos C, Ravald A (2011) Service as business logic: implications for value creation and marketing. J Serv Manag 22:5–22

Grönroos C, Voima P (2013) Critical service logic: making sense of value creation and co-creation. J Acad Mark Sci 41:133–150

Gruen TW, Osmonbekov T, Czaplewski AJ (2007) Customer-to-customer exchange: its MOA antecedents and its impact on value creation and loyalty. J Acad Mark Sci 35:537–549

Gummesson E (2007) Exit services marketing-enter service marketing. J Cust Behav 6:113–141

Han H-S, Lee J-N, Seo Y-W (2008) Analyzing the impact of a firm's capability on outsourcing success: a process perspective. Inform Manag 45:31–42

Heinonen K, Strandvik T, Mickelsson K-J, Edvardsson B, Sundström E, Andersson P (2010) A customer-dominant logic of service. J Serv Manag 21:531–548

Henseler J (2007) A new and simple approach to multi-group analysis in partial least squares path modeling. In: Proceedings of the PLS'07—The 5th international symposium on PLS and related methods, Matforsk, Aas, Norway, 5–7 September 2007

Hoffman RR (1998) How can expertise be defined? Implications of research from cognitive psychology. In: Williams R et al (eds) Exploring expertise. University of Edinburgh Press, Edinburgh, pp 81–100

Kaiser S, Ringlstetter MJ (2011) Strategic management of professional service firms. Springer, Berlin

Kang G-D (2006) The hierarchical structure of service quality: integration of technical and functional quality. Manag Serv Qual Int J 16:37–50

Kellermanns FW, Eddleston KA (2006) Corporate entrepreneurship in family firms: a family perspective. Entrep Theory Pract 30:809–830

Kelley SW, Donnelly JH Jr, Skinner SJ (1990) Customer participation in service production and delivery. J Retail 66:315

Kirby DA, Dylan J-E (1997) Small technology-based professional consultancy Services in the United Kingdom. Serv Ind J 17:155–172

Ko D-G, Kirsch LJ, King WR (2005) Antecedents of knowledge transfer from consultants to clients in enterprise system implementations. MIS Q 29:59–85

Kowalkowski C (2011) Dynamics of value propositions: insights from service-dominant logic. Eur J Mark 45:277–294

Lusch RF, Nambisan S (2015) Service innovation: a service-dominant logic perspective. MIS Q 39:155–175

Lusch RF, Vargo SL, O'Brien M (2007) Competing through service: insights from service-dominant logic. J Retail 83:5–18

Madhavaram S, Hunt SD (2008) The service-dominant logic and a hierarchy of operant resources: developing masterful operant resources and implications for marketing strategy. J Acad Mark Sci 36:67–82

McCarthy JC, Matzke P (2010) The coming upheaval. InTech Services, Forrester Research

Metselaar EE (1997) Assessing the willingness to change: construction and validation of the DINAMO. Doctoral disseration

Mohan K, Urbach N (2012) Do we fully understand the critical success factors of employee portal utilitarianism?—Uncovering and accounting for unobserved heterogeneity. In: Proceedings of the 20th European conference on information systems (ECIS), Barcelona, Spain, 10–13 Jun 2012

Moore GC, Benbasat I (1991) Development of an instrument to measure the perceptions of adopting an information technology innovation. Inf Syst Res 2:192–222

Oesterle S, Buchwald A, Urbach N (2016) Understanding the co-creation of value emerging from the collaboration between IT consulting firms and their customers. In: Proceedings of the 37th international conference on information systems (ICIS), Dublin, Ireland, 11–14 Dec 2016

O'Farrell PN, Hitchins DM (1988) Inter-firm comparison in industrial research: the utility of a matched pairs design. Tijdschr Econ Soc Geogr 79:63–69

Oh H (1999) Service quality, customer satisfaction, and customer value: a holistic perspective. Int J Hosp Manag 18:67–82

Paredes MR, Barrutia JM, Echebarria C (2014) Resources for value co-creation in E-commerce: a review. Electron Commer Res 14:111–136

Park J-W, Robertson R, Wu C-L (2004) The effect of airline service quality on passengers' behavioural intentions: a Korean case study. J Air Transp Manag 10:435–439

Peck F (1985) The use of matched-pairs research design in industrial surveys. Environ Plan A 17:981–989

Pereira CS, Soares AL (2007) Improving the quality of collaboration requirements for information management through social networks analysis. Int J Inf Manag 27:86–103

Richter A, Schmidt SL (2006) Antecedents of the performance of management consultans. Schmalenbachs Bus Rev 58:365–391
Roberts N, Galluch PS, Dinger M, Grover V (2012) Absorptive capacity and information systems research: review, synthesis, and directions for future research. MIS Q 36:625–648
Sandström S, Edvardsson B, Kristensson P, Magnusson P (2008) Value in use through service experience. Manag Serv Qual Int J 18:112–126
Sharma N, Patterson PG (2000) Switching costs, alternative attractiveness and experience as moderators of relationship commitment in professional, consumer services. Int J Serv Ind Manag 11:470–490
Skålén P, Gummerus J, von Koskull C, Magnusson PR (2014) Exploring value propositions and service innovation: a service-dominant logic study. J Acad Mark Sci 43:137–158
Straub DW (1989) Validating instruments in MIS research. MIS Q 13:147–169
Urbach N, Ahlemann F (2010) Structural equation Modeling in information systems research using partial least squares. J Inform Technol Theory Appl (JITTA) 11:5–40
Vargo SL, Akaka MA (2009) Service-dominant logic as a Foundation for Service Science: clarifications. Serv Sci 1:32–41
Vargo SL, Lusch RF (2004) Evolving to a new dominant logic for marketing. J Mark 68:1–17
Vargo SL, Lusch RF (2008) Service-dominant logic: continuing the evolution. J Acad Mark Sci 36:1–10
Vargo SL, Lusch RF (2016) Institutions and axioms: an extension and update of service-dominant logic. J Acad Mark Sci:1–19
Vargo SL, Maglio PP, Akaka MA (2008) On value and value co-creation: a service systems and service logic perspective. Eur Manag J 26:145–152
Varki S, Colgate M (2001) The role of price perceptions in an integrated model of behavioral intentions. J Serv Res 3:232–240
Veit D et al (2014) Business models. Bus Inf Syst Eng 6:45–53
Wang CL (2008) Entrepreneurial orientation, learning orientation, and firm performance. Entrep Theory Pract 32:635–657
Yi Y, Gong T (2013) Customer value co-creation behavior: scale development and validation. J Bus Res 66:1279–1284
Yoon S, Suh H (2004) Ensuring IT consulting SERVQUAL and user satisfaction: a modified measurement tool. Inf Syst Front 6:341–351
Zacharia ZG, Nix NW, Lusch RF (2011) Capabilities that enhance outcomes of an episodic supply chain collaboration. J Oper Manag 29:591–603

Severin Oesterle is a Research Assistant at the Project Group Business & Information Systems Engineering of the Fraunhofer Institute for Applied Information Technology (FIT) and the Finance & Information Management (FIM) Research Center. Furthermore, he is a doctoral student at the University of Bayreuth, where he also completed his Master's degree in business administration. In his research, he focusses on topics of service science, eHealth and digitalization. His work has been published in the proceedings of key international conferences.

Arne Buchwald is Assistant Professor for Digital Transformation and the scientific head of the Center for Digital Transformation at the Strascheg Institute for Innovation, Transformation and Entrepreneurship (SITE) at EBS Business School, Germany. Previously, he was a consultant with Horváth & Partners Management Consultants. He received his doctorate in the year 2016 from the University of Bayreuth, Germany. He studied business administration at EBS Business School and proceeded with his master studies at the School of Business and Economics at Maastricht University, The Netherlands. Furthermore, he gained additional international experience as a visiting scholar at the Stockholm School of Economics (Sweden). His recent research focuses on the digital transformation, bootlegging behavior, and blockchain technology. His work has been published in internationally-renowned journals such as the Journal of Information Technology (JIT) as well as in the proceedings of key international conferences.

Nils Urbach is Professor of Information Systems and Strategic IT Management at University of Bayreuth, Germany, as well as Deputy Director of the Project Group Business and Information Systems Engineering of Fraunhofer FIT and the Finance & Information Management (FIM) Research Center. He has been working in the fields of strategic information management and collaborative information systems for several years. In his current research, he focuses on digital transformation, smart devices, and blockchain, among others. His work has been published in leading academic journals such as the Journal of Strategic Information Systems (JSIS), Journal of Information Technology (JIT), IEEE Transactions on Engineering Management (IEEE TEM), Information and Management (I&M), and Business & Information Systems Engineering (BISE) as well as in the proceedings of key international conferences.

Measuring and Managing the Reputation of Business Consultancies

Volker Nissen and Johannes Dittler

Abstract The consulting business relies on trust between consultants and clients. In a situation where the client has not worked with a particular consultancy before, the positive reputation of this company can act as a substitute for previous personal experience. Vice versa, a negative reputation will be a substantial hindrance for a consulting firm in achieving sustained market success. Thus, creating and maintaining a good reputation is of significant importance for consulting providers. However, reputation is a somewhat cloudy concept that calls for a measurement instrument to determine precisely the status-quo for a given company. Moreover, as only things that can be measured can also be actively managed, measuring reputation is key to close the management circle on this important issue. The current paper presents an approach to measure and actively manage reputation in the domain of business consulting. The basic concept may be transferred to other knowledge-intensive service industries as well.

1 Introduction, Motivation and Research Approach

The consulting market is characterized by a high level of in transparency, which traditionally causes a high amount of transactions costs to gain a market overview and to identify the best consulting offer for certain demand (Neuberger 2002). Main determinants for consulting success are experienced-based trust and reputation (Glückler and Armbrüster 2003). In the field of business consulting, it must be taken into account that the results of the services are difficult to measure and grasp, both during and after the completion of a project. This means that potential customers can only obtain limited information about the quality of the services provided

V. Nissen (✉)
Economic Sciences and Media, Ilmenau University of Technology, Ilmenau, Germany
e-mail: volker.nissen@tu-ilmenau.de

J. Dittler
INVERTO GmbH, Munich, Germany

V. Nissen (ed.), *Advances in Consulting Research*, Contributions to Management Science, https://doi.org/10.1007/978-3-319-95999-3_5

by a business consultancy. As a result, new clients in particular rely primarily on reputation and the associated trustworthiness when selecting consultants for a project within their own company (Jeschke 2015).

Consulting should be viewed as a complex social activity where the success strongly depends on the relationship and interactions between consultants and clients within the consulting project (Coers and Heinecke 2002; Mauerer and Nissen 2014). In a situation, where the client has not worked with a particular consultancy or individual consultant, a positive reputation can act as a substitute for personal experience and create initial trust. It is enormously helpful in consulting sales when your own company is viewed as a trusted advisor (Maister et al. 2001) by (potential) clients. Conversely, it will be a key barrier to sustained success, if your company has a notoriously bad market reputation. Overall, reputation is a key aspect for the long-term success of companies in the consulting industry and successful reputation management is therefore of enormous importance.

Often reputation is viewed as one of the most important levers for shaping the future of companies profitably (Helm et al. 2011), since strategic advantages can be gained from reputation management in relation to the competition (Schwaiger and Raithel 2014; Gray and Balmer 1998). However, in order to establish a functioning reputation management in one's own company and to link the reputation with the generated competitive advantages, it is necessary to develop suitable measuring instruments for the reputation (Davies and Miles 1998).

Consequently, this paper addresses the research question, how an instrument to measure reputation in the consulting industry should look like. This instrument is to be developed on the basis of existing generic measuring instruments and will subsequently be evaluated. A measurement instrument is an artefact in the sense of Hevner et al. (2004). Thus, design science is the research paradigm that fits this objective. In the concrete course of the research process we follow the common Design Science Research Process Model (Fig. 1) according to Peffers et al. (2007). The measurement instrument is intended to offer consultancies an opportunity to

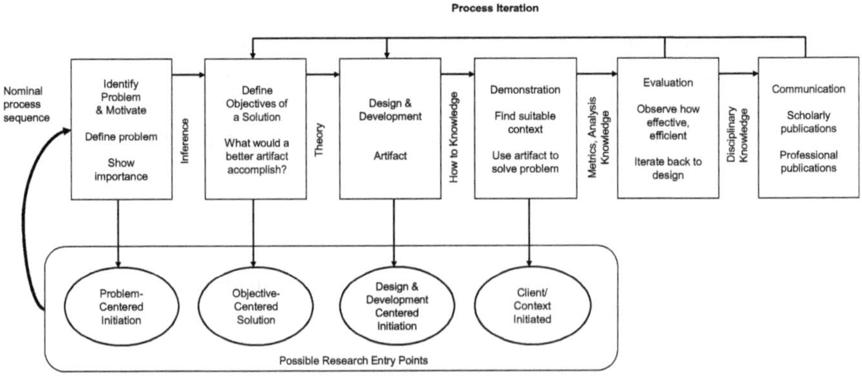

Fig. 1 Design science research process model (Peffers et al. 2007)

measure their reputation and use the measurement to identify the causal relationships and levers for successful reputation management.

2 Reputation Defined

Although there is broad consensus on the strategic importance of reputation, there is no consensus on how to correctly define reputation (Wiedmann 2012). Fombrun et al. (2000) have tried to generate a uniform understanding of the term from these, taking into account the commonalities, and proposed the following definition: "Corporate Reputation is a collective construct that describes the aggregate perceptions of multiple stakeholders about a company's performance". They therefore describe reputation as a collective assessment of a company's ability to provide a good performance to relevant stakeholders. Given that performance is a multidimensional construct, reputation is also expected to be composed of several dimensions on the basis of which stakeholders judge a company's performance (Fombrun et al. 2000). Reputation is the result of the exchange of personal or transmitted experiences between the organization, stakeholders and third parties. Stakeholders are all groups that can influence the success of an organization through their behavior. This can occur immediately or over a longer period, indirectly or directly (Helm et al. 2011). The relevant stakeholders in turn differ depending on the company, industry and other factors. The views of individual stakeholder groups can vary, which means that an organization's reputation is made up of several partial reputations. For example, investors and analysts react much more critically to the failure to meet financial targets than customers, who might hope that the company will be more price-elastic in the short term (Wüst and Kreutzer 2012).

It is striking that reputation is often mistakenly equated with the term image and serves as a synonym for it (Bauhofer 2015; Balmer et al. 1997; Rindova 1997). Image is merely a picture that relevant stakeholders get of an organisation, its services and products. Reputation, on the other hand, has an evaluative character and provides information on the extent to which an organization's performance meets stakeholders' expectations (Wüst and Kreutzer 2012). Reputation can therefore only be built by repeatedly meeting these expectations, whereas image can be 'bought' in the short term through image campaigns (Bauhofer 2015). It can therefore be concluded that the time component plays an important role in differentiating between image and reputation. Developing a reputation takes a lot of time, whereas images can be continuously changed and easily influenced. Image refers to the most current opinion about a company. Reputation, on the other hand, represents a value judgement about the organization that has been built up over a certain period of time.

Despite the differences in the development of image and reputation in terms of duration, in the event of a crisis, considerable damage can be inflicted on both within a very short time (Chun 2005). Ultimately, image can be differentiated from reputation, but the two terms are still connected. Building a sustainable reputation

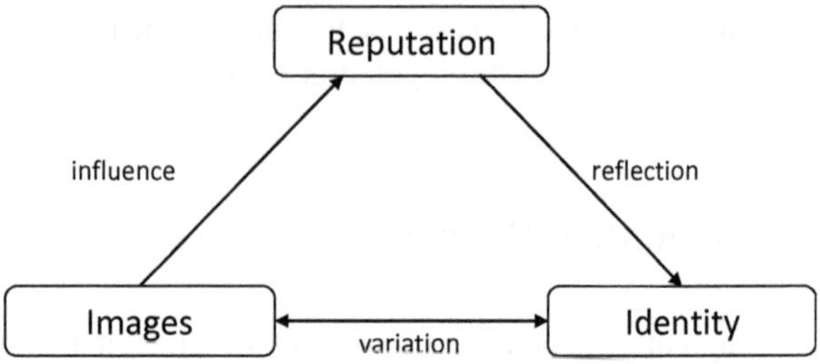

Fig. 2 Relationships between reputation, identity and image [adapted from Whetten (1997)]

requires not only the development of positive images through appropriate communication measures, but also a deserving identity of the organisation, which can be shaped by constant performance, mostly over years (Gray and Balmer 1998). Thus, image and identity can be seen as the main components of reputation (Chun 2005). Identity describes the uniqueness and reality of a company. The basic components are corporate strategy, philosophy, culture and organizational design (Gray and Balmer 1998). It stands for the characteristics of the company and thus represents the company personality (Wüst and Kreutzer 2012; Kirstein 2009). It is not uncommon for a company to have a gap between its identity and image, i.e. there is no correspondence between the perceptions of stakeholders and the values that the company wants to convey from within. To build a stable reputation, however, it is inevitable to close this gap between the two main components of the reputation (Chun 2005).

In summary, it can be concluded that a company's reputation is at best the external reflection of its identity and that short-term images of external stakeholders have a long-term impact on its reputation. Figure 2 should finally show the interplay of the three terms.

3 Reputation Management in Consulting

3.1 General Considerations

Reputation improvements are achieved primarily through active, systematic management of reputation drivers (Bauhofer 2015). Reputation drivers are factors that can have a positive or negative impact on a company's reputation, depending on its performance in the individual categories.

Usually, different reputational drivers are more or less important depending on the stakeholder group. Customers, for example, will largely determine their perception of the company in terms of both the performance and quality of its products and its responsibility for the environment and society, whereas financial success is of paramount importance for financial institutions. Employees, on the other hand, consider the employer positioning and working conditions to be the most important components of their perception of the company (Gray and Balmer 1998). It is necessary to look at both internal and external stakeholder groups and to reconcile their perception of the company.

In order to meet the challenges of reputation management, most changes are being made in the organizational structure, in information communication and in behaviour towards stakeholders (Pruzan 2001). The specific tasks of reputation management must also be clearly assigned to individual persons or a board in order to clearly define responsibilities (Bauhofer 2015). This creates new manager positions that are responsible for reputation management.

The tasks of reputation management should be supported by adequate processes and tools (Pruzan 2001). Without the support of reputation management tools and systems, it is difficult both to prove the correlation between increasing reputation and competitive advantages and to create a clear reputation profile. For the allocation of budget and staff to reputation management, it is necessary to prove these connections and to be able to present a consistent reputation tracking (Davies and Miles 1998). A budget for reputation management is of great importance, as reputation is a form of capital in which investment is also required (Helm et al. 2011). The instrument for measuring reputation resulting from this work is intended to start right here and support reputation management as a tool by making connections clear, revealing a reputation profile and allowing a continuous monitoring of reputation development.

3.2 *Drivers of Reputation in Consulting*

The drivers of reputation can be considered at least partly industry-specific. For consulting providers, the following drivers appear to be particularly relevant.

Service Quality Consulting firms must earn the confidence of their clients with regard to their performance and willingness to perform. Most leading consulting firms attribute their success and reputation to customer confidence in the quality of their services (Jeschke 2007). In addition, the service portfolio and also the innovative strength are decisive for clients when it comes to the selection of consulting services (Lippold 2016). Consequently, a positive reputation can arise if consulting firms offer high-quality and innovative services and the service appears trustworthy to customers (Hagenmeyer 2015).

Client Orientation Satisfied clients can become multipliers, which means that they will share their experiences and recommendations with other market participants without being asked (Niedereichholz 2010; Barchewitz and Armbrüster 2007). The importance of customer satisfaction is also evident from relationship marketing conducted by consulting companies. One of the aims of marketing is to build up consulting satisfaction in client relationships in order to develop strategic competitive advantages (Jeschke 2007). If a consulting firm focuses on the customer's needs and places the customer at the centre of the project, the reputation can be enhanced by the resulting customer satisfaction. Another important factor in customer orientation is the reliability and trustworthiness of the individual consultants (Amann and

Schneider 2015). Trust in the consultant's willingness to perform (Fink and Knoblach 2015) and in the discrete handling of internal company information play a central role for the client.

Employer Brand The quality of the output of a consulting service is often difficult to measure. Consequently, clients increasingly rely on the input side. Consultancies therefore try to provide good consultants and create an acknowledged employer brand in order to use the input quality as a signal for the resulting output quality (Nissen 2007). There is a connection between satisfied clients, satisfied consultants, and employer brand. If consulting employees are satisfied with their work and the work environment, they will tend to perform better and ultimately generate customer satisfaction and loyalty, which in turn leads to an increase in reputation (Chun 2005). If a business consultancy is able to generate a well-known, renowned employer brand through employee quality, satisfaction and development, it increases the attractiveness, competitiveness and reputation with all stakeholders (Lippold 2016).

Competitiveness The reputation driver competitiveness is fundamentally composed of the components of financial performance, competitive position, reactions to new market opportunities and the company's future prospects. Especially in times of many economic crises, the perception of stability and predictability with regard to the upcoming actions of companies has a positive effect on the company's reputation (Wüst and Kreutzer 2012). Financial success and competitive position are particularly important criteria for the stakeholder group of financial institutions (Gray and Balmer 1998). However, since the most important stakeholder group for business consultancies are the clients, competitiveness is a criterion for reputation enhancement, but has a lower importance as other criteria, such as client orientation.

Social and Environmental Responsibility The factor of responsibility for social and environmental issues behaves similarly to the factor of competitiveness in the creation of a positive reputation within consulting companies. Although this factor is becoming increasingly important (Pruzan 2001), other industries are much more affected by this factor. For instance, the reputation of the chemical industry is far more dependent on this factor than consulting. Nevertheless, a pronounced commitment to environmental or social issues leads to an increase in the reputation of companies in all sectors (Brammer and Pavelin 2006).

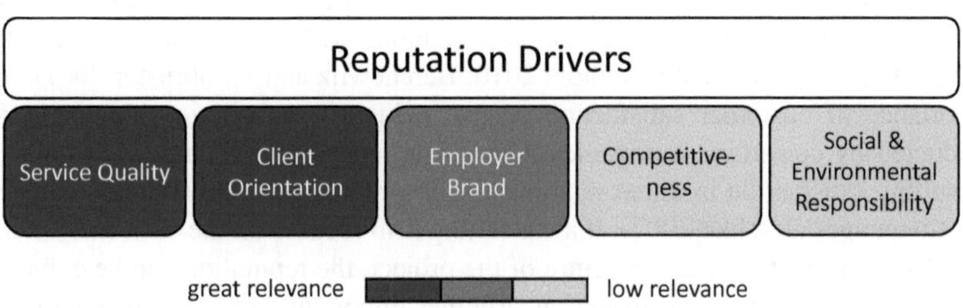

Fig. 3 Reputation drives of consulting companies and estimated relevance

Figure 3 provides a concluding overview of the relevant reputation drivers and their estimated importance for business consultancies.

4 Measuring Reputation: Current Approaches

4.1 Requirements on Reputation Measurement

Unlike a company's sales or profits, reputation is not directly observable and obvious. Due to the importance of reputation, practitioners and scientists alike have in the past dealt with developing a large number of measurement concepts (Schwaiger and Raithel 2014). When developing measuring instruments, it is important to note that reputation cannot be measured one-dimensionally. If stakeholders in the course of a reputation survey can only rate as 'good' or 'bad', it is not possible to explain the reasons for the respective reputation.

For reputation management within the company, this type of measurement does not reveal which levers need to be put in place in order to increase the company's reputation. This example shows that it is necessary to measure reputation multidimensionally, taking into account the different reputation drivers (Chun 2005). In order to enable an assessment of the reputation based on the recognition of strengths and weaknesses of the company, it is necessary to be able to fall back on comparative standards or benchmarks. These can be developed by using a standardised measurement instrument within an industry (Wiedmann et al. 2006).

Reputation can be measured in two different ways. On the other hand, the measurement is based on formative indicators (reputation drivers), which usually result in a strong reputation if they are positive. The positive or negative characteristics of the various formative indicators (e.g. product and service quality, social and environmental responsibility) are measured and the reputation is then calculated. On the other hand, it is also possible to perform the measurement using reflective indicators (reputation reflectors). This involves measuring factors that should be highly pronounced in the event of a positive reputation, e.g. the appreciation of the company or the emotional attachment to the company (Wiedmann 2012).

In general, the following aspects appear essential in the development of a reputation measurement tool:

- Measurement only through systematic studies (e.g. surveys)
- Clear definition of reputation
- Consideration of reputation as a multidimensional construct
- Identification of the relevant reputation drivers
- Identification of relevant stakeholder groups
- Standardization of the measurement concept for the generation of benchmarks
- Decision to measure using formative or reflexive indicators
- Alignment of the instrument to continuous tracking (not problem-based)

4.2 Overview of Selected Reputation Measurement Approaches

Based on literature reviews, the following influential reputation measurement instruments were analyzed as a potential starting point to develop an own approach for the consulting industry:

4.2.1 Fortune's AMAC & GMAC

Until 1997, the reputation ranking of the Fortune magazine 'America's Most Admired Companies' (AMAC) was the only existing one on a global level, but limited to American companies. Since 1997, Fortune magazine has published the Global Most Admired Companies (GMAC) Reputation Ranking, which includes surveys of the reputation of the Global 500 in 24 industries and 13 countries (Schwaiger and Cannon 2004). High-ranking executives from the respective industry are interviewed together with financial analysts about companies in their industry and assess reputation according to eight criteria (including management quality, innovative strength and financial creditworthiness).

4.2.2 Manager Magazine Ranking

Since 1987, Manager Magazine has surveyed company reputation in Germany. CEOs, managing directors and managers are asked by telephone about the reputation of the 100 German companies with the highest turnover. The participants assess the reputation of the companies on a scale of 0–10 taking into account prescribed criteria (e.g. management quality, environmental orientation, price-performance ratio). It is very similar to the reputation ranking of Fortune magazine and forms its German counterpart.

4.2.3 Financial Times WMRC

The Financial Times began to compile a ranking list of the 'Europe's Most Respected Companies' through surveys in 1994. In 1999, they expanded these to World's Most Respected Companies' (WMRC). The ranking is compiled by CEOs from around 50 different countries according to eight criteria (including maximizing customer satisfaction and loyalty, business strategy, product and service quality). The respondents' answers are weighted according to the gross domestic product of the CEOs' home countries (Fombrun et al. 2000).

4.2.4 Corporate Character Scale

This measuring instrument is based on the metaphor of the personification of companies. The items used in the survey usually describe people. The categories to be assessed therefore differ greatly from those of other measuring instruments and include, among others, the competence or recklessness of a company (Davies et al. 2001).

4.2.5 Reputation Quotient (RQ)

Fombrun et al. (2000) developed a measuring instrument called Reputation Quotient (RQ), taking into account the disadvantages of existing magazine rankings. The measurement concept consists of 20 items, separated into six categories. The surveys are conducted in two stages. First, online or telephone surveys are used to identify companies with a particularly good or bad reputation. These companies are then evaluated in a second phase based on six categories (including products and services, vision and leadership, workplace environment). Respondents are randomly selected from a survey database.

4.2.6 RepTrak

The core of this model, developed by the Reputation Institute New York, is the differentiation of measurement into reflexive and formative indicators, which divide the instrument into two steps.

Initially, the reputation is measured by reflexive indicators in the form of the overall RepTrak Pulse value. Trust, admiration, feeling and esteem serve as reputation reflectors. In the second step, characteristics for the relevant reputation drivers are recorded and thus the causal relationships of the reputation are disclosed. The reputation drivers are divided into seven categories (Performance, Products & Services, Workplace, Innovation, Governance, Citizenship and Leadership). Another distinguishing feature compared to other measuring instruments is the consideration of several stakeholders. Data collection is therefore always carried out in company-specific studies among the relevant stakeholders of the respective company (Wiedmann 2012). Overall, this measurement instrument requires substantial effort for application.

4.2.7 Reputation Portfolio by Schwaiger and Cannon

Schwaiger and Cannon (2004) present their reputation portfolio with the aim of measuring and simultaneously explaining reputation. The main distinguishing feature of this instrument is that emotional aspects should be taken into account according to their actual importance. The survey consists of a total of four factors—the quality, performance, responsibility and attractiveness of a company. Within this concept, reputation is divided into cognitive and affective components. The basis of the approach is a structural equation model (Schwaiger and Cannon 2004).

4.2.8 Customer-Based Reputation Scale (CBR)

Walsh and Beatty (2007) developed a scale to measure the customer-specific reputation of companies with a focus on the service sector. The survey is based on five dimensions, which were developed on the basis of Fombrun's RQ approach. These dimensions are customer orientation, good employer, reliable and financially strong company, product and service quality, and finally social and environmental responsibility.

In an assessment, the details of which must be omitted for reasons of space here, these established measurement concepts were evaluated according to specified quality criteria. The result is given in Table 1. The assessment is based, on the one hand, on the generic criteria to compare different tools and systems as identified by Pietsch (2003). These include the following aspects:

- Theoretical base: Describes the theoretical model on which the evaluation procedure is based. The origin or purpose of an evaluation procedure can be derived from the theoretical basis.
- Measurement object: Describes what is measured within the evaluation procedure. In the case of reputation measurement instruments, these can be, for example, the competitive situation, product and service quality, but also the reputation as a whole.
- Source of information: Indicates where the information required for evaluation is obtained.
- Flexibility of approach: Describes the ability of a process to provide correct information under changing conditions. Within this contribution, the relevant framework conditions represent an application in the consulting industry.
- Data collection and evaluation effort: Indicates the effort required during the application of the evaluation procedure.
- Technical support: Evaluates the possibility of a computer-aided collection and/or evaluation of the information and generally the collection technique.
- Presentation, transparency and plausibility: Describes the way the results are presented. This is possible, for example, in the form of key figures, graphs or verbal formulations.

On the other hand, in addition to these general criteria, the assessment of existing reputation measurement approaches is also carried out on the basis of more specific criteria. These appear highly relevant for use in the consulting industry. The following criteria are proposed:

Table 1 Quality assessment of existing measurement approaches (own research)

Criterion	Fortune's AMAC & GMAC	Company ranking of manager magazine	Financial times WMRC	Customer-based reputation scale (CBR)	Corporate character scale	Reputation portfolio by Schwaiger and Cannon	Reputation quotient	RepTrak approach
Theoretical base	3	1	2	4	4	3	4	4
Measurement object	2	2	3	5	2	4	4	4
Source of information	2	2	2	5	3	3	3	4
Flexibility of approach	3	3	3	5	2	3	3	3
Data collection and evaluation effort	4	2	4	4	3	3	2	4
Technical support	4	3	4	4	2	4	3	5
Presentation, transparency and plausibility of results	2	2	2	4	3	4	4	5
Change effort	3	1	3	4	2	3	3	3
Dissemination of approach	5	4	4	3	2	3	5	4
Sum (points)	28	20	27	**38**	23	30	**31**	**36**

Scale 1–5 (5 = best evaluation)

- Change effort: Indicates the effort required to adapt the measuring instrument to the consulting industry, i.e. to what extent special features of the consulting industry are already taken into account. The importance of this criterion is easy to see, as large parts of the existing instrument that has already been evaluated can be retained with less modification effort.
- Dissemination: Describes the awareness for the instrument and the extent to which it or its results are already being used by companies. This criterion is important, as the instrument has already been widely used and thus provides sufficient demonstration of the basic instrument (to be adapted for the consulting industry).

For each criterion, the approaches receive a score between one and five, with one being the worst score and five the best score. A total value is then formed from the points awarded for the individual criteria for each measuring instrument, which represents the final evaluation of the respective approach. The best three generic measurement instruments of reputation are highlighted in bold in Table 1. The best individual approach is the Customer-based Reputation Scale (CBR) of Walsh and Beatty (2007), which in turn was developed from the Reputation Quotient by Fombrun et al. (2000). Thus, CBR will be used as a basis for the creation of our own measurement instrument for reputation in the consulting sector, as described in the following section.

5 Design of a Measurement Instrument for Reputation in the Consulting Industry

5.1 CBR as the Starting Point

While Fombrun's RQ was developed for an application across all industries and company types, the focus of the Customer-based Reputation Scale of Walsh and Beatty (2007) is on service companies and the customer as a central stakeholder. This, and the overall good quality rating of this instrument in the previous section, suggests CBR as a basis for a reputation measurement instrument in the consulting sector.

CBR was developed with the aim of collecting benchmark data in service companies regarding the current reputation and to enable a periodic review of the reputation. CBR is intended to serve as a diagnostic tool that offers service companies the opportunity to identify and eliminate weak points in their reputation. Due to the high acceptance of the RQ, the items of the RQ were also used for the scale development of the CBR. In addition, further qualitative and quantitative research was carried out to complete the measuring instrument.

Based on extensive validation in three types of service companies, the use of a five-dimensional scale has proven itself in CBR: Customer Orientation, Good

Employer, Reliable and Financially Strong Company, Product and Service Quality, and finally Social and Environmental Responsibility. Walsh et al. (2009) have reduced the original measurement tool from 28 items to 15 items in order to minimize the complexity of practical application.

Reputation is measured within CBR using formative indicators, i.e. reputation drivers. The items are evaluated both in their original and shortened form on Likert scales of one to five. The survey's target groups include both potential and current customers, which reinforces the focus on the customer as a key stakeholder (Walsh et al. 2009).

While CBR offers a good starting point to develop a measurement instrument for reputation in the consulting industry, it can not be simply taken over without change for this purpose. One reason is that trust, which is of decisive importance for the consulting business, is not adequately reflected in CBR. But also other factors of relevance in consulting, such as team spirit as an element of a good employer brand, are missing. Thus, in the following the shortened version of CBR will be adapted to reflect the particularities of reputation in the consulting industry.

5.2 General Design Decisions

Due to the work-in-progress character of this research, a full statistical validation of the measurement instrument has not been achieved, yet. However, since the basic structure of our approach is directly derived from CBR, a certain validity of the overall concept is carried over in our opinion. Further validation is achieved by a thorough literature analysis of reputation drivers and other measuring instruments as well as by integrating the results of ten interviews with consulting experts who were asked about an initial prototype in the development process.

Since the CBR in the original version does not offer an option to form an overall reputation score, average values of the assessments within a factor will be formed from the individual items within the new instrument. The calculated average values of the individual factors are then combined with the help of a weighting, depending on the importance of the factor, to an overall reputation score, which ultimately represents the overall result of the measurement. In the final step in the development of the instrument, a proposal for this weighting is therefore drawn up.

It is necessary to decide on a measurement based on formative or reflexive indicators. Since the original instrument is based on a measurement using formative indicators, reputation drivers are also used as indicators within the new instrument. Furthermore, a scale for the evaluation of the items has to be defined.

Here, too, the Likert scales with a rating of one to five from the basic instrument are used. In addition, it was noted in the course of the expert survey that not all items are to be assessed on a Likert scale, as the customer may not have knowledge of certain items. Thereupon the evaluation of the items was supplemented by the answer option "N/A", which is to be selected if an evaluation is not possible due to lack of knowledge. If the customer chooses this option, the item is neglected when calculating the average within the corresponding factor.

5.3 Reputation Factors (Dimensions)

In the course of structuring the measurement instrument, the five original CBR-dimensions will be examined with regard to their importance for the reputation of consulting services. To this end, the reputation drivers for business consultancies highlighted in Sect. 3.2 are compared with those of CBR.

5.3.1 Customer Orientation

When considering the reputation drivers of consultancies, customer orientation has already been identified as an extremely relevant factor, as it has a positive influence on customer satisfaction and thus increases the probability of recommendation or follow-up orders (Niedereichholz 2010). Consequently, the factor 'customer orientation' must be retained in a measuring instrument.

5.3.2 Product and Service Quality

Service quality and client trust in the ability and willingness of consultants to perform well were described earlier as very important reputation drivers for consultancies. Since consultancies only provide immaterial services, the CBR-factor 'Product and service quality' is adopted as 'Service Quality' for the measuring instrument to be developed here.

5.3.3 Good Employer

The term 'good employer' largely overlaps with the 'employer brand' identified as a reputation driver in consulting. The importance of this factor in consulting can be deduced from the assumed relationship between factor input quality and its impact on consulting output quality (see Sect. 3.2). High employee satisfaction generally results in high customer satisfaction within the service sector, as employees tend to perform better (Chun 2005). This ultimately leads to an increase in reputation. Therefore the CBR-factor 'good employer' is kept in our measurement instrument for consultancies.

5.3.4 Reliable and Financially Strong Company

Within Sect. 3.2, competitiveness was identified as another reputation driver. It can be argued that the CBR-factor 'Reliable and financially strong company' basically refers to the same content as the reputation driver competitiveness, but the naming focuses more on financial performance. However, since the items within this CBR-dimension also include issues of future corporate development ("looks like it has strong prospects for future growth") and the competitive position ("tends to outperform competitors") the factor is retained, but the name is changed to 'Competitive company' in our measurement instrument.

Competitiveness can be seen as more of a general factor for reputation enhancement, which is also relevant for business consultancies (Schwaiger and Raithel 2014). Certainly, financial stability, future prospects and the competitive position in a dynamic market are important in enhancing the reputation of consultancies (Wüst and Kreutzer 2012).

5.3.5 Social and Environmental Responsibility

Responsibility for social and environmental issues was also identified as a reputation driver in the course of this work, which is why this factor is also included in the new measuring instrument.

5.4 Reputation Items

The design of the items first considers all CBR-items and their relevance for the reputation of business consultancies. Moreover, it is checked whether the items cover the entire width of a factor and whether there are any overlaps or repetitions between individual items. Each of the items is also examined for meaning and uniqueness. As a matter of principle, the already validated items of the basic instrument are tried to be retained as far as possible and only required changes are made.

5.4.1 Customer Orientation

The CBR-item 'Has employees who treat customers courteously' is also relevant within this factor for consultancies, since customer satisfaction as a prerequisite for long-term consultant-client relationships can be promoted through the behaviour of the consultants. Furthermore, the original CBR-items 'Has employees who are concerned about customer needs' and 'Is concerned about its customers' are also closely linked to customer satisfaction. However, both items are very similar and try to express the focus on customer needs. In our measurement instrument they are combined in the item 'Focuses on delivering value to customers' that expresses the focus on customer needs, both on the part of the consultants and on the part of the entire company. The reliability and discretion of the consultants is also important for the reputation with regard to customer orientation (Amann and Schneider 2015). Due to the information advantage of the consultants and the associated opportunity to behave opportunistically, clients are exposed to the risk that consultants will not use their full performance capacity (Fink and Knoblach 2015). Within the CBR, however, none of the original items covers this topic, which is why an additional item must be introduced that deals with the trustworthiness and discretion of the consultants. This item is 'Has employees who are reliable and act discrete' which is integrated into the factor 'Customer orientation'. Thus, this factor in our measurement instrument initially consists of the following items:

- Has employees who treat customers courteously.
- Has employees who are reliable and act discrete.
- Focuses on delivering value to customers.

5.4.2 Good Employer

Within this factor, it is important to use items that describe a good employer as precisely as possible. CBR uses the items 'Looks like a good company to work for', 'Seems to treat its people well' and 'Seems to have excellent leadership'. Looking at the first item, if a consultancy has a high attractiveness as an employer, this increases the chance of hiring high-quality employees. Thus, the company signals a high input quality. The fair treatment of one's own employees and excellent management within a consulting firm are additional indications for consulting clients that capable employees will prefer such a consulting provider and that there is a high level of employee satisfaction within this consulting firm. Summarizing, CBR's 'Good employer' items reflect the attractiveness of a consulting firm as an employer and the impact on the company's reputation well, which is why they are kept in the new measurement instrument. The factor 'Good employer' thus initially consists of the following items:

- Looks like a good company to work for.
- Seems to treat its people well.
- Seems to have excellent leadership.

5.4.3 Competitive Company

In the original CBR-instrument, the first item in this dimension is 'Tends to outperform competitors'. Transferred to the field of business consulting, the first item is to put the consultancy in comparison with its respective competitors. Since the factors of the instrument should not overlap and a different factor 'product and service quality' exists, this item must be defined in more detail. In our measurement instrument it will deal exclusively with the competitive position in relation to key financial figures and the overall success of the company.

The second original CBR-item 'Seems to recognize and take advantage of market opportunities' deals with the ability of consulting management to identify and build upon market developments in favor of their company. The last original CBR-item is 'Looks like it has strong prospects for future growth'. All three items of the factor serve as signals for a competitive company characterized by financial stability, a good market position and promising future prospects. Having delimitated the focus of the first item, the items within this CBR-factor can be used identically for measuring the reputation of business consultancies. This is due to the fact that CBR is already geared to professional service companies. Furthermore, the items used have already been validated by the antecedent work of Fombrun et al. (2000) and Walsh and Beatty (2007). Consequently, the factor 'Competitive company' initially consists of the following three items:

- Tends to outperform competitors.
- Seems to recognize and take advantage of market opportunities.
- Looks like it has strong prospects for future growth.

5.4.4 Service Quality

The original CBR-items in this dimension are 'Offers high quality products and services', 'Develops innovative services', and 'Is a strong reliable company'. While the first two items basically also apply to consulting companies, the third item appears a bit imprecise and, moreover, overlaps partly with elements of the factor 'Competitive company'. Therefore, the third item was focused more on the key element of client trust in the service quality of the given consultancy as a prerequisite for a good reputation and sales success. In the first item, the notion of product was dropped, as consulting firms offer immaterial services only. Consequently, the factor 'Service quality' consists of the three items:

- Offers high quality services.
- Develops innovative services.
- Offers services I would place my trust in.

5.4.5 Social and Environmental Responsibility

CBR uses the items 'Seems to make an effort to create new jobs' and 'Would reduce its profits to ensure a clean environment'. While in our opinion the first item does build up a connection to social responsibility, it only covers a marginal part of the scope of this broad subject area. For instance, issues such as child labour, minimum wages and inadequate safety standard also belong to this sphere. Through industry and social standards, companies commit themselves to comply with certain social and moral codes of conduct. In order to cover the wide field of social responsibility within the new measuring instrument more adequately, the item 'Supports good causes' previously established in Fombrun's RQ is used here.

Considering the second original CBR-item, without doubt, reducing one's own profit in favour of the environment has an impact on the customer's perception of environmental responsibility, but the issue is not fully reflected by this item. In the extended first version of the CBR the item 'Seems to be environmentally responsible' is used, which is very similar to the item from the RQ 'Is an environmentally responsible company'. Although this item is very general, it reflects the entire scope of a company's environmental responsibility. Thus, the last factor of the measurement instrument suggested in this contribution contains very broad items, but avoids that important aspects of social and environmental responsibility are not taken into account. Accordingly, the factor in the new instrument consists of these items:

- Supports good causes.
- Seems to be environmentally responsible.

5.5 *Initial Design Evaluation Via Expert Interviews*

After a check of the measurement instrument developed so far that resulted in a few verbal simplifications and streamlinings, the next step was to remove inconsistencies and ambiguities and further secure the aptness of the chosen factors and items. For this purpose, ten interviews were conducted with consulting experts. The expert interviews were evaluated using the qualitative content analysis according to Mayring and Brunner (2009). The experts were asked about the following aspects of the instrument:

- Comprehensibility of the items in the instrument
- Subdivision of the instrument into the corresponding factors
- Items within the instrument without relevance for the reputation of consultancies
- Missing items with relevance for the reputation of business consultancies
- Adequacy of the proposed factor weighting

5.5.1 Comprehensibility of the Items

In principle, almost all items within the first prototype of the instrument were considered understandable by the experts surveyed. However, the experts suggested to define the item 'Tends to outperform competitors' of the factor 'Competitive company' more precisely, as it is unclear whether this only relates to financial success and profit, or also to services offered.

Since the factor 'competitive company' is in fact solely concerned with the financial and competitive situation, the item was supplemented by the addition 'according to profit and financial situation' as suggested by an expert. In addition, the item ‘Supports good causes’ of the factor ‘Social and Environmental Responsibility’ was considered difficult to interpret. In this context, two experts felt that the aspects of diversity and integration, which are both part of social responsibility, should be explicitly mentioned. In order to solve these problems, the item ‘Supports good causes’ was extended with corresponding examples. The experts also noted that the item ‘Treats its people well’ from the factor ‘Good employer’ seems fuzzy or even misleading. For this reason, the item was changed to ‘Treats its employees well’ on the basis of a suggestion by an expert, in order to clarify the reference of the item. All other items were considered comprehensible.

5.5.2 Subdivision of the Instrument into the Corresponding Factors

Since all experts considered the subdivision of the instrument into the corresponding factors to be comprehensible and logical, the five factors and the assignment of the items to them were retained.

5.5.3 Items Within the Instrument Without Relevance

Three of the respondents saw the item ‘Has strong prospects for future growth’ as irrational for the reputation building of business consultancies. The experts justified this with the fact that, on the one hand, not every consultancy strives for growth. On the other hand, it is not always in the client’s interest that a business consultancy should be able to demonstrate sustained growth. In some cases, clients even favour consultancies that consist of small teams of experts and will not pursue the goal of greatly expanding them in the future. For this reason, the item ‘Has strong prospects for future growth’ was removed from the final instrument.

In addition, one expert mentioned that a polite attitude towards the customer was not always sufficient. Rather, it is necessary to adapt one’s appearance to the current situation and therefore to behave adequately. For this reason, the item ‘Has employees who treat customers courteously’ was expanded to include ‘and behave adequately’. The remaining items of the instrument were considered relevant for the reputation of business consultancies.

5.5.4 Missing Items

In the course of the expert survey, the financial stability of the business consultancy was highlighted as relevant for reputation. In principle, a reference to financial stability is associated with factor three, but not explicitly mentioned. Therefore, the item ‘Is a financially stable company’ was added to the factor ‘Competitive company’.

Furthermore, it was noted by the experts that the time frame within which a consulting service is provided can be of great importance for the customer. It is therefore not only a matter of high-quality services, but also of ensuring that they are provided within a reasonable time frame. For this reason, the item ‘Offers high quality services’ was supplemented by the addition ‘in adequate time’. Thus, this item combines the quality of services with the time required to provide them.

Trust in the consultant was also considered important. The experts believed that the item ‘Has employees who are reliable and act discrete’ reflects the trust component, but the term “trust” was classified by experts as stronger and more concise than “reliablc”. Therefore, the wording of the item was changed to ‘Has employees who are trustworthy and act discrete’.

5.6 *Proposal for the Weighting Factors*

It has already been discussed in Sect. 3.2 that some drivers appear more important than others for building the reputation of business consultancies. Client orientation and service quality were identified as key points in reputation building for consultancies. Employer attractiveness was also determined to be an important part of the reputation of consulting providers. Although the competitive situation and responsibility for social and environmental issues are relevant aspects, they are less highlighted in the consulting literature than other factors. In the course of the expert survey, the factor ‘Competitive company’ was regarded as more important than responsibility for society and the environment. Furthermore, its importance was emphasized on the same level as a good employer brand.

The importance of the factors and their weighting can therefore be divided into three levels. To keep the instrument simple, the factors receive a weighting between one and three. The proposal for the weighting of the factors is given in Table 2.

This weighting proposal was later confirmed by the experts and considered comprehensible. Although proposals were made to change the weighting of the factors ‘Good employer’ and ‘Social and environmental responsibility’, increases and reductions were proposed to the same extent. The suggested weighting proposal has therefore been retained.

Table 2 Proposal for the weighting of factors (feedback from expert survey integrated)

Factor	Suggested weighting
Customer orientation	3
Good employer	2
Competitive company	2
Service quality	3
Social and environmental responsibility	1

5.7 *Final Measurement Instrument*

Figure 4 summarizes the suggested design of an instrument for measuring reputation in the consulting industry after the expert feedback had been integrated in the design process. The following instructions for use apply:

- The questions are to be answered on Likert scales from 1 (I strongly disagree) to 5 (I totally agree).
- Select the "N/A" box if the question cannot be answered.
- The average is formed from the individual evaluations of the items (excluding N/A answers)
- The overall reputation score is calculated from the average values of the individual factors taking into account the respective factor weightings.
- Explanations of the factors can be found to the right of the evaluation options.

5.8 *Demonstration of the Measurement Instrument*

As part of the Design Science Research process, a demonstration of the applicability and usefulness of the measuring instrument is to be carried out. For an initial demonstration, ten advanced students and alumni of our university were selected to rate three different consultancies by our measurement instrument. With the Boston Consulting Group (BCG), Roland Berger and the German consulting company Integral as sample companies, two in Germany well-known companies and a consultancy with a comparatively lower profile were chosen. BCG and Roland Berger were expected to achieve positive reputation scores. Since Integral is far less known than the others, it could be expected that evaluations would not be equally positive and that more items would be classified as unanswerable by the testpersons.

Before the survey, the concept of the measuring instrument was explained to the testpersons. After the introduction to the instrument, all testpersons felt comfortable to use it. The testpersons were free to obtain information about the respective companies on the Internet before the survey, just as clients also obtain information about potential consulting partners in advance. Table 3 shows the results of the survey.

As expected, BCG and Roland Berger both achieved high reputations. Integral, on the other hand, is in the middle of the scale in terms of overall reputation. BCG achieved a marginally higher reputation than Roland Berger. According to the testpersons, this can on the one hand be attributed to the greater overall fame of BCG. On the other hand, two testpersons mentioned that they linked Roland Berger to the insolvency of the German DIY 'Praktiker' superstores in 2011, which led the testpersons to give this consulting firm a worse rating, especially in the area of service quality.

It is also striking that Roland Berger achieved significantly lower social and environmental responsibility figures than BCG. The reason for this discrepancy is

	1 2 3 4 5 N/A	Average:	Weighting:
Factor 1: Customer orientation			3
Has employees who treat customers courteously and behave adequately.	☐☐☐☐☐ ☐		
Has employees who are trustworthy and act discrete.	☐☐☐☐☐ ☐		
Focuses on delivering value to customers.	☐☐☐☐☐ ☐		
Factor 2: Good employer			2
Is a good company to work for.	☐☐☐☐☐ ☐		
Treats its employees well.	☐☐☐☐☐ ☐		
Has excellent leadership and teamspirit.	☐☐☐☐☐ ☐		
Factor 3: Competitive company			2
Outperforms competitors according to profit and financial situation.	☐☐☐☐☐ ☐		
Recognizes and takes advantage of market opportunities.	☐☐☐☐☐ ☐		
Is a financially stable company.	☐☐☐☐☐ ☐		
Factor 4: Service quality			3
Offers high quality services in an adequate time.	☐☐☐☐☐ ☐		
Develops innovative services.	☐☐☐☐☐ ☐		
Offers services I would place my trust in.	☐☐☐☐☐ ☐		
Factor 5: Social and environmental responsibility			1
Supports good causes (e.g. diversity, integration, safety standards).	☐☐☐☐☐ ☐		
Is environmentally responsible.	☐☐☐☐☐ ☐		

Reputation Score: *(1=worst, 5=best)*	

Customer Orientation:
Customers' perceptions about the degree to which the company and employees aim to satisfy customers needs and put customers in focus.

Good Employer:
Customers' perception as to how the company treats employees and that the company is well-managed and has competent employees.

Competitive company:
Customers' perceptions about degree of competitiveness and profitability.

Service quality:
Customers' perceptions that the company offers trustworthy, innovative, high-quality services.

Social and environmental responsibility:
Customers' perceptions that the company recognizes and acts according to environmental and social responsibilities.

Fig. 4 Suggested instrument to measure reputation in the consulting industry

Table 3 Reputation values (mean) as scored by the testpersons

	BCG	Roland Berger	Integral
Customer orientation	4.0	4.0	3.7
Good employer	4.0	3.6	2.8
Competitive company	4.6	4.2	3.6
Service quality	4.2	3.8	2.3
Social and environmental responsibility	4.2	3.1	3.0
Total reputation score	**4.2**	**3.9**	**3.0**
Values from 1 (minimum) to 5 (maximum)			

the assessment of the item 'Supports good causes', since the other item 'Is environmentally responsible' of the same factor was classified as unanswerable by the majority of respondents at all three consultancies. According to most of the respondents, the reason for Roland Berger's poorer assessment of this item is the explicit mention of diversity and "Woman@BCG" on the BCG website.

When assessing Integral, the difference in the factor 'Service quality' is particularly noticeable, which the testpersons explained with the very short descriptions of the services offered on the website. Furthermore, no empirical studies or innovative products can be found on the homepage as flagships. In comparison with BCG and Roland Berger, the 'Good employer' factor is also much worse at Integral and the items of this factor were very often classified as unanswerable, which the testpersons attribute to missing career information.

Summarizing, at this initial level the applicability of the instrument was confirmed by the test subjects and the results were in line with expectations. However, it was noticeable that each testperson could not rate at least one item of the instrument. The lack of answers to some questions can generally be attributed to the fact that not all testpersons were as familiar with the assessment of business consultancies as the decision-makers in a client company are. As a result, more complete assessments of consultancies are to be expected when the instrument is used in consulting practice.

6 Discussion and Future Research

6.1 Importance of Reputation in Business Consulting

In the course of the ten interviews with consulting experts, the interviewees were also asked how they rated the importance of reputation for consultancies. All respondents considered reputation to be very relevant. The experts identified a good reputation as a strong competitive advantage. However, the experts linked the importance of reputation to the respective project. For smaller, commodity consulting projects, clients focus more on the price component when it comes to selecting a suitable consulting firm (Nissen 2018).

More complex projects, on the other hand, require a lot of know-how and experience, which is why customers will increasingly rely on reputation as a selection criterion for this type of project. Many of the experts even assessed reputation as the most important success factor in generating clients.

6.2 Strength and Weaknesses of the Measurement Instrument

Due to its specialization in business consultancies, the new measuring instrument is able to more accurately reflect the reputation of these companies. Compared to earlier instruments, both the reputation drivers and the weighting of the individual drivers are specially tailored to the consulting industry. Furthermore, our approach to consulting reputation offers the possibility to compare with other companies on a detailed level, and to identify levers for reputation enhancement. It also provides an overall reputation score, and not only results in individual dimensions. Changing the weightings allows for an easy adaption of the instrument at factor level, depending on the particular focus of application and the individual company. By repeatedly carrying out the measurement with the help of the instrument, a consulting firm is able to continuously track its company reputation over time, and check the results of reputation enhancing measures.

However, the current measuring instrument also has some disadvantages that need to be eliminated in future research. In particular, the required level of knowledge of some items to be evaluated in relation to the consulting company is a critical aspect. Without previous personal experience with or in-depth research into the consulting firm, it can be difficult for respondents to evaluate all items of the measuring instrument. Furthermore, it is necessary to validate the measuring instrument appropriately in the course of larger samples in practical applications and to optimize it if necessary. Finally, the design of the measuring instrument in the form of an online tool would greatly simplify the application and, thus, increase the willingness to use the tool in evaluating business consultancies.

6.3 Added Value of the Measurement Instrument in Practice

In the course of the expert survey, all experts were of the opinion that the use of a tool to measure reputation makes sense. Most experts see the added value of the tool in the support of well-founded decision-making, since the measuring instrument provides clear characteristic values for the reputation drivers of a consultancy. Furthermore, the results of the measurement can be used as benchmarks for continuous reputation tracking. In addition, the reputation values can be compared with industry benchmarks (if available) to determine the current competitive position in terms of reputation.

However, half of the experts emphasized that a new measurement instrument can only offer added value compared with existing tools (customer satisfaction analysis, reputation rankings, employer rankings) if it markedly improves upon them. Since these classical instruments focus only on certain areas of reputation, while no holistic measuring is achieved, and causal relationships between reputation drivers and total reputation are missing, the added value of the new instrument can be seen. For instance, customer satisfaction analysis determines the reputation exclusively in the areas of customer orientation as well as product and service quality. Employer rankings, on the other hand, only deal with the company's reputation in the area of employer attractiveness. Reputation rankings are generally in transparent with regard to causal relationships, i.e. how the reputation rank ultimately came about. They are usually based on a survey for the measurement, which is applied in identical manner for all companies in all industries. This can lead to inaccuracies in the measurement, as the industry-specific aspects are not sufficiently taken into account.

In summary, the interviewed experts saw significant added value in the new reputation measurement instrument, particularly for small to medium-sized consultancies without a unique competitive position. Finally, it should be noted that the importance of reputation in a consulting sales process also depends to a large extent on the client (existing or new, internal consulting know how etc.) and the project (size, application area, associated risk etc.) in question.

6.4 Future Research

During the development and especially in the course of the expert survey, we realized that in order to improve reputation management, it might make sense to further specialize the measurement instrument with regard to different consulting fields (e.g. IT consulting, management consulting).

In order to further improve the developed measuring instrument in the future and to prepare it for a broad application in practice, it is also necessary to validate the concept in the form of practical case studies. We therefore encourage consultancies to apply the instrument in their reputation measurements.

7 A Broader View: Setting Up Reputation Management

Setting up a professional reputation management within a consulting company requires more than having a measurement instrument and other supporting tools and systems. Important tasks further include defining processes, organizational structures and roles in reputation management.

7.1 Organizational Setting and Roles

A dedicated organizational framework including roles & responsibilities should be created in the course of setting up an internal reputation management in consulting companies. The supervision for reputation management should be assigned to a person at board level. On the operational level, it is necessary to appoint a head of reputation management who is ultimately responsible for coordinating the tasks and processes of reputation management and (in larger organizations) possibly also acts as a staff manager for employees in reputation management. The detailed organizational structure below the reputation manager will depend on the size of the company, available budget for reputation management, and the need to care for reputation as a success factor in the companies markets.

The operational aspects of reputation management may also be integrated in an existing related organizational unit, particularly in smaller enterprises. In practice, all areas that deal with public relations or with customer acquisition and sales appear suitable, if no dedicated unit for reputation management should be set up. This is due to the fact that these areas are most dependent on the company's reputation or have the greatest influence on it.

7.2 Reputation Management Processes

Before those responsible for reputation management can even get to grips with the current reputation of the company, it is important to create awareness within the company for the importance of reputation. The employees and above all the management level must be sensitized and convinced that reputation is of great importance for the future development and competitive advantage of the company. On the one hand, the commitment of the Management Board and Supervisory Board is necessary to manage reputation. On the other hand, it must be clear to each individual employee that every action and statement can have an impact on the company's reputation. This is the only way to build a targeted reputation.

Once all parts of the company have been sensitized, it is the task of reputation management to determine which reputation or perception should be achieved among the relevant stakeholders. The target reputation is of enormous importance in order to compare the current reputation with the goals and to define the direction of action in reputation management.

However, in order to be able to make comparisons, it is essential to continuously measure the company's current reputation. In general, it is important to consider not only a rough overall reputation, but also the individual components of the reputation, both in the actual and in the target form. For this it is necessary to look at the individual reputation drivers of business consultancies as outlined in this paper. These must be considered in a differentiated way, as the reputation in the individual sub-areas may well differ.

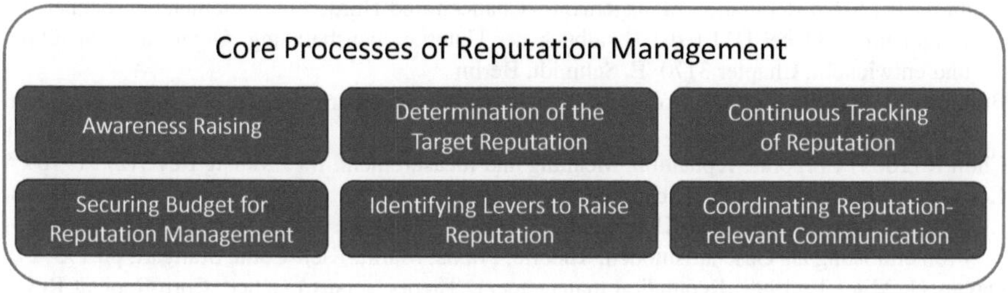

Fig. 5 Main processes of reputation management

Currently it does not appear to be customary in consulting companies to have their own budget available for reputation management. This should definitely be changed as, for example, expenses may be incurred for recording the actual reputation and for communication measures to the public. If these expenses have to be covered by the budgets of other departments, delays and even cancellations can occur, which considerably impairs the ability of reputation management to act in a timely manner. It is therefore fundamentally necessary to apply for a long-term budget for reputation management and use it sensibly.

Furthermore, it is the task of reputation management to identify levers for increasing the company's reputation. These can be seen from measurements of the current reputation or through investigations of benchmarks.

In addition, it is important for reputation management to deal with the company's information distribution and public relations processes. All major (in particular strategic) decisions and information that have to be communicated and which could have an impact on the company's reputation should be reviewed beforehand by reputation management. In this way, negative effects on stakeholders' perceptions of the company can be minimized.

In summary, the activities and processes are broadly diversified and intersect many other areas of the company. Reputation management must therefore work permanently in coordination with other organizational units. Figure 5 finally summarizes the most important reputation management processes to be set up in business consultancies.

References

Amann M, Schneider D (2015) Benchmarking von Unternehmensberatungen. In: Deelmann T, Ockel DM (eds) Handbuch der Unternehmensberatung. Organisationen führen und entwickeln, Chapter 7320. E. Schmidt, Berlin

Balmer JMT, Markwick N, Fill C (1997) Towards a framework for managing corporate identity. Eur J Mark 31(5/6):396–409

Barchewitz C, Armbrüster T (2007) Marktmechanismen und Marketing in der Beratungsbranche. In: Nissen V (ed) Consulting research. DUV, Wiesbaden, pp 217–230

Bauhofer B (2015) Reputation Management—Chancen und Hürden für Unternehmensberater. In: Deelmann T, Ockel DM (eds) Handbuch der Unternehmensberatung. Organisationen führen und entwickeln, Chapter 3170. E. Schmidt, Berlin

Brammer SJ, Pavelin S (2006) Corporate reputation and social performance. The importance of fit. J ManagStud 43(3):435–455

Chun R (2005) Corporate reputation. Meaning and measurement. Int J Manag Rev 7(2):91–109

Coers J, Heinecke J (2002) Die Steuerungsarchitektur in Beratungsprozessen—Kooperationsprozesse von Beratern und Klienten. In: Mohe M, Heinecke J, Pfriem R (eds) Consulting—Problemlösung als Geschäftsmodell. Theorie, Praxis, Markt. Klett-Cotta, Stuttgart, pp 195–218

Davies G, Miles L (1998) Reputation management. Theory versus practice. Corp Reputat Rev 2 (1):16–27

Davies G, Chun R, da Silva RV, Roper S (2001) The personification metaphor as a measurement approach for corporate reputation. Corp Reputat Rev 4(2):113–127

Fink D, Knoblach B (2015) Strategische Planung in der Managementberatung. In: Deelmann T, Ockel DM (eds) Handbuch der Unternehmensberatung. Organisationen führen und entwickeln, Chapter 7310. E. Schmidt, Berlin

Fombrun CJ, Gardberg NA, Sever JM (2000) The reputation quotient. A multi-stakeholder measure of corporate reputation. J Brand Manag 7(4):241–255

Glückler J, Armbrüster T (2003) Bridging uncertainty in management consulting: the mechanisms of trust and networked reputation. Organ Stud 24(2):269–297

Gray ER, Balmer JMT (1998) Managing corporate image and corporate reputation. Long Range Plan 31(5):695–702

Hagenmeyer U (2015) Ethik ist das Fundament einer integren Unternehmensberatung. In: Deelmann T, Ockel DM (eds) Handbuch der Unternehmensberatung. Organisationen führen und entwickeln, Chapter 7610. E. Schmidt, Berlin

Helm S, Liehr-Gobbers K, Storck C (eds) (2011) Reputation management. Springer, Berlin

Hevner AR, March ST, Park J, Ram S (2004) Design science in information systems research. MIS Q 28:75–105

Jeschke K (2007) Die Rolle des Beziehungsmarketings für Beratungsunternehmen. Verhaltenstheoretische Grundlagen und Gestaltungsanforderungen. In: Nissen V (ed) Consulting research. DUV, Wiesbaden, pp 197–212

Jeschke K (2015) Marketingmanagement für Beratungsdienstleistungen—Die Rolle des Branding. In: Deelmann T, Ockel DM (eds) Handbuch der Unternehmensberatung, Chapter 7420. E. Schmidt, Berlin

Kirstein S (2009) Unternehmensreputation. Corporate social responsibility als strategische option für deutsche Automobilhersteller. Gabler, Wiesbaden

Lippold D (2016) Grundlagen der Unternehmensberatung. Strukturen—Konzepte—Methoden. Springer Gabler, Wiesbaden

Maister DH, Green CH, Galford RM (2001) The trusted advisor. Free Press, New York

Mauerer C, Nissen V (2014) Portraying the social dimensions of consulting with structuration theory. J Serv Sci Manag 7(2):110–130

Mayring P, Brunner E (2009) Qualitative Inhaltsanalyse. In: Buber R, Holzmüller HH (eds) Qualitative Marktforschung. Gabler, Wiesbaden, pp 669–680

Neuberger O (2002) Rate mal! Phantome, Philosophien und Phasen der Beratung. In: Mohe M, Heinecke HJ, Pfriem R (eds) Consulting—Problemlösung als Geschäftsmodell. Theorie, Praxis, Markt. Klett-Cotta, Stuttgart, pp 135–161

Niedereichholz C (2010) Beratungsmarketing und Auftragsakquisition, 5th edn. Oldenbourg, München

Nissen V (2007) Consulting Research—eine Einführung. In: Nissen V (ed) Consulting research. DUV, Wiesbaden, pp 3–31

Nissen V (2018) Digital transformation of the consulting industry—introduction and overview. In: Nissen V (ed) Digital transformation of the consulting industry. Extending the Traditional Delivery Model. Springer, Berlin, pp 1–58

Peffers K, Tuunanen T, Rothenberger MA, Chatterjee S (2007/8) A design science research methodology for information systems research. J Manag Inf Syst 24:45–78
Pietsch T (2003) Bewertung von Informations- und Kommunikationssystemen. Ein Vergleich betriebswirtschaftlicher Verfahren, 2nd edn. E. Schmidt, Berlin
Pruzan P (2001) Corporate reputation. Image and identity. Corp Reputat Rev 4(1):50–64
Rindova VP (1997) Managing reputation: pursuing everyday excellence: the image cascade and the formation of corporate reputations. Corp Reputat Rev 1(2):188–194
Schwaiger M, Cannon HM (2004) Unternehmensreputation—Bestandsaufnahme und Messkonzepte. Jahrbuch der Absatz- und Verbrauchsforschung 50(3):237–261
Schwaiger M, Raithel S (2014) Reputation und Unternehmenserfolg. Manag Rev Q 64(4):225–259
Walsh G, Beatty SE (2007) Customer-based corporate reputation of a service firm. scale development and validation. J Acad Mark Sci 35(1):127–143
Walsh G, Mitchell V-W, Jackson PR, Beatty SE (2009) Examining the antecedents and consequences of corporate reputation. A customer perspective. Br J Manag 20(2):187–203
Whetten DA (1997) Where do reputations come from? Theory development and the study of corporate reputation. Corp Reputat Rev 1(1):25–34
Wiedmann K-P (2012) Ansatzpunkte zur Messung der Unternehmensreputation als Grundlage einer Erfolg versprechenden Reputationsmanagementplanung—Das RepTrak-Konzept als Ausgangspunkt und Skizzen zur relevanten Weiterentwicklung. In: Wüst C, Kreutzer RT (eds) Corporate reputation management. Gabler, Wiesbaden, pp 57–101
Wiedmann K-P, Fombrun CJ, van Riel CBM (2006) Ansatzpunkte zur Messung der Reputation von Unternehmen. Journal für Marketing 45(2):98–109
Wüst C, Kreutzer RT (eds) (2012) Corporate reputation management. Gabler, Wiesbaden

Volker Nissen holds the Chair of Information Systems Engineering in Services at Technische Universität Ilmenau, Germany, since 2005. Prior to this, he pursued a consulting career, including positions as manager at IDS Scheer AG, director at DHC GmbH, and CEO of NISSCON Ltd., Germany. In 1994 he received a PhD degree in Economic Sciences with distinction from the University of Goettingen, Germany. His current research interests include the digital transformation of the consulting industry, the management of IT-agility, metaheuristic optimization, and process acceptance research. He is author and editor of 20 books and some 200 other publications, including papers in Business and Information Systems Engineering, Information Systems Frontiers, IEEE Transactions on EC, IEEE Transactions on NN, OR Spectrum, and Annals of OR.

Johannes Dittler graduated 2017 as a Master of Science in Industrial Engineering at Ilmenau University of Technology (Chair of Information Systems Engineering in Services, Prof. V. Nissen). He now works as a consultant for INVERTO GmbH, Munich, Germany.

Development and Handling of Procedure Models for the Selection and Implementation of Business Software

Volker Nissen

Abstract The study presented provides some empirical insights into two core fields of activity in IT consulting. For the selection and implementation of business software, results on the development and handling of procedural models are presented. Such models document the suggested practical steps in corresponding consulting projects. The use of procedure models is well established in consulting practice, at least among the 14 companies surveyed. Apart from some differences in the models' operation due to pragmatic reasons, even small consulting firms behave in this respect in the same way as large consulting providers. Sequential procedure models are mainly used. An orientation towards reference models described in the literature actually takes place. However, such models are always adapted to the individual case of the client. This tailoring of the approach is considered very important for customer acceptance.

1 Introduction and Research Questions[1]

This paper investigates empirically the question of how procedure models for the selection and implementation of business software in consulting firms have been developed and are being handled practically. A procedure model is to be understood as the sequence of all activities that are necessary to carry out a project (Stahlknecht and Hasenkamp 2004). Each of these ends with defined milestones, i.e. decision or approval points with regard to the defined interim results. Procedural models serve to improve process control by reducing the overall complexity of the project, improving the transparency of the process and thus enabling a review of deadlines, cost,

[1]This paper builds on the contributions by Nissen and Simon (2009) and Nissen (2010).

V. Nissen (✉)
Economic Sciences and Media, Ilmenau University of Technology, Ilmenau, Germany
e-mail: volker.nissen@tu-ilmenau.de

V. Nissen (ed.), *Advances in Consulting Research*, Contributions to Management Science, https://doi.org/10.1007/978-3-319-95999-3_6

quality and performance targets. Furthermore, the coordination of project teams and the early detection of errors are facilitated.

As guaranteeing a high-quality service is a central competitive factor (Bruhn 2016), Mieschke (2004) says that consulting firms should apply procedure models for individual project types or consulting topics with the aim of increasing quality.

IT consulting is a primary activity field in 21.6% of about 15,725 consulting firms, which are currently active in Germany (BDU 2017). These companies will briefly be referred to as IT consulting providers. They are more strongly operative oriented than strategy consulting firms (Nissen and Kinne 2008). There are recommended procedure models or descriptions of process sequences in the literature for some activity fields of IT consulting. The development and actual usage of procedure models in consulting does not seem to have been investigated so far. This is supposed to be empirically explained here for the German consulting market. For this purpose, the results of a first, qualitative case study analysis will be presented below (Nissen and Simon 2009).

The contribution is structured as follows: Initially typical topics in IT consulting are briefly introduced. In Sect. 3, these are then classified into one of the three complexity categories (procedure, grey hair and brain projects), suggested by Maister (2003). The selection, respectively implementation of business software will accordingly be classified into the category procedure projects. Such projects are particularly suited for the application of widely standardized procedure models. In Sect. 4 it will thus be empirically investigated, how procedure models are developed and actually used in these two application fields in IT consultings. The contribution is concluded by a brief summary and outlook on the need for more research.

2 Typical IT Consulting Tasks

Based on a comprehensive analysis of 30 established IT consulting providers, a many-faceted portfolio of IT consulting services could be identified. The core activities of IT consulting, most frequently mentioned, are briefly represented below.

- *Software selection*: The consulting field of software selection encompasses the entire process of selecting the most suitable software for the individual company goals. The selection of the 'best' software provider respectively sales partner is, besides the selection of the product, also a component of the activity field. This aspect is thus very significant as the software implementation, following up on the selection process, is frequently conducted together with the same company.
- *Software implementation*: From the consulting firm's point of view, the main task of the software implementation is to introduce (standard) software in a target-oriented and tool-supported manner with the customer's significant involvement so as to achieve optimum long-term benefits (Gabriel and Lohnert 2001). This often includes activities of operational restructuring and process optimization.

- *Information architecture consulting*: The architecture forms, as the fundamental logical model of the information structure, the basis of the company-wide gathered, evaluated and segmented information demand respectively of the required information supply needed for their satisfaction (Heinrich et al. 2004). A wide range of services are offered in this consulting field. They range from advice on the design of an information architecture to support in defining uniform architecture rules and optimizing the architecture of individual software solutions.
- *IT security consulting*: According to the Capgemini study 'IT-trends 2017', raising IT security is an important IT requirement from the top management (Capgemini 2017). A holistic information security management via technical, organizational and physical measures, which forms a wide field for IT consultants, is required to encounter such changes. These include, particularly, the conduction of risks- respectively security analyses to determine the threat potential as well as supporting the conception and implementation of IT security concepts.
- *IT integration consulting*: The current predominant heterogeneous IT landscapes in companies complicate the consistent, efficient support of business processes and require a high amount of maintenance. IT integration consulting deals with all the sub-aspects of an improvement of the integrated information processing in the client's company. These include the process integration regarding the automatization of business processes, the production of a uniform consistent data basis in the framework of data integration, as well as homogenizing and integrating user interfaces of various applications. A typical example of an integration project is the structuring of a company portal.
- *IT strategy consulting*: Strategy development is a sub-task of strategical IT planning (Heinrich et al. 2004). For this purpose, the IT strategy is derived from or aligned with the company strategy (business-IT-alignment) to increase the value of IT for the company. Here, the task of the consulting is the comprehensive support of the client during the design and implementation of an IT strategy.
- *Consulting on IT organization*: This consulting field is closely linked to IT strategy. The IT-specific organizational structure and process organization of the client company is developed in accordance with the strategic guidelines. On the one hand, the consultants can provide the client with guidance on hierarchical classification and internal organizational structure of the 'information processing' organizational unit. On the other hand, the consulting service also deals with the organizationally regulated processes of procurement, initial development, operation, maintenance and further development of the various types of systems. Reference models and frameworks of IT service management, like ITIL, are of great significance here.
- *IT outsourcing consulting*: IT-outsourcing describes the partial or complete transfer of tasks and resources of information processing of a company to one or more legally distinct service providers. Here, it has to be emphasized that activities of IT consulting only refer to the support of the client in the context of preparation and conduction of an outsourcing proposal. The IT consulting provider does not generally render the outsourcing services itself, though.

3 Categorization of Tasks According to Complexity

David Maister suggested a categorization for project types of consulting providers, which has meanwhile gained wide acceptance in the consulting related literature. He differentiated among brain, grey hair and procedure projects (Maister 2003):

- *Brain* projects are characterized by a client problem at the forefront of professional or technical knowledge and extreme complexity. It requires a high professional craft of its staff, since creativity and innovation are essential, while few procedures in these projects are routinizable. This project type requires mainly senior consulting staff and, hence, allows for only a low leverage.
- *Grey* hair projects require a lesser degree of innovation and creativity in the actual performance than *Brain* projects would. While the output must still be highly customized in meeting the client's needs, the problem to be solved is not unfamiliar, and the activities to be performed may be similar to those of other projects, though some judgment and transfer capabilities are essential. Consequently, the fraction of junior consulting staff and, thus, the leverage in these projects can be higher than in *Brain* projects.
- *Procedure* projects address client problems that are very familiar. While there is still a need to customize to some degree, the required steps to solve the problem are somewhat programmatic. Clients often have the ability to perform the work themselves, but turn to consultants, because internal resources are needed elsewhere, or consultants can provide more efficient solutions. The use of procedure models, templates and tools allows for a high fraction of junior staff, leading to a high leverage in this class of projects.

A suggestion, how the mentioned core tasks of IT consulting can be classified, based on their complexity and repetition character according to Maister's categories, is presented in Table 1. Tasks from the category 'procedure project' seem to be especially suitable to structure the project work more efficiently by mostly standardized procedure models. Thus it is not surprising that there are numerous procedure models in the consulting practice, especially for the topics software selection and—implementation.

Table 1 Suggested classification of typical IT consulting tasks into complexity categories

Consulting task within IT consulting	Brain project	Grey hair project	Procedure project
Software selection			×
Software implementation			×
Information architecture		×	
IT security		×	
IT integration		×	
IT strategy	×		
IT organization		×	
IT outsourcing		×	

4 Procedure Models in IT Consulting Practice

4.1 *Method and Data of Survey*

The results presented below are part of an empirical investigation on procedure models done with German IT consulting firms in 2009 (Nissen and Simon 2009). The survey took place in the form of guided interviews with predominantly open questions. Although some time has elapsed since this data was collected, there is good reason to believe that the fundamental aspects addressed in the survey are still valid, and the author would like to share the results with the English-speaking community. The duration of the interviews varied between 45 minutes and two hours. The interview partners were experienced managers with long relevant professional practice. One person per company was questioned. Unlike anonymous online surveys by means of a standardized questionnaire, this qualitative procedure allows queries from both parties, so that misconceptions can be eliminated and the background for an answer can be explained (Mayer 2012).

The number of investigated companies are method-wise moderate compared to large-scaled questionnaire-based studies. First of all, a sample structure was created, which allowed a well-founded sampling. One of the stratification features was the size of the company, which was differentiated as follows: small companies (⍰20 employees), medium-sized (20–500 employees) and large companies (⍰500 employees). Furthermore, the survey was narrowed down to the application of procedure models during the selection and implementation of business software. In this survey, five small, five medium-sized and four large companies participated in the interviews (n = 14, cf. Fig. 1).

To evaluate the interviews anonymously, they were electronically recorded and subsequently transcribed. Due to limited time resources, the transcription was not done verbatim but predominantly analogous.

In the following, a general differentiation between the two considered consulting fields, software selection, and software implementation, will be dispensed with. This seems to be justified, as the handling of procedure models in both fields generally agrees. The impression from the interviews shows that the practical handling of procedure models is largely dependent on the company culture of every consulting house and is less dependent on the task.

A distinction is made between the companies surveyed according to size (number of employees) where this is a differentiating factor in terms of results.

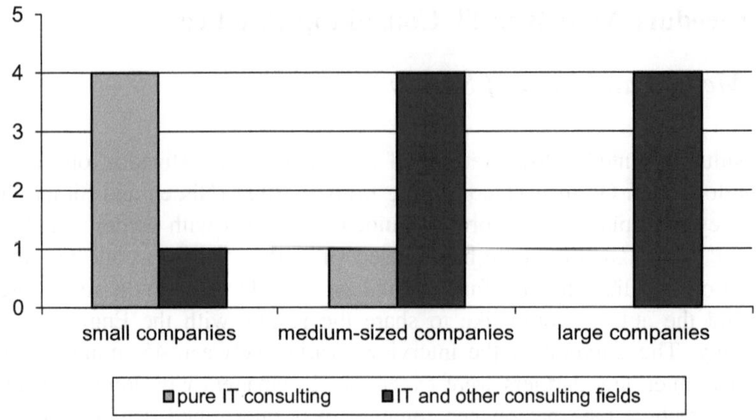

Fig. 1 Distribution of consulting companies in the sample according to size (n = 14)

4.2 *Results and Discussion on the Development of Procedural Models*

4.2.1 Time of Development

All the questioned IT consulting firms use a procedure model in at least one of the two considered application fields (most in both). As of the year 2009, there are three consulting houses, which have already used their procedure models for at least 15 years (cf. Fig. 2). In six consulting houses the models have been used for 10–15 years and four participants stated that the respective procedure model has been used for 5–9 years. One company did not give any details here. These, on average, quite long application periods show that the consulting fields software selection—and implementation, belong to the classical core tasks of IT consulting. Today (2018), they can be classified as procedure projects with according procedural models existing for almost 25 years in some companies.

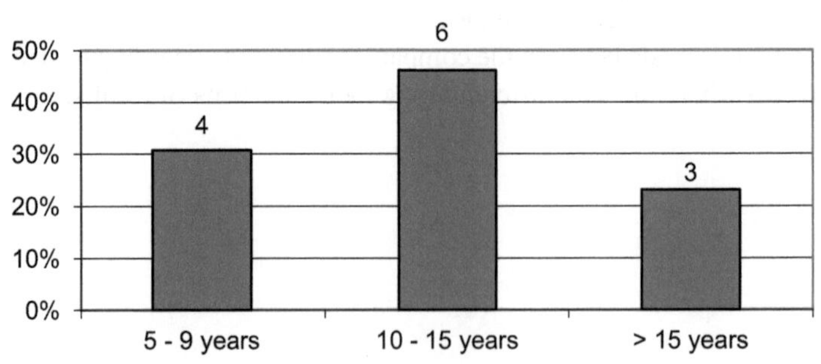

Fig. 2 Duration of application of the procedure models as of 2009 (n = 13)

Fig. 3 Origin of the procedure models (n = 14)

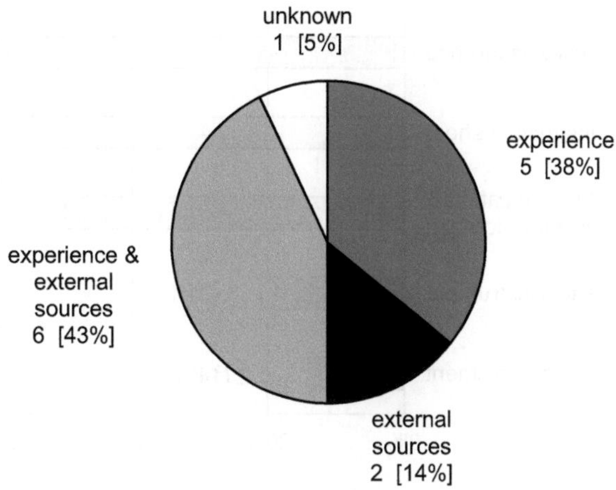

4.2.2 Origin of the Models and Development Process

Companies mainly have two methods available to develop models. Either the gained experiences from the conducted projects are gathered and collectively prepared to form a model—or the company uses external sources and adapts these into own procedure models. These can be established procedures, international standards or scientific literature. Figure 3 shows which of these options the consulting firms surveyed used to develop their procedure models. The results indicate that the know-how gained from practical projects present a valuable basis for the creation of an internal procedure model. In addition, external best practices are evaluated.

The development process for models also differs considerably depending on the size of the company. In consulting firms with few employees, a less formalized but sometimes more creative process takes place, which can be managed by a consultant in addition to the day-to-day business. Medium-sized and large IT consultancies, on the other hand, are experiencing more systematic and formal development. For example, two of the major international consulting firms surveyed here have their own organizational units that are mainly concerned with the development and improvement of procedural models.

4.2.3 Motivation for the Development and Use of Procedure Models

According to the questioned consultants the most important reason for using procedure models is to ensure the consulting quality (cf. Fig. 4). The specification of the work results to be performed and support for quality assurance in the consulting process ensure relatively uniform quality in various projects. Furthermore, a structured procedure improves the transparency of a consulting process and contributes, for example, to safe decisions on software selection by the creation of a profound information basis. Procedure models, therefore, also provide more security to the consulting client.

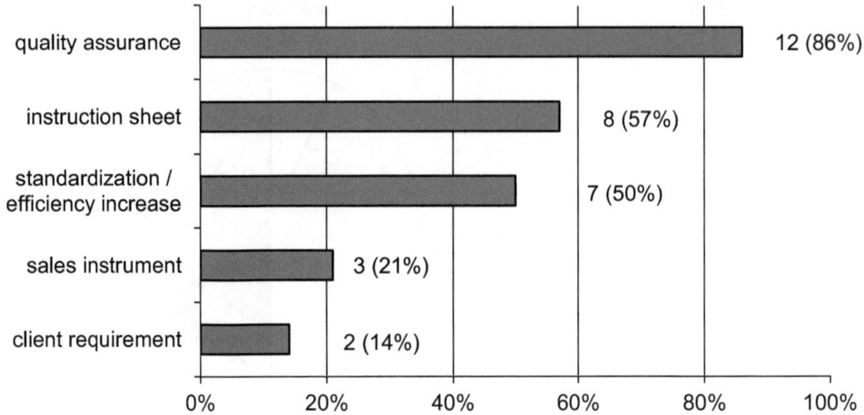

Fig. 4 Motivation for development/use of procedure models (n = 14, multiple answers)

The second most common motive for the development and use of procedure models is their outstanding suitability to serve as an instruction sheet to junior consultants. When all the consultants are familiar with the method to be used, a mutual foundation will considerably facilitate the communication. A uniform basis of understanding with regard to the course of the project is also a critical success factor for the cooperation with the client's employees. A further advantage is seen in the fact that a simple and dynamic team composition is made possible. Since all consultants work according to the same model, new consultants can be called in to the project at any time without having to coordinate subjective working methods and without the need for long team-building phases. This aspect plays an important role, especially for international consulting firms, as it allows global teams to be formed. Finally, procedural models also form the basis for a uniform and high-quality internal training of the new consultants.

Also of considerable importance is the possibility to standardize consulting in terms of workflow and thus to achieve an increase in efficiency in procedure projects. For example, many procedural models include standardized templates, best practices and recommended tools to support the consultants. In spite of the necessary adaptations to the client's situation, this facilitates an accelerated and efficient project execution.

4.3 Results and Discussion on the Handling of Procedure Models

The availability of a procedure model is not a guarantee for a good consulting service. If a consultant has not internalized the method and does not use this method in the project, even the best model will have no added value. The way the company culture is rooted as well as various aspects of the handling of the method in consulting practice will have an influence on the success of a procedure model.

4.3.1 Voluntary or Mandatory Use of the Models

With regard to the voluntary nature of the model application in projects, the survey showed the following picture. In nine of the questioned companies (64%) the application of procedure models is mandatory, in the remaining five companies (36%) one relies on the voluntary use of models by the consultant. Larger companies require the use of their own procedure models rather than smaller companies do (cf. Fig. 5).

The application mandate should not be misunderstood as an 'unconditional constraint'. The consultant is indeed basically encouraged to keep to the given project procedures. On the one hand though, the concrete procedures in the project are always adapted to the actual situation of the client. This can, for example, mean that the procedure model is not completely used. On the other hand, many client companies have their own procedure models, which have to be used by the consultants. In such cases, one tries to adapt the model of the consulting provider or use it complemental.

4.3.2 Documentation of the Procedure Models

Altogether the models in nine of the questioned consulting firms are completely documented and thus explicated. It can be recognized from Fig. 6 that invariably this kind of documentation prevails in all large consultancies. The models are stored in a database or in the intranet, for example, and can be viewed by any consultant and downloaded to their own PC if required. In many cases, the method is also stored

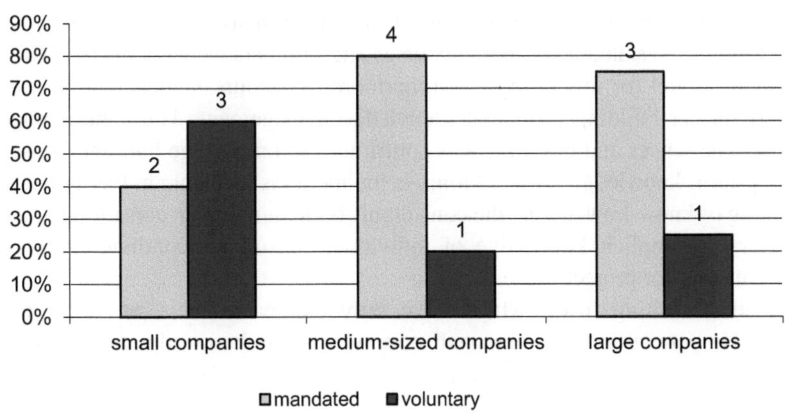

Fig. 5 Voluntary or mandatory use of the procedure models (n = 14)

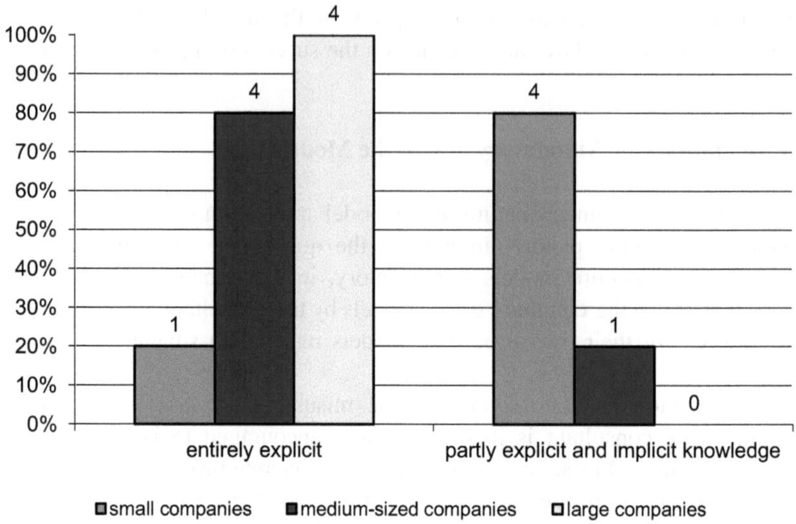

Fig. 6 Documentation of the companies' own procedure models (n = 14)

with templates, best practices and project reports. In five of the consultancies surveyed—mainly small companies—the procedural models were only partly explicated. The forms of this documentation vary from a rough manual, to templates for work results, written project reports in a database, supporting slides, or the presentation of the model on the company website. The main reason for this lower degree of explication in small consulting firms is to be seen in the fact that the consultants there do not actually need any written account due to the in-house development of the model and their own practical project experience. Actual documentation is then carried out for marketing purposes, for example.

The participants, which have fully documented their procedure models in writing, also use them in the sense of knowledge transfer for the initial or further training of the consultants. Five interviewees (two from medium-sized and three from large consulting firms) stated that training courses and seminars were conducted using the procedure model for this purpose. Furthermore, procedure models can be used to support further building blocks of knowledge management. Thus, the storage of project experiences and best practices contributes to knowledge building as well as for long-term knowledge preservation. As the model is available in the intranet, the spreading of know-how among the consultants is encouraged. In consulting practice, however, the implicit knowledge of individual consultants continues to play an important role for project success.

Those consulting firms, which have only explicated their procedure model partially, in general follow a personalization strategy in knowledge management.

4.3.3 Evaluation and Further Development of Procedure Models

Another important aspect of long-term quality assurance is the evaluation of the procedure carried out at the end of each project and the regular further development of the entire model. The clear majority of the consulting firms surveyed (79%) carry out an evaluation of the approach at the end of each project implementation (cf. Fig. 7). The names of this activity vary from 'closing balance', 'final-meeting' and 'de-briefing' to 'lessons learned' or 'feedback', up to 'touch down'. The project key figures, such as adherence to deadlines and costs, are checked in order to draw conclusions about the suitability of the procedure model.

Besides this quantitative control, the positive and negative incidents are collected in the context of a content-related examination of the experiences during the project flow. By means of these qualitative evaluations, deficits within the procedure model can be identified. Furthermore, two consulting providers measure the client's satisfaction by means of questionnaires, or a survey. From this external view additional stimuli can occur.

Though, especially smaller consulting houses do not always conduct explicit evaluations after ending a project, all the interviewees stated that their procedure models are consistently developed further. Usually the rough scheme of the phases is hardly changed in any way. The further development rather refers to details such as updating of best practices, standardization of templates or the improvement of individual methods and tools. The basis of these measures are usually experiences gained from projects. In a large international consulting firm, every employee can participate in collecting ideas (so called brainstorming) and in voting for improvement proposals in the intranet. Furthermore, all the consultants and the people responsible for the methods use scientific literature, publications in magazines or seminar presentations to develop their models further.

4.3.4 Relevance of the Procedure Models for Project Acquisition

With the exception of one self-employed consultant, all the participants stated that the clients approached them about their procedure model during the acquisition phase. The graphical illustration of the answers in Fig. 8 shows, however, that the assessment regarding the eventual relevance in connection with the selection decision for a consulting offer can turn out to be very different. The size of the company is not a relevant factor here.

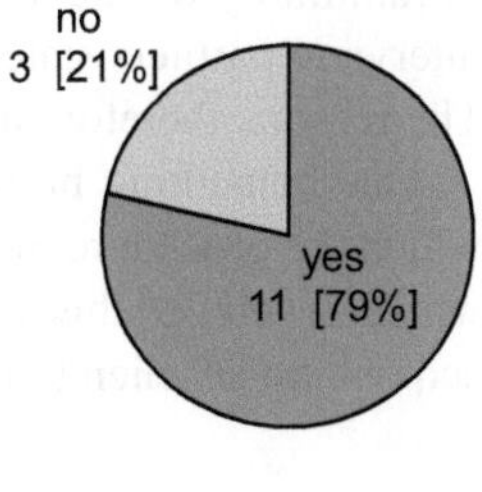

Fig. 7 Regular practical evaluation of procedure models (n = 14)

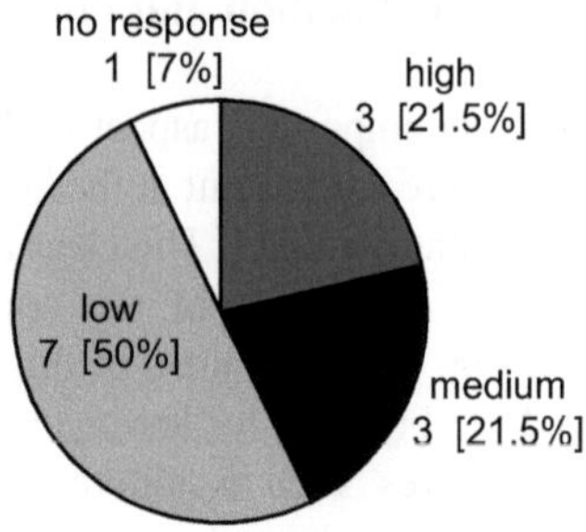

Fig. 8 Relevance of the procedure models for the acquisition (n = 14)

Many clients consider procedure models as the fundamental hand tool used by the consultants. They only form the basis for good consulting services and do not present a unique characteristic. One interview partner even had the opinion that procedure models are overrated as they finally only conform with a generic procedure, despite their very detailed description in some ways. Many of the interviewees agreed that experience, client references, the price, as well as the reputation of the consulting provider are more important criteria for choosing a particular consultancy.

Three participants, however, assigned a high value to procedure models in the context of the acquisition of projects. For reasons of investment- and process security the clients explicitly demand a structured and comprehensive way of working. Concerning this matter, a consultant of a large company reported that the model was a crucial decision criterion in numerous projects. Another interview partner, also from a large consulting reckoned: "In the case of larger projects, it is almost a disqualifier if one does not work with a standardized method". A self-employed consultant was also committed a number of times because of his procedure model, and confirmed a high relevance of the model from both the perspective of the clients as well as from his own perspective. After all, a successful procedure model contributes to the long-period enhancement of the firm's reputation, which again has a positive influence on the client's decision.

4.3.5 Publication of the Models

The publication of one's own procedure model in magazine- and book articles, on one's own web page, or in flyers for the clients, could basically promote the acquisition of projects, as the consulting quality can be presented and the degree of familiarity of one's own company can be enhanced. However, nine (64%) of our interview partners stated that their procedure models are not published (cf. Fig. 9). The reasons therefore are indeed very diverse.

One consulting house abstains from publications, because the public standard, which the procedure model follows, has already been published by the organization, which developed this standard. Other participants did not see any added value for the acquisition of clients in a publication. Finally, the protection of one's own know-

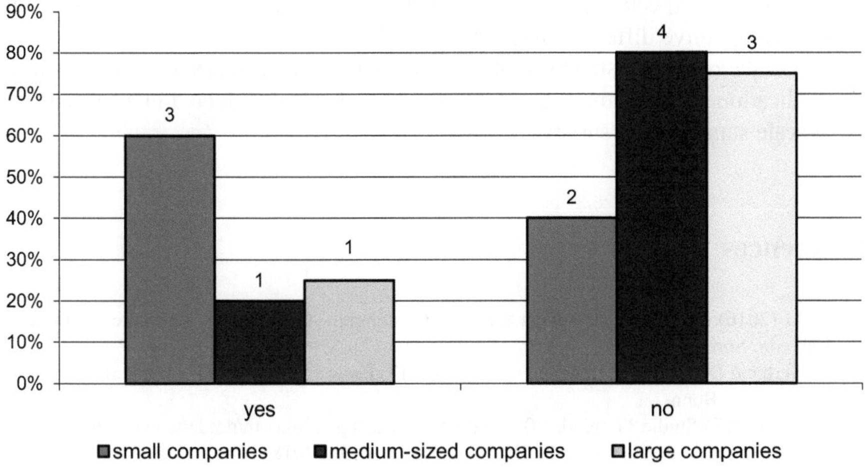

Fig. 9 Publication of the procedure models (n = 14)

how and experience, which went into the procedure model, is frequently a reason why the model is not published. Specifically, the best practices, templates or individual parts of the model are assessed as competitive advantages and should be kept secret to competitors.

The medium-sized and large IT consulting providers follow a more restrictive communication policy regarding their procedure models than the small ones do. One reason for this could be that it is more difficult for small companies to establish new contacts with potential clients from the outset and publishing their procedural models offers an additional opportunity.

5 Conclusions

The study presented here shows that for the two classic IT consulting fields of the selection and implementation of business software, a predominantly long-standing use of procedural models in consulting practice has already been demonstrated. These models derive largely from the consulting firms' own project experience, often drawing on input from external sources such as industry standards and literature. Quality and efficiency targets are the dominant reasons for a model development.

With regard to model handling, it should be noted that especially larger companies are pushing strongly for the application of models in projects, explicating them completely internally but not externally and then using them extensively within the framework of knowledge management. The models have rarely been part of a formal certification process, but they are regularly evaluated and further developed internally. Their relevance for project acquisition is generally considered to be moderate, as they meet the expectations of clients with regard to professional advice rather than being a competitive differentiating factor.

Due to the relatively small sample examined here, the results should be seen as a first indication of the status quo, which should be further evaluated in a subsequent large-scale standardized survey.

References

Bruhn M (2016) Qualitätsmanagement für Dienstleistungen—Grundlagen, Konzepte, Methoden, 10th edn. Springer, Berlin

Bundesverband Deutscher Unternehmensberater (2017) Facts and Figures zum Beratermarkt 2016. Marktstudie, Bonn

Capgemini (2017) Studie IT-trends 2017. https://www.capgemini.com/de-de/wp-content/uploads/sites/5/2017/02/it-trends-studie-2017.pdf. Accessed 30 Jan 2018

Gabriel H, Lohnert S (2001) Implementierung von Standardsoftware-Lösungen. In: Scheer A-W, Köppen A (eds) Consulting—Wissen für die Strategie-, Prozess- und IT-Beratung, 2nd edn. Springer, Berlin, pp 181–210

Heinrich L, Heinzl A, Roithmayr F (2004) Wirtschaftsinformatik-Lexikon, 7th edn. Oldenbourg, München

Maister DH (2003) Managing the professional service firm. Schuster and Schuster, London

Mayer HO (2012) Interview und schriftliche Befragung—Entwicklung, Durchführung und Auswertung, 6th edn. Oldenbourg, München

Mieschke L (2004) Strategisches Geschäftsmodell der Informationstechnologieberatung. DUV, Wiesbaden

Nissen V (2010) Entstehung und Handhabung von Vorgehensmodellen zur Software-Auswahl und Software-Einführung in der IT Beratung. In: Schumann M, Kolbe LM, Breitner MH, Frerichs A (eds) Proceedings MKWI 2010. Universitätsverlag Göttingen, pp 595–610 (CD)

Nissen V, Kinne S (2008) IT und Strategieberatung—eine Gegenüberstellung. In: Loos P, Breitner, M, Deelmann, T (eds) Proceedings „IT-Beratung“ of MKWI 2008. Logos, Berlin, pp 89–106

Nissen V, Simon C (2009) Kernaufgaben und Vorgehensmodelle in der IT Beratung. TU Ilmenau, Chair of Information Systems Engineering in Services. Research reports on consulting 2009–02

Stahlknecht P, Hasenkamp U (2004) Einführung in die Wirtschaftsinformatik, 11th edn. Springer, Berlin

Volker Nissen holds the Chair of Information Systems Engineering in Services at Technische Universität Ilmenau, Germany, since 2005. Prior to this, he pursued a consulting career, including positions as manager at IDS Scheer AG, director at DHC GmbH, and CEO of NISSCON Ltd., Germany. In 1994 he received a PhD degree in Economic Sciences with distinction from the University of Goettingen, Germany. His current research interests include the digital transformation of the consulting industry, the management of IT-agility, metaheuristic optimization, and process acceptance research. He is author and editor of 20 books and some 200 other publications, including papers in Business and Information Systems Engineering, Information Systems Frontiers, IEEE Transactions on EC, IEEE Transactions on NN, OR Spectrum, and Annals of OR.

How to Design, Implement, and Manage Accepted Business Processes

Volker Nissen and Thomas Müllerleile

Abstract Business process related consulting accounts for a substantial part of the total consulting turnover. However, the positive results that are frequently associated with business process management can only be achieved through triggering of the process by its users and the correct execution by the process operators. Unfortunately, business scandals in various domains have shown that people sometimes do not execute their processes according to given standards or do not use existing processes at all. This failure in process execution can lead not only to suboptimal performance but also to life threatening disasters. By circumvention of official channels, individuals within the company create shadow organizations. Thus, unofficial processes and shadow IT systems emerge, which run alongside the official organization. This in turn has several disadvantages, among others increased complexity and lack of transparency, compliance risks and higher costs. It is, therefore, of crucial importance for clients and consultants alike to understand, why people accept or dismiss official business processes. This contribution proposes a theoretically as well as empirically founded model to explain why some processes are practiced, and others not. Thus, when designing or implementing process changes in the course of consulting projects, these results offer guidance and support for consultants as well as clients.

1 Introduction and Motivation

Consultants are often hired for tasks of business process design, optimization, standardization or harmonization. In fact, organizational consulting, which includes these topics amongst others, recently accounted for 43.5% of the total consulting

V. Nissen (✉)
Economic Sciences and Media, Ilmenau University of Technology, Ilmenau, Germany
e-mail: volker.nissen@tu-ilmenau.de

T. Müllerleile
Technische Universität Ilmenau, Ilmenau, Germany
e-mail: thomas.muellerleile@tu-ilmenau.de

V. Nissen (ed.), *Advances in Consulting Research*, Contributions to Management Science, https://doi.org/10.1007/978-3-319-95999-3_7

turnover in the German market, with an annual growth rate of 7.5% (BDU 2017). But what makes a successful business process?

Business processes are designed as a blueprint for delivering services or the production of goods. Business Process Management (BPM) and process optimization are a way for many companies to master the current economic challenges. Process innovations, the exploitation of cost reduction potentials and increasing customer satisfaction are common goals. However, these positive effects can only occur if the corresponding processes are accepted, lived and implemented correctly.

Unfortunately, in operational practice, process design is often not geared to the needs of the process participants. As a result, those affected experience a certain degree of frustration when initiating or carrying out the process. The trouble may be so great that the process is not (again) triggered. Alternatively, the execution of a process is changed or completely bypassed. Such behaviour can have serious consequences, as demonstrated by the extreme case of the Tokai-Mura nuclear accident due to an unauthorised deviation in the filling process of the reactor (IAEA 1999). Workarounds (Alter 2014) are thus created in day-to-day operations. Shadow organizations and shadow IT (Behrens 2009) can develop. This counteracts efforts in the areas of quality management and governance, risk and compliance (GRC). From a business informatics perspective, these developments hamper data consistency and create unnecessary organizational overhead.

Unaccepted processes are a risk for organizations. Thus, Frei et al. (1999) identified three negative effects in the banking sector that were caused by process deviations. These include a decline in customer satisfaction, a poorer image and more complaints. Tsikriktsis and Heineke (2004) show empirically for the aviation industry that process deviations correlate negatively with customer satisfaction. Bendoly and Cotteleer (2008) attribute process deviations to an insufficient and unsuitable IT infrastructure. Conversely, Markus and Keil (1994) argue that the non-use of IT systems is due to inadequate process design. Ultimately, the task is to design accepted processes underpinned by efficient IT systems. In practice, often consultants are hired to support the design and optimization of business processes, or help implementing associated ERP-systems.

It can be argued that wherever process deviance occurs, the process in its current form is not technically feasible or not accepted by its stakeholders. In general, the value delivered by a business process depends on the social interaction patterns of its members. This indicates that business processes possess inherent social properties that should be taken into account when processes are designed and implemented in organizations (Müllerleile and Nissen 2014). Given these circumstances, it is of particular interest to consultants and clients alike, to understand why process deviance occurs.

In designing and optimizing processes in organizations often the topics effectiveness and efficiency are in focus. Insufficient attention is given to the person who ultimately performs these processes. Process acceptance research addresses this issue by taking into account social aspects of process execution and investigates what the acceptance of business processes generally depends upon. As a result the foundations of a process acceptance theory have been developed on an empirical basis (Müllerleile and Nissen 2014; Müllerleile et al. 2015; Nissen et al. 2016; Ritter et al. 2016; Nissen and Müllerleile 2017). In particular, factors influencing process acceptance were identified. These results are potentially very useful to create the right conditions for correct process execution in business. The remainder of this paper describes such foundations of a model of process acceptance.

2 Basic Terms and Related Work

2.1 Business Processes

According to Becker et al. (2012) a process is a completely closed, temporal and logical sequence of activities which are required to work on a process-oriented business object. A business process is a special process that is directed by the business objectives of a company and by the business environment. It should be noted, however, that here a quite mechanistic view is taken, where a process converts inputs by transformation steps into outputs. Although such a process definition allows the development of appropriate modeling notations, the process is perceived primarily as a technical problem, with organizational and social dimensions being subordinate. We will argue in our paper that this is a too restricted perspective. Moreover, too little attention is paid to the fact that operational processes are subject to change.

Melao and Pidd (2000) extend the process concept by adding a social dimension and view it as complex, dynamic systems. This implies that processes interact with the external world and are therefore subjected to social and technical interferences. Inversely, as social constructs, properties can be assigned to business processes. Thus, business processes implement a normative statement for their stakeholders. The inherent social properties, which are assigned by subjects, exposed to the process, result directly from process design.

Processes are carried out by individuals who have different goals, values and expectations. It follows that individuals, based on their experiences and perceptions, construct and interpret processes differently. As a result, the same process is perceived differently by different participants.

2.2 Acceptance and Process Acceptance

Acceptance is always an issue where normative statements, e.g. social or legal norms, are implemented, and is therefore discussed at great length in the context of philosophy and the social sciences. Acceptance, in general, expresses that something or someone, or a behaviour, was, is, or can be approved by another person. Acceptance can be partitioned into three different dimensions. These dimensions are the acceptance subject, which constructs the acceptance, the object to be accepted, and the context in which the acceptance takes place (Lucke 1995). These dimensions can be further explicated. The subject exhibits, based on its value system, a general potential for accepting something. The object to be accepted, therefore, has to possess certain acceptability in the context of the value system of the subject. For example, consuming meat, as an acceptance object would not incorporate a general acceptability for a vegetarian, the acceptance subject.

It follows that acceptance is no inherent property of an object that has a timeless validity. Rather acceptance is actively constructed within this field of tension as a result of a mutual process by the involved parties and represents the result of an act of rational insight and inner conviction (Lucke 1995).

Process acceptance is defined here as an attitude of a process stakeholder towards a process. This attitude results in acknowledging and approving the process as designed, which in turn leads to a process conformal behaviour. A lack of process acceptance may lead to process deviance. If process acceptance is missing, process stakeholders may not trigger, be inclined to change, or circumvent the process. While these deviations from the official process may be positive, neutral, or negative in their overall effect, a deviation will always work against standardization efforts. Thus, it can be stipulated that if process acceptance is missing, this can be considered a negative interference variable for executing the process.

2.3 Concepts Related to Process Acceptance Research

One approach to identify process deviance is to employ process mining, or, more specifically, conformance checking (Rozinat and van der Aalst 2008). This technique allows for comparing the existing process model with the event log of the same process in the supporting information systems. If there is an event log available for the process under analysis, it can be used to reveal what the process deviance consists in. A further development are deviance mining methods (Nguyen et al. 2014), which can distinguish between normal and deviant process runs by identifying and classifying process patterns (e.g. step X occurs before step Y).

This technology is particularly useful if process logs are available to generate valuable insights on how process deviance occurs. However, reasons leading to the deviation may require a social understanding of the events, which may not necessarily be accessible by algorithms. Also, process mining may only be applied to logs of previously executed and recorded processes. If a process lacks acceptance among its stakeholders, it is unlikely that the process is triggered at all. Therefore, no information can be recorded in process logs. Additionally, not all processes generate process log data. Reasons might include that the underlying information system does not generate log data or that processes include tasks, which cannot be mapped to an underlying information system. This is especially true for processes in the service industry, where customer interaction is often personal.

In general, the value delivered by a business process depends on the social interaction patterns of its stakeholding subjects. Subject-oriented business process management (S-BPM) focuses on subjects, which are responsible for any process variance and their collaboration via structured communication in business processes

(Fleischmann et al. 2012). The subject-oriented approach to business process management as a new field of BPM study underlines the importance of behavioristic aspects as compared to only functional ones. The key difference of methods and tools of this approach is that they are oriented towards end users and create business applications based on the developed model. The S-BPM concept allows modeling and analyzing a business process, and immediately executing it in a form convenient for the end users.

While the mentioned concepts help to better understand *where* people deviate from predefined processes (process mining), respectively support looking at business processes from the viewpoint of their end users (S-BPM), it appears fair to state that a true understanding of the factors influencing process acceptance and process deviance have not been achieved with either of these techniques.

Empirical research on software process improvement (SPI) adoption yielded several critical success factors (Niazi et al. 2006). These include top management support, training, awareness, and the allocation of resources. Also, possible demotivational factors were identified by Baddoo and Hall (2003), including a lack of feedback, high workloads, time pressure constraints, and cumbersome processes.

In BPM, literature on the social aspects of processes remains scarce. A notable exception is research presented by Antunes and da Cunha (2013). They transfer the results of research on SPI problems to the field of business process management. Four dimensions are evaluated (Motivation, Understanding, Value, and Effort) to understand why people ignore processes or see them as a burden. Antunes and Cunha propose a model, based on a questionnaire, to identify pain points in business processes. However, they only present results from two case studies and acknowledge the scarce literature available. Possible other influential factors are not discussed.

The field of Information Systems (IS) is heavily influenced by acceptance research. Especially the Technology Acceptance Model (TAM) (Davis 1989) and its successors, such as the model by Venkatesh and Bala (2008), which try to give an explanation on why some technologies are accepted while others are not, has had a profound impact on the whole IS field. However, the TAM and similar models have drawn much critique regarding their relevance and usefulness for future technology or system design (Bagozzi 2007). In process modelling, acceptance has not yet been discussed at length.

Complementing TAM research in IS, concepts from marketing or service management may be applied. Processes deliver services to customers, therefore, research on SERVQUAL (Parasuraman et al. 1988) and other measurement systems on service quality may be relevant to research. The five dimensions of SERVQUAL (reliability, assurance, tangibles, empathy and responsiveness) cannot be transferred completely to BPM, because they emphasize the personal traits of the employee who delivers the service. However, some properties, such as reliability and responsiveness, can be understood as process traits.

3 Foundations of a Theory of Process Acceptance

3.1 Research Goal

The goal of our research is to develop a theory of process acceptance, and thus attempt to propose an independent theory in a defined area of business informatics or process management. This is to be based on the guidelines of Gadenne (1999) for the development of theory. Based on the question of why processes are not accepted, nomological hypotheses that can be bundled in one theory are to be made explicit. This results in an intersubjective verifiability and possible conditions of falsification. For the construction of this theory empirical quantitative (experiments) as well as design oriented methods (artifact creation) are used.

3.2 Theoretical Starting Point

Already in the 1980s, Ajzen (1985) provided a general explanation for human behaviour with his theory of planned behaviour. This theory, as well as a detailed literature analysis on the subject of process deviations, serves as a basis for us to develop a theory of process acceptance. Figure 1 adapts core thoughts of Ajzen's theory to the case considered here of the correct execution of a defined process.

The behavior of an employee regarding the execution of a process depends on his or her intention to execute the process correctly, which in turn is influenced by three determinants: the employee's attitudes to the process, the influence of the social environment and the perceived ease (possibility) to execute the process correctly. Thus, employees have the intention to carry out processes correctly when they have a positive attitude towards this process, when they feel social pressure from other people to do so and when they believe they can carry out the process. From the intention to execute a process correctly, a corresponding behavior will occur if the

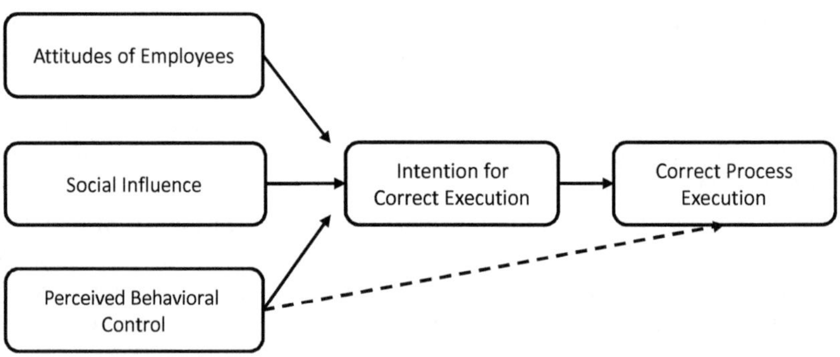

Fig. 1 Adaptation of core aspects of the theory of planned behaviour (Ajzen 1985) on the correct execution of processes

person sees good opportunities of performing what is visualized in Fig. 1 by the dashed line.

First of all, the behavior during the process execution depends on the employee's attitudes (Ritter et al. 2016). These in turn depend, among other things, on the possible consequences of one's own behaviour. As an example, let us consider that an employee should trigger an internal purchase order for a material in a process using an IT system. The official delivery time is two working days. Unofficially, the employee also has the possibility to call his colleagues and place the order without an IT system. In this case the delivery time is two hours. The consequence of this unofficial process is assessed more positively because of the shorter waiting time, which means that attitudes towards the official process are more negative. The setting also depends on the process culture. A culture characterised by openness, trust, clear goals and comprehensible interrelationships supports the positive attitude of employees to a defined process. If the employee is aware of the interrelationships, i.e. the effect his behaviour has on the company, other departments or employees, there is no tendency to deviate from the process. The benefits of the official process tend to be recognised.

The employee is also subject to social influence by managers and colleagues. If the managers are accepted and their expectations in dealing with processes are clear, this tends to lead to a correct process execution. If all other colleagues adhere to the process, a subjectively felt pressure arises to carry out this process correctly.

However, even if the employee's attitude towards the process is positive and the social impact is conducive to correct execution, there can still be deviations in the process execution. Employees must also be able to perform this process correctly. If the process has only arisen in theory and cannot be put into practice, the official process cannot be lived. The same applies if necessary information or other resources for execution are missing. If the employee in the example above has no time to wait two days for an order, he or she will try to circumvent the process. In the same way, it is necessary that the process participants have the appropriate skills and abilities to carry out the process. If this is not the case, for example due to lack of training, the process is tended to be circumvented.

The theory of Ajzen's planned behavior provides a first indication of why employees behave differently in processes than they should. On the other hand, this theory is very general and limited in its significance in the specific context of process acceptance. It is therefore necessary to investigate in more detail which influencing factors are effective in business processes (Müllerleile et al. 2015).

3.3 Method and Data

3.3.1 Expert Interviews

To address our research question, a series of 21 semi-structured interviews were conducted at two sites of a major automotive supplier. This form of interview is well suited for exploratory research (Kramp 2004). Literature recommendations for guidelines and interview execution were followed (Helfferich 2009). The guide addresses aspects of process design, implementation and questions about the daily routine of process execution. It was validated in a pre-test by two scientists with four test persons. This included the question of whether process-differentiated behaviour would be played down by respondents for reasons of social desirability. This assumption was not confirmed neither in the pre-test nor in the interviews. Interestingly, the opposite was observed. The importance of the research question was underlined by the great interest of the interview partners, who were very pleased to be able to report on process problems.

The interviews were conducted for several processes and at different hierarchy levels. Thus, statements about entire processes, from beginning to end, could be made and analyzed from different perspectives. After a rough process description had been worked out with the interviewee, the process was discussed in detail and special features and process deviations were discussed. Care was taken not to influence the interlocutor in the answers, rather the interviewee was encouraged to describe freely.

The sample of respondents was built up step by step according to the snowball principle (Biernacki and Waldorf 1981). Care was taken to select only those conversation partners who were well integrated into their respective processes. The 21 respondents all come from the same company in the automotive industry, but from two different plants and different areas (production planning, production, logistics, services, accounting). Both process managers and process executors were included in the sample. Some of the respondents had a commercial and some a technical background. All talks were personally held between March and August 2014. They lasted between 45 and 90 min. The interviews were recorded, then transcribed and analyzed in detail.

3.3.2 Data Analysis

The data analysis after the transcription of the interviews took place in two steps. First, the text was annotated with Open Coding. In a few words, these codes represent the central statement of a text passage (Corbin and Strauss 1990). Codes from previously edited interviews should be reused in later texts of the same research context (Hruschka et al. 2004). A common codebook was used to increase intercoder reliability.

In the first step, the analysis of the interviews resulted in 364 codes, which were supplemented by memos to provide further information on the context and meaning of a code. Memos can also contain initial considerations on the formulation of hypotheses. 230 memos were added to the codes in our case. In the second step, all codes were combined and grouped into categories. The result is a code hierarchy of categories and sub-categories. Finally, these categories were annotated with properties resulting from the underlying codes.

Further insights could be gained from the subsequent axial coding. The codes that have already been identified are regrouped by drawing links between categories and sub-categories (Strauss and Corbin 1990). In this way, it is possible to identify relationships that affect the phenomenon under investigation. The coding recommendations of Strauss (1987) were followed. The Open and Axial Coding resulted in the following factors of process acceptance. These will later be used as treatment variables in experiments on process acceptance.

3.4 Results

3.4.1 Overall Model Structure

The evaluations provided an overall structure for the process acceptance phenomenon, with which the identified influencing factors of the process acceptance can be brought into a logical structure. In addition, the interviews revealed that process deviations are a common phenomenon in the context under consideration. Reasons can be divided into four categories, two of which (design, implementation) can be attributed to process preparation and another two (execution, controlling and change) to process execution (see Fig. 2). The factors in each category were further structured according to the respective acceptance dimension: subject (process participants or stakeholder groups), object (process) and context (organization, business process environment). In the following, the respective acceptance factors are discussed in these three dimensions.

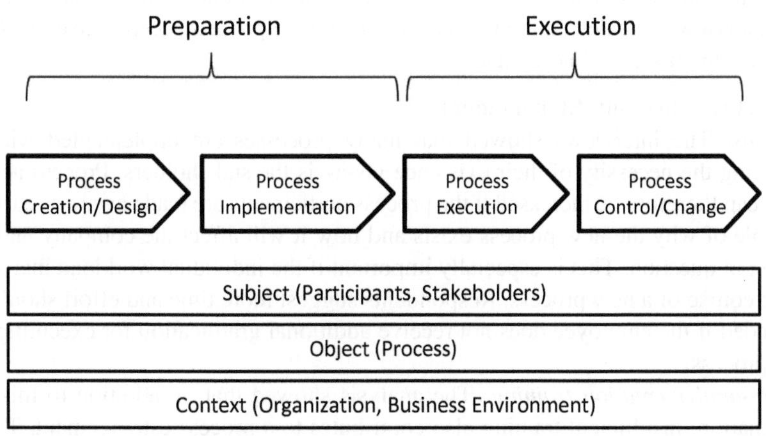

Fig. 2 Overall structure of process acceptance

3.4.2 Process Creation/Design

The process design encompasses all the steps necessary to create a process. This includes the acquisition of information about the process to be designed, e.g. through interviews, and its modeling with relevant modelling techniques. For this category, the data analysis provided only influencing factors of process acceptance in the subject's area.

Subject (Participant, Stakeholder)
Stakeholder involvement: The results underline the importance of integrating future process participants into the process design. However, this will not always be possible. Nevertheless, respondents stressed that all stakeholders of the process in question (including process customers) should be integrated into this phase. In this way, an exchange of experience is initiated and diverse perspectives are included. In addition, employees accept a self-designed process more easily than one from above. This is all the more so if other employees at the same hierarchy level are also included.

Dissemination of involvement: Process acceptance increases when employees know that other employees (in particular, employees at the same hierarchy level) were involved in the process design.

3.4.3 Process Implementation

This phase concerns all activities related to the actual implementation of the business process in its functional environment. This also includes the training of employees and communicative activities to make the new process known to all stakeholders. The interviews revealed that the influencing factors of process acceptance come from all three dimensions of acceptance.

Subject (Participant, Stakeholder)
Reasons: The interviews showed that many processes are implemented without justifying the necessity of their existence vis-à-vis the stakeholders. Process acceptance can therefore be increased if the process participants are made aware as early as possible of why the new process exists and how it will affect the company and the person in question. This is especially important if the individual workload increases in the course of a new process. Respondents suggest more time and effort should be expended if the employee does not receive additional gratification for executing the new process.

Pre-implementation training: The analysis showed that, in addition to missing information, insufficient training also contributes to a process estrangement. Training courses facilitate the transition to new processes, which can also be supported by the early distribution of information on new processes.

Peer group involvement: If a peer group as a whole is subject to executing a new process, process acceptance is larger than when individuals are singled out. Further increases in process acceptance may be achieved, if members of the group are included in the process creation. Additionally, a short social distance between members of the peer group may further increase process acceptance.

Process guide: Targeted and personal instructions on the new process (process guidance) can have a positive effect on the level of process acceptance. Such a guide should be involved in the process itself and preferably originate from the same hierarchy level.

Object (Process)

Transparency: Almost all interview partners expressed the desire to be informed about all details of a process, such as the process model or the process description. Great importance is attached to process instructions and clear communication regarding responsibilities.

Structure: A well-structured and/or less complex process leads to greater process acceptance. An increase in complexity from the perspective of a process participant is easier to accept if the complexity for another process participant decreases more than proportionately.

Context (Organization, Business Environment)

Implementation strategy: The analysis showed that a step-by-step introduction leads to more acceptance, as the employees can become better acquainted with the new process. This is all the more true the greater the workload for the individual increases as a result of the process.

Implementation context: Processes introduced in a comparatively chaotic context suffer from low acceptance. For example, hasty and forced process implementations have a negative effect.

Information strategy: The way in which the stakeholders of a process are informed about changes has a clear impact on process acceptance. Process participants appreciate it when information is communicated early, personally and officially.

3.4.4 Process Execution

The analysis again showed that all three dimensions of acceptance are significant at this stage, as is outlined below.

Subject (Participant, Stakeholder)

Interdependence/number of process participants: The involvement of several people creates dependencies between the individual actors of a business process. The more participants, the more interfaces there are and the more information has to be exchanged. The absence or non-availability of individual participants can have a negative effect on the activities of other actors, e.g. by creating idle times. The interviewees regarded idle times as negative. Since a large number of process participants and/or dependencies increase the probability of process interruptions, process acceptance decreases in this case.

Effects of the hierarchy: Respondents pointed out that working with hierarchically higher ranking persons is a mental burden. Therefore, a process in which many different hierarchy levels interact with each other tends not to be well accepted.

Number of organizational units involved: The interview participants stated that different organizational units often follow different goals. Therefore, when members from different business units carry out a process cooperatively, they are influenced by these different target systems in their actions. This can lead to conflicts of interest, which in turn have a negative effect on process acceptance.

Responsibility: Process acceptance is negatively influenced, if organizational units interfere with the process. A shared process may lack clear responsibilities. Keeping processes contained increases their internal cohesion, which will result in higher efficiency and acceptance. It makes sense to define a process expert as a contact person to other stakeholders in the process.

Communication: For respondents, personal communication between the process stakeholders is an essential enabler for process conformal behavior. Other forms of communication were classified as inefficient in this sense. Therefore, the management should carefully consider how the communication of the process participants is organized.

Object (Process)

Feedback on the process: The results show that a process is more likely to be accepted if it is designed to provide participants with feedback on the process status. Incorporating instructions as a self-help system for the process user increases the acceptance of the process further.

Failure tolerance: Process stakeholders feel more comfortable executing processes tolerant to errors and late changes. Thus, if a process implements self-healing features or fail-safe measures it is more likely to be accepted.

Task heterogeneity: Stakeholders appreciate the diversity of tasks within a process. Thus processes, which exhibit highly repetitive tasks, will be ill accepted.

Perceived process length: The interview participants expressed the desire for well-defined, manageable processes. It can therefore be assumed that comparatively short and logically structured processes meet with higher acceptance.

Standardization: Cross-departmental process standardization contributes to acceptance. However, if too many exceptions are allowed, its value as a standard is called into question and acceptance decreases.

Context (Organization, Business Environment)

Cross-process consistency: Respondents expressed their dissatisfaction with exceptions to certain processes. More generally speaking, the whole process landscape should have a certain degree of consistency. It can therefore be concluded that a process that complies with all applicable standards is better accepted.

Organizational overhead: Sometimes processes require additional organizational inputs, such as approvals or decisions, which could be formalized in the form of business rules. Processes with high organizational overhead were perceived by the respondents as cumbersome. Thus, processes, which require a low amount of input from other instances that cannot be formalized as business rules, will be more accepted.

Time and resource constraints: If a process is excessively restricted in terms of execution time or available resources (e.g. tools), this leads to dissatisfaction and resistance. This results in a desire for deviations from the specified process, such as shortcuts. Appropriate allocation of required resources and execution times therefore leads to improved process acceptance.

Bureaucracy: Respondents complained about processes where a large number of forms have to be filled in. Processes that are organized in a very bureaucratic manner and that practically do not allow for flexibility encourage process deviations and impair process acceptance.

3.4.5 Process Control/Change

The business and organizational environment in which processes take place evolves, and thus the processes themselves, are subject to the need for change. Good, systematic change management is important for process acceptance.

Subject (Participant, Stakeholder)

Stakeholder inclusion: It is easier to accept a change in an existing process if many stakeholders are involved in the change to the process.

Object (Process)

Stability/process age: Interviewees value the ability to master a process. Therefore, a long-lasting, well-established process meets with a higher acceptance of its stakeholders.

Context (Organization, Business Environment)

Ignorance of management: Not only subordinate process participants circumvent standards according to personal preferences. Management also ignores defined processes, which is often the result of conflicting goals. If these deviations become the unofficial standard, the original process flow receives less attention and its acceptance decreases.

Process maintenance: Implemented processes are easier to accept if they are 'well maintained'. This includes permanent key performance indicator measurement, control, clear responsibilities, and continuous improvement. The interviewees felt that, in the absence of such efforts, their labour would be wasted.

Table 1 summarizes the influencing factors of process acceptance identified in our study.

Table 1 Key factors for process acceptance (Müllerleile et al. 2015; Nissen et al. 2016)

Phase	Subject	Object	Context
Creation/ Design	Stakeholder involvement, dissemination of involvement		
Implementation	Explain reasons, pre-implementation training, peer group involvement, process guidance	Transparency, structure	Implementation strategy, implementation context, information strategy
Execution	Interdependence, hierarchy, no. of organizational units involved, responsibility, communication	Process feedback, failure tolerance, task heterogeneity, perceived process length, standardization	Cross process consistency, organizational overhead, time and resource constraints, bureaucracy
Control/ Change	Stakeholder inclusion	Process stability/Process age	Management ignorance/override, process maintenance

4 Discussion and Practical Implications

The results show that process acceptance is influenced by different forces and that their influence varies along the process lifecycle. First of all, acceptance is mainly determined by factors of the process subject and the process itself. Later, during process execution and maintenance, context variables become increasingly important. In general, the process implementation and the execution phase incorporate the most factors. Some factors that promote acceptance, such as the strong involvement of stakeholders in virtually all life-cycle phases, seem quite obvious. However, it should not be forgotten that even here, in practice, serious mistakes are often made. This applies in particular to the communicative tasks in BPM. Stakeholders are keen to be informed, but this communication should take place via the official channels. Unfortunately, managers often avoid direct communication with their employees, especially if unpleasant information is to be disseminated.

During the implementation and execution phases, the process properties are of great importance for process acceptance. Here, poor process design is particularly evident. The results of the interviews show that employees value processes as normative structures for their daily work routines. If this function is endangered by chaotic or inconsistent process contexts, process acceptance suffers. The establishment of a coordinated, process-oriented organizational structure is therefore of great importance.

In general, process acceptance can be improved by influencing three basic factors. These are the attitudes and behavior of the process subjects, the process properties and the properties of the process context. The first option offers potential for short term benefits, e.g. by adapting incentive systems. The second option, changing process properties, requires redesigning processes, and thus offers potential for medium term benefits. The third option, changing the organizational culture, is a strategic effort, and may only yield benefits in the long run.

Measures such as introducing real-time process feedback, reducing the number of process participants and protecting against the risk of errors in the process can increase process acceptance. These recommendations can be implemented by adding process patterns to existing processes. For example, a pattern that communicates the present state of the process to its stakeholders can improve process acceptance. Further, it is conceivable that different stakeholders receive different state information. Additionally, process simulation can help to detect unnecessary interdependencies, and fail-safe mechanisms can be implemented during the process design phase by providing additional information. These measures can be especially useful for processes, which are partially outside the organizations' scope of control, e.g. processes that include the customer.

Other findings are quite worrisome, for example a large number of interviewees deemed non personal communication ineffective to establish process conformal behavior. Here, conflicts with the realities of a networked world arise, in which it is often necessary to use telecommunications tools instead of face-to-face communication.

If the influencing factors of process acceptance determined here are not taken into account during the life-cycle of a process, non-compliant behavior of the process participants is more likely. This has negative consequences for efforts with regard to governance, risk and compliance management, because any process execution deviating from the defined standard (even if it should have a positive effect) eludes active management.

Only the correct execution of processes can guarantee their desired consequences. Deviations can have far-reaching consequences, including impairments of quality, safety and competitiveness. In the interviews, one interlocutor referred to the concrete example of the legal consequences of an ad-hoc logistics process modified by the management. This process deviation led to customs investigations because of embargo violations in foreign business. It resulted in additional work and a risk for the company which would not have occurred in the specified process.

Management should take measures to ensure or increase acceptance of relevant processes in the company. It is important here to design the incentive systems in order to influence the behaviour of employees in the direction of correct process execution (e.g. measuring quality instead of piecework). Employees should also be involved at an early stage and comprehensively in the design and implementation of processes. Another way is to change the properties of the process itself. For example, process acceptance increases when the process informs the participants of its current status. Another possibility is to change the process context. In this way, the long-term goal can be aimed at building a process-oriented corporate culture.

All in all, it is advisable to take greater account of the social aspects and thus the people who carry out processes in process design and process management, so that defined processes can be put into practice.

5 Measuring Process Acceptance: Case Study Results

The factors influencing process acceptance were developed and tested in various projects and case studies. Subsequently, the results of a case study in the field of e-mobility are briefly presented, where the process as acceptance object was in focus (Müllerleile et al. 2016). The objective of this study was twofold. On the one hand, an instrument to empirically measure process acceptance was tested in the form of a questionnaire. On the other hand, it was of particular interest to prove in practice that the change of treatment variables leads to a measurable change in process acceptance.

The application scenario was charging an electric car in two different ways, one with cable and the other one inductively without cable. These experiments took place in November 2015 in a pilot plant for e-mobility in Stuttgart, Germany. 60 subjects, an equal numbers of men and women, interested in e-mobility participated in the experiment.

In both cases, the subjects initially got into the electric car and drove 15m to the charging station. Thereafter, the participants got out and conducted the loading process according to specifications. Then they drove the car back to the starting point and got out. The first group performed at first cable-based charging and then inductive charging. The second group did exactly the opposite.

After completion of the second charging process, a questionnaire was filled in by all participants. The item content was derived from the results shown above, the influencing factors of process acceptance, and the literature on the various dimensions of acceptance (Reichwald 1978; Dethloff 2004; London 1976). The items were either associated with the affective, cognitive or conative dimension of acceptance. Therefore the measurements reflected how the subjects experienced the process, how they thought about it, and whether they were willing to carry out the respective process again.

Questionnaires were split in two groups for analysis, the first rating cable based charging, after being exposed to inductive type charging, and the other rating inductive type charging after being exposed to cable based charging. The data, resulting from this balanced, randomized design, with two independent variables on a nominal scale, was evaluated through an analysis of variance (ANOVA).

Table 2 summarizes the results. Upon first inspection, prominent outcomes include the absence of significant results for sex and the interaction effect in all three models. This means that a preference for the charging type, in any construct, is completely independent of the sex of the subject. Most striking results, and those of primary interest in this study, are that there does exist a charging type preference in all three dimensions of acceptance. P-values are smaller than 5% for the factor charging type across all three dimensions of acceptance and smaller than 1% for the cognitive and conative dimensions. This indicates that electrical vehicle users feel better (affective dimension) when charging via the inductive process, think that (cognitive dimension) the inductive process is better and have a higher intent of repeating (conative dimension) the induction based charging process.

Table 2 ANOVA-results (analysis of variance) for two charging scenarios (Müllerleile et al. 2016)

Dimension	Affective			Cognitive			Conative		
	Sum of squares	(DF)	F-stat.	Sum of squares	(DF)	F-stat.	Sum of squares	(DF)	F-stat.
Charging type	18.96	(1)	4.362*	28.17	(1)	7.668**	39.19	(1)	10.149**
Sex	1.44	(1)	0.331	0.00	(1)	0.001	1.10	(1)	0.285
Interaction	0.21	(1)	0.047	0.04	(1)	0.011	0.00	(1)	0.001
Residuals	217.39	(50)		183.66	(50)		193.04	(50)	

Significance of p-values: ** = 0.01, * = 0.05

More generally, the results of this case study show that it is possible to vary selectively treatment variables and measure the impact on process acceptance. Thus the basis is provided to use a completed process acceptance theory for providing design recommendations that will contribute to better accepted business processes in practice. However, field studies like the one described here require a high effort. Thus, a method was sought-after which would similarly allow to change treatment variables and measure the impact on process acceptance on a less difficult and expensive basis. IT-enabled experimental process research (Nissen et al. 2016) addresses this issue successfully.

6 IT-Enabled Experimental Process Research: A New Approach to Investigate Process Acceptance

An important aspect from the subject-oriented approach to business process management is to understand why subjects accept business processes and, thus, trigger and execute them, or why they dismiss and circumvent them. In a next step, it is important to clarify the effect sizes precisely. The results could be incorporated in a general, empirically validated model of process acceptance. Such an understanding would be helpful in designing processes that people accept. Basically, this can be done through explorative empirical research, as was shown above. Field studies in business organizations can be conducted, as was also done in (Müllerleile and Nissen 2014) as an example. However, such a form of study is expensive, time-consuming and there are methodical problems (Döring and Bortz 2016).

We suggest proceeding in a different way to look at the effect size and mode of action of factors influencing process acceptance, in particular by applying a quantitative IT-based lab research approach. Our methodology is based on setting up process acceptance experiments that allow for a more objective investigation at reduced time and cost, as compared to classical field studies. In lab experiments process users are subjected to processes with different parameter values derived from the identified acceptance factors. Since these processes are executed in an IT-based process engine, participants really 'experience' the process in its different facets.

Moreover, influential factors from the lab experiments can be studied in the real world later on. By using a mixed approach of quantitative and qualitative methods, and because other researchers can repeat the lab experiments more easily than field studies, the validity of the research approach as a whole is elevated (Wohlin et al. 2012).

The proposed approach relies on advantages of crowdsourcing (Howe 2006). Crowdsourcing is an interactive form of value-added services using modern information and communication technologies. Distinctive feature of crowdsourcing include the breakdown of large tasks into small parts that can be fulfilled by qualified volunteers all over the world using the internet. Generally, workers solve their tasks in short term, and either non-paid or for a low price, which can be extremely profitable or helpful for a company or initiating person. Crowdsourcing offers an interesting platform to implement subject-oriented IT-enabled experiments in process acceptance research. Currently, the only widely known platform that allows conducting such social experiments is Amazon Mechanical Turk (Kittur et al. 2008). More specifically, we suggest using the following approach for experimental IT-enabled process research (Nissen et al. 2016):

- The process experiment employs crowd workers through a crowdsourcing platform such as Amazon Mechanical Turk (AMT). Mechanical Turk supports the acquisition of volunteers and implementation of the process experiments. Basically, a large number of workers interact independently with an executable process that is implemented using BPMN[1] process models.
- Process control must be arranged by using a software application that manages the business process (workflow engine). The process models are loaded into and run in this engine.
- Through the REST[2] interface of the process engine interaction with the process is facilitated. The interaction takes place on the user's side with a web application on HTML5/AngularJS base. All components are integrated into a server application that provides the necessary infrastructure.
- Treatment variables with which the worker interact can be changed individually or together, resulting in different process variants. The acceptance for these process variants is then measured. More specifically, after the worker was exposed to a process, he fills in a questionnaire as a measurement tool. The collected data are complemented with demographic information and stored in a database for later analysis.
- The outcome can be used to determine cause-effect relationships of treatment variables and the acceptance for a given process. This in turn can be exploited in practice to design, implement and manage processes better and to adapt them in a meaningful way to the process participants and the context.
- It is intended to publish the software under an OSS license later and present it to the research community.

In Fig. 3 the abstract experimental setup is depicted.

To implement the approach non-functional and functional requirements were established, which formed the basis for developing a software prototype. The prototype conceptual model as an UML sequence diagram can be seen in Fig. 4.

Very briefly, in the experiment that tests the prototype, a picture analysis was to be performed by the participants on Amazon Mechanical Turk. This experiment was selected because it is easy to implement and therefore suitable to test the prototype. The aim of this experiment was to reveal which way is the more convenient for

[1]BPMN (Business Process Model and Notation) is a graphical representation for specifying business processes in a business process model.

[2]REST (Representational State Transfer) is an architectural pattern to interact with web services by using HTTP calls.

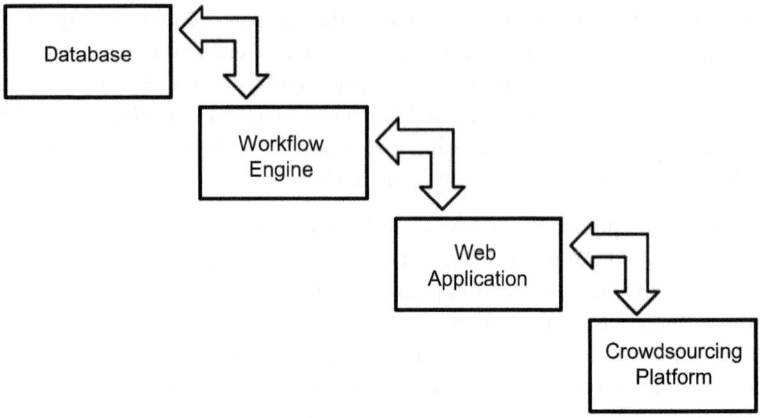

Fig. 3 Abstract model of experimental setup as interconnected IT applications (Nissen et al. 2016)

participants—answering questions about a given picture step by step or answering several questions at the same time (connected). In other words, testing two process variants similar in idea, but different in process steps.

The experiments themselves are developed as HTLM/Javascript applications. The integration with AMT is achieved by posting an ad for the experiment on the AMT workers page. If an AMT worker accepts the task, he is redirected to the experiment and the subsequent measurement instrument, which evaluates the workers process acceptance. After finishing the experiment, a token is generated which enables the AMT worker to claim the task as finished and to get paid.

The proposed process acceptance experiments rely on interacting with the process engine where the process steps are implemented. This interaction is provided by BonitaNG, a module library for AngularJS. Data from the participants of the experiment is collected using web forms while they perform the process steps. After going through the process, the data is transferred as a set of variables to the Mongo database and stored there for further analysis. More details can be found in Nissen et al. (2016).

7 Conclusions, Limitations, and Future Research

Business processes and the management thereof can create value for companies. This expected contribution of BPM may only unfold if the processes are executed as designed. A decision not to trigger the business process or to modify it during execution depends on the subject's process acceptance. It is thus self-evident that ill-accepted processes impact process governance and quality management efforts negatively.

When designing and optimizing processes in companies and other organizations, the focus is usually on effectiveness and efficiency. The human being who finally

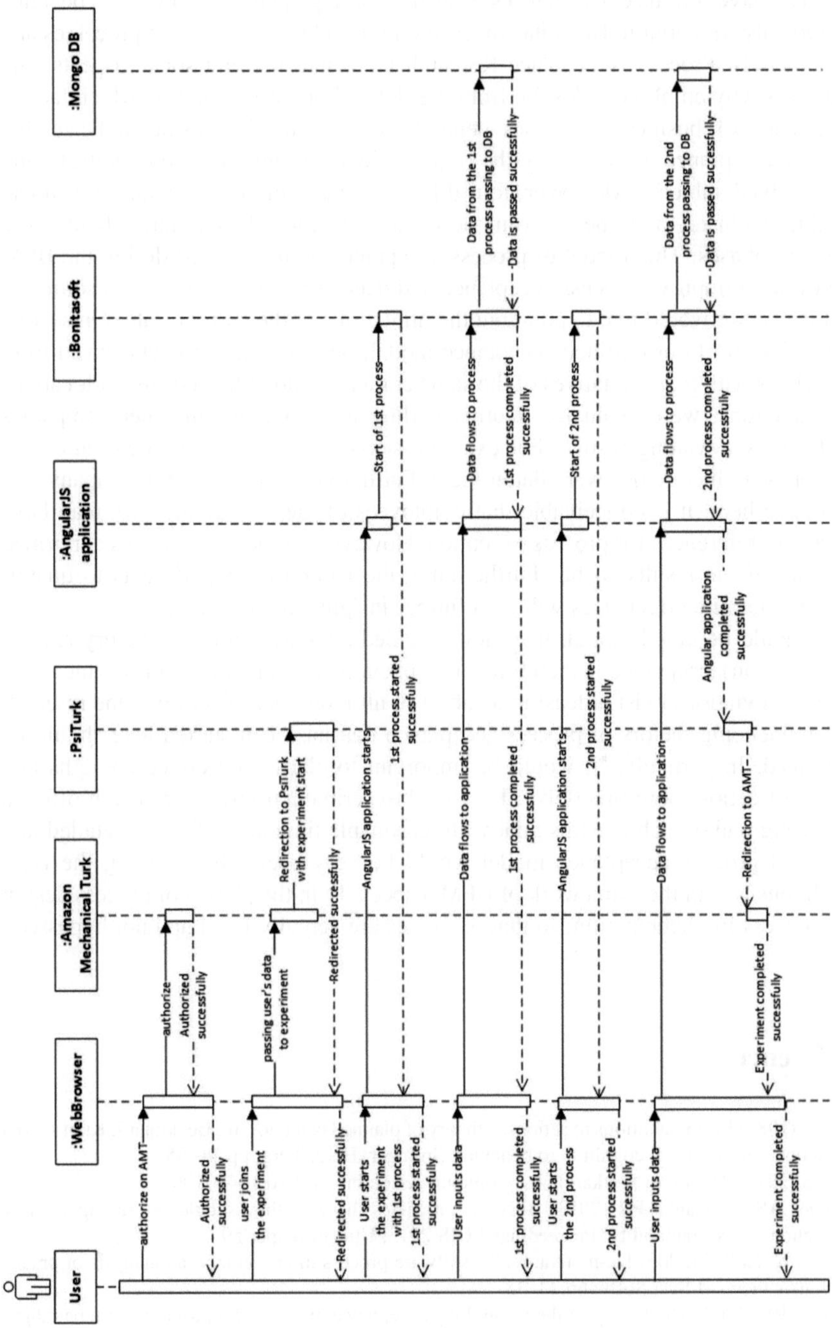

Fig. 4 Prototype conceptual model as UML sequence diagram (Nissen et al. 2016)

carries out these processes is often neglected. However, ignoring process instructions can have serious consequences in terms of safety, quality and business benefits. Historically, research in BPM has focused on the technical aspects of processes and their models. Process Acceptance Research takes into account social aspects, and addresses why employees deviate from pre-defined processes, and on which factors acceptance of business processes depends in general. Our results indicate that process acceptance is formed by the organizational context, the process itself, and the involved subjects. Moreover, four different phases in process management can be differentiated, and the relevant acceptance factors change throughout these different phases. This model of process acceptance could be used during the BPM life-cycle to improve process acceptance and decrease waste of process resources.

Finally, we would like to point out the limitations of the current state of research. In the design of our outlined acceptance model, only qualitative data derived from interviews with representatives of the same company, albeit from different locations and functions, were evaluated. Corresponding investigations in other companies could show deviating results. For example, some context effects would change if the company hierarchies were flatter there. Furthermore, an industrial company was examined here. It is conceivable that employees of the service industry may have different preferences for process execution. However, further case studies confirmed the core of the results so far. Furthermore, the laboratory experiments to quantitatively measure effect sizes will gain further insights in the future.

It should be noted that all interviews yielded similar, non-contradictory results. Process (non)acceptance is therefore a real phenomenon and problems of undesired process deviations exist at least in a subset of all industries. Therefore, the research into influencing factors of process acceptance that has been started here should be continued. In particular, it would be important to clarify the effect strengths and modes of action more precisely. IT-enabled experimental process research offers a promising path to achieve this goal with reasonable time and effort. A detailed and validated process acceptance model would be very useful for creating the right conditions within the framework of BPM, especially in the phases of process design and process implementation, so that processes are actually lived and not bypassed.

References

Ajzen I (1985) From intentions to actions: a theory of planned behavior. In: Beckman J, Kuhl J (eds) Action-control: from cognition to behavior. Springer, Heidelberg, pp 11–35

Alter S (2014) Theory of workarounds. Commun Assoc Inf Syst 10:1041–1066

Antunes AS, da Cunha PR (2013) Business processes the way they should be: tuning for low friction and sustainability. Proceedings ECIS 2013, Utrecht, Paper 59

Baddoo N, Hall T (2003) De-motivators for software process improvement: an analysis of practitioners views. J Syst Softw 66:23–33

Bagozzi RP (2007) The legacy of the technology acceptance model and a proposal for a paradigm shift. J Assoc Inf Syst 8:244–254

BDU (2017) Facts & figures zum deutschen Beratungsmarkt 2016/17. BDU e.V., Bonn

Becker J, Kugeler M, Rosemann M (2012) Prozessmanagement: Ein Leitfaden zur prozessorientierten Organisationsgestaltung, 7th edn. Gabler, Wiesbaden
Behrens S (2009) Shadow systems: the good, the bad and the ugly. Commun ACM 52:124–129
Bendoly E, Cotteleer MJ (2008) Understanding behavioral sources of process variation following enterprise system deployment. J Oper Manag 26:23–44
Biernacki P, Waldorf D (1981) Snowball sampling: problems and techniques of chain referral sampling. Sociol Methods Res 10:141–163
Corbin JM, Strauss AL (1990) Grounded theory research: procedures, canons, and evaluative criteria. Qual Sociol 13:3–21
Davis FD (1989) Perceived usefulness, perceived ease of use, and user acceptance of information technology. MIS Q 13:319–340
Dethloff C (2004) Akzeptanz und Nicht-Akzeptanz von technischen Produktinnovationen, Berlin
Döring N, Bortz J (2016) Forschungsmethoden und Evaluation für Human- und Sozialwissenschaftler, 4th edn. Springer, Berlin
Fleischmann A, Schmidt W, Stary C, Obermeier S, Brger E (2012) Subject-oriented business process management (S-BPM). Springer, Berlin
Frei FX, Kalakota R, Marx LMM (1999) Process variation as a determinant of service quality and bank performance: evidence from the retail banking study. Wharton, Working Paper, pp 97–36
Gadenne V (1999) Der kritische Rationalismus und die Rolle von Theorien in der Wirtschaftsinformatik. In: Schütte R, Siedentopf J, Zelewski S (eds) Wirtschaftsinformatik und Wissenschaftstheorie. Working Paper No. 4, PIM-Institut, Universität GH Essen, pp 5–21
Helfferich C (2009) Die Qualität qualitativer Daten. Wiesbaden
Howe J (2006) The rise of crowdsourcing. Wired Magazine, June 2006
Hruschka DJ, Schwartz D, St. John DC, Picone-Decaro E, Jenkins RA, Carey JW (2004) Reliability in coding open-ended data. Field Methods 16:307–331
International Atomic Energy Agency (1999) Report on the preliminary fact finding mission following the accident at the nuclear fuel processing facility in Tokaimura, Japan. TR, Vienna
Kittur A, Chi EH, Suh B (2008) Crowdsourcing user studies with mechanical turk. In: Proceedings of the SIGCHI conference on human factors in computing systems (CHI'08). ACM, New York, pp 453–456
Kramp M (2004) Exploring life and experience through narrative inquiry. In: de Marrais KB, Lapan SD (eds) Foundations for research: methods in education and the social sciences. Routledge, Mahwah, NJ, pp 103–121
London KR (1976) The people side of systems. New York
Lucke D (1995) Akzeptanz: Legitimität in der Abstimmungsgesellschaft. Leverkusen
Markus ML, Keil M (1994) If we build it, they will come: designing information systems that people want to use. Sloan Manag Rev 35(4):11–12
Melao N, Pidd M (2000) A conceptual framework for understanding business processes and business process modelling. Inf Syst J 10:105–129
Müllerleile T, Nissen V (2014) When processes alienate customers: towards a theory of process acceptance. In: Nonopoulos A, Schmidt W (eds) Proceedings S-BPM one. Ingolstadt, LNBIP, pp 171–180
Müllerleile T, Ritter S, Englisch L, Nissen V, Joenssen D (2015) The influence of process acceptance on BPM: an empirical investigation. Proceedings of the 2015 I.E. 17th conference on business informatics (CBI 2015), pp 125–132
Müllerleile T, Martinovic D, Joennssen D, Orner M, Grimm M, Nissen V, Reuss H-C (2016) Fully charged: process acceptance of different ev charging processes. Available at SSRN: http://ssrn.com/abstract=2834600
Nguyen H, Dumas M, La Rosa M, Maggi FM, Suriadi S (2014) Mining business processes deviance: a quest for accuracy. Proceedings of "On the move to meaningful internet systems" (OTM 2014), LNCS 8841, Berlin, pp 436–445
Niazi M, Wilson D, Zowghi D (2006) Critical success factors for software process improvement implementation: an empirical study. Softw Process Improv Pract 11:193–211

Nissen V, Müllerleile T (2017) Prozessakzeptanzforschung. Warum manche Prozesse gelebt und andere umgangen werden. In: Corsten H, Roth T (eds) Handbuch Dienstleistungsmanagement. Vahlen, München, pp 1049–1073

Nissen V, Müllerleile T, Kazakowa E, Lezina T (2016) Analyzing process acceptance with IT-enabled experimental research. Vestn Econ (3):109–129

Parasuraman A, Zeithaml VA, Berry LL (1988) SERVQUAL: a multiple-item scale for measuring consumer perceptions of service quality. J Retail 64:12–40

Reichwald R (1978) Zur Notwendigkeit der Akzeptanzforschung bei der Entwicklung neuer Systeme der Bürotechnik. Working Paper, Hochschule d. Bundeswehr, München

Ritter S, Müllerleile T, Nissen V (2016) Akzeptanz – der Schlüssel für gelebte Prozesse. Qualität und Zuverlässigkeit 61(4)

Rozinat A, van der Aalst W (2008) Conformance checking of processes based on monitoring real behavior. Inf Syst 33:64–95

Strauss LA (1987) Qualitative analysis for social scientists. Cambridge University Press, Cambridge

Strauss AL, Corbin JM (1990) Basics of qualitative research: grounded theory procedures and techniques. Sage, Newbury Park, CA

Tsikriktsis N, Heineke J (2004) The impact of process variation on customer dissatisfaction: evidence from the U.S. domestic airline industry. Decis Sci 35:129–142

Venkatesh V, Bala H (2008) Technology acceptance model 3 and a research agenda on interventions. Decis Sci 39:273–315

Wohlin C, Runeson P, Höst M, Ohlsson MC, Regnell B, Wesslén A (2012) Experimentation in software engineering. Springer, Berlin

Volker Nissen holds the Chair of Information Systems Engineering in Services at Technische Universität Ilmenau, Germany, since 2005. Prior to this, he pursued a consulting career, including positions as manager at IDS Scheer AG, director at DHC GmbH, and CEO of NISSCON Ltd, Germany. In 1994 he received a PhD degree in Economic Sciences with distinction from the University of Goettingen, Germany. His current research interests include the digital transformation of the consulting industry, the management of IT-agility, metaheuristic optimization, and process acceptance research. He is author and editor of 20 books and some 200 other publications, including papers in Business & Information Systems Engineering, Information Systems Frontiers, IEEE Transactions on EC, IEEE Transactions on NN, OR Spectrum, and Annals of OR.

Thomas Müllerleile is a research assistant at the Chair of Information Systems Engineering in Services (Prof. Dr. Volker Nissen) at the Technical University of Ilmenau. His research focuses on business process management. It examines the acceptance of business processes and the question of why business processes fail.

An Empirical Study on the Work-Life-Balance in German IT Consulting: With a Focus on Female Consultants

Volker Nissen and Frank Termer

Abstract The age pyramid in Germany and gender aspects have recently led many industries to call for an increase in the proportion of women among their employees. However, IT consultancies still find it difficult to adequately exploit highly qualified womens' potential when recruiting and bonding them. Our thesis is that deficits in the perceived work-life balance of the consultants are essential for this. On the basis of an empirical study, consisting of an online survey and subsequent telephone interviews with experts, the status of the topic of work-life balance in IT consulting firms is examined. This article focuses on the situation of female IT consultants and shows that the consulting industry can improve the work-life balance of female IT consultants through additional efforts and thus increase their attractiveness also for women starting their careers.

1 Introduction[1]

The provision of consulting services with the aim of improving the use of information processing (IP) or information technology (IT) at a client company is referred to as IT consulting. Whereas in the past the trend of intensive search for suitable personnel for the consulting industry was already recognizable, the demographic change will continue to pose a challenge for consulting companies in the future concerning the recruitment and retention of highly qualified employees. The reconciliation of work and private life, as a paraphrase for the concept of work-life balance

[1]This paper builds on Nissen and Termer (2011, 2014), and Termer and Nissen (2012).

V. Nissen (✉)
Economic Sciences and Media, Ilmenau University of Technology, Ilmenau, Germany
e-mail: volker.nissen@tu-ilmenau.de

F. Termer
Bitkom, Berlin, Germany
e-mail: f.termer@bitkom.org

V. Nissen (ed.), *Advances in Consulting Research*, Contributions to Management Science, https://doi.org/10.1007/978-3-319-95999-3_8

(WLB),[2] is generally assigned a key role here (Kaiser et al. 2010; Rustemeyer and Buchmann 2010).

In Germany, women are strongly underrepresented in IT-related jobs. In 2015, the percentage of women working in IT companies was only 15% (Anonymous 2017). Additionally, in fields of study relevant to IT jobs, only low numbers of women can be seen. Thus IT professions belong to a number of other professions being confronted with gender-specific differences. Clearly, problems of WLB are relevant in other developed countries, too, and the "war for talent" is an international phenomenon (Duxbury 2008; Felstead et al. 2002; Pocock et al. 2010; Wooden et al. 2009).

Empirical examinations in the past have focused either on the topic of WLB without explicit reference to IT consulting, e.g. Klimpel and Schütte (2006), Czurlok (2007), or on the area of women in consulting without or with only a slight reference to WLB, e.g. Hördt (2002) and Grass (2006). In linking the two subject areas, the study we have carried out examines the central research question as to whether the existing potential of highly qualified, female employees for the IT consulting industry can be better exploited in the future by means of adequate WLB measures. The focus on female consultants is based on the assumption that the compatibility of family and children in particular with women's careers is considerably more challenging, due to the still prevailing classical distribution of roles (Kastner 2010). In addition, the urgency to connect both things successfully becomes more and more important with the increasing age of female consultants due to biological reasons, such as whether or not they want to have children. As the consulting job implies a very high degree of professional strain, effective concepts for a good WLB are necessary to counteract a small percentage of women and a high fluctuation (Kaiser et al. 2010) in the German consulting sector. Our work can also be seen in the context of the discussion in Germany to enforce a quota of women in management positions by law. This would require knowing in more detail the requirements of women in terms of work-life balance measures.

The presentation of the initial situation is followed in this article by an overview of the methodological approach and data of the study. Section 3 presents the main findings from the perspective of female consultants as well as HR management, followed by a discussion of the results and conclusions. Section 5 provides a critical summary and highlights practical implications as well as further research needs.

2 Method and Data

The contribution is based on the study 'Work-Life-Balance for women in IT consulting (WoBaFIT)', which was conducted from September 2010 to April 2011 (Nissen and Termer 2011; Termer and Nissen 2012). Although some time has elapsed since the data was collected, we have no reason to believe that the situation concerning WLB has fundamentally changed at consulting providers in the meantime.

[2]Concerning the discussion about different definitions of WLB, we refer to Felstead et al. (2002), Pocock et al. (2010) and Schobert (2007).

Methods of empirical-qualitative, exploratory research were used with the aim of generating verifiable hypotheses. Results are based on a triangulated approach with online-questionnaires and expert interviews, thus combining quantitative and qualitative methods (Schnell et al. 2013) to explore a research field that has not received much attention so far. The persons of interest were female IT consultants, as well as HR managers in IT consultancies. Descriptive data analysis methods were applied to the data from the online-questionnaires.

The data collection was based on a two-stage procedure (Döring and Bortz 2015): First an online survey was carried out and then telephone interviews were conducted. The principle of snowball sampling was used to attract survey participants. Existing contacts to the sought-after experts in the consulting scene were used and further participants were gained through their contacts and recommendations in the network of those addressed. Thus, it was possible to reach 331 people and win 268 of them to participate in the online survey. Since only fully completed questionnaires were used, a total of 170 (155 consultants and 15 HR managers) could be used for the evaluation. Afterwards, 22 consultants and 8 HR managers agreed to participate in a telephone interview.

The online questionnaire was designed with reference to other comparable studies (cf. Klimpel and Schütte 2006; Czurlok 2007), and contained questions dealing with topics such as WLB, career, and working conditions. With the help of 20 corresponding questions, the perceptions of the two target groups were collected and confronted. The consultants were asked a total of 32 questions, while HR managers were asked 24. These were predominantly closed questions and opinion questions in multiple choice form.

The results of the online survey were incorporated into the design of interview guidelines. With their help, issues were highlighted which could only be investigated unsatisfactorily by means of a standardized survey (open questions) or which arose as a result of the online survey. The expert interviews (Mayer 2012) carried out by telephone in this way in a second stage as a special form of the guideline interview were converted into transcripts and coded. The use of an interview guide made it possible to systematically evaluate and compare the data obtained. The results were prepared using structured content analysis (Mayring 2015).

3 Results

3.1 Attitude Towards Work-Life-Balance

3.1.1 Concept of Work-Life-Balance

The term WLB was interpreted by female IT consultants very broadly (cf. Fig. 1). In the online study, the areas relationship and profession were cited equally and together with the aspect health were "definitely" seen as part of the topic area WLB. The answers "friends", "family/children", "hobbies" and "sports" also met with high approval. "Travelling", further "professional training" and "cultural

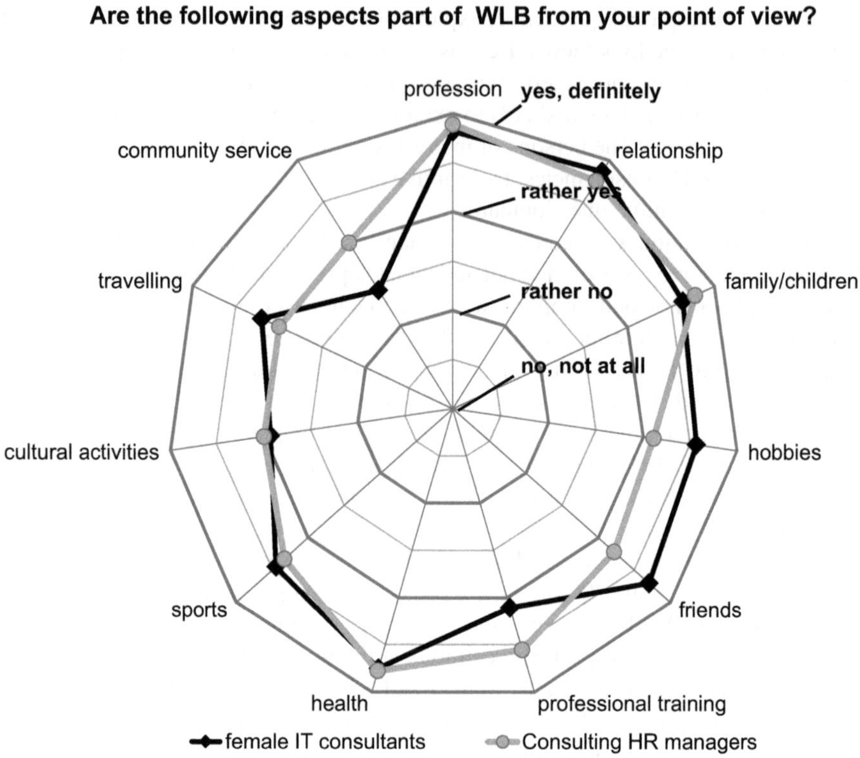

Fig. 1 Topic areas cited as being part of work–life balance

activities" were also connected to WLB, but 20% of the interviewees did not see them as being a part of their WLB.

"Community service" is the only aspect which is not seen as part of the participants' WLB. In addition, the last four aspects were evaluated ambivalently. Here, the answers range from "yes, definitely" to "not at all".

In the guided interviews we can see that WLB is described differently by every individual consultant, and that every person has individual and differing emphases. Terms cited relatively often in relation to WLB were "feeling of well-being", "inner contentment" and "balance". Particular emphasis was placed on the fact that the importance of the different areas in a WLB vary over time and in the course of a consulting career.

In the beginning, family/children is deemed less important, especially for young IT consultants working in this field for only a few months or a few years. But after some years of working life, the desire for family and children becomes stronger; hence this area becomes more important in the field of WLB. According to older IT consultants, this aspect then loses its importance when their children have become more independent and leave their parents' home. After this, areas such as hobbies, culture and travelling gain increasing interest.

The term WLB was also described in great detail by HR managers and all the areas offered as an answer were added to the subject area WLB (cf. Fig. 1). However, it becomes clear that the topics of profession, relationship, family/children and health rank ahead of all other possible answers. In these four areas, the degree of agreement also coincides with the responses of the interviewed IT consultants. Larger deviations are evident in the areas of hobbies and friends, where HR managers clearly underestimate the importance assigned by IT consultants, as well as in the areas of professional training and community involvement, which in turn are overestimated.

As a supplement to the survey, the view of the HR managers was confirmed in the interviews. There were very different opinions: For example, one HR manager stated that WLB is "not an issue" in the company, since it is a matter of fact and therefore one does not have to talk about it or specify the term in detail. On the opposite side, it was also stated that WLB is actively approached and is in demand, especially when recruiting new staff.

3.1.2 Strive for Work-Life-Balance

To determine the potential of WLB measures for the recruitment of women and for the bonding of female IT consultants, we asked whether IT consultants actively strive for a balance between their professional and private life, and whether their profession makes the realization of a private WLB possible at all (cf. Table 1). A total of 95% of the interviewed IT consultants said that they actively strive for a balance between their professional and private life. However, 59% also said that their profession does not really enable them to realize a private WLB. Only 4% said that the balance strived for is made possible by their profession, while a further 4% do not strive for any active WLB.

Several reasons were mentioned in the interviews as to why the consulting profession does not make a personal WLB realistic. An active WLB is often connected to regular activities during the week (e.g. family life, sports, meeting friends, etc.). Due to the predominantly project-oriented work at the customer's site, these private things are often only possible on weekends, which is seen as limiting

Table 1 Striving for and realization of work-life balance among female IT consultants

	Does your profession make the realization of your personal WLB possible?				
Do you actively aim for a balance between your professional and private life?	No information (%)	Yes (%)	Somewhat (%)	Not really (%)	Not at all (%)
No information (%)	0	0	1	0	0
Yes (%)	0	4	26	31	4
Somewhat (%)	0	0	8	20	1
Not really (%)	0	1	0	3	0
Not at all (%)	0	0	0	0	0

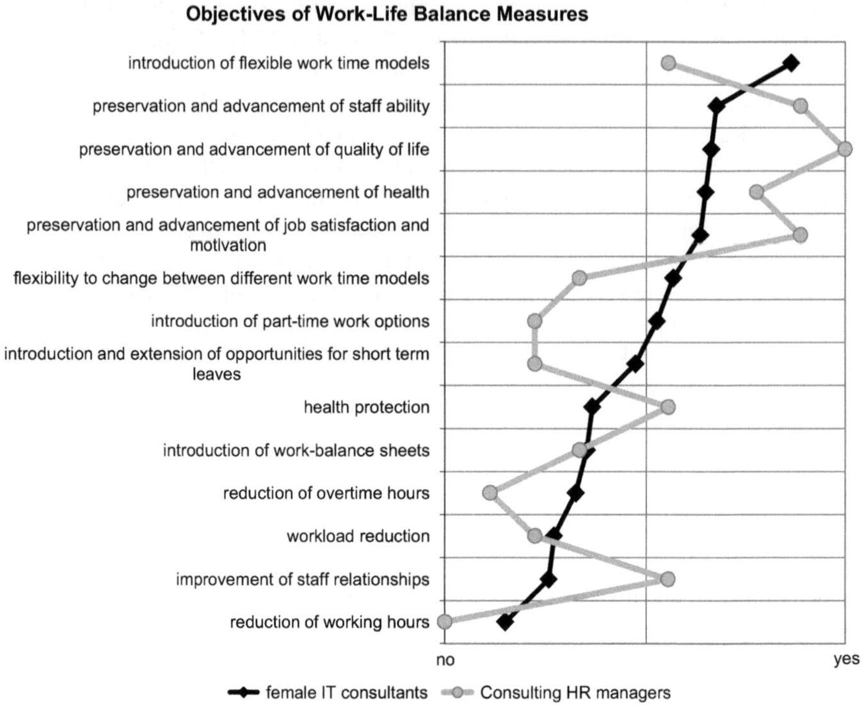

Fig. 2 Objectives of WLB measures

for the realization of a WLB. Furthermore, the readiness to enable flexible overtime hours at short notice also makes the projectability of an active private WLB difficult. As a result, the consulting profession generally offers rather bad WLB conditions.

3.1.3 Objectives of Work-Life-Balance Measures

To successfully implement WLB for the employees of a company, HR managers can choose from a number of measures that have already been developed (Kaiser et al. 2010). However, the concrete implementation depends on the identified or desired objectives of such measures. Asked what goals WLB measures should pursue, a differentiated picture emerged between IT consultants and human resources managers (cf. Fig. 2).

From the point of view of IT consultants, the organization of working time should be an important aim of WLB measures. This could be the establishment of flexible working time models, the flexibility to change between different working time models or the possibility to flexibly exit from working for a short time. This view is clearly underestimated by HR managers.

Both groups surveyed consider the objectives of maintaining and advancing quality of life, health and staff ability/performance as well as increasing job

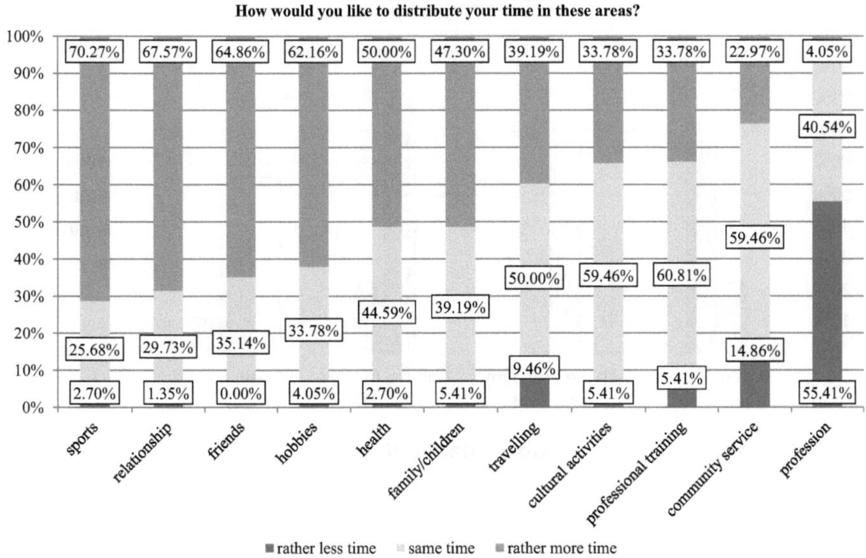

Fig. 3 How consultants would like to distribute their time

satisfaction and motivation to be important, although in some cases these points are more strongly emphasised by HR managers. For HR managers, reducing or preventing health complaints and the improvement of staff relationships are also goals, which consultants do not formulate.

In the interviews with HR managers, the aim of WLB measures was mainly seen in the combination of work and life, so that there is no contradiction here, but these areas are seen as complementary. In some IT consulting firms, the success of WLB measures is already measured by specific key figures such as the fluctuation rate.

3.2 *Implementation of Work-Life-Balance in Consulting*

3.2.1 How Consultants Would Like to Distribute Their Time

An important starting point for the organization of WLB measures is the distribution of available time. IT consultants were asked how they would like to spread their time to different areas. Here it can clearly be seen that the area "profession" is the only one for which the consultants would like to spent less time than they actually do (cf. Fig. 3), whereas they would like to have more time for all the other areas (sports, relationship, friends, hobbies, health, family/children)—or at least the same time (travelling, culture, community service and further professional training).

In addition, the desire to reduce the time they currently spend on working is confirmed by the interviews. In these, we asked the consultants about their level of

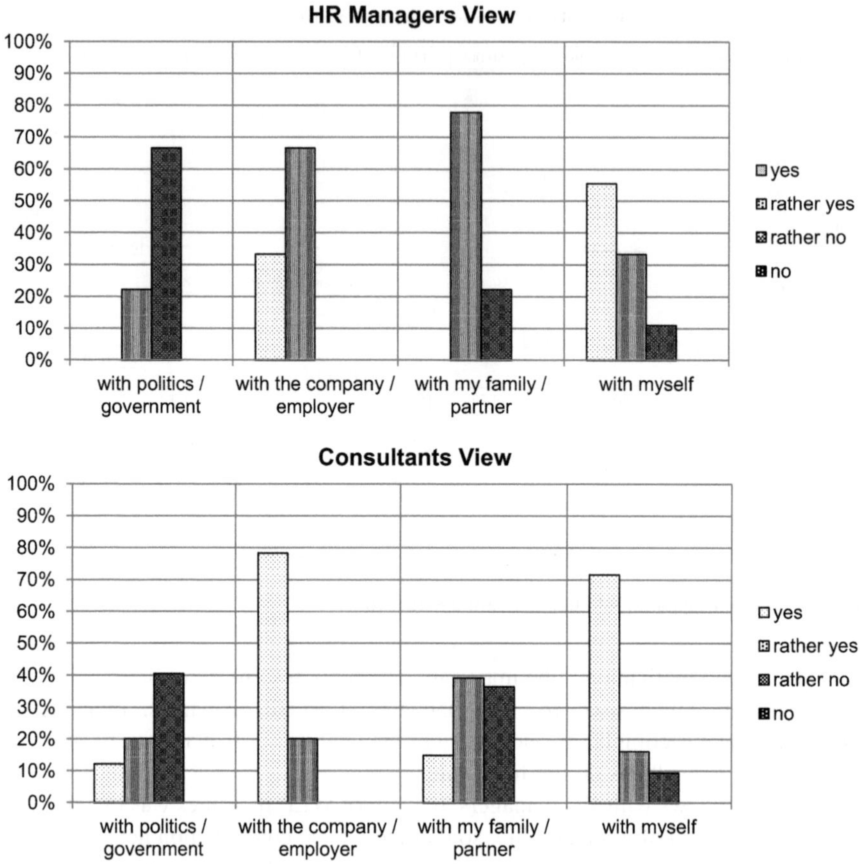

Fig. 4 Where the responsibility for introducing and implementing WLB-measures is seen

satisfaction with their current WLB. Those consultants that were clearly unsatisfied said that this feeling is due to "long working days" and "long commutes to work", so that things like friends and hobbies become downgraded. Not a single consultant judged their current situation as optimal. Other reasons given for the wish to spend more time with other things were the negative consequences already experienced with regards to health problems, problems with one's partner and the estrangement of friends.

3.2.2 Responsibility for Introducing and Implementing WLB-Measures

The answers to the question of who should be responsible for implementing WLB measures (cf. Fig. 4) make it clear that, according to IT consultants and human resources managers, several parties should assume joint responsibility. At the global level, however, it is noticeable that this primary responsibility is not transferred to

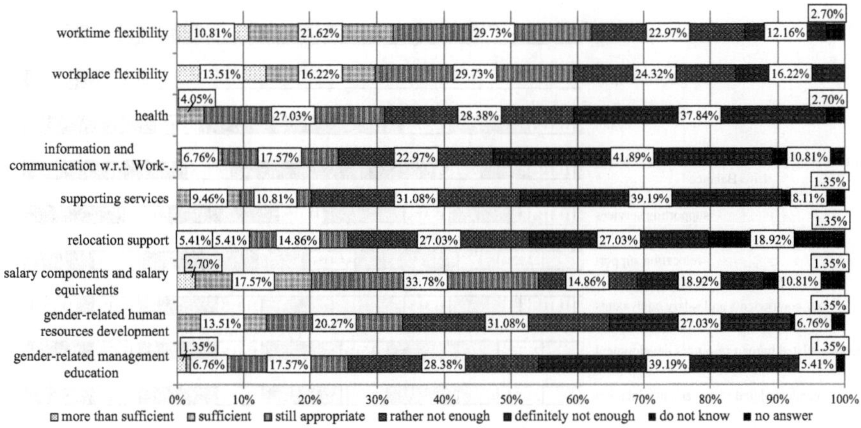

Fig. 5 How consultants see the range of work-life-balance measures offered by their companies

politics or the government. Rather, it is first of all the companies, or rather the employer, and the individuals or employees themselves to whom responsibility is assigned.

Secondly, however, a partial responsibility is also attributed to the family or partnership environment of an individual, with IT consultants presenting a more differentiated picture here, as HR managers do. After all, just below 40% of the surveyed consultants tend not to see any responsibility for the family or the partner. It can therefore be concluded that both groups, consultants and employers, should and want to assume joint responsibility for the introduction and implementation of WLB measures.

3.2.3 Consultants' View on Available WLB-Measures

The next question looked at how consultants judged the range of work–life balance measures offered by their respective companies (cf. Fig. 5). Only flexibility in the place of work, flexibility and the organization of working time and salary components were seen as appropriate or better by more than 50% of female IT consultants. Measures concerning so-called supporting services (e.g. daily shopping or laundry services), the gender-related education of managers and human resources development, and information and communication about WLB and health were seen as inadequate by more than 60% of the interviewees.

When we asked in the interviews which WLB measures are offered by the employers we received a mixed picture. On the one hand, some IT consultants said that a widespread range of measures was available to the employees, but only partial offers are made when explicitly requested by the employees. However, many employees do not know that WLB measures were even available—and so they never

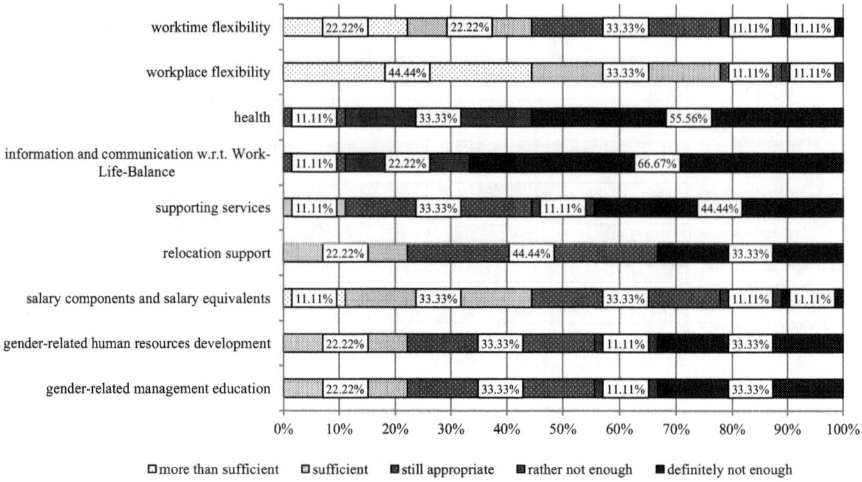

Fig. 6 How HR managers see the range of work-life-balance measures offered by their companies

ask for them. On the other hand, half of the IT consultants said that no official offers for WLB exist.

3.2.4 HR Managers' View on Available WLB-Measures

HR managers were also asked how the actual provision of WLB measures is viewed by them in their own companies. Compared to the responses of the IT consultants, the overall results show a much more positive picture (cf. Fig. 6). Certain areas are identified as underrepresented or not implemented at all, such as information and communication on WLB, as well as supporting services and health. But the areas of workplace flexibility and worktime organisation and flexibility are seen as being implemented extensively or even very extensively with over 65% and over 50% agreement in the responses. This is interesting in that it is precisely these two areas which were cited by consultants as deserving of further improvement. For HR managers, this means that they view the situation too positively. Despite the level of implementation achieved, they should not draw the conclusion that they can stop or reduce efforts to make work location and working hours more flexible. There is a differing opinion among HR managers in the areas of gender-related management education and HR development, and there is no discernible majority tendency.

On the whole, it should be noted that HR managers represent a more positive picture of the scope of the WLB measures offered in comparison with the consultants and thus overestimate the perception of the efforts made so far and possibly even have a transfigured view of them. Nevertheless, HR managers are aware of the fact that many areas are not yet sufficiently addressed.

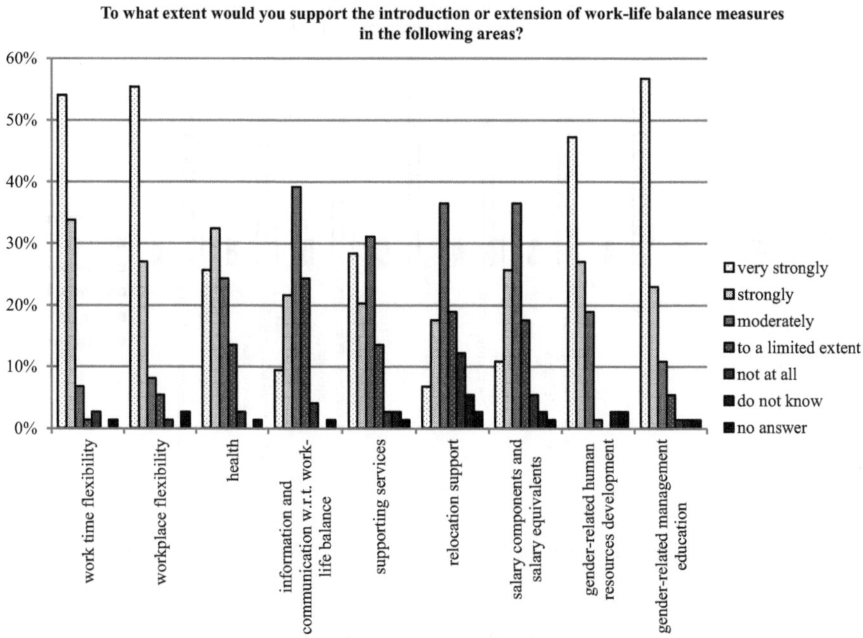

Fig. 7 How consultants believe work–life balance measures should be further developed

3.2.5 What Measures Should Be Offered in the Future According to Consultants

Female IT consultants would like to have more measures to improve their WLB (cf. Fig. 7). According to more than 80%, organization and flexibility in relation to working time and working place is seen as either important or very important, as well as the area of gender-related manager education (approx. 80%) and HR development (approx. 75%). The smallest need was expressed for relocation support, with less than 30% thinking that an extension is important, while 12% did not think it was important at all.

In addition to these figures, the desire for "more flexibility" was expressed often in the interviews. The excessive emphasis on "financial and material values in salary" was seen as negative in comparison to the consideration of "weak factors", which were seen as an important field of development. Furthermore, a change of culture was seen generally as an important factor in IT consulting for upgrading the importance of WLB measures.

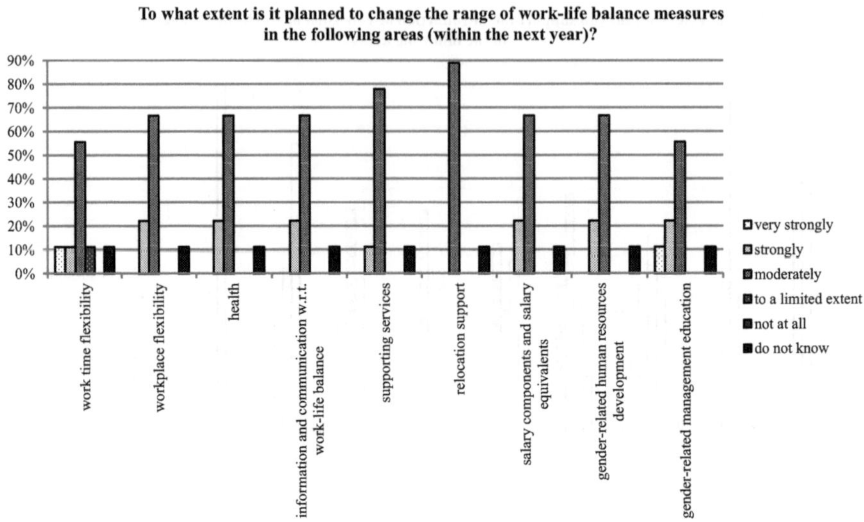

Fig. 8 How HR managers envision the future development of WLB-measures in their companies

3.2.6 How the Provision of WLB-Measures Will Develop According to HR Managers

The HR managers surveyed should also provide information on how the range of WLB measures offered should develop in the future (cf. Fig. 8). The main result of this question shows that the majority of all areas are aiming to maintain the status quo within the period of 1 year. It was said only sporadically that a small or even a strong expansion of the measures was planned. One HR manager also consistently stated that he did not know what the future development was going to look like, and another HR manager replied that the scope of measures in the area of worktime organization and flexibility should even decrease slightly.

If one compares the statements of the HR managers with the wishes of the IT consultants, it becomes apparent that HR managers massively underestimate the view of the IT consultants. There have been clear requests for the expansion of measures, but HR managers are only planning medium changes and want to stick to the status quo. In the overall view, this result comes as a surprise, since HR managers consider the status quo in sum to be insufficient (cf. Fig. 6). This suggests that in general, the topic of WLB in IT consulting firms is generally considered to play only a subordinate role from the perspective of HR management and that the priorities have been shifted in favour of other HR management tasks. As a frequent reason for the weak expansion of WLB measures, it was stated in the telephone interviews that extensive WLB measures already existed, but employees did not make use of them and therefore no expansion will follow. From the point of view of some HR managers, consultants would rather be remunerated on a monetary basis. This

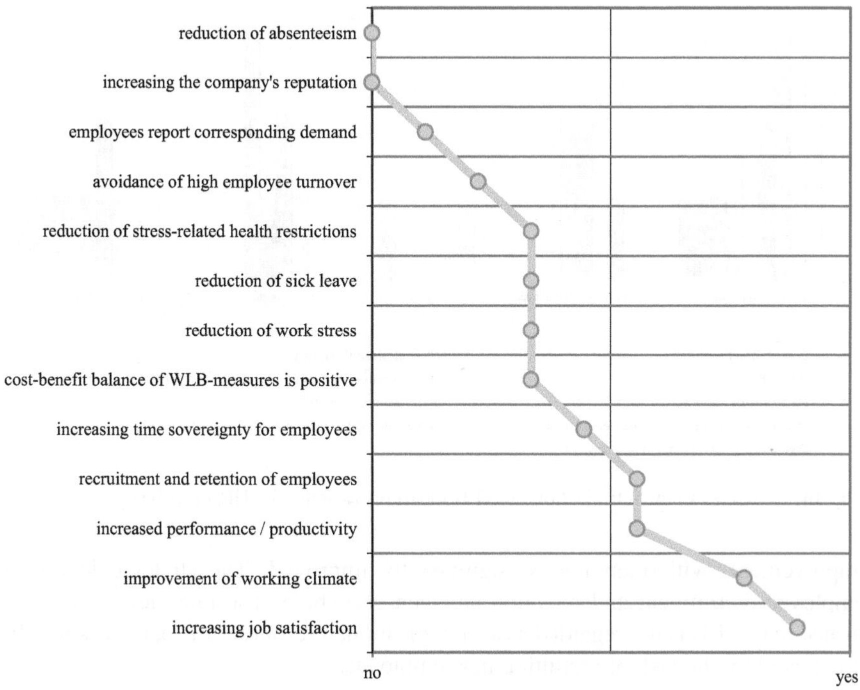

Fig. 9 Reasons why consulting providers introduced WLB-measures

view was contradicted by other HR managers who wish to prioritize WLB measures at a very high level and therefore to expand them accordingly in the future.

3.2.7 Why IT Consulting Firms Introduce WLB-Measures at All

If consulting firms describe the scope of their own WLB measures as rather inadequate, see themselves as being jointly responsible for the issue, but do not plan to expand the measures in the future, for what reasons were or will such measures be introduced anyway (cf. Fig. 9)?

To a large extent, the HR managers interviewed here argued with regard to the well-being of employees and the working atmosphere in the company. This is followed by an increase in performance and productivity, but also an improvement in the recruitment and retention of employees. On the other hand, the reduction of absenteeism or a positive effect on the image of the consulting firm are not cited as reasons for introducing WLB measures. Similarly, the avoidance of high employee fluctuation or a personal desire on the part of employees does not constitute grounds for consulting companies to offer WLB measures.

It can be seen that WLB measures are more attributed to the support of 'soft' labour factors. This explains why the status quo, even if it offers potential for

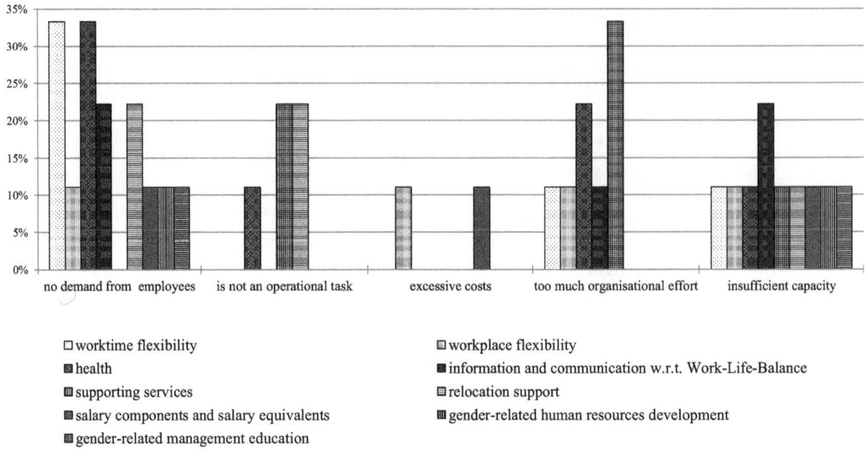

Fig. 10 Obstacles to the introduction of WLB-measures as stated by HR managers

improvement, will often not be significantly improved. The strategic levers in employee recruitment and retention are seen elsewhere. The interviews also confirmed that WLB is not regarded as a strategic human resources issue, but is strongly dominated by the task of recruiting new employees.

3.2.8 Obstacles to the Introduction of WLB-Measures

The question as to what obstacles prevent the introduction of WLB measures (cf. Fig. 10) shows that there are no individual obstacles to the introduction of WLB measures, but rather that it is a bundle of reasons which stand in the way of a general implementation of WLB measures. High costs do not play a major role as an obstacle. Rather, there is a problem with the implementation of WLB measures at a broad level. For some measures, the reason cited is generally too much organisational effort (e.g. supporting services). This makes it clear once again that HR managers focus on other topics and that WLB measures are not considered to be a necessary complementary element.

Lack of demand from employees was surprisingly often cited as a reason why WLB-measures are not implemented at a broad scale. There seems to be a general communication problem here, whereby female IT consultants (and possibly also male consultants) do not even approach their wishes and needs in the area of WLB to HR managers. Thus, it can be concluded that employees need to communicate more strongly with the staff managers of their employer if they want to use WLB measures, as otherwise there is a risk that corresponding requirements cannot be identified.

If one takes a closer look at the individual WLB measures, it is noticeable that the area of staff and management education in gender-related aspects in particular is a suitable starting point for approaching the topic of WLB from both sides.

Shortcomings in these areas have been identified by consultants as well as HR managers. Consultants would like to see an improvement here, and from the perspective of HR managers, there are no major obstacles to this. From these answers, the anchoring of WLB in the areas of staff and management education can be seen as the lowest common denominator between IT consultants and HR managers.

Some participants supplemented individual answers to this question. The following additional obstacles were identified: (a) lack of customer acceptance, (b) WLB measures were not strategic success factors and (c) the size of the company prevented the introduction of WLB measures. All in all, however, such further obstacles were only mentioned in isolated cases.

4 Discussion

4.1 The Consultants' Perspective

The "war for talent" provides opportunities for the well-qualified workforce. Since there is a shortage of skilled workers, their position is strengthened in relation to employers. Consequently, knowledge workers can basically place demands on their work environment. To render these demands tangible for female IT-consultants was a primary goal of our study.

Female IT consultants summarize a number of life fields under the term WLB (cf. Fig. 1). WLB is described as a system where the aim is to gain satisfaction in the fields involved, and where no field is neglected or subordinated to another. Indeed it is very clear that a metaphorical balance (equal weight) between working life and private life is only strived for by a small number of female IT consultants. In fact, individual situations are cited which may change during one's lifetime.

It is quite clear why the first priority among WLB measures has been the establishment of flexible worktime models (cf. Fig. 2), as the current distribution of worktime among IT consultants is very unbalanced (cf. Fig. 3). It dominates the occupancy of the IT consultants massively, which is quite in line with the findings of others in the literature (cf. Bailyn 1997; Duxbury 2008). It should be noted that working longer hours than preferred can have a significant negative impact on well-being (Wooden et al. 2009), while the health and well-being of the workforce has important economic implications (Brinkley et al. 2009).

Some possible starting points to improve the situation from the point of view of IT consultants are offers concerning the organization and flexibility of worktime and the workplace (cf. Fig. 7). According to female IT consultants, consulting companies in these fields still have the potential for change, although the efforts made up until now are seen as insufficient (cf. Fig. 5). All in all it has to be said that all fields of WLB measures in their current state are perceived as underdeveloped and it can be questioned whether the profession has sufficiently established WLB at all.

If we look at the wishes of the female IT consultants, several already existing possibilities to organize worktime and the workplace have proved to be usable. With the help of work-time accounts (balance sheets), temporal part-time working with differing work hours or long-term exits (sabbaticals), long-term time potentials could be established, so that spare time could then be used for other fields of life. One possibility for short-term needs could be the rectification of the working day, which means that the employees do not have to work during a fixed period of time but in individual blocks. In order to achieve this, it would be necessary to have a more flexible concept of what constitutes the "workplace". For some jobs it is not necessary for the consultant to be personally within the company, but can instead establish themselves in a home office or even telework. In general, the concept of "virtual consulting services" could be explored and implemented, e. g. by using IT to reduce attendance times or the need for on-site IT consultants.

To remain attractive for women in the long term, consultancies should keep new career models in mind so as to encourage individual development without necessitating longer working hours, journeys or long-term absences. This would result in the knowledge of female IT consultants being maintained in the company over the long term.

4.2 The HR Managers' Perspective

The results of the WoBaFIT study show that from the perspective of the consulting firms, WLB is not assigned a particular priority among all HR management tasks, and therefore supports other studies (Strack et al. 2009). Recruiting is one of the topics mentioned by most HR managers in this context, which clearly dominates all other tasks. From the perspective of the interviewed IT consultants, however, it can be assumed that WLB measures have the potential to attract more women for a career in the IT consulting industry and to keep women in this sector longer. However, it seems that management consultancies have not (yet) recognized the desire of consultants for better WLB measures.

However, what exactly is the reason for this is not essential for further steps. It should be noted that a possible reciprocating of the WLB initiative between consultants (consulting firms simply do not offer enough WLB measures) and HR managers (consultants simply do not report a corresponding need for WLB measures) is not helpful in the whole issue. On the contrary, both parties should look for common starting points that could be identified by the study. A first step would be to increase the awareness of managers and staff responsible for human resources in the area of WLB and to develop an appropriate information and communication policy in this area. Management (e.g. those responsible for HR) and consultants should start an intensive dialogue to consider the need for a better WLB in the profession. The wish to include the topic into manager education (cf. Fig. 7) highlights the fact that such an exchange does not take place in the way at present (from the point of view of female IT consultants).

In relation to the above findings, it makes sense to question the current practices around the organization of work time and the workplace of consultants, and thus to develop more flexible approaches for consulting services. The possibilities to "virtualize" consulting should be elaborated so as to provide services independently from time and place, with the innovative use of information techniques playing a key role. Existing structures and procedures should be reviewed to take into account the necessary flexibility already at the beginning of the project planning. Certain project tasks could then be planned and defined as part-time or off-site jobs.

If consulting firms underestimate the importance of WLB measures or deliberately assign a low priority to the topic area, the associated risks must be weighed up. In addition to the "soft" factors, such as employee dissatisfaction or low loyalty to the company, the high costs that can arise as a result of non-observance of the WLB should be mentioned. For example, direct costs can arise from the loss of employees, the payment of severance payments upon leaving the company and the replacement of positions. Incorrect entrepreneurial decisions or unused opportunities can also lead to considerable indirect costs if they are attributable to neglected WLBs of managers (Stock-Homburg and Roederer 2009; Stock-Homburg 2011).

A welcome side-effect of better enabling WLB within the consulting industry is an improved image. This would make the job description more attractive for highly qualified women and men in general, so that WLB measures can be a building block in solving the shortage of skilled workers and gaining a strategic advantage over competitors in the competition for future employees. Some consulting companies are aware of the relevance and the potential of WLB, and new ideas are being developed on the ways to broaden WLB concepts in consulting companies (cf. Rustemeyer and Buchmann 2010). These should be looked at critically, be further developed and completed with reference to the consulting sector or adapted to individual companies.

5 Summary, Limitations and Future Research

In our view, well-trained woman should be recruited and promoted by consulting companies more than is the case today. As pointed out in our study, this would require solving some of the most pressing WLB issues that women in consulting experience. Summarizing our results, we come up with the following theses:

- For female IT consultants, reaching a WLB mainly means the compatibility of job and family.
- The current role of an IT consultant makes an active implementation of WLB impossible.
- The employer plays an important role in developing a personal WLB for female IT consultants. However, the WLB measures offered by consulting companies at the moment are not sufficient. Consequently, the potential of well-qualified women is not yet fully recognised and deployed in the consulting sector today.

- Clearly, the current and future demographic situation will make it more and more difficult (particularly for small and medium-sized consulting companies without a brand name) to employ the personnel they require. The extension of WLB measures may support the recruitment of highly qualified women for IT consulting and enforce their ties to the company. For this reason, the topic should be prioritized more by the consulting management.

The present study is based on a comparatively moderate sample of consultants and HR managers. Therefore, it may be that the results are not completely representative, especially in detail. Furthermore, it cannot be ruled out in anonymous surveys that distortion is caused by the fact that people misunderstand questions. Due to the additional interviews we were able to rule out this problem at least in the cases of our interview partners.

Clearly, WLB is not a topic that concerns only women. The changing roles in family life suggest that more and more men will make use of WLB measures, but this was not the focus of our study. We have not looked at differences with male consultants. As such, further studies will also need to look at how male IT consultants' ideas differ in comparison to their female colleagues.

Moreover, our empirical basis is female consultants in Germany. Although, issues of WLB are of international relevance, the situation can differ in detail, when one looks at consulting companies in other developed societies. Consequently, it would be useful to repeat the survey in other countries and compare the results with our findings.

Finally, older workers represent another underrated pool of skilled workers that could be recruited and deployed more intensively by the HR departments of consultancies. Again, measures of work-life balance will play an important role to leverage existing opportunities here. This offers another interesting field of research with immediate practical implications.

References

Anonymous (2017) https://www.deutschland.de/de/topic/wirtschaft/frauen-in-it-berufen. Accessed 18 Jan 2018

Bailyn L (1997) The impact of corporate culture on work-family integration. In: Parasuraman S, Greenhaus JH (eds) Integrating work and family: challenges and choices for a changing world. Quorum, Westport, pp 209–231

Brinkley I, Fauth R, Mahdon M, Theodoropoulou S (2009) Is knowledge work better for us? Knowledge workers, good work and wellbeing. The Work Foundation

Czurlok J (2007) Erfolgsfaktor Work Life Balance. http://www.familienbewusste-personalpoltik.de/fileadmin/fba/download/Pilotstudie_Erfolgsfaktor_Work_Life_Balance.pdf, 2007. Accessed 12 April 2011

Döring N, Bortz J (2015) Forschungsmethoden und Evaluation in den Sozial- und Humanwissenschaften, 5th edn. Springer, Berlin

Duxbury L (2008) Work-life balance in Australia in the New Millennium: rhetoric versus reality. http://www.beaton.com.au/

Felstead A, Jewson N, Phizacklea A, Walters S (2002) Opportunities to work at home in the context of work-life balance. Hum Resour Manag J 12(1):54–76

Grass B (2006) Karrierechancen von Frauen in der Unternehmensberatung. FH Bonn-Sieg, Rheinbach

Hördt O (2002) Frauen in der Unternehmensberatung – Empirische Analyse zur geschlechterspezifischen Segregation. DUV, Wiesbaden

Kaiser S, Reindl C, Stolz ML (2010) Work-life-balance in professional service firms. In: Kaiser S, Ringlstetter MJ (eds) Work-life-balance. Springer, Heidelberg, pp 67–81

Kastner M (2010) Work-life-balance für Extremjobber. In: Kaiser S, Ringlstetter MJ (eds) Work-life-balance. Springer, Heidelberg, pp 1–27

Klimpel M, Schütte T (2006) Work-life-balance – eine empirische Erhebung. Rainer Hampp, Mering

Mayer HO (2012) Interview und schriftliche Befragung – Entwicklung, Durchführung, Auswertung, 6th edn. Oldenbourg, München

Mayring P (2015) Qualitative Inhaltsanalyse – Grundlagen und Techniken, 12th edn. Beltz, Weinheim

Nissen V, Termer F (2011) Work-life-balance bei Frauen in der IT-Unternehmensberatung. Technical report (in German), University of Technology Ilmenau, Institute of Business Informatics

Nissen V, Termer F (2014) Women and their work-life balance in German IT consulting. In: Rode JA, Wulf V (eds) Proceedings gender IT 14 – gender and IT appropriation (Siegen 2014), European Society for Socially Embedded Technologies. ACM Digital Library, pp 1–9

Pocock B, Skinner N, Pisaniello S (2010) How much should we work? The Australian Work and Life Index 2010. University of South Australia Centre for Work + Life, Adelaide

Rustemeyer H, Buchmann C (2010) Erfolgsfaktor work-life-balance bei der Unternehmensberatung A.T. Kearney. In: Kaiser S, Ringlstetter MJ (eds) Work-life-balance. Springer, Heidelberg, pp 165–179

Schnell R, Hill PB, Esser E (2013) Methoden der empirischen Sozialforschung, 10th edn. Oldenbourg, München

Schobert DB (2007) Grundlagen zum Verständnis von work-life-balance. In: Esslinger AS, Schobert DB (eds) Erfolgreiche Umsetzung von work-life-balance in Organisationen. DUV, Wiesbaden, pp 19–33

Stock-Homburg R (2011) Work-life-balance als Herausforderung: Burnout im Topmanagement. Forschung & Lehre 18:842–843

Stock-Homburg R, Roederer J (2009) Work-life-balance von Führungskräften: Modeerscheinung oder Schlüssel zur langfristigen Leistungsfähigkeit. Personalführung 2:22–32

Strack R, Caye J, Zimmermann P, von der Linden C, Thurner R, Haen P (2009) Creating people advantage: how to tackle the major HR challanges during the crisis and beyond. The Boston Consulting Group, Boston

Termer F, Nissen V (2012) Work-life-balance – Strategische Waffe des HR-managements in der IT-Unternehmensberatung? In: Mattfeld D, Robra-Bissantz S (eds) Proceedings of MKWI 2012. GITO, Berlin, pp 369–380

Wooden M, Warren D, Drago R (2009) Working time mismatch and subjective well-being. Br J Ind Relat 47:147–179

Volker Nissen holds the Chair of Information Systems Engineering in Services at Technische Universität Ilmenau, Germany, since 2005. Prior to this, he pursued a consulting career, including positions as manager at IDS Scheer AG, director at DHC GmbH, and CEO of NISSCON Ltd, Germany. In 1994 he received a PhD degree in Economic Sciences with distinction from the University of Goettingen, Germany. His current research interests include the digital transformation of the consulting industry, the management of IT-agility, metaheuristic optimization, and process acceptance research. He is author and editor of 20 books and some 200 other publications, including papers in Business & Information Systems Engineering, Information Systems Frontiers, IEEE Transactions on EC, IEEE Transactions on NN, OR Spectrum, and Annals of OR.

Frank Termer is Head of Software at Bitkom (German Association for Information Technology, Telecommunications and New Media e.V.). After studying Business Informatics at the Otto-von-Guericke University Magdeburg, he worked from 2006 as an IT Consultant and carried out projects in business process and IT service management. He was primarily responsible for companies in the energy industry, financial services and public administration. From 2010 he worked as a research assistant at the Technical University of Ilmenau in the field of Business Informatics for Services. There he focused his research on issues of strategic IT management. During this activity, numerous publications on the subjects of IT agility, enterprise architecture management, business process management and business IT alignment emerged. Since 2015, he has been responsible for the committees of the software competence area at Bitkom. He designs, organizes and moderates committee events and is responsible for the thematic development of these committees as well as their content-related positioning within the Bitkom and for the communication of the positions towards politics and the public.

Part III
Consulting Fields and Approaches

Systemic Consultancy, Theory and Application

Martin Hillebrand and Stefan Mette

Abstract Systemic consultancy has gained in presence and influence in organizations in recent years. The theoretical foundations were developed in the 1980s, and the set of corresponding consulting instruments has since grown significantly on the architecture, design and tools levels. A concrete example illustrates the approach and procedure.

1 Theory

It is amazing to see how systemic consultancy has developed in recent years from an innovative form of consulting into a true commodity. This statement definitely applies at least in the German-speaking world. While criticism from the business sector might have been loud in the pioneering years of the 1980s and 1990s (Königswieser and Exner 2004; Simon 2007; Wimmer 2004), when systemic was at times even "translated" into systematic, the term "systemic" is now virtually a standard prefix in the development sector (c.f. systemic strategy development, systemic school development, systemic coaching).

We are convinced that the VUCA (Volatility, Uncertainty, Complexity, Ambiguity) world and the political instability have contributed to this trend. And we take a closer look at further relevant trends like digitalization in the case study described in this article.

But to set the scene, we would like to begin by taking a look at the different theories that have influenced systemic organizational consulting.

M. Hillebrand (✉)
CO(13), Berlin, Germany
e-mail: m.hillebrand@co13.eu

S. Mette
BNP Paribas Personal Finance, Bremen, Germany
e-mail: stefan.mette@ymail.com

V. Nissen (ed.), *Advances in Consulting Research*, Contributions to Management Science, https://doi.org/10.1007/978-3-319-95999-3_9

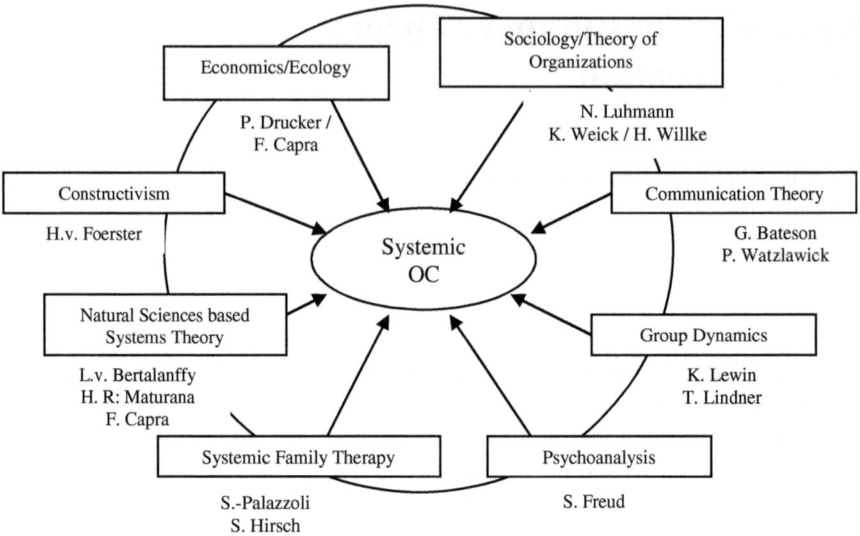

Fig. 1 Influences on our understanding of systemic organizational consulting (Königswieser and Hillebrand 2005)

1.1 Theoretical Foundations (In Brief)

The term "system" comes from the Greek and literally means "to stand—together". It refers to the whole, the coming together of the individual parts. And as Aristotle once said: The whole is more than the sum of its parts. This essentially sums up what lies at the core of "systemic": the look at the whole and at the interaction of its parts.

We will resist at this point the temptation to provide a description of the emergence of systems theory (details of which can be found, for instance, in Königswieser and Hillebrand 2005), and would like instead to introduce just a few of the key thinkers who have had a fundamental influence on systemic consulting (see also Fig. 1).

We encounter the biological understanding of systems (in particular Maturana and Varela 1987) in the consulting context in the principle of the self-organization of systems (homeostasis = self-organization and autopoiesis = self-producing, self-maintaining). The actions of each system are thus considered meaningful if they contribute to its continuation.

Niklas Luhmann (1984) translates this notion to communication in social systems. Similar to the self-reproduction of living organisms, "social" systems also only perceive things that are compatible and fit with them. This behavior makes sense because it significantly reduces complexity and, in doing so, very often ensures survival.

Communication theorists like Gregory Bateson (1951) or Paul Watzlawick (Watzlawick et al. 2000) and cognitive psychologists like Jean Piaget (1992) look, in turn, at the effect of feedback on behavior. Asking yourself the following

Table 1 Mechanistic and systemic views of the world (Königswieser and Hillebrand 2005)

Mechanistic view of the world	Systemic view of the world
Objectivity, one truth, fixed laws	Construction of reality, many "truths", theses
Right–wrong, guilty–innocent	Context-dependent, usefulness, connectivity
(External) control	Self-control, self-organization
Linear cause and effect chains	Multiple reciprocal effects, feedback loops
Measurable, fixed difference	Being different, changing
Linear progression, changing	Development, changing and maintaining, unblocking
Formal logic, no contradiction, exclusion	Integration of conflicting views, involvement
Hard facts, rational relationships	Integration of hard and soft factors (emotions, intuitions, communication processes)
Roles: doers, leaders and followers, manipulation	Roles: motivators, gardeners, enablers, development guides, coaches
Methods: instruction, orders, commands, learning by trial and error	Methods: listening, asking questions, dialog, discussion, reflection, learning to learn

questions opens up a first feedback loop in human learning: "Have I been successful with my actions or not? Did I achieve what I wanted to achieve? If not, can I do something differently?" Feedback gives us the opportunity to be "more successful". But we can also reflect on whether our goals, desires, or values are coherent in the given situation and thus open up a second learning loop. This learning to change underlying values and assumptions is known as double loop learning.

Family therapy has had a strong influence on the repertoire of interventions used in systemic organizational consultancy. Again, the basic idea here is that we should not focus solely on the individual in difficult situations but should instead look at the complete family system, the broader context, the interactions between the members. Paradoxical interventions, reframing and circular questions are particularly important instruments in systemic consultancy, especially when it comes to unravelling difficult situations and rigid loops. Mara Selvini Palazzoli and her colleagues at the "Milan school" (Selvini Palazzoli et al. 1978 also provided us with a first translation of systemic family therapy to the organizational context through their book *The Hidden Games of Organizations* (Selvini Palazzoli et al. 1988).

The systemic view of the world moves away from the mechanistic or mechanical model and the belief in objectivity. It uses multiple perspectives, emphasizes self-organization and thus offers a possible answer to complexity and uncertainty (see also Table 1).

This distinction is also fundamental when it comes to differentiating between traditional business process and systemic process consulting. The roots of traditional business process consulting lie in the mechanistic view of the world, in the conviction that there is one unequivocal truth. Accordingly, clear goals—and also brilliant strategies—are important. The consultants develop the best solution for the client, which must then be implemented consistently. The consultants guide the client through the process and provide the necessary contextual logic and consistency. The necessary authority is supplied by the board/executive management team.

Systemic process consultants, on the other hand, believe that the client can break down the blockages itself. The results are thus always co-creations between the consultant and the client, and the implementation of the solutions forms an integral part of the process from the outset.

2 From Theory to Practice

In systemic consultancy, these theoretical concepts become visible in four different forms, namely the architecture of change processes, the design of workshops and the use of tools in concrete work settings (as the three core levels of intervention) as well as, of course, the attitude of the consultants.

The starting point for all such consulting processes is always the client—and their needs naturally differ greatly. Typical examples of the types of clients we work with and the problems they seek to resolve include a bank that wants to improve its sales organization and internal cooperation activities, an automobile manufacturer who wants to achieve a team-oriented performance culture after some particularly lean years, an energy supplier who received "poor" ratings in an internal staff survey and wants to rectify the situation, or an NGO who would like to cope better with its growth and become a more professional organization.

In nearly all cases, such projects are about initiating a development process that turns the people affected into active participants and working in unison with the organization to find appropriate solutions. This joint work begins right at the very start of the process, when we sit down with the client to develop a joint plan of action.

2.1 Architecture

In our consulting processes, we refer to the overall concept and plan as the *architecture*. Which groups with which functions work where and when? This provides us with an overview of where the possibilities might lie.

Like a good architect, we work with the client to plan what is needed, set the objectives, and define the budget. This is a joint, cooperative process—a delicate balancing of the expertise of the consultants with the wishes and expectations of the client.

In the increasingly fast-moving world of modern business, we always find it useful to establish a plan for a full year. This gives sustainability to the consulting project and also paves the way for deeper changes. If workshops are only arranged sporadically, there is a greater tendency not to address difficult topics and conflicts to ensure that normal, everyday business is not disrupted. But in our experience, all projects face crises at some point—and these are almost always necessary to achieve real change. A carefully planned architecture ensures that things keep moving.

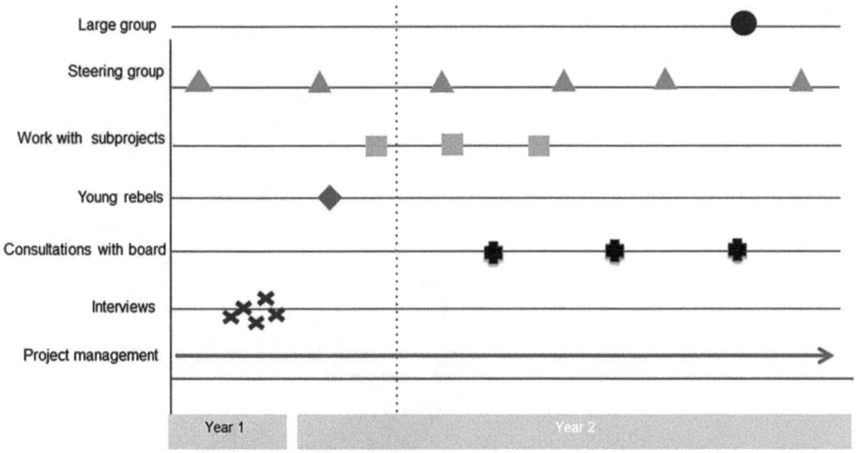

Fig. 2 An architecture for improved sales performance

To illustrate what we mean by this, we will now describe some of the key elements of such an architecture in more detail. Figure 2 provides an example of an actual architecture planned with one of our clients, namely a large-group event for over 100 branch managers and managing directors. The individual elements of this architecture are explained in detail below.

System Diagnosis A first essential step is the so-called system diagnosis. For this purpose, group interviews with members of staff in the client organization are used to gather information on the client system through dialog. It is useful here to include a broad mix of people in terms of age, function, position in the hierarchy, etc. This intervention encourages dialog in the organization and is also a form of introspection and self-reflection.

After the interviews, the consulting team sits down and forms hypotheses: What is the logic behind the client system? What latent patterns can be seen? What can we use as levers for change in the organization? The results of this hypothesis-building work are often translated into pictures (see Figs. 3 and 4).

2.1.1 Mirroring

The mirroring of the interview results is an important step in establishing trust with the client system. All results are presented to all interviewees in a group session lasting around 2 h. The actual presentation itself takes about 1 h and is followed by an opportunity for the participants to discuss the results. How well do these images reflect our organization (on a scale of 0–100)? What corresponds to our own impressions? What do we find irritating?

Fig. 3 The human interface between IT and the operative units is missing

Fig. 4 Here, the customer is still king

From a consulting perspective, a concurrence rate of 70–80% is helpful, because it indicates that a good balance has been achieved between connectivity and irritation, i.e. between expected results and new perspectives.

Dialog and feedback is also important at this stage, particularly when an organization has already worked with many consultants. It serves to demonstrate that it's all about working together to change and shape the future.

2.1.2 Core Team

The core team is the driving force in the change process. Ideally, the core team will contain a good mix of people with decision-making power, people who are affected by the change, experts and people with informal influence. It should also reflect the various age groups, seniorities, genders and other relevant differences in the organization. In this way, the core group serves as a "microcosm" of the organization—it includes multiple perspectives and thus has greater relevance.

The core team develops appropriate measures based on the system diagnosis (and corresponding hypotheses). In larger projects, individual subprojects and teams are set up for the individual fields of action. In smaller projects, the ideas are developed in the core team itself and implemented as pilot projects.

In the course of the project, the core team is also responsible for keeping an ear to the ground and establishing feedback loops, i.e. for monitoring the change and reporting back to the sponsor(s).

2.1.3 Subprojects

The subprojects work on the leverage topics identified in the system diagnosis and the work with the sponsors (e.g. leadership, cost reductions). This is where the actual work that will set the system in motion is done. It is also where the necessary interventions are conceived and put forward to the core team.

2.1.4 Large-Group Events

Working with large groups is a *sine qua non* in holistic change processes. At such events, large numbers of people come together in one room and simultaneously see how and in what direction the organization could—and should—develop. Alongside presentations and keynote speeches by the directors or the core team, such events also offer a platform for dialog in smaller groups. This creates a sense of togetherness and a collective new start.

It is important to see such events not as singular elements, but as part of an overall architecture, otherwise they would just be nice events with no lasting effect (Königswieser 2000; Seliger 2015).

2.1.5 Sponsors/Work with Top Management

There is an old Viennese saying that goes: "When you sweep the stairs, you always start at the top." The same applies to a change process—it also begins with top management. In addition to their role model function, top management also have to demonstrate that they are team players. The credibility of the project depends greatly on their actions: Do they set an example and practice the new values? Do the new principles provide guidelines for managers? How do they communicate and enter into dialog? Do they recognize and support cross-departmental issues?

It should also not be forgotten that even the members of top management need time and space to consider these questions and to develop—both as individuals and as a team.

2.1.6 Work in the Consulting Team

High quality work on the part of the consultants is a key factor for the success of a consulting project. In our approach, we very deliberately always work in pairs, because we also need feedback and the opportunity to reflect in order to provide professional support. And we frequently formulate hypotheses and suppositions to help us understand what is going on in the system and determine which interventions would be beneficial.

The above serve merely as a brief example of the different architecture elements in change processes. But there are, of course, plenty more that could be used—e.g. "young rebels" (groups set up to think laterally and speak their minds), train the trainer, coaching—depending on the situation (for further examples see Königswieser and Hillebrand 2005).

2.2 Designs

We refer to the actual format of an individual architecture element—e.g. the agenda for a workshop, the plan of action for a steering group or the team in a subproject—as a *design*. Essentially, designs are the architecture elements in practical form. Some designs are more complex and are developed in loops, like multi-day large-group events with large numbers of participants. Others are more simple, such as a short 6-minutes status report.

2.2.1 Example Design: A Workshop

How do we go about, for example, designing a workshop? What aspects should be included on the agenda? Based on our hypotheses and reflections, a workshop will be designed along five dimensions, namely the practical/content, social, spatial, time and symbolic dimensions.

Practical/Content Dimension The topics and content that will be handled in the project are, of course, determined by the brief. But when precisely these different topics will be handled in a workshop is determined when setting the agenda. This also provides certainty regarding the topics that will be handled and how.

Transparency is always important when working with groups. Letting people experience something for themselves takes precedence over theory inputs. A hearing with the management team is more exciting—and thus has a more lasting effect—than a PowerPoint presentation. A sketch portraying a strength or a weakness in the organization opens up a new perspective and thus also different scope for solutions. It is often only then that latent issues can become open to discussion.

Social Dimension The question of who should attend a workshop is usually already determined through the architecture. Important for the social dimension are the work formats that will be used in a workshop: plenary discussions, subgroups (4–8 people), small groups (3–4 people), pairs and solo exercises. Plenary situations offer the advantage of greater transparency and shared development but they can also become tiring because not everyone gets the opportunity to speak. Subgroups are advantageous when working on practical or content issues, while small groups encourage openness and trust-building. Outdoor/park constellations, and especially walks in pairs, are good for discussing personal issues and development and for transferring things back to the everyday work situation. Solo exercises are a good way of preparing for group exercises or for reflecting on what has been learned.

Time Dimension Less is definitely more. In the hectic modern world of business, we frequently experience that there are too many topics on the agenda and not enough time to discuss them all in the necessary depth and with the required level of intensity. The amount of time allocated to an exercise determines the subsequent depth with which the topic will be handled. We also see breaks as "unstructured" work time. The participants continue talking about the topics and have the opportunity to discuss them in a different way. Evening sessions are good for personal development issues, like values and attitude, and for feedback exercises. Beneficial, in-depth exchange is then also achieved, particularly in small groups.

Spatial Dimension Should I organize the event in the company's offices or at an external venue? The latter enables the group to work without distractions and allows the participants to clear their minds. But holding a workshop at an external venue does require additional effort (travel time, costs). The furnishing constellation in the room naturally also has an effect. Placing the seats in a circle permits a more open and flexible form of working than if the participants are seated at a table or tables. It is also important to ensure that everyone can see and hear what is going on in a large-group event. And last but not least, the size of the room is important: How large (or small) does it need to be to accommodate the particular purpose of the workshop?

Symbolic Dimension This dimension runs through all of the other four dimensions. Having the project leader open the workshop instead of the consultants is not only good from a practical/content perspective, it also signalizes that it is the organization, and not the consultants, that is taking the lead. If the individual workshops in a series always begin with an introductory round ("How am feeling today?"), it immediately becomes clear that the people also matter here. If the organization arranges a "Fuck-up Night", at which all manner of different failures and flops are recounted, it becomes obvious that the organization also learns from its mistakes. At large-group events in particular, the participants are extremely sensitive when it comes to this dimension. Accordingly, we always recommend sounding out the design in advance with a so-called sounding group.

We likewise always recommend a five-step approach to planning designs like workshops:

1. Gather and share information.
2. Form hypotheses: What is going on under the surface?
3. Set the direction(s): Where do we want to go? What do we want to achieve?
4. Gather elements and ideas for the agenda.
5. Define the timing and plan the detailed design.

Table 2 shows an example agenda for a large-group event as part of a customer orientation values process.

Many organizations are spread around the globe, making face-to-face meetings costly and time-consuming. Yet contact, dialog and exchange within an organization remain essential. Since many such meetings now take place in the virtual world (e.g. Skype, Webex, Zoom), many of our design elements—and, of course, also the architecture elements—can likewise be used in a virtual setting (see Gärtner et al. 2014).

2.3 *Tools*

Systemic organizational consultancy has developed its own toolkit from multiple sources and concepts. Many of these tools have been drawn and adapted from (family) therapy contexts (see Schlippe and Schweitzer 2003). Some of the key basic tools include, for example, reframing, splitting, positive connotations, the good in the bad and paradoxical interventions (see Königswieser and Hillebrand 2005).

Questions also play a special role in our consulting work. We ask questions almost continuously in the consulting process—at the first meeting, during the system diagnosis, at large-group events or in workshops.

In addition to supplying information, questions can also serve as a call to the respondent(s) to rethink an issue. This requires helpful questions and often also a setting that is open to such an approach. It also generally requires the use of open questions: "How would you describe the cooperation between managers?" "Where do you think there is room for improvement?". This not only supplies information, it also builds up a relationship of trust between the consultants and the client. And then there are the circular questions, the "high art" of asking questions, e.g. What would my colleagues say? How would our customers describe us?

The key purpose of systemic questions is to identify relevant differences and thus gather valuable information. Asking questions also calls for consultants to be archaeologists and not inquisitors—i.e. to demonstrate an attitude that incorporates genuine curiosity and an acceptance of the results.

Table 2 Example agenda for a large-group event

When	What	Who	Materials
10.00	Intro by board, incl. goals/context/attitude Customer orientation, moderation, orientation day	Board Moderation: Co13	Slides
10.15	Input on customer orientation Presentations by actual customers	Film; board customer (à 10–15 minutes each); Seating: in a circle	Film, slides
10.40	Group introductions Group exercise: discussion of initial understanding of customer orientation	16 circles of 9 seats; Moderation: implementation team	Flipcharts for orientation issues
11.50 12.00	Input on our customer orientation Interviews in previously defined tandems 0–0	Customer/supplier	Slides, handout
12.45	Lunch		
13.30 14.00	Evaluation of customer/supplier interviews (1 min. each on content and process) Moderation notes basic customer orientation principles/characteristics Selection of core theme/characteristic for customer orientation from the group	Implementation team Seating: in circles In big letters on flipchart with description	2–6 principles on cards; flipcharts
14.10	Look at the organization: Where are we strong? Where do we need to develop? Scale of 0-100. Flash feedback in groups.	Flipcharts distributed around the room; Seating: in circles	All
14.35 14.50	Customer orientation initiative process: 15 minutes Questions/feedback on process (seats in circles) Implementation ideas noted down on cards	Project leader Mod: implementation team	Slides, cards
15.10	Feedback in prev. customer/supplier tandems What have I learned today? What I am taking away with me? What will I do to promote customer orientation in my own setting?	Find partners Murmuring (à 7 minutes)	–
15.30	Back to home group: Spotlight on the day/process/issue/people	Moderation, Co13	–
15.50	Final remarks/close of event	Board	

The following examples illustrate how systemic questioning techniques work in practice:

(a) **The absent others**

How would the works council describe the situation?
What would customers say about the situation?

Such questions provide an insight into the assumptions about the others and open up new perspectives.

(b) **Percentage questions**

How satisfied are you with the development of the organization on a scale of 0–100?

How strongly do you assess the need for change in the organization on a scale of 0–100?

This requires people to take a position and makes soft topics measurable. It also allows us to determine how "difficult" or "problematic" the topic is considered to be.

(c) **Expectation questions**

What do you expect of the consultants? What should they do and what shouldn't they do?

How has the relationship to customers changed as a result of the new product?

What do you expect from this workshop?

These questions help to achieve clarity regarding relationships.

(d) **Aggravation questions**

What would you need to do to make the problem worse?

What would be worse if the problem were resolved?

These questions consider the functional aspects and relativize the problem. Care should be taken here not to come across as cynical.

2.4 Attitude

Tools are then particularly effective when the consultant has the right attitude. Appreciation and trust in the ability of organizations to develop is the basis of all our consulting work.

The attitude of the consultant is a fundamental factor for success and is more important than any use of tools. Only when I reflect on my own values and images of the world, but also my mistakes, limits, strengths and weaknesses, can I increase my own effect and effectiveness. This means that I constantly have to work on myself. Work in the consulting team, supervision and collegial intervision are all key elements of professional consulting work.

For us, attitude is evident in action, and we have therefore developed the following set of 13 commandments for our consulting practice.

1. Observe carefully and try to understand.
2. Ask respectfully, listen and try to understand.
3. Pay attention to the whole, the unsaid, the context.
4. Be conscious of your own perception filters; work with colleagues who are different to you.
5. Form hypotheses, reflect in loops, think in terms of solutions.

6. Draw on multiple perspectives to increase the courses of action open to the system.
7. Choose your interventions carefully; pay attention to the spatial, temporal, contextual, social and symbolic dimensions.
8. Work with your client to develop a shared image of the future—both for the project and the organization.
9. Slow down and create space for dialog, development and feedback.
10. Irritate and sensitize people to patterns in the organization and how it handles contradictions and complexity. Establish the parameters for a successful, insightful approach to mistakes.
11. Enjoy your work and the people you work with, provide advice to the whole system, and remain neutral.
12. Be positive. Set the focus on meaning and values, on the question "Why?"
13. Be useful and make an impact!

3 Systemic Change in Practice

Many corporate business models are facing enormous pressure to change as a result of digitalization. In the banking sector, many customer processes are being digitalized, and customer expectations are changing: on average, around half of all customers now use digital platforms to manage their finances. Many banking transactions can now be completed quickly and easily online. It is now quicker and cheaper to do bank transfers or purchase or sell shares via a bank's online banking system. Customers are constantly being offered new products and services, which are taken off the market just as quickly again if they do not work. In addition, new market players who focus on the digitalization of the individual business processes in financial processes—so-called Fintechs—are putting pressure on established financial services firms with their innovative products and rapid speed of innovation.

These changed customer processes and expectations and accelerated rates of innovation can no longer be accommodated in the established business processes and traditional organizational structures of conventional banks. They are too unwieldy, too hierarchical, and frequently do not have the right staff to handle the new demands. They need flexible, collaborative forms of working, new organizational models, and also new staff with different skills profiles. In concrete terms, this means that people—and this applies just as much to management as it does to staff—who have worked for years or even decades in traditional management and organizational structures, and whose behaviors and characters have been shaped accordingly, need to be helped into the new digital world. Designing products radically from the customer perspective requires new—and different—personal and professional skills. Change becomes a permanent task for everyone (Gratton 2011).

So what does all this have to do with systemic consultancy? The answer in itself is simple: In the modern world of dynamic markets and rapid speed of change, companies will ultimately only remain competitive if they are able to let go of their traditional, mechanistic ideas of business and embrace a more systemic view of the world.

3.1 Case Study: Human Resources

Let us now take a closer look at the practice of change using the example of an HR department. In our chosen case study, the transformation of HR is about improving the internal customer focus through the digitalization of the business process and the introduction of standardized HR products and processes. It is also about supplying innovative consulting formats to support management and staff in dealing with pending—and probably disruptive—changes. It is about leadership in a network-based organizational structure at different locations in different time zones and about new working hours models. And it is also simply about people, who need support and new skills to deal with the change on a personal level.

Many HR departments find it difficult to translate the consequences of the digitalization of business models into modern HR work that produces measurable results. The process of transforming HR from an administrative, task-based role to that of a modern business partner has been ongoing since the mid-1990s and appears to be taking longer than was originally anticipated: "The HR function has been transforming for nearly 20 years—but with uneven results" (Kern 2013). Actual practice in many organizations ultimately tends to be mixed. From an organizational structure perspective, many companies have adapted Dave Ulrich's three-legged model, which divides the HR function into three segments (shared services, business partners and centers of expertise; Ulrich 1997), even if the interfaces are frequently not clarified and the distribution of roles and tasks remains blurred. They often also lack modern, market-oriented HR processes, products and staff that can adequately handle the new roles and tasks. Overall, many HR departments react too slowly to new parameters. Indeed, according to a study by Mercer, 62% of HR departments in Europe find it difficult to assume a decidedly strategic role that provides added value for the company. While 66% of HR staff see themselves as strategic partners, only 38% of them are actually also involved in their company's strategy planning process (Kern 2013). On the whole, analyses and surveys regularly show that these areas of modern HR work are considered by all players in a company to be both relevant and important. Leadership, change, competence management and coaching always lie at the top of the internal agenda. More recently, "Reskilling the HR function" even made it into the Top 3 of the Deloitte Human Capital Index: 66% of the companies surveyed see a need here for urgent action, i.e. HR departments will have to adapt more quickly to changing conditions if they want to survive as independent business units (Deloitte 2014).

The building blocks of modern HR work—clear focus on the business, up-to-date products and processes, and capable staff—have long been clear. Yet the conclusions on the state of many HR departments remain critical. What are the reasons for this, and what contribution can systemic consulting make in this regard? How can successful transformation be achieved?

We are of the firm conviction that the systemic approach offers a set of tools that can bring the desired results. Change projects have to be designed in a way that combines the planning and strategic work with personal reflection and learning processes as well as consistent communication between management and staff. So how precisely did we go about planning the transformation of the HR division in this case study? What did the architecture for the change project look like?

3.1.1 The Analysis of the Status Quo

The willingness of company management to realign the HR function was an important basis for the start of the change project and a central factor for its success. What was the best architecture for this step? (Königswieser and Exner 2004) The spokesman for the management board was the sponsor of the change project. The first step was to conduct a candid analysis of the status quo and develop a shared picture of challenges faced. An ad hoc working group was set up for this purpose and served as the steering group for the strategy process. The composition of this steering group was a key success factor for the joint activities. It was made up of members of staff who had a fresh and open opinion of the status quo, were experts in their respective fields and had predominantly not held management positions in the previous system.

Three perspectives have to be considered in this phase of the analysis. Nagel (2009) refers to these as navigation instruments in the change process:

1. The examination of the relevant system environments, in our case, the consequences of the digitalization of bank business models and their effects on the world of banking.
2. The analysis of the inner world to identify the existing strengths and weaknesses and render the ability of the organization to realize change tangible.
3. The look to the future, i.e. the development of future scenarios in order to establish options for the future positioning of the HR function.

Interviews were carried out with external experts to intensify our understanding of the relevant system environment. These included traditional business consultants from international consulting firms and experts from other companies who had also worked on modernizing the HR function as well as coaches and organizational consultants who were familiar with the company from an internal perspective.

To explore the inner workings of the company and understand the logic behind its previous approach to change, intensive discussions on the strengths and weaknesses of the work of the HR department to date were held in the steering group during the strategic analysis. The (self-)examination and diagnosis of the organization both proved to be helpful interventions in this regard. It was important to understand how the organization dealt in general with mission-critical demands, what patterns of behavior were evident in response to change and which levers had proved successful in the realization of change projects (Königswieser and Exner 2004).

A corresponding questionnaire was drawn up as the basis for the interviews with the management team, the internal customers, the works council and the external experts. All in all, interviews were conducted with around 5% of the workforce (it is important in the case of a large organization to identify the right people to interview in order to obtain a balanced picture). An online survey also proved to be a useful instrument and enabled us to involve a large number of employees. In addition to the methods chosen for this project, there are a host of different intervention instruments that can be used in the diagnosis of the status quo (Nagel 2009). The following list offers a few examples of the questions used:

- On a scale of 1–4, how would you rate the recruiting process for new staff? What is/was good? (Please give a maximum of three examples.) What do we need to improve? (Please give a maximum of three keywords.)
- On a scale of 1–4, how would you assess the salary and bonus system?
- On a scale of 1–4, how would you assess the annual appraisal meeting?
- Which facts/figures/data do you use in your management role?
- When you think about the current HR department, what image comes into your mind?
- Please give three adjectives that in your opinion best describe the current corporate culture.
- Imagine that you were in charge of the HR department for a day. Which three projects would you give priority to and what would be the first thing you would change?

The involvement of many stakeholders and the intensive discussion process within the steering group provided a solid base for a valid assessment of the existing situation. Everyone had the chance to contribute his/her "truths" and there was intense wrangling over which of the shared conclusions should be presented to the sponsor. At the same time, this work established a solid relationship of trust and an open atmosphere of debate. So what were the key results?

- The basic administrative processes (e.g. salary payment) worked.
- The internal customers criticized the HR department's lack of clear focus, sluggish completion of task and overall lack of customer focus. Satisfaction depended largely on the personal commitment of individual members of the HR team.
- The organizational structure and the processes had basically developed over time and were characterized by unclear roles and task descriptions. This led to a great deal of dissatisfaction among the affected members of staff and a high level of fluctuation.
- While options were in principle available (e.g. in the fields of personnel development, talent management or Compensation & Benefit), they were not aligned to the company's strategic goals.

- The effects of the digitalization of the business model on daily work, the strategic focus of HR and demographic change had hitherto been totally ignored.
- The cooperation with the works council was hitherto based on hostility and confrontation, not on cooperation and trust. Important topics for the future (e.g. with regard to working hours) had not been worked on.

This first step in the analysis of the status quo was also important because it revealed a significant discrepancy between how the management of the HR department saw its work and how it was seen by company management and its "customers". In this case, these different perceptions of the status quo were discussed at the mirroring of the results. This provided an indemnified picture of the current situation, which served as the basis for the strategic realignment and ultimately led to changes in work priorities, the organization and the people involved. Incidentally, this approach works both in large international groups as well as in medium-sized companies, since the link to the status quo is established. The potential for optimization becomes clear in every case and can then be used as the basis for the strategy development.

3.1.2 Picturing the Future

Strategy is the bridge between the present and the future (Nagel 2009). The candid analysis of the status quo established in the first step of this project allowed a "letting go" of previous truths and created space for the development of the new strategy and for the shaping of the future. What is the goal of this initial step? In an ideal situation, it results in a strategy that includes the substantive focus, the (usually) necessary organizational changes and an initial time plan. In our case, the actual strategy document to be approved by the board was prepared by the steering group and was discussed regularly with the project sponsor. The document itself follows the logic applied in the analysis phase: Processing of the external factors and their effect on the company, results of the analysis of the status quo, conceptualization of future projects and initial implementation plan.

The next step is to have the new strategy approved and adopted by the board. Here, the procedure will depend on the size of the team, the political situation and the prior level of involvement of the individual board members. Ideally, a shared image of the future will already have been established in advance and will enjoy the broad support of all concerned. If this is the case, approval and adoption is usually just a formality.

As you will recall, in our example, the strategy was developed outside the existing hierarchy and without those responsible in a separate steering group. This can lead to irritation and uncertainty among those who were previously responsible for such activities. Accordingly, once the strategy has been approved and adopted, it is extremely important to inform all members of staff in detail and to involve them in the implementation phase.

3.1.3 Enabling and Ensuring Implementation

The implementation of a strategy is a long-term endeavor and is frequently linked with a restructuring of the organization with the engine still running (Nagel 2009). It requires:

1. The planning and realization of substantive changes like, for instance, the introduction of a new target agreement system or agile cooperation models.
2. The realization of organizational and process changes.
3. Accompanying measures for those members of staff who have to drive the changes forward, but also for those who are actually affected by them.

Successful implementation projects need an architecture that takes account of the particular challenges of this phase. Sound project management and good project planning are prerequisites for a successful implementation. In our case study, each subproject now had to be designed and specified in detail. How precisely should we go about achieving the desired changes (e.g. the introduction of a new salary or target agreement system)? When it came to the redesign of HR products, we only fell back on external consultants in exceptional circumstances. In most cases, the new products (e.g. the new target agreement system) were designed in internal working groups made up of customers, staff representatives and members of the HR team. This gained them acceptance and made sure they tied in with the previous corporate culture.

Organizational and process changes are an important variable when it comes to improving the quality of the services provided by an HR department. As already mentioned, many organizations nowadays base their organizational structure on Dave Ulrich's three-legged model (Ulrich 1997). We also opted for this model and introduced a new business partner department as internal service provider for customers, a department that focuses on product development (e.g. talent management or Compensation & Benefit systems) and a service department that provides the necessary IT infrastructure for employee self-service, payroll and administration.

Many companies have adopted this model in recent years, but not always with success: Simply changing the sign on the door and calling HR a business partner is not going to work. Accordingly, we decided to work at length on the content of the roles, the necessary attitudes and the processes involved. The roles—business partner, consultant, and service partner—were defined in a joint process and then tried out in practice. At the same time, a process working group was established as a central architecture element. This working group was tasked with adapting all HR processes to the new organizational structure. This revealed that the new roles were not yet fully workable and led to conflicts during process definition regarding their actual implementation.

Accordingly, reflection and feedback loops were regularly incorporated into the process workshops. This led to the development of an attitude in the team that was shaped by listening, asking questions, dialog, discussion and joint learning. Hard and soft factors were integrated into this process, which ultimately resulted in clear substantive solutions and a new quality of cooperation and cohesion, which was also evident to customers.

This approach was accompanied by a coaching process for the management team. This team learned in turn to address open issues and latent conflicts and to work together to find solutions. This gradually led to the establishment of a culture of greater trust and cooperation. As a result, managers were able to act not just as superiors, but as sources of inspiration and coaches to their staff.

3.1.4 Summary

Strategy development and implementation is a joint learning process (Gratton 2000). Sustainable and successful implementation is helped by a transformation architecture that combines sound project management, clear organizational and process parameters with a joint learning and development process that results in customer-oriented products and processes and a new quality of work both within the organization and with its customers.

Systemic consultancy offers diverse, versatile and well-founded methods for organizational development. The systemic approach has moved on from its pioneering phase at the start of the twenty-first century and is now in broad use. Alongside the well-founded theory and differentiated methods, the systemic attitude is the key to success. And given the current trends and dynamics in society and business, this attitude is even more important than ever before.

References

Bateson G (1951) Communication. The Social Matrix of Society. W.W. Norton, New York

Deloitte (2014) Global human capital trends

Gärtner H, Hillebrand M, Isermann W (2014) Virtuelle Zusammenarbeit etablieren. Ein Werkstattbericht aus dem Unternehmen Sennheiseser. Organisationsentwicklung, pp 57–67

Gratton L (2000) Living strategy: putting people at the heart of corporate purpose. Prentice Hall, London

Gratton L (2011) The shift. The future of work is already here. Harper Collins, London

Kern D (2013) HR organization effectiveness. Mercer Consulting

Königswieser R (2000) Das Feuer von Großgruppen. In: Königswieser R, Keil M (eds) Das Feuer großer Gruppen. Klett-Cotta, Stuttgart, pp 30–44

Königswieser R, Exner A (2004) Systemische Intervention, 8th edn. Klett Cotta, Stuttgart

Königswieser R, Hillebrand M (2005) Systemic consultancy in organisations. In: Concepts-tools-innovations. Carl-Auer, Heidelberg

Luhmann N (1984) Soziale Systeme. Suhrkamp, Frankfurt

Maturana HR, Varela FJ (1987) The tree of knowledge: the biological roots of human understanding. Shambhala, Boston

Nagel R (2009) Lust auf Strategie. Workbook zur strategischen Strategieentwicklung. Schäfer Poeschel, Stuttgart

Piaget J (1992) Einführung in die genetische Erkenntnistheorie. Suhrkamp, Frankfurt

Schlippe A, Schweitzer J (2003) Lehrbuch der systemischen Therapie und Beratung. Vandenhoeck & Rupprecht, Göttingen

Seliger R (2015) Einführung in Gossgruppen-Methodik. Carl-Auer, Heidelberg

Selvini Palazzoli M, Boscolo S, Cecchini G, Prata G (1978) Paradoxes and counterparadoxes. Aronson, New York

Selvini Palazzoli M, Anolli L, di Blasio P, Giossi L, Pisano I, Ricci C, Saci M, Ugazio V (1988) The hidden games of organizations. Routledge, New York

Simon F (2007) Einführung in die systemische Organisationsberatung. Carl-Auer-Verlag, Heidelberg

Ulrich D (1997) Human resources champions. Harvard Business School Press, Boston

Watzlawick P, Beavin JH, Jackson D (2000) Menschliche Kommunikation. Formen, Störungen, Paradoxien, 10th edn. Hans Huber Verlag, Berne

Wimmer R (2004) Organisation und Beratung. Carl-Auer-Verlag, Heidelberg

Martin Hillebrand studied Psychology in Würzburg, Albany (NY, USA) and Oldenburg and holds a qualification in client-centred psychotherapy according to Rogers as well as long-term systemic consultant training. After completing his studies, Martin Hillebrand first worked for a consultancy company for a number of years. He then spent 4 years in an expanding multi-utility company, working in the fields of personnel and organisational development, further training, strategic personnel management and company development. His main areas of activity are designing and supporting complex and sustainable change processes as well as the development of strategies, including in particular their implementation. He also trains change managers and consultants both nationally and internationally. Martin Hillebrand is managing partner of CO(13), Gruppe für systemische Beratung: www.co13.eu.

Stefan Mette is an experienced manager with a strong focus on the modernization of HR functions in various industries, nationally and internationally. Currently Division Head of Human Resources, Brand & Corporate Communication, Administration at BNP Paribas Personal Finance in Germany, Dr. rer. soc, Tübingen University, Dipl. Verwaltungswissenschaftler, Constance University, M.A. (USA), Rutgers University, Management Development Programm, ESSEC Business School, Paris, Coach and organizational developer and member of the German Society of Supervision (DGSv).

Open Management as Management Innovation: Thoughts About New Business and Disruption in Consulting

Stephan Friedrich von den Eichen, Kurt Matzler, and Julia Hautz

Abstract Based on the management innovation of "Open Management" the authors explore chances as well as risks in view of management consulting. It becomes evident that most companies cannot find their way to "Open Management" without external support. Prima vista, good times for consultants. A closer look reveals: What companies currently need is not provided by traditional consultants. And traditional consultants will not be able to support companies on their way to "Open Management". There will be others who will rule this game...

1 Surprising Evidence...

In April 1989, Martin Chalfie, Professor of Biology at the Columbia University, went to hear a lecture, in which he was not even really interested. This lecture was about the process through which jellyfish produce visible lightening and rely on bioluminescence. Stimulated and inspired by the jellyfish, a new idea struck Chalfie. If he could connect the GFP-gene (the gene which drives the bioluminescence) to another random gene, it would be possible to observe its movements. Nobody had come up with this idea before. This lecture should change Chalfie's life. He was awarded the Nobel Prize and was able to provide a very important new tool to the world of science (Klein 2013). Is this a story of a coincidence leading to pioneering discovery? No, the message is a different one.

S. Friedrich von den Eichen (✉)
Innovative Management Partner, Munich, Germany

University of Bremen, Bemen, Germany
e-mail: friedrich.v.d.eichen@imp-consulting.de

K. Matzler
Innovative Management Partner, Free University of Bolzano, Bolzano, Italy
e-mail: kurt.matzler@unibz.it

J. Hautz
IMP Network of Excellence, University of Innsbruck, Innsbruck, Austria
e-mail: julia.hautz@uibk.ac.at

V. Nissen (ed.), *Advances in Consulting Research*, Contributions to Management Science, https://doi.org/10.1007/978-3-319-95999-3_10

But let us have a look on another case first. Goldcorp, a Canadian gold mine, was confronted with bankruptcy around the millennium. The outputs were low and the company was not profitable. At this time, CEO McEven came up with an unconventional new approach: "What if we publish our entire geological knowledge on the web, make it available to everyone and ask the world where we could find gold based on this information?" McEven and his idea were seen a naïve and were smiled at. Some even called him crazy. But actually he got suggestions and ideas from all over the world from a wide range and diversity of participants: geologists, students, consultants, mathematicians, … 110 sources of gold were identified—more than 8 billion ounces of gold were extracted. The biggest surprise was the winner of the competition. It was neither a geologist, neither an engineer, nor a scientist specialized on mining. His name was Nick Archibald, and he was CEO of Fractal-Graphics Ltd in Australia. He had never been in gold mine or even in Canada before. But he had very specialized knowledge in a different area: His corporation was specialized in the production of 3D computer simulations and 3D visualization of data. This experience and knowledge was worth a lot of gold (Tapscott and Williams 2008)—in the true sense of the word.

What can we learn from these two cases?

1. First, pioneering solutions are always a coincidence? Coincidence may play a role, especially if it meets—following Pasteur—with a prepared mind (Pasteur 1933). But another factor is decisive here: the willingness and capability to be open. If someone is open for impulses, if someone is open for new perspectives, which could not have been identified by himself, this enables him to connect dots, which have not been connected before (Friedrich von den Eichen 2016).
2. The second finding is, that in order to find revolutionary ways, expert knowledge in the respective discipline is not enough. Rather it is important to transfer solutions from one context to a completely different one and apply it there. 90% of successful business model innovations are nothing more than the transfer (or the reconfiguration) of patterns from different industries (Gassmann et al. 2013). In this context we refer to "cross-fertilization" (Matzler et al. 2016).
3. Finally, rarely groundbreaking ideas and revolutionary approaches are provided by an individual. It is essential to specifically use and benefit from the "wisdom of the crowd". This includes access to external knowledge. And this includes relevant methods and the capability to transform (external and internal) knowledge into specific solutions.

These three insights have multiple implications. In the following, we will focus on three perspectives: implications for strategy and innovation in organizations, implications for the value added by (management-) consulting and implications for positioning of consulting firms and their business models.

2 Implications for Strategy and Innovation

Please imagine: A manager who died in the 1960s, returns to earth just for a few hours. He would be astonished about what has changed: In the meantime we have been on the moon, we print various objects with 3D-printers, we are guided by voices within our cars, we make videos and even do the shopping with our smartphone. But he would even be more surprised if he would visit our corporations. Basically, hardly anything has change there. Despite rapid and tremendous economic and technological progress in the last decades and dramatic changes in markets and consumer behavior, conventional management methods, tools and approaches have remain the same and seem to be relicts from stone age (Hamel and Breen 2007).

Does the following situation sound familiar to you? The strategy department comes up with long-term predictions or even scenarios. The corporate center sets strategic goals. The business units develop their strategic plans accordingly. These plans are discussed with the corporate center. Then everything is sent back to the business units for revision until the plans are finally approved. This is followed by the budgeting process. Budgets also need to be approved. At the end of this (time consuming) planning period the strategy quite often does not really match the situation—and the process starts again with a deviation analysis (Matzler and Friedrich von den Eichen 2015). This process, previously developed, communicated and distributed by consultants has its roots in in the beginning of "Corporate Strategy" from the 60s and early 70s (Friedrich von den Eichen 2000). Back then, decision makers had enough time to intensively engage with changes in their environment, to thoroughly analyze different alternatives and to make sound and profound decisions. Back then, the world was less complex. It was sufficient to be familiar with your own industry, selected competitors and the relevant technologies. Today corporate strategy is facing different challenges (Matzler et al. 2016):

- Technologies are developing at exponential pace
- Industry boundaries are becoming permeable and disappear
- New actors compete with different business models
- Information is rapidly transferred, knowledge is ubiquitous and transparency increases

Strategy, done in the traditional way, is too slow to meet these new conditions. Typically it is limited to an inner circle of top management teams and is kept secret (Whittington et al. 2011; Matzler and Friedrich von den Eichen 2015). This closed and secretive approach does not allow diversity of perspectives and cross-fertilization, described above. But these are essential requirements for organizations to be able to cope with more complex and fast changing environments, to grow, to renew and to tap into new businesses. "No matter who you are, most of the smartest people work for someone else". With this sentence Bill Joe of Microsystems has characterized the open movement in 1990: No organization possess all the knowledge necessary to solve problems or to develop good strategies. Even if you engage

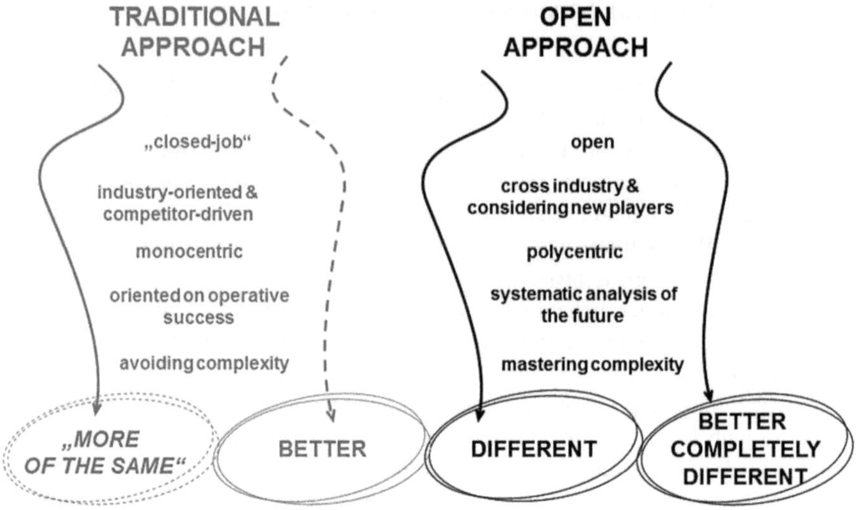

Fig. 1 Traditional strategy approach vs. open strategy approach

the best experts, the capability to solve problems and creativity are limited through professional mind-sets, and routines of employees shaped by history, organizational values and path dependencies of strategic decisions (Hautz 2017; Sydow et al. 2009).

The principles and concepts of Open Innovation, introduced by Henry Chesbrough (2003), describe a shift of paradigm from closed to open innovation approaches. These principles seem to provide promising opportunities also for strategic management. And they become even more relevant if the goal of your strategy is not only to increase efficiency but rather evolutionary or disruptive innovation (Matzler et al. 2014; Friedrich von den Eichen et al. 2016; Hautz et al. 2017) (cf. Fig. 1).

To sum up:

- New approaches are created (most likely) through “cross-fertilization. This “fertilization” is enabled if boundaries are crossed—boundaries of your own discipline, organizational boundaries, industry boundaries. This is true for the development of new technologies but also for identifying new fields of application for already existing technologies.
- If you would like to achieve breakthroughs, you need to escape established patterns in strategy and innovation (Christensen et al. 2011). At the end, technological breakthroughs which should lead to successful innovations require management innovations. If organizations do not succeed in these management innovations by opening up their strategy and innovation, they will fail in their corporate renewal.
- “Open Management” describes the transfer of the principles of the Open Innovation philosophy to strategic management. “Openness” is thereby not restricted

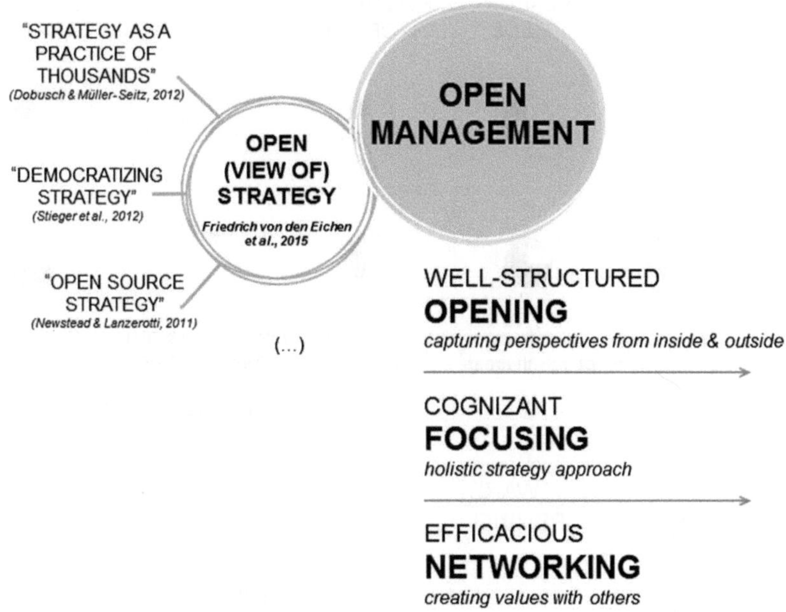

Fig. 2 The concept of Open Management

to generating and collecting new ideas at the front end of the process, but is applied across the entire strategic management, from strategic analyses to the detection of search fields, the evaluation of options, and the detailing and implementation of strategy (cf. Fig. 2).

- This "Open Management" is already applied in practice. This is shown by comparing the degree of openness of strategy projects of the management consultancy IMP between 2010 and 2016. A few years ago, e.g. "competence audits" were substantially based on an inside-out perspective. Today, organizations rely much more on an external, expert-based evaluation of their competence/ technology portfolio. The same is true concerning the "strategic search fields" and "innovation target areas". Today only few organizations rely on their internal capabilities to identify new growth areas. The more radical and disruptive, the more organizations are willing to open up (cf. Fig. 3).

3 The Value-Added of Management Consulting

Technological breakthroughs require "Open Management"—or more precisely: Technological breakthroughs will not lead to successful innovations (or new business) without management innovations. But organizations are hardly able to manage the transformation to Open Management on their own. Large companies might have

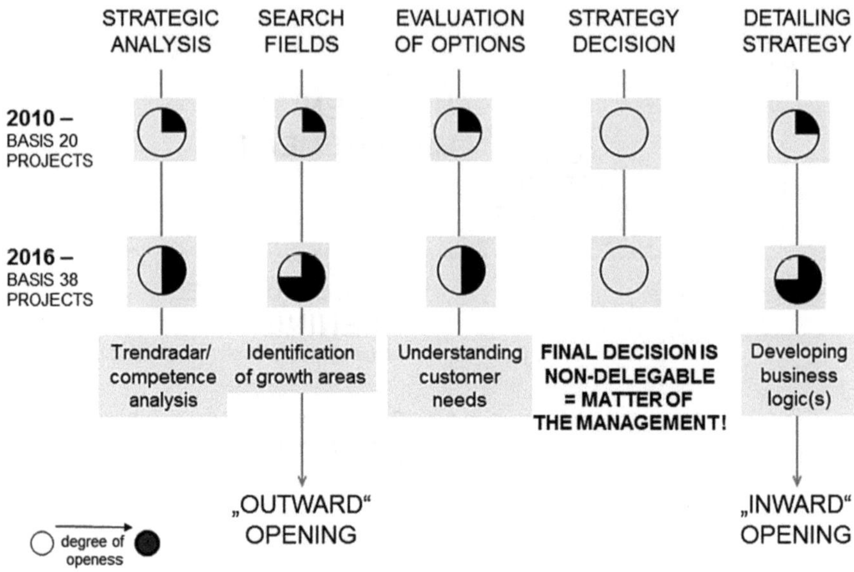

Fig. 3 Degree of openness in strategy projects "consulted" by IMP in 2010 resp. 2016

access to external knowledge, but they lack methods, structures and cultural capabilities to use and leverage these sources of knowledge for cross-fertilization. Small- and medium-sized companies additionally lack access to external expertise beyond their existing core business. Good times for consultants?

For decades, the perception of the value proposition of a consultant (supply) and the reasons why organizations buy these services (demand) was pretty clear: The consultant—in his view the "Mr. Automotive", the "Mr. Health Care", or the "Mr. Pulp & Paper"—is an expert in his particular industry. He is part of the system. He is familiar with the rules of the game in the respective industry. He is familiar with the players and familiar with their strengths and weaknesses. And he knows a lot about threats and opportunities in "his" industry. During the years he might have worked for most companies in "his" industry. This expertise makes him precious for organizations. But only as long as companies follow the excellence and benchmark approach. This paradigm has dominated thinking and acting for years and has justified the role of consultants in nearly all industries. But if the goal is no longer to increase efficiency but rather (non-core) growth and (radical) innovation, a different perspective needs to be adopted. Both columns on which the value proposition of traditional consulting is based on—industry expertise and outstanding capabilities of individuals—collapse. What are the reasons?

In best case, industry-focused consulting results in "being better" than competition based on the common performance indicators. It concerns the optimization of core business compared to direct competitors. At the end this leads to "industry-typical" solutions and a convergence of business models within an industry. But, if organizations want to differentiate by being different, industry expertise is not a critical success factor.

If organizations have additionally internalized that "not all smart people are working for us" they will realize that a heterogenous crowd is much more capable to find smart solutions than a individual. Organizations will not ignore brilliant minds, but the lonely genius will lose importance compared to the crowd. So, Mr. "X-Industry" will lose his unique position and his impact.

It is obvious that companies need support to apply the Open Management philosophy. This might be a chance for additional consulting business. However, first one need to clarify (a) which kind of support is really needed and (b) who has the ability to provide this support. In this context the "role-of-consultant-framework" might be helpful (Friedrich von den Eichen 2005, 2017).

To be open means to adopt new perspectives. Openness includes to see a situation (but also oneself) with different eyes. Empirical evidence shows that organizations are reluctant to open up proactively. Many are only willing to react to articulated needs (market research), manifested dissatisfaction (complaints) or massive pressures (financial markets). Some organizations might be willing to open up, but do not know how. With it, some lack the willingness to be open, others the capability. And some even lack both. Being open comes at some costs. Openness disrupts the status quo and disturbs "common sense". It takes time and requires management resources. Based on our projects we have gained the experience that openness has to be achieved against the strive for efficiency. Management needs to be confronted with the "useful investment" in openness. If openness is perceived as a process, it becomes visible where support is indicated. Hypotheses concerning the future of the company need to be formulated. These hypotheses should be translated into pictures. Others, especially externals, should add their understanding of the future. So, openness is also about networking and gaining access: Access to creativity, access to knowledge, access to lateral thinkers, lead experts and lead users. Traditional consultants cannot support this "open" processes, because their access is limited to the boundaries of "their" respective industry. But again, support is needed. Consultants create added value by acting as networkers, facilitators and catalysts bringing together external and internal knowledge.

Consultants should no longer promote their promise to reduce complexity. In contrast, in the future, value will be created through helping organizations to escape their comfort zone. To give an example: A consultant could confront organizations with (simulated) disruptive attacks by integrating external parties. If a consultant is doing a good job, top management will see more risks afterwards. However, they will also be aware of new opportunities. To do so individuals and organizations have to be motivated to share knowledge and information. In addition, appropriate methods and their skillful application are required to be able to absorb, channel and make use out of the knowledge of the crowd. This knowledge can be applied to develop future scenarios, to detect opportunities, to evaluate technologies or to understand customer needs. In general someone is needed who provokes and makes clear how disruptions can destroy the existing core business. As irritator a consultant can create added value. This, however, is a role, which is in contrast to traditional consulting.

Openness offers a diversity of signals. The challenge here is to identify patterns. To derive strategic options based on this patterns, to define strategic directions and—based on that—to develop and implement sustainable business models. Despite their efforts regarding creativity, strategy and focus, many companies are not doing a good job. At first glance, "traditional management" and "Open Management" seem to be pretty close. But having a deeper look, for example on a "competence analysis", it becomes obvious that Open Management has different requirements. If we assess the existing competence profile within distinctive "closed" clusters, e.g. within the top management teams or within the R&D departments, this will lead to quite homogeneous results. However, if we open up this analysis and also Externals are asked for their assessments, things become very different. On one hand, competencies which organizations have been sure of, will lose their impact. On the other hand new, unexpected (and so far hidden) competencies will be discovered. This was also the case in an SME with its roots in producing printing machinery. This organization was not aware of a capability, which allows solving a critical issue in the context of fuel cells. The same with a traditional company in producing textile machinery. The competency discovered by externals to infuse super absorber into strings provides access to the "high-margin" market of medical products. If a consultant wants to add value here, he first needs to be familiar with "open methodologies". Second, he needs, what we call instinct. Instinct means to be able to imagine what can be done based on competencies, but also concerning the existing willingness and capabilities of organizations for new ventures without having too much organizational reluctance. Value is created by consultants in addition if they are able to enforce discipline: discipline to avoid the premature abolishment of alternatives, and to rather invest additional efforts; but also the discipline to avoid endless repetitions and discussions, and instead consciously exclude alternatives. Helping to achieve this delicate balance can be of great support. In sum, an external supporter has to take the role of a navigator, who provides the appropriate methods, tools and experience to ensure that the organization stays on course. This is also in contrast with traditional consulting.

By applying Open Management unique requirements are revealed. In order to be able to meet these requirements, companies with complementary competencies have to collaborate. On the one hand this needs "design competence"—the capability to create completely new ecosystem of value creation. On the other hand, "operating excellence" is required to run the business with several value adding partners. Networks are polycentric structures, which cannot be managed via hierarchy and control. It is a critical success factor of Open Management to master this complexity. Some "guiding principles"—in the sense of a common understanding of strategic roles, ambitions and values—might provide useful direction. Besides this, a corporate strategy—this time on a network level—has to be formulated: Who is part of the network? How is value-added defined by the network partners? Based on which logic is added value distributed among the partners? The overall goal of Open Management is a creative domino with complementary competencies of like-minded partners, through which new value is created for (hopefully) all who are engaged. This requires that someone takes the role of an integrator. This role has multiple facets. It does not only concern the coordination of value contributions of the business partners. It is also about integrating the multi-level support-offer of the start-up economy including accelerators, incubators, company builders, venture capitalists, and others. At the moment, especially SMEs are lacking a comprehensive understanding who provides which services, how to make use of these services and to harmonize the start-up philosophy (fail often, but fail early) with the willingness of corporate innovation to transfer the company to its future. Here again the consultant can provide value through transparency, choosing appropriate facilitators and helping the organizations to set up an appropriate open ecosystem of innovation, which fits to the specific challenge of the company.

Finally, beyond the activities mentioned above, a consultant may also be actively engaged in innovation (content-wise). As a co-innovator he takes up ideas on his own in accordance with the principles of an incubator. By integrating external expertise, he transfers ideas into sustainable business logics, prepares market entry and takes care of a smooth start of the "new business". Co-innovators takes entrepreneurial risk, but also participates in the opportunities of the new business.

4 Business Models in Consulting

Consulting business is not free of competition. On the contrary. An increasing demand in professional services during the last decades has attracted new competitors. And this is typical for this industry: The number of competitors is increasing through "cell division", this means new consultancies emerge through spin-offs from already existing ones. At the same time, the high margins in consulting business attract additional supply from the "neighborhood": Chartered accountants, advertising agencies, HR consultants, university departments, IT service firms and many others try to find their way into the market.

Market saturation, more demanding and learning customers combined with difficult economic environments cause new challenges for the consulting industry. Strategic management, which so far has been sold as a consulting service to clients, become now a topic for consulting firms themselves. Quite often consulting firms are very similar. But the more homogenous, comparable and even reproducible consulting services are, the lower the margins. By focusing on rapid growth, many consultancies have overstretched their portfolios. And the smaller the firms are, the broader is often the range of services they offer.

In this context, positioning and especially focusing become essential. Considering "more focus" consultancies choose different paths. Some focus on particular industries (e.g. consulting for banks, consulting for energy and utilities, ...). Others concentrate on functional services (e.g. supply chain consulting, experts in purchasing, . . .). And still others specialize on particular methods (e.g. scenario consulting, CRM consulting, . . .).

All that is already known. But with Open Management we have to build on the cornerstones of strategy discussion within consulting—and could finally add a new chapter. This new approach impacts consulting in two ways. On the one hand it has an influence on the opportunities: Digitization and digital disruptions, cross-fertilization and cross industry innovation, business model innovation and—overall—Open Management, all these concepts "smell" like new business for consultancies. These concepts might even bear the potential for a new consulting hype. Here, consultants can benefit from their "real" core competence: creating appropriate bundles of solutions and then, convincing clients that only by following this way their survival can be ensured. On the other hand, the new dynamics including Open Management also have an impact on risks: What has been seen as a trigger for radical change for clients now also influences the consulting industry. The dynamics, which have substantially disrupt industries such as steel or publishing, now also transform the consulting industry. Christensen et al. (2013) point out that for the time being the established consulting firms could rely on intransparency of the market and on their own agility. But these advantages disappear. What we might add with respect to Open Management: Also new actors can be found of the playground who follow different rules of the game.

This becomes apparent if we analyze the business model of a consulting company,[1] which focus on the role of a Co-innovator. Differences compared to traditional consulting company appear—and also the barriers, which need to be overcome if you want to enter this market.

The positioning of a co-innovator differs from a traditional consultant. This can be seen in the value proposition of a co-innovator: He intends to enable new business. Therefore, he is not only interested in consulting projects, rather his intention is to find a way—based on a common understanding of the initial situation—which most likely allows innovation to succeed. This could be a consulting project—driven by Open Management philosophy. This could also be the advice to "outsource" an idea and let it grow within an external innovation ecosystem. But focusing also is a topic for co-innovators, but in a different way. Their strategic arena is well defined. For example, in the case of IMP (Innovative Management Partners) the goal is to achieve sustainability either through targeted interventions in the existing business models of the client or through new, adding or replacing business logics. The focus is not achieved by a specialization on industries or functions. It is achieved by strictly concentrating on a particular customer need. The customer-oriented and comprehensive understanding of the customer needs drive the service portfolio of the co-innovator in respect of content and the way of delivery of the service (commission of appropriate innovation partners, innovation projects, incubator activities).

---

[1]In terms of methodology we further apply on the IMP Business Logic Approach. For analyzing, designing and implementing a business logic, the following dimensions are crucial: positioning, product and service architecture, value chain logic, go-to-market logic and revenue logic (Bailom et al. 2011; Matzler et al. 2013).

Co-innovating—and this leads us from the service architecture to the value chain logic—is based on an open consulting approach. If a consultancy wants to convince clients on Open Management, it needs to apply this philosophy on oneself. For this approach the access to external knowledge is crucial. In the case of IMP a network of more than 1.500 experts, classified in different clusters, give access to knowledge (= IMP Network of Excellence). The inclusion of external expertise is realized case by case, based on the specific competences required and through an elaborated evaluation and selection process.

Also the go-to-market approach of co-innovators follows their own logic. A co-innovator cannot rely on a well-known "brand", which could open doors. He has to rely on feedbacks and word-of-mouth. His "door openers" are successful lighthouse projects, which illustrate how he enables new business. Agility is trump for the co-innovator. Through trial and error he learns from project to project, which creates an important and uncatchable advantage. He cannot afford difficult and complex procedures. His structure is quite similar to cells. Based on the particular challenge, internal resources are combined with external experts, facilitators, and the customer system. His thoughts and actions are close to the "lean start-up philosophy". But from his point of view entrepreneurial agility is not in conflict with sustainable value creation, he is rather eager to find a balance between both concepts.

The services of the co-innovator and his way of "consulting" consequently result in a different revenue logic. The co-innovator is no longer payed on a daily rate or "value price", he bears entrepreneurial risks and participates in successful development of the new business.

To sum up, a co-innovator is an own specie in the consulting industry. Analyzing his business it becomes apparent that co-innovators attacks the traditional consulting firms merely from the bottom. He is neither as big nor as shiny as the established consulting firms, but through accumulated experience in the handling of new ways of innovation ("trial and error") he becomes a more and more powerful and valuable alternative. Co-innovators themselves build on the Open Management philosophy. He exploits different sources of knowledge via his network of excellence, which is expanding project by project. Already this new profile indicates substantial barriers, which make it (almost) impossible for traditional consulting firms to offer Open Management as one of their services.

- Earmark: If someone has developed a particular image and invested resources to be perceived in this way—in the case of traditional consulting this includes deep industry knowledge, ruthless optimization of core processes and personal expertise—he will lose credibility if he abandons these values and advocates almost the opposite. Here also quickly established incubator approach is of no help.
- Service portfolio and standardization: traditional consulting is not about finding an appropriate solution for a specific problem. The sequence "problem first—then the solution" is changing often. The "art" of consulting is to standardize services and then convince as many customers as possible that they have a problem, which matches the existing solution—even if customers are not aware of their problem

yet. Open Management is not really compatible to standardization and not the playground for consulting factories.

- Networking and control: Many consulting firms already have their troubles coordinating the internal matrix between "industry practices" and "functional practices". First, networking—Open Management is based on—also requires networking within organizations. Second, networking with externals (experts, research institutes, thought-leaders. . . .) is in contrast with hierarchy and control of resources, advertised by traditional consulting. In addition, Open Management requires a high level of agility. Organizational size and scope are no longer critical factors, as they bring rigidity and cause complex decision making.
- Consultant profiles and values: Open Management is less a matter of education and more a matter of mindset. The "cool distance" often practiced by traditional consultants is replaced by topical (and emotional) infights. Co-innovators think and result-oriented. Traditional consultants are not familiar with such an approach. They balance their efforts against the customer satisfaction, because this might be the best way to be able to sell more consulting services. Open Management is not about working for costumers but is about working together with customers. This is different. A co-innovator is required to have an entrepreneurial mindset—including risk taking. Current business models of consultants do not consider such an orientation.

5 Take Aways

- Breakthrough innovations can be fostered by cross-fertilization.
- Cross-fertilization requires openness. Hence, technological breakthroughs are not feasible without management innovation.
- Open Management is a management philosophy, which requires openness along the entire strategy process, from idea generation to implementation of business model.
- Open Management is a management innovation, which does not happen on its own. It needs external support—at first sight good times for consultants.
- By taking a closer look, it becomes apparent that (traditional) consultants cannot provide the support needed by organizations on their transition to Open Management.
- As always, consultants might argue: There is nothing, which cannot be fixed by consultants. But this time things seem to be different. With respect to Open Management we have identified substantial hurdles for traditional consulting. Added value is created through externals, who act as
  - *irritators*—disrupting the common sense of organizations about their future
  - *networkers*—giving access to external expertise
  - *catalysts*—integrating internal and external knowledge
  - *navigators*—helping to stay on track

- *integrators*—managing the heterogeneous contributions of multiple value adding partners
- *co-innovators*—being familiar with all these roles an even going beyond, by taking entrepreneurial risks.

Traditional consulting is not compatible with these roles and the respective business model behind.

- Successful will be those, who are adapting their methods & actions according times and according to external conditions (Machiavelli). In the case of Open Management organizations might be able to do so—at least "with a little help" from externals. Traditional consultants are less likely to succeed in adapting their service portfolio. There will be other winners—bad times for (traditional) consultants, good times for co-innovators.

References

Bailom F, Friedrich von den Eichen S, Anschober M (2011) Die Dimensionen der Geschäftslogik sind systemisch zu betrachten! Komplex? IMP Perspect (2):29–34

Chesbrough HW (2003) Open innovation. The new imperative for creating and profiting from technology. Harvard Business School Press

Christensen C, Matzler K, Friedrich von den Eichen S (2011) The innovator's dilemma. Warum etablierte Unternehmen den Wettbewerb um bahnbrechende Innovationen verlieren. Vahlen Verlag, Munich

Christensen C, Wang D, van Bever D (2013) Consulting on the cusp of disruption. Harvard Business Review (October)

Dobusch L, Müller-Seitz G (2012) Strategy as a practice of thousands? Academy of Management Best Paper Proceedings

Friedrich von den Eichen S (2000) Quo vadis strategisches management. In: Hinterhuber HH et al (eds) Das neue strategische management, 2nd edn. Gabler, Wiesbaden, pp 7–30

Friedrich von den Eichen S (2005) Der Berater und seine Rollen. In: Kirsch, W. (Hrsg) Grenzen der Strategieberatung. Haupt, Bern, pp 369–383

Friedrich von den Eichen S (2016) Wie zukunftsfähig ist die Zukunftsarbeit unserer Unternehmen? Vortrag im Rahmen der BMWI-Industriekonferenz 2030, Berlin

Friedrich von den Eichen S (2017) Neue Spielregeln für Consultants. Harvard Business Manager (March)

Friedrich von den Eichen S, Matzler K, Anschober M (2016) Open strategy – die Zweite. IMP Perspect (7):99–105

Gassmann O, Frankenberger K, Csik M (2013) Geschäftsmodelle entwickeln: 55 innovative Konzepte mit dem St. Galler Business Model Navigator. Carl Hanser Verlag, Munich

Hamel G, Breen B (2007) The future of management. Harvard Business School Press

Hautz J (2017) Opening up the strategy process – a network perspective. Manag Decis 55(9):1956–1983

Hautz J, Seidl D, Whittington R (2017) Open strategy: dimensions, dilemmas, dynamics. Long Range Plan 50:298–309

Klein G (2013) See what others don't – the remarkable ways we gain insights. Public Affairs, New York

Matzler K, Friedrich von den Eichen S (2015) Leadership 2.0: Fünf Thesen zur erfolgreichen Führung in Zeiten des Web 2.0. IMP Perspect (5):57–70
Matzler K, Bailom F, Friedrich von den Eichen S, Kohler T (2013) Business model innovation: coffee triumphs for Nespresso. J Bus Strateg 34(2):30–37
Matzler K, Füller J, Koch B, Hautz J, Hutter K (2014) Open strategy – a new strategy paradigm? Strategie und Leadership. Springer, Berlin, pp 37–55
Matzler K, Bailom F, Friedrich von den Eichen S, Anschober M (2016) Digital Disruption: Wie Sie Ihr Unternehmen auf das digitale Zeitalter vorbereiten. Vahlen Verlag, München
Newstead B, Lanzerotti L (2010) Can you open-source your strategy? Harvard Business Review (October)
Pasteur VR (1933) Œuvres de Pasteur. vol 6: Maladies virulentes, virus-vaccins et prophylaxie de la rage. Masson, Paris
Stieger D, Matzler K, Chatterjee S, Ladstätter-Fussenegger F (2012) Democratizing strategy: how crowdsourcing can be used for strategy dialogues. California Management Review 54(4):1–26
Sydow J, Schreyögg G, Koch J (2009) Organizational path dependence: opening the black box. Acad Manag Rev 34(4):689–709
Tapscott D, Williams AD (2008) Wikinomics: how mass collaboration changes everything. Penguin Books, New York
Whittington R, Cailluet L, Yakis-Douglas B (2011) Opening strategy: evolution of a precarious profession. Br J Manag 22:531–544

Stephan Friedrich von den Eichen has studied engineering and business administration at the University of Karlsruhe and the University of Mannheim. His research visits include the University of St. Gallen, the University of Innsbruck, and the University of California, Berkeley. After 25 years in "traditional" Management Consulting he joint IMP (Innovative Management Partner) in 2009. As Management Partner he has positioned IMP as a Co-Innovator. Applying the Open Management "philosophy" and based on a proven methodology (IMP Business Logic Approach) IMP has successfully implemented several disruptive innovations in the market—for SMEs as well as for multinational corporations. SFvdE is a professor of business administration, especially business model innovation at LEMEX, University of Bremen, and author of numerous books and articles.

Kurt Matzler is professor of strategic management at the Free University of Bolzano and academic head of the Executive MBA program at the Management Center Innsbruck (MCI). His research focuses on strategy, innovation, co-creation and business model innovation. He was guest professor or visiting scholar at the Wharton School of business, University of Pennsylvania, Fairfield University Connecticut, Southeast Missouri State University, Bocconi University, Milano. He is author and editor of more than 20 books an author of more than 200 academic articles published in journals such as Strategic Management Journal, Global Strategy Journal, MIS Quarterly, Journal of Product Innovation Management, MIT Sloan Management Review, California Management Review, Journal of Economic Psychology, Technovation, Creativity and Innovation Management, Journal of Economic Psychology, Marketing Letters, Industrial Marketing Management. Kurt is heading the IMP Network of Excellence, a viable network of more than 1.500 experts (with clusters as "Technology Scouts", "Lead Experts", "Digital Disruptors", "Lead Customers", "Academic", Entrepreneurs/Strategy" and "Lateral Thinkers") on which the IMP philosophy of open management consulting is based on.

Julia Hautz is assistant professor of strategic management at the University of Innsbruck and member of the IMP Network of Excellence. Her research focuses on strategy and innovation. In particular she is interested in patterns and determinants of corporate strategy and openness in innovation and strategy processes through crowdsourcing, social networks or online communities. She has been a visiting scholar at the University of Bath, UK and the Said Business School at the University of Oxford, UK. She is a co-editor of a recent Special Issue on Open Strategy in Long

Range Planning. She has published her research in multiple academic journals including Strategic Management Journal, Global Strategy Journal, Long Range Planning, Journal of Product Innovation Management, British Journal of Management, Creativity and Innovation Management, Journal of Interactive Marketing, Harvard Business Review, Harvard Business Manager, Business History Review and Management Decision. Her research has been awarded with multiple prizes including a promotion "sub auspices", the Creativity and Innovation Management best paper award, and the Journal of Interactive Marketing best paper award.

Sustainability Consultancies and Their Contribution to Sustainable Development

Lisa Hannemann

Abstract Advancing and responding to the political guiding principles of sustainable development will require the engagement of all actors in society. Increasingly, private enterprises purchase consulting services to address sustainability challenges. To date, there has only been limited research to investigate the characteristics of these sustainability consulting services. Using website analysis and qualitative interviews with experts from the largest management consulting firms operating in Germany, this paper identifies the most prevalent sustainable development topics among sustainability consulting services. It also outlines their conceptions of sustainability and how consulting firms perceive their role as potential promotors of sustainable development.

1 Introduction

Over the past 30 years, multiple agreements have been adopted at transnational level with the aim of promoting sustainable development. These are foremost political instruments. However, they also affect the practices and routines of companies (Williams 2015). The United Nations (UN) Sustainable Development Goals (SDGs) were adopted in September 2015, and the private sector is considered to have a key role to play in their implementation (UN General Assembly 2015). This point has also been emphasized in Germany's approach to SDG implementation, formalized in the National Sustainable Development Strategy (Bundesregierung 2016a, b). Companies therefore face the challenge of translating complex political and societal objectives into operational concepts and measures.

In recent years consulting firms around the world have built up expertise and extended their portfolios to meet the challenges of sustainable development and offer solutions. As a result, a new market for sustainability consulting has emerged in the consulting sector. This is no minor development, as independent sustainability

L. Hannemann (✉)
University of Oldenburg, Oldenburg, Germany

V. Nissen (ed.), *Advances in Consulting Research*, Contributions to Management Science, https://doi.org/10.1007/978-3-319-95999-3_11

departments within multi-national consultancies have been established. In Germany alone, 18.4 billion euros were spent on strategy, organization and process consulting in 2015, accounting for 68% of total sales of consulting services in the country (BDU 2016). Those areas cover, inter alia, the topics of corporate strategy, innovation, procurement and supply chain management, all of which are increasingly called on to incorporate sustainable principles and practices. Consulting projects related to corporate social responsibility (CSR) generated sales of 3.2 million euros (BDU 2016).

Due to their expertise and specific service offerings, consultancies have become an interface between the political guiding principles of sustainable development and the private sector. Experts from the consulting sector therefore play a significant role in shaping sustainable development. Consequently, the industry has a responsibility to take on this role (Martinuzzi 2003).

This paper examines the consulting practices of the largest consulting firms operating in the German market in the area of sustainability consulting, and evaluates their contribution to sustainable development. The following three questions are raised and answered:

1. What sustainable development issues are addressed by consulting services?
2. What basic conception of sustainability underlies these consulting services?
3. With regard to their role in shaping sustainable development, what role do consultancy firms assume and what barriers do they face?

2 Theoretical Foundations

2.1 Concepts of Sustainable Development

The political and normative guiding principle of sustainable development has been continuously developed since the 1970s. Key milestones in sustainability policy include the Brundtland report by World Commission on Environment and Development (WCED) in 1987, the United Nations Conference on Environment and Development in Rio de Janeiro in 1992 and its Agenda 21, and the Rio follow-up process with the Rio+20. During the latter, there were demands for starting negotiations of action-oriented, measurable but legally non-binding goals for sustainable development (von Hauff 2014). These SDGs were adopted by 193 UN Member States on 25 September 2015 at the Sustainable Development Summit in New York (IISD 2015).

To date, it is the 1987 Brundtland definition that has been most widely used to define sustainable development:

“Sustainable development is development that meets the needs of the present without compromising the ability of future generations to meet their own needs” (WCED 1987, p. 41).

Today, 17 goals, 169 targets and 230 indicators covering five thematic areas—people, planet, prosperity, peace and partnership (UN General Assembly 2015)—make up the Agenda 2030. It provides a new framework for the guiding principles of sustainable development. In this context, it is Article 67 that addresses the private sector and calls on "all businesses to apply their creativity and innovation to solving sustainable development challenges" (UN General Assembly 2015, p. 31).

In the social sciences, the concept of sustainable development is mainly discussed from a macroeconomic perspective. The Brundtland definition of sustainable development, with its significant scope for interpretation, has provided the basis for several controversial debates in the field of economics (von Hauff 2014). These surround four issues: (1) conceptions of human nature, (2) understandings of justice, (3) dimensions of sustainability and (4) strategies for sustainable development. As the first two discourses are highly abstract and remote from the operative level, the subsequent analysis will focus solely on the two latter aspects.

Ecology, economy and society are considered as the three pillars or three dimensions of sustainable development (von Hauff 2014). Ecological sustainability refers to the preservation of ecosystems. Nature is considered as the basis for all human activity and therefore also of all economic activity. However, supporting, provisioning and regulating services can only be secured in the long-term if excessive use is prevented. Ensuring economic sustainability involves strengthening economic power while securing a certain quality of life. Social sustainability encompasses, among other things, matters of justice and equality of opportunity and capability (Sen 1980) as well as social and societal cohesion between institutions and humanity (von Hauff 2014). In the three pillars concept, these dimensions are considered equally important for the realization of sustainable development (von Hauff 2014). In the business context, these assumptions have been established as a "triple bottom line" (Elkington 1994), and this model is also widely used in the political sphere (von Hauff 2014). Ecological economists are especially critical of this equivalence between the three dimensions. They advocate for an overarching environmental guiding principle, which comprehends the economic system as a subsystem of the ecosystem. The social dimension is largely ignored in these debates (von Hauff 2014).

With regard to strategies for relieving the pressure on ecosystems, efficiency, consistency and sufficiency are regarded as the "triumvirate" for achieving sustainability (Leitschuh et al. 2013). The first strategy aims to increase the efficiency and productivity of the energy and natural resources used. In business practices, it is the most common strategy due to advantageous cost savings, but is also the strategy most strongly associated with rebound effects—when actual resource savings fall short of potential resource savings due to behavioral or other systemic responses (von Hauff 2014). A consistency strategy, also called eco-consistency or eco-effectiveness, involves optimizing material cycles and natural ecosystems with economic practices that cause the least possible disruption (Huber 2013). This strategy includes approaches such as closed loops, waste prevention and recycling of materials. While the first two strategies are heavily influenced by technological progress, sufficiency strategies set limits on economic growth and focus on cultural change processes. Sufficiency stands for an alternative conception of well-being which, in a new way of calculating profit, places the social optimum above the individual maximum. It also aims to achieve a balanced relationship between tangible goods and intangible needs (Linz 2013). By promoting changes in production and consumption patterns, it aims to ensure economic activities and lifestyles take place within planetary boundaries (Fischer and Grießhammer 2013). This approach is particularly supported by post-growth economists. Their idea of an economic system for sustainable development works without growth and is based on concepts such as sufficiency, subsistence economy, de-globalization and de-monetarization (Paech 2012).

2.2 *Sustainability Consulting*

Just as sustainable development has risen up the political agenda over the recent decades, resulting in new agreements and the creation of new institutions, a new market has emerged in the consulting sector, called eco-consulting (Birke et al. 2003; Martinuzzi 2003) or sustainability consulting (Mohe and Pfriem 2003; Reineke and Bock 2007). In this paper, sustainability consulting is understood as:

> Consulting services, designed to provide companies and other organizations with expertise and tools to actively manage the social and environmental impacts of entrepreneurial activity (Reineke and Bock 2007).

The subject of sustainability consulting falls into the business consulting research discourse. Focuses within consulting research include theoretical-conceptual basic research, strategy and management consulting and studies of large consulting companies (Nissen 2007). Within consulting research, only a few scholars have investigated subjects such as the environment, sustainability or sustainable development. With regard to the role of consultancies, Thomas (2011) notes that the absence of key players distinguishes the environmental consulting segment from the rest of the consulting market. He points to internationally established consulting firms, which offer environmentally oriented consulting within their strategy consulting. However, none of them has achieved a dominant market position (Thomas 2011; Martinuzzi 2006). According to Fink and Knoblach (2007) (see also Heuermann and Herrmann 2003), business consultants are simultaneously "trendsetters" (Fink and Knoblach 2007). They are able to accentuate specific perceptions and practices with their clients and legitimize them using success examples. This can lead to the application and diffusion of new guiding and management principles. Martinuzzi (2003) points out that it is consultancies rather than research institutes that are companies' preferred partners in the context of eco-consulting, sustainable development and efficient sustainability policy. He identifies six consulting functions—information and awareness, optimization, diffusion, networking, moderation and feedback—that characterize consulting firms as an interface between the political guiding principles of sustainable development and entrepreneurial practice. Paech (2005, p. 114) interprets these functions in such a way that they "must form the core of a sustainability-oriented consulting" (Paech 2005).

The consulting sector has not been given enough attention in the literature regarding its contribution to sustainable development (Martinuzzi 2003). The annual surveys produced by the Association of German Management Consultants (BDU) about the German consulting market do not cover sustainability issues sufficiently, only listing them under the heading of "Corporate Social Responsibility" (BDU 2016). The SDG Engagement Survey (PwC 2015) provides information about the relevance of sustainable development topics for business practices. However, there is no backcoupling on the relevance of SDGs to consulting portfolios.

Qualitative studies on conceptions of sustainability are available for other research subjects that are not part of the consulting sector (Carew and Mitchell 2002). One component of the research project SUMMER—SUstainable Markets eMERge—from the University of Oldenburg was an analysis of 50 sustainability-oriented consultancies' publications and webpages, using the three dimensions and strategies for sustainable development (Paech 2005). The Massachusetts Institute of Technology and the Boston Consulting Group (BCG) regularly assess the opinion of experts and executives on how selected companies perceive sustainability using qualitative and quantitative methods (Berns et al. 2009; Kiron et al. 2012). A similar study is also conducted by the UN Global Compact and Accenture Strategy as part of their CEO Study (Lacy et al. 2012). However, there is still no research devoted to how the consulting firms themselves conceive sustainability.

Martinuzzi et al. (2002) and Martinuzzi (2003) published papers on the roles and functions of consultancies and their potential contribution to the political guiding principles of sustainable development, suggesting that consultancies should also be considered part of the governance structures for sustainable development. However, his ideas—such as the six consulting functions introduced earlier—were not further developed. Outside the specific field of sustainability consulting, Caroli (2007) assigns functions and roles to consultancies in line with those proposed by Martinuzzi. At the same time, he laments that there is a lack of academic literature focusing on the interaction between consultants and their clients, narrowing down the functional contribution of consulting.

This literature review, using journal databases and applying backward and forward review of citations (Webster and Watson 2002), might not cover the entire discourse. However, given the dates of the majority of publications and the lack of follow-up work based on these research contributions, it can be presumed that sustainability consulting remains a minor topic within the consulting research discourse. This article seeks to take up the topic again so as to close a research gap concerning the relationship between sustainable development and the role of business consultancies, with a particular focus on the key players in the German consulting market.

3 Methods and Data

There was no review of existing hypotheses. Rather, this study took an exploratory approach and examined the role of management consultancies in the implementation of sustainable development. Although the SDGs were agreed and are being implemented internationally, to narrow down the scope of this research, this study focused exclusively on consulting activities in Germany.

3.1 Data Collection

To further limit the object of research, sustainability consultancies were selected based on their size, measured in annual turnover. As no overview of turnover data is available for specialized sustainability consultancies and their services (BDU 2016), the selection was made using the overall turnover of management consultancies. The research is also limited to consultancies operating in Germany. Accordingly, the companies examined are among the 25 highest-revenue management consultancies as of 2012[1] (Lünendonk 2013) and have specific expertise in the field of sustainability consulting.

To collect the data, an analysis was first conducted of the websites of the 25 -highest-revenue management consultancies in Germany according to Lünendonk (2013), focusing on specific and independent industry expertise or service competence in sustainability within the organizational structure of the consulting firm. This step served to limit the scope of the research. The portfolios were then analyzed using a qualitative content analysis (Kuckartz 2016). For the second phase of qualitative data collection, interview requests were sent to the partners at the selected consulting firms with sustainability expertise. Using a semi-standardized interview guide, 30-minutes telephone interviews were then conducted with six experts—consultants in mid to high-level management—from six different sustainability consulting units. Other consultancies were either unavailable for interview or did not offer sustainability services in the first place. Of the interviewees, three of them spoke on behalf of audit firms, later referred to as "Audit Firm One" (AF1), "Audit Firm Two" (AF2) and "Audit Firm Three" (AF3) and three on behalf of strategic consultancies, later referred to as "Strategic Consultancy One" (SC1), "Strategic Consultancy Two" (SC2) and "Strategic Consultancy Three" (SC3). Data evaluation was again carried out via qualitative content analysis (Kuckartz 2016).

[1]More recent available data depicts only global revenue (Lünendonk 2017).

Table 1 Portfolio analysis—codes for the first research question

#	Specificity	Criterion	Code (incl. example)
1	Service	Independent product/expertise according to one of the 17 SDGs or can be assigned to a SDG based on the subsequent description	SDG No._Service (12_Service)
2	Service	Independent product/expertise according to one of the 169 targets or can be assigned to a target based on the subsequent description	SDG No. Target No._ Service (12.2_Service)
3	Reference	Description of a service/practice refers to an SDG/target	SDG No. or SDG No. _Target No. (12 or 12.2)

Table 2 Conception of sustainability—codes for the second research question

#	Issue	Criterion	Code (applicable to each criterion)
1	Dimension	Economy Ecology Society Other	Major role/secondary role/minor role/increasing/decreasing
2	Strategy	Efficiency Consistency Sufficiency Other	

3.2 *Data Analysis*

For each consultancy, a profile was created in MAXQDA, which included the website texts and transcripts of the expert interviews. These were then coded and evaluated within the scope of the qualitative content analysis proposed by Kuckartz (2016). The author assigned all codes during several review sessions of the text material, to ensure a consistent methodological approach in the sense of intra-coder reliability (Mayring 2012).

Each of the three research questions was given its own code system, whereby the criteria originated from deductive, inductive-deductive or completely inductive approaches. The codes are presented in Tables 1, 2, and 3. For the first research question, the 17 SDGs and 169 targets provide the theoretical framework (UN General Assembly 2015) regarding sustainable development themes and services. The formation of categories was done a-priori. Thus, deductively, different codes were allocated when consulting services responded to a specific SDG or target, or when there were references to individual goals as part of a service description (Table 1). This distinction made it possible to depict the diversity of the SDGs within the portfolios and, at the same time, to make statements about the specificity or quality of an SDG within the consulting portfolio.

To discuss the second research question, viewpoints from the academic discourse (von Hauff 2014) were contrasted with statements by the interviewees. For this, categories were created using deductive and inductive approaches (Kuckartz 2016). The code system covers the sustainability definition, the three dimensions of

Table 3 Shaping sustainable development—codes for the third research question

#	Functions (Martinuzzi 2003)	Criterion	Code
1	Information and awareness	Raising the awareness among decision-makers	Decision-makers
		Addressing (the necessity of) environmental strategies	(Need of) environmental strategy
		Depicting elements of a sustainability strategy	Elements of sustainability strategy
		Giving impulses for dealing with sustainability topics	Impulse
2	Optimization	Nomination of methods, based on lead in knowledge/know-how, leading to economies of scale in application	Know-how
		Reference to process optimization	Process optimization
3	Diffusion	Reference to external standards/guidelines/regulation	Standards
		Designation of own tools/practices	Tools
		Contribution to the development and dissemination of (market-specific) sustainable solutions	Development of solutions
4	Networking	Reference to cooperation between several actors within a project/topic/challenge	Cooperation
		Promoting (cross-industry) exchange	Exchange
5	Moderation	Setting up voluntary guidelines/codes of conduct	Voluntary guidelines
		Communication with internal and external stakeholders	Stakeholder communication
		Improving relationships (in conflict situations)	Relationship management
6	Feedback	(Scientific) reflection on sustainability practices	(Scientific) reflection
		Cooperation with politics	Cooperation politics
		Active engagement and agenda setting	Agenda setting
			Other

sustainability, and the three strategies for the implementation of sustainable development. Deductive categories were based on the variables economy, ecology and society with regard to the dimensions, and efficiency, consistency and sufficiency with regard to the strategies. In a second step to create the categories, the inductive phase, sub-categories were created by working with the text material. Within each sub-category, the ordinal gradations "major role, secondary role, minor role" were introduced to indicate the significance of each strategy or dimension. The gradations "increasing" and "decreasing" were used to show how trends were changing in importance. The residual category "other" was also created to exploit the method's explorative potential (Table 2). The question of the sustainability definition was approached in an explorative manner. Correspondingly, the creation of categories was based entirely on the text material, according to the inductive creation of categories (Kuckartz 2016).

To answer the third research question, the functions of sustainability-promoting consulting defined by Martinuzzi (2003) served as a framework, which was then expanded both deductively and inductively using the interview material (Table 3). The question of which barriers influence sustainability consulting was explorative in nature and thus categories were formed inductively based on the material.

4 Results

4.1 Sustainability as Part of the Consulting Portfolio

During the first data collection phase, 10 of the 25 highest-revenue management consultancies in Germany were identified as having in-house expertise related to sustainability and services in sustainability consulting: Accenture Strategy, A.T. Kearney, Bain & Company, BearingPoint, The Boston Consulting Group, Ernst & Young, KPMG, McKinsey, Oliver Wyman and PricewaterhouseCoopers (Table 4).

The portfolio analysis showed that Sustainable Production and Consumption (SDG12), Economic Growth (SDG 8), Climate Action (SDG 13), Renewable Energy (SDG 7) and Infrastructure (SDG 9) are the most important topics related to sustainable development within their consulting services. Except for SDG 9, this trend was confirmed later in the interviews. The results from the expert interviews led to the following key findings for each research question.

4.2 Incremental Innovation: Incorporating Sustainability Themes into Consulting Portfolios

The consultancies were either aware of or addressed in their services 15 of the 17 SDGs, with SDG 10 (Reduced inequalities) or SDG 14 (Life below water) not featuring. As in Fig. 1, the SDGs are addressed overall and through specific sub-goals (according to service specificity #1 or #2 respectively, see Table 1). A particularly high specification of consultancy services exists for:

- SDG 12 Consumption and Production, in particular SDG 12.2 (Resource efficiency in production), SDG 12.6 (Sustainability reporting), SDG 12.7 (Sustainable procurement), SDG 12.8 (Education for sustainable development) as well as the overall goal SDG 12, focusing on supply chain management,

Table 4 Sustainability consulting expertise in highest-revenue management consultancies in Germany

#	Consultancy	Turnover in Germany 2012 in million euros (Lünendonk 2013)	Employees in consulting in Germany 2015 (brand eins 2015)	Internal labeling of sustainability expertise
1	McKinsey & Company Inc.	>600.0	1300	Sustainability and Resource Productivity
2	The Boston Consulting Group GmbH (BCG)	490.0	1500	Sustainability
3	KPMG AG WPG	403.0	2400	Sustainability Services
4	PricewaterhouseCoopers AG WPG (PwC)	315.2	2000	Sustainability Services
5	Accenture GmbH	296.0	6000	Sustainability
6	Oliver Wyman Group	280.0	n.a.	Sustainability Center
7	Bain & Company Germany	256.0	650	Sustainability
8	A.T. Kearney GmbH	252.0	405	Sustainability
9	Ernst & Young GmbH WPG (EY)	248.3	794	Climate Change and Sustainability Services
10	BearingPoint GmbH	225.0	1400	Sustainable Development

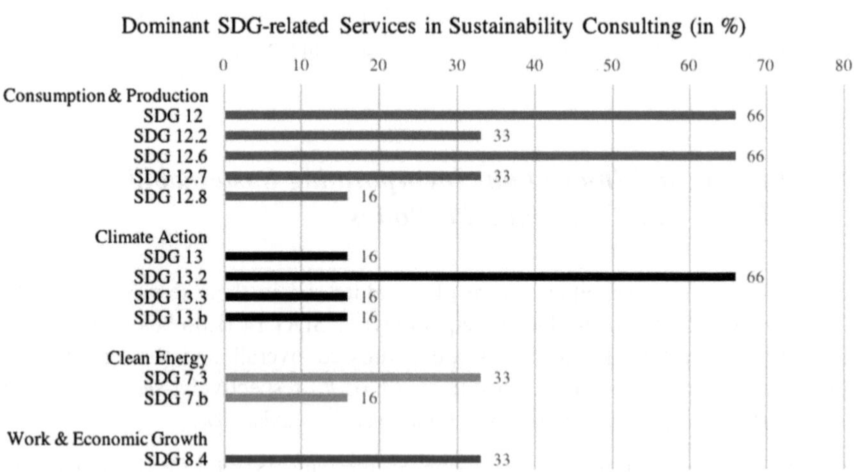

Fig. 1 Most dominant SDG-related services in sustainability consulting

- SDG 13 Climate Action, in particular SDG 13.2 (Climate change measures), SDG 13.3 (Awareness on climate change) and 13.b (Raising capacity for climate change-related planning and management),
- SDG 8 Economic Growth, in particular SDG 8.4 (Resource efficiency in consumption and production and decoupling of economic growth from environmental degradation), and
- SDG 7 Clean Energy, in particular SDG 7.3 (Energy efficiency) and SDG 7.b (Development and expansion of modern energy services).

Prevalent consulting services that do not directly relate to the SDGs but address sustainability issues in a broader sense are:

- Sustainability strategy as an overall theme of consulting services, and
- Measurability or monetarization of the overall societal impact of companies.

Through "incremental innovation" (Birke et al. 2003, p. 97), consultancy firms are using their growing sustainability expertise to innovate and gradually complement and extend their core competences with sustainability-related services. In the audit firms, this was reflected in their focus on sustainability reporting and climate reporting. At one of the major strategy consultancies, the focus lay more on sustainability strategy: "The topic of strategy is extremely exciting for us because it is the core of what we do anyway" (SC1). This linking of the sustainability department and the core themes of a consulting firm was also clear at a consultancy firm focusing on technology and digitization: "Since we are the world leaders in the topic of digitization [...] we link the SDGs to digital solutions [...]" (SC2).

4.3 *Triple Bottom Line, Ecology and Efficiency as Framework for Sustainability Consulting*

Definitions of sustainability vary (Fig. 2). One consulting firm advocated a broad understanding, saying that: "[. . .] principally, everything that is oriented towards the

Code System	SC1	SC2	SC3	AF1	AF2	AF3	SUM
Definition							0
Context dependent	■						1
Client dependent	■		■				2
Long term success	■	■				■	3
Economic success	■	■				■	3
Integration of socio-ecological aspects	■	■					2
Compatibility of three dimensions				■	■	■	3
Extension of decision making variables		■			■		2
Other							0
Future-oriented			■				1
Spatial and time dimension					■		1

Fig. 2 Definitions of sustainability

Code System	SC1	SC2	SC3	AF1	AF2	AF3	SUM
Dimensions							0
Economy							0
Economy_major role	■		■	■			3
Economy_minor role						■	1
Ecology							0
Ecology_major role	■	■		■	■	■	5
Ecology_secondary role			■				1
Society							0
Society_major role		■		■	■		3
Society_minor role			■				1
Society_increasing		■				■	2
Other							0
Economy as core of overall consulting activities	■	■	■			■	4

Fig. 3 Dimensions of sustainability

future viability of a company is fundamentally subject to the concept of sustainability" (SC3). Most commonly, sustainability was defined as long-term economic success that is also compatible with the ecological and social dimensions. This fits strongly with the "Triple Bottom Line" concept from Elkington (1994) as this interviewee emphasizes: "We assume the holistic concept of sustainability, which includes the social and the environmental component but also the compatibility with economic aspects" (AF1). References to the Brundtland definition were made to at least some degree due to the emphasis on the long-term perspective. There was strong awareness of the goal of socially and environmentally compatible economic growth (WCED 1987).

Out of the three dimensions of sustainability, achieving economic goals was considered as the core objective of the overall consulting market. With regard to sustainability expertise, there was the most focus on consulting activities related to the ecological dimension. Five out of six of the consultancies have a focal point here. Second and equal in importance were the economic and societal dimensions, which three of the six interviewees considered relevant. The social dimension is expected to increase in importance (Fig. 3).

In the academic discourse, efficiency, consistency and sufficiency are considered three possible strategic approaches for achieving sustainable development. However, they are regarded as irrelevant as guiding principles for consulting practices: "When discussing with customers, we seldom speak about consistency and sufficiency strategies, since these are abstract textbook concepts" (SC2). When connections are made between consulting activities and strategies, "economic mainstream" thinking (von Hauff 2014, p. 19) dominates due to a clear focus on efficiency strategies. Consistency strategies play a role in some cases for business model innovation or in combination with circular economy approaches. Sufficiency strategies are not used but could gain importance due to digitization trends, as they provide new ways of using goods, services and resources. Accordingly, one interviewee predicts: "Efficiency will always be important, but perhaps less important. Overall, we are moving away from the traditionally strong efficiency theme to more sufficiency and consistency" (SC2) (Fig. 4).

Code System	SC1	SC2	SC3	AF1	AF2	AF3	SUM
Strategies							0
Efficiency							0
Efficiency_major role	■	■		■			3
Efficiency_decreasing		■					1
Consistency							0
Consistency_secondary role	■	■		■			3
Consistency_increasing		■					1
Sufficiency							0
Sufficiency_secondary role	■			■			2
Sufficiency_increasing		■					1
Other							0
Little relevance of academic framework	■	■	■		■	■	5
Client dependent	■		■	■	■	■	5
Context/industry dependent	■				■		2

Fig. 4 Strategies for sustainable development

4.4 Know-How and Awareness-Raising for Sustainable Development

Consultancies cover most of the functions proposed by Martinuzzi (2003)—information and awareness, optimization, diffusion, networking, moderation and feedback—whilst the awareness of their own potential for promoting sustainable development varies with the functions.

The consultancies' lead in knowledge and know-how is particularly well-known. Here, consulting firms see their most important contribution and the most important leverage in promoting sustainable development (optimization function). Likewise, consultancies consciously promote exchange (networking function) and encourage customers to engage with sustainability topics (information and awareness function).

The data revealed that the consulting firms tended to view cooperation with policymakers (feedback function) as an opportunity to overcome obstacles within their own consulting work. Consequently, this function could be used more purposefully to promote sustainable development. The same applies to taking on a moderating role in the development of voluntary agreements (moderation function), which is the least pronounced function across all consulting firms.

Audit firms mainly incorporate sustainability principles into their consulting practice by working with external standards, guidelines and responding to regulation. Strategic business consultancies are more alert to trends in the private sector, such as the emergence of new business models. They develop and disseminate their own sustainable solutions (diffusion function) (Fig. 5).

The main barriers to sustainability consulting are missing incentives, or inconsistent or even "unambitious and inadequate regulation" (SC2). Businesses also need a stronger strategic approach to addressing sustainability challenges, and company leadership awareness on the impact of entrepreneurship on environment and society. Sustainability is still commonly assigned to corporate communication departments and quickly disappears from the agenda "[...] as soon as there are other urgent

Code System	SC1	SC2	SC3	AF1	AF2	AF3	SUM
Functions							0
Information and awareness	■	■	■	■	■	■	6
(Need of) environmental strategy		■				■	2
Impulse	■	■	■	■	■	■	6
Elements of sustainability strategy				■		■	2
Decision makers		■		■		■	3
Optimization	■	■	■	■		■	5
Process optimization		■	■	■			3
Know-How	■	■	■	■		■	5
Diffusion	■	■	■	■	■	■	6
Development of solutions	■	■					2
Tools	■	■	■			■	4
Standards				■	■	■	3
Networking	■	■	■	■	■	■	6
Exchange	■	■	■	■	■	■	6
Cooperation	■			■	■		3
Moderation				■	■	■	3
Voluntary guidelines				■	■	■	3
Stakeholder communication				■	■		2
Relationship management							0
Feedback	■	■	■	■	■	■	6
Agenda setting			■	■	■		3
Cooperation politics			■	■		■	3
(Scientific) reflection	■	■	■	■			4

Fig. 5 Functions of sustainability consultancies

economic issues" (AF3). Finally, there is a need to further translate the complex guiding principles of sustainable development to the business and entrepreneurial context. According to one audit firm, ensuring sustainable development will require an "overall process of social change" (AF2), in which companies are no longer judged solely on the basis of economic factors, the maximization of personal benefit is no longer considered paramount, and the triple bottom line becomes the guiding principle (Fig. 6).

Code System	SC1	SC2	SC3	AF1	AF2	AF3	SUM
Barriers							0
From politics							0
Contradicting regulation		■	■	■	■		4
Weak enforcement of regulation		■		■			2
Missing incentives/regulation			■			■	2
From businesses							0
Impact awareness		■		■	■		3
Market restraints	■	■	■		■		4
Strategic relevance of sustainability		■	■	■		■	4
Beliefs	■	■					2
Conceptional							0
System change					■		1
Limits of consultants			■	■	■	■	4
Complexity vs. applicability		■	■	■	■	■	5
Other	■						1

Fig. 6 Barriers to sustainability consulting

5 Discussion of Findings

The analysis highlighted consulting firms' strong focus on SDG 12 (Production and Consumption). It is clear from the comparison with consulting and business practices that SDG 12 is assigned less importance in business practices, only ranking after SDG 8 (Economic Growth), SDG 9 (Infrastructure) and SDG 13 (Climate Action) (PwC 2015; Steenblock 2016). As economic aspects are a key component of consulting practices overall, it can be assumed that the companies do offer consulting services that contribute to economic growth as defined by SDG 8. However, they have not been linked to sustainability expertise so far. Key political objectives, namely SDG 2 (Zero Hunger), SDG 6 (Water and Sanitation) and SDG 7 (Clean Energy) (UN General Assembly 2012), are underrepresented in consulting services. Nevertheless, it is not possible to make conclusive statements about consulting firms' contribution to the implementation of the guiding principles of sustainable development, since this study focuses exclusively on consulting activities in Germany whilst the SDGs are international political goals.

One critical finding was the lack of innovation of sustainability services in consultancies. At present, consulting firms are mainly expanding their core competences to include aspects of sustainability rather than broadening their competences to take into account further functions, such as those proposed by Martinuzzi (2003), or even raising normative questions about their contribution to sustainable development. At the same time, Birke et al. (2003, p. 114) perceive "sustainability-oriented development, application and dissemination of concepts such as eco-efficiency and eco-rating" as an opportunity to mainstream sustainability consulting in consulting practices. Hence, the current trend of establishing sustainability oriented services close to consultancies' core competences can be understood as key moment in integrating sustainability into consulting portfolios overall.

The interviewees viewed global developments, such as international climate protection agreements and the SDGs, as providing an external impetus that shaped their firm's consulting practices or sustainability portfolio. Nevertheless, the audit firms emphasized developments in public opinion and the adoption of new standards as important. In contrast, the strategic business consultancies are increasingly stimulated by the private sector when it comes to "first mover advantages" (SC1) and the innovation of business models. These observations were summarized by an interviewee as follows: "Contrary to our colleagues in the audit sector, we are not influenced by regulation. The auditors certainly see demand increase when laws are changed. This is less the case with us. We work innovatively and are growth-oriented" (SC2). Implicitly, however, political developments are still significant for sustainability consulting practices, as was observed in the early days of sustainability consulting: In the mid-1990s, shortly after the United Nations Conference on Environment and Development in Rio de Janeiro, one of the audit firms discussed for the first time introducing the examination of non-financial information as a new service. Ten years later, two strategic consultancies followed and established sustainability expertise. At the same time, the first German National Sustainable

Development Strategy was launched and the German Council for Sustainable Development (RNE) convened. Its first chairman was also a member of the advisory board at one of the consulting firms. In the late 2000s, expertise was established across all the other interviewed consulting firms. This was well timed to link with the 15th United Nations Climate Change Conference and the Copenhagen Agreement (UNFCCC 2014), as well as the first publication of the ISO standard 26000 on CSR (ISO n.d.). These developments therefore show that policy-making can have an impact on consulting practices.

Management consultancies place a clear focus on efficiency strategies to support sustainable economic growth. According to the UN, this principle, whereby economic growth is decoupled from environmental degradation, is central to achieving the sustainability targets (UN General Assembly 2015). Consistency strategies only played a role in this study in the context of business models inspired by the principles of the circular economy. The use of just these two strategies—efficiency and consistency—would not be considered sufficient by strong sustainability advocates—they would require the application of sufficiency strategies (von Hauff 2014). According to Thomas (2011, p. 176), current consulting practices reflect practices in businesses, which also tend to focus on "ecologically rational environmental (cost) management". The analysis of the SUMMER research project also identified efficiency as the most significant sustainability principle within sustainability-oriented consulting. This project took place over 10 years ago (Paech 2005), showing that the characteristics of sustainability consulting have evolved little over the last decade. Consultancies view sustainability as an approach that can enable their clients to move away from established thinking patterns, as well as an opportunity to expand the horizons of their decision-making towards more societal and environmental aspects. However, academic concepts are not fundamental to their practice, serving rather as ideas. Solutions are primarily developed in line with client requirements, with normative aspects playing a secondary role.

The evaluation of the functions proposed by Martinuzzi (2003) makes it possible to assess the extent to which the consultancies promote sustainable development, as they responded to the functions with varying degrees of awareness. Some functions are pursued explicitly and deliberately, while others seem to be adopted unconsciously. This can be seen in how the interviewees did not mention a large number of functions in response to questions about the role of consultancies in the implementation of sustainable development. Rather, they spoke about the functions when speaking about the measures their firms used to tackle external challenges and obstacles to sustainable development, or in other, completely different contexts. For example, the majority of audit firms approach decision-makers in order to sensitize them to sustainability topics (information and awareness function), develop their own tools, advise on external standards (diffusion function) or encourage collaborations (networking function), for example on joint projects between NGOs and the private sector. As introduced earlier, in the sense of Fink and Knoblach (2007), sustainability experts from management consultancies act as "trendsetters". They raise the profile of sustainability issues and reaffirm practices with decision-makers by highlighting best practices and successes. In this way, they contribute to the discussion and diffusion of new tools and management principles, and promote sustainable development. Nevertheless, it seems as though consultancies are in some respects unaware of their own ability to promote sustainable development in the sense proposed by Martinuzzi (2003). The feedback function, in particular with regard to cooperation with the political sphere, is mostly viewed as an opportunity to overcome obstacles within their own work, rather than as a channel for proactively shaping a progressive sustainable development agenda. Nonetheless, some interviews did indicate an emerging awareness that consulting firms could potentially exert some normative influence and play a role in shaping sustainable development. According to one strategy consultancy, it is possible to show "[...] that within our current economic system, there are certainly more possibilities for integrating ecological and social aspects into core business and core decisions" (SC2). For an audit firm, there is "[...] a high connectivity to society that results in a very high responsibility for where and what signals we send into society" (AF2). Martinuzzi (2003) sees particular potential for consultancies to promote sustainable development in the least pronounced function—the moderation function—because they act as facilitators at interfaces within and between companies. The results of this research show that consulting firms are least aware of this function, meaning it offers significant opportunities for increasing their impact and role in shaping sustainable development.

Within the consulting firms, the importance of sustainability expertise was predicted to either remain constant or, more likely, increase in future. Today, sustainability consultants account for only a very small proportion of consulting firm employees, ranging between 1% and 6%. In some consultancies, investments have been made in recent years as this expertise is considered to be a key business area. For example, one audit firm is convinced that sustainable development will become "one of the most important strategic issues" (AF2) while an interviewee from another firm stated: "This is also the expectation on a global scale [...] and has resulted in the expansion and investment in this area over the past few years" (AF3). However, according to one major strategy consultancy, sustainability will not remain a separate field of expertise for much longer. As sustainability becomes more and more important in all areas, "[. . .] we will soon find that we do not explicitly call it sustainability; rather it will be seen as the new standard" (SC1). This interviewee supported his statement by pointing out that sustainability-driven social developments will lead to business models becoming outdated, and developments such as the electrification of the transport sector or more environmentally conscious consumer behavior will then "transform business models" (ibid.). However, statements relating to such a vision for the guiding principle of sustainable development were also cautious. Translating political principles into business practices has only taken place slowly in the past and is a process "[. . .] which does not happen overnight, but is long-term" (AF3). Nevertheless, the interviewees are optimistic due to "[...] the concept of sustainable development [being] conceived as an opportunity" (SC2). Whether consultancies contribute in the sense of Fink and Knoblach (2007), converting sustainability into a trend that may later be superseded by another trend, or whether they are effective in the sense suggested by Rogers (2003), contributing to the diffusion and establishment of the concept, was not the focus of this research. This question can therefore not be conclusively assessed at present. However, it is safe to say that consultancies are contributing to some degree to the "thematization and expansion" (Fink and Knoblach 2007, p. 98) and to the "take-off" (Rogers 2003) of the sustainability concept in the business world. Kiron et al. (2012, p.3) even argue in their executive study that "sustainability nears a tipping point".

The complexity of the concepts underlying the guiding principle itself is also generally understood to pose a key external challenge for the advancement of sustainable development. On the one hand, this is good for the consulting business, as companies typically rely on consulting firms to provide knowledge and reduce complexity. These types of services and tasks contribute significantly to how consultancies perceive themselves. Nevertheless, one interviewee lamented that the latest scientific findings are not always used in consulting or business practices. Equally, science rarely serves to prompt changes in consulting practices. Strengthening cooperation between consulting firms, the science community, and other actors, for example from the political sphere, could help to operationalize concepts like the SDGs, make them more applicable and contribute to the mainstreaming of sustainability practices. At the same time, sustainability policy is exposed to an "interest policy" (Schaltegger 2003, p. 147). Changing goals, shifting ecological, social and economic challenges, and the difficulty of addressing a broad range of stakeholders' demands make designing and implementing policy for sustainability a complex regulatory project (Schneidewind 2003). Thomas (2011, p. 192) emphasizes the importance of the public authority for sustainability and the environment: "The central role of the public sector as a sponsor and client in environmental consulting is a significant differentiation between other consulting segments". In addition, government can "set standards as a leader, pioneer and key player" (ibid.). Such leadership is also being demanded by consultancies, and especially by auditing firms. In this case, practitioners and the scientific community have common demands.

6 Conclusion

With their expertise and independent sustainability consulting departments, the "hardly questioned and controlled (quasi-) institution [management consultancy]" (Birke et al. 2003, p. 25) stands as a promoter of sustainable development. In the fields of production and consumption, climate action, sustainability strategies and measuring companies' overall societal impact, consultancy firms mainly use efficiency and consistency strategies and advance the ecological dimension of sustainable development. At present, management consultancies do not have an official political mandate to promote sustainable development. However, considering consulting firms as part of the governance structures for implementing the SDGs could be an effective way of optimizing the impact they can have in promoting sustainability policies (Martinuzzi 2003). By using the latest scientific findings, cooperating with political stakeholders and integrating their experience and expertise, management consultancies can play a strong role in diffusing the guiding principles of sustainable development and therefore the implementation of the 2030 Agenda.

References

BDU (2016) Facts and figures zum Beratermarkt 2016/2017. https://www.bdu.de/media/278823/bdu_facts_figures_2017.pdf. Accessed 03 Mar 2017

Berns M, Townend A, Khayat Z, Balagopal B, Reeves M, Hopkins MS, Kruschwitz N (2009) The business of sustainability. Findings and insights from the first annual business of sustainability survey and the global though leaders' research project. In: MIT Sloan Management Review. Special Report. http://sloanreview.mit.edu/reports/the-business-of-sustainability/. Accessed 15 May 2017

Birke M, Schwarz M, Göbel M (2003) Beratungsthema Unternehmensnachhaltigkeit: Künftige Herausforderungen für Umweltmanagement und Öko-Consulting. Ed. Sigma, Berlin

Brand eins (2015) Brand eins Thema. Unternehmensberater. Der Branchenreport von brand eins Wissen und Statista 2(3):86–121

Bundesregierung (2016a) Bericht der Bundesregierung zum high-level political forum on sustainable development 2016. Stand 12.06.2016. https://www.bmz.de/de/zentrales_downloadarchiv/Presse/HLPF-Bericht_final_DE.pdf. Accessed 03 Nov 2016

Bundesregierung (2016b) Deutsche Nachhaltigkeitsstrategie. Neuauflage 2016. Entwurf Stand 30.05.2016. https://www.bundesregierung.de/Content/DE/StatischeSeiten/Breg/Nachhaltigkeit/0-Buehne/2016-05-31-download-nachhaltigkeitsstrategie-entwurf.pdf?__blob=publicationFile. Accessed 03 Nov 2016

Carew AL, Mitchell CA (2002) Characterizing undergraduate engineering students' understanding of sustainability. Eur J Eng Educ 27(4):349–361

Caroli T (2007) Unternehmensberatung als Sicherstellung von Führungsrationalität? In: Nissen V (ed) Consulting Research. Unternehmensberatung aus wissenschaftlicher Perspektive. Deutscher Universitätsverlag (Gabler Edition Wissenschaft), Wiesbaden, pp 109–126

Elkington J (1994) Towards the sustainable corporation: win-win-win business strategies for sustainable development. Calif Manag Rev 36(2):90–100

Fink D, Knoblach B (2007) Unternehmensberater als Modemacher. In: Nissen V (ed) Consulting research. Unternehmensberatung aus wissenschaftlicher Perspektive. Deutscher Universitätsverlag (Gabler Edition Wissenschaft), Wiesbaden, pp 89–108

Fischer C, Grießhammer R (2013) Mehr als nur weniger. Suffizienz: Begriff, Begründung und Potenziale. Öko-Institut Working Paper 2/2013. https://www.oeko.de/oekodoc/1836/2013-505-de.pdf. Accessed 19 Dec 2016

Heuermann R, Herrmann F (2003) Unternehmensberatung. Anatomie und Perspektiven einer Dienstleistungselite. Franz Vahlen, München

Huber J (2013) Konsistenz – Schlüssig für Nachhaltigkeit. In: Leitschuh H, Michelsen G, Simonis UE, Sommer J, von Weizsäcker EU (eds) Jahrbuch Ökologie 2014. Deutsche Umweltstiftung, Hirzel, Stuttgart, pp 55–63

IISD (2015) United Nations sustainable development summit 2015. Highlights for Friday, 25 September. http://www.iisd.ca/post2015/summit/enb/25sep.html. Accessed 24 Nov 2016

ISO (n.d.) ISO 26000 – social responsibility https://www.iso.org/iso-26000-social-responsibility.html. Accessed 25 Apr 2017

Kiron D, Haanaes K, Reeves M, von Streng Velken I, Audretsch M, Kruschwitz N (2012) Sustainability nears a tipping point. MIT Sloan Manag Rev 53(2):69–74

Kuckartz U (2016) Qualitative inhaltsanalyse: methoden, praxis, Computerunterstützung, 3rd edn. Beltz Juventa, Weinheim

Lacy P, Haines A, Hayward R (2012) Developing strategies and leaders to succeed in a new era of sustainability: findings and insights from the United Nations Global Compact-Accenture CEO Study. J Manag Dev 31(4):346–357

Leitschuh H, Michelsen G, Simonis UE, Sommer J, von Weizsäcker EU (eds) (2013) Jahrbuch Ökologie 2014. Deutsche Umweltstiftung. Hirzel, Stuttgart

Linz M (2013) Suffizienz – unentbehrlich für Nachhaltigkeit. In: Leitschuh H, Michelsen G, Simonis UE, Sommer J, von Weizsäcker EU (eds) Jahrbuch Ökologie 2014. Deutsche Umweltstiftung, Hirzel, Stuttgart, pp 44 – 54

Lünendonk (2013) TOP 25 der Managementberatungs-Unternehmen in Deutschland 2012. http://luenendonk.de/wp-content/uploads/2013/05/LUE_Liste_u_PI_2013_Managementberatung_f1605131.pdf. Accessed 28 Oct 2016

Lünendonk (2017) Lünendonk-Liste 2017: Führende Managementberatungs-Unternehmen in Deutschland. http://luenendonk-shop.de/out/pictures/0/luenendonk_listepi_managementberatung_2017_f240517(1)_fl.pdf. Accessed 20 Aug 2017

Martinuzzi A (2003) Beratung für nachhaltiges Wirtschaften. Von der Öko-Nische am Consultingmarkt zum Instrument einer effizienten Nachhaltigkeitspolitik. In: Linne G, Schwarz M (eds) Handbuch Nachhaltige Entwicklung. Leske + Budrich, Opladen, pp 493–505

Martinuzzi A (2006) Beratungsprogramme für Nachhaltiges Wirtschaften — Institutionelle Innovationen im Grenzbereich von Umweltökonomie und Umweltmanagement. In: Pfriem R, Antes R, Fichter K, Müller M, Paech N, Seuring S, Siebenhüner B (eds) Innovationen für eine Nachhaltige Entwicklung. Deutscher Universitätsverlag, Wiesbaden, pp 171–200

Martinuzzi A, Schubert U, Zachhalmel R (2002) Sustainability consulting in Europe. Berater auf dem Weg zur Nachhaltigen Entwicklung? Forschungsschwerpunkt Nachhaltigkeit und Umweltmanagement, Wien, pp 1–17

Mayring P (2012) Qualitative Inhaltsanalyse — ein Beispiel für Mixed Methods. In: Gläser-Zikuda M, Seidel T, Rohlfs C, Gröscher A, Ziegelbauer S (eds) Mixed methods in der empirischen Bildungsforschung. Waxmann, Münster, pp 27–36

Mohe M, Pfriem R (2003) Sustainability consulting. Nachhaltige Perspektiven für Klienten und Berater? In: Linne G, Schwarz M (eds) Handbuch Nachhaltige Entwicklung. Leske + Budrich, Opladen, pp 507–520

Nissen V (2007) Consulting research – Eine Einführung. In: Nissen V (ed) Consulting research. Unternehmensberatung aus wissenschaftlicher Perspektive. Deutscher Universitätsverlag (Gabler Edition Wissenschaft), Wiesbaden, pp 3–50

Paech N (2005) Nachhaltiges Wirtschaften jenseits von Innovationsorientierung und Wachstum: Eine unternehmensbezogene Transformationstheorie. Metropolis, Marburg

Paech N (2012) Befreiung vom Überfluss. Auf dem Weg in die Postwachstumsökonomie. oekom, München

PwC (2015) Make it your business. Engaging with the sustainable development goals. https://www.pwc.com/gx/en/sustainability/SDG/SDG%20Research_FINAL.pdf. Accessed 20 Apr 2017

Reineke RD, Bock F (eds) (2007) Gabler Lexikon Unternehmensberatung. Gabler, Wiesbaden

Rogers E (2003) The diffusion of innovations, 5th edn. The Free Press, New York

Schaltegger S (2003) Nachhaltigkeitsmanagement im Spannungsfeld von inner- und außerbetrieblicher Interessenspolitik. In: Linne G, Schwarz M (eds) Handbuch Nachhaltige Entwicklung. Leske + Budrich, Opladen, pp 147–158

Schneidewind U (2003) Symbolsysteme als Goverance-Strukturen für nachhaltiges Wirtschaften. In: Linne G, Schwarz M (eds) Handbuch Nachhaltige Entwicklung. Leske+Budrich, Opladen, pp 135–146

Sen A (1980) Equality of what? In: McMurrin SM (ed) The Tanner Lecture on Human Values. University of Utah Press, Salt Lake City, UT, pp 197–220

Steenblock R (2016) Sustainable development goals in der deutschen Wirtschaft. Analyse und Auswertung zum Stakeholder-Dialog. In Cooperation with the Deutsche Netzwerks Global

Compact, econsense – Forum Nachhaltige Entwicklung der Deutschen Wirtschaft and Fountain Park. http://www.fountainpark.fi/wp-content/uploads/2016/11/SDGs-in-der-deutschen-Wirtschaft-Finaler-Report.pdf. Accessed 26 Apr 2017
Thomas E (2011) Der Umweltberatungsmarkt in Deutschland. Ansätze einer Marktanalyse. Z Manag 6(2):171–199
UN General Assembly (2012) Secretary-general's initial input to the open working group on sustainable development goals. https://sustainabledevelopment.un.org/content/documents/1494sgreportsdgs.pdf. Accessed 02 May 2017
UN General Assembly (2015) Transforming our world: the 2030 Agenda for Sustainable Development. Entwurf des Ergebnisdokuments des Gipfeltreffens der Vereinten Nationen zur Verabschiedung der Post-2015- Entwicklungsagenda. https://www.destatis.de/DE/Methoden/2030Agenda/TransformingOurWorld.pdf?__blob=publicationFile. Accessed 15 May 2017
UNFCCC (2014) The Copenhagen climate change conference. December 2009. https://unfccc.int/meetings/copenhagen_dec_2009/meeting/6295.php. Accessed 25 Apr 2017
Von Hauff M (2014) Nachhaltige Entwicklung. Grundlagen und Umsetzung, 2nd edn. De Gruyter Oldenbourg, München
WCED (1987) Our common future. http://www.un-documents.net/our-common-future.pdf. Accessed 23 Nov 2016
Webster J, Watson RT (2002) Analyzing the past to prepare for the future: writing a literature review. MIS Q 26(2):xiii–xxiii
Williams A (2015) Aligning with the sustainable development goals. In: Rodney I, Schaltegger S (ed) Proceedings of the first WBCSD and EMAN joint international sustainability accounting symposium in Geneva, pp 116–117. http://eman-eu.org/wp-content/uploads/2016/04/Proceedings_EMAN_2015_Bridging-Corporate-and-Academic-Contributions.pdf#page=116. Accessed 15 May 2017

Lisa Hannemann, M.A., graduated in Sustainability Economics and Management from the University of Oldenburg, Germany. From 2014 to 2016 she worked as a research assistant for Prof. Bernd Siebenhüner at the Department of Ecological Economics. She holds a Bachelor degree (B.A.) in International Cultural and Business Studies from the University of Passau. Her research interests include environmental governance, strategic sustainability management, sustainable development and sustainability consulting.

Part IV
Consulting Clients and Market

Consulting Industry and Market Trends: A Two-Sided View

Christoph Treichler

Abstract The consulting market is in its notably first major turmoil since its inception approximately 100 years ago. Driven by technological and economic shifts leading to newly evolving needs and expectations and buying behaviors of clients the consulting market has to find its appropriate responses. This article looks at the way the current changes, often referred to as the area of Consulting 4.0, impact client demand, buying patterns and the collaboration between client organizations and consultants as well as the competitive dynamics on the supply side across incumbent traditional consulting firms (like the large strategy consultants, the Big Four and the system integrators) and the emerging start-up consulting service providers and innovative newcomers.

1 The Customer View on Consulting

1.1 Trends in Consulting Demand

1.1.1 The «Game Changing» Factors

A lot has been thought and written about the consulting industry since Harvard Business Review published an article written by Clayton M. Christensen, Dina Wang and Derek van Bever, titled Consulting on the Cusp of Disruption (Christensen et al. 2013). For decades, the management consulting's fundamental business and operating model has not changed significantly. It has always been based on the superior knowledge, resources and skilled personnel to help clients deal with their most challenging problems and to recommend smart solutions. But what exactly is meant by the «cusp» or by the disruptive forces which are argued to threat and reshape the traditional business model of consulting companies? According to Christensen early signs of disruptive patterns in the consulting industry are the

C. Treichler (✉)
Cardea AG, Zurich, Switzerland
e-mail: christoph.treichler@cardea.ch

V. Nissen (ed.), *Advances in Consulting Research*, Contributions to Management Science, https://doi.org/10.1007/978-3-319-95999-3_12

emergence of new entrants with nontraditional business models which reduce costs and increase efficiency of consulting services delivery through technology, streamlined workflow, and alternative staffing models.

But there are additional «game changing» factors on the side of client organizations which basically allow disruptive and new business models for consulting services being accepted in the consulting market:

1. Client organizations have become increasingly savvy about hiring and deploying consulting companies. This is owed to the fact that they increasingly have hired former consultants and therefore have moved more and more work in-house which formerly has been outsourced to consulting firms and that increasing cost pressures have forced clients to watch their professional services costs and to adopt a more critical selection process when deploying external consulting resources.
2. Triggered by newly emerging technologies («digitization») and the more complex challenges client organizations face in a globalized, volatile and unsecure environment client demand has shifted dramatically. A major area of focus for many clients is the use of emerging technologies to transform their businesses and operating models.

1.1.2 Novel Opportunities and Possibilities

As the long-time and renowned incumbents in the consulting industry attempt to come to terms with the shift in client demand, clients complain that traditional service providers are unable to meet their rapidly evolving needs and expectations. Client organizations are calling on consulting service providers to focus on providing services that are able to solve their most prevalent business issues. The digitized world dissolved the boundaries between three traditional lines of consulting: strategy, technology, and marketing and design. The changing economic environment, on the other hand, requires fast, fundamental and complex transformations of clients' business models, value chains and product/service offerings. Client demand therefore shifts the consulting's competitive dynamic: When clients realize that there are inadequacies in traditional consulting capabilities and that they can benefit from greater speed, responsiveness, and control, they are willing to engage with alternative, more agile consulting service providers or smaller consulting service providers which specialize in supplying one specific aspect in the client engagement.

With new entrants or consulting companies developing innovative services the consulting market offers clients novel possibilities and chances to buy new types of consulting services. The emergence of disaggregated or modular services leads clients to seek «best-of-breed» expertise and approaches, reducing their reliance on solution-shop providers and enabling them to choose the most effective and efficient solutions, in terms of time, value and money. Although, according to a study conducted by the meta-consulting firm Cardea, clients tend to rely more often on large, international consulting firms for larger-scale strategic projects (Cardea 2016), the importance of scale and brand of a consulting company is decreasing. A study conducted by the internet marketing service firm Technova revealed that of those clients questioned, 86% indicated that they were currently exploring partnerships with innovative new companies (Parakala 2015). This especially applies to consulting demand and services related to improving customer experience and business model change with the use of emerging digital technologies.

1.1.3 Disappearing Boundaries and Differentiation

The consulting service providers' responses to this shift in client demand involve that traditional boundaries between market segments are disappearing and, as a result, consulting service offerings are converging. The past years have seen a growing convergence between the worlds of management consulting, technology consulting and creatives (marketing, brand and communication agencies). Management consulting and technology service companies are rapidly bolstering their design and digital skills, whereas agencies with their heritage in marketing and design are building their consulting capabilities in the area of strategy, organizational and process consulting and adding them to their creative portfolio. As a consequence, the consulting industry becomes even more competitive and significantly fragmented with a wide variety of consulting firms, ranging from the global management consulting and advisory firms to a large number of niche players and individual/independent consultants. Apart from the differences in size and scale, there exists a wide variety in the positioning and differentiation of the various consulting firms. There are firms that focus on a variety of issues in the same market such as the large management consulting firms, as there are firms that focus on a specific domain, such as information technology or a specific functional link of the value chain.

The good thing is: There are many choices for buyers of consulting services. The bad thing: The differentiation among consulting firms is so minimal. According to the above cited study, lack of differentiation between the major consulting firms in all categories is an issue for 83% of clients. They do not see delivery capability as a differentiator, because all major consulting service providers are considered equally capable of doing the work (Parakala 2015). To find the right consultants for their businesses is still a major concern of client organizations, to be able to meet the rapidly evolving needs and expectations of client organizations is increasingly a challenge for consulting service providers.

1.1.4 Challenges of Procuring Consulting Services

A recent exploratory study conducted by the meta-consulting firm Cardea across large corporations and SMEs from different industries and countries in Europe revealed four factors that will significantly change client organizations' buying behavior when procuring consulting services (Cardea 2016):

1. Almost two third of those clients surveyed stated that it is difficult or very difficult for them to find the right consultants for their businesses. This perception is even more significant because only few reported that they know how to improve the screening, evaluation and selection processes when hiring consulting service providers.
2. Over 70% of the clients surveyed said that digital media and channels are gaining importance for seeking out potentially eligible consulting service providers. Only 20% of consulting companies though have a defined strategy and concept how to market their services and capabilities via these channels, making it difficult for clients to find them in the marketplace.
3. Over 50% of the decision makers questioned reported that their expectations have not been met by the consulting companies they have deployed. Clients complain most about that consulting service providers do not deliver on their promises (58%), that consulting service providers lack implementation skills (42%) and that the consultants which are assigned to projects lack adequate experience (37%).
4. The «Big Four» advisory houses (KPMG, PwC, Deloitte, and EY) are perceived to be least focused, unable to exactly communicate and clarify how they intend and are able to support their clients' businesses. A majority of decision makers at client organizations cannot clearly assess for which kind of projects these kind of consulting companies or services are most eligible. While for strategy work a majority of clients still relies on the capabilities of the traditional strategy consulting firms (68%), they are increasingly turning for assistance to boutique firms, IT consulting firms and freelancers for operational and transformation projects (Fig. 1).

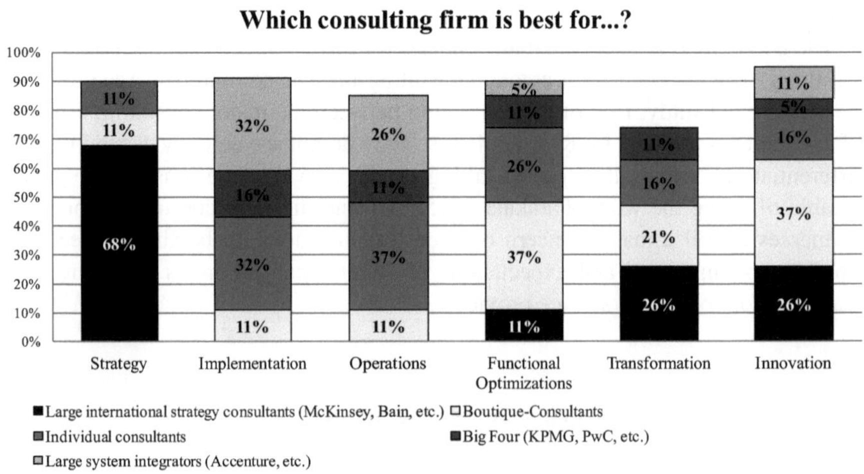

Fig. 1 Clients' perception of the eligibility of consulting companies (Cardea 2016)

The wider variety of choices and the growing sophistication lead clients to reduce their reliance on «integrated solution shops» and to shift their attention also to smaller, specialized consulting service providers.

1.1.5 Buying Consulting Services Beyond Scale, Brand and Expertise

Yet, the answer to the question what client organizations are looking for when choosing a consulting company does not limit itself to the factors of size and scale. Decision makers at client organizations are weighing a variety of factors in deciding which consulting company to engage for a specific mandate. When selecting a consultant, buyers of consulting services are looking first for the right set of team expertise, skills, functional and industry knowledge. A good consultant should have experience with the challenges or opportunities the client company is facing. For any consultant to be successful in helping a client company, though, the consulting firm's approaches, methodologies and provided roles must fit with the client's project requirements and needs. So, in the increasingly competitive world of consulting, client organizations differentiate consulting companies not only by their specialization (i.e. their functional and industry/market expertise)—if they even can, because, as already mentioned, clients often see very similar levels of ability in each of these attributes—, but increasingly by a dimension which relates to the way a consultant works: that means, not by what a consulting company does, but by how it does it. Asking clients about which attributes of consulting companies they value most now and in the future, shows clearly this shift in clients' expectations when working with consultants (Fig. 2). Not only a consulting company's expertise, best practice know-how, functional capabilities and resources are important (all factors which potentially can be assessed before a project engagement), but increasingly attributes such as delivery to promises, pragmatism and solution orientation which only can be assessed having entered into a collaboration with a consulting company or by independent analysts (Cardea 2016). Notably, this general shift in clients' expectations towards these more «soft facts» applies similarly to all of the researched consulting categories (strategy & operational management consulting, IT consulting) and types of consulting firms (from large, international consulting firms to boutique consulting firms and independent consultants).

1.1.6 The Difference Between «High-Value» and «Low-Cost» Consulting

Although many of the features clients value most when working with consultants seem to strongly underpin the fact that clients want to buy more from specialized niche firms because the latter are thought to fulfil these specific expectations better than their bigger rivals, further analysis suggests the situation is more complex. Both consulting firms and buyers of consulting services predict that the consulting market is split into three major segments (Cardea 2017):

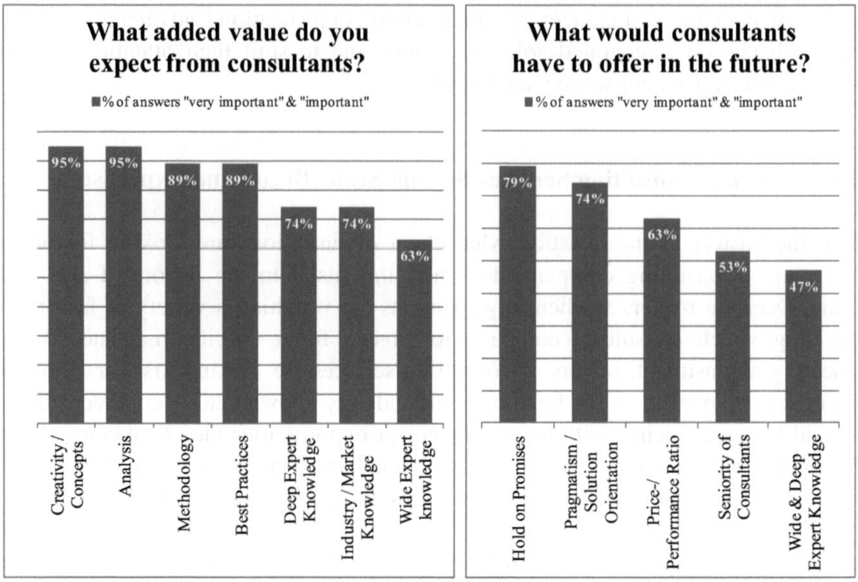

Fig. 2 Client expectations towards consultants (Cardea 2016)

- High-value strategy consulting
- Large-scale transformation consulting
- Spot-consulting/high-value specialist consulting.

High-value strategy consulting is needed when clients do not know what the underlying causes to their problems or challenges are, and so are not able to specify their needs or to identify a solution to their problems. In this case, it is partly true that clients which are less confident about the problem and the work needed are more tempted to use a big brand consulting firm, following the notion that scale and brand is a proxy for quality. Partly, however, it is also true that clients in this situation are much less clear about which consulting firms they should work with. High-value consulting largely depends on the ability to think and act in a creative and informed way about complex issues, a capability that for a long time has been the exclusive space of the large international strategy houses. The current «ambivalence» of clients which are seeking out eligible consulting companies in the high-value market stems from the perception of clients that the traditional consulting service providers are struggling to come to terms with the shift in their demand, and therefore are unable to meet their newly evolving needs and expectations. Highly creative and forward-thinking solutions require more-experienced consultants, multi-disciplinary issues and projects require the consulting firms to bring deep and specific expertise to bear, and end-to-end consulting services (from analysis, strategy/concept to implementation) require flexible delivery models. If the strategy (and other large, integrated) consulting firms want to fulfill all of these client needs they would have to adapt their business models. But even if the large consulting brands manage to provide a holistic «one stop shopping» offering to their clients (e.g. by sub-branding the different pieces of integrated consulting services), they will lack the ultimate credibility in the eyes of their clients because «most clients dislike the idea of buying a range of different specialist services from a single source on the time-honored grounds that a consulting firm which is a jack of all trades is inevitably a master of none» (Czerniawska 2012). This fact is also underpinned by the responses of clients to a survey conducted by the meta-consulting firm Cardea: The survey revealed that in the eyes of their clients the multi-specialists do not (yet) seem to hold their promise: More than 2/3 of clients perceive the multi-specialists to be lacking breadth and depth of specialized expertise (Cardea 2016).

Transformation consulting, also referred to as «low-cost consulting» (Czerniawska 2016), on the other hand, involves solving familiar problems with highly specialized, standardized and ultimately commoditized consulting services. When solutions are known and projects are better defined clients are more able to take control over the work to be done, the approach and outcome. Consequently, they will seek out consulting service providers which exactly match their specific requirements and they will no longer be willing to pay the fees of big consulting firms. However, the transformation consulting market is not without its own challenges: From our research and experience we know that clients prefer to turn to specialist boutique consultants when looking for specialized (e.g. functional) expertise (Cardea 2016). So, although clients seem to pull the two ends apart and make a clear differentiation between high-end and transformation consulting, today's challenges on the strategy or the operational side of clients' businesses tend to foster the convergence of the two consulting markets: strategy does not go without transformation, and both strategy and transformation increasingly do not go without technology (especially in the emerging digital world where technology has far reaching implications on business strategies and new business and operating models as well as digitization/ automation of processes). Strategy and transformation consulting and projects today require the elements of all three. That's why almost all of the management and IT consulting service providers (the big as well as the smaller ones) are trying to offer (or build) a range of different services to cover all aspects necessary to solve today's challenges of their clients.

1.1.7 In Search of Cost-Effective Alternatives

In their attempt to link strategy, technology and transformational consulting services consulting companies of all kind will put pressure on their traditional business models, a topic which we elaborate more in the next section. What's more important here, taking into account the disappearing boundaries between the consulting market segments and the converging consulting service offerings it makes sense to introduce a third dimension of consulting work: high-end specialist consulting. This is the consulting segment where the disruptive forces are most evident with new entrants in the consulting market which are devising a different type of consulting. Although these alternative firms may not be able to deliver the entire value proposition of traditional consulting firms, they specialize in supplying one specific link in the value chain and—even more important—are offering innovative types of consulting services and delivery models with certain advantages to clients such as greater speed, responsiveness, pragmatism and lower costs than their more traditional competitors. Mostly, but not only, on the back of digital, non-traditional consulting firms are adopting new approaches to consulting, introducing innovative methodologies and tools such as «Rapid & Agile Prototyping», (Innovation) Labs, Accelerators, Design Thinking, «Lean Start-up Approaches» or data- and analytics-enabled consulting such as «Asset Based Consulting». All of these new ways of consulting are geared to better meet the evolving needs of clients and to reduce the amount of human intervention and consultants' involvement compared to what the traditional consulting model requires.

1.2 The Impact on Client Organizations

The outlined trends in consulting demand have a significant impact on client organizations: how they identify, evaluate, select and measure consulting companies and their services in the future.

1.2.1 A Highly Fragmented and Diverse Consulting Landscape

The consulting services industry is highly competitive and fragmented. Competition takes place among a large number of diverse consulting service providers including business operations consulting firms, financial consulting firms, management consulting firms, accounting firms, technical and economic advisory firms, regional and specialty consulting firms and independent professional resources. The emerging growth in multi-disciplinary projects forces consulting service providers of all kind to diversify and expand their consulting service portfolio in order to be able to provide end-to-end consulting services in a specific domain and/ or to resolve complex issues by accommodating multi-specialist skills under one roof. This almost every time involves consolidating broad and deep expertise in strategy, operations, and technology. Traditional product and market segmentations, as shown in Fig. 3 for the US consulting market, will obviously lose importance because the traditional boundaries between the single solutions are blurring. While this exemplary segmentation covers only management consulting services, the same applies also to other consulting categories such as IT consulting services.

One can also observe a series of business model innovations that could reshape the way consulting firms engage with clients in the future. Today, the consulting market offers more than just «classic» consulting services. Many consulting firms are offering innovative business models and solutions for a variety of clients' challenges and needs. The emergence of «disaggregated» services leads clients to

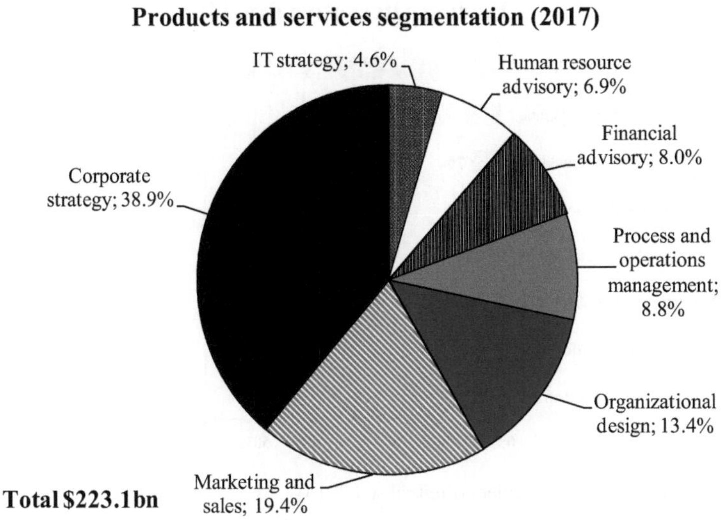

Fig. 3 Services segmentation in the US consulting market (IBISWorld 2017)

seek «best-of-breed» expertise and approaches, reducing their reliance on solution-shop providers and enabling them to choose the most appropriate solutions.

The wide variety of available solutions and consulting services truly offers advantages for buyers of management consulting services: there are many choices for buyers of consulting services. But it also bears a risk: it is almost impossible for client organizations to keep the big picture up and to know which consultant has the needed skills or the right approach. Since differentiation among consulting firms is so minimal, buyers of consulting services often do not know how potential consulting firms can help them with their needs. It's difficult for them to figure out who is good in what and who is right for their business and challenges.

1.2.2 Looking for the «Best Match»

When selecting a consultant, buyers of consulting services are looking for a variety of factors and features which a consulting company should be able to bring to a project. Primary selection criteria have not changed much recently: Team expertise and skills, knowledge of industry, existing relationships, past performance, service offering, and flexibility/ responsiveness still rank under the top 10 buyers selection criteria (Frederiksen 2013). Some clients will always buy the cheapest option, no matter the performance. However, higher prices are not always a proxy for better quality neither. Consider what is best buy: A consulting firm/service that offers an optimal combination of delivery, outcomes, price, quality and other benefits in meeting a buyer's specific need.

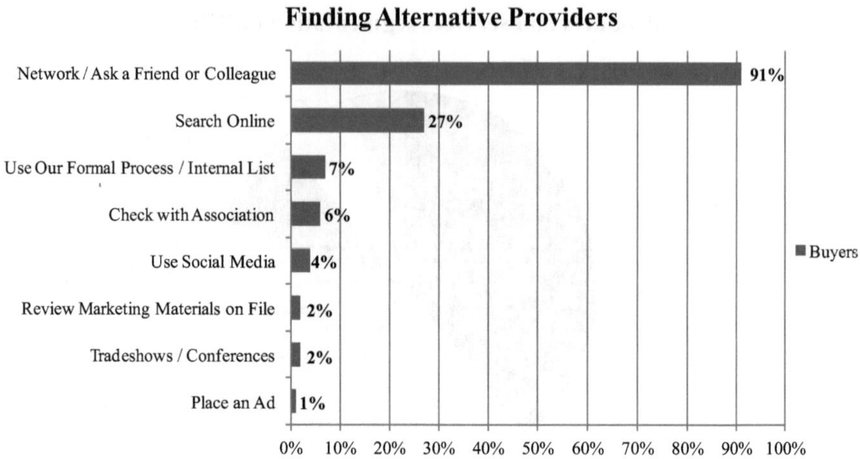

Fig. 4 Finding alternative providers (Frederiksen 2013)

1.2.3 How to Find the Right Consulting Company

The process of finding a new consulting service provider starts with looking for alternatives. A study conducted by the Hinge Research Institute found out that only 7% of buyers of consulting services feel that they already know all the alternatives that they need to consider or rely on resources that approach them (Frederiksen 2013). For the rest, their search for alternatives follows a pattern shown in Fig. 4.

A remarkable fact is that across the diverse mechanics how buyers of consulting services find providers, online techniques have eclipsed many of the more traditional methods. The diversity and accessibility of information online has made online search increasingly fundamental. A majority of clients and buyers of consulting services rely on digital market places and communities, B2B networks such as LinkedIn and Xing as well as search engines as most commonly used online sources of information when looking for prospective consulting firms (Cardea 2017). Given the fact that clients' procurement organizations will look for more efficient and effective ways to procure consulting services, the use of (such) technologies will gain further importance. Probably also since in the age of platform economy specialized software-based platforms aiming at increasing the productivity and ease of screening and selecting consulting services for clients are emerging (such as gocatalant.com, focusing on independent experts, or consultingsearcher.com, focusing on corporate consulting companies).

2 The Consultant View on Consulting

Whereas consulting firms have traditionally relied on talent to drive success in client engagements, one can observe a series of business model innovations that could reshape the way consulting firms engage with clients in the future. Technological innovations available today augment, and in some cases, replace manual effort with tools and software that allow for new business and delivery models, automation, and cost-efficient consulting services.

2.1 Consulting Business Models Under Challenge

On the supply side of the consulting market, there are two major things that currently happen:

1. The emerging «modularization» of the consulting industry, i.e. a shift in consulting's competitive dynamic from the primacy of integrated solution shops, which are designed to conduct all aspects of the client engagement, to modular providers, which specialize in supplying one specific link in the value chain—at a fraction of the costs of traditional consulting, with greater speed and beyond the traditional project-based model.
2. The ongoing consolidation within the consulting market.

One of the drivers for consolidation in the consulting sector has been international consulting firms seeing challenging conditions with many of their key markets flat or in decline. Looking for continuous growth they have embarked on a strategy to become multi-specialists/one-stop-shop providers of consulting services. On the other hand, consolidation is triggered by newly emerging technologies («digitization») and the more complex challenges client organizations face in a globalized, volatile and unsecure environment. The digitized world dissolved the boundaries between three traditional lines of consulting: strategy, technology, and marketing and design. The changing economic environment, on the other hand, requires fast, fundamental and complex transformations of clients' business models, value chains and product/service offerings.

2.1.1 The Changing World of Consulting

Rising competition due to lower growth rates in the consulting market, the emergence of new entrants which are challenging and undermining the position of longtime leaders and, finally, the evolving client needs and expectations have caused many consulting companies to start rethinking and reshaping their business models and consulting service offerings.

- *Convergence of strategy, operations, design and technology:* Mainly due to the upcoming work consulting firms must do around digitization of their clients' businesses the traditional boundaries between management and technology consulting are blurring. Since consulting service providers are seldom able to build these new capabilities (either in the area of management consulting or technology) fast enough internally, they are partnering with or buying specialized providers to be able to offer genuinely integrated services. The examples of consulting firms which have been rapidly launching new digital consulting divisions are manifold. A quick scan over the last 5 years of the consulting arena reveals an acquisition frenzy where design and digital firms are being acquired by large management consulting and IT services firms: Deloitte acquired Ubermind, PwC the digital creative consulting firm BGT, Accenture picked up design firm Fjord, McKinsey bought Agility, BCG acquired Strategic & Creative and—just recently—Maya Design, Wipro bought Danish agency DesignIT, only to name a few. These acquisitions have given rise to new practices focused on services to help clients exploit the opportunities of new technologies such as big data and analytics, customer experience, digital marketing, interactive design, new products and services and automation of processes. The digital consulting era is still in its infancy. Consulting firms are likely to launch even more outcomes-focused services as clients demand faster and more tangible results for their consulting spend. As execution speed becomes a defining factor in who wins, clients will pay less for slide decks and frameworks and more for actual products and solutions (Desai 2016).
- *Commoditization:* Commoditization describes a state when products and services become less differentiated. The key effect of commoditization is that it reduces the pricing power of the provider: Buyers care less about who they buy from and they will tend to buy the cheapest. Consulting services become commoditized when clients are starting to see no differences in the services of consulting firms. When clients believe that many consulting firms are capable of offering the same service, they will substitute one firm for another. Price competition and falling margins are the obvious results. In addition, with client organizations' increasing sophistication about consulting services allowing them to do more and more work themselves, the value added of a consulting service provider for this kind of work decreases because its superior topic or methodological expertise and knowledge does not count anymore. It's possible that clients will still rely on consulting support for this kind of tasks—because working with a consultant can speed up things or can overcome internal barriers—but they will not be willing to pay the expensive premium prices of prestigious consulting service providers. Compared to a decade ago, a greater proportion of consulting work has been commoditized—e.g. cost analysis/benchmarking, change management, business process management—leaving clients with the power to reduce the scope and cost of work they outsource to consulting firms. That's also one of the reasons why on-demand freelance consulting and eco-systems (i.e. «virtual» marketplaces that connect talented independent and skilled persons with clients who need their

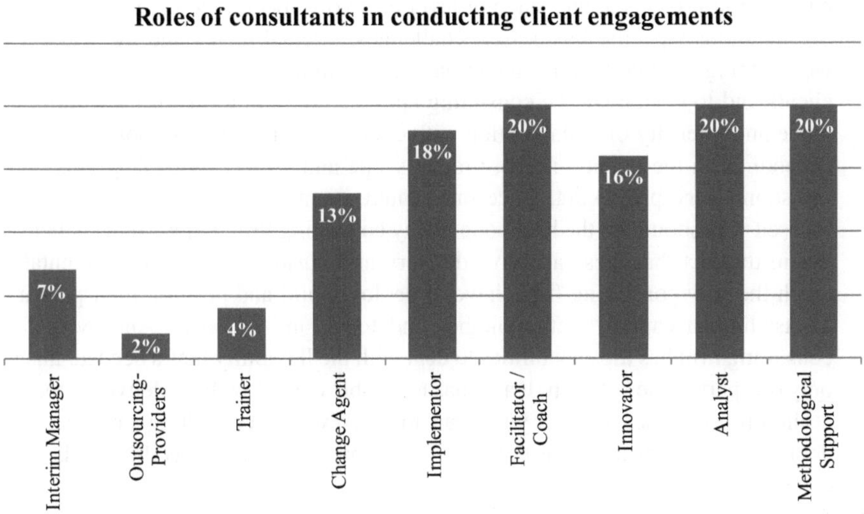

Fig. 5 Clients' Role Expectations towards Consultants (Cardea 2016)

services) are on the rise, allowing client organizations to buy flexibly («on demand») tailored expertise at highly competitive rates.

- *Multiple consulting roles:* The focus of a consultant's work varies depending on the managerial challenges or required project tasks. The typical functional roles involved in client engagements revolve around information gathering/analysis, design and conceptualization (problem solving) and implementation support. This basically has not changed over the last years since these functional roles are closely tied to the common phases of a consulting project from analysis to implementation. At the heart of these different roles must be different people and skills, however, because the way these tasks (or roles) have to be accomplished today have changed. Consulting companies will differentiate themselves by providing both broad and deep role expertise (Fig. 5): (1) Through their ability to gather data with greater speed, thoroughness and accuracy and to provide tools and deep analytics skills to deal with large amounts of unstructured data on the inside and outside (e.g. customer insights) of their client companies. (2) Through their excellent ability to solve problems and to find solutions requiring more creative and innovation skills and methodologies (e.g. design thinking, open innovation). (3) Through their ability to implement complex solutions in a dynamic environment involving a combination of consulting, people («transformational»), technology and entrepreneurial skills.
- *Flexible consulting delivery and business models:* Since clients tend to disaggregate consulting services, both the large multi-specialists (or «one stop shops») and smaller consulting firms have to respond by applying customer focused delivery and business models. More and more, it's not the services the consulting firms offer that differentiate them, but rather the way in which they serve their customers. Successful consulting firms are likely to be those that are capable of

engaging in projects at any stage or level of involvement, aligned with the client organizations' specific businesses, challenges, internal teams and the way they work. Being flexible then means to have different delivery options available for clients and to customize the consulting approach (e.g. in terms of team staffing, mode and intensity of collaboration with clients, pricing models, tools provided) depending on the client's needs, project scope and project dynamics. This may not sound very provoking, since one would assume that acting in a customer focused way should be the backbone of any consulting firm, but the real challenge lies in the fact that these adaptive delivery and business models fundamentally touch the way consulting firms have to deploy, build and develop their primary assets: human capital, methodologies and tools, and products. And even if a consulting firm has the capabilities to deal with the flexibility that's needed, this is only one part of the solution. It also has to be able to deploy these delivery models at the drop of a hat. Clients will want to work with a consulting firm that can demonstrate its instance response to their organizations' specific needs and expectations.

- *Asset based solutions:* McKinsey has often been cited to be one of the first movers having identified a dramatic need for change and having unbundled its services to provide tools and offerings outside the traditional project-based model (Christensen et al. 2013). Others recently have been following this trend by building or expanding their solution- or asset-based offerings (e.g. Deloitte Products & Solutions, KPMG Asset Business, BearingPoint Asset Based Consulting, Accenture Software). The major reason why asset-based consulting is an important trend is that it involves taking some of the tasks that consultants have traditionally performed using their personal skills and expertise and productizing them, turning them into tools that can be used repeatedly for client engagements, at a fraction of the cost and providing a clearer ROI and more control for clients. Although it will not replace traditional consulting with its reliance on talent completely, the proportion of the consulting market which could be taken over by a new breed of intelligent machines could be significant (Czerniawska 2017).

2.2 *The Impact on Consulting Organizations*

Although the use of consultants and consulting firms has been prevalent for long and will continue in the future, the practice of consulting, the nature of assignments consulting organizations undertake, the value they (must) generate for their clients, and the way consulting firms are organized and managed will change at least to certain extent. The case for change for consulting firms depends on a number of factors, including a consulting firm's size, organization, services, client and sector portfolio and, of course, the extent to which it has already changed.

2.2.1 Need for Greater Differentiation

A consulting firm's value proposition has partly transformed from (only) providing smart people to solve clients' problems to providing clients access to the consulting firm's knowledge base, tools and methodologies. It also begins to shift towards less knowledge-based factors such as speed, flexibility, independence/control and solution orientation. As competition intensifies due to the ongoing consolidation and the entry of heterogeneous players in the market, there is a significant need for consulting firms to define their unique identities and to differentiate themselves from the rest, in an increasingly fragmented industry. Aggressive competition in the market for commoditized consulting services is seriously impacting the profitability of many consulting companies. Unless consulting firms put much more effort in developing a strategy and the ability to clarify exactly how they intend to support their clients' businesses in a differentiating and value-adding way they will face immense price pressures. With a greater proportion of consulting work being commoditized, the urge for consulting firms to differentiate themselves not only in terms of their (functional or technical) competences and capabilities, but increasingly in terms of how they collaborate with clients (e.g. bring in greater speed, help clients to co-create solutions, etc.) will be higher. Although this particularly applies for the lower-cost consulting market where clients consider the majority of consulting service providers to be equally capable of doing the work, it will also play a greater role in the high-value consulting market.

2.2.2 Flexible Access to Specialist Skills

The consulting industry has clung for many years to a pyramid model in which consulting teams are made up of a very small number of very senior people (managing the relationship with the client and overseeing projects) and a much larger number of junior staff doing the doing. Since clients generally expect more senior people and hardly are willing to pay high rates for junior consultants, the pyramid structure is gradually being challenged. Many consulting firms therefore have started to strengthen their «middle layers» by hiring more staff with former line or consulting experience, so turning their pyramids into diamonds or triangles. But, since there is increasingly a demand for flexibility (i.e. there may be clients that are commissioning very large projects and are hiring large amounts of external resources for some projects, whereas for other projects they want to buy best of breed high-caliber expertise), the future is not about a choice between pyramids or diamonds so much as it is about the flexibility to offer clients both (Source for Consulting 2013).

Especially for the larger consulting firms it will be a challenge to accommodate alternative staffing models within the same company and with the existing staff, respectively. Allowing clients to have flexible access to specialist skills for smaller engagements that not require the common structure of consulting project teams can put significant pressure on the existing organizational and business models of consulting firms. It's a fact that even the large, multi-specialist consulting firms usually do not have a «mass» of equally high-caliber experts in a specific area of competence and these scarce resources have to be allotted to a more less wide client portfolio. Second, it's not given that clients are willing to pay the higher fees of senior experts of prestigious consulting firms for projects that have a smaller scope of work, are better defined and do not have a large value at risk. Notably, because for projects with these attributes today clients are able to find alternative consulting service providers that are specializing in assembling leaner project teams or providing single resources from a pool of highly experienced independent consultants at a small fraction of the cost of traditional competitors.

2.2.3 Brand, Reputation and Visibility

It is generally easier for consulting firms to build a good reputation and brand recognition with existing clients than to generate leads for engagements with new clients. This is illustrated by the results of a survey conducted by the meta-consulting firm Cardea asking consulting companies about how they think they are perceived by existing and new clients (Cardea 2017). Although the survey participants feel that their current clients are well aware of their consulting brands, brand visibility and recognition in the market as a whole were consistently rated lower. This seems to create a challenge for consulting firms since visibility is so much important for the success of a consulting firm. For that reason, consulting firms should focus on strategies that increase their brand visibility not only for current but also for prospective clients. Lack of transparency and knowledge about what consulting firms actually do and who they serve seem also to be a challenge for buyers of consulting services. Especially when it comes to specialist know-how, consulting buyers find it difficult to explore visible and credible external consultants (Fig. 6).

When clients are becoming much more selective and modular about what they are buying, are seeking innovative solutions and increasingly are exploring partnerships

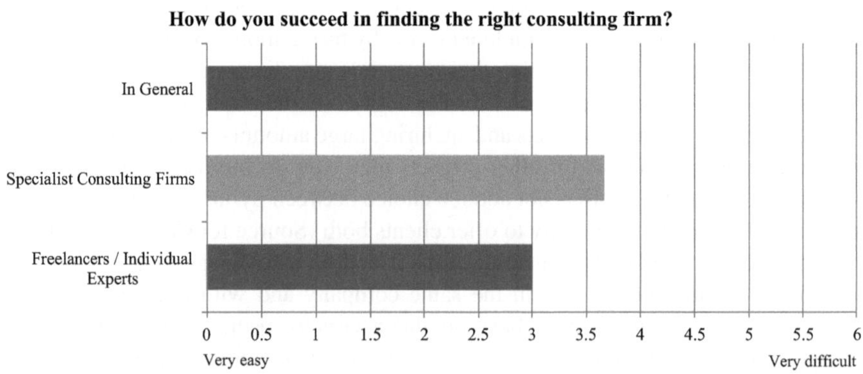

Fig. 6 Difficulties encountered in seeking out consultants (Cardea 2017)

with innovative new consulting companies, it is becoming more and more crucial for incumbent consulting companies to stay «top of mind» and to enhance their marketplace visibility of their full (innovative) service portfolio, skills and expertise. Although personal client relationships are still the most important success factor for the future growth of consulting firms, the second most important factor is brand (brand recognition, positioning, and reputation), closely followed by visibility and ease of being found (Cardea 2017).

It's interesting to note that, according to research of the Hinge Research Institute, consulting service providers tend to overestimate the interest of existing clients. Only 18% of buyers of consulting services rated the consultants' services as very important to addressing their challenges, 46% saw them as not being very relevant. In addition, fully two thirds of buyers of consulting services admit that they do not know all the services a consultant provides and therefore do not know how a consultant can help them (Frederiksen 2013).

2.2.4 Digitization of Marketing

The Internet has finally arrived for the business-to-business market. Centralized markets for B2B commerce over the Internet will create unprecedented levels of market transparency and lower the cost of procurement (Morgan Stanley Dean Witter 2000). The availability of digital media and online channels has already remarkably changed how buyers of consulting services look for prospective consulting firms. The diversity and accessibility of information online has made tools such as online search increasingly fundamental. Among the online techniques used by buyers of consulting services digital market places and portals have eclipsed more traditional methods such as search engines and social media channels (e.g. LinkedIn).

Besides building and maintaining longer and stronger client relationships and relying on traditional marketing techniques and channels, online marketing strategies become more and more key for consulting firms in order to boost further growth. Digital marketing differs from traditional marketing in that it involves a wider range of marketing instruments (such as search engine advertising, search engine optimization and inbound marketing activities) and channels (such as social media, digital market places and communities) which help consulting clients search for and explore consulting firms and their services and allow consulting firms to increase their visibility and brand reputation in the web.

With diminishing opacity of the consulting industry, being market-oriented is increasingly essential for consulting firms, and not only for their clients. Choosing the right sales and marketing strategies and approaches is essential for growing one's consulting firm. This is similarly true in the era of advanced digitalization. As our research shows, it seems though that consulting companies did not yet find the right recipe for their digital marketing strategies (Cardea 2017). Consulting firms are well advised to exploit the opportunities which modern digital platforms, inbound marketing, online lead generation and performance marketing can provide.

2.2.5 And the Winners Are...

Every consulting category or segment has service providers who out-perform their competitors by a significant margin. These service providers have managed to differentiate themselves in terms of leadership, culture, client engagement, service offering and pricing, business strategy, innovation and people management (Parakala 2015). It is always a mix of factors which can make a consulting company succeed (or fail) in the market. Of all the characteristics of the successful consulting firm of the future, flexibility is arguably the most significant because it challenges the very foundations on which many firms are built (Source for Consulting 2013).

Flexibility involves the ability of consulting firms to respond to the rapidly evolving clients' needs and expectations in every aspect related to improving customer value and to helping them transform their businesses and solve their most prevalent business challenges. Probably it is too early to say whether the models of the integrated management and technology one-stop shops (including the large strategy houses, the Big Four or the technology integrators), the specialized niche boutique consulting firms, the start-ups or the associated networks of freelance consultants are most capable of providing the most compelling business offering to clients. Size and investment power will probably favor the large consulting companies to respond to new market environments, on the other hand, the agility of the smaller consulting companies will help them to adapt quickly and increase time-to-market. That's why there will probably always be a consulting service provider which will be able to fill the gap and deliver new services to clients where other service providers are unable to meet client expectations.

2.2.6 Consulting 4.0

The term Consulting 4.0 borrows from the various industrial revolutions (from industry 1.0 to industry 4.0), but is far from being as clearly defined. However, similar to the fourth industrial revolution, Consulting 4.0 is proclaimed to have begun, spurred by interconnected digital technology. However, Consulting 4.0 is more than the digitalization of the consulting industry. Consulting 4.0 describes the fundamental change of an industry which for a long time has escaped the need to respond to the threats of disruption.

The factors which led to these disruptive changes in the consulting industry have been described in detail in this article. The question arises, though, whether Consulting 4.0 marks the future of consulting or is just a temporary trend. The expertise which is expected from a consultant has not changed a lot in recent years: A consultant has to bring in and demonstrate specific methodological know-how, expertise in an industry or industries as well as functional areas. New challenges, new client needs and demands require more, however. Much of management consultants' value lies in their functional know-how and expertise, the real value from a consulting engagement however is increasingly received by the ability of the consultant to influence and improve the operations or direction of a client's business in the long run through innovative, actionable solutions in a complex market environment for a fair or adequate price. This generally requires multiple specialist know-how due to the current requisite to bundle strategy, operations, marketing and technology assistance, conceptual and implementation support as well as software-based data collection (i.e. analytics, predictive analytics) and consultative data interpretation.

The consulting industry's market leaders—strategy consultants, IT consultants and system integrators or the Big Four—take the chance to position themselves as multi-specialists, sometimes by eagerly acquiring smaller specialist consulting firms. Likely, smaller consulting companies on their own, with their deep specialist know-how and/or innovative business models and solutions, could be well-positioned to make a remarkable amount of work in nearly all sectors as clients realize the possibilities for wide-ranging change, major transformation, and the rethinking of business models in order to help them thrive in the markets of the future.

The management consulting industry has come to a stage at which it has to cope with increasingly demanding and sophisticated clients and therefore has to partly re-invent itself by finding and offering new and innovative solutions, services and values for its buyers of consulting services. The traditional management consulting model will not be completely replaced in the future, but it will be permanently augmented and complemented through new services, products and business models—calling for more adaptivity of the consulting firms. The players and available solutions in the consulting market therefore have become and will continue to be even more and increasingly varied. To be able to navigate through this consulting service provider jungle in the consulting market, transparency is needed. For clients which seek out the right consultants for their businesses this will be one of their major challenges for now and the future.

References

Cardea (2016) Trends in the consulting market 2016. Cardea AG. https://www.consultingsearcher.com/eng/Cardea-competence-centre/The-consulting-market/Executive-Survey-Consulting-Market-Trends. Accessed 28 Jun 2017

Cardea (2017) Digitization of consulting 2017. Cardea AG. https://www.consultingsearcher.com/eng/Cardea-competence-centre/The-consulting-market/Survey-Digitization-of-Consulting-20163. Accessed 28 Jun 2017

Christensen CM, Wang D, van Bever DCM (2013) Consulting on the cusp of disruption. Harv Bus Rev 91(10):106–114

Czerniawska F (2012) Multi-disciplinary consulting: the best thing since sliced bread? http://www.sourceglobalresearch.com/blog/2012/07/23/multi-disciplinary-consulting-the-best-thing-since-sliced-bread. Accessed 26 Jun 2017

Czerniawska F (2016) Agility and the unknown unknowns. http://www.sourceglobalresearch.corm/blog/2016/06/07/agility-and-the-unknown-unknowns. Accessed 27 Jun 2017

Czerniawska F (2017) #3: Five big numbers for 2017. http://www.sourceglobalresearch.com/blog/2017/03/07/3-five-big-numbers-for-2017. Accessed 28 Jun 2017

Desai F (2016) The rise of digital consultancies. https://www.forbes.com/sites/falgunidesai/2016/03/23/the-rise-of-digital-consultancies/#35270ebe6a79. Accessed 28 Jun 2017

Frederiksen LW (2013) How buyers buy: management consulting services. Hinge Research Institute. https://hingemarketing.com/library/article/how_buyers_buy_management_consulting_services#. Accessed 28 Jun 2017

IBISWorld (2017) Management consulting in the US: market research report. March 2017. https://www.ibisworld.com/industry-trends/market-research-reports/professional-scientific-technical-services/professional-scientific-technical-services/management-consulting.html. Accessed 28 Jun 2017

Morgan Stanley Dean Witter (2000) The B2B internet report. Collaborative commerce equity research North America, April 2000. https://pdfs.semanticscholar.org/6286/7b15820a5dfb1d0c5c90dd03df45710777fe.pdf. Accessed 28 Jun 2017

Parakala K (2015) Global consulting and IT service providers trends, an industry perspective. Technova. http://www.technova.com.au/global-consulting-and-it-service-providers-trends-an-industry-perspective/. Accessed 28 Jun 2017

Source for Consulting (2013) The consulting firm of the future. Source for Consulting Services Ltd. http://edenmccallum.com/pdfs/Consulting_Firm_of_the_Future_2013.pdf. Accessed 28 Jun 2017

Christoph Treichler is managing partner and founder of Cardea AG, a meta-consulting firm which assists clients with searching, evaluating and selecting consulting companies, and recognized expert on strategic trends in the consulting market and in sourcing and deploying consulting services. He's also significantly involved in developing and running the innovative, digital platform for consulting services consultingsearcher.com.

The Development of Interpersonal Trust Between the Consultant and Client in the Course of the Consulting Process

Christian Mauerer

Abstract This research work investigates the development of interpersonal trust between the client and the consultant during the consulting process. It gives a conceptual outline of the trust building dimensions in the consultant-client relationship in terms of propensity to trust, perceived trustworthiness and the conditions of the trust situation with referring to the integrated trust model of Mayer, Davis and Schoorman. The research findings are enhanced by a qualitative practical investigation to provide a further context-specific concretization. Even though the implications from the practical investigation are in main parts congruent with the conceptual findings, it turned out that trust as a social mechanism is difficult to be grasped during practical interviews, why a conceptual foundation is indispensable to capture the total trust spectrum. This work shows that the trustworthy factors of abilities, integrity and benevolence are relevant for building interpersonal trust between the consultant and client, whereas a lack of ability-related trustworthiness cannot be compensated by the others. It is identified that signaling same-goal-orientation with the client and demonstrating a supportive role for the client's interests are key factors for building trust by the consultant. It is also highlighted that a transparent working approach of the consultant is vital to reduce the client's uncertainty and to promote trust building.

1 Significance of Trust in the Consulting Process

Consulting is often characterized as a trust object. The client needs to rely on the expertise promised by the consultant in advance of the project and the consultant's performance is also difficult to be evaluated even after finishing the project (Woratschek 1996; Mohe 2003). The lack of trust is considered as a main cause for failures of consulting engagements. The trust matter has gained increasing relevancy for the client company and, consequently, for the consultancy when, at the same time of a growing consulting market, also the number of unsuccessful

C. Mauerer (✉)
Technische Universität Ilmenau, Ilmenau, Germany

V. Nissen (ed.), *Advances in Consulting Research*, Contributions to Management Science, https://doi.org/10.1007/978-3-319-95999-3_13

consulting projects as well as frivolous behavior of the consultants significantly increased (Greschuchna 2006).

Consulting in the sense of this research contribution is defined in accordance to Nissen as follows (Nissen 2007):

> Consulting is a professional service that is provided by one or more persons, who typically have the required expertise to solve the problem at hand and are hierarchically independent of the client organization. The consulting engagement is limited in time, financially compensated and has the objective to define, structure and analyze business issues of the client organization interactively with the client's employees and to develop corresponding solutions as well as to implement them in close cooperation with the client if requested.

Despite the various areas of consulting engagements, there are certain characteristics that are typical for consulting services. The nature of consulting is seen as a weakly pre-determined and complex domain. The actual consulting service as the product is to be concretized while the consulting processes are carried out based on interactions between the consultant and the client. The way to the final consulting result is significantly driven by several bases of expectations from both the client and consulting organization (Jacobsen 2005). A certain portion of risk is always inherent to consulting projects, what originates from the structural input-output uncertainty that is typical for services with incorporating the external factor (Maleri 1997).

Consulting as a service has an intangible character, which implies a high portion of contingencies (Jacobsen 2005). Glueckler and Armbruester have identified institutional uncertainty and transactional uncertainty as the two most significant types of uncertainty in the consulting sector (Glückler and Armbrüster 2003). Institutional uncertainty derives from the lack of formal institutional standards like industry principles and codes of conduct. Transactional uncertainty stems from confidentiality of information, service-product characteristics and the interdependent and interactive character of the co-production of consultants and client (Glückler and Armbrüster 2003). The consultant's possibilities of opportunistic behavior and moral hazard make the client feel uncertain (Gillespie 2003). There is substantial risk during the consultant engagement that his actions and decisions are to the detriment of the client organization. The client is faced with the hazard of hidden intentions by the consultant, which could only be revealed after the contracting phase when the consulting project is in progress (Kralj 2004). This is in one line with the further typical agency problems of hidden actions (opportunistic behavior of the consultant) or hidden characteristics (inadequate expertise and capabilities of the consultant) (Barchewitz and Armbrüster 2004).

Irrespective of the actual role of the consultant, whether he acts more as a coach or as an expert, the consulting situation is always determined by the clash of two parties. Consequently, the interactions between consultants and clients and, hence, the focus on individuals are the crucial drivers for consulting success. Constant communication is required to ensure that the specific context of the client organization can be incorporated into the development and implementation of solutions (Sommerlatte 2000). Consulting is thus about forming relationships. The consultant needs to create a productive and sustainable relationship with the individuals of the client's company to achieve success (Coers and Heinecke 2002).

The high interaction need during a consulting process is the reason why a trustful cooperation has a significant impact on the consulting process (Jeschke 2004). A certain level of personal proximity is to be admitted by the client to enable the consulting engagement to deliver results that are specific for the client context. However, the consultant's own economic interest to maximize profit through the engagement and the hazard of opportunistic behavior indicate the need for caution and control. The client is therefore faced with critical attribution problems of what level of freedom can be granted to the consultant (Müller et al. 2006). As mentioned, these problems are not controlled by a superior instance like an industry authority. Due to that fact, trust is a critical dimension in the relationship between consultant and client and therefore has an existential role in the consulting processes (Höner 2008). Studies by Covin and Fisher analyzing the success of consulting projects have shown that a lack of trust is the frequent cause for a failure of a consulting engagement (Covin and Fisher 1991). Dean points out that trust should not only be seen as a soft factor, but also as a hard prerequisite for the consultant to enable transformations and impact in the client organization. The consultant's profound expertise and methodologies would not have any effect if they cannot flow into a sound and trustworthy client-consultant relationship (Dean 2005).

2 Research Context, Specification and Methodology

2.1 Basic Perspectives on the Comprehension of Trust

The investigation of interpersonal trust development in the constellation of the consultant-client relationships requires first to constitute the relevant conceptual basis for that research matter. The trust phenomenon is scientifically approached by different disciplines, why there is no consistent comprehension of the trust terminology and, consequently, no overall conception of trust that is universally accepted (Ripperger 2003; Jehle 2001; Klaus 2002). In the academic literature there are numerous definitions for trust. Castaldo has identified 72 different approaches for that definitional matter (Castaldo 2002). For the present research work the essential scientific cornerstones of the trust research are mentioned.

The groundwork of trust research was made within the psychological discipline with the primary focus on the characteristics of individuals. In that regard, the preconditions for interpersonal trust have been investigated and it is argued from a behavioral-oriented and preference-oriented perspective (Klaus 2002). This psychological orientation was predominantly influenced by the behavioral-oriented studies of Deutsch, who provided major contributions with his experiments in the fields of game theory when investigating the motivational effects of cooperative, competitive and individualistic patterns on the decisions of individuals in different situations of interactions (Deutsch 1958, 1960). Trust in the conception of Deutsch is interpreted as observable, situation-dependent and voluntary behavior of individuals (Deutsch 1962). Deutsch stated that "...the problem of trust arises from the possibility that if, during cooperation, each cooperator is individually oriented to obtain a maximum gain at minimum cost to himself (without regard to the gains or costs to the other cooperators), cooperation may be unrewarding for all or for some" (Deutsch 1960).

Next to the psychological perspective the sociological view on trust enhances this conception with perceiving trust as a feature in social relationships (Moorman et al. 1993). Luhmann provided a fundamental contribution to the trust conception in this sociological perspective (Luhmann 1989). In conjunction with his system-theoretical comprehension, Luhmann perceived trust as a mechanism to reduce complexity (Luhmann 1989) which occurs through the adoption of specific expectations about the future behavior of the interaction partner. This positive expectation is selected amongst a range of possibilities. Complexity is absorbed by trust as someone who grants trust acts as if the trustee's actions are to a certain extent predictable (Lane 1998). Trust is thus perceived as mechanism that overcomes "the problem of time" with bridging uncertainty in the face of imperfect information. Due to the given problem of time and knowledge, trust is a risky investment because it requires a risky pre-commitment (Luhmann 1979).

In 1995, Mayer, Davis and Schoormann provided a significant contribution to the comprehension of trust in the economic science (Mayer et al. 1995). The term "willingness to be vulnerable" is in the focus of their trust conception. Their model of trust, which is relating to the trust phenomenon in dyadic organizational interaction processes, has been frequently apprehended also in other disciplines of trust research (Kilduff 2006). Mayer et al. considered trust between individuals and also discussed attributes of the trustor, the trustee, the specific situations as well as the behavior that follows a trust relation. As a result, their model integrates determinants, effects and feedback mechanism of trust. In course of their investigation, Mayer et al. integrated insights from trust conceptions of different disciplines and portrayed them in the organizational context. Their comprehension of trust is applicable to any relationship with a person that is assumed to act intentional. The constitutive element of trust is hereby seen in the perception that the trustee can deliberately choose his reaction. This implies that the trustee has always the possibility to honor the granted trust relation or to disappoint it (Mayer et al. 1995).

2.2 Trust Conception for This Research Work

The trust comprehension in this research work refers to the trust concept of Mayer et al. This model concurs with the given thematic consulting context that suggests to investigate trust based on both the characteristics of individuals as well on the level of social relationships between the involved individuals. The conceptual model therefore allows considering the processual perspective of trust development and its dynamics that take effect in the different developing stages of the consulting project. One of the crucial conceptual orientations of their model is that they perceive trust to go beyond a pure dispositional facet that is "trait-like", but to be also an aspect of relationship. This implies that trust varies across relationships (Mayer et al.

2007). Moreover, the trust model of Mayer et al. integrates both multi-level and cross-level approaches of trust that allow the investigation of interpersonal trust relations within an organization as well as between two separated organizations, as being relevant for the consulting context (Mayer et al. 2007).

The trust model of Mayer et al. has seen significant scientific dedication in consecutive research works, both in empirical and theoretical terms (with showing more than 16,000 scientific citations in Google Scholar by May 2017). Mayer et al. took on these substantial scientific reflections with formulating a subsuming research work in 2007 that also integrates advances and further concretizations of their trust model (Mayer et al. 2007).

Mayer et al. basically defined trust as follows:

> The willingness to be vulnerable to the actions of another party based on the expectation that the other will perform a particular action important to the trustor, irrespective to the ability to monitor or control the other party (Mayer et al. 1995).

In their model they highlighted the importance of the propensity to trust. If there is no information about the interaction partner available, the propensity to trust determines the portion of trust from the trustor. The propensity to trust hereby describes a generalized expectation with regard to the trustworthiness of another person, which is stable throughout different situations. Propensity to trust is assumed to influence how much trust one has for a trustee prior to the availability of data on that particular party (Mayer et al. 1995).

If information about an interaction partner is available then the granted trust depends on the perceived trustworthiness of the specific trustee as well as on the trustor's propensity to trust. In their model they assumed that trustworthiness can be explained through a function of perception about the ability, benevolence and integrity of the trustee. If the trustor feels that one of those components is only weakly shaped at the potential trustee, this impairs the potential to build up a trust relation (Mayer et al. 1995).

The fundament of a trust decision of human beings is characterized as "risk taking in relationship", which is assumed to be a function of trust and the perceived risk (Mayer et al. 1995). Based on the consequences of a trustful behavior the trustor modifies the perceived trustworthiness of the trustee. The outcome of the "risk taking in the relationship" results in an updating process of the original estimation of the ability, benevolence and integrity of the trustee. Any negative or positive feedback from the interaction has therefore direct effect on the trust relation for the subsequent situation of interaction (Mayer et al. 1995).

With constituting the relevant conceptual baseline and definition of trust for this research work, it is also vital to delimit trust from other essential conceptual terms. Mayer et al. hereby differentiate trust from *cooperation*, *confidence* and *predictability*. With regard to *cooperation*, the distinction to trust is often misconstrued. Trust can frequently lead to cooperation. However trust is not a necessary precondition for it, as cooperation does not always put a party on risk. To bring the cooperative behavior in relation with trust, there needs to be vulnerability as a hard pre-requisite (Mayer et al. 1995). There is also an amorphous relation of trust with the term *confidence* in the history of trust research. Mayer et al. hereby integrate the proposed conceptual distinction of Luhmann when he argued that for trust a relevant portion of risk needs to be recognized and assumed, while this is not the case with confidence. With the trust decision one chooses an action in preference to others in spite of the possibility of being disappointed by others. With confidence one does not consider alternatives (Mayer et al. 1995; Luhmann 1988). Next to this, both trust and *predictability* are means of uncertainty reduction. As trust refers to the risk the trustor has based on the vulnerability that is subject to the trustee's behavior, predictability is mainly driven by general and external factors that let the counterparty derive the probable behavior of the other (Mayer et al. 1995).

2.3 Research Specification

Based on the comprehension of trust as quoted in the previous section this research work investigates interpersonal trust in the consultant-client relationship during the consulting process and dedicates to the following research question:

> What are the influencing factors for interpersonal trust development between the consultant and the client during the consulting process?

Hereby, the interpersonal trust position is regarded as dependent variable. For that purpose it will conceptually break down the examination of the interpersonal trust relation in the trust building factors of propensity to trust, perceived trustworthiness and the conditions of the trust situation. The investigation of perceived trustworthiness will be further segmented in its determining factors of personal characteristics and behavior-related factors. An embedment in the specific context of the consulting process is essential to ensure that the findings consider the concrete social environment. The role of the consultant defines his position and his level of power in the consultant-client relationship and, therefore, delineates the potential social context in which a trust situation can occur.

A target-oriented and meaningful investigation of that thematic research focus also requires the delimitation of aspects that are not considered as scope of investigation. This research work concentrates on the interpersonal dimension of trust between the consultant and the client. It does not take up the generation and the dynamics of organizational or systemic trust towards the client organization or the consultant organization, which might be constituted by their reputation or by the experience-based trust with the organization as such. Organizational trust, however, is integrated in this research work to the extent that it has deriving character for the interpersonal trust relation. Moreover, this research work focuses on the trust development during the actual consulting project. It does not refer to a relationship between the consulting organization and the client organization beyond that process. As a consequence of that, the effect of trust at the client's selection process of consultants is not a part of this work. Further-on, this research concentrates on those consulting projects that require a minimum level of interaction between the consultant and the client to produce the consulting result. The explanations and findings of this work will be less meaningful for consulting projects in which the consultants act mainly independently, what might be the case when the consultant is engaged as assessor or independent surveyor.

After having specified the research focus, related work will now be reviewed.

2.4 Related Work

Greschuchna provided an investigation of trust in the consulting context. She focused primarily on the hiring phase of consulting services from the perspectives of small and mid-sized client companies, which were also the basis of her empirical investigation. The objective of her research work was the analysis of the role of trust in the selection process of a consulting company by the clients. It was about to determine which factors influence the client's perception of trust towards the consultancy at the initial contact and what impact trust has on the engagement decision. She primarily investigated what driving factors in conjunction with organizational trust towards the consulting company do matter. Greschuchna stated that she sees further need to investigate trust during the actual consulting process phase and specifically the dynamics of trust between the client and the consultant (Greschuchna 2006).

A further contribution to the investigation of trust was elaborated by Mencke focusing on trust in social systems and consulting. He provided an analysis of the fundamentals of trust in social systems and applied this to the consulting processes carried out at small- and mid-sized companies. His analysis approach was driven by the system-theoretic orientation. This theoretic orientation bases on the assumption that social complexities and, therefore, social mechanisms such as trust cannot be controlled or influenced by the individuals (Mencke 2005). Due to his theoretic orientation, he could not fully explain the relevancy of interpersonal dynamics and characteristics for the development of interpersonal trust.

In the book "The trusted advisor" Maister, Green and Galford provided practical guidelines for consultants how to achieve a trusting relation with the client in the consulting process. The statements quoted in the book originate from the authors' own consulting experiences. They gave meaningful insight how consultants could behave in various situations in order to build or maintain a trustworthy position. In case studies and training sections they provided concrete instructions how to deal with clients. Using a practical model they illustrate the steps the consultant would need to take in order to establish and develop a trustful relationship (Maister et al. 2000). This literature represents a valuable practical source of insights into trust development, but the authors do not relate to a specific theoretical model or empirical evidence.

2.5 Research Methodology

Trust is perceived as a complex research object, as it needs to be considered in the wide set of psychological and sociological perspectives. The trust relation as a social facet of the individuals is difficult to be measured and reflected. This suggests that research on interpersonal trust requires a respective theoretical dedication in the first stage. The elaboration of profound statements about the influential factors for the trust relation in the consultant-client relationship has to integrate trust into the social scheme of consulting processes. Only based on that social-analytical framework, one is in a position to capture a holistic picture about the trust relation and the dynamics of trust during the consulting process. Theory-building from a pure quantitative empirical approach would not capture the total of social complexity that is inherent in the interactions of human agents of a consulting project.

Next to that, a qualitative practical analysis is conducted for the purpose of enrichment and concretization of the research topic. For that empirical investigation, it is not intended to conduct an overall empirical validation of hypotheses derived from the theoretic statements. Instead, the empirical approach follows an open explorative consideration of the research topic and is, in general, consecutive to the theoretical conception that has guiding and structuring character for the design of this empirical part. This practical investigation is conducted by using the qualitative approach based on semi-structured expert interviews referring to real practical experiences in consulting projects. Hereby, four consultants and four client employees that have at least 5 years direct experience of involvement in various consulting projects were interviewed.

3 Conceptual Specification of Interpersonal Trust Development in the Consultant-Client Relationship

This section outlines the application of the trust model of Mayer et al. on the interpersonal trust development between the consultant and the client. To investigate the mechanism of the trust building the individual characteristics of the client and the consultant as interaction partners, their relationship as well as situation-specific aspects have to be taken into consideration. The individual characteristics of the interaction partners have to be reflected by the propensity to trust on the side of the trust subject as well as the trustworthiness of the trust object (Mayer et al. 1995, 2007).

3.1 Occurrence of a Trust Situation

With investigating how the development of interpersonal trust between the consultant and the client occurs, it is vital to outline the context in which a trust situation happens. It will be described how the conceptual understanding of the trust relevancy in this research work is represented by the situations in the course of the consultant-client relationship.

The fundament of a trust decision is characterized in the applied model as "risk taking in relationship", which is assumed to be a function of trust and the perceived risk (Mayer et al. 1995). Therefore, trust becomes relevant in those situations that are uncertain with regard to an outcome of an event or behavior. The conceptual analysis of trust building therefore refers to situations in which *subjective uncertainty* on side of the consultant or client as potential trustor is given. Basically, the consulting process is affected by various aspects of uncertainty. As basically pointed out in Sect. 1, consulting as a service has an intangible character, which results in structural input-output risks and therefore implies a high portion of contingencies (Jacobsen 2005). Also the consultant has to cope with subjective uncertainty in the relationship with the client. There is uncertainty concerning the quality and correctness of information he is given by the client employees as well as the expertise and competencies of the client that matter for the consulting project. Next to this, there is also uncertainty for the consultant that his engagement is misused by the client for the political game within the client organization or that the client follows hidden motives with the consultant engagement. As a result the analysis of trust building refers to those situations of the consultant-client relationship in which the consultant and the client are faced with subjective uncertainty about the motives and intentions and consequently the behavior of the other party.

The next aspect of a potential trust situation is that the potential trustor is *vulnerable* when entering a trust situation, as that could cause potential damage to him (Mayer et al. 1995). Here, only the perceived vulnerability matters, which originates from the individual assessment of potential positive or negative outcomes of the respective situation (Späth 2007). On the client side there is a substantial risk of damage since the client has to cope with the economic consequences of the consulting outcome. Moreover, potential damage could also occur to the level of individuals of the client organization, when the outcome of a consulting project results in the loss of allocative or authoritative resources for some client employees. Damage for the consultant can arise regarding their reputation and the loss of potential follow-up business. This might be caused by an unsuccessful consulting outcome due to sanctioning behavior of the client employees or the misuse of the consulting role.

A further important requirement can be derived from the trust definition of Mayer et al. with referring to the term "*willingness*" to be vulnerable. This implies that there needs to be *freedom to decide* on part of the trustor. Trust as a social mechanism can only be granted when the consultant or the client in the role of a trustor can make the trust decision voluntarily. The trusting consultant or client need to have the possibility to determine on their own how to behave in the context of the trust situation. This refers to their freedom to decide how they dispense the level of control and supervision towards the interaction partner. Consequently, those situations of consultant-client interactions are not to be comprehended as trust situation in which it is predetermined or prescribed how they have to behave. Trust as intentional construct will for instance not evolve in situations in which the client employee is e.g. directed by hierarchical authorities or processual instructions of the client organization to act or behave in a certain way. Overall it has to be stated that the trust decision cannot be enforced.

3.2 Propensity to Trust of the Trust Subject

The interpersonal trust building is at first grounded on the characteristics of the trustor as the actor who is supposed to give trust to somebody in a specific situation. Interpersonal trust has its fundament in the personality disposition of that trustor. This personality disposition is approached by Mayer et al. as the propensity to trust. It has influence on how much trust the trustor has for a trustee unless he has direct and relevant information about the interaction partner available. Propensity to trust is also described as the general willingness to trust others and has high relevance in terms of building initial trust (Mayer et al. 1995). As soon as further information about the interaction partner is available this experience will successively undermine the significance of propensity to trust (Nooteboom and Six 2003). Accordingly, Mayer et al. state that "time" generally plays an important role in the meaningfulness of the variables in the model. Propensity to trust, as a dispositional quality, would be an important factor at the very beginning of the relationship, whereas judgements of ability and integrity would form relatively quickly in the course of the relationship (Mayer et al. 2007).

Therefore, in a consultant-client relationship the degree of trust that can evolve is at first determined by that propensity to trust. This is a characteristic of the trusting consultant and client. They show higher propensity to trust when they have inner security in the sense that they have the respective level of self-assurance that enables them to encounter the potential disappointment of the trust relation with fortitude. Propensity to trust as a stable "within-party factor" of the trusting consultant and client therefore determines the likelihood that they will trust the interaction partner unless they made direct experience with each other in the consulting process (Mayer et al. 1995). It describes the general willingness of the consultant or the client to trust others. As people in general differ in their inherent propensity to trust, this also refers to the variety of different personalities that come up in the role of the consultant and the client. The propensity to trust depends on the different developmental experiences, personality types and cultural backgrounds of the individual client employees and consultants. Some of them could show the extreme case of frequently granting blind trust, whereas some of them show unwillingness to trust also in favorable circumstances during the consulting project (Mayer et al. 1995).

Propensity of trust has particular significance for trust building when the client and consultants have only a low spectrum of information available about each other. In a lot of projects, the client and the consultant come together as two strangers, as the consultant is temporarily engaged for solving a specific problem of the client organization and he is considered as an outsider of the client organization. This leads to the situation that in many cases the consultant and client do not know each other when the consulting project starts. Propensity of trust is therefore ascribed with high relevance in terms of building initial trust in the entry phase of the consulting process. With evolvement of the relationship between the consultant and the client, situation-specific patterns and experiences gain in importance. Certainly, the context of missing acquaintance does not apply in situation where the consultant is engaged for a follow-up project. Here, the dominance of propensity to trust for an initial trust building is compensated already by the direct knowledge of each other.

Propensity to trust is considered to be a relatively stable personal feature of the respective consultant and the client acting as trustor. It is regarded as to be hardly influencable. The dynamics of interpersonal trust position in course of the consulting process is therefore rather driven by the actual trustworthiness of the trust object as well as situation-specific factors. However for empirical investigations of trust situations the propensity to trust needs to be taken into account as it provides important insight into the sources of trust building in the respective situation.

3.3 Trustworthiness of the Trust Object

Next to the propensity to trust, the decision whether trust can be granted is essentially determined by attributes of the interaction partner as trust object (trustee). The emergence of trust in a relationship is hereby not necessarily triggered by the actual goodness of the trustee's character, motives or intentions. Instead, it is crucial how the potential trustor perceives those attributes. The perception of those attributes determines the level of trustworthiness and consequently the potential of building trust to the interaction partner (Mayer et al. 1995). Mayer et al. provided a meaningful subsumption of factors for trustworthiness based on their interdisciplinary trust research (Mayer et al. 1995). They resume that the following three characteristic dimensions of the trustee determine his trustworthiness: *ability, integrity and benevolence* (Mayer et al. 1995). Each characteristic "... contributes a unique perceptual perspective from which to consider the trustee, while the set provides a solid and parsimonious foundation for the empirical study of trust for another party" (Mayer et al. 1995).

The question if and to what extent interpersonal trust between the consultant and the client can be built is significantly determined by that trustworthiness of the potential trustee. Also here it is crucial how the trustor perceives those trustworthy attributes of the interaction partner with utilizing the available information to build either positive or negative expectations of the behavior of the other. The trustworthy attributes then guide the consultant and the client in the trust decision whether the other has the intention and motives that the resulting actions will not cause damage to the trusting consultant and client or even result in a beneficial state for him. The trustee is then also expected to relinquish opportunistic behavior.

Ability as an attribute of the interaction partner refers to the skills, competencies and characteristics that enable him to have influence within some specific domain. For the relevancy of trustworthiness, this domain needs to be important for the consulting project. This might refer to competence in some functional area in which related project tasks are to be carried out. However, this also implies that this trustee could have little aptitude, training or experience in another area that does not matter for that specific consulting process and the trust situation (Mayer et al. 1995). Based on the conceptual understanding, a trust situation is given regarding the correct statement of the consultant and the client about their abilities. Trust becomes thus relevant when the actual abilities of the interaction partner cannot be fully assessed and one has to rely on information from the interaction partner himself or from a third party. Here, trust refers to the reliability of information about the interaction partner's abilities, whereas confidence describes the belief that those abilities are actually sufficient to achieve a result in the specific situation.

Ability has high significance as the client has the expectation that the consultant brings in specific knowledge, skills and expertise to solve the client's problem, to improve the organizational or processual conditions or to enable the client to achieve innovation in his business. The consultant's abilities play thus an important role for the consulting outcome. The input of the consultant does not just refer to technical knowledge and experiences, but also to generic methods and skills (Kieser 1998). As a result the client's perception of the consultant to be trustworthy is determined by the degree the consultant demonstrates that he possesses the required expert knowledge, problem solving competency, methodical skills and other abilities that are needed to support the consulting process and to (co-)produce the consulting outcome. In the consulting context, the perception of abilities is assumed to have higher weight in comparison to integrity and benevolence. Mayer et al. argue that benevolence and integrity by itself are insufficient to build the absolute fundament of trust, since a well-intentioned person who lacks in ability may not be considered as having the respective portion of trustworthiness (Mayer et al. 1995). The reliability of information about the consultant's ability has particular relevancy in the early phases of the consulting project, when the client cannot yet refer to own meaningful experiences from the interactions with the consultant. At the beginning of the consulting process the consultant is therefore required to signal his actual abilities to enhance trustworthiness. Here, the reputation of the consulting organization is assumed to contribute to the client's perception of ability-based trustworthiness, too. On the opposite side, abilities are also an essential influencing factor to evaluate the client's trustworthiness by the consultant. The consultant is dependent on the functional expertise and knowledge of the client to ensure that the consulting outcome meets the specific requirements of client organization. As many consultants primarily focus on providing methodologies, it has particular relevance that the concretization to the client organization can be achieved, which requires the integration of the client's expertise. It is assumed that the dependency on the client employee's abilities is primarily relevant when the consultant acts in a coaching role focusing on the facilitation of the solution finding by the client.

As a next factor of trustworthiness, Mayer et al. subsumed several behavior-related attributes to the *integrity* dimension. Integrity is assumed when the trustor has the perception that the trustee adheres to a set of principles that the trustor finds acceptable, whereby both the adherence and the acceptability are important. It is referred to McFall (1987) who argued that an interaction partner could strictly follow one principle (e.g. strong focus on profit seeking), which however does not provide the perception of integrity to the trustor in that context as this principle is not acceptable for him. Besides this, integrity also encompasses virtues of reliability in terms of consistency of the party's past actions, credible communication about the trustee from other parties, belief that the trustee has a strong sense of justice, and the extent to which the party's actions are congruent with his or her words. For the evaluation of trustworthiness the perceived level of integrity matters instead of the reasons why the perception is formed (Mayer et al. 1995). The relevant set of principles that need to be adhered in the consulting context to demonstrate integrity are dominated by the client's expectations that the consultant is striving to reach the goals of the consulting project, while he acts in professional manner and on behalf of the client's interests. Vice versa, the consultant expects the client to give him the respective support to reach the goals and not to misuse the consulting engagement. Openness is considered to be an elementary driver for the perceived integrity in behavior why it can be seen as central component for personal trustworthiness (Brückerhoff 1982). For openness the consultant and client request a free flow of information in their relationship and that they do inform each other in complete manner. The significant impact of disclosure of information to the interpersonal trust development has been underlined by Morgan and Hunt (1994), while also Aulakh et al. (1996) have shown in their study that there is a significant positive correlation between the extent and quality of information exchange and the development of interpersonal trust. Interpersonal trust between the consultant and the client is therefore influenced by the client's willingness to share the respective information in terms of organization-specific information, functional and industry-specific knowledge with the consultant that is needed to produce the consulting outcome (Das and Teng 1998; Lorbeer 2003).

Next to this, integrity is also demonstrated by honesty and truthfulness (Neubauer and Rosemann 2006; Kumar 2000; Lorbeer 2003). Both behavioral characteristics create a situation that the consultant and the client can rely on the given statements and provided information of the counterparty. Implicated honesty and truthfulness moreover give them essential orientation for acceptance of information, while the positive perception of those attributes is also seen as mechanism to reduce the uncertainty and complexity within the consulting process. Honesty of the interaction partner does also include the expectation of the client and the consultant to receive negative feedback if it is required (Seifert 2001). A further important dimension of integrity refers to the consistency of the consulting interaction partners with regard to his behavior. Based on consistent behavior the trustor can derive reliability and predictability out of it. This increases the perception of security and thus enhances the trustworthiness, as it will be interpreted as indicator for the future behavior of the interaction partner (Lewicki and Bunker 1996; Lorbeer 2003). The trustor hereby expects that his interaction partner will remain constant in what he has pronounced and presented as the prospect. If the client frequently changes his opinion about matters presented by the consultant for alignment or approval, this might lead to an increased demand for reconciliation with the client on the consultant side. On the other hand, consistency is also a strong requirement on the client side with a certain link to the consultant's neutrality: The consultant appears as neutral when he is constant in his opinion and does not change it in discussions with different stakeholder of the client organization.

Benevolence is the third category for the perception of trustworthiness. It is characterized by Mayer et al. as "... the extent to which a trustee is believed to want to do good to the trustor, aside from an egocentric profit motive." Benevolence therefore suggests that the trustee has some specific proximity to the trustor and there is a positive orientation to him. High benevolence of the potential trustee is thus, for example, inversely related to his motivation to lie. It basically captures virtues of altruism and loyalty (Mayer et al. 1995). Benevolence basically contributes to the development of interpersonal trust in the consultant-client relationship when it is assumed that the trustee has generally good motives and intentions for the other party in context to the consulting project as the social platform. Benevolent behavior requires that the client and the consultant in the role as trustee do not solely follow egocentric goals. Instead, they have a general favorable attitude towards the other. When the consultant wants to be attributed with benevolent characteristics it requires him to be aware of the interests and needs of the respective client employees. This is a prerequisite for the consultant that he can respect and take care of the client employees' situation, and that he does not unconsciously carry out an action that is to the detriment of the client's interest (Gambetta 1998). However, the sole knowledge of the client's interests is not regarded to be sufficient. It is required that the consultant actively demonstrates concern about the prosperity of the client employees (Shaw 1997). Consultants can actively express the respective concern if they involve the client employees and incorporate their proposals and feedback, but also offer their direct and individual support. Overall, the client needs to have the perception that the consultant subordinates his own interests to the client's interests. This is why the signaling of same-goal-orientation with the client is considered as essential. The client then senses emotional safety when he believes that even without being in steady contact with the consultant, his actions are basically aiming at common goals. At such a state, the client is also assumed to be ready to reduce his control demand over the consultant. Conversely, benevolent attributes are also relevant for the perceived trustworthiness of the client, as the consultant also has some face-saving and reputational interests. For a successful consulting outcome the consultant needs to have first and foremost a clear view of the real motives and goals of the consulting engagement. Clearly communicated motives and goals contribute positively to the trust generation. When the client demonstrates respect to the role of the consultant, he does not exploit him with abnormal task overloads and does not misuse him, then benevolent attributes of the client are acknowledged. This contributes to interpersonal trust building as fairness regarding the consultant's engagement is signaled.

3.4 Situation-Specific Factors

Next to propensity to trust and the trustworthiness, the potential and actual degree of trust in a relationship is further driven by the situation-specific factors. Those furthermore moderate the influence of the other personal determinants, as Mayer et al. state that the context of the situation helps to determine the perceived level of trustworthiness (Mayer et al. 1995). To analyze the situation is therefore of critical relevance as trust is understood as social mechanism reflecting the constellation between the interaction partners. The consideration of situation-specific factors has a long tradition in the trust research. The initial fundament has been provided by Deutsch with his investigation in context of the Prisoner's Dilemma studies and the examination of trust in those different situations for the interaction partners (Deutsch 1958, 1960). Mayer et al. further approach the situation-specific context with arguing that even though the level of trust determined by ability, benevolence, integrity and propensity may be constant, the specific consequences of trust will be determined by contextual factors. Those factors can refer to the stakes involved, the balance of power in the relationship, the perception of the level of risk and the alternatives available to the trustor. Perceived ability will change with the dynamics of the situation that requires that ability. A similar coherence is seen with regard to integrity that is also affected by the counterparty's action. A decision of the counterparty may appear inconsistent with earlier decisions, why his integrity might be questioned when knowing nothing about the situation. The trustor's perception and interpretation of the context affect both the need for trust and the evaluation of trustworthiness. Changes in such factors like the political climate and the perceived volition of the trustee in the situation can cause a reevaluation of trustworthiness. A basic situation-related facet is the level of risk. Risk itself is assumed to have impact on the trust building, as the propensity to trust decreases (ceteris paribus) with an increasing level of perceived risk in a situation. This bases on the fact that trust can only mediate subjective certainty to the trustee but does not create objective certainty to him. As risk is inherent in the behavioral manifestation, one does not need to risk anything in order to trust, however, one must take a risk in order to engage in a trusting action (Mayer et al. 1995).

The interpersonal trust development between the consultant and the client requires risk-taking. Such situation is characterized by a certain level of dependence of the consultant and the client on his counterparty. The level of risk determines the perceived vulnerability of the consultant or the client. The portion of risk of the participants of the consulting project varies in the course of the consulting process and dependents on the respective situations as well as is linked to the role of the consulting participant. In accordance to that, also the required level of interpersonal trust diversifies. The buyer of the consulting engagement who typically works on the executive or middle management level is usually the direct addressee of the consulting outcome. He bears a high business and organizational risk that the consulting outcome is an objectively and comprehensively elaborated result. Business-related dimensions dominate his risk spheres. Similar for the managing partner of the consultancy, since his main risk areas are seen in the violation of the overall relationship between the consulting and the client organization as well as the potential damage of the overall reputation of the consulting firm. Next to this, the consulting project leader and the client project leader are also seen to be highly dependent on the progress of the consulting process as there is usually high success-related personal attribution towards these roles. Participants of the consulting project on lower levels from the client organization (functional or processual experts, supporting personnel) as well as from the consulting organization (junior and senior consultants) are considered to have more individual-related risks in context of the consulting project, e.g. regarding their status in the client organization, allocated resources or the individual performance evaluation of the consultant.

In general, the weights of the three trustworthy dimensions ability, benevolence and integrity are assumed to vary in the course of the consulting process and also depend on the situation and the concerned personalities (Shaw 1997; Mayer et al. 1995; Seifert 2001). The higher the benevolent components of the trust relation between the consultant and the client are and the more direct experiences have been made between the interaction partners, the more robust is the portion of interpersonal trust. This leads to the situation that e.g. inconsistent behavior of the trustee would not necessarily result in a complete breach of the trust relation (Lewicki and Bunker 1996).

4 Practical Findings About Development of Interpersonal Trust in the Consultant-Client Relationship

At this stage the research matter of interpersonal trust development in the consulting process is enhanced by practical insights from expert interviews. The subsumption of the interviews is basically structured analogously to the conceptual trust model in the previous chapter with referring to the factors of trustworthiness in terms of ability, integrity and benevolence. As this investigation focuses on explanations and drivers that promote the interpersonal trust development specifically during consulting processes, the trustor's propensity to trust as a dispositional facet of the individual was regarded as static attribute and has therefore not seen a separate consideration, but has been mentioned in the interviewee profiles below. Moreover, as shown in Sect. 3.4, situation-specific factors have influence on the significance of the various trustworthy attributes. This is why they were integrated and reflected in the respective sections of trustworthiness in that practical subsumptions.

For the selection of interviewees it was tried to consider different levels and roles of the consultants, the same as for different hierarchical levels of client employees involved in consulting processes. For instance, client employees acting in expert roles, as project manager or the "buyer"/"ordering client" were interviewed. On the opposite side, consultant interviewees with advanced career levels (senior consultant, consulting project manager) were selected, enhanced by a consultant acting as a freelancer. Next to this, also the required intensity of interactions between the consultant and the client varied in the consulting projects. The type of consulting projects the interviews based on are however quite homogeneous, as all projects relate to expert-oriented consulting concepts. Moreover, most consulting projects had an IT- and process-oriented thematic focus. Regarding the reference consulting projects of the interviews it needs to be highlighted that there is no integrated investigation of specific consulting projects from both the consultant and client side in parallel. Instead different projects were used as reference point for the consultant and client interviewees.

Tables 1 and 2 give an overview of the interviewee's profiles selected for the roles as consultant or client:

Table 1 Interviewee profiles of consultants

	Consultant 1	Consultant 2	Consultant 3	Consultant 4
Consulting experience	7 years	6 years	5 years	11 years
Consultant level	Senior consultant	Senior consultant	Senior consultant	Freelancer
Consulting company	Large international IT consulting company	Large international management consultancy	Large international audit and advisory company	Consulting freelancer
Self-assessment of propensity to trust	In general high propensity to trust	High/moderate propensity to trust	Low propensity to trust	Moderate level of propensity to trust
Type and scope of project	IT system implementation	Implementation of IT-system for risk management	Central project management for finance project	Integration of business segment after carve-out
Role of interviewee	Project manager	Project manager	Sub-project leader in project office	Sub-project leader (processes)
Profile of client company	Manufacturing industry, 14,000 employees, Germany	Banking industry; 3500 employees, Germany	Banking industry; 23,000 employees, Germany	Pharmaceutical industry; 4500 employees, Ger + US
Duration of project	6 months	1 year	1 year	3 years

Table 2 Interviewee profiles of clients

	Client 1	Client 2	Client 3	Client 4
Stated experience with consultants	15 years	6 years	5 years	7 years
Role in client company	Expert in finance department	Project manager/Programme leader	Functional expert controlling	Project manager in treasury organization
Client company	Large international bank	Large international bank	E-commerce	International electronic manufacturer
Self-assessment of propensity to trust	In general low propensity to trust	In general high propensity to trust	In general moderate propensity to trust	Moderate level of propensity to trust
Type and scope of project	Finance-IT platform implementation	Finance-IT platform implementation	Introduction of new purchasing process	Implementation of payment system
Role of interviewee	Functional expert	Client project manager	Functional expert (controlling)	Client project manager
Profile of client company	Banking industry; 23,000 employees	Banking industry, 23,000 employees	Internet industry, 360 employees	Electronic industry, 370,000 employees
Duration of project	6 years	5 years	9 months	1.5 years

4.1 General Significance of the Personal Level for Trust Building in the Consulting Project

In conjunction with the interviews conducted for this empirical investigation of interpersonal trust in the consultant-client relationship, also insights have been retrieved that indicate the general significance of the personal level between consultant and client for the trust building. Those relate to the overall significance of the research topic, and are therefore discussed in the following.

The interview with *CLIENT-4* has indicated that person-related attributes do outcompete the brand of the consulting firm in building the trust relation between the consultant and the client. The client (a project manager of the client organization) stated that "ultimately, it doesn't matter which brand the consultant is working for. Consulting is an absolute people business". The consulting brand, however, could be helpful to signal reliance in the first instance, e.g. it could reduce a certain level of uncertainty in non-transparent markets. But the consulting brand is not considered to automatically create a credit of trust by the client at the beginning of the consulting project. *CLIENT-1* confirmed this by stating that knowing from which consulting company the consultant comes from is not necessarily important for the creation of interpersonal trust towards this consultant. She further emphasized the importance of personal characteristics and personal abilities for the generation of interpersonal trust. The reputation of the consulting company is considered to be more relevant for inferring confidence into the abilities, particularly the knowledge of the consultancy, as stated by *CLIENT-3*. He (functional expert) further highlighted that for trust building in the consultant-client relationship human aspects are much more crucial. *CONSULTANT-1* gave an important differentiation of the trust matter in context of the consultant-client relationship: He stated that the trust context "needs to be further distinguished between the trust on a personal level (e.g. honesty) and the competencies. One can say that one trusts an interaction partner's abilities, but not him as a person". *CONSULTANT-1* moreover noted that the size and reputation of the consulting company have no essential effect on interpersonal trust building during the consulting process. Instead, he also highlighted the significance of personal characteristics, as "the client wants the personality. This relates to the character of the person. And it is also completely independent whether you come from a large or small consulting company". This perspective is also shared by the other interviewed consultants, as *CONSULTANT-2* has indicated that for trust it is important to have a personal relationship, and not only competency-related factors are crucial. Also in the interview with *CONSULTANT-4* it has been noticed that trust development during the consulting process is seen personal-oriented and independent from the consulting organization's reputation.

4.2 *Trust Generation Through Reliance on Ability*

With discussing how ability-related aspects are addressed in the interviews, the conceptual approach for this research work needs to be recapped: ability plays a role in the trust development in so far the trustor grants trust that the interaction partner made correct statements about his abilities or the information about his abilities are valid. As highlighted in Sect. 3.3, the question whether these abilities are actually sufficient to solve the existing problem rather refers to the matter of confidence. This problem of demarcation of trust from confidence to the abilities is exemplarily visible in the interview with *CLIENT-1* (functional expert). She argued that it is positive for trust when the consultant is on the same competency level, and is therefore in the position to challenge the client. She furthermore honored the functional competency of the consultant, which would contribute to the quality of the consultant-client cooperation and argued that it is beneficial if she can also learn something from the consultants. Overall, she focused on the importance of the actual personal abilities to develop trust to the consultant. These statements need to be contrasted with the trust conception as stated above, and do therefore rather relate to the confidence in the abilities of the consultant.

As trust is assumed to be developed by relying on the information about the consultant's abilities, a trusting relation can evolve when the consultant as interaction partner can confirm that he actually possesses the relevant abilities. This can be proved with successfully delivered working results by the consultant (*CLIENT-4*). The client's uncertainty about the consultant's abilities can also be compensated when the consultant demonstrates ability on a regular basis (*CONSULTANT-2*).

Hereby, intensive interaction experiences between the consultant and the client are considered to promote the building of interpersonal trust (*CONSULTANT-3*). This experience-based trust resulting from good deliverables of the consultant reduces the control demand of the client over the consultant (*CONSULTANT-4*). Moreover, trust towards the consultant grows if the consultant constantly confirms that he has his work packages under control (*CLIENT-2*).

Comparing the results from this practical investigation with the conceptual outline in Sect. 3.3 it can be resumed that the matter of ability is particularly considered with the functional expertise of the consultant, as well as the ability to deliver good results. The last aspect indeed incorporates also other facets of the consultant's abilities like methodological or social skills. Those, however, have not been addressed directly by the interviewees. The interviews pointed out that it is important to demonstrate the respective abilities on a regular basis in order to contribute to the interpersonal trust relation. However there were no findings that ability-related trustworthiness is specifically important at the early phases of a consulting project, as conceptually outlined in this work. Next to this, it can also be noted that the matter of ability is rather discussed with regard to the consultant. Even though in some case the interviewer tried to trigger the discussion about the relevancy of the client's abilities during the consultant interviews, this has not been taken on much by the interviewed consultants why it can be reasoned that the client's abilities do not play a significant role for the client's trustworthiness.

4.3 Trust Generation Through Integrity

The interviews revealed several basic behavioral patterns of the interacting partners that promote an integrity-based trust building. Overall, *CONSULTANT-2* mentioned basic integrity-related behavior of the client as very important to build up trust.

More specifically, honesty is considered to be one essential virtue for the interactions within the consulting project. *CONSULTANT-1* stated that for building trust, one of the most important things is "to be open and honest". When the consultant has a shortage in certain knowledge required for the consulting project, then it is important to reveal this in order to receive trust from the client. Also *CONSULTANT-3* experienced that the client's perception of a trustworthy consultant is promoted if he is honest in such a situation. If there is a knowledge gap on the consultant side that comes up in the interactions with the client employees, he considers it as "a legitimate process to request other consulting colleagues for that matter and to provide the client the respective response afterwards. This rather helps to develop trust on the client side, instead of giving the client a pseudo answer or an answer that is obviously wrong". Moreover, honesty of the consultant to confirm his trustworthiness is also highly relevant when it comes to admitting failures that occurred on his side during the consulting process. However, admitting failures is also a critical topic for the consultants, as it would potentially discredit the consultant's role in the consulting project. Therefore, admitting failures is a matter which consultants "as external service provider do usually deploy in dosed manner towards the client. Such things would rather not be expressed in written form, like in e-mails, but more (...) in personal conversations". Next to this, there were hints in the interviews that also honesty on the client side promotes trust building by the consultant. Also here trust development is promoted when client employees are admitting failures (*CONSULTANT-4*). *CONSULTANT-2* confirms this and states that "clearly, one has to say that honesty of the client is certainly the most important virtue to build up trust. But it is difficult to assess whether somebody is honest or not". Interestingly, the matter of honesty is not a matter that has been brought up by the client employees during the interviews. Apparently, the honesty of the consultant is considered to be a virtue that should be taken for granted. Exemplarily, *CLIENT-2* immediately led over to other specific aspects when the discussion of consultant's honesty was intended.

Further important findings in the interviews that refer to integrity-related facets of trustworthiness can be categorized as transparency and openness. *CLIENT-1* indicated that the consultant has to ensure traceability in his working to promote his trustworthiness. Signaling transparency to the client is also highly valued by *CONSULTANT-1*. "When he recognizes that the client is uncertain then the consultant has to try to involve the client as much as possible into the consulting work." It can also help to "provide the client with daily status updates" about the work of the consultant and to answer his questions in detail to reduce his uncertainty". *CONSULTANT-1* further resumes that it is one of the most important virtues to be open. *CLIENT-3* also highlights that it is critical that the consultant makes transparent what his goals and motives are. This should confirm the client that the consultant does not have a "hidden agenda". He furthermore underlined the importance of openness and transparency of the consultant to provide certainty to the client, as it has great significance for the client to know "that the consultant is not going in the wrong direction, since he is naturally lacking certain specific processual knowledge of the client organization". *CONSULTANT-3* also considers this aspect as vital for maintaining a trust relation to the client, as it is required to "steadily show open and direct communication to the client", also with regard to possible failures made on the consultant side. *CLIENT-3* emphasized that openness of the consultant towards the client organization is required in several respects. Hereby, a trusting consultant should be ready for open discussion with the client about ideas and proposals. Additionally, he underlined that consultant's openness also means that he takes the opinions of the client employees into consideration. He refers to a concrete personal project experience in which "the consultant has refused to take the opinions of functional departments of the client organization into consideration. Moreover, this consultant declined to accept the decisions of the clients based on further information". This led to non-acceptance of the consultant and trust problems. It is therefore of critical importance for the consultant to adopt the feedback of the client organization to maintain the trust relation to them.

In the same line, openness and transparency are also perceived as important virtues for the trustworthiness of the client employees. *CONSULTANT-4* hereby said that trust development is promoted when client employees also reveal background information and direct feedback to the consultant. “When the client employees admit that there are specific problems on their side, and if they tell you things that shouldn’t actually be told, then this is seen as clear indication that client employees try to build up a trusting relation to the consultant”. In that context the trustworthiness of the client employees is also enhanced when they show directness towards the consultant. Hereby *CONSULTANT-3* stated that “to straightforward people on the client side that are open about their opinions and the consultant knows what their attitude is, it is more likely to build-up trust”. As an opposite, it is perceived to be negative when the client uses devious tactics and does not allow the consultant to gain full insight into the relevant set of information. Next to this, further trustworthy attributes are recognized in the interview with *CLIENT-3*. For him it is very important that the consultant shows authentic behavior during the consulting project. He further states that the consultant is required to assume a neutral position within the client organization during the consulting process.

When contrasting the practical findings of integrity-based trustworthiness with the conceptual outline done in Sect. 3.3 it turns out that the interview results basically suggest very similar dimensions for integrity-based trust development. In that regard, particularly the attributes of openness, honesty and truthfulness have been stated, whereas there were no hints regarding the relevancy of consistent behavior of the consultant. Honesty was highlighted as an important attribute for the consultant’s trustworthiness specifically from the consultant interviewees, whereas there was interestingly no respective emphasize from the client interviewees. It is assumed that the consultant’s honesty is rather taken as granted by the client when engaging a professional service. The interviews also pointed out that honesty in the consulting project is getting crucial when failures made during the project have to be admitted. Moreover there was also further concretization provided regarding openness, as next to the stated client’s request of direct involvement and participation into the consulting project, it has been highlighted that transparency of the consultant’s approach and work steps is crucial for building interpersonal trust. This requires the consultant to go in regular alignment with the client, which in turn gives the client inner security about the consultant.

4.4 Trust Generation Through Benevolence

With conducting the interviews, also benevolence-related factors for determining the trustworthiness were revealed. *CLIENT-4* stated that a trusting client is “somebody with whom he gets along also on a personal level and with whom he talks the same language”. This also indicates that consulting is seen foremost as a “people-business”. *CLIENT-1* also refers to the importance of benevolence in the consultant-client relationship and considers a good communication between them as indication for that. *CONSULTANT-2* emphasized that trust to the consultant is also to a great part a matter of sympathy, which is also expressed by the extent of personal communication. “An individual unconsciously trusts a likeable person more than a non-likeable person... why sympathy plays an important role". The matter of sympathy has also been underlined by *CONSULTANT-3* in that regard. Furthermore, *CONSULTANT-3* also highlighted that when doing a client a favor this also promotes the perception of benevolence-related trustworthiness. Finally, it has also been indicated by *CONSULTANT-4* that a trust offer with proactively demonstrating trust can also have positive effect on the trustworthiness of this interaction partner.

Moreover, the interviews have also revealed that benevolence of the consultant is also by a large extent expressed through the perception of the same-goal-orientation between the consultant and the client. The client needs to get the feeling that the consultant follows the same goals and motives (*CLIENT-3*). The consultant has to demonstrate that he is on the same side (*CONSULTANT-1*). The consultant, therefore, needs to show proactivity and to demonstrate that he thinks with the client. "If the consultant thinks outside the box, he thinks with the other and acts with foresight, then this is enormously helpful for building trust to the consultant" (*CLIENT-4*). It is also honored when "the consultant questions certain things and also raises criticism against the client" (*CLIENT-1*). To demonstrate benevolence by the consultant, "it is better to show definiteness instead of being reserved and not provoking potential annoyance". The interviewee moreover highlighted that a trust-based cooperation requires the feeling that the consultant represents the same views (*CLIENT-1*). *CLIENT-2* (project manager in the client organization) has also stated that trust towards the consultant is promoted if the consultant demonstrates that he is thinking the same way as the client, and gives hints to the client about improvement potentials on his own initiative. Trust is particularly promoted if the consultant "pro-actively gives statements on existing problems, provides recommendations, thinks as oneself and has not solely his own business interests in focus" (*CLIENT-2*). For a consultant to be able to support the goals and motives of the individual client employees, it is also required to discover the interests and the political positions of the client employees to initiate the trust building (*CONSULTANT-1*). It was also mentioned that the aspect of benevolence could particularly be demonstrated when the consultant gives support to the client in extraordinary situations. This promotes the feeling of solidarity on the client side, exemplarily when the consultant offers extra working hours to help the client in solving an individual critical issue (*CLIENT-4*).

During the interviews further findings for benevolence regarding the hierarchical status of individuals were made. Hereby *CONSULTANT-2* stated that client employees with a high hierarchical level are considered to be less trustworthy compared to client employees acting in expert roles. Moreover, *CONSULTANT-4* indicated that young client employees with high claim for career development are assumed to have generally lower trustworthiness for the consultant, as they frequently show opportunistic behavior. Conversely, trust building towards consultants is also seen in dependence to their roles and levels; (Senior) Managers are assumed to be primarily business-driven, what decreases their general level of benevolence and trustworthiness. In that regard, freelancing consultants are assumed to be less career-oriented, thus this increases their trustworthiness.

Comparing the practical findings with the conceptual outline in Sect. 3.3 it can be subsumed that those go into the same direction for determining benevolence-related trustworthiness. The facets of loyalty and altruism are pointed out also in the interviews. Thus, the interviews highlighted the importance of same-goal-orientation and direct personal support to develop trust. It has been shown that a trust offer given by one party is often a fruitful step into a mutual trusting relationship between the consultant and the client. It has been revealed that the quality of communication between the consultant and the client is a good indicator of how much benevolence-driven trust is given. Otherwise, there were no direct hints about the importance of fairness for the trust building, e.g. with regard to avoidance of consultant's misuse in the client organization. Additional insights have been provided concerning the relevancy of the hierarchical level for the trust relations in the consulting context.

5 Concluding Remarks on Research

This research work has investigated the factors for interpersonal trust development with referring to the conceptual model of Mayer et al. as well as subsuming practical findings from expert interviews. The latter followed an open explorative approach to identify generic explanations for trust building between the consultant and the client based on the interviewee's overall experience. Future research should aim for concretizing the results further through integrated case studies that comprise several participants of a certain consulting project in order to reflect the specific project context on both the consultant and client in parallel. The investigation is to be deepened with observing the various attributes of trustworthiness in the complete course of the consulting process. Here, also the individual's propensity to trust as a dispositional facet as well as the situation-related aspects like risk positions are to be captured to further derive findings in the respective trust environments. Moreover, those dynamic observations will also provide further explanation about the influence and weighting of the trustworthiness attributes in the course of the consulting project. A limitation of practical research findings of this work is seen in the relatively low number of interview partners as well as in the selection of consulting projects, which mainly referred to expert-oriented consulting engagements. Consecutive research work should also integrate the practical investigation of coaching roles or consulting projects focusing on organizational development.

References

Aulakh PS, Kotabe M, Sahay A (1996) Trust and performance in cross-border marketing partnerships: a behavioral approach. J Int Bus Stud 27(5):1005–1032

Barchewitz C, Armbrüster T (2004) Unternehmensberatung. Marktmechanismen, Marketing, Auftragsakquisition. Deutscher Universitätsverlag, Wiesbaden

Brückerhoff A (1982) Vertrauen. Versuch einer phänomenologisch-idiographischen Näherung an ein Konstrukt. Dissertation, University Münster

Castaldo S (2002) Meanings of trust: a meta-analysis of trust definitions. Working paper presented at 2nd conference of the European Academy of Management (EURAM), Stockholm, Sweden, 09–11 May 2002

Coers J, Heinecke J (2002) Die Steuerungsarchitektur in Beratungsprozessen – Kooperationsprozesse von Beratern und Klienten. In: Mohe M, Heinecke J, Pfriem R (eds) Consulting – Problemlösung als Geschäftsmodell. Theorie, Praxis, Markt. Klett-Cotta Verlag, Stuttgart, pp 195–218

Covin TJ, Fisher TV (1991) Consultant and client must work together. J Manag Consult 6(4):11–19

Das TK, Teng BS (1998) Between trust and control: developing confidence in partner cooperation in alliances. Acad Manag Rev 23(3):491–512

Dean DR (2005) Arbeiten mit Managementberatern: Bausteine für eine erfolgreiche Zusammenarbeit. In: Petmecky A, Deelmann T (eds) Arbeiten mit Managementberatern: Bausteine für eine erfolgreiche Zusammenarbeit. Springer, Berlin, pp 13–17

Deutsch M (1958) Trust and suspicion. J Confl Resolut 2(1):265–279

Deutsch M (1960) The effect of motivational orientation upon trust and suspicion. Hum Relat 13 (1):123–139

Deutsch M (1962) Cooperation and trust: some theoretical notes. In: Jones MR (ed) Nebraska symposium on motivation, Lincoln, pp 275–319

Gambetta D (1998) Can we trust? Making and breaking cooperative relations. Basil Blackwell, Oxford

Gillespie N (2003) Measuring trust in working relationships: the behavioral trust inventory. Working paper presented at annual meeting of the Academy of Management, Seattle, USA, 01–06 Aug 2003

Glückler J, Armbrüster T (2003) Bridging uncertainty in management consulting: the mechanisms of trust and networked reputation. Organ Stud 24(2):269–297

Greschuchna L (2006) Vertrauen in der Unternehmensberatung: Einflussfaktoren und Konsequenzen. Deutscher Universitätsverlag, Wiesbaden

Höner D (2008) Die Legitimität von Unternehmensberatung: Zur Professionalisierung und Institutionalisierung der Beratungsbranche. Metropolis, Marburg

Jacobsen H (2005) Der Kunde in der Dienstleistungsbeziehung. Beiträge zur Soziologie der Dienstleistung. Verlag für Sozialwissenschaften, Wiesbaden

Jehle R (2001) Aufbau und Absicherung von Vertrauenspotentialen durch Kommunikationspolitik: Instrumente, deren Anwendung und Relevanz im Marketing klein- und mittelständischer Investitionsgüterhersteller. Lang, Frankfurt am Main

Jeschke K (2004) Marketingmanagement der Beratungsunternehmung. Deutscher Universitätsverlag, Wiesbaden

Kieser A (1998) Immer mehr Geld für Unternehmensberatung – und wofür? Organisationsentwicklung 17(2):62–69

Kilduff M (2006) Editor's comments: prize-winning articles for 2005 and the first two decades of AMR. Acad Manag Rev 31(4):792–793

Klaus E (2002) Vertrauen in Unternehmensnetzwerken: eine interdisziplinäre analyse. Deutscher Universitätsverlag, Wiesbaden

Kralj D (2004) Vergütung von Beratungsdienstleistungen: Agencytheoretische und empirische Analyse. Deutscher Universitätsverlag, Wiesbaden

Kumar N (2000) The power of trust in manufacturer-retailer relationships. Harv Bus Rev 74 (6):92–106

Lane C (1998) Theories and issues in the study of trust. In: Lane C, Bachmann R (eds) Trust within and between organizations: conceptual issues and empirical applications. Oxford University Press, Oxford, pp 1–30

Lewicki RJ, Bunker B (1996) Developing and maintaining trust in work relationships. In: Kramer R, Tyler T (eds) Trust in organizations. Sage, Newbury Park, pp 114–139

Lorbeer A (2003) Vertrauensbildung in Kundenbeziehungen. Ansatzpunkte zum Kundenbindungsmanagement, Deutscher Universitätsverlag, Wiesbaden

Luhmann N (1979) Trust and power. Wiley, New York

Luhmann N (1988) Familiarity, confidence, trust: problems and alternatives. In: Gambetta D (ed) Trust: making and breaking of cooperative relations. Blackwell, Oxford, pp 94–107

Luhmann N (1989) Vertrauen: Ein Mechanismus der Reduktion sozialer Komplexität, 3rd edn. Enke, Stuttgart

Maister DH, Green CH, Galford RM (2000) The trusted advisor. Simon & Schuster, London

Maleri R (1997) Grundlagen der Dienstleistungsproduktion. Springer, Berlin

Mayer RC, Davis JH, Schoorman FD (1995) An integration model of organizational trust. Acad Manag Rev 20(3):709–734

Mayer RC, Davis JH, Schoorman FD (2007) An integration model of organizational trust: past, present, and future. Acad Manag Rev 32(2):344–354

McFall L (1987) Integrity. Ethics 98(1):5–20

Mencke C (2005) Vertrauen in sozialen Systemen und in der Unternehmensberatung. Eine Grundlagenanalyse und Hinweise für eine vertrauenssensible Beratungspraxis am Beispiel größerer mittelständischer Unternehmen. Gabler, Wiesbaden

Mohe M (2003) Klientenprofessionalisierung. Strategien und Perspektiven eines professionellen Umgangs mit Unternehmensberatung. Metropolis, Marburg

Moorman C, Deshpand R, Zaltman G (1993) Factors affecting trust in market research relationship. J Mark 57(1):81–101

Morgan P, Hunt SD (1994) The commitment-trust theory of relationship marketing. J Mark 58 (3):20–38

Müller W, Nagel E, Zirkler M (2006) Organisationsberatung: Heimliche Bilder und ihre praktischen Konsequenzen. Gabler, Wiesbaden

Neubauer W, Rosemann B (2006) Führung, Macht und Vertrauen in Organisationen. Kohlhammer, Stuttgart

Nissen V (2007) Consulting research – Eine Einführung. In: Nissen V (ed) Consulting research: Unternehmensberatung aus wissenschaftlicher Perspektive. Deutscher Universitätsverlag, Wiesbaden, pp 3–38

Nooteboom B, Six F (2003) The trust process in organizations: empirical studies of the determinants and the process of trust development. Edward Elgar, Northampton

Ripperger T (2003) Ökonomik des Vertrauens: analyse eines Organisationsprinzips, 2nd edn. Mohr Siebeck Verlag, Tübingen

Seifert M (2001) Vertrauensmanagement in Unternehmen: eine empirische Studie über Vertrauen zwischen Angestellten und ihren Führungskräften. Hampp, München

Shaw RB (1997) Trust in the balance. Building successful organizations on results, integrity and concern. Jossey-Bass, San Francisco

Sommerlatte S (2000) Lernorientierte Unternehmensberatung. Modellbildung und kritische Untersuchung der Beratungspraxis aus Berater- und Klientenperspektive. Deutscher Universitätsverlag, Wiesbaden

Späth JF (2007) Interpersonelles Vertrauen in Organisationen. Eine empirische Untersuchung der Einflussfaktoren und Verhaltenswirkungen. Peter Lang, Bern

Woratschek H (1996) Die Typologie von Dienstleistungen aus informationsökonomischer Sicht. Markt 35(1):59–71

Christian Mauerer After finishing his study of business administration, he has worked for 7 years with Deloitte Consulting, lastly as Managing Consultant with the major of business transformation and outsourcing. Subsequently, he joined Continental Automotive GmbH where he was engaged for 3 years to further establish the Business Consulting unit of the corporation. Currently he is working in the organizational development unit of a major business unit of Continental.

How to Successfully Position New Consulting Services with Clients: Insights from the Theory of Planned Behavior

Volker Nissen and Tino Machts

Abstract Consulting providers, which want to launch new products and services on the market, differing from the service spectrum they have provided so far, are confronted with two groups of problems. On the one hand, there are difficulties during the product development phase, because of insufficient own resources and competences. On the other hand, there are problems to win clients for these new products. Both aspects will be discussed in the following contribution. The focus though will be on the client-related problem. To explain this problem, established social psychological models will be used. This aims at a deeper understanding of the correlations and also gives practical design guidelines. We use an IT consulting company as an example. This company wants to market supplementary services in the fields of management consulting in the future.

1 Fundamentals[1]

A variety of aspects can be the object of business consulting. For instance, strategy consulting tries to establish long-term competitive advantages for the client. IT consulting is, however, primarily operatively oriented, where aspects of clients' digital information processing are the center of consulting themes. Organizational questions, business processes and project management support are typical focus areas of organization consulting, which has a close connection to the strategic decision level, as well as to IT-technical process support. The terms of strategy- and organization consulting are often combined as management consulting.

[1]This paper builds on and extends the contribution by Nissen and Machts (2009).

V. Nissen (✉)
Economic Sciences and Media, Ilmenau University of Technology, Ilmenau, Germany
e-mail: volker.nissen@tu-ilmenau.de

T. Machts
Rudolf-Breitscheid-Str. 2 b, Jena, Germany
e-mail: tino.machts@googlemail.com

V. Nissen (ed.), *Advances in Consulting Research*, Contributions to Management Science, https://doi.org/10.1007/978-3-319-95999-3_14

Management consulting accounts for the majority of consulting turnover in Germany (BDU 2018).

There are in particular two reasons why it can be interesting for an IT consulting company to extend its portfolio to management consulting. Firstly, one is involved in new projects of the client at an earlier stage and at the same time a relational network can be established on a high management level. Therewith one hopes for better chances to obtain orders for the IT-core business. Secondly, the margin in management consulting is clearly higher than in IT consulting, which makes this consulting field attractive. IT consulting providers are, though, confronted with many difficulties when they try to supplement their service offers with management consulting. The reasons can roughly be differentiated into resource-related, internal problems on the one hand, and the difficulties to win clients for these new services on the market, on the other hand. The latter will be predominantly looked at in this contribution. In the process we will pursue the following research questions:

1. What are the determinants of a client's behavior in the case of novel, potentially unexpected consulting products of an existing provider?
2. How can the consultant sales force influence the client's behavior in a targeted manner?

It should be emphasized that this contribution does not assume a complete changeover, but rather a supplement to existing consulting products of a company. Methodically the results particularly base on an analysis of established social psychological theories from which implications for the consulting sector are derived. From the perspective of resources, a general overview on possible reasons, which may prevent consultancies to successfully develop and render novel consulting services, is given in the following section. Subsequently we focus on the problem to win clients for new services. In addition, we look at the determinants of human behavior to identify starting points, which makes it possible to rectify negative conceptions and preferences of clients in the marketing and sales process of new consulting products.

2 Resource Barriers

Generally, consulting firms which would like to provide service products on new themes, often struggle with resource-related obstacles in their own companies. In this context, organizational knowledge and organizational learning abilities represent core competences of a consulting company. They are specific skills in accordance with Prahalad and Hamel (1990), which allow providers to successfully position their services on markets. Organizational competences are becoming core competences, when the criteria of strategic relevance (differentiation factor in competition) and organizational complexity (in the sense that it is difficult for the competitor to imitate the novel service) are fulfilled (Probst and Raub 1998).

The core competence-approach, originally developed for manufacturing industries, can be transferred to knowledge intensive service companies, where the "production skills" are determined by human capital. In the original contribution by Prahalad and Hamel (1990, p. 90) it already becomes clear that "people [...] embody competence". As a consequence, it is seen as one of the main tasks of consulting management to create terms under which the competences can be established and expanded.

The management of an IT consulting provider that wants to advance into the field of management consulting therefore has to establish the missing core competences. In the short-term, this can for example happen by company mergers and cooperations, if the build-up would be too lengthy on its own. However, potential integration or coordination problems with the partner company need to be considered. The option to buy a foreign management consultancy, moreover, demands considerable financial power, which means that for most of the mid-sized IT consulting companies this option is not applicable. It is also possible to supplement ones own competence portfolio by means of employing experienced management consultants (who possibly bring along suitable clients or at least have a relevant personal network). Attempting to quickly multiply the knowledge and skills of new employees internally, it is thus possible that there may be acceptance problems amongst the IT consultants, who may not be interested in developing further into this direction. Here it has to be considered that professional content, consulting methodology, average project duration, as well as communication and working style in management and IT consulting clearly differ (Nissen and Kinne 2008). The internal training of methods cannot replace relevant project experience. From the perspective of IT consulting, it also needs to be considered how a new management consulting unit should operate on the market and relate to existing business.

Significant difficulties can derive from the path-dependency of the development opportunities of a company considering its own historical development course. Individual conditions and developments in the past of a company make it possible to acquire certain resources. In management consulting, these are above all knowledge and skills. Deviating conditions on the development path of competitors often do not offer a comparable opportunity to acquire the respective resources. When answering the important question which new knowledge an organization can most easily acquire, both Cohen and Levinthal (1990) as well as Kogut and Zander (1992) indicate that the closeness of already existing foreknowledge in the company is decisive.

In this context, Cohen and Levinthal (1990, p. 128) use the concept of absorptive capacity, which is defined as the "[...] ability to recognize the value of new information, assimilate it, and apply it to commercial ends." Boudreau (2003) describes the absorptive capacity of a company as a form of knowledge enabler. The capability to assess and use external knowledge is particularly dependent on the amount of similar knowledge, which is already available in the organization. Here a dynamic self-enforcing (cumulative) effect arises. In this way, a dependency of the absorptive capacity of a company on its historical development path is explained. The absorptive capacity, therefore, forms an immaterial strategic resource (Barney 1991), which has a significant influence on the innovation skills of a company. It generally develops as a side-product of corporate activities including research efforts, production processes (consulting projects) and training measures. Should though, knowledge be acquired and integrated, which is far removed from the current foreknowledge within the organization, then specific investments in the absorptive capacity are necessary. A lack of investment in management consultancy skills in the past has therefore created a low absorptive capacity of IT consulting firms in this area, making it difficult to quickly build up such new competences.

The concept of combinative capabilities (Kogut and Zander 1992) of a company is rather similar to the concept of absorptive capacity. New knowledge arises from the recombination of already existing capabilities. Organizational learning particularly happens in those areas, which are close to the present practices of a company. From this perspective, the learning capabilities as well as the opportunities for further development of a company also depend on its historical path. Thus, IT consulting providers who wish to create and sell new services that are very different from their past portfolio, are hindered by resource-related problems. Additionally, established management consultancies may have certain strategic resources available compared to potential new competitors, which present further barriers for entering the market. For example, an outstanding reputation in the market is to be considered here.

Even if resource-related obstacles can be overcome, the problem how to find clients and how to convince them to use the novel consulting services remains. On the one hand, these difficulties are related to the fact that the purchasers (clients) for management consulting services are usually different from those for IT consulting. This means that a new sales relationship must be established even with existing customers. On the other hand, the previous profile of the IT consulting firm, independent of the actual competence in management consulting issues, leads to an image on the client side that hinders a commission. This aspect is discussed in more detail in the following section.

3 Client-Related Obstacles

Consulting clients determine the capability potential of an IT consulting to provide services initially on the base of their own experiences with the company during earlier projects (if these do exist). They also listen to the assessment of a trusted third party (Glückler and Armbrüster 2003) or look at the image of the company on the market. As the focus of the activities in many IT consulting companies is on the selection, respectively the implementation of enterprise software (Nissen and Simon 2009), clients notice the strength of such consulting firms particularly in the realization of IT-solutions. Clients though, do not see the strength of the company in conceptual design (e.g. process optimization) before the implementation of software takes place, or in the capability of providing strategic consulting. Therefore, the clients do not even contact the company, if commissions for management consulting may be awarded, or they show barely any inclination to purchase new consulting services, even when an acquisition talk has taken place. For consulting firms, this raises the question of how they can increase the willingness of clients to buy new services. This is basically the question of the determinants of behavior and the possibilities for influencing it.

The theory of planned behavior (TPB) of Ajzen, very influential and empirically largely validated in social psychology, helps to understand the determinants of behavior (Ajzen 1985, 1991, 2005, 2008; Ajzen and Gilbert Cote 2008). Very briefly, in this model, three major factors influence human action: a favorable or unfavorable evaluation of the behavior (attitude toward the behavior), perceived social pressure to perform or not perform the behavior (subjective norm), and the perceived capability to perform the behavior (behavioral control). The combination of these three factors (their relative importance can vary depending on the behavior and the population) leads to a behavioral intention. This intention is an indicator of how strongly an individual will try to behave in a specific way. The stronger the intention regarding a specific behavior is the more probable is the performance of this behavior. The basic requirement for the intention to be effective is though, that an individual is free to choose to perform or not perform a specific behavior. Moreover, it is generally not possible to measure all aspects of actual behavioral control, as information on factors that facilitate or impede the performance of the behavior in question is lacking. However, to the extent that people are realistic in their judgements, a measure of perceived behavioral control serves as a proxy for actual control.

Hence the two central requirements for goal-directed behavior are motivation and possibility. The coherences within the model are shown in Fig. 1.

In the TPB, the first determinant, i.e. the attitude determines to which degree an individual is inclined or reluctant to show a desired behavior or to perform this behavior. In this context the accessible behavioral beliefs of a given person are responsible for the formation of a specific attitude toward the behavior in question. Behavioral beliefs are the beliefs of a person that the performance of an action either has a specific benefit, or may also have a disadvantage. Specifically, the positive or negative emphasis on an outcome (result) acts proportionally on the attitude regarding the behavior.

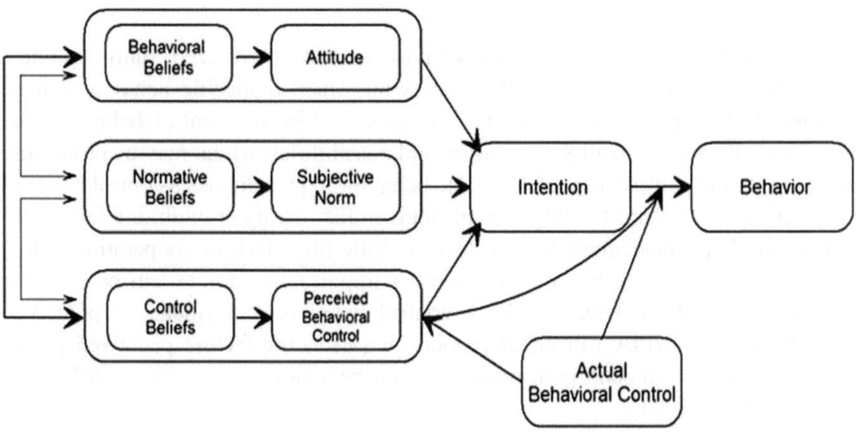

Fig. 1 Coherences in the theory of planned behavior according to Ajzen (2008)

If the purchaser of the client has, for example, the belief that an IT consulting firm is inadequately qualified for management consulting and, hence, the probability for failure is high, this logic will result in a negative attitude towards commissioning such themes, and the behavioral intent will be influenced correspondingly. According to Ajzen the attitude (A) of a person toward a particular behavior is directly proportional (symbol $\propto$) to the sum of the strengths of the relevant behavioral beliefs (b) multiplied with their associated positive or negative outcomes (e). This leads to the following formula (Ajzen 1991):

$$A \propto \sum b_i e_i \tag{1}$$

The second determinant is a social factor, the subjective norm. This determinant is closely linked to the environment of the individual. Potential social expectations, group- and society pressure, social rules, social or society roles or one's own role in the company are included in this factor. Here the socialization learned mechanisms are effective. Via the subjective norm social aspects regarding a performance or a refusal of an action, are determined. The individual weighs whether the desired behavior is viewed positively or negatively by his or her social environment. Thus, if a purchaser fears that by commissioning an IT consultant with issues of management consulting will not be understood by his superior or external stakeholders of the company, he will rather not do it.

The behavior is thus also dependent on the expected social result. Negatively assessed social results are rather inhibiting, whereas positively associated results will have a constructive influence on the performance of an action. The following equation will explain the coherence between normative beliefs and the subjective norm. The subjective norm (SN) is directly proportional ($\propto$) to the sum of the accessible normative beliefs (n), which are multiplicatively linked to the respective motivation (m) of the individual to direct himself at the referent individual or group concerned (Ajzen 1991).

$$SN \propto \sum n_i m_i \tag{2}$$

The third determinant is perceived behavioral control (perceived control on one's own behavior), which describes the ease, with which a specific behavior can be performed. This is dependent on the accessible subjective control beliefs of the individual. They refer to all the resources and possibilities, which may be promoting or inhibiting the performance of a specific behavior. Ajzen defines a control belief as a person's subjective probability that that a given facilitating or inhibiting factor will be present. Thus, inadequate knowledge, too little time, lack of cooperation, a low hierarchical position, or the absence of other important resources can be negative control factors of the behavior. Each control belief (c) contributes to perceived behavioral control (PBC) in direct proportion ($\propto$) to the factors perceived power (p) to facilitate or impede performance of the behavior, leading to the following equation (Ajzen 1991):

$$PBC \propto \sum c_i p_i \tag{3}$$

The basic rule is that the more positive the attitude, the higher the expected social result based on positively associated subjective norms and the higher the perceived control of a person over his or her own behavior, the greater the intention of the individual and thus the likelihood of a particular behavior. The relative weightings of the individual components vary from situation to situation or behavior to behavior, but the basic components remain the same (Ajzen 1991).

The theory of planned behavior does not explain all the procedures and determinants for the behavior of people. Ajzens himself acknowledges an element of incompleteness (Ajzen and Gilbert Cote 2008). For instance, an overwhelming number of aspects play a role during the perceived behavioral control, so that single attitudes may move into the background. External unforeseeable factors can prevent a behavior despite a high intention. Spontaneous behavior is not discussed at all in Ajzen's theory. The effect of time aspects shows a larger influence than realized by Ajzen. Individuals prefer the performance of behavior, where the intention and action are close together. Nevertheless, the theory of Ajzen allows some conclusions, and it provides starting points to influence the consulting clients' behavior and hence to improve the chances of an IT consultant to successfully position his proposals of management consulting.

Firstly, the model implies that an adaption of a particular client's behavior is possible via the insights and targeted influence of behavioral determinants in the model of Ajzen. "[...] behavioral intervention must try to change the beliefs that, according to the theory, ultimately guide performance of the behavior" (Ajzen 2018). Here the matter is, in particular, the various forms of beliefs as well as the attitude. A basic requirement is to know these exactly to convince clients of new service proposals, which they are skeptical about.

Secondly, the theory underlines the fact that it is necessary to speak to the hierarchically high positioned people in the consulting company. The more power the contracting authority at the client (purchaser) has, the more liberties this person has to decide on his or her behavior. This again implicates that a change in the thinking of the higher management has to start happening as the chances to overcome psychological barriers are particularly high here. Since the contracting authorities for management consulting are often located higher up in the client's hierarchy than those for IT consulting, the problem here is how to establish contact with this level of decision-makers at all. If the direct effort to address this level by the sale of the IT consultancy is little promising, at least three more indirect ways can be pursued:

1. The contractor for IT consulting is part of the social network of the contractor for management consulting and establishes the connection through personal intervention (internal recommendation). Alternatively, another personal contact of the IT consultancy to the client can be used to obtain a sales appointment.
2. The contractor of management consulting is in the client's steering committee for IT-projects. There a high-ranked representative of the IT consulting provider can establish contacts himself and build a sales relationship at the right hierarchical level.
3. Contact to the contractor for management consulting can be established in a more general context (e.g. at an industry fair or at a training seminar).

Thirdly, the professional-social environment and the personal situation of the potential purchaser on the client's side, has an important influence on his behavior. It is thus also essential to know these facts, should a change in behavior be successfully brought about. It is rather difficult to obtain such information from new clients. This leads to the fourth insight of the TPB. It is necessary to start with the distribution of new consulting services to existing customers, as more detailed information on the above-mentioned issues is usually available. The reputation and references achieved with orders from existing customers can then be used to place orders with new customers or with existing customers who were previously skeptical.

4 How Consulting Sales Might be able to Influence the Preconditions of Client Behavior According to Ajzen

4.1 Possibilities to Influence Control Beliefs

Starting points to influence control beliefs must concentrate on making it easier for the customer's decision-makers to place an order for new types of consulting services (e.g. in the area of management consulting) with IT consulting.

First, it is certainly the right approach to concentrate sales efforts on a high management level as lower levels do not have the hierarchical power to commission new types of consulting services to a provider without many relevant references.

Second, a consulting salesman should initially make sure that he makes an appointment with the client, without having any time pressure, as insufficient available time can influence the perceived behavior control of the client, which means that it can lead to a negative intention. It is necessary to conduct the sales talk in such a way that all knowledge deficiencies the decision-maker may have on newly gained management consulting capabilities concerning the IT consulting company, are comprehensively removed. It has to be shown how the competence profile of the consulting firm has been extended by the necessary knowledge and skills.

Furthermore, it is of great significance to observe project chances with the client at an early stage, so that the possibility for a commission does still exist. It is much easier to obtain relevant information early, when one is already working on an IT consulting project at the client on site. Ideally the need for management consulting directly results from the requirement analysis of the IT project—e.g. the preparation of an ERP implementation can clearly show that upstream process standardization and harmonization or the development of an IT security concept would be appropriate. Naturally, this assumes that the IT consulting provider has the essential know-how available to realize this need so that it can immediately stand in as a solution provider.

4.2 Possibilities to Influence Normative Beliefs

The commission of a novel consulting proposal presents a risky venture, virtually an experiment from the perspective of the client. Here it is the consultant's task to convince the decision-maker (consulting purchaser) that his professional surrounding (in particular superiors or external stakeholders) should rather evaluate the chances of a commission than its risks. Therefore, the advantages of a commission have to be evident and substantial for its environment. Ultimately the decision-maker has to be provided with arguments that he can use to convince key people in his professional surrounding to approve commissioning the IT consulting provider with new types of consulting services, such as management consulting. It is therefore necessary that in the acquisition phase consulting sales has a clear picture of the individuals and social groups that make up the relevant professional surrounding of the consulting purchaser.

On the other hand, the client must have a widely rooted confidence in the particular IT consulting provider to even consider commissioning new types of services. Such confidence is usually based on a long-standing and successful cooperation between the client and the consultancy. When pilots for novel consulting proposals are searched for, only those regular clients should be spoken to, where it is known or can be assumed that the professional environment of the consulting purchaser there tends to allow experimentation or is willing to take risks if incentives are sufficient.

4.3 Possibilities to Influence Behavioral Beliefs

The behavioral beliefs ("conceptions"), i.e. the subjective evaluations of the behavior results (benefit, damage) and the consequent attitudes towards the behavior, are the most important starting points to achieve behavior changes on the client's side and successfully get a commission for new types of consulting services. To do this, one plausibly has to convince the decision-maker that the commission will have advantages. At the same time, it is an objective to adjust one's own company image in the eyes of the client. In our case, this means that an IT consultancy must convincingly convey the competences in its new types of consulting services, such as management consulting, to the client.

Frequently, the sales representative of an IT consulting firm will be confronted with significant acceptance problems when trying to convince buyers for management consulting of new consulting services. Ideally, the sales meeting should be conducted by a proven management consultant who has recently joined the staff of the IT consulting firm, but who has already worked successfully with the client in question at a previous employer. Then the purchaser's own experiences with this person are already available and there is a personal basis of trust, which is a good starting point for a successful acquisition.

It would also be particularly trustworthy, if the IT consultancy has employed experienced management consultants with corresponding competences (and possibly own, useable reference clients), or if appropriate companies are bought, which have a significant share in a planned project. The cooperation with a suitable consulting partner can also demonstrate convincingly that essential competences can be provided. It is less convincing though, if the competence building is supposed to be successful under one's own steam alone (and without a suitable project basis).

Generally it would be helpful if the IT consulting firm in question was able to demonstrate knowledge on management consulting in the context of a previous project with the respective client. In this way, it is conceivable that during an IT consulting project deficiencies in the conception of an upstream management consulting project (e.g. lacking practicability on the IT level) are revealed and improvement proposals made. When the IT consultancy has already rendered free additional services from the field of management consulting to the client, it is also possible to convince the client of one's new skills and establish an internal reference. Moreover, it is also very useful to receive recommendations from a third party, who the client rates as competent and trustworthy, something called networked reputation (Glückler and Armbrüster 2003). Accordingly, the client will be prepared to put this recommendation in the place of his own experiences.

Low daily rates, free services and comparable special terms are additional pecuniary incentives for the client toward commissioning. Free services can however be seen as ambivalent. Firstly, one does not know how serious the client's interest is (only something, which is expensive, is valuable). Secondly, the client may very quickly get used to free services and possibly demand more services without adequate payment.

In this context it could be important in future, that IT consulting providers due to their IT competence can, in general, more easily and efficiently provide virtualized forms of consulting to clients than management consultancies. The aim of virtualization is to reasonably reduce the amount of face-to-face interaction between consultant and client by the suitable use of information and communication technologies (Nissen 2018). It can thus be referred to as the strategy for digital transformation of the consulting business. Technology-fueled tools and digital products can distinguish a provider from its competitors by optimizing and sustainably extending the service-portfolio. Moreover, virtualization can offer new starting points to lower ones' own costs and recover marginal scope.

To win a client for new services, the IT consulting firm can also argue that they supply all services from one source, establishing a form of "one-stop-shopping". This makes it clear that management consultancy services should complement and not be completely detached from the already established IT-related consulting topics of an IT consultancy. Therefore, depending on the current focus, it is to a varying degree useful and promising for different IT consulting firms to offer additional management consulting services. If for example a firm initially conducts an optimization of the business processes with the client and then subsequently supports these optimized processes with an IT solution, it is credible that the IT-practicability of the conception is secured to save error costs and repetition efforts. In practice, problems at the interface of process conception and IT implementation often occur when several consulting houses are employed in different phases of an overlapping consulting context. However, the fact that IT consulting tends to be commissioned by the IT-organization, management consulting by the top management, can sometimes lead to an overarching solution provider being unacceptable to the parties involved.

IT consulting can demonstrate its speed-related advantages over competing management consultancies if, for example, it has already been possible to build up the necessary in-depth, company-specific knowledge within the framework of preliminary projects for the task at hand, but not by competitors.

4.4 Ways to Effectively Implement a Behavioral Intervention

It has to be decided then, which beliefs (referring in particular to behavioral beliefs) of the client can be changed most effectively by a behavioral intervention on the decision-maker's side, and how this intervention should be methodically conducted through the consulting company. However, TPB only gives general action guidelines, without giving any detailed recommendations. It is even explicitly pointed out that there are no limitations on the part of TPB referring to the applicable psychological intervention method on the beliefs and attitudes of people. Generally though, the measures for a given communication situation should be matched to the client (personal conversation under four eyes, discussion in a group, presentation at a conference). Different situations require different methods (Fishbein and Ajzen 2005).

The stronger pronounced a client's belief is, and the more positively or negatively the results of the corresponding behavior are associated, the stronger this belief influences the intention towards the relevant behavior. When clients' attitudes have to be changed, either the intensity of the behavioral belief, or the assumption about the anticipated results can be considered as an object of change. However, it has to be noted that it will possibly not be enough to change one or two beliefs to achieve the required behavioral adaption. Possible interactions between different beliefs of the client (see arrows in Fig. 1) should also be considered here. "Only when the balance of beliefs in the total aggregate shifts in the desired direction can we expect a change in attitude toward the [desired] behavior" (Ajzen 2018).

A possibility to change a client's belief, which is explicitly mentioned in Ajzen's theory, is persuasive communication. For example, the aim may be to promote the creation of new beliefs on the client side by providing focused information from the consulting sales representative. It has been empirically proven that this is often simpler than changing existing beliefs. The new information though must be accurate, because otherwise the client might realize in the long term that he was deceived. This would lead to a reversion of the behavior, which often relapses behind the old (undesired) state (Ajzen 2018).

One of the most researched and certainly also one of the most useful models for changing attitudes from the domain of persuasive communication is the Elaboration-likelihood-model (ELM) of Petty and Cacioppo (1986). The ELM essentially deals with the question which kinds of information, under which circumstances, will sway a person to change his or her attitudes. Here two ways are differentiated, which can achieve changes. If a person has the capabilities (resources) and motivation to listen carefully and is willing for active, cognitive processing of the provided information, then the quality of the presented arguments will decide whether the arguments will be rejected or accepted. When the arguments are accepted they can be integrated in the context of preliminary knowledge on the considered attitude theme. On this so-called central path of persuasion, a long-lasting, stable change of attitude will develop.

The quality of the arguments on the so-called "peripheral path" of persuasion is negligible compared to the central path. Here, peripheral attractions, such as the reputation of the consulting company or the attractiveness, credibility and competence of the discussion partner are in the foreground. If they are convincing, then they will also lead to a change of attitude. These are, though, unstable and less reliable regarding the prediction of the actual behavior. Both paths, central and peripheral, can be followed at the same time.

A conscious attentiveness and processing of the consultant's arguments are thus the key to a lasting change of attitudes on the client's side. An active discussion about the arguments between the client and the consultant will, for instance, be impeded by the following: a too complex or lengthy presented consulting offer, too little personal relevance of the contents for the counterpart, the distraction of the client by other stimuli or inadequate willingness and capability to submit to a cognitive effort. Peripheral impressions will then become dominant.

In comparison, such clients, who intensively like to mentally deal with problems and arguments, are fully concentrated and feel a high personal concernment on the addressed topic, can rather be swayed to change their attitude via the central path of strong arguments and high quality of communication. This change of attitude will then be relatively lasting. Herewith it becomes clear, how important it is that the consultant gets to know the cognitive characteristics of his discussing partner and his actual personal situation, respectively that he assesses the situation spontaneously and correctly, before a sales talk begins. This underlines the above made statement that it is sensible to initially supply new consulting offers to existing clients because a lot of detail information is already known about them.

The change of attitude and consequently intention does not automatically lead to the desired change in behavior. Therefore, it is essential to establish a strong connection between the changed attitude and the behavior of the target person (Gollwitzer 1999). This can happen particularly when the consulting provider supports the client in developing a plan that is as concrete as possible, which determines when, where and how the intended behavior is realized.

5 Summary and Conclusions

Consulting providers, which intend to launch new consulting products, differing from the service spectrum they have provided so far, are confronted with two groups of problems. On the one hand, there are difficulties during the product development phase, because of insufficient own resources and competences. On the other hand, there are problems to win clients for these new products. Regarding the latter problem, Ajzen's theory of planned behavior can lead to valuable insights for consulting sales. Table 1 summarizes central insights from the application of Ajzen's model to consulting.

Table 1 Options to influence a consulting client according to Ajzen's behavioral model

Control beliefs	Concentrate sales activities on higher management level, as lower levels do not have the hierarchical power to commission new types of consulting services to a provider without many relevant references.
	Avoid time pressure on the client's side during a sales talk.
	Identify project chances for new theme areas early enough (use previous project for orientation and influence).
	Eliminate knowledge shortcomings of the client regarding the new product spectrum and expanded competence profile of the consulting provider and substantiate these in a credible way.
Normative beliefs	Select clients as pilots, who are happy to try out new products and are prepared to take risks.
	Select clients as pilots, who have already established a large and widely rooted interorganizational trust basis with the consulting provider in question (long-standing business partners).
	Collect information about the decision maker's relevant professional surrounding (peer group, external stakeholders, etc.). Provide this person with arguments with which he can justify a commission in his relevant professional environment.
Behavioral beliefs	Pre-sales/marketing should be conducted or at least supported by experienced management consultants (newly employed or "additionally bought"), who are ideally known to the client from earlier projects and who the client feels positive about (personal trust).
	Use opportunities to demonstrate new competences already in running projects and this way establish an internal reference at the client.
	If possible, obtain a recommendation from a third party that is trustworthy in the eyes of the client (networked reputation).
	Present the advantages of the assignment in a structured manner (costs, quality, speed). Select pilot clients for new services in such a way that there are synergies with existing or upcoming client IT consulting tasks.
	Ensure that the solution from one source ("one-stop shopping") is both acceptable to business departments and the IT of the client, and that it is indeed seen as an advantage.
	Argue in an understandable and reliable way (no exaggerations or empty promises). The consultancy must indeed have the essential competences available.
	Already name key-people in the sales phase. These persons should be selected in such a way that the client trusts them and is convinced of their skills.

Certainly, the primary factor to influence a client is his attitudes, or rather behavioral beliefs. Control beliefs and normative beliefs of a contracting authority are generally more difficult to access for consulting sales. Nevertheless, there are also approaches of influencing them as was shown in the main body of this contribution.

References

Ajzen I (1985) From intentions to actions: a theory of planned behavior. In: Kuhl J, Beckmann J (eds) Action-control: from cognition to behaviour. Springer, Heidelberg, pp 11–39

Ajzen I (1991) The theory of planned behavior. Organ Behav Hum Decis Process 50:179–211
Ajzen I (2005) Attitudes, personality, and behavior. Open University Press/McGraw-Hill, Milton-Keynes
Ajzen I (2008) Consumer attitudes and behavior. In: Haugtvedt CP, Herr PM (eds) Handbook of consumer psychology. Lawrence Erlbaum Associates, New York, pp 525–548
Ajzen I (2018) Behavioral interventions based on the theory of planned behaviour. http://people.umass.edu/aizen/pdf/TPB.intervention.pdf. Accessed 18 Jan 2018
Ajzen I, Gilbert Cote N (2008) Attitudes and the prediction of behavior. In: Crano WD, Prislin R (eds) Attitudes and attitude change. Psychology Press, New York, pp 289–311
Barney J (1991) Firm resources and sustained competitive advantage. J Manag (1):99–120
Boudreau JW (2003) Strategic knowledge measurement and management. In: Jackson SE, Hitt MA, DeNisi AS (eds) Managing knowledge for sustained competitive advantage. Jossey-Bass, San Francisco, pp 360–396
Bundesverband Deutscher Unternehmensberater (BDU e.V.) (2018) Facts and figures zum Beratermarkt 2017. Marktstudie, Bonn
Cohen WM, Levinthal DA (1990) Absorptive capacity: a new perspective on learning and innvoation. Adm Sci Q (1):128–152
Fishbein M, Ajzen I (2005) Theory-based behavior change interventions: comments on hobbis and sutton. J Health Psychol 10:27–31
Glückler J, Armbrüster T (2003) Bridging uncertainty in management consulting: the mechanisms of trust and networked reputation. Organ Stud 24:269–297
Gollwitzer PM (1999) Implementation intentions: strong effects of simple plans. Am Psychol 54:493–503
Kogut B, Zander U (1992) Knowledge of the firm, combinative capabilities, and the replication of technology. Organ Sci 3:383–397
Nissen V (2018) Digital transformation of the consulting industry – extending the traditional delivery model. Springer, Berlin
Nissen V, Kinne S (2008) IV- und Strategieberatung – eine Gegenüberstellung. In: Loos P, Breitner M, Deelmann T (eds) Proceedings der Teilkonferenz "IT-Beratung" der MKWI 2008. Logos, Berlin, pp 89–106
Nissen V, Machts T (2009) Probleme und Lösungsansätze bei der Entwicklung und Positionierung neuartiger Beratungsangebote. In: Fischer S, Maehle E, Reischuk R (eds) Proceedings INFORMATIK 2009, GI, LNI P-154, 2009, vol 487, pp 3730–3744
Nissen V, Simon C (2009) Kernaufgaben und Vorgehensmodelle in der IV-Beratung. Forschungsbericht zur Unternehmensberatung 2009-01, TU Ilmenau, Institut für WI
Petty RE, Cacioppo JT (1986) The elaboration likelihood model of persuasion. In: Berkowitz L (ed) Advances in experimental social psychology. Academic, New York, pp 123–205
Prahalad CK, Hamel G (1990) The core competence of the corporation. Harv Bus Rev 68(3):79–91
Probst G, Raub S (1998) Kompetenzorientiertes Wissensmanagement. Zeitschrift für Führung und Organisation (3):132–138

Volker Nissen holds the Chair of Information Systems Engineering in Services at Technische Universität Ilmenau, Germany, since 2005. Prior to this, he pursued a consulting career, including positions as manager at IDS Scheer AG, director at DHC GmbH, and CEO of NISSCON Ltd, Germany. In 1994 he received a PhD degree in Economic Sciences with distinction from the University of Goettingen, Germany. His current research interests include the digital transformation of the consulting industry, the management of IT-agility, metaheuristic optimization, and process acceptance research. He is author and editor of 20 books and some 200 other publications, including papers in Business & Information Systems Engineering, Information Systems Frontiers, IEEE Transactions on EC, IEEE Transactions on NN, OR Spectrum, and Annals of OR.

Tino Machts is project manager in the field of strategy, online marketing and design at an e-commerce agency in Jena and is an expert for product information management, master data management and content management. He studied business informatics at the Technical University of Ilmenau with focus on the areas of consulting research, European commercial law, human resources management and strategic business management. After completing his studies, he expanded his consulting expertise at a software company, working as a consultant and project manager for numerous software implementations in international companies. He acquired extensive knowledge in the areas of process management, risk management and ICT Management.

Part V
Future of Consulting

On the Current State of Digital Transformation in the German Market for Business Consulting

Volker Nissen, Anne Füßl, Dirk Werth, Kristina Gugler, and Christian Neu

Abstract Among many other industries, the digital transformation has also reached the consulting and IT services sector for some time. Not only client-side projects for the redesign of digital business models are carried out, but also consultancies face the challenge of rethinking their own business and delivery models in order to remain competitive. To determine the current status and future developments of the digital transformation in business consulting, an empirical study was conducted in the German market in summer 2017. A total of 233 usable answers were evaluated. This article summarizes the main results. Although there is an advance on an earlier study from end of 2015, low-virtualized consulting technologies are still predominantly used in a primarily supportive function. Highly virtualized consulting tools and tasks, such as complex analytical applications, cognitive systems and self-service consulting apps, despite their disruptive potential, remain marginal phenomenons up to now.

1 Competition in the Consulting Industry Is Changing

Even though the total turnover in the consulting industry is increasing from year to year, the competitive conditions for consulting companies are also changing rapidly (Nissen 2018). On the one hand, this is due to the latest developments in the field of innovative technologies, which are used by successful new digital entrants. On the other hand, however, substantial changes and changing requirements on the customer side can also be observed. In view of new challenges and changed framework

---

V. Nissen (✉) · A. Füßl
Economic Sciences and Media, Ilmenau University of Technology, Ilmenau, Germany
e-mail: volker.nissen@tu-ilmenau.de; anne.fuessl@tu-ilmenau.de

D. Werth · K. Gugler · C. Neu
AWS Institut, Saarbrücken, Germany
e-mail: dirk.werth@aws-institut.de

V. Nissen (ed.), *Advances in Consulting Research*, Contributions to Management Science, https://doi.org/10.1007/978-3-319-95999-3_15

conditions, consultants should always critically review their service portfolio and rethink the traditional, complex face-to-face consulting model.

The digital transformation can be described as a process of change that arises through the use of digital technologies and their effects. It has a holistic effect on the economy and society as well as everyday life (Mertens et al. 2017; Cole 2017; Matt et al. 2015). With the rapid development and spread of new technologies in almost all areas of the global economy, companies are faced with the challenge of rethinking their own business model due to changed market situations (Peitz and Waldfogel 2012; Downes and Nunes 2013).

Meanwhile, the same disruptive forces that have already changed the business models of other industries have begun to seriously influence the consulting and IT services sector (Parakala 2015). Like their clients, consulting firms face a digital transformation process that leads to partially or completely virtualized processes, adapted organizational structures and digital business models. A sustainable competitive advantage can arise when consulting firms use new technologies to innovate their consulting processes. Technology-based tools and digital products can differentiate a consulting provider from its competitors by optimizing and sustainably expanding its service portfolio. Digital consulting services can offer new starting points to reduce one's own costs and to regain leeway in the economic margin.

By rethinking the delivery model of consulting, interaction with clients can be redesigned and new customer segments can be opened up. A promising approach to achieving these goals is virtualization. Consulting is traditionally a personnel-intensive business. Consultants are usually sent to customers to interactively solve business problems on site. In comparison, a virtual process is a process in which physical interaction disappears. The transition of a physical process to a virtual process is called process virtualization (Overby 2008). Central virtualization mechanisms are digitization and networking. Virtualization is ubiquitous today. Online banking and social media are just two examples that show that virtualization is now playing an increasingly important role in everyday life. Virtualization is a trend that also consulting firms should apply to their own business processes. In view of the market challenges, the virtualization of consulting services can be an innovative strategy to ensure sustainable business success. The goal of virtualization is to sensibly reduce personal interaction between consultants and clients through the use of information and communication technologies (ICT) (Christensen et al. 2013; Greff and Werth 2015; Nissen et al. 2015). It can therefore be described as a strategy for the digital transformation of the consulting business.

Virtual services can complement classic business consulting services in order to optimize performance and supplement the existing service portfolio and delivery options. New digital business models for consulting can be introduced in the course of virtualization, which increase the efficiency, agility and effectiveness of consulting services. In connection with a standardization of consulting services, the door to fully automatic consulting solutions is opened in some areas.

Virtualization can extend the reach to new markets that would otherwise not be suitable or geographically accessible for traditional forms of consulting (Nowak 2015). Virtualization can also be the cornerstone for new forms of collaboration and integration with clients, bringing both opportunities and risks (Nissen et al. 2018b).

However, consulting firms that do not or only superficially deal with the topic of their own digital transformation run the risk of falling behind the competition. Demographic change and the increasing war-for-talents provide further arguments to investigate the possibilities of digitization in the consulting industry.

While some of the established consulting firms have recognized the signs of the times and initiated digital transformation initiatives (McKinsey Solutions and Bearing Point Asset-based Consulting are examples), most companies in the German market for business consulting were recently still in the early stages of digitizing their own company, as the results of a study from December 2015 showed (Nissen and Seifert 2016). In most consulting firms, for example, the focus was on a low form of virtualization, in which technologies are only used to reduce travel times, increase the personal productivity of consultants, or improve the quality of existing services.

In order to determine the current progress and future developments in the digital transformation of business consultancies, a follow-up study was carried out in August/September 2017 (Nissen et al. 2018a). This study is a cooperation between the Bundesverband Deutscher Unternehmensberater e.V. (Federal Association of German Business Consultants, BDU), the Ilmenau University of Technology (Department of Information Systems Engineering for Services, Prof. V. Nissen) and the AWS Institute for Digital Products and Processes gGmbH in Saarbrücken (Head: Prof. A.W. Scheer and Dr. D. Werth). In addition to comparing the progress of development with the first study, the aim was also to explore how future billing models can be designed as a consequence of digital consulting technologies (Deelmann 2009). Further aspects of interest included to what extent the professional requirements and qualifications of business consultants are changing, the importance of critical aspects such as privacy and data security in digital consulting projects, and why management consultancies choose the digital route for the delivery model of their consulting services (Nissen 2018; Nissen et al. 2018a). Another special feature compared to the study conducted earlier was that, in addition to a survey of consultants, representatives of the client side were also surveyed this time. This article presents results and insights of the current study from the consultants' point of view.

2 Consultant Perspective

2.1 *Method and Data*

The questionnaire is based on the procedure and guidelines for formulating questions according to Bagozzi (1996). With the help of the software EFS Survey of Questback GmbH, the questionnaire was created as an anonymous online survey. In a two-stage pretest, researchers from the Faculty of Economics and Media at Ilmenau University of Technology were involved. In a second round, experts from the BDU survey group submitted their comments on the draft questionnaire. After the optimization of the questionnaire, the survey was opened for official participation on July 17th, 2017. For this purpose, 10,000 members of the BDU as a whole were

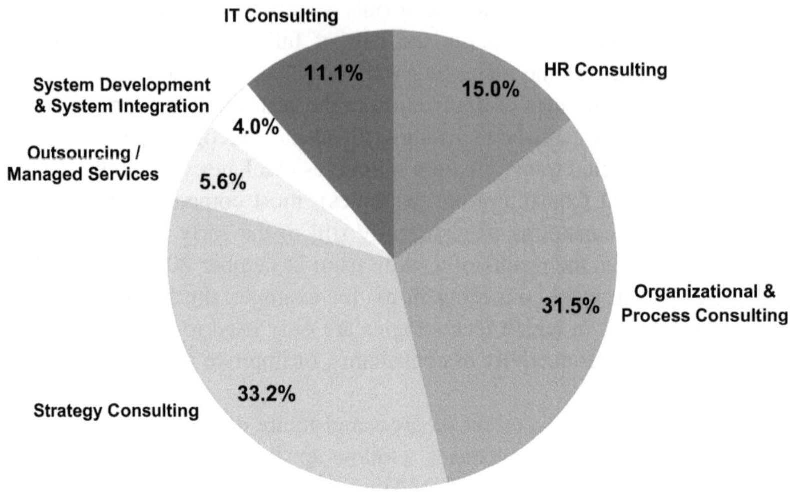

Fig. 1 Consulting field (n = 233)

invited to participate in the survey by e-mail via a link. By September 30th, 2017, a total of 336 respondents had participated (response rate 3.36%). Excluding very incomplete answers, 233 usable data sets were found, which is considered sufficient within the scope of the chosen objective. The sample is structured according to consulting field, company size, client industry, age distribution and gender as well as consulting experience.

The classification of the sample according to the four core consulting fields corresponds largely to the usual market shares according to facts and figures of the BDU (2017), whereby strategy consulting is slightly overrepresented and organizational consulting is slightly underrepresented (Fig. 1).

In terms of enterprise size, both individual consultants and representatives from micro enterprises (2–10 employees), small enterprises (11–50 employees), medium enterprises (51–250 employees) and large enterprises (>250 employees) participated (Fig. 2). Overall, it can be noted that sample is primarily characterized by micro and small companies with few employees as well as individual consultants. This reflects the situation in the German consulting market quite (BDU 2017).

Furthermore, the sample can be described by socio-demographic characteristics such as age, gender and work experience. Analysis of the age distribution by gender showed that more than half of the respondents are male and on average between 46 and 60 years old (Fig. 3, left). In addition, the age distribution of business consultants shows that the smallest proportion (2.7%) of those surveyed are in the under-30s age segment. Overall, the majority of respondents have 10–25 years of consulting experience (Fig. 3, right). This result was also to be expected, as decisions on issues of digital transformation in consulting companies are made by senior management.

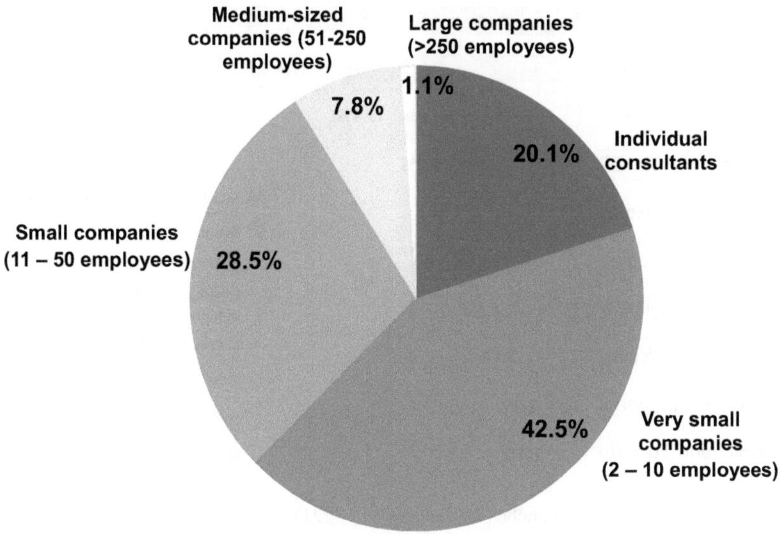

Fig. 2 Sizes of company (n = 233)

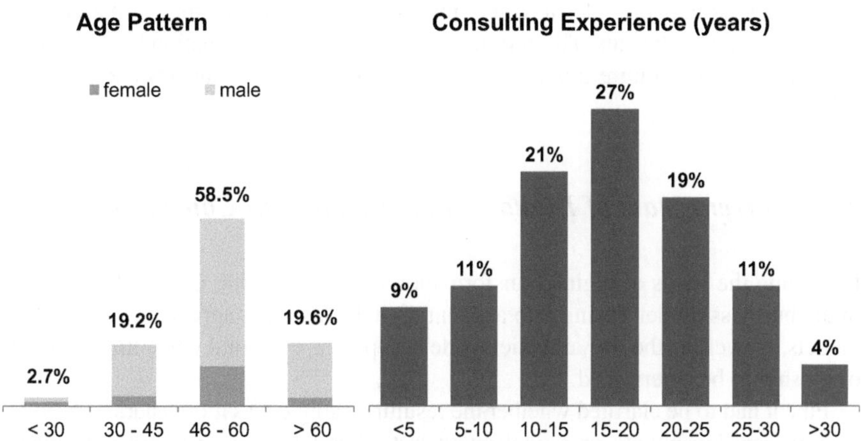

Fig. 3 Distribution of age and gender (n = 224) as well as consulting experience (n = 215)

With regard to the distribution of client industries, it can be seen that the usual market shares according to the regular facts and figures study of the BDU (2017) are also apparent here. Only in the financial services sector the value does not correspond to the market share of approx. 20.0%. This could be due to the additional summary category 'Services (no focus)', but the sector as a whole is still adequately represented in the sample (Fig. 4).

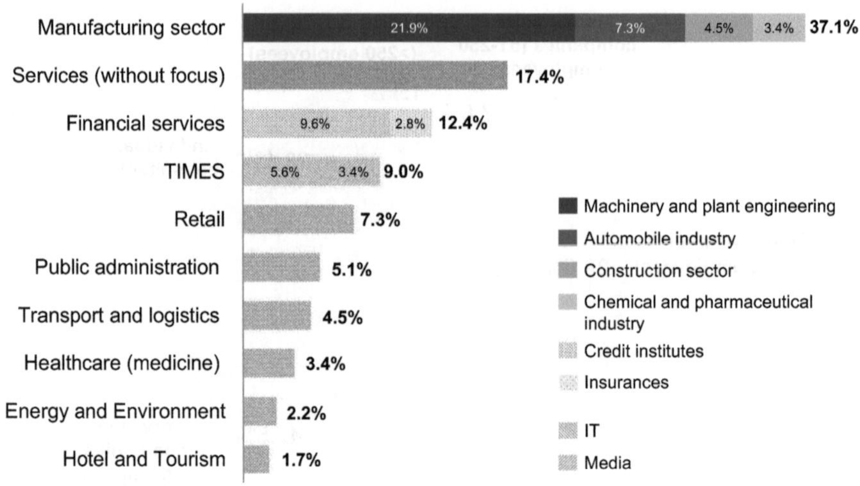

Fig. 4 Distribution of client branches of industry (n = 221)

The sample thus provides a largely representative picture of the German market for business consultancies. The current status of digital transformation in the German consulting market, future trends and developments for consultancies are presented below.

2.2 Current State of Digital Transformation in Consulting

Regarding the status of digital transformation in the consulting market, the changes in the business model, taking into account digital consulting approaches and billing models, as well as the use and client-side acceptance of digital consulting technologies should be determined.

First it had to be clarified whether the resulting sample was more characterized by face-to-face consultants or digital enthusiasts. Digital enthusiasts are consultants who are highly sensitized to new technologies and are always prepared to change their consulting behavior through digital technologies.

The evaluation of the results shows that the majority of respondents are still more likely to belong to classic face-to-face consulting (Fig. 5). The proportion of those who classify themselves as digital enthusiasts or precursors is highest in the IT consulting field at 9.5% (Fig. 6). In strategy, organizational and process consulting, the shares of digital enthusiasts are 3.6% and 1.7%, respectively. According to the sample, there are currently no digital enthusiasts in the area of HR consulting and outsourcing/managed services. This distribution can be attributed to the varying degrees of thematic relevance to digital technologies in the various fields of

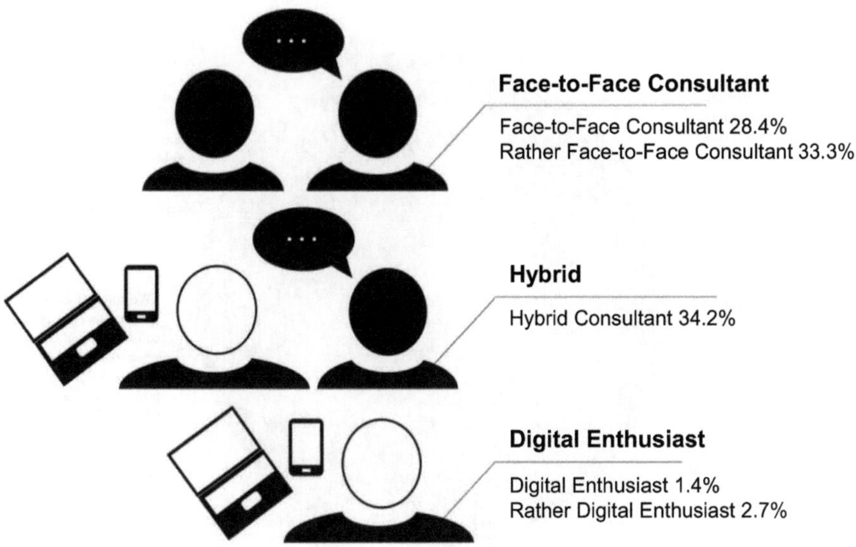

Fig. 5 Consultant personality type (n = 222)

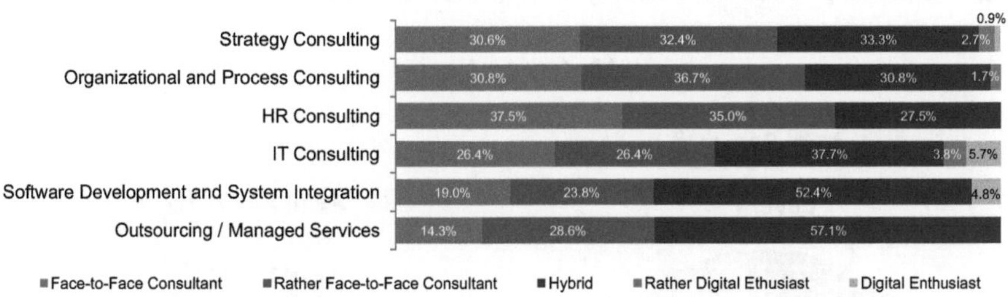

Fig. 6 Consultant personality type in the different consulting fields (n = 222)

consultancy, as well as to the age structure of the sample with a small proportion of younger consultants.

The virtualization of consulting services represents a transformation process in which in the simplest case individual consulting services and in the highest expansion stage the entire business model of business consulting is digitally transformed. Nissen and Seifert (2016) defined a corresponding maturity model of virtualization with four stages (Fig. 7). In the first study from end of 2015, the majority of the consulting providers surveyed were still at levels 1 and 2 of this maturity model (Fig. 8). In order to find out to what extent progress has been made in this area in the meantime, the maturity level was also surveyed in the current survey.

According to the current survey, 26.4% of respondents stated that the progress of virtualization in their company corresponds to level 1. 48.1% are most likely to identify with level 2 and 23.1% with level 3. 2.4% of respondents said they had reached the highest level 4 of maturity (Fig. 8). Compared to the market situation at

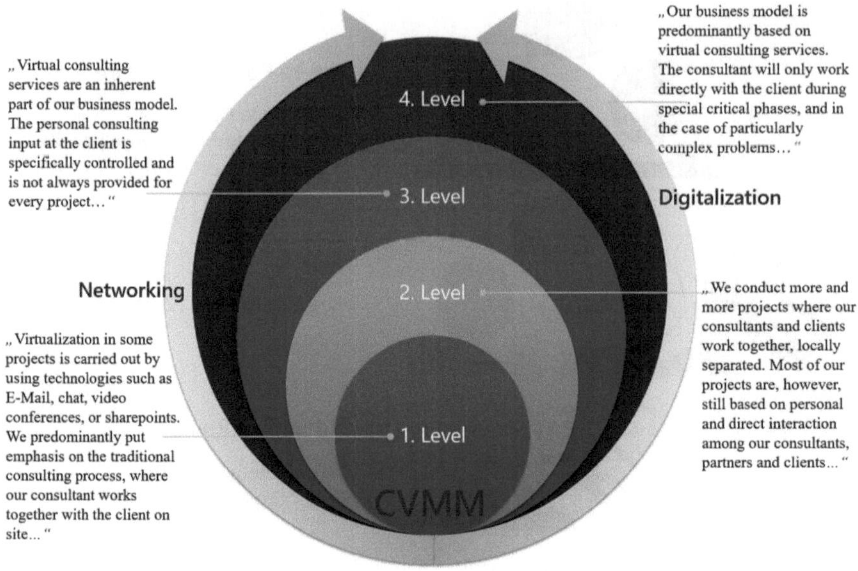

Fig. 7 Consulting virtualization maturity model (Nissen and Seifert 2016)

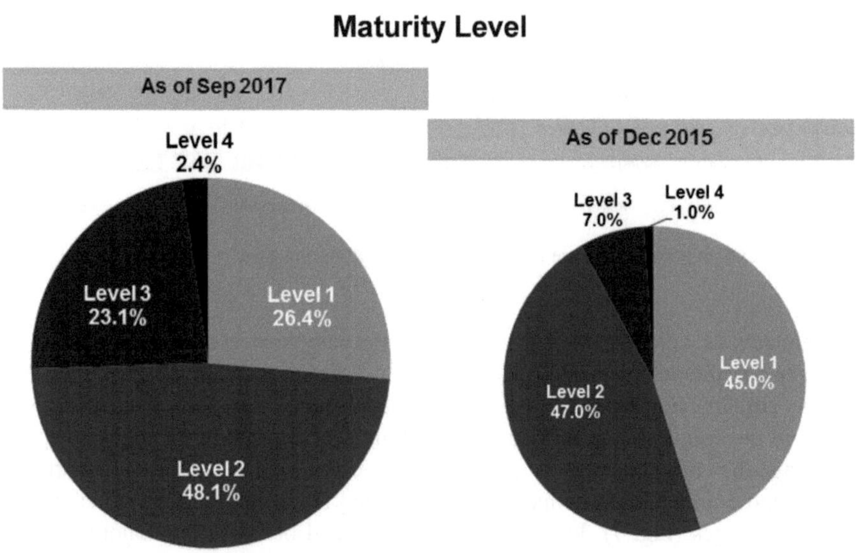

Fig. 8 Maturity levels of consultancies in Germany as of September 2017 (n = 212) and December 2015 (Nissen and Seifert 2016)

the end of 2015, the share of level 3 has thus risen significantly from 7.0% to 23.1%. At the same time, level 1 shows a decline of 18.6%. Level 2 remained largely unchanged. At level 4 there was more than a doubling, albeit at a low level.

Werth and Greff (2018) distinguish four digital consulting approaches: Under the 'core only consulting' approach, the information-based segments (often not in the central area of service) of consulting services are separated from the 'physical' segments that require personal interaction between consultant and client. This gives the supplier the opportunity to implement these parts efficiently and scalably with the help of information and communication technologies. Examples of this are communication via audio/video conferences, scheduling via Doodle or invoicing via web-based portals. The 'platform consulting' approach is characterized by the externalization of resources and the use of the potential of a sharing economy. This is achieved through the use of digital marketplaces to select suitable consultants (people-oriented mediation) or alternatively the mediation of consulting products (product-oriented mediation). One example is the placement of freelancers via digital marketplaces (e.g. Clarify.fm). The 'self-service consulting' approach provides digital consulting solutions, such as consulting apps or digital assessments for assessing the current situation and problem analysis for clients. These are used largely autonomously by customers. One example is BestPrax.de as online benchmarking for dental practices. The fourth consulting approach 'algorithmic consulting' automates individual consulting tasks, such as the analysis and processing of large amounts of data and structured presentation of the results in the form of ready-to-use presentation slides or process models. Data and process mining techniques are examples in this area (e.g. the solutions of Inspirient and Celonis).

The current empirical study shows that more than half of all respondents claim to already follow the core-only consulting approach (Fig. 9). This is comparatively easy to implement and automates support functions in the actual consulting

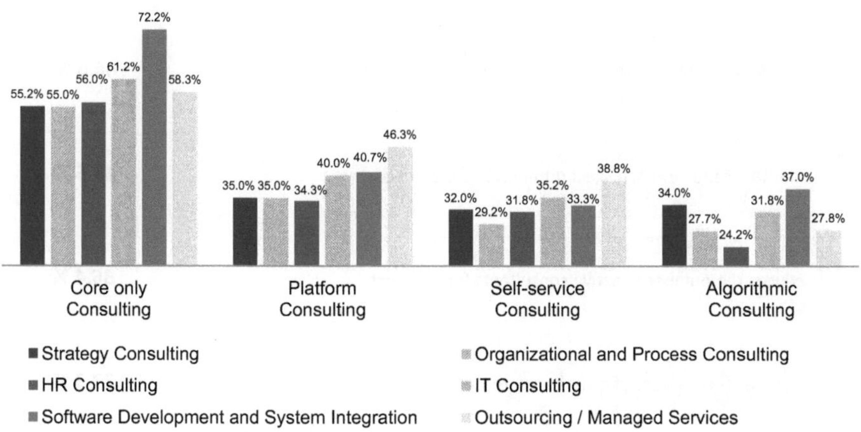

Fig. 9 Digital consulting approaches in the different consulting fields (n = 222)

environment. However, the approaches of platform consulting, consulting self-services and algorithmic consulting have so far been used less frequently in day-to-day consulting in Germany. This seems contradictory to the previously described progress of virtualization, where the majority of respondents already ranked in levels 2–3 of the maturity model. The results on the use of digital consulting approaches suggest a lower degree of virtualization in German consulting firms than previously stated. Overall, consultants from IT-related consulting fields use digital consulting approaches most frequently, which can be explained by the high affinity for technology already existing there.

The process of virtualizing consulting services requires the targeted use of digital consulting technologies. To this end, the study participants were asked why their consulting firms integrate such consulting technologies into their day-to-day consulting activities. Furthermore, it was necessary to find out which concrete consulting technologies are currently being used and how the survey participants would assess the client-side acceptance of the respective digital consulting technologies.

According to all those surveyed, the integration of digital consulting technologies into day-to-day consulting activities has a more positive impact on qualitative key figures such as company image or project success than on certain quantitative key figures (number of active consultants/project, number of orders acquired). The detailed results are shown in Fig. 10.

The majority of respondents use established distributed or cloud-based technologies, such as audio/video conferences, chats or document management systems with a low degree of virtualization. About half of the study participants also use

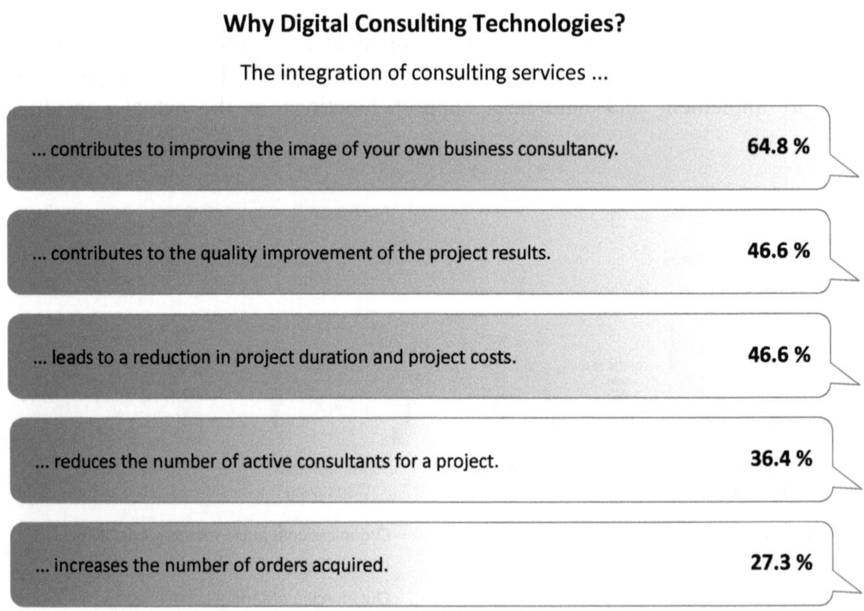

Fig. 10 Key figures on the effect of digital consulting technologies (n = 192)

Fig. 11 Use of digital consulting technologies (n = 218)

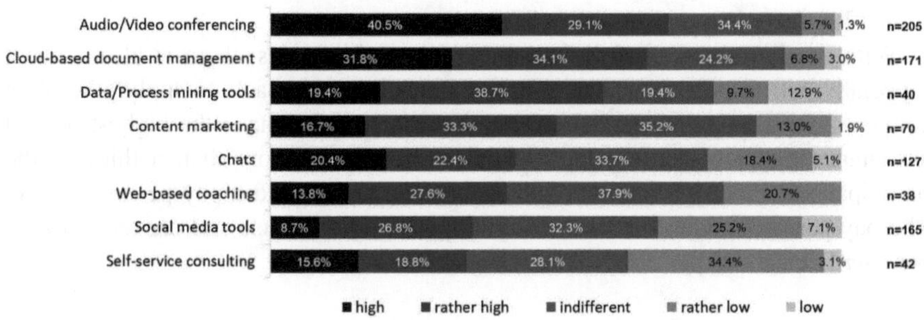

Fig. 12 How consultants assess client-acceptance of consulting technologies

search engine optimization and social media tools to increase their own reputation. Self-service consulting (18.0%), product configurators (3.0%) and expert platforms (10.3%) are currently used less in business consulting. The use of complex analytical tools (e.g. data mining and process mining applications) and crowdsourced consulting approaches with a high degree of virtualization is hardly common. The use of other consulting technologies is shown in Fig. 11.

The consultants consequently rate the client-side acceptance of well-established audio/video conference tools and cloud-based document management as high (Fig. 12). Content marketing, chats and web-based coaching are seen as medium

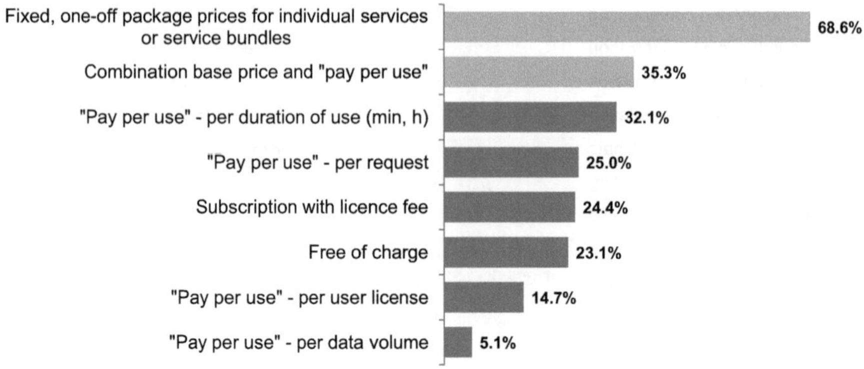

Fig. 13 Acceptance of new billing models for virtualized forms of consulting (n = 197)

to rather highly accepted by clients. Surprisingly, the acceptance for data and process mining technologies is also rated relatively high, which, however, are still hardly used in practice today, as Fig. 11 shows. Thus, it can be assumed that such approaches will be increasingly introduced to the market in the near future.

Social media technologies and self-service consulting, on the other hand, are rated comparatively lower on the client side, which explains the relatively moderate implementation of client self-service approaches by consultants in particular. However, social media technologies are quite common in consulting practice for reputation enhancement (Fig. 11), while customer acceptance is not clearly seen positively (Fig. 12)—there is a certain contradiction here.

With the introduction of digital consulting technologies, there is also a need, especially with a high virtualization of the consulting approach, to apply other than conventional time billing models. One-off package prices have the highest overall acceptance of all consulting representatives surveyed. More than a third of the participants still accept the combination of a base price and a pay-per-use option. The pay-per-use models are valued higher per duration of use and per request than per user license and per data volume (Fig. 13).

2.3 *Trends and Future Developments*

Within the framework of trends and future developments in the context of the digital transformation of consulting, the topics of data security and privacy, necessary changes of consultant qualifications, the relevance of various forms of digital transformation and global market changes were the focus of the survey.

Aspects of data security and privacy when using digital consulting technologies are considered to be of above-average importance in all phases of a consulting project (Fig. 14). The respondents showed a clear approval of more than 68% across all project phases. In the project phases of problem analysis, as well as problem

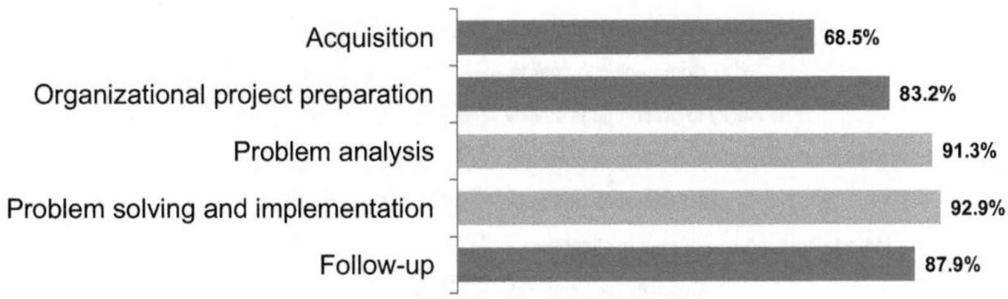

Fig. 14 Relevance of privacy and data security aspects (n = 191)

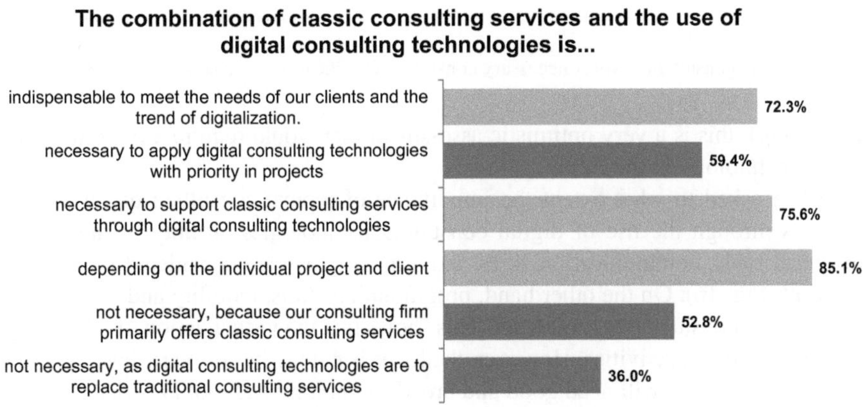

Fig. 15 What consultants think about combining classical with digital forms of consulting (n = 187)

solving and implementation, the relevance is particularly highly valued, as this is where the internal aspects of the client are most clearly in focus.

In order to determine the importance of digital consulting technologies compared to traditional face-to-face consulting in the German consulting market, study participants should evaluate selected statements according to their consent (Fig. 15). On average, the majority of respondents (approx. 85%) feel that the adjustment of the combination 'classic—digital' depends on the individual project and client. Digital consulting technologies should primarily support traditional consulting services (approx. 75% approval). Currently, more than half (approx. 53%) of all respondents still offer predominantly classic consulting services and see no need to integrate digital consulting technologies there. This group of sceptics is opposed by a second group of optimists. For example, 36% of those surveyed consider a combination of traditional and digital consulting services to be unnecessary because they are convinced that digital consulting technologies will completely replace traditional consulting services in the future. This view is particularly widespread in the fields of IT-related consulting, software development and system integration. In view of the still moderate use of advanced digital consulting technologies (e.g. data and process mining tools, see Fig. 11) and innovative consulting approaches (e.g. crowdbased

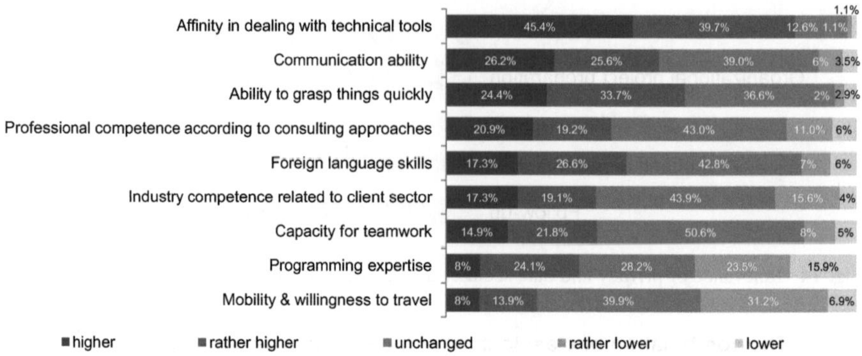

Fig. 16 How consultants expect necessary consulting qualifications to change (n = 183)

consulting), this is a very optimistic assessment that would require a more massive use of technology in the future.

When asked to what extent the importance of typical consultant qualifications changes through the use of digital consulting technologies, affinity in the use of technical tools, communication skills and a quick grasp are considered to be more relevant (Fig. 16). On the other hand, programming skills, mobility and willingness to travel are considered less relevant. This shows that the virtualization of consulting should save travel activities. However, the focus is not on the software developer but on consultants who will need good and broad technology and tool knowledge in the future in order to be able to assess which measures of virtualization of consulting make sense and can be implemented under given project conditions. The ability to work in a team as well as professional and industry-specific consulting skills will remain important in the future.

The digital transformation of business models in the consulting market can be divided into different forms. Nissen (2018) differentiates five types of digital business model transformation for consulting firms (see Fig. 17). A distinction is made between evolutionary and disruptive transformation of business models through innovative technologies. The digital evolution describes a step-by-step transformation that affects individual components of a business model. Whereas digital disruption represents the complete replacement of a previous classical service in the consulting context by new digital approaches and technology innovations.

Overall, the respondents regard all forms of digital business model transformation as fundamentally relevant for the consulting business. According to this, a general rethinking of the consulting market is discernible. The potential of technology-based solutions is recognized and it is clear that one's own business models should be critically reviewed. In direct comparison, however, the forms of digital evolution are considered more relevant than the forms of digital disruption (Fig. 18). This ultimately limits risks, but may also mean that opportunities are seized too late or missed.

There is still disagreement outside the consulting industry about the right approach to digital transformation. For example, Clauß (2016) recommends an

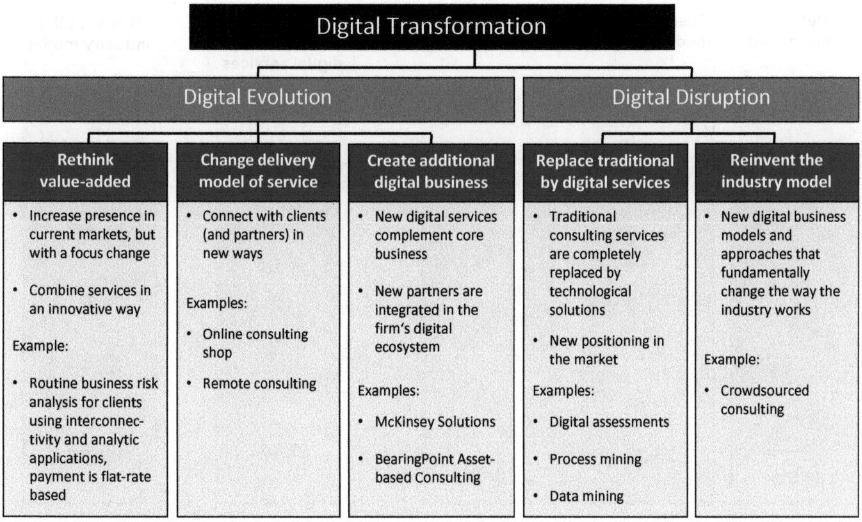

Fig. 17 Five types of digital business model transformation in consulting (Nissen 2018)

iterative process of change by 'thinking big but starting small', as business models are very complexly structured. On the other hand, Klimmer and Selonke (2016) report on the basis of their own empirical studies that many of their interview partners have decided to 'turbo-entry' into the topic. They have launched major projects that build as much as possible on the knowledge and ideas of the workforce.

In addition, current trends in the consulting market were recorded by asking participants their opinions on the use of innovative consulting approaches such as open communities and crowdsourced consulting (Fig. 19). The results of the survey show that open communities and expert platforms contribute to an improved exchange of knowledge and experience between consultants (54% approval). However, crowd consulting and consulting marketplaces also lead to increased competition in the consulting market (54% approval). Less than half (40%) of those surveyed agree that evaluation opportunities in consulting marketplaces contribute to improving the image of their own business consultancy. Furthermore, only 32% are of the opinion that the disruptive new consulting approaches are increasingly triggering cooperations and company mergers between consulting firms.

Perhaps most surprisingly, only 30% of respondents believe that technology-based consulting providers are entering the market as new competitors. While many technology-driven newcomers currently consider established consulting firms as their focus customers and offer tools to automate subtasks in classical consulting processes, this should not distract from the fact that the same tools (the data analysis tool by Inspirient as an example) could very well also be used meaningfully by large consulting clients and thus lead to direct competition with established consulting providers.

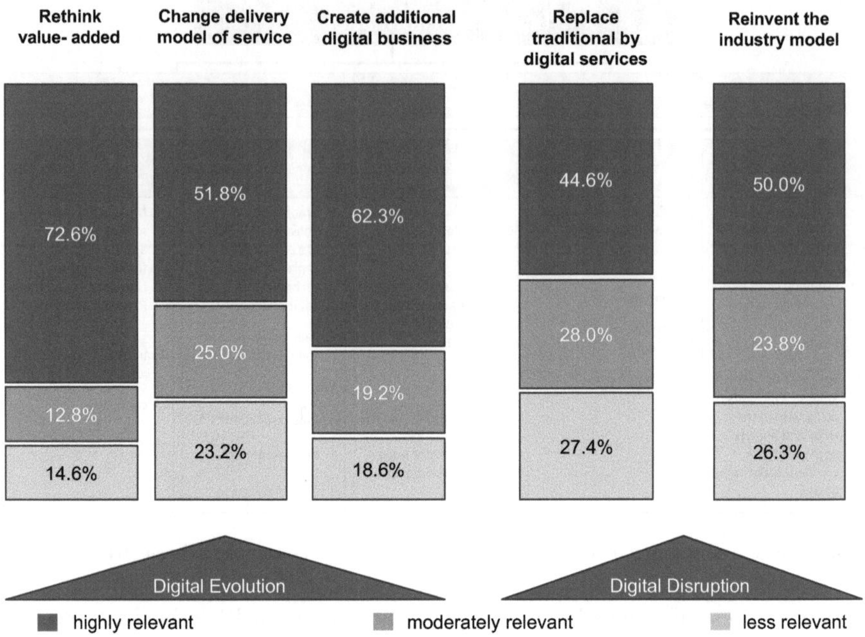

Fig. 18 Digital evolution of business model more relevant than digital disruption (n = 183)

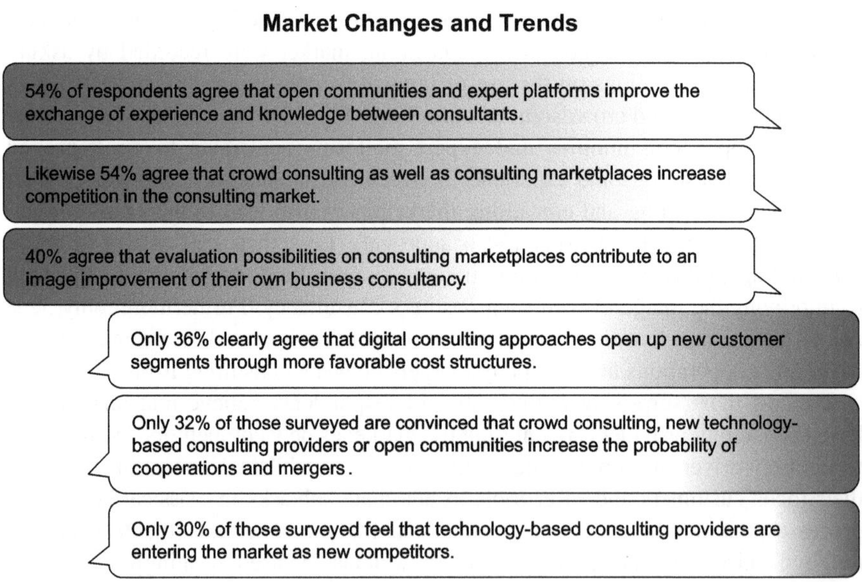

Fig. 19 Current trends in the consulting market (n = 175)

Only 36% of respondents clearly agree that digital consulting approaches open up new customer groups through more favorable cost structures. Here the potential could be misjudged, since the virtualization of consulting services often leads to a significant increase in the scalability of consulting and lowers costs. On the one hand, this allows margins to be regained, which is of particular interest for commodity consulting services. On the other hand, however, target groups that would not normally afford classical consulting also come to the fore. The digital assessment solution BestPrax.de may serve as an example here, with which dental practices can be benchmarked in the sense of strategy consulting, but at a small fraction of the costs of a personal strategy consultant.

3 Summary of Results as Quick Facts

Quick Fact 1

The majority of respondents associate themselves with traditional face-to-face consulting, with the proportion of digital enthusiasts in software development as well as IT consulting being higher.

Customers are sometimes further ahead than their consultants in terms of technology affinity. The acceptance for digital consulting services often seems to be fundamentally given on the client side. Consulting firms should make use of this and be more open to digital change, also with regard to their own processes. The ultimate goal is to develop meaningful synergies between classic face-to-face consulting and digitization technologies. In order to further integrate digitization technologies into consultants' daily work, it would be helpful if customers could specifically address their demand for such a technology application.

Quick Fact 2

Compared to the BDU study at end of 2015, there has been significant progress in the degree of maturity in the virtualization of business consulting.

However, this optimistic picture is clouded if one takes a closer look at the actual use of consulting technologies (see Quick Fact 3). The good result of the consultants' self-assignment to one of the four levels of our maturity model must therefore be regarded as tending to be too optimistic.

Quick Fact 3

The actual use of digital consulting technologies and digital consulting approaches focuses primarily on established communication, documentation and groupware applications.

Highly virtualized complex solutions, such as data and process mining or consulting apps in a form of client self-service remain the exception, as do crowdsourced consulting approaches. There is still great potential for development in this area among consulting firms, especially as clients are certainly showing acceptance in many of these areas.

Quick Fact 4

The client-side acceptance of complex data and process mining technologies is rated surprisingly high among consultants, although they are hardly used in practice.

Business consultancies should gain targeted experience with technology-based consulting approaches, some of which can be attributed to artificial intelligence, and expand their specialist knowledge in these areas. Especially the use of analytical applications and cognitive systems in the consulting process promises massive competitive advantages in the future, as the quality of consulting can be increased, the cost situation improved and project times shortened.

Quick Fact 5

According to those surveyed, the integration of digital consulting technologies has a more positive influence on qualitative key figures (image, project success) than certain quantitative key figures (number of active consultants/project, number of orders acquired).

From an overall perspective, however, it is also important to keep an eye on positive changes in quantitative project-related key figures and to address these in a targeted manner in marketing in the long term. From the clients' point of view, for example, quantifiable advantages can be perceived and marketed in the form of more favorable price structures and project results that are available more quickly.

Quick Fact 6

One-off package prices and the combination of base price and variable cost rate (pay-per-use models) are preferred as new billing models for digital consulting technologies.

Due to the digital change of the consulting offer, consulting companies face the challenge of changing their previous billing models and adapting them to digital services. Currently, package prices and a combination of base price and variable cost rate make the most sense.

When using digital consulting services, clients of consulting projects are faced with new price calculations that are not based on previous consulting rates. Pay-per-use models are expected to provide use-oriented and thus more favorable price structures for individual digital consulting services.

Quick Fact 7

The consultants surveyed consider data security and privacy to be of above-average importance in all phases of a consulting project. In the project phases of problem analysis as well as problem solving and implementation, the relevance is rated most strongly on average with over 90%.

This topic offers business consultancies a still very high need for discussion and threatens to become a central obstacle to the development and distribution of digital consulting services. Suitable measures must be designed here to protect the client's internal affairs.

Quick Fact 8

For 85% of the respondents, a combination of classic and digital consulting services depends primarily on the project and the respective client. Digital consulting technologies should mostly support traditional consulting services (>75% of respondents). 36% of the consultants even expect the complete replacement of classic consulting services by digital technologies.

In the short term, the use of digital consulting technologies in combination with classic face-to-face consulting seems to become the standard, whereby the mix is made dependent on the respective project and client. In the long term, however, the share of digital technologies in consulting projects should increase and successively replace selected traditional consulting services. This can already be seen today, for example, in the use of powerful data and process mining tools.

(continued)

Clients who have understood the potential of technology-driven consulting approaches will demand an increased use of such technologies in future consulting projects, whereby recourse to personal consulting should be possible if necessary.

Quick Fact 9

A stronger affinity in dealing with technical tools as well as communication skills and a quick comprehension are considered to be more relevant consultant qualifications in the future. On the other hand, programming skills as well as mobility and willingness to travel are considered less relevant in the future by the consultants surveyed. Other qualifications remain largely as important as with traditional forms of consultancy.

Innovative digitization technologies require fewer programming skills on the part of consultants, but a stronger affinity to the technology, which requires a quick grasp and strong communication skills in order to offer and implement digital consultancy services in a meaningful and comprehensible way in the consulting project. At the same time, the willingness to travel is less demanded in comparison to classical consulting.

Quick Fact 10

The clear majority of those surveyed agrees with the relevance of digital business model transformations in business consulting. Forms of digital evolution are considered more relevant than forms of digital disruption.

Business models have to undergo a critical review and technological potentials for digital reorientation in the consulting market have to be recognized and used. Less radical approaches to changing or supplementing existing business models are associated with lower risks and are thus suitable for gaining initial experience with the digital transformation of one's own services and processes. However, the opportunities (with increased risks at the same time) in the area of digital disruption of business models are higher.

Quick Fact 11 (Summary of Further Assessments)

Open communities and expert platforms contribute to an improved exchange of knowledge and experience in consulting. At the same time, crowd consulting and consulting marketplaces increase competition in the consulting market. Only 30% of those surveyed believe that technology-based consulting providers are entering the market as new competitors. Likewise, only a third suspect more favorable cost structures through digital consulting approaches.

Consulting firms should not lose sight of digital newcomers as direct competitors in the consulting market, as they can build up an interesting offer for clients through automated approaches and intelligent technologies. Digital consulting approaches, especially in connection with cloud technologies, scale better than traditional, personnel-intensive consulting, which leads to better cost structures and thus also enables lower prices. Even though technology-based newcomers in consulting often focus on established consulting firms as clients for their tools and services, this will not prevent them from approaching consulting clients directly in the medium term.

For clients, new consulting services and providers are entering the market, opening up new approaches for consulting. As a result, customer groups that have so far refrained from consulting services for cost reasons could also benefit from digital consulting services.

References

Bagozzi RP (1996) Principles of marketing research. Reprint. Blackwell Business, Cambridge

BDU (2017) Facts and Figures zum Beratermarkt 2016/2017. BDU e.V., Bonn

Christensen CM, Wang D, van Bever D (2013) Consulting on the cusp of disruption. Harv Bus Rev 91(10):106–114

Clauß T (2016) Digitale Geschäftsmodelle gestalten. Wirtschaft Nordhessen 3:16–17

Cole T (2017) Digitale Transformation. Warum die deutsche Wirtschaft gerade die digitale Zukunft verschläft und was jetzt getan werden muss! 2nd edn. Verlag Franz Vahlen, München

Deelmann T (2009) Internetberatung-Einige Überlegungen zu Möglichkeiten einer sinnhaften Vollautomation von Beratungsleistungen. In: Fischer S (ed) Informatik 2009. Im Focus das Leben – Beiträge der 39. Jahrestagung der Gesellschaft für Informatik e.V. (GI), Bonn, pp 3745–3759

Downes L, Nunes PF (2013) Big bang disruption. Harv Bus Rev 91(3):44–56

Greff T, Werth D (2015) Auf dem Weg zur digitalen Unternehmensberatung. IM+ io – Das Magazin für Innovation Organisation und Management (1):30–34

Klimmer M, Selonke J (2016) Digital leadership. Springer, Berlin

Matt C, Hess T, Benlian A (2015) Digital transformation strategies. BISE 57(5):339–343

Mertens P, Bodendorf F, König W, Schumann M, Hess T, Buxmann P (2017) Grundzüge der Wirtschaftsinformatik, 12th edn. Springer Gabler, Berlin

Nissen V (2018) Digital transformation of the consulting industry – introduction and overview. In: Nissen V (ed) Digital transformation of the consulting industry – extending the traditional delivery model. Progress in IS. Springer, Cham, pp 1–58

Nissen V, Seifert H (2016) Virtualisierung in der Unternehmensberatung. Eine Studie im deutschen Beratungsmarkt. BDU e.V., Bonn

Nissen V, Seifert H, Blumenstein M (2015) Virtualisierung von Beratungsleistungen: Qualitätsanforderungen, Chancen und Risiken der digitalen Transformation in der Unternehmensberatung aus der Klientenperspektive. In: Deelmann T, Ockel DM (eds) Handbuch der Unternehmensberatung, Kz. 7311. Erich Schmidt Verlag, Berlin

Nissen V, Füßl A, Werth D, Gugler K, Neu C (2018a) Zum aktuellen Stand der digitalen Transformation im deutschen Markt für Unternehmensberatung. BDU e.V., Bonn

Nissen V, Seifert H, Blumenstein M (2018b) Chances, risks and quality criteria of virtual consulting. In: Nissen V (ed) Digital transformation of the consulting industry – extending the traditional delivery model. Progress in IS. Springer, Cham, pp 137–151

Nowak S (2015) Karibik ohne Strand und Sonne – Wie digitale Beratung Projekte in außergewöhnlichen Regionen ermöglicht. IM+io 2:74–79

Overby E (2008) Process virtualization theory and the impact of information technology. Organ Sci 19(2):277–291

Parakala K (2015) Global consulting and IT service providers trends, an industry perspective. Technova

Peitz M, Waldfogel J (2012) The Oxford handbook of the digital economy. Oxford University Press, Oxford

Werth D, Greff T (2018) Scalability in consulting: insights into the scaling capabilities of business models by digital technologies in consulting industry. In: Nissen V (ed) Digital transformation of the consulting industry – extending the traditional delivery model. Progress in IS. Springer, Cham, pp 117–135

Volker Nissen holds the Chair of Information Systems Engineering in Services at Technische Universität Ilmenau, Germany, since 2005. Prior to this, he pursued a consulting career, including positions as manager at IDS Scheer AG, director at DHC GmbH, and CEO of NISSCON Ltd, Germany. In 1994 he received a PhD degree in Economic Sciences with distinction from the University of Goettingen, Germany. His current research interests include the digital transformation of the consulting industry, the management of IT-agility, metaheuristic optimization, and process acceptance research. He is author and editor of 20 books and some 200 other publications, including papers in Business & Information Systems Engineering, Information Systems Frontiers, IEEE Transactions on EC, IEEE Transactions on NN, OR Spectrum, and Annals of OR.

Anne Füßl is a doctoral candidate at the Group for Information Systems Engineering in Services at Technische Universität Ilmenau, Germany. Her research interests focus on the development of a learning and decision-making knowledge model (iKnow) to support consulting services in the context of digital transformation. In 2015, Anne has already contributed to the research and development of the knowledge model iKnow in two publications. She holds a Master's degree in Business Information Systems Engineering, was a student assistant and worked as product manager at Magnitude Internet GmbH for an online portal.

Dirk Werth is managing and scientific director of the AWS-Institute for digitized products and processes, a private independent non-profit research center focusing its research on digitization of businesses and society. Before, he worked at the German Research Center for Artificial Intelligence (DFKI) for more than a decade, where he served in different management positions. He has been responsible for numerous international and national research and consulting projects in the area of innovation by ICT technologies. He holds diplomas in Business Administration and in Computer Sciences as well as a PhD in economics.

Kristina Gugler is a junior researcher at the AWS-Institute for digitized products and processes in Saarbrücken/Germany.

Christian Neu studied business administration as well as business informatics at Saarland University. After being a research associate in the field of business intelligence and analytics, he worked as a senior technology-consultant on national and international implementation projects in the medical and pharmaceutical industry. He is currently responsible for Industry 4.0 research at the AWS-Institute for digitized products and processes in Saarbrücken/Germany where he acts as a project manager for digitization projects.

Digital Transformation and IT Topics in the Consulting Industry: A Labor Market Perspective

Frank Bensberg, Gandalf Buscher, and Christian Czarnecki

Abstract Information technologies, such as big data analytics, cloud computing, cyber physical systems, robotic process automation, and the internet of things, provide a sustainable impetus for the structural development of business sectors as well as the digitalization of markets, enterprises, and processes. Within the consulting industry, the proliferation of these technologies opened up the new segment of digital transformation, which focuses on setting up, controlling, and implementing projects for enterprises from a broad range of sectors. These recent developments raise the question, which requirements evolve for IT consultants as important success factors of those digital transformation projects. Therefore, this empirical contribution provides indications regarding the qualifications and competences necessary for IT consultants in the era of digital transformation from a labor market perspective. On the one hand, this knowledge base is interesting for the academic education of consultants, since it supports a market-oriented design of adequate training measures. On the other hand, insights into the competence requirements for consultants are considered relevant for skill and talent management processes in consulting practice. Assuming that consulting companies pursue a strategic human resource management approach, labor market information may also be useful to discover strategic behavioral patterns.

1 Introduction

Enterprises are continuously confronted with changes of market requirements, customer demands, and technological conditions. The ability to continuously adapt to those changes is an important driver for sustainable success (Hanna 2010). In this

F. Bensberg (✉)
Osnabrück University of Applied Sciences, Osnabrück, Germany
e-mail: f.bensberg@hs-osnabrueck.de

G. Buscher · C. Czarnecki
HfT Leipzig University of Applied Sciences, Leipzig, Germany
e-mail: gandalf.buscher@hft-leipzig.de; czarnecki@hft-leipzig.de

V. Nissen (ed.), *Advances in Consulting Research*, Contributions to Management Science, https://doi.org/10.1007/978-3-319-95999-3_16

context, a transformation is as a fundamental change of an enterprise's value propositions, structures, and/or technologies (Rouse 2005; Lahrmann et al. 2012). Major drivers for transformations are innovations, globalized markets, as well as mergers and acquisitions (Aier and Weiss 2012). IT innovations enable efficiency increases through automation but also the realization of new business models (Ward and Peppard 2002). Actually, topics like Big Data, Internet of Things (IoT), and Cloud Computing are discussed as IT enablers of the digital transformation (e.g. Buyya et al. 2009; Balandin et al. 2015; Trovati et al. 2015; Czarnecki and Dietze 2017). In this chapter, those topics are summarized as *transformational IT topics* (Lucas et al. 2013).

To utilize their transformation potentials, enterprises often rely on the professional services of IT consulting firms, whose core task is to improve the enterprise's information systems (Niehaves and Becker 2006; Nissen and Simon 2009). Those consultancy services are conducted by IT consultants, who are high-qualified professionals with the necessary skills to design customer-specific IT solutions. With respect to increased technology dynamics and the associated knowledge dissemination, IT consulting firms are expected to acquire specialists—related to innovative consulting topics—in order to stay competitive (Deelmann and Mohe 2006; Polster 2012). In this context, a labor market analysis helps to identify skill profiles for IT consultants.

The findings of this contribution provide transparency about the labor market demand for IT consultants, which can be used in order to gain further insights into the structural developments of the consulting sector (Christensen et al. 2013). Furthermore, academics in information systems can use the findings to align study programs with labor market requirements. As a contribution to both—IT consulting firms and academia—the following questions are researched:

1. What is the topical focus related to IT consultants demanded on the labor market?
2. What is the relevance of the transformational IT topics in those demands?
3. Is the digital transformation of the client's business a separate field of activity for IT consultants?

These questions are answered based on an analysis of job vacancies, which provides findings on job-related and individual requirements of institutions (Grob and Lange 1995; Sailer 2009). The method is also attractive from a research-economic perspective, as the empirical basis is publicly accessible via job portals in digital form. Although various labor market analyses on IT professions are available, a dedicated study on IT consultants and transformational IT topics is a new research field. The results presented here are a revised and updated version of an own study that was published in the MKWI 2016 conference proceedings (Bensberg and Buscher 2016).

In order to answer the above research questions, this chapter presents the results of an exploratory, large-scale job opening analysis, which focuses on IT-related requirements of consultants. In Sect. 2 related work is discussed, and the research methodology and empirical basis is illustrated. The subsequent sections discuss the concrete results of the empirical analysis. Section 3 provides the topical focus of the market labor demand in IT consulting (research question 1). Section 4 explains the relevance of transformational IT topics (research question 2), and Sect. 5 illustrates the specialist demands related to transformation activities (research question 3). The chapter closes with a summary and conclusion (Sect. 6).

2 Methodology and Empirical Basis

2.1 Related Work and Research Positioning

Job advertisement analyses are a common approach with a long tradition in the field of information systems (IS) research. They are used in the context of competence research in order to identify qualification requirements for IT professions descriptively (Gallivan et al. 2004). While up to the 1990s mainly job advertisements from print media were used as an empirical basis (Grob and Lange 1995), recent research uses the possibility of extracting data from job portals (Webb 2006; Debortoli et al. 2014). Recent studies focus on the discussion about the relevance of hard and soft skills for IT professions (Litecky et al. 2004) and on new qualifications required by evolving technological developments, such as Cyber Security (Potter and Vickers 2015) as well as Business Intelligence and Big Data (Bensberg and Buscher 2014; Debortoli et al. 2014). However, job advertisement analyses are mainly based on small-scale samples as well as manual data collection (Harper 2012).

A large-scale study is presented by Litecky et al. (2012). They have collected and analyzed 640,000 job advertisements for IT professionals from US job portals. According to this study, the increasing spread of ERP systems has led to an increased demand of IT specialists with business competences in the functional areas. The authors state that there is a drastic change in the structural development of specialist needs, and recommend the integration of business competences in adequate IS curricula. Another large-scale study with more than 40,000 German-language job advertisements derives various occupational areas for IT specialists (Bensberg and Vogel 2013). IT consultants—with a share of 20% of all analyzed job advertisements—are one of the occupational areas identified in this study. However, no further differentiation of competences and topical requirements for IT consultants is provided there.

From a methodical perspective, job advertisement analyses are mostly related to the tradition of content analysis, which provides a quantifying analysis of texts (Berelson 1952). Quantitative content analysis uses a priori defined categories to provide a theoretical grounded classification of text items (Harper 2012). However, this approach does not recognize structural developments in the database, such as the emergence of new competence requirements. Furthermore, job opening analyses often ignore rare terms in the database due to the methodological framework used (Litecky et al. 2012; Debortoli et al. 2014). Potentially interesting results remain disregarded, which limits the explorative generation of new findings.

In order to allow an exploratory answer to the initially articulated research questions, the analysis utilizes a lexicometric, corpus-driven research approach. This research approach is able to uncover unknown linguistic structures and connections, and therefore anticipates the problems of content-analytical approaches (Keil 1965). The implementation uses basic lexicometric methods, such as the frequency, correlation and concordance analysis of words or word sequences, and the analysis of co-occurrent terms (Dzudzek et al. 2009; Ignatow and Mihalcea 2016). To generate the necessary document corpus, a mainly automated data collection based on web crawling is used to ensure that a high number of job openings is considered.

2.2 Data Collection and Structure

In order to gain insights into labor market requirements, job advertisements from job portals represent a detailed and up-to-date data source. From a methodological point of view, this paper employs an exploratory job advertisement analysis, which is structured according to the generic job mining process depicted in Fig. 1.

The empirical basis of job advertisements for this study was collected in the period from June 24, 2014, to March 19, 2017. The collection of these text items was carried out using a set of web crawlers, which periodically searched the job portals for new job advertisements and transferred them into a local database. The collection was focused on job portals that publish job advertisements for IT specialists. These include public job portals, such as Jobserve, LinkedIn and Monster, but also company-specific job portals from selected companies in the IT sector (e.g. SAP, IBM, Microsoft) and consulting firms (e.g. Accenture, Capgemini). In addition, the job portals of DAX-listed companies were crawled. Figure 2 shows the top 20 list of crawled job portals by number of collected job advertisements. These top 20 portals represent more than 98% of all crawled vacancies.

Within the data collection period, 318,391 vacancies have been collected whose job title refers to consulting activities (**consul**). By using the similarity-based

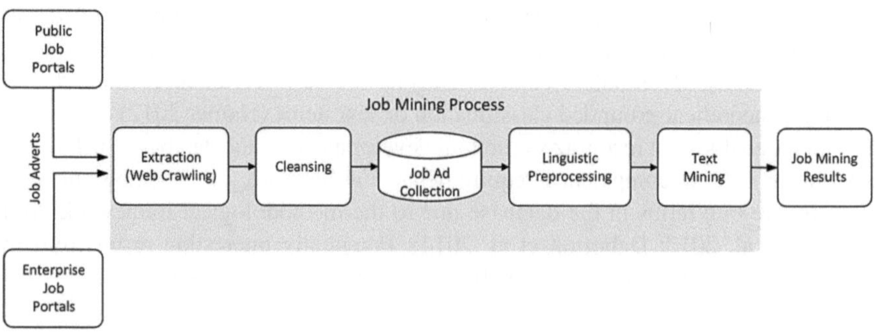

Fig. 1 Job mining process

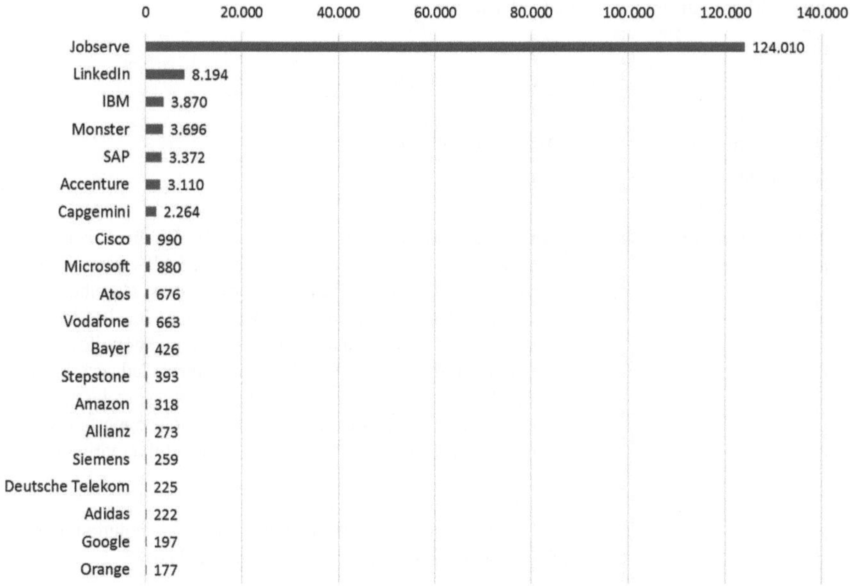

Fig. 2 Crawled portals (Top 20) by number of collected job advertisements

duplicate detection (Manku et al. 2007), approximately 39% of the job advertisements were excluded, so that n = 194,423 job advertisements resulted. By use of automatic language detection, English language job advertisements were selected, such that the net data finally amounts to n = 156,365 job advertisements. Main content-related attributes of the underlying data structure are exemplary illustrated in Table 1.

2.3 *Analysis Method*

Starting point of the analysis were the job titles. A sample analysis of the job titles showed that this attribute defines specific areas of activity and/or software products and thus supports screening processes of applicants (Posthumus 2015). Therefore, a frequency analysis combined with an analysis of co-occurrent terms was conducted on the job titles. As a result, frequent terms were identified that shape the topical demand in IT consulting (research question 1).

In order to explore the importance of the individual transformational IT topics (research question 2), search queries with appropriate keywords for the topics were formulated. These queries were executed on both the job titles as well as the job descriptions. The results deliver insights into the diffusion of the individual topics. For each transformational IT topic characteristic terms have been derived from the job vacancies.

Table 1 Major attributes of job advertisements

Attributes	Exemplary content
Job title	SAP SD consultant
Employment type	Full time
Hiring organization	Accenture/Software engineering
Job location	Prague
Readout job portal	Accenture
Job description (incl. tasks and requirements)	For anyone serious about a career in SAP, Accenture is hard to beat. We are a recognized global leader in SAP solutions and services, with a 30-year track record of success. No other organization than Accenture can combine the same level of industry and functional process insight and technology know-how with broad global resources. You will receive unrivalled access to the most advanced methodologies and technologies, including the latest software releases from SAP. This is your opportunity to build and expand your skills to a higher level than virtually anywhere else. What will be your responsibility? **Implement new or maintain existing business solution in SAP SD/IC area based on user requirements analysis** [...]

Finally, it was examined to which extent digital transformation of the client's business is an independent area of IT consulting (research question 3). For this last research question the use of the term *transformation* has been analyzed in the job titles. The results offer different directions of transformation and their characteristics within IT consulting.

The analysis was conducted by using the corpus analysis program AntConc (Anthony 2013) as well as the text mining system IBM Watson Explorer (Zhu et al. 2014). The results are presented in the following three sections.

3 Topical Focus of the Demand for IT Consultants

As part of the frequency analysis on the job vacancies, a list of words was generated, which was subsequently corrected based on stop words (e.g. and, a). Furthermore, words have also been ignored which were expected in the job titles (e.g. consultant, consulting, consultancy) or which did not provide any topical value (e.g. London, Senior, Principal). From the resulting word list, the leading eight words have been selected for the co-occurrence analysis at field level. The results are shown in Fig. 3.

The results show that most of the demand (cf. column 3) is related to specific expert knowledge in technical areas. Only up to 11.4% of all job vacancies are focused on general business and management consulting (6.6% business and 4.8% management). And even in those business-focused demands the co-occurrence analysis (cf. column 4) shows the requirement of technical competences, such as

Frequent Word	Frequency Absolute	Frequency Percentage
SAP	31,026	19.8 %
Technical	10,659	6.8 %
Business	10,255	6.6 %
Security	10,222	6.5 %
IT	9,867	6.3 %
Oracle	7,921	5.1 %
Management	7,499	4.8 %
Data	6,978	4.5 %

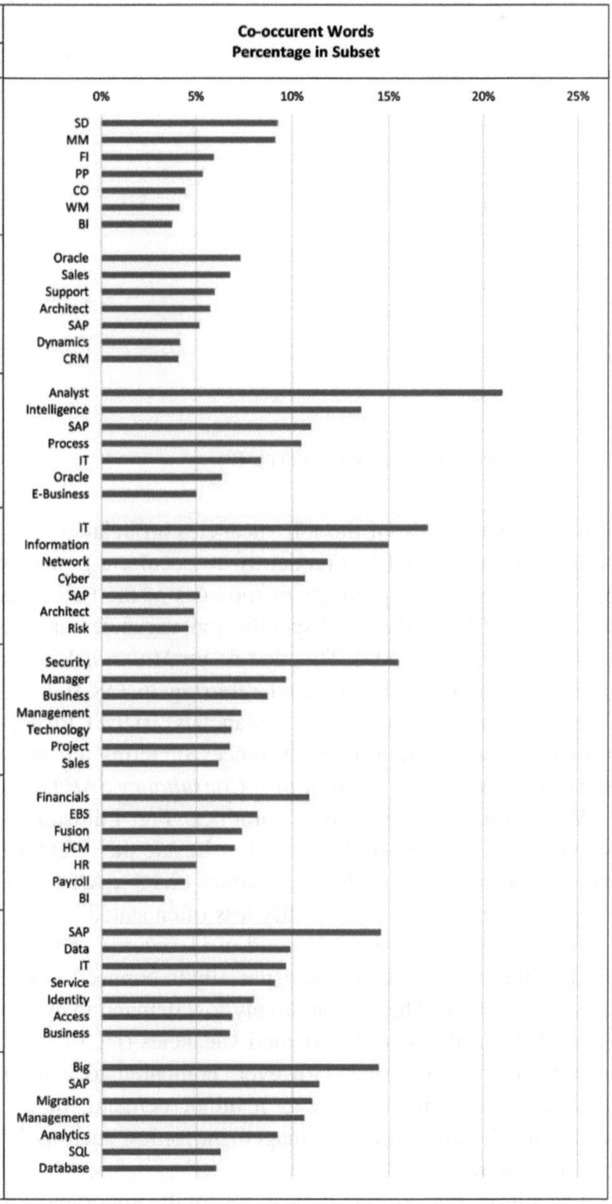

Fig. 3 Frequent words in job titles and co-occurrences

SAP, e-business, data, and IT. This indicates that pure generalists form only a minor demand in the IT consulting labor market.

Moreover, a significant demand for experts in the field of IT consulting is focused on specific software products of the two brands SAP and ORACLE. Figure 3

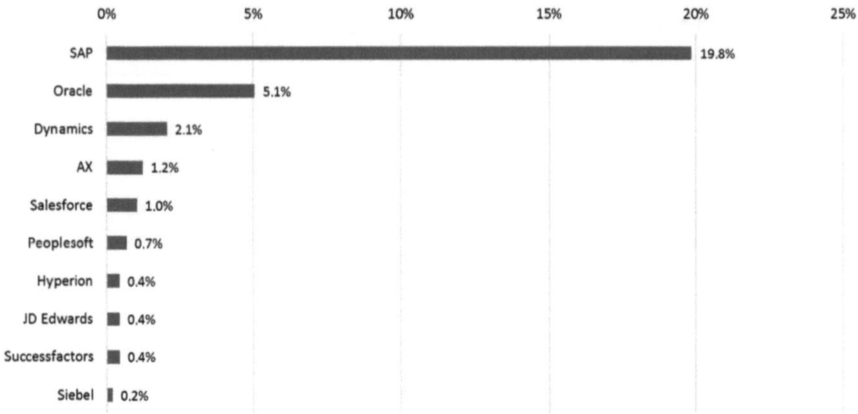

Fig. 4 Software brands in job titles (Top 10)

illustrates that 19.8% of the job vacancies are related to SAP, while 5.1% refer to products from ORACLE. Frequently co-occurrent terms are in particular related to the concrete software products or modules of the two software brands. The results show that 9.3% of the SAP-specific job vacancies are associated to the *Sales & Distribution* module (SD). The module for *Material Management* (MM, 9.1%) is of similar importance. The demand referring to ORACLE is more focused on the *Financial Management* module (Financials, 10.9%). Please note that within a single job advertisement multiple occurrences of terms are possible, for example, *SAP SD/MM Consultant* or *IT Auditor—Consultancy SAP/ORACLE*.

With respect to other software products, Fig. 4 illustrates a top ten list of software brands that were used in the job titles. Beside the reference to SAP and ORACLE, other software brands such as Dynamics (2.1%), AX (1.2%), Salesforce (1.0%), or Peoplesoft (0.7%) are significantly less often stated.

Another topical focus is the field of IT security. The term *security* was found in 6.5% of the job vacancies, and especially in connection with the terms *IT*, *information*, and *network*. The comparatively low demand in cyber security is interesting—only 10.7% of the security-oriented vacancies (i.e. 0.7% of all job advertisements) refer to the virtual space. However, compared to a prior analysis this area has increased. Furthermore, there is a minor demand for a combination of security with general technical and management topics, such as SAP, IT architecture, and risk management.

In addition, Fig. 3 offers indications for the importance of analytical activities and information systems in IT consulting. This is particularly evident in job titles with business reference: 21.0% of these vacancies are based on business analysts and 13.6% on business intelligence. Although, to a much lesser extent, this is underlined by the vacancies with data reference. In addition consultants with a topical focus on *(SAP) Data Migration*, *Big Data*, and *Data Analytics* are required, what already delivers some evidence for the relevance of transformational IT topics for the client business.

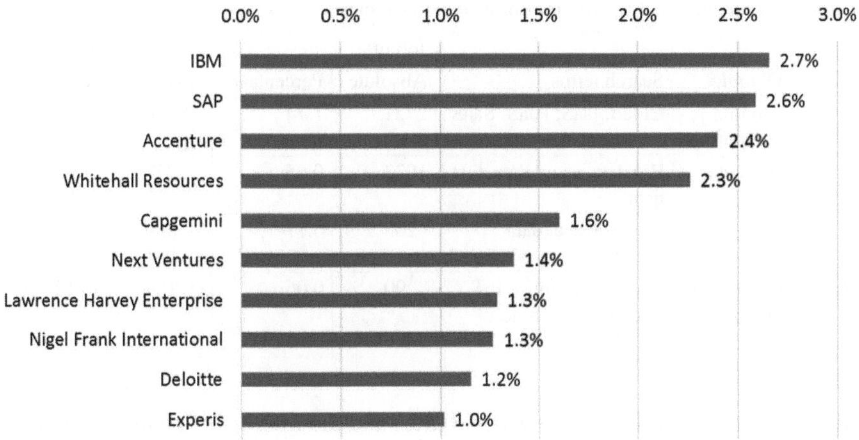

Fig. 5 Hiring organizations (Top 10)

As the hiring organization is included in the collected data, statements about the demand side are possible (Fig. 5). Based on the total amount of job vacancies per organization, the ten organizations with the highest demand represent a total of 17.6%. Among software companies (*IBM, SAP*), full service and IT consulting firms like *Accenture*, *Capgemini* and *Deloitte* create high demands. In addition, recruiting companies (e.g. *Whitehall Resources*, *Next Ventures*, *Lawrence Harvey Enterprise*) are also in search of IT consultants to find suitable personnel for their client businesses.

From a geographical perspective (job location), the vacancies focus on Great Britain (38.9%), the USA (17.7%) and Germany (4.1%). This geographical distribution results from the selected set of job portals (Fig. 2) and is biased towards Jobserve as an originally UK-focused portal for IT-jobs.

Based on this analysis the relevance of transformational IT topics is discussed in the next section.

4 Relevance of Transformational IT Topics in IT Consulting

For the analysis of transformational IT topics, search queries on job titles and job descriptions with corresponding search terms were executed. The used search terms and corresponding results are shown in Table 2.

The table shows that *Cloud Computing* has reached the highest demand. While only about 1.7% of job titles refer to the topic of Cloud or the related services (IaaS, PaaS, SaaS), this topic is mentioned in 13.8% of the job descriptions. Hence, a certain degree of maturity can be stated with respect to the demand for specialists. The other three topics have a significantly lower demand. *Big Data* occurs in 3.3% of

Table 2 Frequency analysis for transformational IT topics

Rank	IT topic	Search terms	Job title		Job description	
			Absolute	Percentage	Absolute	Percentage
1	Cloud computing	Cloud, IaaS, PaaS, SaaS	2721	1.74	21,596	13.81
2	Big data	Big data, smart data, fast data	1023	0.65	5237	3.35
3	Data science	Data science, data scientist	265	0.17	850	0.54
4	Internet of things	Internet of things, IoT, Machine2Machine, M2M	90	0.06	184	0.12

all job vacancies, while *Data Science* (0.5%) and the *Internet of Things* (0.1%) are only mentioned rarely.

A further analysis of the four subsets of job vacancies provides additional characteristics for each transformational IT topic. Based on a correlation analysis (Nasukawa and Nagano 2001) the terms typically used in the job advertisements of the respective transformational IT topic were identified. The results are shown in Fig. 6.

The identified terms show, which competences and which product knowledge are required for IT consulting activities in the related professional environment:

- The IT consulting market related to *Cloud Computing* seems to focus on the products *Azure*, *Amazon Web Services (AWS)*, and *VMWare* with competences in the fields of storage, virtualization, and automation. With respect to a prior study (Bensberg and Buscher 2016), the combination of development and operations (*DevOps*) and *Private Cloud* are newly requested competences with still a low demand.
- A much stronger thematic concentration is apparent in the analytical topics of *Big Data* and *Data Science*. Significant preferences for individual analytical software products (*Hadoop*, *Hive*), programming languages (*Python*, *Java*, *R*), and concepts (*Analytics*, *Machine Learning*, *Data Mining*) were identified.
- The demand related to the *Internet of Things* is characterized by technical concepts related to devices and telecommunications networks (*TCP/IP*, *Carrier*, *Cisco*). Furthermore, functional competences in manufacturing and Big Data are requested.

From a quantitative perspective, the overall results indicate that currently the transformational IT topics—with the exception of Cloud Computing—have a small relevance for the labor market of IT consulting. However, compared to prior data (Bensberg and Buscher 2016) the demand has slightly increased.

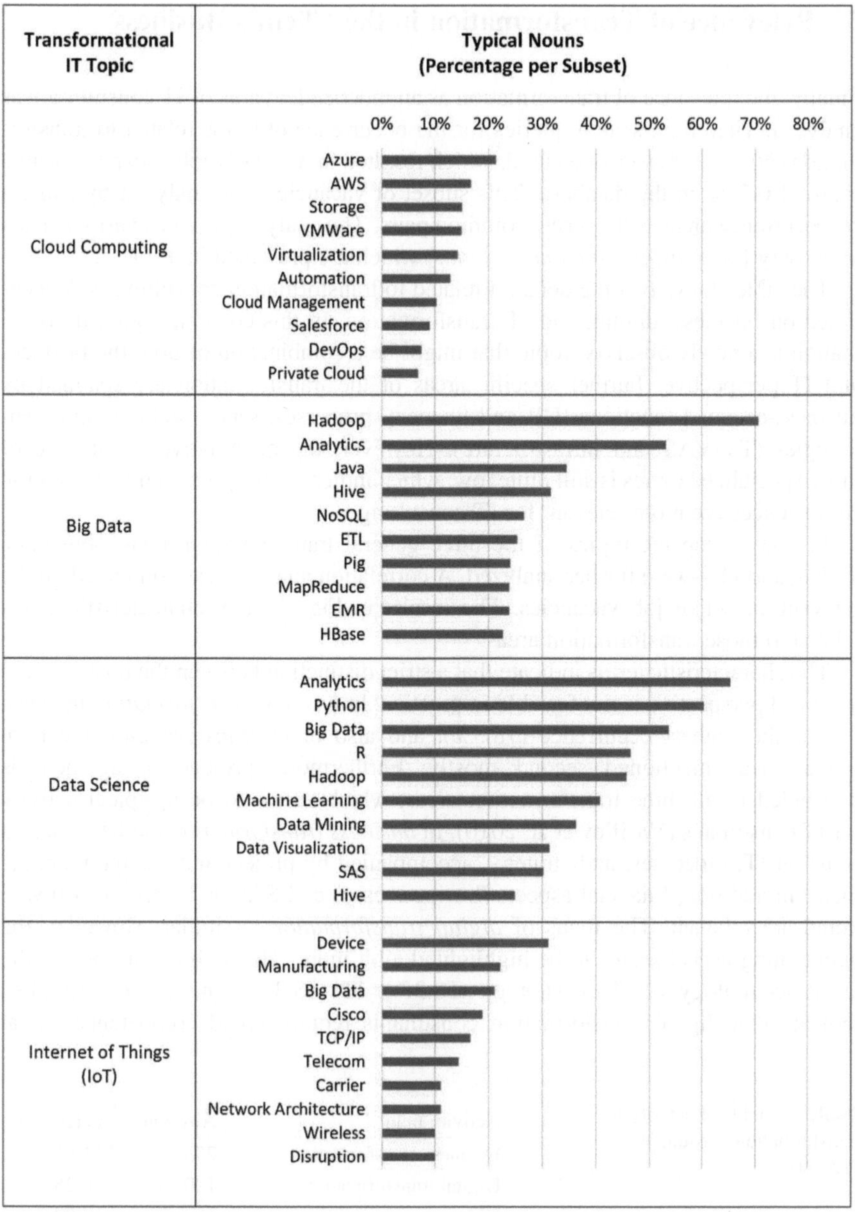

Fig. 6 Typical terms associated with transformational IT topics

5 Relevance of Transformation in the Client's Business

Finally, the relevance of transformation as an independent area of IT consulting was analyzed. Therefore, search queries for the occurrence of terms related to transformation (**transfor**) were executed, which resulted in n = 1171 job vacancies with a share of 0.75% in the database. This subset of vacancies was analyzed by using a co-occurrence analysis to derive common pairs. The analysis provides various fields of activity for *transformation consultants*, which are presented in Table 3.

The table shows that the demand related to transformation consulting is concentrated on business, digital, and IT transformation. In this context, digital transformation is a newly observed topic that might be a combination of both the business and IT perspective. Further specific areas of the transformation are spanned by business-oriented functions (HR and finance), processes, services/cloud, and technologies (TV/VAS and infrastructure). However, the quantitative occurrence of those specialized topics is still quite low, which indicates that general transformation competences are more relevant for IT consulting.

In a next step the topics of the three general transformation areas—business, digital, and IT—were further analyzed. A correlation analysis was conducted on the relevant subset of job vacancies. The results in Fig. 7 show characteristic terms related to those transformation areas.

The characteristic terms indicate that a strict distinction between the business and technical perspective is not feasible in practice. In *business transformation* the term IT has the highest occurrence (78.3%), and also in *IT transformation* the term process was mentioned second mostly. Furthermore, project management is demanded in all three transformation areas, which seems to be a typical activity for IT consultants (Vasil'ev et al. 2010). In *business transformation* the focus seems to be on IT, processes, and strategy, accompanied by project and change management. In addition, financial aspects (business case) and SAP as a specific software brand are relevant. The focus of *digital transformation* is similar. However, the overarching aspect seems to be highlighted a bit more. The high occurrence of the terms technology (76.7%), strategy (58.3%), IT (58.3%), and process (53.3%) indicate that digital transformation consultants require broad competences in at

Table 3 Fields of activity for transformation consultants (Top 10)

No.	Activity field	Absolute	Percentage
1	Business transformation	253	21.61
2	Digital transformation	120	10.25
3	IT transformation	105	8.97
4	HR transformation	55	4.70
5	Process transformation	19	1.62
6	Financial transformation	18	1.54
7	Service transformation	14	1.20
8	Cloud transformation	12	1.02
9	TV/VAS transformation	11	0.94
10	Infrastructure transformation	9	0.77

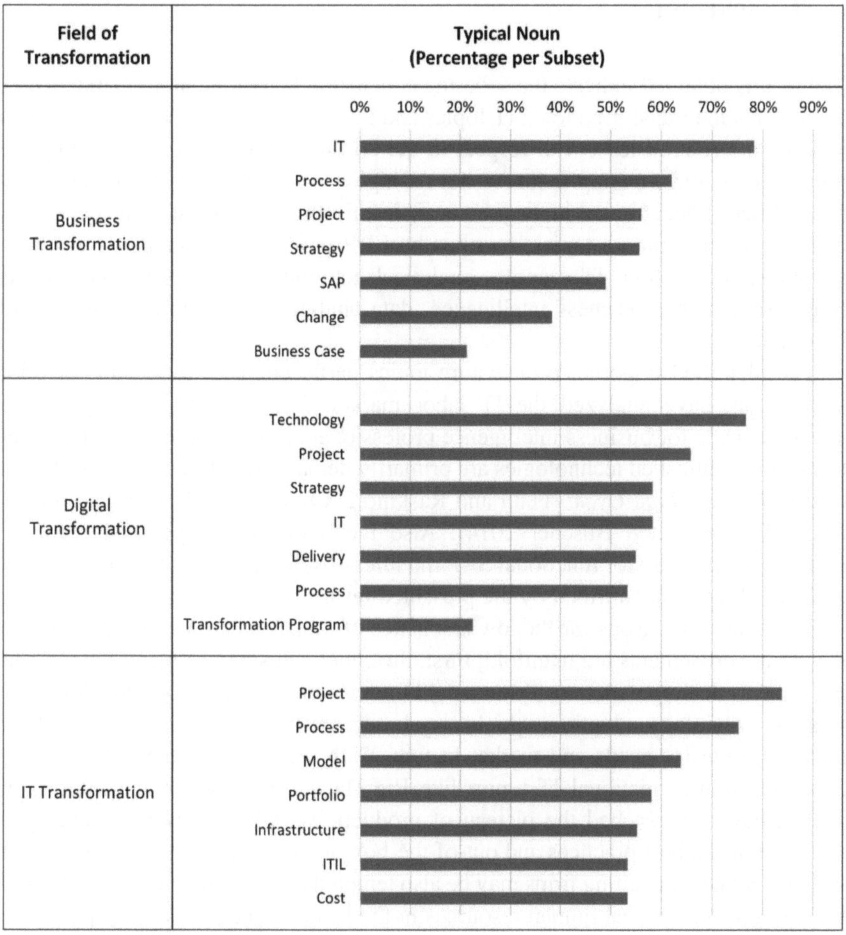

Fig. 7 Typical terms for selected transformation activities

least two of those areas, such as a combination of technology and processes. In addition, the implementation (project, delivery, transformation program) is of high relevance. In IT transformation technical skills (model, infrastructure, ITIL) are requested in the job vacancies. However, also project management (83.8%), processes (75.2%), and costs (53.3%) are relevant competences in this field.

In summary, the findings indicate that transformation is an independent and broad field of activity in IT consulting, however—similar to the previously discussed IT topics—there is still a relatively small amount of dedicated job advertisements. Furthermore, digital transformation was identified as a separate topic in IT consulting. However, the specific competence requirements in all three transformation area—business, digital, and IT—are quite similar.

6 Conclusion

The results obtained indicate the sobering conclusion that in the labor market for IT consultants the transformational IT topics and the digital transformation play only a subordinate role, at least with respect to the considered analysis period. Only the topic of *Cloud Computing* seems to have a higher significance, which is shown by the number of occurrences in the job vacancies. Furthermore, most of the demand is concentrated on mature topics, such as the ERP products of established software suppliers. In addition, IT security, analytical activities, and information systems (business analysts, business intelligence, data analytics) are also becoming more important.

The identified importance of mature topics partly confirms the results of prior studies that have analyzed the IT labor market. For example, a study of job advertisements for business intelligence professionals from 2014 states that competences for established technologies are primarily demanded, while innovative topics of the *Gartner Hype Cycle* (Fenn and Raskino 2008) are of only marginal importance (Bensberg and Buscher 2014). Also the demand for specialists of ERP systems—especially for functional SAP modules—is discussed in literature (Litecky et al. 2012) and is confirmed by the presented results.

The potential reasons for the low resonance of transformational IT topics within the job advertisements are manifold. First, the client's business demand for consulting projects dealing with transformational IT competences may be on a low level due to slow technology adoption, which may be driven by low perceived technology maturity, industry needs and market factors. With regard to Gartner's hype cycle approach, transformational IT topics like Big Data, Data Science and Internet of Things have not reached the plateau of productivity, which presumes developed methodologies, best practices and out-of-the-box product suites (Steinert and Leifer 2010). Second, consulting firms may be also tempted to develop core staff instead of searching for additional human resources in the labor market, which—in particular for hype technologies—are likely to be scarce and costly. For instance, consulting staff which is already specialized in mature technologies like Business Intelligence and Data Warehousing can likely develop to work on new IT topics like Big Data and Data Science. This tendency may be additionally supported by the observation, that the consulting industry itself is going through a deep transformational process (Christensen et al. 2013). Finally, it has to be underlined that our database covers very different types of hiring organizations. Besides genuine consulting firms (e.g. Accenture, Capgemini) and software companies (e.g. IBM, Microsoft) there are numerous recruiting firms searching for consultants. We follow the hypothesis that recruiting firms are predominantly in search of competences concerning mature IT topics (e.g. qualifications for ERP-systems from SAP/ORACLE) which already achieved a high degree of standardization. We have to test this hypothesis by further segmentation of the labor market for consultants, in particular by taking into account the different types of hiring organizations.

The findings obtained in this contribution can be used for the design of trainings and education activities in order to increase the employability of graduates. For example, it is advisable to supplement the education in ERP or IT security with consulting-specific skills and competences, such as techniques for effective customer communication (Wang and Chen 2006). Furthermore, the focus areas identified in Sect. 3 should be integrated into dedicated IT consulting courses which can be further differentiated by selected transformational IT topics (Sect. 4).

In addition to the improvement of educational offerings, the results achieved can support the skill management of consulting firms (Deelmann and Loos 2004). Even though the exploratory analysis could not provide differentiated competence profiles, the identified topics offer reliable indications for the competences demanded on the IT consulting market (cf. Figs. 3, 6, and 7). In the course of a further analysis, these terms could be examined with regard to their linguistic context, in order to derive typical consulting activities. These can subsequently be integrated into the formulation of target competence profiles in order to support the analysis of competence gaps and the development of competences (Granados and Erhardt 2012).

Regarding the contribution to consulting research (Nissen 2007), it should be considered that the explorative analysis—so far—allows only limited conclusions about the acquisition behavior of genuine IT consulting firms. As discussed above, a significant proportion of the demand for IT consultants is handled by software and recruiting companies. In the course of further analyses, it is necessary to investigate which topics are actively promoted by leading actors in the consulting sector. The available database provides a suitable empirical basis for this purpose, which could be a comprehensive starting point for future research.

References

Aier S, Weiss S (2012) Facilitating enterprise transformation through legitimacy – an institutional perspective. In: Mattfeld DC, Robra-Bissantz S (eds) Multi-Konferenz Wirtschaftsinformatik 2012 – Tagungsband der MKWI 2012. GITO Verlag, Braunschweig, pp 1073–1084

Anthony L (2013) Developing AntConc for a new generation of corpus linguists. In: Proceedings of the Corpus Linguistics conference (CL 2013), pp 14–16

Balandin S, Andreev S, Koucheryavy Y (eds) (2015) Internet of things, smart spaces, and next generation networks and systems. Springer International Publishing, Cham

Bensberg F, Buscher G (2014) BI-Stellenanzeigenanalyse 2014-Was der Arbeitsmarkt von BI-Fachkräften erwartet. In: BI-Spektrum, Online Karriere Special. Online Karriere Special 2014. http://www.tdwi.eu/fileadmin/user_upload/zeitschriften//2014/Online_Karriere_Special/bensberg_buscher_OKS_2014.pdf

Bensberg F, Buscher G (2016) Digitale transformation und IT-Zukunftsthemen im Spiegel des Arbeitsmarkts für IT-Berater – Ergebnisse einer explorativen Stellenanzeigenanalyse. In: Tagungsband zur Multikonferenz Wirtschaftsinformatik (MKWI) 2016. Technische Universität Ilmenau, pp 1007–1018

Bensberg F, Vogel D (2013) IT-Kompetenzbarometer–Was der Arbeitsmarkt von IT-Fachkräften erwartet. In: e-learning & education (eleed). eleed, Iss. 9., Open Access Journal. https://eleed.campussource.de/archive/9/3575

Berelson B (1952) Content analysis in communication research: Foundations of communication research. Free Press, Glencoe

Buyya R, Yeo CS, Venugopal S (2009) Cloud computing and emerging IT platforms: vision, hype, and reality for delivering computing as the 5th utility. Futur Gener Comput Syst 25:599–616. https://doi.org/10.1016/j.future.2008.12.001

Christensen CM, Wang D, van Bever D (2013) Consulting on the cusp of disruption. Harv Bus Rev 91:106–114

Czarnecki C, Dietze C (2017) Reference architecture for the telecommunications industry: transformation of strategy, organization, processes, data, and applications. Springer International Publishing, Cham

Debortoli S, Müller O, vom Brocke J (2014) Comparing business intelligence and big data skills: a text mining study using job advertisements. Bus Inf Syst Eng 6:289–300. https://doi.org/10.1007/s12599-014-0344-2

Deelmann T, Loos P (2004) Skill-management in einer Unternehmensberatung - Praxisbeispiel. GI Jahrestagung 2:322–326

Deelmann T, Mohe M (eds) (2006) Selection and evaluation of consultants, 1st edn. Hampp, München

Dzudzek I, Glasze G, Mattissek A, Schirmel H (2009) Verfahren der lexikometrischen Analyse von Textkorpora. In: Glasze G, Mattissek A (eds) Handbuch Diskurs und Raum: Theorien und Methoden für die Humangeographie sowie die sozial- und kulturwissenschaftliche Raumforschung, 2nd edn. Transcript, Bielefeld

Fenn J, Raskino M (2008) Mastering the hype cycle: how to choose the right innovation at the right time. Harvard Business Press, Boston, MA

Gallivan MJ, Truex DP, Kvasny L (2004) Changing patterns in IT skill sets 1988-2003: a content analysis of classified advertising. ACM SIGMIS Database 35:64–87. https://doi.org/10.1145/1017114.1017121

Granados A, Erhardt G (2012) Corporate agility organization-Personalarbeit der Zukunft: wertschöpfende Personalmanagementprozesse im Unternehmen verankern. Springer

Grob HL, Lange W (1995) Zum Wandel des Berufsbildes bei Wirtschaftsinformatikern: Eine empirische Analyse auf der Basis von Stellenanzeigen. Westfälische Wilhelms-Universität, Münster

Hanna N (2010) Enabling enterprise transformation: business and grassroots innovation for the knowledge economy. Springer, New York

Harper R (2012) The collection and analysis of job advertisements: a review of research methodology. Libr Inf Res 36:29–54

Ignatow G, Mihalcea R (2016) Text mining: a guidebook for the social sciences. Sage, London

Keil R-D (1965) Einheitliche Methoden in der Lexikometrie. Int Rev Appl Linguist Lang Teach 3:95–122

Lahrmann G, Labusch N, Winter R, Uhl A (2012) Management of large-scale transformation programs: state of the practice and future potential. In: Aier S, Ekstedt M, Matthes F (eds) Trends in enterprise architecture research and practice-driven research on enterprise transformation. Springer, Berlin, pp 253–267

Litecky C, Arnett KP, Prabhakar B (2004) The paradox of soft skills versus technical skills in is hiring. J Comput Inf Syst 45:69–76. https://doi.org/10.1080/08874417.2004.11645818

Litecky C, Igou AJ, Aken A (2012) Skills in the management oriented IS and enterprise system job markets. Proceedings of the 50th annual conference on computers and people research (SIGMIS-CPR '12). ACM Press

Lucas HC, Agarwal R, Clemons EK (2013) Impactful research on transformational information technology: an opportunity to inform new audiences. MIS Q 37(2):371–382

Manku GS, Jain A, Das Sarma A (2007) Detecting near-duplicates for web crawling. In: Proceedings of the 16th international conference on World Wide Web. ACM, pp 141–150

Nasukawa T, Nagano T (2001) Text analysis and knowledge mining system. IBM Syst J 40:967–984. https://doi.org/10.1147/sj.404.0967

Niehaves B, Becker J (2006) Design science perspectives on IT-consulting. MKWI Tagungsband, pp 7–17

Nissen V (ed) (2007) Consulting research: Unternehmensberatung aus wissenschaftlicher Perspektive, 1st edn. Dt. Univ.-Verl, Wiesbaden

Nissen V, Simon C (2009) Kernaufgaben und Vorgehensmodelle in der IV-Beratung. Forschungsberichte zur Unternehmensberatung. Univ.-Bibliothek Ilmenau

Polster T (2012) Innovation in Beratungsunternehmen: eine managementorientierte Perspektive. Springer Gabler, Wiesbaden

Posthumus J (2015) Use of market data in the recruitment of high potentials: segmentation and targeting in human resources in the pharmaceutical industry. Springer Gabler, Wiesbaden

Potter LE, Vickers G (2015) What skills do you need to work in cyber security?: A look at the Australian market. ACM Press, pp 67–72

Rouse WB (2005) A theory of enterprise transformation. Syst Eng 8:279–295. https://doi.org/10.1002/sys.20035

Sailer M (2009) Anforderungsprofile und akademischer Arbeitsmarkt: die Stellenanzeigenanalyse als Methode der empirischen Bildungs- und Qualifikationsforschung. Waxmann, Münster

Steinert M, Leifer L (2010) Scrutinizing Gartner's hype cycle approach. In: Technology management for global economic growth (PICMET), 2010 Proceedings of PICMET'10: IEEE, pp 1–13

Trovati M, Hill R, Anjum A (eds) (2015) Big-data analytics and cloud computing. Springer, Cham

Vasil'ev RB, Kalyanov GN, Levochkina GA (2010) Directions of strategic IT consulting. Autom Remote Control 71:1718–1726. https://doi.org/10.1134/S0005117910080205

Wang ET, Chen JH (2006) Effects of internal support and consultant quality on the consulting process and ERP system quality. Decis Support Syst 42:1029–1041

Ward J, Peppard J (2002) Strategic planning for information systems, 3rd edn. Wiley, Chichester, West Sussex

Webb GK (2006) The market for IS and MIS skills and knowledge: analysis of on-line job postings. Issues Inf Syst 7:253–258

Zhu W-DJ, Foyle B, Gagné D (2014) IBM Watson content analytics: discovering actionable insight from your content. IBM Redbooks

Frank Bensberg is Professor of Information Systems at the Faculty of Economic and Social Sciences at Osnabrück University of Applied Sciences. After receiving the doctoral degree and the qualification to lecture in Information Systems from the University of Münster, he worked at the Hochschule für Telekommunikation Leipzig, Germany. Focal research areas are digitization, big data, data mining, job mining and text analytics.

Gandalf Buscher studied business informatics at the Hochschule für Telekommunikation Leipzig and works as an integration manager at Deutsche Telekom AG. Central working areas are business analytics, big data and job mining. The focus is on new, agile methods for increasing the efficiency of product development in the context of digitization. Gandalf Buscher authored numerous publications. In addition, he is an ambassador of Deutsche Telekom AG and gives his experience to young academics.

Christian Czarnecki is Professor of Information Systems at the Hochschule für Telekommunikation Leipzig, Germany. During his academic career, he received a Doctor of Engineering from the University of Magdeburg. He has extensive practical experience in different consulting companies and has managed numerous transformation projects in Europe, North Africa, and the Middle East. His research includes digital transformation, process management, and enterprise architectures. In the industry organization TM Forum he is involved in the further development of the reference model enhanced Telecom Operations Map (eTOM). His work has been published in leading academic journals, in proceedings of international conferences, and in various books.

Consulting in the Age of Digital Transformation

Ferdinando Piumelli

Abstract Consulting is becoming an increasingly attractive job for many IT graduates. The demand for innovative digital solutions without involving permanent IT staff is growing in enterprises. Even though the professional field of consultants has experienced strong growth in recent years, and this will not change in the foreseeable future, it is difficult to meet the demand for well-trained consultants. The two main reasons for this are the deficit in number of experts caused by demographic transformation, and the current generation Y with its particular expectations and wishes for work environment and working conditions. New demands of advancing digitalization are also placed on consultants: away from pure professional competence towards a holistic, goal-oriented and creative consulting. To meet the IT-demands of companies under these new conditions, the present solutions range from employing freelancers to outsourcing. This article presents another solution, which promises greater efficiency and meets the evolving requirements of the consulting industry simultaneously.

1 Working Environment in the Age of Digital Transformation

Digitalization has occupied not only different areas of work, but virtually every area of life—from mobility to medicine and finance. Buying a train ticket via app, booking an appointment online or managing your own bank account on the smartphone is no longer a fantasy for the future, but has long been the present. Whole industries have been modified by the digital transformation: video rental stores went extinct and streaming portals took over the music market. Your own car is no longer just a means of transport, but almost as smart as our mobile phones. Even these few examples show the profound changes digitalization entails in all areas of life and work.

F. Piumelli (✉)
mindsquare GmbH, Bielefeld, Germany
e-mail: piumelli@mindsquare.de

V. Nissen (ed.), *Advances in Consulting Research*, Contributions to Management Science, https://doi.org/10.1007/978-3-319-95999-3_17

The speed of digitalization has grown exponentially over the past decades. As early as the 1960s, Gordon Moore described the doubling of computer performance every 2 years in Moore's Law, the law named after him (Meckel 2008). According to this law, computers will work just as fast as the human brain in 2024, that is in less than 7 years. At the same time, technological performance is becoming more and more cost-effective—in the development stage and for end users. In 2046, according to Moore's law, we will reach technological singularity, which means all existing artificial intelligence shall exceed the globally available human reasoning potential.

Due to the continuous emergence of new technologies and their further development, a completely new kind of work will emerge. Unfettered by time and space, it is increasingly possible to deal with all work-related topics via digital channels. This ranges from online applications to mobile CRM applications and logistics applications as well as mobile management of working hours and employee data. Company-owned smartphones are provided nowadays for employees to easily process mails or switch to video conferencing.

Because of this rapid digital development, we speak of the second modern era. Based on the first modern era—the industrial revolution with its replacement of muscle power by machines—the second modern era describes the replacement of human reasoning power by digital machines, such as computers (Klotz 1996).

If companies want to become or remain successful in the future, they must use digital technologies and develop digital business models. The high demand for new technologies turns every company into an IT company. Therefore, well-educated computer scientists are indispensable for many companies.

In practice, however, especially in small and medium-sized businesses, it has been shown that the budget to retain corresponding employees in the long term as well as the option of presenting themselves as attractive employers to very well-trained computer scientists is usually not available. The core competency of most companies is not in IT, and therefore the options for further growth for computer scientists are limited. For example, the main business of a bank is managing money, and operating economic activities with this money. Nevertheless, it is just as important for a bank to design and deploy digital innovations as it is the case, for example, for a pure IT company.

Because of this discrepancy between a growing demand and a lack of resources for an independent IT division, it has become more economical for many companies to break down their expertise in technology into services and to procure these services only as needed, e.g. by hiring IT consultants for a specific project or time frame.

2 Deficit in Experts in IT-Consulting

With the increasing demand for IT solutions, consulting is a professional field with a promising future. The BDU study from 2016 shows: turnover has nearly doubled over the last 10 years at stable prices (Fig. 1).

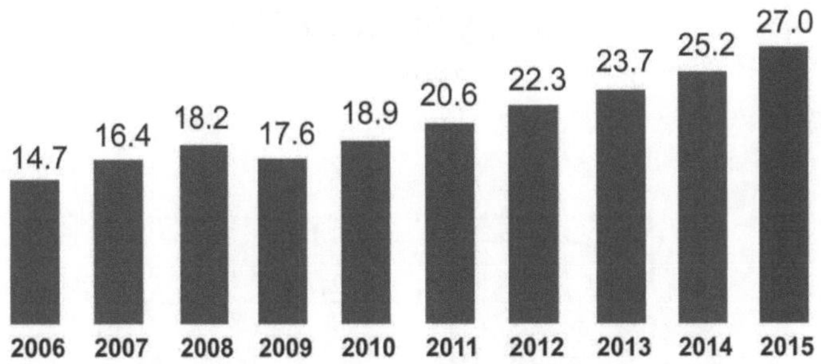

Fig. 1 Growth of consulting turnover in Germany from 2006 to 2015 (in billion euros) (BDU 2016)

Facing a massive deficit in IT experts, companies are becoming increasingly dependent on consultants to meet their needs. Three major reasons contribute to the increasing deficit in experts. On the one hand, demographic transformation is a factor that reduces the number of potentially suitable candidates. On the other hand, companies have to adapt to the changed demands of the generation Y if they want to attract young professionals. In addition, requirements for IT consultants have changed; only a fraction of the job applicants and professionals are still eligible for this job now.

2.1 Demographic Transformation

As already mentioned, in addition to the increasing digitalization, the demographic change is another challenge that companies are facing. We are living longer and longer and at the same time Germany's population is declining which leads to a massive shift in age pyramids with serious consequences for the job market (Destatis 2015).

In 2015, the Federal Statistical Office recorded 13.2 million people in Germany (Destatis 2015) in the age group of 22–34-years—which are of particular relevance for consultancy. Considering that a MINT degree is necessary to be successful in IT consulting, this limits the number of possible employees in this area even further. In comparison, 20 years earlier—in 1995—there were still approx. 17 million people to be allocated to this relevant age group (Destatis 2015). A glance into the near future in 2024, when computing power will have reached the capacity of the human brain, indicates a further shrinkage in the relevant group. By then, only 11.9 million people will be aged 22—34 (Destatis 2015).

If we reach technical singularity in 2046, decline is unmistakable. Only 10.1 million people will be in the relevant age group by then (Destatis 2015). Compared to 2015, the number of potential specialists will drop by a further three million people. The shift in age structure and the impact of population decline are illustrated in Fig. 2.

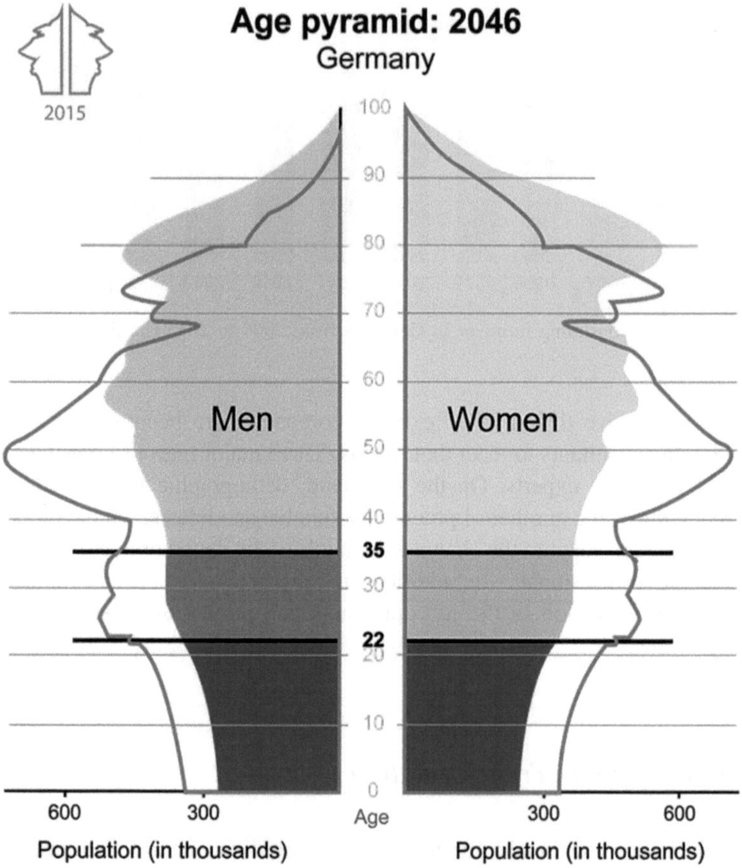

Fig. 2 Development of the population in 2015 and 2046 (Destatis 2015)

The relevance of demographic transformation and the impact on the job market are evident in this figure. A decline by almost 25% of the group of 22–34 year olds represents a particular challenge for companies. It is therefore necessary for them to intensify their recruiting activities. Not only do employees apply to companies, but companies also have to apply as attractive employers to potential new employees.

Job requirements for consultants change due to the demographic transformation and specific needs, requirements and desires of generation Y. What this exactly means is elaborated in the next section.

2.2 *Expectations of the Generation Y*

Generation Y describes the successor generation of generation X or baby-boomers (Signium 2013). This makes generation Y one of the youngest generations in the job market. Due to their small number, today's young professionals of generation Y are highly courted by companies (Petry 2015). This fight for well-trained specialists is therefore also known as "War for Talents" (Signium 2013).

A special feature of generation Y is already reflected in its name: The letter Y points to the generation's tendency of questioning everything and not accepting anything as self-evident any longer (Dahlmanns 2013). Generation Y belongs to the first generation that has grown up with digital media and techniques. Therefore, the term "digital natives" is often used. Since digital media had a strong influence on those young professionals during their teenage years, they have no fear or scepticism towards new and innovative technologies (Dahlmanns 2013). Thus, it is self-evident for them to learn new knowledge or to go into an exchange of knowledge using digital media. The concepts of information- and knowledge-based society have also been established based on this fact.

Employees belonging to generation Y want a meaningful and, above all, fulfilling work. It is important for those individuals to be perceived and valued as individuals (Signium 2013). Their credo is: successful is who is happy. This can be achieved mainly by meeting their wishes as well as the needs. This also includes the reconciliation of family and career and a good work-life balance. This is true for both genders, since social roles of men and women in the generation Y changed compared to previous generations. It is no longer the single-income earning man and the housewife, but often a double-income household, in which the husband is more and more concerned about education and household (Signium 2013).

In addition, gaps in CVs are less important for generation Y than it was previously the case. The strong individualism of this generation is also reflected in their résumés (Parment 2013). Loyalty to employers has declined sharply, they eagerly leave jobs in search of a better employer (Buck et al. 2002). This means companies have to keep those young professionals of generation Y loyal with special incentives and cater more and more to their individual needs, such as a good work-life balance.

At the same time, the negotiating position of the generation Y is almost never the opposite of the company. Since they belong to a persuaded minority, they are in a position to make demands. Companies need to deal with them if they want to hire the best young specialists, create innovations and gain a competitive advantage.

2.3 *New Requirements*

The digital transformation leads to various changes in the job profile of IT consultants. Since IT is increasingly becoming a part of a company's strategic core, more and more computer scientists are necessary for consultations instead of business management graduates. Deep understanding of technology is indispensable in achieving outstanding consulting results. In addition to the pure programming performance, computer scientists have to develop additional distinctive consulting skills. However, this can be learned with the right methodology in a relatively short time, unlike well-founded IT competencies that business graduates cannot acquire in an online course along the way.

Companies are demanding less and less pure programming skills but are rather looking for stocktaking and joint solution finding. In addition to excellent professional competencies, the focus is shifting to personality and social skills. Credibility, reliability and relationship management are essential if consultants want to be successful in their careers. Maister et al. (2001) have already impressively described the role of these various competencies in consultancy in their book, "The Trusted Advisor". The Trusted Advisor model is extremely helpful in training inexperienced MINT-graduates in the shortest possible amount of time to become trustworthy consultants, thus laying the foundation for a career as a successful IT consultant.

It is important to clarify why particularly young computer scientists between 22 and 34 years are so much in demand. The reason lies in biology. At the beginning of one's career, creativity is often at its peak (Becker 2010) and it is creativity that is needed to create digital innovation to meet the economic challenges. While older computer scientists and consultants are thinking based on their experiences in existing patterns, job starters bring an impartiality that makes it easier to develop completely new solutions.

3 Ways to Mitigate the Deficit in Experts

Taking into account the situation described above, it is often the most economical solution, particularly with regard to digital transformation, to outsource IT expertise and work with well-trained IT consultants. Various models have been established for this kind of cooperation. In the following, four models with their individual advantages and disadvantages are discussed.

3.1 Outsourcing of Individual Projects

One option is to outsource individual projects. This is particularly lucrative if it is a one-time project, where it is not worthwhile to build in-house expertise, or the IT department has no free resources at its disposal. It would be much bigger of an investment to get the same quality results with newly built in-house resources than hiring a professional service provider with years of experience in the subject. In this case, hiring an external specialist is the optimal and most cost-efficient solution. The company does not have to commit itself to other employees in the long term. It benefits from relatively low costs and the experience of the service providers (best practices). However, the flexibility can also be disadvantageous because the expertise of the service provider is lost with the completion of the project and if the project framework is not defined in advance, there is a risk of cost explosion. This must be observed during the selection of the service provider or before the end of the project to guarantee handover and transfer of knowledge.

3.2 *Outsourcing of Entire Processes*

In addition to outsourcing individual projects, it is also possible to outsource entire processes. The most famous distinction here is offshore (from the Central European perspective: Asia) and nearshore (from the Central European perspective: Eastern Europe). In both cases, entire development departments are handed over to other companies. The big advantage: organizations can keep their existing resources free for their core business without engaging them for other areas. However, there are relatively many disadvantages. This includes a lack of continuous improvement of processes as well as an inflexibility of the service often strongly linked to defined processes. As a result, a return on invest only emerges after a prolonged, smooth running of the process. Similarly, in practice it has been shown that disputes are very likely to arise between the two parties involved. This is often due to different motivations and goals of company and outsourcing service provider.

3.3 *Body Leasing*

Body leasing is the third most common model for cooperation with external (IT) service providers in addition to the already described versions of outsourcing. A temporary worker or freelancer is paid at a predefined hourly or daily rate for the actual working time he has rendered. After completion of the task or reaching a certain time or cost limit, the external employee can be released again without complications.

More and more companies are opting for the use of body leasing. On the one hand, because the offer of experienced and qualified specialists is at least as important as any topic in the IT area; but on the other hand, also because this form of cooperation offers maximum flexibility and companies make only minimal commitments.

Since the work is paid on an hourly basis, the risk of cost explosion is much lower compared to outsourcing of complete processes. Depending on the requirements, an external employee can also be booked over several projects. This creates long-term working relationships between specialists and companies, in which the skilled worker increasingly acquaints himself with the company and their specific requirements and, similar to a permanent employee, is integrated into the respective task regime.

What initially sounds attractive to companies also has some disadvantages. For example, no continuous advanced training is guaranteed here, since every freelancer himself takes care of it. Similarly, mediation through agencies should be viewed critically, if they tend to focus more on their commission rather than on the needs of the companies when placing a freelancer. Cooperation with pure sales agencies is therefore not recommended. Last but not least, there is a risk of legal and financial consequences for body leasing companies, should an apparent self-reliance of the skilled employees be established (IHK 2017). In general, body leasing has proven to be worthwhile when long-term tasks—from about 3 months onwards—are to be assigned.

3.4 Professional Employer Organization (PEO)

Professional Employer Organizations work similar to traditional consulting companies. This corporate model has been a long-standing practice in the USA where it has developed in the 1960s (Klaas et al. 2000, 2005). It is ideal to resolve the role-based conflict of interest between specialized employees (i.e. IT consultants) and top management and is widely used in different industries. Its model can be explained quite simple using the example of an IT PEO.

The management of a company selling whatever kind of product has in particular the commercial success in view. The company has an IT department but it can be economically feasible to not always invest in seminars for IT employees and newest technology. IT employees on the other hand have different and partly contrary interests: They want to gain and deepen expertise in their field of technology and innovate instead of working basic IT issues. A conflict between IT employee and management is pre-programmed, at least if the employee is ambitious.

PEOs offer a solution and are able to resolve this conflict of interest as far as possible. A PEO acts as a company specializing in the respective area of expertise, in the example as a company for IT experts in a certain area of technology. Companies conclude contracts with a PEO if a certain need arises, for example, for a very specific new IT product or if they want to optimize their business processes by implementing new digital solutions. The PEO then coordinates the realization of the purchased service or project. In this way, the management can continue to focus on their core business: the strategic management and the overall success of the company. At the same time, the PEO provides best conditions for IT experts and offers them optimal working modalities, for example, relevant professional training.

PEOs like consulting companies are especially helpful for companies wanting to innovate and invest in projects for digital transformation. As most companies can't afford to employ highly trained experts full-time, working with PEOs only when needed is a cost efficient solution. Besides when hiring a PEO, companies benefit from experts' experiences with different projects and industries and their best practice approach instead of solely relying on knowhow of their own employees.

In this regard, Professional Employer Organizations work similar to conventional consulting companies: They send consultants to clients to solve a specific problem, evaluate a certain situation or conduct a defined project. The experts are permanently employed and benefit from all the advantages associated: financial security and regular advanced training. But there is one major difference. PEOs put career interest and well-being of their consultants first whereas traditional consulting companies view them rather as a human resource.

While consulting companies often do not consider personal preferences in regard to regions, duration of projects or career paths, PEOs offer flexible career opportunities and try to match individual interests and business goals. Besides continuing education supporting each consultant on his personal career path as best as possible is a key characteristic of PEOs. As a result of this strategy, PEOs not only create highly-trained consultants but also extremely engaged ones. And as personal satisfaction fosters job performance, the corporate model of PEO is not an altruistic but rather a very economic and efficient answer to the rising demand in IT services and digital innovation. Compared to other available options, it is probably even the best option available especially for small and medium sized companies to thrive in the age of digital transformation.

4 Case Study of Mindsquare GmbH

Common for a long time in the USA, the PEO model is still largely unknown in Germany. mindsquare GmbH is one of the first IT companies in Germany to be organized as a PEO.

mindsquare was founded in 2007 as a PEO in SAP and Salesforce consulting. It has been awarded the EU Promotion Prize while regularly achieving top placements at the Great Place to Work competition. Feel-good management plays a key role and builds a corner stone of the company culture. It includes regular team events or company celebrations but it goes beyond. To ensure a friendly and safe working environment, feel-good management at mindsquare includes i.e. core value seminars as part of the onboarding processes where consultants learn about integrity, life balance and maintaining respectful relationships.

In order to achieve excellent results for its clients, mindsquare works with only the best IT graduates in Germany. In a multi-stage application process, the best 3% of graduates are selected. During an assessment centre, soft skills such as, communication talents, team skills, etc. are tested in addition to professional competence.

All new entrants initially complete a 6-week trainee program including SAP certification at mindsquare. Afterwards, the employees are given the option to go through a 2-year managerial training program in order to ensure appropriate career advancement opportunities. Continuous professional and personal advanced development is one of the core values of mindsquare GmbH.

Depending on individual orientation, employees are given the option to choose from 9 areas, in which they wish to work. Employees achieve real top performance only if they are intrinsically motivated and are enthusiastic about their subject field. How mindsquare uses the concept of PEO is shown in Fig. 3.

The consultants with their technical knowledge and expertise are employed directly at mindsquare. They find optimal working conditions in their professional

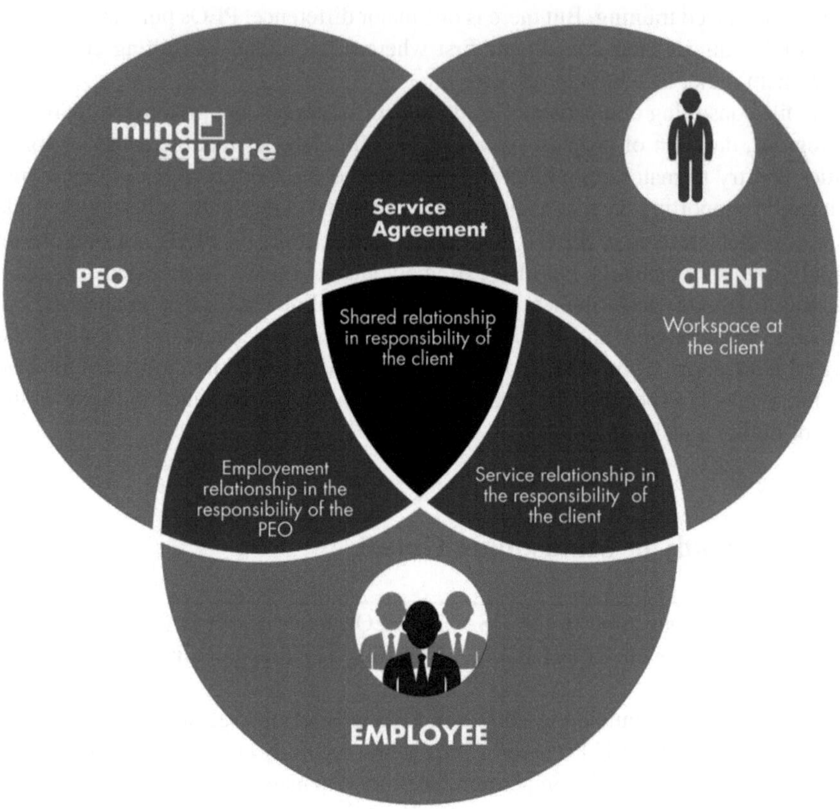

Fig. 3 Concept of the PEO using the example of mindsquare

field. The core business of mindsquare is in its area of work; consultants receive many advanced training opportunities and benefit from a feel-good management tailored to the interests of computer scientists. With simultaneous job security, they have the option to gather a lot of experience in a short time through different clients and projects.

Companies have the option to procure the service of excellently trained consultants from mindsquare to carry out joint projects with them. Customers no longer need to build specific in-house expertise or hire new employees for projects. Entire business areas can be partially transferred to PEOs. They are free to choose whether they appoint consultants on a time and material basis or outsource entire projects including management. Companies use either mindsquare consultants in order to be able to focus on their core business, while strategic future projects are implemented by mindsquare experts in projects, or they employ consultants for their day-to-day business to implement in-house competition-critical strategic advanced development themselves.

Not only medium-sized companies, but also national and international corporations are increasingly relying on mindsquare's services. 22 of the DAX30 companies are among mindsquare's customers for SAP and Salesforce. In times, when it is extremely difficult to find highly trained computer scientists, companies can waive complex job application processes for areas that are not in their core business. Instead, they resort to a PEO that has already taken over the quality selection. Working with a PEO, not only to solve their own weaknesses in IT and are able to initiate innovation, but they also save time and money in the long run as regular innovation is increasingly important to remain competitive.

The example of mindsquare shows that the concept of PEO can also be successfully implemented in Germany and particularly in the field of consulting. This is also proved by the figures of mindsquare: since the foundation, the company has recorded an annual growth rate of 40% in sales and employees, and it was only in May 2017 that mindsquare was awarded as one of the best consulting companies in Germany in a study by the economic magazine Brand Eins and Statista (Brand Eins 2017).

5 Conclusion and Outlook

In summary, it can be said that the effects of digital transformation in combination with the progress of demographic transformation are serious. Not only will there be fewer and fewer specialists, but generation Y, with their very special wishes and needs, will also have to be taken seriously. This is especially true if it is important for companies to retain long-term qualified employees. The points shown here are also increasingly changing the professional field of consulting. Companies have various options to access external service providers. These include the assignment of individual projects, the transfer of entire processes or the body leasing model. Each option has its own advantages and disadvantages. Their use should be considered and adapted depending on the individual company situation.

The global economy is undergoing a profound transformation process. This is an opportunity and a challenge for IT consulting in Germany. On the one hand, demand for technological innovation has grown exponentially, but on the other hand there is a lack of qualified computer scientists in Germany. As a result, the majority of the most innovative companies i.e. Google, Facebook, Uber, Airbnb where not founded in Germany but in Silicon Valley. While German engineers and IT developer succeed in optimizing processes using digital solutions and artificial intelligence, true innovation made in Germany is rare. Whether Germany succeeds in catching up with the already existing gap in digitalization will depend decisively on whether extensive course corrections are implemented in the education system in order to qualify the age cohorts with low figures of birth to future-oriented professional fields.

Short-term relief is provided by PEOs which fulfil the requirements of generation Y in terms of optimal career conditions while simultaneously offering a resource-friendly way for companies to benefit from and create technological innovation.

Now, it is important to gather more comprehensive practical experiences with this model and to establish further alternative models in order to enable sustainable economic growth under the changed framework conditions of the digital transformation.

References

BDU (2016) Marktstudie "Facts and Figures zum Beratermarkt 2015/2016" https://www.bdu.de/media/174314/charts-pressemappe-auswahl.pdf. Accessed 24 Mai 2017

Becker M (2010) Optimistisch altern! In: Ritz A, Thom N (eds) Talent Management. Talente identifizieren, Kompetenzen entwickeln, Leistungsträger erhalten. Gabler, Wiesbaden, pp 39–56

Brand Eins Thema (2017) Consulting – Der Branchenreport von brand eins Wissen und Statista – die besten Berater 2017. J Manag (6):117

Buck H, Kistler E, Mendius HG (2002) Demografischer Wandel in der Arbeitswelt. Chancen für eine innovative Arbeitsgestaltung. Fraunhofer IAO, Stuttgart

Dahlmanns A (2013) Generation Y und Personalmanagement. Hampp Verlag, Mering

Destatis (2015) Koordinierte Bevölkerungsvorausberechnung für Deutschland. https://service.destatis.de/bevoelkerungspyramide/#!y=2046&a=22,35&o=2015v1&g. Accessed 19 Apr 2017

IHK (2017) Scheinselbstständigkeit. https://www.frankfurt-main.ihk.de/recht/themen/arbeitsrecht/scheinselbstaendigkeit/. Accessed 17 May 2017

Klaas BS, McClendon JA, Gainey TW (2000) Managing HR in the small and medium enterprise: the impact of professional employer organizations. Entrep Theory Pract 25(1):107–107

Klaas BS, Gainey TW, McClendon JA, Yang H (2005) Professional employer organizations and their impact on client satisfaction with human resource outcomes: a field study of human resource outsourcing in small and medium enterprises. J Manag 31(2):234–254

Klotz H (1996) Die Zweite Moderne. C.H. Beck, Munich

Maister DH, Green CH, Galford RM (2001) The trusted advisor. Free Press, New York

Meckel M (2008) Corporate communication 2.0. In: Meckel M, Schmid BF (eds) Unternehmenskommunikation. Gabler, Wiesbaden, pp 471–492

Parment A (2013) Die Generation Y. Mitarbeiter der Zukunft motivieren, integrieren, führen, 2nd edn. Springer Gabler, Wiesbaden

Petry T (2015) Market study – head-hunting in Germany. https://www.bpm.de/sites/default/files/petry_bpm_headhunting_studie_210x297mm_final_web.pdf. Accessed 17 May 2017

Signium (2013) Generation Y – Das Selbstverständnis der Manager von morgen. https://www.zukunftsinstitut.de/fileadmin/user_upload/Publikationen/Auftragsstudien/studie_generation_y_signium.pdf. Accessed 19 Apr 2017

Ferdinando Piumelli is a successful entrepreneur, founder of 11 start-ups and angel investor. His business focuses on three major subjects to enable companies to thrive in the era of digital transformation: strategic management consulting, process consulting, IT consulting and Software development. His biggest company mindsquare has received several awards, i.e. Best Place to Work Award and Best Consulting 2017 Award. Ferdinando Piumelli has been working as a strategy consultant for digital transformation and as an executive coach with DAX30 companies and medium-sized enterprises for the past 15 years.

Case Study: Digital Consulting for Dental Practices by Benchmarking

Christian Stummeyer

Abstract Owners of dental practices are entrepreneurs, but often lack comprehensive business knowledge. Thus, they often would need advice from a professional business consultant. However, given the revenue size of a common dental practice, fees for a professional management consulting project are simply not in financial reach for most dentists. By conducting a benchmarking study of a dental practice using an online platform, the dentist gains access to a proven consulting method and recognizes a clear and objective perspective on strengths and improvement potential for the practice. For the very first time, a professional benchmarking is available at an affordable base price. In addition, standardized consulting services can be booked on top for reasonable prices.

1 Consulting for Dental Practices

1.1 Challenges for Dentists

A typical dental practice in Germany with only one dentist working in the practice generates a yearly "revenue" between 300,000 and 800,000 €, and a pre-tax profit between 100,000 and 300,000 € for the owner (Kassenzahnärztliche Bundesvereinigung 2016; BestPrax 2017). A dental practice is typically a small company and employs several employees. Thus, the dentist is—besides the role of a medical doctor—an entrepreneur by running the practice, but often has an insufficiency of profound business knowledge, as the studies are mainly focused on medical topics.

Today, dentists with own dental practices face many challenges:

C. Stummeyer (✉)
Technical University of Ingolstadt, Ingolstadt, Germany
e-mail: christian.stummeyer@thi.de

V. Nissen (ed.), *Advances in Consulting Research*, Contributions to Management Science, https://doi.org/10.1007/978-3-319-95999-3_18

- The costs for employees, material and infrastructure are increasing year by year.
- The compensations, paid by healthcare providers and patients, are not evolving in the same way as the related costs, leading to lower margins.
- The competition of acquiring "attractive" patients is becoming harder.
- An adequate amount of time for a professional management of the own dental practice is missing.
- Achieving a good work-life balance is getting increasingly difficult.

When it comes to the point, where the entrepreneur asks himself, how to master all the challenges and do business better, business consulting seems to be an option. But for most dentists, a highly paid management consultant with daily rates of 3000 € and more and an optimization project with a 30-day duration is not a realistic option, as the project fees would absorb a major share of the practices's yearly profit. Thus, a more affordable and "standardized" form of business consulting is needed to improve the dental office.

1.2 Automatic Dental Practice Benchmarking as Possible Solution

Conducting a benchmarking study could be a possible solution: Benchmarking is a proven management approach for implementing best practices at low costs and it is a newer concept in the healthcare system. Benchmarking made its first appearance in the healthcare system in 1990 with the requirements of the Joint Commission on Accreditation of Healthcare Organizations (JCAHO) in the United States, which defined it as a measurement tool for monitoring the impact of governance, management and clinical and logistical functions.

In practice, benchmarking also encompasses:

- regularly comparing indicators (structure, activities, processes and outcomes) against best practitioners,
- identifying differences in outcomes through inter-organizational visits,
- seeking out new approaches in order to make improvements that will have the greatest impact on outcomes, and
- monitoring indicators (Ettorchi-Tardy et al. 2012).

If a dentist wants to analyze the economic performance of his practice and wants to compare with best practice dental offices, he often contacts his tax advisor. The tax advisor usually uses statistics of other medical practices—not necessarily dental practices—and looks for offices within the same range of revenue. With this basic information, some tax advisors try to answer e.g. the question, if the cost structure of a practice is okay or not. This leads to a situation, where a lot of dental practices, which are e.g. in the same range of 1.0 to 1.5 million euros revenue, are compared. However, a highly specialized dental practice in a metropolis with only one dentist and a revenue of 1.3 million euro has a very different cost structure compared to a basic dental practice with three dentists in a rural area without specialization with the same revenue.

Given that, the idea of performing an automatic benchmarking procedure based on an online platform for dental practices was born in 2008. The company BestPrax GmbH was founded 2009 in Munich by a former management consultant, who had the idea to provide standardized benchmarking for dental practices, which goes beyond the traditional comparison of tax advisors and tax service companies. To master the challenges and to get transparency of the current economic situation of the own dental practice, BestPrax offers benchmarking for dental practices in Germany using an online platform. Based on management facts and pre-defined key performance indicators, the owner of a dental practice learns how his practice is performing compared with the average, as well as to the leading practices in the relevant peer group ("similar practices"). This leads to an excellent transparency for the individual dentist (Zahnarzt Wirtschaft Praxis 2009).

The owner of the dental practice now can easily identify the strengths, which are the basis of competitive advantage. And also, he recognizes in which dimensions his own practice falls short and, hence, where he can realize potential for improvement. This is all achieved with very little effort for the dentist and at a price that is by far lower than the usual daily rate of a management consultant.

2 Benchmarking as a Digital Consulting Service

2.1 The Benchmarking Approach

The company BestPrax developed the first online-based benchmarking approach in Germany, which focusses only on dental practices. The participant—or customer—of the benchmarking procedure is the owner of the dental practice. He has to register on the website by entering a valid e-mail address. After this, the participant receives a so-called "practice cipher" which allows an anonymous analysis of the data. The dentist then gains access to the benchmarking cockpit, where the relevant data can be entered (Fig. 1).

To perform the benchmarking exercise of the dental practice, data and information in three main parts are necessary, always reflecting the prior year (BestPrax 2017):

- **Dental practice:** e.g. structure of practice, infrastructure, number of dentists and their focus areas, employees, capacity of dentists and employees, yearly revenues
- **Economic analysis:** e.g. revenue and cost structure including cost categorization, considering profit centers (if available), e.g. own laboratory
- **Medical cases:** e.g. number of treated patients, number of different key dental services (e.g. professional dental cleanings, implants, root canal treatments)

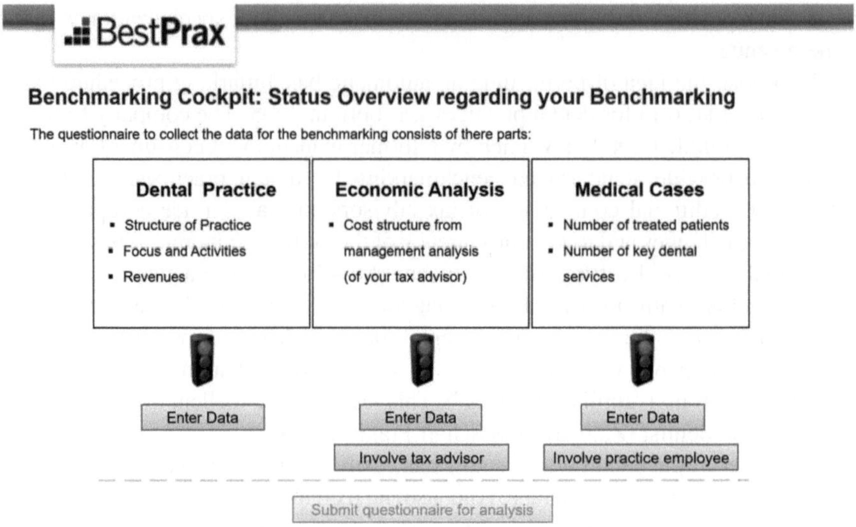

Fig. 1 Benchmarking cockpit with traffic lights (©BestPrax)

To enter the data, the format of an online questionnaire is used (Fig. 2). The user receives background information and definitions regarding the necessary data and can save the inputs at any time.

Whilst the first part of the questionnaire "dental practice" is usually filled in by the owner of the practice, the second part "economic analysis" can be filled in by the tax advisor of the practice. The online platform provides an automated e-mail workflow to acknowledge the tax advisor and ensures that the data provided by the tax advisor is integrated into the practice data. Usually a practice manager or another employee of the practice provides the data for the third part "number of medical cases". The platform supports their contribution and collaboration in data entry, too (BestPrax 2017).

A key objective by designing the benchmarking platform is to make the data entry as short and smooth as possible for the owner of the dental practice. To fill in the first part, the practice owner needs approximately 25–30 min. The data entry of the tax advisor in part two usually lasts between 15 and 20 min, the data entry of the practice manager for part three also between 15 and 20 min. For part three there is often an additional time frame for gathering the data regarding the numbers of medical cases in the IT systems of the practice necessary.

After all relevant data has been filled in, the benchmarking cockpit displays three green traffic lights. At this point, the participating owner must authorize all data—also the data provided by tax advisor and practice manager—and submits the data to perform the automatic benchmarking procedure by BestPrax.

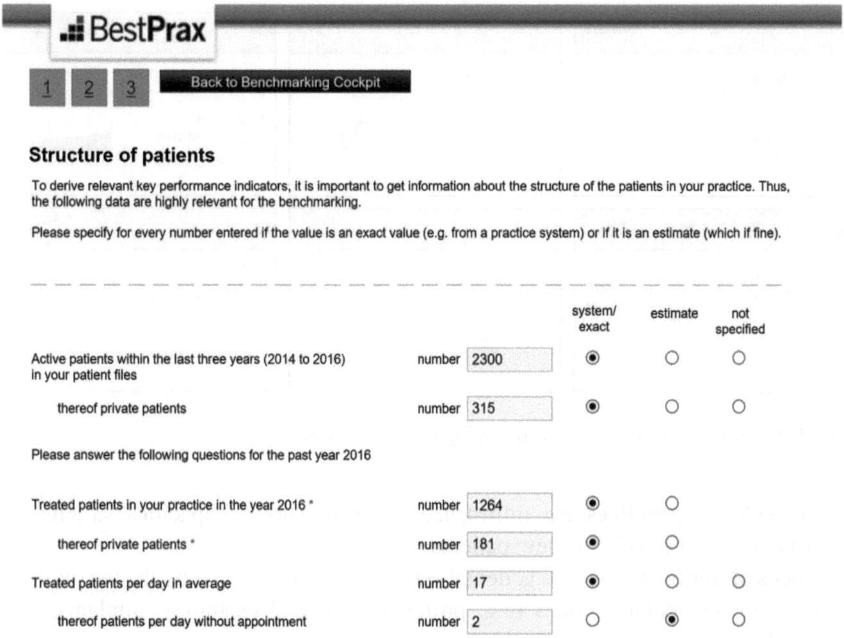
BestPrax

1 2 3 Back to Benchmarking Cockpit

Structure of patients

To derive relevant key performance indicators, it is important to get information about the structure of the patients in your practice. Thus, the following data are highly relevant for the benchmarking.

Please specify for every number entered if the value is an exact value (e.g. from a practice system) or if it is an estimate (which if fine).

			system/ exact	estimate	not specified
Active patients within the last three years (2014 to 2016) in your patient files	number	2300	◉	○	○
thereof private patients	number	315	◉	○	○
Please answer the following questions for the past year 2016					
Treated patients in your practice in the year 2016 *	number	1264	◉	○	
thereof private patients *	number	181	◉	○	
Treated patients per day in average	number	17	◉	○	○
thereof patients per day without appointment	number	2	○	◉	○

Fig. 2 Example of the online questionnaire (excerpt)

2.2 *The Core Elements of Benchmarking*

The benchmarking method is based on aggregating data of all participating dental practices of a dedicated year into the so-called "joint benchmarking pool". Within this joint benchmarking pool, a sub-pool is determined for each dental practice. This sub-pool comprises practices, which are comparable in terms of

- structure of practice,
- focus of dental services,
- size (revenue and capacity).

Thus, it is ensured that practices are only compared to offices of equal rank based on the characteristics just mentioned ("peer group")—and not on a calculated average of all practices. In addition, an algorithm makes sure that every sub-pool has a sufficient number of practices that allow a benchmarking procedure, which is statistically significant.

After compiling the results, every practice receives a document with more than 50 pages, covering and benchmarking the following six areas (Fig. 3) (Bestprax 2017):

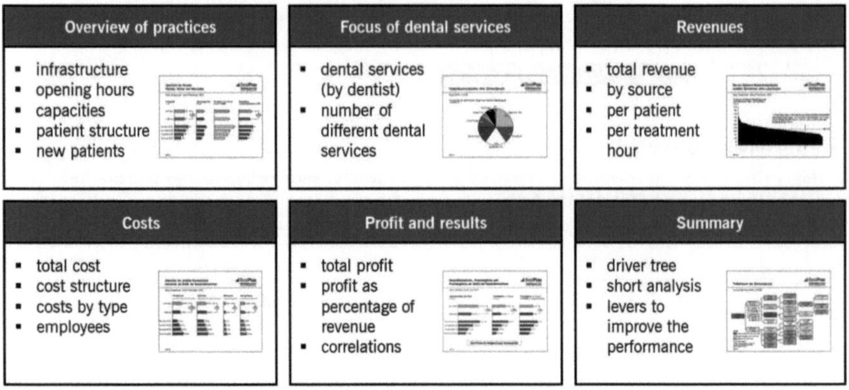

Fig. 3 Six areas covered in the benchmarking report (overview)

- **Overview of practices:** e.g. infrastructure, opening hours, capacities, structure of patients, treated patients, new patients.
- **Focus of dental services:** e.g. dental services by practices and by dentist, number of different dental services (e.g. professional dental cleanings, implants, root canal treatments).
- **Revenues:** e.g. total revenues of practice, revenues by sources, revenues per patient, revenues per treatment hour.
- **Costs:** e.g. cost structure, costs by type, employees, employees per treatment hour.
- **Profit and results:** e.g. total profit of dental practice, profit as percent of revenue, different correlations.
- **Summary:** e.g. driver tree for the dental practice with traffic lights, written short analysis of the practice, levers to improve performance.

A key result of the benchmarking study is the driver tree for each dental practice, which is an in-house development by BestPrax according to the idea of the DuPont-System of Financial Control. The driver tree highlights strengths and weaknesses by using traffic light colors (Fig. 4). Dimensions, in which the practice is already good and better than similar peer group practices, are marked in green. Dimensions, where the practice is slightly worse, are marked yellow and if the performance is significantly worse, the color red is used. This color coding system makes it easy for a dentist to focus on the fields where the practice needs improvement.

In detail, all relevant key performance indicators (KPIs) of a dental practice are considered in the benchmarking study. In total, more than 50 KPIs are analyzed. A selection of them is mentioned in Fig. 3 on an overview level. An important KPI for each dental practice is the production (revenue) of a dentist per treatment hour. Figure 5 shows this KPI—revenue per dentist treatment hour—as a selected example.

The participant gets to know the value of each KPI for his dental practice. In addition, this value is set into relation with the mean of all practices participating in

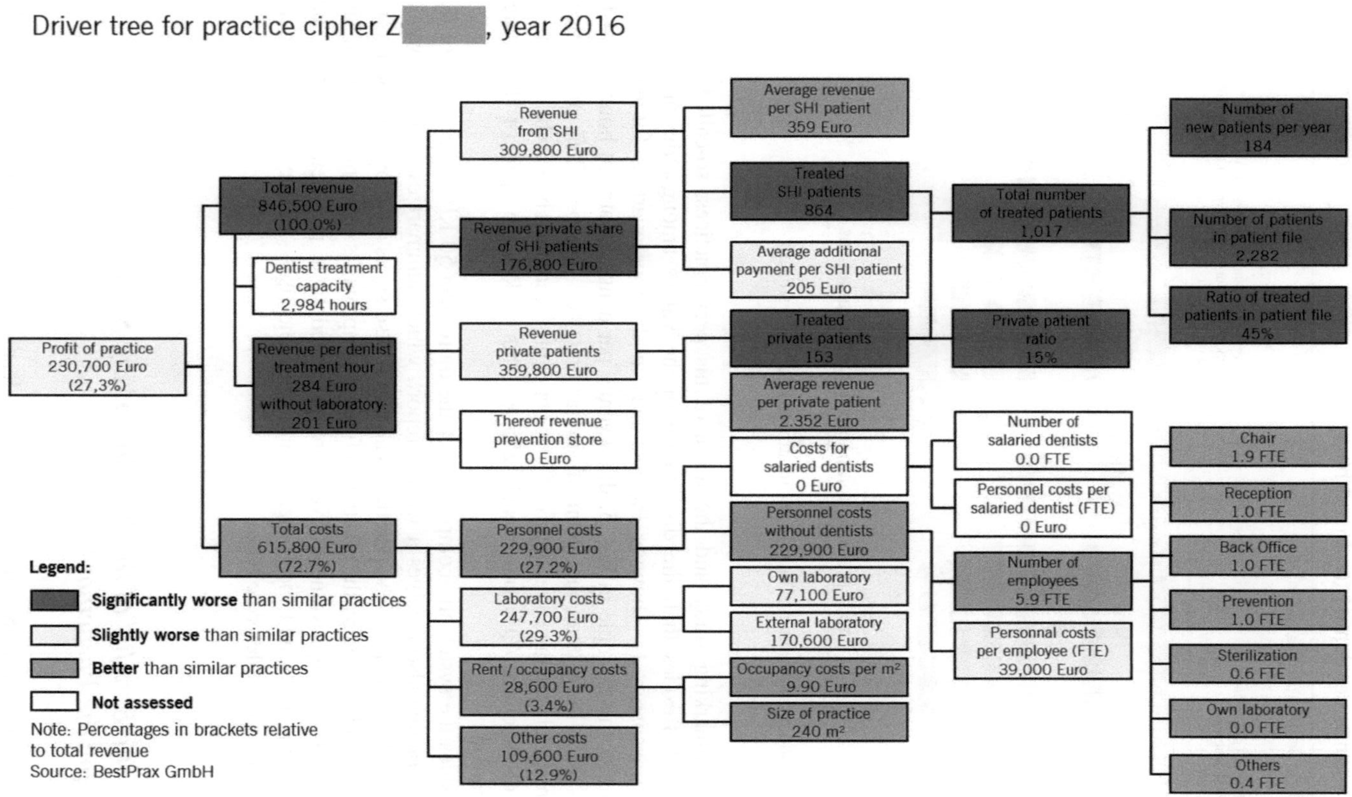

Fig. 4 The driver tree of a dental practice (©BestPrax)

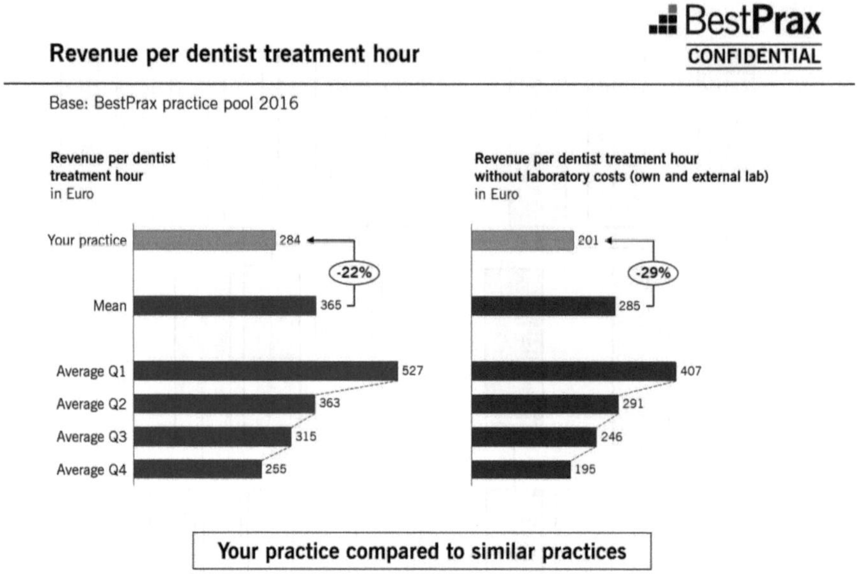

Fig. 5 Production/revenue of dentist per treatment hour (©BestPrax)

the benchmarking study and the mean of his peer practices, so-called "similar practices". Besides that, the distribution of the values amongst the practices is made transparent by showing the averages in the four quartiles for each KPI. Regarding the example in Fig. 5, the revenue per dentist treatment hour is 284 €, that is 22% lower than the mean of similar practices. The best 25% of practices (Q1) realize in average a revenue of 527 € per dentist treatment hour, while the worst 25% of practices (Q4) only reach 255 €. This makes the span of the values transparent.

Besides the systematic comparison of the more than 50 KPIs, the owner of the dental practice also receives a written report, which summarizes strengths, weaknesses and potentials of the practice. The report also states a list of concrete levers, which should be used by the practice in future to improve its economic situation. The report and the improvement levers are generated by a proprietary system that analyses the KPIs and their interdependencies and uses—besides other dynamic elements—a complex rule base.

2.3 *The Benefits of the Benchmarking Study for the Participant*

Benchmarking is a proven method, which leads to several core benefits for the participating dentist (Zahnarzt Wirtschaft Praxis 2009):

- Providing fact-based transparency of the economic situation of the dental practice from an external perspective.
- Identification of levers to improve the dental practice.
- Setting realistic objectives for the dental practice.
- Driving the implementation of improvement measures.

Many owners of a dental practice have been running their "business" for many years and have a gut feeling where the practice has strengths and weaknesses. But indeed, they appreciate the objective, fact-based view on the practice from an external perspective. On one hand, this provides additional confidentiality besides the gut feeling, on the other hand, in most cases unseen strengths and weaknesses are revealed and additional potentials are identified by the benchmarking procedure.

Thus, concrete levers with the biggest impact for the dental practice can be identified. The playing field for improvement levers is very large, e.g.

- increasing the number of new patients by optimizing the practice marketing activities,
- increasing the revenue per dentist treatment hour by optimizing internal processes in the practice,
- lowering the personnel costs by optimizing practice organization,
- improving work-life balance by delegating administrative tasks,
- increasing practice revenue and profit by raising the amount of patients, who get a professional tooth cleaning,
- and many, many more.

For most levers identified, the owner of the dental practice is able to set a realistic goal for the future—as he knows the current situation in his practice, but also has transparency of best practices in similar dental practices from the benchmarking study.

Thus, the owner can begin with the implementation of the measures. Benchmarking is a method that should be used on a regular and continuous basis to see the development of the levers over time (Tracy 2016). This means, the progress can be tracked, by taking part in the benchmarking procedure on a regular—yearly—basis.

In addition, the way the benchmarking study is conducted, BestPrax offers many advantages for the participants (BestPrax 2017):

- Conducting the benchmarking procedure in a secure way, the identity of the practice stays anonymous.
- Time-efficient way to conduct the benchmarking study.
- Cost-efficient way, as the base price for benchmarking starts at 469 € (net base price in 2017).
- The participating owner of the dental practice also receives 5 education credits. In Germany, each dentist is obliged to earn 125 education credits (so-called "Fortbildungspunkte") within every 5-year period—in average 25 education credits per year—by participating in special trainings to ensure that his knowledge stays state of the art.

3 The Business Model Automatic Benchmarking

3.1 The Revenue Model

The BestPrax business model clearly focuses on

- one core product—benchmarking,
- one clear target group—dentists with own practice and
- one defined region—Germany.

As there are more than 50,000 dental practices in Germany, the market potential seems to be attractive. The participation in the benchmarking study currently costs 469 € (net base price in 2017) for the practice. If the dentist decides to obtain more services, this price increases, e.g. for

- the "plus package" with support for entering the benchmarking data (849 €) or
- the "premium package" with the benefits of the "plus package" and additional consulting services: two longer consulting phone calls based on the results of the benchmarking study with a seasoned expert (2490 €).

Thus, by using the online platform, a professional benchmarking procedure for dental practices is available at an affordable price for the very first time. Moreover, additional professional consulting services can be booked on top (BestPrax 2017).

As benchmarking is a method, which should be used on a regular basis to see the development and adjust the measures and levers over time on a continuing basis (Tracy 2016), many dental practice owners have decided to take part in the benchmarking study year by year. This leads to a revenue stream, which is partly predictable from recurring customers, but of course, it is necessary to deal with a yearly churn rate in business planning and to gain new dental practices to ensure further revenue growth.

3.2 Marketing and the Consulting Ecosystem

To win and maintain dentists as customers, a broad range of marketing activities is required. It is a clear advantage, that the marketing activities can be focussed on a clearly defined target group: dentists with an own practice. For the acquisition of new customers, generating awareness and interest for the consulting product benchmarking is key. This can be done e.g. by

- public relations and press releases in dentist journals and magazines (print and online),
- paid ads in dentist journals and magazines (print and online),
- participation (booths) at special fairs and exhibitions for dentists,
- lectures at dentist conferences and meetings,
- joint marketing activities with dental societies (e.g. mailings, e-mailings),

Fig. 6 Benchmarking for dental practices explained in a video (©BestPrax)

- partnerships with tax advisors and practice consultants, who are specialized on dentists and use benchmarking as a value-adding product in their work and
- online marketing activities (Google search for relevant keywords).

The benchmarking product runs on a digital platform. This means that in the case that the interest of a dentist is gained, the prospective customer will most likely come across the website. On the website, comprehensive information about the approach, product and benefits for dentists have to be provided. In addition, to ensure a good conversion rate, a video in which benchmarking is explained, is prominently presented on the website. The video helps also to build trust and credibility, as the product and the digital consulting services get a "personal face" by the presentation of the Managing Director himself (Fig. 6).

In addition, activities to trigger the interest of customers who have participated in the last year—or in the years before—are necessary. A suitable measure to address these groups are e-mail campaigns to reactivate the existing customer base in order to ensure a high number of participating dental practices.

3.3 *Benefits for the Consulting Firm*

The automatic benchmarking procedure brings a proven method of business consulting to a customer group, which had only rare access to this method in the past. By doing this, BestPrax is addressing a new group of customers for real strategic consulting.

The advantages for the consultant are obvious: A scalable management consulting product is offered and the revenue scales with the number of benchmarking assignments. As the benchmarking report is mainly the result of algorithms and data processing, employee time doesn't limit the growth.

And if a customer wants to get additional services ("plus package", "premium package"), these standardized consulting offers can be performed and delivered by a consultant sitting in the BestPrax office using telecommunication infrastructure (telephone, skype, etc.)—without travelling times and expenses.

4 Summary and Outlook

The approach of bringing benchmarking, a proven method of management consulting, to the dental practices has attractive benefits for both, customers and the consulting company. The owner of a dental practice profits from the fact-based practice comparison and gets insight on how to improve the economic situation of his practice. The service is offered for a—compared to traditional consulting projects—low fix price. And furthermore, the consulting company BestPrax addresses a new group of customers with a highly scalable management consulting product.

The core business model reaches limitations, when it comes to a point where the owner of a dental practice understands the benchmarking results and the proposed levers, but has no idea how to implement the optimization measures and needs a more regular on-site project support. In this case, traditional consultants with a focus on dental practices can help. They can use the results of the benchmarking study and define concrete objectives, measures and an action plan.

Thus, there is clearly potential for the future development of the BestPrax business model. As the automatic benchmarking study is not limited to dental practices in Germany, the core product could be offered in other countries with a significant size. Also, the service could be extended to other medical practices, and maybe even beyond the medical sector. Service providers such as lawyers or tax advisors represent an interesting target group. Anyhow, besides understanding the new region or industry and setting up a suitable benchmarking methodology, it is always a substantial marketing challenge. Let's be curious, what the next business model extension will be—but, one thing is for sure: the market potential for this type of digital consulting service is clearly evident.

References

BestPrax (2017) Das BestPrax®-Benchmarking für Ihre Zahnarztpraxis. https://www.bestprax.de/. Accessed 01 Aug 2017

Ettorchi-Tardy A, Levif M, Michel P (2012) Benchmarking: a method for continuous quality improvement in health. https://www.ncbi.nlm.nih.gov/pmc/articles/PMC3359088/. Accessed 01 Aug 2017
Kassenzahnärztliche Bundesvereinigung (2016) Jahrbuch 2016: Statistische Basisdaten zur vertragszahnärztlichen Versorgung, Cologne, Zahnarzt Wirtschaft Praxis, pp 114–141
Tracy E (2016) Benchmarking a dental practice for success. http://www.oregondentalcpas.com/blog/featured-stories/benchmarking-a-dental-practice-for-success/. Accessed 01 Aug 2017
Zahnarzt Wirtschaft Praxis (2009) Wie Benchmarking Ihre Praxis besser macht, 6/2009, pp 24–25

Christian Stummeyer is holder of the chair "Business Informatics and Digital Commerce" at the Technical University of Ingolstadt, his focus areas in research and teaching are e-commerce and digital business models. After graduation in business (Diplom-Kaufmann), he earned a PhD (Dr. rer. pol.) in Business Informatics and started his career as Management Consultant at The Boston Consulting Group in Dusseldorf. He was member of the international management circle of SIEMENS AG in Munich and is a successful founder and e-commerce entrepreneur. Besides his role as professor, he acts as trusted advisor to large and medium-sized companies regarding digital strategy, e-commerce and digital transformation consulting.

Transformation of Consulting for Software-Defined Businesses: Lessons from a DevOps Case Study in a German IT Company

Rainer Alt, Gunnar Auth, and Christoph Kögler

Abstract Digital transformation is occurring across all industries and leads to the presence of information technology (IT) in business processes, products/services and business models. Consulting companies are important enablers in this transformation and contribute knowledge on the (re)design of strategies, processes and systems. At the same time, this involves a change in consulting itself, since the classical distinction of consulting sectors is increasingly blurring. To compete in digital innovation, consulting companies require IT knowledge, in particular, in the domain of software. In view of a growing "softwarization" of products and services, this chapter argues that consulting companies need to establish skills in efficiently providing software-based solutions. This represents an opportunity for traditional consulting companies, but also for traditional software companies to move towards consulting. Based on agile software engineering methodologies, this chapter conceives DevOps as a promising approach for linking customer requirements with software development and operation. A case study from the German IT company T-Systems Multimedia Solutions is used to formulate a more generic implementation model as well as experiences, which in turn contribute to enhancing the body of knowledge in the DevOps field.

R. Alt (✉)
Leipzig University, Leipzig, Germany
e-mail: rainer.alt@uni-leipzig.de

G. Auth
Hochschule für Telekommunikation Leipzig, Leipzig, Germany
e-mail: gunnar.auth@hft-leipzig.de

C. Kögler
T-Systems Multimedia Solutions GmbH, Dresden, Germany
e-mail: christoph.koegler@t-systems.com

V. Nissen (ed.), *Advances in Consulting Research*, Contributions to Management Science, https://doi.org/10.1007/978-3-319-95999-3_19

1 Consulting for Software-Defined Businesses

Supporting organizations in establishing, maintaining and improving their competitiveness is a key element of consulting companies. Over the years, the consulting market has grown from an estimated USD 205 billion in 2011 to USD 251 billion in 2016 with the main segments strategy, operations, financial advisory, human resources and technology (Consultancy.uk 2017). According to this source, the largest market segments are operations and financial advisory with 28% each, followed by technology with 20% of global market share and strategy as well as human resources with 12% each. This distinction of the consulting market is reflected in many projects, when organizations first mandate strategy consultants, then operational consultants and, finally, technology consultants to develop and to implement new solutions. Even in the technological field multiple consultants are often employed, for example, when an IT company is engaged in an implementation project where another consultant has previously conducted the selection of a business software product (Niehaves et al. 2006). While there is a rationale for contracting different consultants (e.g. higher specialization, reduced dependencies), the downside of engaging multiple specialized consultants and the increased importance of information technology (IT) became apparent in the observation of Iyer et al. (2006, p. 211), whereas "information technology and the hope and frustration of implementing IT has further fueled the growth in the management consulting industry. In recent times, consultants have moved away from the traditional role of just giving advice to actively participating in implementation of ideas and technology."

Today, IT is an inherent element of future solutions and cannot be regarded as something that requires attention only after the formulation of strategic and operational concepts. Within this digital transformation or this move to digitization (Nambisan et al. 2017), software plays a particularly important role. In his well-known statement from 2011, the co-author of the Mosaic webbrowser and the co-founder of Netscape, Marc Andreessen, has asserted that "software is eating the world" (Andreessen 2011). He recognized that IT is not limited to traditional information businesses, such as the publishing and media industries, but that software-related innovations have the power to change the products and processes of more or less all industries. In this process, most organizations are bound to be transformed towards software-defined businesses where existing business processes or entire value chains are profoundly changed or being replaced by new ones. This is reflected in the growth rate of the so-called "global software-defined anything market", which is estimated at 31% between 2016 and 2022, representing USD 28 billion in 2022 (Marketsandmarkets 2017). Examples may be found in the financial sector with the fintech innovations (Alt et al. 2018) as well as in the automotive sector with interconnected vehicles (car-to-car and car-to-infrastructure communication) and the networked production known as Industry 4.0. With its potential to change industry structures, the digital transformation means that every company is also bound to become a software company (Forşgren and Kersten 2018), but vice versa software companies, such as Google or Microsoft, also have the opportunity to penetrate many industries, e.g. the automotive and media industries.

This development implies changes for the established "consulting chain". In particular, creating new innovative IT-based solutions requires that consulting companies are not only able to translate technological potentials into strategies and operations, but that they also efficiently master the IT value chain. Thus, IT consultants are not only expected to act as passive service providers who receive the "business blueprint". Instead, they need to capitalize their technological skills and evolve to drivers of value creation using software-based business solutions (Krüger and Teuteberg 2016). The move towards software-defined businesses represents an opportunity for traditional companies to enter other fields of consulting since the ability to quickly provide early prototypes in the innovation process as well as to quickly develop and deploy reliable software releases is among their key competencies. While all consulting companies have an opportunity to position themselves as solution provider for software-defined businesses, the single-case study (Yin 2014) in section three suggests that IT companies with skills in software development and operation are in a position to also offer consulting services in the operations and partly even in the strategy field. The case presented below provides an in-depth view how this company has leveraged its skills in software development and IT operation using the DevOps approach. The design of this case study is based on two main research questions:

1. What are the potentials of DevOps in software-defined consulting projects?
2. What are the implications for transforming IT companies towards consulting via DevOps?

2 Transformation of a Software Company with DevOps

2.1 Idea and Emergence of DevOps

DevOps is a rather new concept that aims to leverage skills in the areas of software development and operations. It originates from the observation that for software developers, the responsibility for their deliverables tends to terminate with the user acceptance test and the release of the software for the operating environment.[1] The subsequent installation and configuration in the operating environment (deployment) is then the task of operations in the IT department. In many companies, software development and operations are not only functionally separated, but it was observed that both areas also work differently. Decoupled departmental thinking occurring in so-called silos was recognized as harmful to collaboration between development

[1] See, for example: Process Release & Deployment Management in ITIL (IT Infrastructure Library) or ISO/IEC 16350:2015 Application Management.

units and operations units in IT, as in the case of classical development units and production units in the manufacturing industry (Zarnekow et al. 2006).

While software engineering as well as IT management (ITM) have seen many improvements over the last decades, significant shortcomings remain. On the one hand, prototyping and agile approaches, such as Scrum, have reduced weaknesses of the traditional waterfall development model, but barriers to the IT departments, which are traditionally responsible for developing and operating IT services, still exist. On the other hand, IT service management (ITSM) methodologies, such as the IT Infrastructure Library (ITIL) recommend transition phases in terms of a handshake between development and operations, but there remains a fixed point where responsibility is handed over. As soon as development fails to adequately take care of the requirements of operations for a smooth launch, problems arise that may delay or hamper the deployment and thus lead to a negative user experience. Frequent problems are, for example, the delayed provision of releases by development, errors in the releases and/or the deployment, as well as missing or incorrect documentation, such as regarding the necessary installation steps or the operating environment (Disterer 2011).

DevOps has emerged as a collection of best practices and tools designed to counteract typical problems between development and operations teams, to improve collaboration between stakeholders, and, ultimately, to enhance end-user experience and customer satisfaction. At the same time, DevOps practices may also contribute to productivity (Brown et al. 2016) since they incorporate the approach of continuous software delivery (Humble and Farley 2011; Humble 2018), which is based on the model of a pull system for operations management in manufacturing, as known from just-in-time manufacturing (Slack et al. 1995). Willis (2010) has formulated four basic principles for DevOps, which have become widely known under the acronym CAMS (Humble and Molesky 2011; Lwakatare et al. 2015):

- *Culture* denotes a change towards a shared responsibility to deliver high quality software among all participants.
- *Automation* refers to establishing an automated chain of delivery from development, testing, implementation and operation.
- *Measurement* implies that all activities follow predefined objectives, which are controlled permanently and are linked towards improved business value.
- *Sharing* defines the collaboration between all participants and comprises the exchange of knowledge as well as the use of appropriate tools and infrastructures.

These principles illustrate the broad nature of the DevOps concept. On the one hand, it consists of general issues, such as culture and sharing, that determine the efficient collaboration among all parties involved, i.e. internal team members (consultants, developers, operators) as well as representatives from the customer organization. On the other hand, DevOps also stipulates specific infrastructural and project management issues, such as an integrated delivery pipeline consisting of specialized software development and management tools, and measurements along the software life cycle. This comprises coding, building, testing and a repeated deployment in different environments before the tested application is delivered or deployed into the operating environment (John et al. 2017). Where in the past, only specific team members could carry out the necessary steps manually, DevOps strives to automate the delivery pipeline as completely as possible, thereby creating reductions in time required and error rate.

2.2 Case Study T-Systems MMS

The use of DevOps in the context of innovative consulting projects will be shown in a case study from T-Systems Multimedia Solutions GmbH (T-Systems MMS). Founded in 1995, T-Systems MMS is a full service provider for digital transformation based in Dresden (Germany) and six national locations throughout Germany. As a fully owned subsidiary of T-Systems International GmbH, it is part of the Deutsche Telekom Group and offers services from strategy to solution for business customers. T-Systems MMS combines software and technology expertise in e-commerce, social business, marketing, big data, mobile solutions, retail and industry. In 2016, the company had an annual turnover of 154 million euros and employed more than 1500 people, who were particularly active in the fields of consulting, software development, testing and deployment as well as in service management for complex internet applications. As a classic IT service company, T-Systems MMS has been involved in digitization for a long time already, although this competence was earlier referred to as "web innovations" and "digital change". Today, digitization and digital transformation projects are the core of the company's value proposition, both internally and in collaboration with its customers. To develop its own consulting approach T-Systems MMS initiated a DevOps program, which explicitly aims to improve the company's offering in the area of innovative digital services. The case first illustrates the initial situation at T-Systems MMS and the motivation for the DevOps program, which is followed by a description of the use of DevOps in customer projects and of the infrastructure that has been established.

2.3 Initial Situation at T-Systems MMS

The introduction of DevOps at T-Systems MMS was primarily driven by customer requirements arising from digital transformation projects, namely mobility and agility as well as the timely availability of new services. Customers of T-Systems MMS are usually active in the B2C business segment, i.e. they offer services directly to the end customer via the internet, for example, in the form of mobile applications, shopping portals and self-service portals. Their goal is to sustain competitiveness against innovative incumbents and, especially, new competitors (e.g. start-up businesses, IT providers, such as Amazon, Google and the like). For this purpose, T-Systems MMS was increasingly not only faced with developing and operating software solutions, but also became involved in consulting projects that included the discussion of strategic potentials and the (re)design of operational processes. Besides enhancing the consulting portfolio and improving the skills in innovative strategic

Table 1 Departments of CU BT & E at T-Systems MMS

Department	Responsibilities
IT service delivery	• Operations, maintenance and enhancement of servers (physical, virtual), databases, storage and network infrastructure • Root cause analysis of problems as well as problem solving, identification and prevention • Support for planning, designing and implementing internal IT systems within project teams • Operation of central development-supporting applications for the realization of customer value within the R2S process cluster
Office services	• Service desk, clients, reception, system and telecommunication technology, facility management • Flexible working environment, in particular room concept, workplaces, buildings, technology and services as well as space management strategy and optimization of floor utilization • Operation and administration of basic infrastructure as well as provisioning of meeting and conference rooms
Process improvement and excellence	• Process and quality management, in particular, management systems, processes, audits, assessments and certifications • Customer, service and program management, project planning and improvement of internal processes, services and applications • Information security, data protection and compliance

and operational solutions, the goal was also to link these with an integrated development and operation environment. For this purpose, T-Systems MMS set up a dedicated DevOps project initiative. An important driver of this program was the T-Systems MMS' corporate unit "Business Technology and Excellence" (CU BT & E), which is the internal IT department of T-Systems MMS with three (sub)departments (see Table 1).

In recent years, CU BT & E already underwent the transition from an internal service provider to an internal innovation driver. Among the previous projects was the digitization of internal processes, which has not only improved their speed and quality, but which has also enabled the broad adoption of mobile and location-independent work—both being important for supporting the core processes of many consulting companies. At T-Systems MMS, these core processes were formulated in five clusters comprising cross-sectoral collaboration, close cooperation with customers, agile change management as well as consulting along the entire development process (R2S in Fig. 1). For quality reasons, various certifications have been achieved that range from information security through software development to IT service management and the test and integration center. In addition, the ITSM standard ITIL is used both in the internal IT department and in consulting projects that involve the operation of web applications.

Within the DevOps program, T-Systems aimed to create an environment that enabled the support along the entire software life cycle. It should also allow providing consulting for increasingly fundamental as well as evolutionary developments of the products and services taking place in close collaboration with customers. This meant that in addition to ensuring the stable operation of current

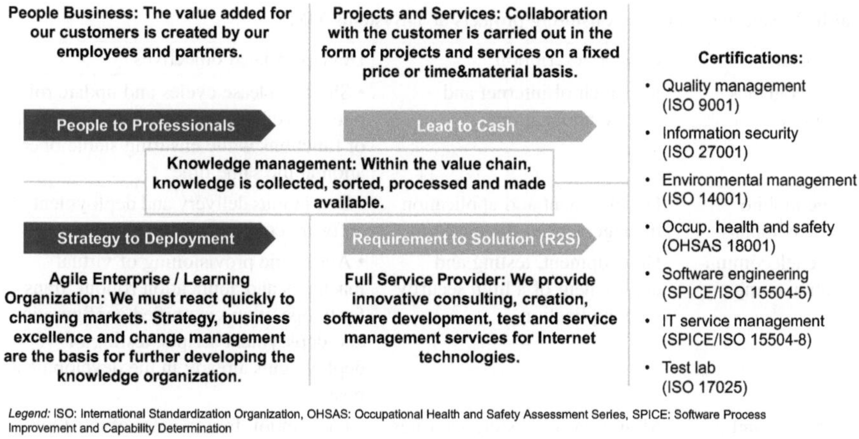

Fig. 1 Core business process clusters of T-Systems MMS

versions, the ability to detect errors early and to quickly eliminate them in ongoing developments was important. Traditional product development and release cycles have shown deficits in guaranteeing this speed, especially in the light of new infrastructure concepts such as cloud, virtualization, containerization, infrastructure as code (Spinellis 2012) and automation tools for continuous delivery and deployment (Chen 2017).[2] This included to:

- align the tools that were already in place for software development. For example, T-Systems MMS has been using agile approaches for some time in software development, testing and operation. However, these different tools and frameworks were used independently and were not part of an overall delivery pipeline.
- enhance the ideas of ITIL, which formulates guidelines for supporting the service life cycle. However, ITIL is focused at the certification of individuals and not organizations. In addition, DevOps should also be applicable not only for IT services, but also for IT-based business services in consulting with customers.
- initiate a transformation program for the entire enterprise. According to the CAMS principles, the DevOps program was a corporate effort, which comprised cultural as well as infrastructural issues. Compared to previous agile and ITIL approaches the DevOps program was more comprehensive.
- establish competencies for supporting customers in the generation of innovative solutions. For this purpose, the design thinking methodology was adopted in multiple consulting projects.

[2]Infrastructure as Code (IaC) applies to software scripts, which aim at achieving a rule-based automation of the configuration of virtual and physical infrastructure components, such as servers.

Table 2 Selected DevOps consulting projects at T-Systems MMS

Customer	Project description	DevOps-related objectives
Large logistics company	Relaunch of internet and mobile applications	• Shorter release cycles and update roll-outs as well as continuous development of functions while ensuring stable operation at the same time
Large mobile phone company	Development and application management of the platform	• Continuous delivery and deployment of software components
Large telecommunication company	Development, testing and deployment of a high security web application	• Automatic provisioning of virtual machines and application rollout, transfer to operation via unified configuration and deployment scripts, testing of deployments already in the development phase
Global oil and gas company	Migration of existing websites into a new business environment	• Interruption-free transfer of existing websites into new operating environment • Service availability of 99.9% • Deployment management with monthly releases • Comprehensive testing and quality management • Service-oriented service monitoring and reporting
Large system supplier in material management	Replacement and rebuilding of a complex e-commerce solution	• High availability and scalability of the solution

2.4 *DevOps in Customer Projects*

T-Systems MMS has applied DevOps principles in more than 20 consulting projects. As shown in the five selected customer projects in Table 2, these projects involved the (re)design of business applications, which were developed in DevOps teams consisting of representatives of customer(s), business consultants, developers as well as experts from IT operation. All projects used the delivery pipeline that allowed scalable development, testing and operation processes on different cloud platforms based on preconfigured scripts. In the case of software development, the current state was automatically compiled into a deliverable artifact via a standardized build process and tested automatically in the subsequent step. Unit tests, automated technical, regression and security tests, as well as technical quality tests ensured the fulfilment of all existing and newly added functional and non-functional requirements. Finally, if the user acceptance tests were completed successfully, the software could be installed automatically "at the push of a button" and within minutes on the test or real operating environments.

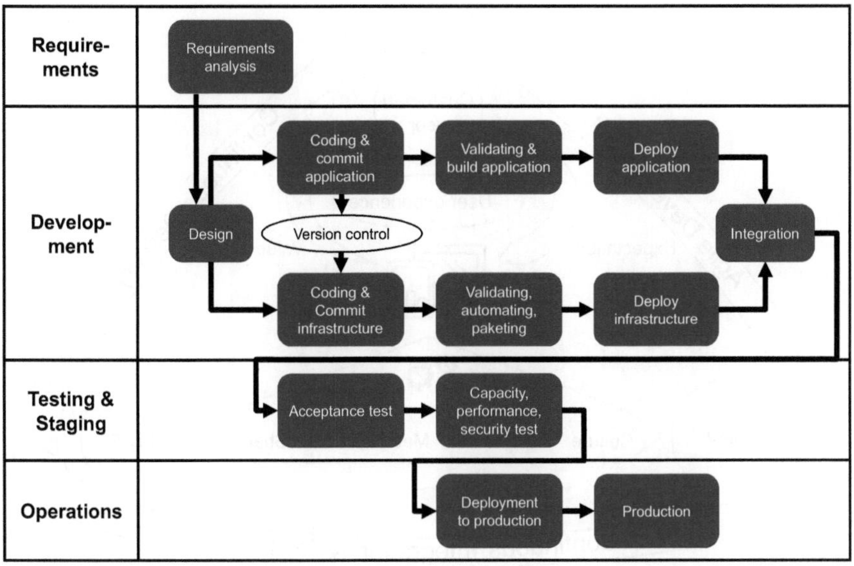

Fig. 2 Delivery pipeline of T-Systems MMS

2.5 *IT Infrastructure for DevOps*

The technological infrastructure for DevOps comprises a three-layer architecture. The basic layer consists of various internal and external cloud platforms and products for supporting the infrastructure operation. The specific automation logic for DevOps is included in the middle architecture layer. It manages all automation scripts, rules and tools for the individually implemented, continuous process chaining in a central repository and makes it available to all DevOps employees. The top layer provides services to support software development, testing, and operations, with the operation being primarily based on service level agreements (SLA). This is embedeed in an overarching architecture, which together with quality assurance as well as documentation ensures the continuous development of the architectural layers. Figure 2 depicts the MMS delivery pipeline implemented in the middle architectural layer along the DevOps phases used in the process cluster "Requirements to Solutions" (R2S) (see Fig. 1). For the automation of the delivery pipeline, T-Systems MMS has developed its own DevOps framework, which provides the required services and their components according to the infrastructure as code principle.

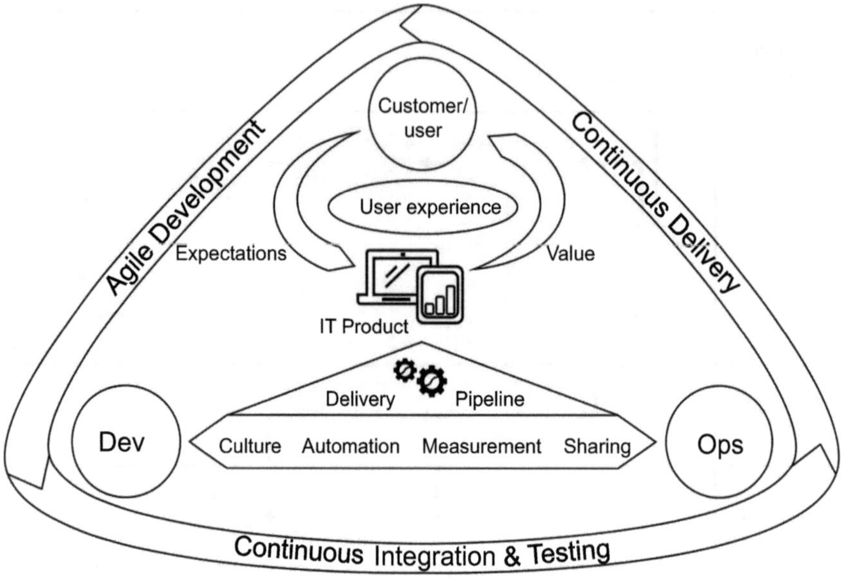

Fig. 3 Enhanced DevOps framework

3 Learnings from the Transformation Using DevOps

The case showed that DevOps had a dual role at T-Systems MMS. First, DevOps was used to move the software and IT provider more towards consulting. Second, the experiences obtained from the internal transformation were also applied in consulting projects with customers. The following summarizes these learnings regarding the main areas of change, the process model applied in the transformation project and the challenges that were observed.

3.1 Dimensions of the Transformation

For a software and IT company, DevOps may be understood as a missing link between agile development on the one hand and high-frequency service delivery during ongoing operations on the other. This should result in customer-oriented end-to-end processes with increased innovation cycles, which in turn are linked with reliable business continuity. The introduction of DevOps was also expected to lead to a transformation towards consulting since a positive user experience on the customer side represented the ultimate goal of applying DevOps. Thus the first observation on transformation recognized DevOps not only as a combination of "development" and "operation", but also included the "customer". Figure 3 shows this enhanced DevOps framework, which links the three core participants via a continuous delivery, development as well as integration and testing process. The delivery pipeline designed along the DevOps principles is the basis for quickly creating software prototypes, products and services that are needed in software-defined consulting projects.

Since the concepts of continuous integration, testing and delivery originate from the domain of software engineering, it might suggest that DevOps is only primarily applicable for technology consultants. However, the case study also suggests a link to the concept of continuous innovation (CI) (Ries 2011). By integrating and developing the various "continuous concepts" along an agile development process, DevOps creates the prerequisites for continuous innovation in a software-based product context (Fitzgerald and Stol 2017). CI points at a more comprehensive implementation of DevOps principles as part of a digital transformation strategy focused on innovation. Similar to design thinking, CI conceives an iterative value creation approach where the creation of innovative digital solutions also implies an early availability of software prototypes. Ideally, these minimal viable products (MVP) already offer sufficient benefit to convince (potential) customers to mandate the full concept to the consulting company. MVPs are known to follow the small batches principle (Limoncelli 2016) and to be continuously enhanced in minute steps, each development progress being delivered directly to the customer. In this process, CI is linked to the delivery pipeline, which includes the close collaboration among customers, consultants and/or developers. It follows the observation from companies, such as Etsy or Netflix, which could identify and eliminate errors earlier and more easily than with large-scale releases in large time intervals (Denning 2015). In addition, the high degree of control over these small product adaptations is believed to increase the resilience of the overall system. New features may also be implemented in an experimental way without explicit customer requirements in order to test promising ideas directly with the customer. The control capability also includes the possibility to reverse changes "at the push of a button", if they do fail to prove beneficial. From the point of view of the four CAMS principles, the transformation at T-Systems MMS revealed:

- In the *culture* dimension, cross-departmental collaboration as well as stronger involvement of the customer in the development work was a central feature of the DevOps program. The basis was a cultural change in the organizational areas involved, which should motivate all stakeholders to assume greater responsibility for the product and customer needs.
- The *automation* and *measurement* dimensions were closely interrelated, as not only process support, but also system-based measurement (Forsgren and Kersten 2018) by time stamps and automated quality tests has improved with the continuous pipeline support through several development tools. Overall, DevOps had positively affected the ratio of agility and speed of delivery in projects while ensuring reliability. This was reflected, for example, in the reduced lead-time for the successful launch of new releases, which has decreased from several months to a few days or even hours in DevOps mode. It resulted in cost savings of up to 75% for customers, as parallel development and test environments were

necessary for shorter periods than before. In conjunction with the other DevOps measures, automation has increased the customer's speed of innovation and, in particular, has accelerated the start of operation for new innovative developments. It was emphasized that customers as well as the internal ITM should be enabled to test, learn and further improve their innovations in practice by shortened periods for project setup, development and start of operation. Both statements from customers as well as involved T-Systems MMS employees confirmed the achievement of this goal.

- In the *sharing* dimension, conflicts between the development department as well as between the service managers and administrators prior to the introduction of DevOps should be addressed. Often, quality assurance had to ensure that no major problems could arise in this mixture of conflicting objectives. With the introduction of DevOps, it was possible to reduce the target conflicts by considering the essential operating requirements (e.g. security, load distribution, logging, monitoring) early on during agile development. The DevOps introduction may also be regarded as a change management process since the tasks included the development and implementation of a communication strategy to provide as much information as possible about the new approach without overburdening employees. Among the communication tools used were expectancy queries as well as events, such as the internal MMS DevDays event, and self-produced video clips.

3.2 DevOps Transformation Process

The internal implementation of DevOps at T-Systems MMS was considered a long-term program that should be constantly enhanced from internal as well from external consulting feedback. It should thus be considered a strategic investment by management and an opportunity for the internal IT departments to assume an active role in this transformation. At T-Systems MMS, the implementation of the CAMS principles was operationalized in seven transformation tasks (see Table 3). Referred to as value packages (Foegen et al. 2007), each task denotes small, self-contained improvements, which aim to realize a specific benefit in the current daily business and shall prevent that employees are overburdened. The procedure follows the observation (e.g. in ITIL) that incremental improvements are conducive to creating a positive feedback.

Since T-Systems MMS had a long tradition of applying Scrum in its software development process, it was obvious to design an agile process model also for DevOps. The perspective on customer value in Scrum matched the company's appreciation of its own employees, who were considered as customers of the DevOps@MMS program. In the first place, the value packages were designed from the point of view of employees, especially in development and operations. For implementing the program, a matrix organization consisting of a core team of six full-time people with five roles (program manager, senior experts, DevOps architect,

Table 3 Transformation tasks for introducing DevOps@MMS

Transformation task	Description
1. Collaboration model	• Definition of vision, roles, responsibilities, processes and terminology • Common understanding of the impact of DevOps on IT
2. Integrated task management	• Development of an integrated management system for holistic management of tasks, bugs, incidents, changes and problems • Unified processes and tools for development, testing and operation
3. Continuous delivery	• Process design and alignment to enable continuous software delivery, including configuration management, continuous integration, testing and deployment • Agility from development (Dev) via test to operations (Ops)
4. People empowerment	• Identification and realization of necessary training (e.g. with regard to technical innovations) • Investment in employees, cooperation models, new tools, curiosity and innovation
5. Infrastructure provisioning	• Selection, implementation and development of tools • Identification of the smallest common multipliers for standardization • Definition of software-defined infrastructure and integrated platform services
6. Pipeline automation	• Selection, implementation and development of tools • Standardized automatic setup, technical testing and delivery • Compiling, building and deploying of software at any time
7. Organizational implementation	• Defining organizational structures, roles and rules of the game • Transfer of knowledge between Ops and Dev

change manager, quality manager) was created. In addition, about 90 experts from the line organization participated in the work streams. The fact that a member of the board was heading the program's steering committee reflects the support of top management. At the beginning of the program, a process model was designed that combines a waterfall-like phase-oriented frame with agile sprints (see Fig. 4). The DevOps@MMS process model may thus be considered a hybrid of plan-driven and agile approaches. Each value package passes through six sequential phases and after each phase the steering committee decides on the approval for the next phase:

- *Initiation:* An extended kick-off for each value package is conducted, which comprises core team members, other team members and stakeholders from business units. In the consulting projects, representatives from the customer side are participating from the beginning.
- *Planning:* After the steering committee has approved the start for the value package, the planning phase starts with the first sprint. Among the activities are a requirements, a stakeholder and a risk analysis as well as a definition of the scope for the value packages. The solution is formulated with clear acceptance criteria.
- *Prototyping:* After the planning phase, the prototyping phase aims to implement, document and review the solution. Key performance indicators are defined and approved by the steering committee.

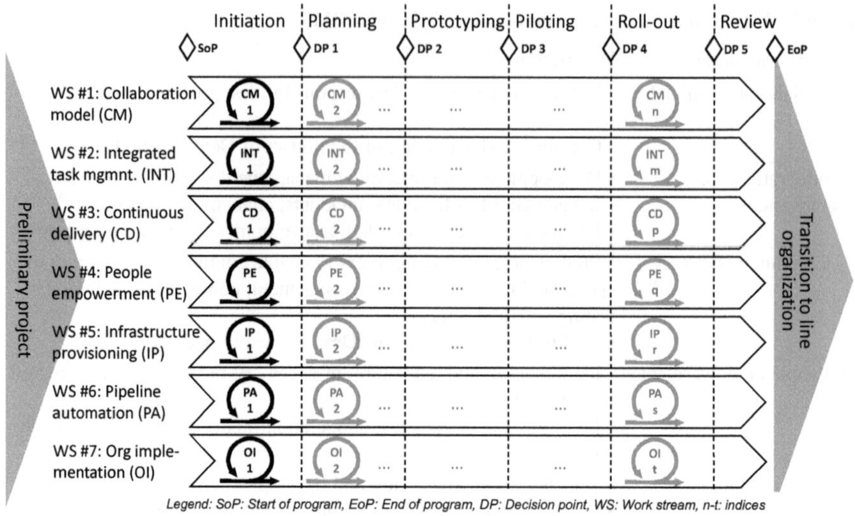

Fig. 4 Hybrid process model for implementing DevOps

- *Piloting:* Following prototyping, the developed solution is piloted in selected projects. It is examined whether the solution can be implemented broadly and whether quality-relevant effects need to be considered.
- *Roll-out:* After validation in the pilot system, the company-wide roll-out starts. The solution is either implemented as binding or recommended as best practice. If training measures are required for users, they are planned and implemented.
- *Review:* The aim of the review phase is to ensure that deviations are identified, analyzed and correction or improvements are implemented.

Following the hybrid model, all activities regarding a certain value package are integrated into a work stream for this package. Each work stream consists of agile sprints according to Scrum with a time box of four weeks. The number of sprints in each phase depends on the work load for implementing the respective value package. The Scrum roles are then performed as follows: the steering committee acts as product owner, a member of the core team as Scrum master and other team members as development team. Since the program is designed as a temporary structure, it terminates with the transition of all its results into the line organization.

3.3 Challenges in Implementation and Lessons Learned

During the introduction of DevOps at T-Systems MMS and the accompanying transformation towards a software-consulting company, multiple challenges were observed. First, obtaining knowledge on the DevOps approach was difficult due to the early development stage of DevOps. In view of the lack of trainings, certification

Table 4 Learnings from DevOps case study

DevOps principle	Success factors from case study
Culture	• Integrated end-to-end view on the software process and close involvement of the customer • Top management support • Setting up a dedicated DevOps project organization • Focus on value packages • Interaction-oriented workspace concepts
Automation	• Development of an automation architecture • Definition of delivery pipeline services with SLAs • Design of a delivery pipeline for automation logic • Link of internal and external cloud platforms as foundation
Measurement	• Formulation of transparent requirements to avoid measurement conflicts • Definition and measurement of DevOps metrics • Design of project-specific DevOps stacks • Use of tools for measurement and visualization
Sharing	• Establishing of skills among the employees • Transfer of knowledge between internal and external projects • Cooperation with external experts • Definition of an integrated change management process
Overall	• Digitization of administrative and support processes • Definition of process areas and targets • Certifications in the fields of development and operation

or literature on DevOps in German, primary sources of information were limited to internet resources (e.g. presentations, conference and blog contributions) as well as publications by analysts. In addition, the context of a large corporation enabled the search for colleagues with DevOps experience in other areas as well as the identification of internal best practices in the collaboration with external experts.

The second challenge was the high-level nature of the DevOps principles. Since reference artifacts and integrated continuous development tools were not available, the DevOps projects represented individual configurations of existing innovation and software development tools. Establishing an aligned tool portfolio ("DevOps stack") was recognized as an important next step for leveraging DevOps in consulting projects.

Third, the complexity of parallel development, test and deployment cycles made it difficult to obtain an overview of all improvements. To address this challenge, T-Systems MMS has initiated a DevOps dashboard for its customers, which was intended to graphically visualize all releases throughout the entire process chain (i.e. from technical requirements to regular operations), to adapt itself automatically to end devices (e.g. laptops, browsers, tablets or smartphones) and to be configurable for different user groups. In the future, providers and customers could create different views on the relevant phases in the DevOps process chain.

Finally, learnings may be formulated from the factors that positively affected the implementation of DevOps at T-Systems MMS along the CAMS principles (see Table 4). They show requirements that are important for the transformation towards more consulting, i.e. customer interaction. These consulting projects should feature some prerequisites for applying DevOps. With short cycles, which are typical for mobile apps, shop portals, customer self-care portals or new digital and fast-changing business models, investments in DevOps are expected to pay off more quickly. For example, in the app stores of major vendors, such as Apple and Google, release cycles from a few days to a maximum of weeks are the rule, and apps that are not updated in this frequency, are quickly considered obsolete and less valuable according to T-Systems MMS customers. In this environment, the benefits of a DevOps environment should be higher than in the case of the classic enterprise software, which typically features longer release cycles.

4 Conclusions

This chapter has described how a software and IT company has used the opportunity of software-defined business to move into consulting. The development is driven by digitization, which is spreading across all industries and forces businesses to adopt innovative business models, products and processes more quickly than ever before. By reducing the entry barriers in many industries and by changing customer requirements towards quick and reliable solutions, the established specialization in the consulting industry is bound to change. With software at its core, digital transformation initiatives depend heavily on a deep understanding of how to design and implement customer value-oriented software life cycle processes. For software companies, this not only implies to leverage competences and resources of all relevant internal departments, but especially to establish the ability to quickly (further) develop products and services.

DevOps has been characterized as a young and promising approach to tackle the transformation towards more consulting for a software and IT company. It enhances existing agile methodologies to create environments where participants from various internal and external departments—including the customer organization—collaborate. The case study showed that DevOps is strategic in nature and that it links the development of IT solutions, which are often innovative in nature, with their operation. Since DevOps is rather a philosophy than an elaborated methodology, each company is required to develop an individual adaptation until standardized process models, templates and comprehensive tools become available (Roche 2013). Since research and certifications on DevOps are still emerging, offering DevOps skills for other software companies could be another business segment for consulting. For these software and IT companies the transformation will not occur "overnight". A DevOps program requires long-term preparation and should be embedded in the entire organization. This understanding as a comprehensive organizational change, the implementation as a strategic program and the early involvement of internal and external partners were important success factors for the introduction of DevOps at T-Systems MMS. Especially an aligned and flexibly adaptable delivery pipeline is important for a sustainable competitive advantage. A development similar to the diffusion of agile methodologies may be expected, which were regarded as pure software engineering approaches in the beginning.

In summary, the single-case study presented in this research was helpful to answer the two research questions. First, DevOps may be considered an approach that contributes to implementing innovation for software-defined business environments, which sustains the transformation towards more consulting. It involves methodologies from innovation management that aim at creating innovative solutions by providing quick prototypes and also allows to develop and to deploy software releases that use new technologies more efficiently. The projects conducted in the case company confirmed this for new mobile and web applications. Second, the case shows that (IT) consulting companies need to transform themselves for DevOps. The learnings observed along the four CAMS principles illustrate that substantial change is required regarding culture, organization and infrastructure. From a process viewpoint, the concept of value packages was suggested and combined with an established process model from agile development. While the case study shed light into more details of the still high-level DevOps methodology, the single-case research clearly has limitations. This applies to investigating DevOps implementations in other consulting organizations, to analyzing the costs and benefits of DevOps more quantitatively as well as to derive architectural configurations of the DevOps tool stack. Ultimately, this may create a competitive advantage for IT companies in the consulting market.

References

Andreessen M (2011) Software is eating the world. Wall Street Journal (20 Aug 2011). http://www.wsj.com/articles/SB10001424053111903480904576512250915629460. Accessed 24 Feb 2017

Alt R, Beck R, Smits M (2018) FinTech and the transformation of the financial industry. Electron Mark 28(3). https://doi.org/10.1007/s12525-018-0310-9

Brown A, Forsgren N, Humble J, Kersten N, Kim G (2016) 2016 State of DevOps report. Puppet and DORA. https://puppet.com/resources/whitepaper/2016-state-of-devops-report. Accessed 10 May 2017

Chen L (2017) Continuous delivery: overcoming adoption challenges. J Syst Softw 128:72–86

Consultancy.uk (2017) Consulting industry – global. http://www.consultancy.uk/consulting-industry/global. Accessed 13 Aug 2017

Denning S (2015) New lessons for leaders about continuous innovation. Strateg Leadersh 43(1): 11–15

Disterer G (2011) ITIL-basierte Inbetriebnahme neuer Anwendungen. HMD – Praxis der Wirtschaftsinformatik 48(2):48–57

Fitzgerald B, Stol K-J (2017) Continuous software engineering: a roadmap and agenda. J Syst Softw 123(1):176–189

Foegen M, Solbach M, Raak C (2007) Der Weg zur professionellen IT – Eine praktische Anleitung für das Management von Veränderungen mit CMMI, ITIL oder SPICE. Springer, Berlin

Forsgren N, Kersten M (2018) DevOps metrics. Commun ACM 61(4):44–48

Humble J, Farley D (2011) Continuous delivery. Addison-Wesley, Upper Saddle River, NJ

Humble J, Molesky J (2011) Why enterprises must adopt DevOps to enable continuous delivery. Cutter IT J 24(8):6–12

Humble J (2018) Continuous delivery sounds great, but will it work here? Commun ACM 61(4): 34–39

Iyer G, Ravindran S, Reckers PMJ (2006) Procurement of IT consulting services and firm-specific characteristics. J Assoc Inf Syst 7(4):207–240
John W, Marchetto G, Nemeth F, Skoldstrom P, Steinert R, Meirosu C, Papafili I, Pentikousis K (2017) Service provider DevOps. IEEE Commun Mag 55(1):204–211
Krüger N, Teuteberg F (2016) IT consultants as change agents in digital transformation initiatives. In: Nissen, V et al. (eds) Proceedigs of Multikonferenz Wirtschaftsinformatik (MKWI) 2016, pp 1019–1030
Limoncelli TA (2016) The small batches principle. Commun ACM 59(7):52–57
Lwakatare L, Kuvaja P, Oivo M (2015) Dimensions of DevOps. In: Lassenius C et al. (eds) XP 2015, LNBIP 212, pp 212–217
Marketsandmarkets (2017) Software-defined anything market by technology (SDN, SDDC, & SDS), service (integration & deployment, consulting, managed services), deployment mode (cloud & on premise), vertical, and region – global forecast to 2022. http://www.marketsandmarkets.com/Market-Reports/software-defined-anything-market-19947525.html. Accessed 27 Aug 2017
Nambisan S, Lyytinen K, Majchrzak A, Song M (2017) Digital innovation management: reinventing innovation management research in a digital world. MIS Q 41(1):223–238
Niehaves B, Klose K, Becker J (2006) Governance theory perspectives on IT consulting projects: the case of ERP. e-Serv J 5(1):5–26
Ries E (2011) The Lean Startup: how today's entrepreneurs use continuous innovation to create radically successful businesses. Crown Business, New York
Roche J (2013) Adopting DevOps practices in quality assurance. Commun ACM 56(11):38–43
Slack N, Chambers S, Harland C, Harrison A, Johnston R (1995) Operations management. Pitman Publishing, London
Spinellis D (2012) Don't install software by hand. IEEE Softw, July/August 2012, pp 86–87
Willis J (2010) What Devops means to me. https://blog.chef.io/2010/07/16/what-devops-means-to-me/. Accessed 28 Dec 2016
Yin RK (2014) Case study research – design and methods, 5th edn. Sage, Los Angeles
Zarnekow R, Brenner W, Pilgram U (2006) Integrated information management – applying successful industrial concepts in IT. Springer, Berlin

Rainer Alt is a full professor for Business Information Systems at Leipzig University, Germany. He earned a master's degree in business administration from the University of Erlangen-Nuremberg, Germany, and received a Ph.D. as well as a postdoctoral degree (habilitation) from the University of St. Gallen, Switzerland. Before assuming his current position, he was a visiting researcher at the University of California, Irvine, a senior consultant at Roland Berger in Germany, and an assistant professor at the University of St. Gallen. His research focuses on interorganizational information systems and methodologies for business innovation.

Gunnar Auth is a full professor for Business Information Systems at Leipzig University of Applied Telecommunications, Germany. He completed his master's degree in business information systems at the University of Bamberg, Germany, and received a Ph.D. from the University of St. Gallen, Switzerland. He started his professional career as an internal consultant at DaimlerChrysler where he worked in several management positions in logistics, operations and quality management. Before assuming his current position, he was IT director and representative of the CIO board at Leipzig University. His research focuses on IT project management, IT service management and information management.

Christoph Kögler heads the Innovation Department at T-Systems Multimedia Solutions GmbH, one of the leading European Internet solution providers. He has more than two decades of leadership and project management experience in multimedia, telecommunications and media industries, most of the time primarily in the areas of business development and innovation management. Christoph is certified as a Project Management Professional® and as trainer of SRI Internationals Five Disciplines of Innovation® program. As a recognized expert in the topic of innovation management, he coaches start-ups and intrapeneurs and is a regular speaker at national and international conferences.

Robo-Advisory: Opportunities and Risks for the Future of Financial Advisory

Dominik Jung, Florian Glaser, and Willi Köpplin

Abstract Without professional advisors, taking financial risks is a challenging task for most private households (retail investors). Across countries, digital financial advisory services, in particularly robo-advisors, are becoming more popular in retail and private banking. These tools support their users in financial decision-making, like risk-measurement, portfolio selection, or rebalancing. Recent studies suggest that in the long-term, they could supplement human financial advisory. This work illustrates the key concepts of this (r)evolution, and discusses strengths, weaknesses, opportunities and risks of robo-advisory. The results suggest that robo-advisors have a huge potential to shape the future of the financial advisory industry, despite the fact that there is still a lot of potential yet to be exploited.

1 The Rise of Robo-Advisory

In order to assess the status quo of the digital transformation in the German consulting market, demand and usage of digital services in nearly all parts of consumers' lives keeps increasing—including banking activities such as online debit accounts and online payments, which are the norm rather than the exception now (Praeg et al. 2015, 2016). As part of progressive digitalization, growing e-commerce business and the new opportunities introduced by algorithmic trading, so called robo-advisors entered the market, providing a fully automated investment experience for a large range of potential customers (Jung et al. 2017, 2018a; Sironi 2016). These digital advisors do not only create and invest into a portfolio, shaped by the individual risk preference of the investor, but also manage the portfolio afterwards, being aware of market changes and changes of asset characteristics, and prevent biased financial decision-making (Jung et al. 2018b). This seems to make it a

D. Jung (✉) · F. Glaser · W. Köpplin
Karlsruhe Institute of Technology (KIT), Karlsruhe, Germany
e-mail: d.jung@kit.edu; florian.glaser@kit.edu

V. Nissen (ed.), *Advances in Consulting Research*, Contributions to Management Science, https://doi.org/10.1007/978-3-319-95999-3_20

potential substitute for the use of personal advisors, not least because it may shrink management fees from 0.89 to 0% as analysed in the U.S. (Schapiro 2017). In addition, it makes advisory services accessible to not only wealthy clients but also investors with lower investable amounts.

The potential of the robo-advisory concept, as seen by venture capitalists and other investors, is huge. For example, in 2015 venture capitalists invested approximately $300 million in the business, believing in the disruptive potential they obtain (Wong 2015). Furthermore, some forecasts even see robo-advisory adding up to over 10% of the whole wealth management industry in 2020 as Kocianski (2016) states. These statements and the fact that digitalization still is one of the most recent trends, makes it interesting to investigate the concept of robo-advisory by examining its key characteristics and discussing the future potential for advisory and consulting research.

Therefore, we formulate the following research question:

RQ1 *How can robo-advisors shape the financial advisory industry, what are harmful and what are helpful factors?*

The remainder of the paper is structured as follows: In Sect. 2, we give an overview considering the term "robo-advisory", addressing the historical development of financial advisory, and the key functionalities of robo-advisors. The subsequent chapter is concerned with evaluation of the robo-advisory concept, employing a strategic analysis on strengths, weaknesses, opportunities and threats of the business, followed by a conclusion.

2 State-of-the-Art of Financial Advisory

The financial advisory industry is facing a major change in their traditional advisory business. New, innovative participants joined their business in recent years, driven by the continuing development of information technology, as well as the need to bring transparency and accessibility into the long-time established traditional wealth management. In the subsequent sections of this chapter, we outline how financial advisory has changed over the past decades, and investigate the concept of robo-advisory. In particular, we analyse general functionalities and characteristics, differences and peculiarities in comparison to established advisory setups, as well as recent market developments concerning the financial advisory industry.

2.1 Financial Advisory

The main purpose of the financial advisory industry is to help individuals or institutions to make proper investments, meeting individual investment goals of investors considering long or short term investment horizons. This definition goes hand in hand with the definition of investment advice. As stated in the European MiFID, investment advice represents "the provision of personal recommendations to

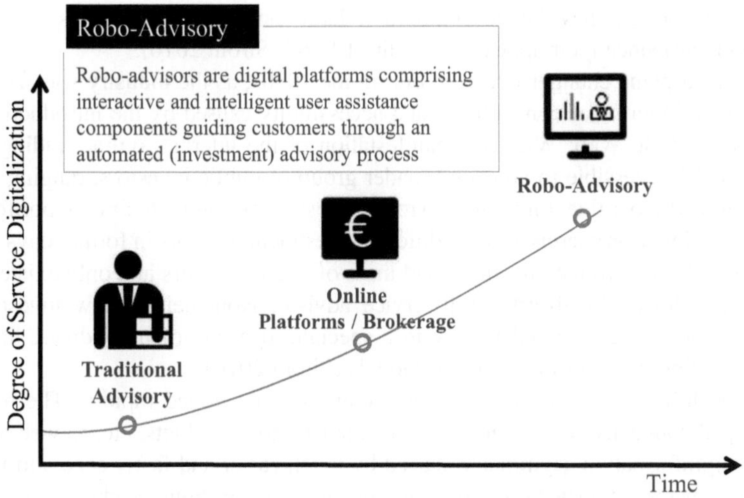

Fig. 1 The digitalization of financial advisory services towards digital platform (Jung et al. 2018a; Sironi 2016).

a client, either upon its request or at the initiative of the investment firm, in respect of one or more transactions relating to financial instruments" (Cocca 2016 p. 47).[1]

Traditionally, only very affluent investors enjoyed the experience of individual investment advice, not least because of the exorbitant fees commonly charged for this kind of advice. Nevertheless, the market for financial advisory is changing constantly and recently opened for low-budget investors (Jung et al. 2017). During the past decades certain events are likely to have triggered those changes, as illustrated in Fig. 1. In the US, which can be considered the main market for financial advisory, the very beginning as it is known today took place in the 1950s. Personal financial advice and wealth management in general were exclusive and highly expensive services targeting so called ultra-high net worth individuals (having a net worth higher than $30 million in 1950) as the only potential investors who could afford personal advice, usually represented by rich families (Sironi 2016).

A major change regarding accessibility of financial services took place in the 1970s as financial advisories opened to the US middle class by introducing discount brokers. Discount brokers are cheaper than traditional financial advisors, as they do not provide real investment advice, but simply execute buy and sell orders at a reduced commission. This was revolutionary, as the stock market was now accessible to a much broader range of potential investors. Discount brokers still play an

[1]The Markets in Financial Instruments Directive (MiFID) is a regulation set up by the EU seeking to improve the competitiveness of EU financial markets, by creating a single market for investment services and activities, and to ensure a high degree of harmonized protection for investors in financial instruments (European Securities and Markets Authority 2007).

important role as they "have acquired a large portion of AUM (assets under management) since their appearance in the 1970s" (Sironi 2016).

The next game changer occurred during the 1990s, as the industry was facing a big change in terms of connectivity and accessibility caused by the introduction of the World Wide Web. With the manifestation of the internet, online trading was theoretically accessible to an even broader group of public investors, ranging from high net worth to affluent investors to retail investors managing their own portfolios. Human dialogue as exercised by traditional investment advisors in former days, now seemed to be subordinate for the broad mass of retail investors and only existed for investors who could afford a full-service advisor. Nonetheless, new investment opportunities were confined mostly to a specialized group of individuals, limited to those being trading-orientated individuals (Sironi 2016).

In the following years, information technology developed rapidly. The highly developed connectivity through computers, smartphones, tablets, etc. as well as the declining information asymmetry caused by much easier and faster access to information, lowered transaction costs significantly. Algorithmic trading (so called AlgoTrading) emerged, representing fully automated investment vehicles and providing new opportunities to potential investors. Nowadays, not only technological changes but also an unprecedented familiarity with social media and digital tools, especially seen in millennials, triggered a radical shift in behaviour of individuals (Sironi 2016). These developments are the antecedents of new entrants who are about to revolutionize the market by simplifying user experience, lowering fees and contextually develop new investment strategies for potential investors - the so called *robo-advisors* (Nicoletti 2017).

2.2 Robo-Advisory

The term *robo-advior* may initially trigger thoughts of a humanoid robot giving financial advice, which is correct to only a limited degree. There is no physical presence of a robot, but a virtual. Robo-advisors are digital platforms that comprise interactive and intelligent user assistance components, using information technology to guide customers through an automated financial advisory process (Jung et al. 2018a; Sironi 2016; Ludden et al. 2015). Breaking down recent robo-advisor conceptualizations (Jung et al. 2018a; Tertilt and Scholz 2017; Sironi 2016), robo-advisors differ from traditional advisory services in two conceptual levels (customer assessment and customer portfolio management) as outlined in Table 1, and described below in more detail.

The disruptive potential of robo-advisors induced by these key aspects has several implications. First, a consequence of the fully automated customer profiling and investment process is the considerably low fee structure and minimum investment (Jung et al. 2017). For example, in Germany the minimum investment amount ranges from 0 € to 10,000 € (Dorfleitner et al. 2017). Consequently, the raise of robo-advisors resulted in a new low-budget investor class that has not been served by

Table 1 The key characteristics of robo-advisors (Jung et al. 2018a)

Customer assessment	*Private households as target segment:* • The target segment is independent of actual wealth • No customer screening or pre-selection process • Public online platform, simple registration process
	Automated customer profiling: • Self-reporting to quantify an individual's profile • Questionnaires to measure the risk attitude • Preferences, goals, special interests measured by self-assessment questionnaires
Customer portfolio management	*Automated investment process:* • The whole investment process of robo-advisors is automated and requires no human activity for profiling/portfolio management. • Asset allocation is based on quantitative optimization • Portfolio rebalancing: active (client interaction)/passive (quantitative only) • Portfolio strategy assessment: Dynamic (adjustments by customer)/ static (fixed after initial process)
	Passive investment products: • No actively managed financial products to reduce costs • Instruments with transparent cost structure • Common choice: exchange-traded funds (ETF), exchange-traded commodities (ETC)

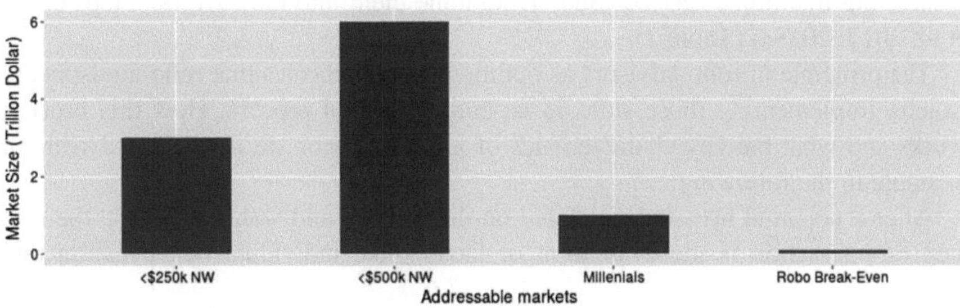

Fig. 2 $16–$40 billion of assets for robo-advisors to reach break-even compared to potential size of addressable markets (Wong 2015) (Addressable markets are 'Millennials', households with less than $250,000 of net worth and households between $250,000 and $500,000 of net worth)

traditional financial advisors before. Second, millennials (people born mid-1990s to early 2000s) are a primary target group of robo-advisors, as they constitute an investor group rather attracted by using technology than discouraged by it like older investors (Sironi 2016). According to Fig. 2, the market potential is large considering the millennial investor group shown. Because the estimated break-even is much smaller than the potential market, and therefore the opportunity for robo-advisory firms to make a profit, this is rendering the market attractive to firms newly entering the market (Gauthier et al. 2015; Wong 2015). To sum up, the main reasons for robo-advisors being able to be disrupt traditional advisory business are the cheapness, simplicity to access, and the attractiveness towards new customers such as millennials and tech savvy investors.

To reach a considerably large range of investors, stand-alone robo-advisors like Betterment or Scalable Capital started with this untapped market of tech savvy low-budget investors. Afterwards, they started targeting affluent and high net worth investors, having about $250,000 of net worth (NW) and more, hence starting to steal customers from traditional advisors (Sironi 2016). Nowadays, traditional wealth management advisors increasingly integrate robo-advisory solutions into their business models. The most popular examples of this hybrid advisory structure are Vanguard Personal Advisor Services and Schwab Intelligent Portfolios. At the beginning of 2017 they were the largest robo-advisors, with $47 billion and $10.2 billion of total AUM (Statista 2017). The next sections are illustrating a more detailed examination of functionalities provided by robo-advisors.

2.3 *Financial Advisory and Robo-Advisors*

Robo-advisory services provide an alternative approach to traditional financial advisory. Robo-advisory has adapted and digitalized traditional phases and fulfils basic functionalities of financial advice in wealth management (Cocca 2016). But, contrasting traditional services, they recombine them into three overall steps (Jung et al. 2017, 2018a) (Table 2):

The principle of robo-advisors as outlined above indicates that robo-advisors are exactly implementing those steps in an entirely digital process. How this process works and what the key characteristics of a robo-advisor are is illustrated with an example in the following:

After a potential investor registered on the website and wants to invest, the first step of interaction is the evaluation of factors like individual risk aversion and

Table 2 The activities of robo-advisors across the advisory process (Jung et al. 2018a)

Robo-advisor process	Advisory activities (based on Jung et al. 2017; Cocca 2016; Sironi 2016)
Configuration	1. Financial advisory initiation 2. Customer profiling, identifying investment needs and objectives 3. Customer assessment, measure risk and investment profile of the client based on profiling and by automated/cognitive self-assessment (age, risk tolerance, investment amount)
Matching	1. Defining investment strategy 2. Implementing the defined strategy 3. Long-term model portfolio (visualization of investment proposal) 4. Money management (intern, extern, hybrid)
Maintenance	1. Monitoring and rebalancing of portfolio, reverting to optimal model portfolio 2. Performance and communication (push/pull, event-driven, narrative, digital,. . .), customer retention and information

Table 3 Overview of the three main categories and subcategories for customer assessment and profiling of robo-advisors [adapted from Tertilt and Scholz (2017)]

Category	Variables of the customer profile
General information	Income, investment amount, job description, source of income, spending, time to retirement, type of account, working status
Risk capacity	Dependence on withdrawal of investment amount, income prediction, investment amount/saving rate ration, investment amount/total capital ratio, investment horizon, liabilities, saving rate, total capital
Risk tolerance	Age, association with investing, association with risk, choose portfolio risk level, comfort investing in stock, credit based investments, dealing with financial decisions, degree of financial risk taken, education, ever invested in risky asset for thrill, experience of drop/reaction on drop/max drop before selling, family and household status, financial knowledge, gender, investment experience, investment goal, investor type/self-assessment risk tolerance, preference return vs. risk

investment horizon, which are needed later on for the construction of the suggested portfolio. This routine requires the investor to answer a prepared questionnaire with questions varying between companies and countries (for an overview see Tertilt and Scholz 2017). A summary of different categories and subcategories for questionnaires is given in Table 3. Though Tertilt and Scholz (2017) indicate that some of the questions do not have a measurable impact on the subsequently generated choice of equity portfolios, they are the basis for later asset allocations and investment proposals.[2] Schwab Intelligent Portfolios is an example for using a questionnaire to assess an investors' risk preference, whereas Wealthfront Inc. uses a behavioural approach asking only a few questions with multiple possible answers (Park et al. 2016 ; Wealthfront Inc. 2017). The assessment of individual risk aversion and other factors in this step is essential for the further suggestion of individual portfolio structure.

The use of questionnaires without an initial personal consultation is a big change compared to traditional wealth management services. Additionally, with the use of a questionnaire the investor is given a feeling of making a logical choice of a portfolio, which is less because of a third party's recommendation, but more because of logical choice of their own opinions (Sironi 2016). The procedure following the completion of the questionnaire and submitting it passes fully automatically.

In the next step, each robo-advisor uses different approaches for selecting appropriate asset classes (e.g. stocks, bonds, currencies, commodities) according to each individual investor's profile. Asset class selection is based on the answers of the questionnaire and may take into account individual risk preference, goal types, tax-conditions, and more. For instance, a goal type could be the building of retirement savings and hence imply a longer overall investment horizon. Another example is a highly risk-averse person who is likely to prefer bonds with high credit ratings

[2]The pros and cons of using questionnaires are outlined during the SWOT analysis in the next chapter.

than in individual stock listings, as the default risk of such bonds is very low. For a less risk averse individual, U.S. stocks may be included in a portfolio to a larger extent, because of the high capital growth, inflation protection and tax efficiency attributes (Lam 2016). The tax efficiency attributes of robo-advisors will be outlined in Sect. 3.1. In summary, the challenge for a robo-advisor is to adequately capture these preferences and goals from a digital interaction with the customer who might not be able to precisely state his preferences or biased when trying to do so.

The assets are mainly represented by selected exchange traded funds, passively tracking market benchmarks. They are predominantly used, as robo-advisors mostly rely on passive indexing strategies when investing in different asset classes. They consider ETFs to be the best choice as they are cheap, provide good market liquidity and minimize tracking error, compared to actively managed funds (Lam 2016).[3] Moreover, continuous rebalancing can be done automatically and investors are linked to market trends instead of trying (but often failing) to gain more return through active asset management as Arnott et al. (2000) show. Active management would attempt to achieve above market returns by trading or shorting the constituents of an index, based on rules, sentiment, or portfolio managers' views (Sironi 2016). Passive mutual funds are also less usual, because ETFs can be traded at any time on open markets, facilitating automated portfolio rebalancing and tax-loss harvesting (Sironi 2016).[4] Furthermore, each robo-advisor has multiple ETFs for each asset class, to shift between them when, for example, the estimated volatility of one asset is considerably larger than the estimated volatility of a substitute asset. A variation of the passive indexing strategy of most robo-advisors is "direct indexing", in which the underlying stocks of ETFs are indexed, to achieve even more advanced tax-harvesting purposes, which is outlined in more detail in the following chapter.[5]

After successfully identifying which asset classes should be considered, proper portfolio weights for the different asset classes must be chosen, as they indicate how much of a specific asset relative to the others should be included in the target portfolio. The most prominent and modern approach on estimating optimal and therefore efficient portfolio weights is manifested in the modern portfolio theory (or mean-variance analysis) (Markowitz 1952). Basically, modern portfolio theory constitutes a mathematical framework considering a set of risky assets and calculating portfolios for which the expected return is maximized for a given level of portfolio risk (Lam 2016).[6] Though there exist many different approaches compared

[3]A tracking error describes the difference in return between the index fund and the index itself.

[4]To name some of the most prominent assets used, one of the stock ETFs Betterment uses is the 'Vanguard U.S. Total Stock Market Index ETF' and one of the bond ETFs is BlackRock's 'iShares Short-Term Treasury Bond Index ETF' (see Betterment portfolio structure https://support.betterment.com/customer/en/portal/articles/2347714-what-bond-etfs-are-used-in-the-betterment-portfolio?_ga=2.194102186.600542314.1497271052-1668747052.1496058254, last accessed on 10.07.2017).

[5]See www.wealthfront.com/tax-optimized-direct-indexing, last accessed on 10.07.2017.

[6]For a compact summary on the function principles and limitations of mean-variance analysis see Lam (2016).

to the basic model, most robo-advisors are using modern portfolio theory or an alteration of it to determine portfolio weights for the predetermined asset classes (Lam 2016). In a first step expected returns and volatilities of the different asset classes must be estimated, which is usually done by analysing the assets' historical returns and volatilities. After the determination of the different capital market assumptions is completed, mean-variance optimization is done. The optimization is based on the risk profile previously identified from the questionnaire of the investor considering the correlations in between the different asset classes. In the end, this approach leads to the successful estimation of portfolio weights (Lam 2016).

After the investment is conducted, "algorithmic rebalancing" provides stability of the portfolio weights and therefore the risk-level, by shifting investments among asset classes to revert towards its predefined risk long-term equilibrium, when the weights of the portfolio change. This can be triggered by high and low performance of individual assets or by external factors like for example down going markets. Rebalancing rules are different among various robo-advisors. There can be rules of discrete schedules (e.g. once a month), which has the disadvantage of reacting poorly to fast changing environmental factors. Referring to Lam (2016), a more prevalent rebalancing rule is to use thresholds rather than time-based rebalancing. In this rebalancing model, the weights of asset classes are adjusted when reaching certain thresholds. For example, if stock ETFs returns are reaching a certain upper limit, they cause a difference in portfolio weights compared to the long-term equilibrium. Subsequently, some of the stock ETFs are sold and put into other asset classes to get back to the previous weight combination of asset classes. With this approach, each investor stays invested in their specific risk level, not needing to pay an active investment manager for doing this job. Furthermore, if risk preferences of an investor change over time, the rebalancing techniques also adjust the portfolio towards the new target allocation. This can be the case if, for example, an investor suddenly has a lot more money, resulting in lower risk-aversion (Lam 2016).

Finally, continuous monitoring and 24/7 accessibility is a given feature of robo-advisors, differentiating them from traditional wealth manager services according to Sironi (2016). To summarize, the key benefits of the investment process of robo-advisors are the personalized approach of using questionnaires, the suggestion of a portfolio based on academic evidence, the simple use, automated rebalancing as well as continuous monitoring of investments.

3 SWOT Analysis of Robo-Advisory

In the following, we rely on a "strengths-weaknesses-opportunities-threats" or SWOT analysis (Helms and Nixon 2010) as a methodological tool to investigate the complex market situation and strategic elements of the current robo-advisory market. Hence, we outline the strengths and weaknesses of robo-advisors, as well as the external factors it is facing, represented by opportunities and threats to reduce the

Table 4 Overview of the key characteristics of the SWOT analysis of robo-advisory

	Helpful positive characteristics	Harmful negative characteristics
Internal	*Strengths* • Lower fees and minimum investment • Tax-loss harvesting • Investment experience • Portfolio construction by algorithms and automated rebalancing • Less emotional decision making	*Weaknesses* • Investment costs are not minimized • Conflict of interests • Poor assessment of risk tolerance and lack of personalization • No personal contact • Unfulfilled fiduciary duty
External	*Opportunities* • Ubiquity of Digital Services • Opportunity to standardize and integrate • Goal-based investing • Complement traditional advisors	*Threats* • Competitive environment • No acceptance of users • Possible threat from regulators • Bearish market and crisis

quantitative complexity of driving forces. The purpose of this SWOT analysis is to critically analyse the advantageousness of robo-advisory and to show what potential robo-advisory is unlocking to transform financial advisory as we know it today. Table 4 provides an overview of the key points discussed in the following.

3.1 *Strengths*

Lower Fees and Minimum Investment Two of the key strengths of robo-advisors are the comparably low fee structure and low minimum investment requirements (Glaser et al. 2018, Jung et al. 2017). Taking the U.S. market as an example, minimum investments for robo-advisory services start at $0 as Meola (2017) shows. Furthermore, fees are also substantially lower because robo-advisors predominantly invest into ETFs who often have the advantage of an inherent low-cost structure. In some cases, U.S. robo-advisors advertise "zero fees" as reported by Gauthier et al. (2015). Nonetheless, the upper limit for direct fees for robo-advisory in the U.S. market is 0.89% by the U.S. advisor Vanguard Personal Capital Services for investment amounts below $1 billion (Schapiro 2017). Meola (2017) shows that the fee structure of many robo-advisors is regressive and inversely correlated to the invested amount (that is larger investments lead to lower fees in percentages and vice versa).

The low fee structure and the low minimum investment of robo-advisors are real game changers in financial advisory, as traditional advisors charge fees ranging from 1% to 3% of the portfolio value for their services (Mercadante 2017). A new field of potential low-budget investors can be accessed, previously not noticed by traditional advisory firms. Additionally, high net-worth investors are potential targets, as they could see the opportunity to increase profits by reducing fees, assuming that the provided service is of equal quality.

Tax-Loss Harvesting Another feature is that robo-advisors are tax-loss harvesting in some countries (e.g. in the U.S.). The rationale is to sell securities at a loss, take the proceeds and buy a highly positively correlated substitute asset.[7] The capital losses can then be realized and offset against other capital gains to create a tax saving amount. With this approach, investors can profit in two ways. First, the tax saving amount can be reinvested to generate a compounding of the tax saving. Second, due to the different tax rates for long- and short-term capital gains, tax rate arbitrage can be conducted.[8] Overall, the risk-return-profile is maintained because of the high correlation between both the sold and the bought security, but additional gains are generated. This method is only suitable for long term-investors as both compounding of tax savings and tax-arbitrage due to different tax rates are solely realizable in the long-run (Lam 2016).

Most robo-advisors are using this tax gap on ETF basis to buy and sell highly correlated ETFs. Nevertheless, advisors such as Wealthfront advance to even more sophisticated methods by applying the concept of "direct indexing", where not the ETFs but their underlying individual stocks are bought and sold. This makes tax-loss harvesting even more effective and a useful approach on generating additional gains. Wealthfront suggests that with "direct indexing" it is possible to add as much as 2% to annual investment performance compared to vendors not using tax-loss harvesting.[9]

Tax-loss harvesting is value-adding for long-term investors compared to individual investments as tax matters can be outsourced, without the need to consult an expensive personal advisor. Nonetheless, the usefulness of tax-loss harvesting is limited to countries using different tax rates for long- and short-term capital gains. In Germany, for example, a uniform tax rate prevents tax arbitrage of this type.

Investment Experience The entirely digital approach of robo-advisory is an advantage regarding the ease of use. Especially in times where smartphones, tablets and other wearables are ubiquitous, this concept seems to be promising. In particular, millennials and people with a high affinity to technology are targeted here. Furthermore, due to the transparency and graphical presentation provided on the advisors' websites, the consumers feel that they can understand the offer without ambiguity, are granted easy access to the platforms and feel they can afford it (Sironi 2016). This single-mindedness of robo-advisory is also manifested in the questionnaires, as with answering them investors perceive the model portfolio more as a logical choice of their own opinions rather than as an external advice given by a financial advisor (Sironi 2016).

Established Algorithms and Automated Rebalancing Portfolio optimization of most robo-advisors is based on modern portfolio theory using eminent approaches

---

[7]It is not possible to buy the exact same security as this would be a 'wash sale' and not permitted in the U.S. (see https://www.sec.gov/answers/wash.htm, last accessed on 10.07.2017).

[8]Long-term (>1 year holding time of the investment) tax rate on capital gains is higher than the short-term tax rate in the U.S. Therefore tax-arbitrage can be done by not realizing capital gains before a holding time of 1 year (Lam 2016).

[9]See https://www.wealthfront.com/tax-optimized-direct-indexing, last accessed on 10.07.2017.

from Markowitz (1952) and alterations thereof. The advanced risk management resulting from its use becomes apparent by taking a look at the performance of robo-advisors. A study conducted by Reher and Sun (2016, Robo advisers and mutual fund stickiness. Unpublished manuscript, last modified https://pdfs.semanticscholar.org/75d1/7b81485eaf6a6f6a214242a6dfdc7bf9ec59.pdf. Accessed 01 Nov 2016) shows that they outperform both self-managed as well as mutual fund portfolios (on a risk adjusted basis). This speaks for the modern portfolio theory as well as for the passive investment strategy of robo-advisors. Nonetheless, they also investigated the "mutual fund stickiness" of investors to mutual funds, that is, investors do not seem to switch to robo-advisory even when robo-advisors apparently generate higher profits. Furthermore, though modern portfolio theory is highly contemporary, there are still difficulties in the assessment of short-term strategies, which indicates that robo-advisors are more valuable in the long-run as in the short-run (Nicoletti 2017). The concept of automated rebalancing, which formerly had to be done by active managers, also speaks for robo-advisors. As Lam (2016) indicates, active managers may not keep pace with changing weights of asset classes in a customer portfolio, resulting for instance from higher returns in one of the asset classes. This can lead to return slippage and delayed risk adjustment, which is avoided by robo-advisors.

Less Emotional Decision Making The last major strength of robo-advisory services, however, is concerned with the emotionality of investors. Average investors may build a portfolio and when the market turns down for some reason they immediately panic and sell it. With this habit of buying-high and selling-low they may miss potential rises in prices after they sell the securities (Traff 2016). A study of Vanguard shows that financial advisory can outperform regular retail investors by up to 3%, which is partly because professional investor are less emotionally driven (Kinniry et al. 2016). In accordance with these findings robo-advisors are likely to be advantageous as they are not driven by emotions. If markets go up or down, algorithmic trading algorithms should prevent them from making 'wrong' choices and furthermore should help to stick to a consistent risk level.

3.2 Weaknesses

Investment Costs Are Not Minimized The aspect of low fees compared to traditional advisory firms as outlined in the last chapter, is also facing criticism. Fein (2015) criticizes robo-advisors for advertising their products to be "low fee" or "zero fee" services which does not necessarily have to be true. She states that "robo-advisor users typically bear the cost of brokerage, transaction, and other fees and expenses, whether directly or indirectly, and thus contribute to the robo-advisor's compensation" (Fein 2015). Though fees of robo-advisors are comparably low because of the low-cost structure of ETFs and no need of advisory personnel, Fein's investigation seems to be argumentative. As robo-advisors still have to defray costs and moreover have intentions to run a profitable business, with real 'zero fees' charged to the customer this is not possible. Indirect fees are often not explicitly shown in the investment dashboards, and hence masked as lower returns of investor portfolios.

Furthermore, Fein (2015) states that robo-advisors reserve the right to change the fees at their discretion. This can be an indication for advisors using the low-fees as an initial feature to attract new customers until they have a large enough customer base and increasing the fees afterwards to generate higher profits.

Conflict of Interests A report from FINRA (2016) is calling attention for customers of robo-advisory services to be aware that robo-advisors do not necessarily eliminate conflicts of interest present in personal financial advisory—quite the contrary might be true.[10]

Robo-advisors maintain relationships to affiliated brokers, clearing firms, custodians and other firms to provide the service of automated investment to their customers. Fein (2015) investigated these relationships to identify whether conflicts of interests between customers and robo-advisors are a present issue. For instance, she identified that some companies do use brokers of their choice, demanding a higher price than favourable for the customer (Fein 2015). This indicates that a share of the higher price is kept as profit by the robo-advisor. Especially for "zero fees" robo-advisors, this conflict of interest seems to be present. If they would not exploit the possibilities of indirect fees they would not generate any revenue. In particularly, some robo-advisors are disclosing that they "may have an interest or position in securities that are recommended to clients" which indicates an additional conflict of interest like commission payments for these instruments (Fein 2015). Consequently, there exist conflicts of interest on two conceptual levels: firstly, concerning the affiliated brokers, and secondly concerning the selection of recommended assets.

Since conflicts of interest potentially exist in the received investment advice, customers of robo-advisory services should assess whether those conflicts compromise the objectivity of investment advice given by the robo-advisor. However, this assessment might be as challenging as managing the portfolio yourself. It is worth noting, that these conflicts of interest are quite similar to those that are present in traditional financial advisory.

Poor Assessment of Risk Tolerance and Lack of Personalization A commonly expressed point of criticism refers to the risk assessment of robo-advisors based on prepared questionnaires. A report of the SEC and FINRA (2015) alerts investors that the questionnaires they fill to identify what individual investment strategy suits best, is often not taking into account the individual goals and may be based on incorrect additional assumptions, incomplete information or circumstances not relevant for the

[10]The Financial Industry Regulatory Authority is regulatory institution in the U.S. mainly concerned with participants in securities trading (see www.finra.org/about, last accessed 16.07.2017).

investors (for example age, time horizon and individual goals).[11] Cocca (2016) shares this view, assessing the simplicity of risk tolerance questionnaires as 'natural' limit in the development of robo-advice.

Furthermore, Tertilt and Scholz (2017) recently added research regarding the use of questionnaires to assess risk levels. They found that of the robo-advisors they investigated, which are based in Germany, the U.S. and the U.K., only 60% of the asked questions have an impact on the risk categorization. In addition to that, they found robo-advisors to give similar equity recommendations as human advisors, challenging the claim of robo-advisors to be per se more valuable and unbiased than traditional financial advisors.

Having a look at the rebalancing mechanisms of robo-advisors, lack of personalization and (possibly) wrong advice are also present. The rebalancing rules outlined in Sect. 2.3 are fairly simplistic and therefore limitedly suitable (Sironi 2016). For example, Schwab Intelligent Portfolios ignores individual requirements and inserts the investor into a one-size-fits-all rebalancing algorithm (Marotta 2015).

To summarize, it seems that due to the lack of personalization in risk assessment and rebalancing, robo-advisory does not meet the need of investors with moderately complex requirements so far.

No Personal Contact One of the main features of robo-advisors is that there is no need for a personal advisor anymore. On the one hand, this can be an advantage as fees are getting lower and advisory services are brought to a broader mass of customers. On the other hand, the question arises whether impersonal investment advice is something a customer actually wants (Jung et al. 2017). Regarding a survey conducted in Italy in 2016, 49% of the polled persons would not use robo-advisory services without the support of an in-person consultant and only 11% are willing to rely on an autonomous robo-advisor (Nicoletti 2017).

Especially in wealth management, where traditionally high net worth clients are present, personal contact seems to be more important, as for example "a customer may feel more willing to talk about the consequences of the sudden passing away of their wife when the long-time advisor of the family addresses this delicate issue with due care, whereas a robo-advisor might send a change of text of the testament contract by e-mail on the basis of the calculated probability of such a scenario" (Cocca 2016). This example illustrates the difficulty of not having a personal relationship with the financial advisor. Moreover, clients are left to their own devices when they try assessing whether the provided investment strategies meet their needs and goals (Fein 2015).

Unfulfilled Fiduciary Duty In the U.S., under the Fiduciary Standard of Care, broker-dealers are obliged to act in their clients' best interest when giving financial

[11]The SEC (U.S. Security Exchange Commission) is an independent exchange supervisory authority in the U.S. overseeing securities trading in the U.S. (see https://www.sec.gov/Article/whatwedo.html).

advice.[12] Though not giving personal advice, a robo-advisor also acts as an advising fiduciary under the Investment Advisers Act of 1940 and is obliged to meet the fiduciary standards (SEC 1940). Due to the lack of personal investment advice, in a more recent study Fein (2015) investigates the fiduciary implications following this shortage.

She indicates that robo-advisors do not provide overall portfolio analysis because they assess investments in isolation (for each asset class) and do not develop an overall investment strategy on behalf of the client. Moreover, Fein (2015) states that robo-advisors only limitedly consider individual client conditions or other external factors, which can lead to fatal consequences, for example in plummeting market scenarios. Finally, she concludes that only professionally trained advisors can reliably manage portfolios (Fein 2015).

3.3 *Opportunities*

Ubiquity of Digital Services The financial industry and wealth management is in constant demographic and technological change. Consequently, behaviour of consumers is also shifting. People are pervasively connected via smartphones, tablets, notebooks and other devices, everywhere at any time. Especially younger generations grow up with technology and are therefore much more used to it (Sironi 2016). Today's digitalization of every day's life provides good foundations for robo-advisors to establish in a market that is dominated by conventional wealth and asset management institutions. The strategy of choice in this environment seems to be reaping the cost reductions enabled by technology while still acting as an expensive intermediary (Cocca 2016). Robo-advisors are quitting this concept of intermediality.

Indeed, Gauthier et al. (2015) states that robo-advice is explicitly targeting the younger, tech savvy generation. Cocca (2016) shows in his study that 30% of respondents of a survey conducted in Europe can imagine to use a purely automated investment advisor, whereas this percentage rises to 45% when excluding the population at age 60 or above as they tend to stick to their accustomed habits. The potential market represented by millennials is currently below $2 trillion in the U.S., which is significantly lower compared to the total AUM of the asset management industry. However, the market keeps growing year by year alongside the degree of digitalization of societies (Wong 2015).

Opportunity to Standardize and Integrate Apart from services like portfolio rebalancing and automated asset allocation robo-advisors currently provide, the wealth managements' industry offer is still considerably larger. They provide services of higher complexity which are hard to standardize and mass-customize by

[12]Broker-dealers are individuals or firms doing both executing investments on their clients' behalf (broker) and trading for its own account (dealer).

robo-advisors, including for example cross-border tax-advice, which is not only considering different national tax laws but also international tax law and individual tax arrangements among countries. The full integration and combination of financial, legal and tax issues on an international scale is a very complex process, where a large number of degrees of freedom appear (Cocca 2016).

Nonetheless, the opportunity to standardize and integrate more complex services is a key factor in attracting more customers currently relying on a traditional personal advisor. As Cocca (2016, p. 51) states, "the question of who can bring together a comprehensive total offering is currently in the background, but it is likely to be very relevant in the future". Established traditional advisors launching individual advisors or acquiring stand-alone robo-advisors may have an advantage here, as they have decades of experience considering wealth and asset management practices and knowledge.

Goal-Based Investing The simple approach of assessing customers risk profiles using questionnaires and applying concepts of the modern portfolio theory for portfolio optimization has been discussed previously. To prospectively solve these problems of simplification, assuming the market volatility to be the setscrew of return, the philosophy of goal-based investing is the long-term goal of the robo-advisory business, as it differs fundamentally from mean-variance optimization concepts. Following goal-based investing, the individuals themselves, composed of multiple individual values, investment goals, priorities, time horizons and risk profiles, are the centre of attention (Sironi 2016). As every human differs in the combination of the previously stated attributes, a much more individual model must be developed to reach a high degree of personalization and optimally meet customer needs.

Gauthier et al. (2015) as well as Ludden et al. (2015) see high future potential of advanced personalization of robo-advisory services, not least because of contemporary technological developments like big data analytics to assess goals and fears of investors. Rudimentary aspects of advanced personalization are already implemented in some robo-advisors. Motif Investing, for example, gives the investor the opportunity to choose between three "impact portfolios", namely "sustainable planet", "fair labour" and "good corporate behaviour". Each of these investment tracks chooses only assets meeting one of the three previously chosen individual goals mixed up with mean-variance optimization.[13] This is only a first step towards goal-based investing, as there is a severe limitation on numbers of goals and no such individual goals as for instance college savings, planned home purchases, retirement, protection needs, etc. included, but in the long-run, robo-advisors will head the direction of goal-based investing as Sironi (2016) states.

Complement Traditional Advisors The low amount of AUM currently held by stand-alone robo-advisors is a problem for them, as it seems that they do not attract enough high-net worth customers. Although they have high growth rates, the current

[13]See https://www.motifinvesting.com/products/impact-portfolio, last accessed 03.07.2017.

total market share of the wealth management market attributable to robo-advisors is still below 1% in 2016 (Cocca 2016). This is not necessarily crucial, as Wong (2015) states the break-even of robo-advisors to be considerably low, but they act in a competitive area and have lots of marketing costs to increase their reach and to acquire new customers (Sironi 2016). According to Burnmark (2017), it costs a US robo-advisor $389, on average, to acquire a customer, while the average account size of $27,000 only produces a revenue of $90.

A possible solution for this problem could be the combination of aspects or even whole businesses of traditional and robo-advisory. Gauthier et al. (2015) analysed potential scenarios of interactions between stand-alone robo-advisors and existing traditional advisors. One part of their study considers the partnering of existing robo-advisors and banks which is beneficial for both, as wealth managers can offer robo-advised portfolios and robo-advisors profit from existing knowledge and client base of wealth managers. Sironi (2016) also recognized this development, appropriately naming it a transformation "from B2C robo-advisors to B2B2C robo-4-advisors". Betterment and its platform "Betterment 4 Advisors" is a recent example of this, providing the integration of robo-services for traditional advisors.[14]

Sironi (2016) also notices the transformation of existing robo-advisors to B2B business models, providing cloud services for financial institutions that want the technology of robo-advisory but do not have the capabilities to build their own solution. Furthermore, robo-advisors could extend their portfolio and include also personal advisors, to attract customers not willing to rely only on implemented algorithms. For example, Betterment announced to add live advisors to its offering, available to investors with AUM of $100,000 or more, making it a hybrid service (Anderson 2017).

3.4 Threats

Competitive Environment A future threat for every robo-advisor in the market is the high competition they are facing. According to Burnmark (2017), in Europe currently more than 70 robo-advisors exist, each of them following similar investment principles. Moreover, in the U.S. there exist even more than 200 robo-advisors, each competing for customers. This competitiveness is currently mostly restricted to domestic markets, but if regulatory environments, investment practices and other barriers to entering foreign markets change, international competition will rise, and smaller companies will face U.S. companies, which are considerably larger in terms of AUM (CB Insights 2017).

Furthermore, stand-alone robo-advisors are recently facing robo-advisors founded by traditional advisory firms. Introduced in 2015, Schwab Intelligent Portfolios and Vanguard Personal Advisor Services, which are such robo-advisors,

[14]See https://www.bettermentforadvisors.com/, last accessed 03.07.2017.

gradually overtake the largest US FinTechs, Betterment and Wealthfront, in terms of AUM (Malito and Zhu 2016). Primarily, this is a result of the large customer base which traditional advisors already have when launching their own robo-advisor. This can be a major threat for stand-alone robo-advisors as they need time to acquire a competitive customer base and become profitable. Wong (2015) investigated when robo-advisors start getting profitable and states that the break-even client asset level for robo-advisors ranges from $16 billion to $40 billion, which is 8–20 times the current client asset level of leading robo-advisory firms, which suggests that most advisors are likely to be underfunded at this stage. Therefore, most of the current stand-alone robo-advisors will face strong competition, and hence will hardly survive the next decade without adjusting to the changing market conditions by enhancing their customer base and increasing their profitability.

No Acceptance of Users As emphasized before, the shift in behaviour and increasing affinity to technology is indicating millennials as an attractive target for robo-advisors (Gauthier et al. 2015). Nevertheless, this does not necessarily mean that a broad mass of potential users will actually consider robo-advisors as a real opportunity compared to retail investing or a personal advisor.

Following a survey conducted by Ludden et al. (2015), they indicate that 77% of the surveyed wealth management clients trust their financial advisors. Moreover, 81% say that face-to-face interaction is important. This indicates that personal advisory service is still a highly desired feature of financial advisors. Furthermore, they take up the position that current robo-advisors do not meet the needs of investors with complex financial lives, as the implemented approaches for, e.g., risk assessment are too plain (Ludden et al. 2015).

A study conducted by Reher and Sun (2016, Robo advisers and mutual fund stickiness. Unpublished manuscript, last modified https://pdfs.semanticscholar.org/75d1/7b81485eaf6a6f6a214242a6dfdc7bf9ec59.pdf. Accessed 01 Nov 2016) shows that mutual fund holders stick to their mutual fund investment, even when a comparable robo-advisor significantly outperforms the mutual fund. This is an indication for the missing trust in robo-advisors, though it may also be attributed to other reasons such as higher costs or laziness to switch investments. As a result, robo-advisors are starting to launch hybrid solutions, providing a personal advisor besides the robo-advisory service. For instance, Betterment recently introduced a call centre of certified financial planners to monitor accounts and provide advice.[15]

The argument of trust is also discussed by Cocca (2016), stating that, eventually, it will depend on the individual preferences of customers to receive advice based on an algorithm or provided in person. Nonetheless, the question of broad acceptance of the robo-advisory concept in the future remains uncertain, constituting a potential threat for the business.

[15]See http://www.wealthmanagement.com/technology/betterment-pivots-toward-human-robo-hybrid, last accessed on 10.07.2017.

Possible Threat from Regulators Recently, many institutions and individuals uttered rising concerns regarding regulation of digital investment advisory for several reasons. For instance, Fein (2015) is concerned about potential conflict of interests, the lack of personal advice and utters fiduciary concerns as outlined in Sect. 3.2. Furthermore, Novick et al. (2016) provide a good overview about which institutions recently addressed concerns regarding regulation on robo-advisors. FINRA (2016) and SEC and FINRA (2015) raise concerns regarding supervision of algorithms, conflicts of interest, practices on customer profiling and automatic rebalancing, showing that there is a need on advanced regulation of robo-advisors. Moreover, under the fiduciary rule released by the Department of Labor (2016), U.S. digital advisors "need to evaluate whether they need to make changes in their programs to ensure that they are compliant with ERISA fiduciary requirements".

Baker and Dellaert (2017 p. 4) also see a need of regulators represented by lawyers, economists, and behavioural scientists already involved in financial services regulation, to extend their range of competencies "to understand enough about computer and data science to craft and apply new regulatory strategies". They also mention the need to regulate robo-advisors because of the new scale of risks, as all of their investors follow similar algorithms (Baker and Dellaert 2017).

These recent developments and rising concerns about regulation on digital investment advice constitute a potential threat for the robo-advisory industry. If regulation gets stricter in the future, this could have impacts on profitability due to increased compliance costs.

Bearish Market and Crisis A point many investors are concerned about is that currently established robo-advisors never experienced a crisis or bearish market. Among others, Fein (2015) states, that she is concerned about how a robo-advisor will perform in a market downturn. Traff (2016) argues that robo-advisors have the advantage of making practically no emotionally-driven decisions, and would perform better than a retail investor or even a traditional financial advisor, as both carry individual emotional and cognitive biases. This can be illustrated with a recent example. In 2016, during the referendum on the Brexit in the U.K., many investors panicked and sold their positions impulsively, missing the later opportunity of rising stock prices. This is avoided by robo-advisors, as they stick to the predefined risk determination, reallocate between certain assets and asset classes and do not panic in similar situations. This can be an opportunity for robo-advisors.

Nonetheless, the question how robo-advisors will perform in extreme market downturns like during the financial crisis in 2008 remains unanswered. Consequently, it is unclear whether trust in robo-advisors is big enough to not sell their positions proactively, even in times of extreme market shifts or if a personal advisor is considered more trustworthy in such situations.

4 Conclusion

In the preceding discussion, we gave an overview about the changing landscape of financial advisory as well as the functionality and market developments of robo-advisory. Furthermore, we critically analysed the robo-advisory concept, outlining current strengths and weaknesses as well as opportunities and threats. We outlined robo-advisors to be an innovative, new approach that is transforming financial advisory as it is known today. However, there is still a lot of potential yet to be unlocked.

Being investment approaches with low costs, high transparency and good performance compared to mutual funds, as Reher and Sun (2016, Robo advisers and mutual fund stickiness. Unpublished manuscript, last modified https://pdfs.semanticscholar.org/75d1/7b81485eaf6a6f6a214242a6dfdc7bf9ec59.pdf. Accessed 01 Nov 2016) show, they address the low-wealth investor group which has not been targeted by incumbent wealth and asset management firms. Furthermore, most robo-advisors rely on passive index investment strategies in combination with amendments of the modern portfolio theory introduced by Markowitz (1952), thus relying on a scientific approach. Nevertheless, robo-advisors face a lot of scepticism, especially from regulatory authorities. They have raised concerns regarding conflict of interests, the poor assessment of risk tolerance, the missing personal contact and consequentially the unfulfilled fiduciary duty towards investors and regulatory authorities.

On the other hand, regarding future developments, there are opportunities to be leveraged by robo-advisory. The shift in behaviour due to the intensified use of electronic devices might render robo-advisory more attractive for investors in younger generations. Furthermore, goal-based investing and the individual modelling of goals, values and time horizons might be the next steps taken by robo-advisory. Opportunities of business transformation of stand-alone robo-advisors emerge through cooperation with existing financial institutions in order to switch from B2C models to B2B2C, as Sironi (2016) pointed out.

Despite these promising upsides, there are threats the industry is facing. First, the environment is getting increasingly competitive. Considering Europe, there exist more than 70 individual robo-advisors, each of them competing in the same potential market (Schapiro 2017). Second, it is unclear whether users will accept fully automated investment devices, without any personal contact. Third, regulation can be a future threat as authorities like FINRA or the SEC recently uttered their concerns (SEC and FINRA 2015; FINRA 2016).

Consequently, the rise of robo-advisory has just begun, and it is questionable to what extent it defends its existence facing bearish markets for the first time. Many questions regarding design, implementation and regulation are still unanswered and therefore robo-advisory research is still in its infancy (see Jung et al. 2018a for an overview).

References

Anderson T (2017) More robo-advisors are adding a human touch to their services. http://www.cnbc.com/2017/01/31/more-robo-advisors-are-adding-that-human-touch.html. Accessed 10 Jul 2017

Arnott RD, Berkin AL, Ye J (2000) How well have taxable investors been served in the 1980s and 1990s? J Portf Manag 4:84–93. https://www.firstquadrant.com/system/files/0003_How_Well_Have_Taxable_Investors_Been_Served_0.pdf. Accessed 10 Jul 2017

Baker T, Dellaert B (2017) Regulating robo advice across the financial services industry. ERIM report series research in management in Erasmus Research Institute of Management. https://repub.eur.nl/pub/98312. Accessed 10 Jul 2017

Burnmark (2017) The US still has the robo-advisor lead. Burnmark. http://www.burnmark.com/wp-content/uploads/2017/Burnmark%20Report%20April17.pdf?utm_source=Triggermail&utm_medium=email&utm_campaign=Post%20Blast%20%28bii-fintech%29:%20The%20US%20still%20has%20the %20robo-advisor%20lead%20%E2%80%94%20SWIFT%20continues%20to%20battle%20Ripple %20%E2%80%94%20Standard%20Chartered%20teams%20up%20with%20startups&utm_term=BII%20List%20Fintech%20ALL. Accessed 10 Jul 2017

CB Insights (2017) A wealth tech world: mapping robo-advisors around the globe. https://www.cbinsights.com/blog/robo-advisor-global-fintech-map/. Accessed 10 Jul 2017

Cocca TD (2016) Potential and limitations of virtual advice in wealth management. Capco Inst J Financ Transform 44:45–57 https://www.capco.com/insights/capco-institute/~/media/Capco/uploads/articlefiles/file_0_1479204971.pdf. Accessed 29 May 2017

Department of Labor (2016) Conflict of interest final rule. https://www.dol.gov/agencies/ebsa/laws-and-regulations/rules-and-regulations/completed-rulemaking/1210-AB32-2. Accessed 13 Jul 2017

Dorfleitner G, Hornuf L, Schmitt M, Weber M (2017) FinTech in Germany. Springer, Cham

European Securities and Markets Authority (2007) MIFID and MIFIR. https://www.esma.europa.eu/policy-rules/mifid-ii-and-mifir. Accessed 10 Jun 2017

Fein ML (2015) Robo-advisors – a closer look. SSRN Journal. https://papers.ssrn.com/sol3/papers.cfm?abstract_id=2658701. Accessed 12 Jun 2017

FINRA (2016) FINRA reports on effective practices for digital investment advice. http://www.finra.org/newsroom/2016/finra-reports-effective-practices-digital-investment-advice?utm_source=feedburner&utm_medium=feed&utm_campaign=Feed%3A+FINRANews+%28FINRA+News%29. Accessed 18 Jun 2017

Gauthier V, Laknidhi V, Klein P, Gera R (2015) Robo-advisors: capitalizing on a growing opportunity. Deloitte. https://www2.deloitte.com/us/en/pages/consulting/articles/robo-advisors-capitalizing-on-growing-opportunity.html. Accessed 31 May 2017

Glaser F, Iliewa Z, Jung D, Weber M (2018): Towards designing Robo-advisors for inexperienced investors with experience sampling of time-series data, In: Proceedings of the Retreat on NeuroIS 2018, Vienna.

Helms MM, Nixon J (2010) Exploring SWOT analysis – where are we now? A review of academic research from the last decade. J Strateg Manage 3(3):215–251

Jung D, Dorner V, Weinhardt C, Pusmaz H (2017) Designing a robo-advisor for risk-averse, low-budget investors. Electron Mark

Jung D, Dorner V, Glaser F, Morana S (2018a) Catchword robo-advisory – digitalization and automation of financial advisory, business and information systems engineering (BISE)

Jung D, Erdfelder E, Glaser F (2018b) Nudged to win - Designing robo-advisory to overcome decision inertia. In: Proceedings of the 26th European Conference on Information Systems (ECIS 2018)

Kinniry F, Jaconetti C, DiJoseph M, Zilbering Y (2016) Putting a value on your value: quantifying Vanguard advisor's alpha, Vanguard. https://www.vanguard.com/pdf/ISGQVAA.pdf. Accessed 18 Jun 2017

Kocianski S (2016) The robo-advising report: market forecasts, key growth drivers, and how automated asset management will change the advisory industry. Business Insider. http://www.businessinsider.de/the-robo-advising-report-market-forecasts-key-growth-drivers-and-how-automated-asset-management-will-change-the-advisory-industry-2016-6?r=US&IR=T. Accessed 10 Jun 2017

Lam JW (2016) Robo-advisors: a portfolio management perspective. Yale College. http://economics.yale.edu/sites/default/files/files/Undergraduate/Nominated%20Senior%20Essays/2015-16/Jonathan_Lam_Senior%20Essay%20Revised.pdf. Accessed 13 Jun 2017

Ludden C, Thompson K, Mohsin I (2015) The rise of robo-advice: changing the concept of wealth management. Accenture. https://www.accenture.com/_acnmedia/PDF-2/Accenture-Wealth-Management-Rise-of-Robo-Advice.pdf. Accessed 03 Jun 2017

Malito A, Zhu E (2016) Top 5 robo-advisers by AUM. http://www.investmentnews.com/article/20160225/FREE/160229960/top-5-robo-advisers-by-aum. Accessed 10 Jul 2017

Markowitz H (1952) Portfolio selection. J Financ 1:77–91. http://onlinelibrary.wiley.com/doi/10.1111/j.1540-6261.1952.tb01525.x/full. Accessed 10 Jul 2017

Marotta DJ (2015) Schwab intelligent portfolios: services not provided. https://www.forbes.com/sites/davidmarotta/2015/04/12/schwab-intelligent-portfolios-services-not-provided/#3cabf148a231. Accessed 29 May 2017

Meola A (2017) Robo investing reviews: performance and fees comparison. http://www.businessinsider.de/bis-robo-investing-reviews-performance-and-fees-comparison-2017-1?r=US&IR=T. Accessed 10 Jul 2017

Mercadante K (2017) Robo-advisors vs. financial advisors – which one should you use? https://investorjunkie.com/41363/robo-advisors-vs-financial-advisors/. Accessed 17 Jun 2017

Nicoletti B (2017) The future of FinTech. Springer, Cham

Novick B, Lu B, Fortin T, Hafizi S, Parkes M, Barry R (2016) Digital investment advice: roboadvisors come of age. Blackrock. https://www.blackrock.com/corporate/en-at/literature/whitepaper/viewpoint-digital-investment-advice-september-2016.pdf. Accessed 03 Jun 2017

Park JY, Ryu JP, Shin HJ (2016) Robo-advisors for portfolio management. Adv Sci Technol Lett 141:104–108. http://onlinepresent.org/proceedings/vol141_2016/21.pdf. Accessed 10 Jul 2017

Praeg C-P, Schmidt C, Bauer W (2015) Trendstudie Bank und Zukunft – Aufbruch zu neuen Kundenerlebnissen und Services in der digitalen Oekonomie. Fraunhofer, Stuttgart

Praeg C-P, Schmidt C, Bauer W (2016) Trendstudie Bank und Zukunft 2016 – Neue Wege gehen. Fraunhofer-Institut für Arbeitswirtschaft und Organisation (IAO). Fraunhofer, Stuttgart

Schapiro K (2017) Backend benchmarking – the robo report Q1 2017. https://theroboreport.com. Accessed 10 Jul 2017

SEC (1940) Investment advisers act of 1940. https://www.sec.gov/about/laws/iaa40.pdf. Accessed 13 Jul 2017

SEC and FINRA (2015) Investor alert: automated investment tools. https://www.sec.gov/oiea/investor-alerts-bulletins/autolistingtoolshtm.html. Accessed 29 May 2017

Sironi P (2016) FinTech innovation: from robo-advisors to goal based investing and gamification. The Wiley Finance Series. Wiley

Statista (2017) FinTech: personal finance https://www.statista.com/download/outlook/whiterpaper/FinTech_Personal_Finance_Outlook_0217.pdf. Accessed 08 Jul 2017

Tertilt M, Scholz P (2017) To Advise, or not to advise – how robo-advisors evaluate the risk preferences of private investors. SSRN J. https://papers.ssrn.com/sol3/papers.cfm?abstract_id=2913178. Accessed 12 Jun 2017

Traff JD (2016) The future of the wealth management industry: evolution or revolution? MBA submission, Massachusetts Institute of Technology. https://dspace.mit.edu/handle/1721.1/104548. Accessed 05 Jun 2017

Wealthfront Inc. (2017) Wealthfront investment methodology white paper: determining your risk. https://research.wealthfront.com/whitepapers/investment-methodology/. Accessed 08 Jul 2017

Wong MM (2015) Hungry robo-advisors are eyeing wealth management assets: we believe wealth management moats can repel the fiber-clad legion. Morningstar. http://fsc.org.nz/site/fsc/files/FAAR%202015/Morningstar%20%20Hungry%20Robo-Advisors% 20Are%20Eyeing%20Wealth%20 Management%20Assets%20We. . .pdf. Accessed 03 Jun 2017

Dominik Jung is a researcher in the group Electronic Markets and User Behaviour at the Karlsruhe Institute of Technology (KIT), and the Karlsruhe Decision & Design Lab (KD2Lab), Germany. He earned a Bachelor of Science and a Bachelor of Arts from the Technical University of Ilmenau, Germany, and a Master of Science from each Karlsruhe Institute of Technology and University of Hagen, Germany. His research focuses on Decision Support Systems, and Behavioral Decision Making, and has been published in top international outlets such as Electronic Markets, or Business & Information Systems Engineering.

Florian Glaser is a research group lead of the group Electronic Markets and User Behaviour at the Karlsruhe Institute of Technology (KIT), Germany. He is a scientific consultant at the Stuttgart Stock Exchange. His research focuses on different aspects of digital platforms like Blockchain, Social Trading and Robo Advisory. His research has been published, for example, in by the European Systemic Risk Board, the Journal of Information Technology (JIT) and in conference proceedings of ECIS and HICSS.

Willi Köpplin is a Masters student in Industrial Engineering and Management at the Karlsruhe Institute of Technology (KIT), Germany. Furthermore, he earned a Bachelor of Science in the same-named subject at the KIT. In his studies he is focusing on Financial Service Design and Statistics. Besides his studies he works as a research assistant at the Department for Finance and Banking (FBV).

MIX
Papier aus verantwortungsvollen Quellen
Paper from responsible sources
FSC® C105338

If you have any concerns about our products,
you can contact us on
ProductSafety@springernature.com

In case Publisher is established outside the EU,
the EU authorized representative is:
Springer Nature Customer Service Center GmbH
Europaplatz 3, 69115 Heidelberg, Germany

Printed by Libri Plureos GmbH
in Hamburg, Germany